THE BOOK OF
FOOTBALL
QUOTATIONS

Phil Shaw is a sports journalist who has written for the *Independent, Independent on Sunday, Guardian, Observer, Daily Telegraph, Sunday Telegraph, Scotland on Sunday, Time Out* and *Backpass* magazine. He has compiled nine editions of *The Book of Football Quotations* over the past 30 years, the first five in collaboration with the late Peter Ball. Among the major sporting events on which he has reported are five World Cups and four European Championships. Phil is a native of Leeds and now lives with his wife Julie in Staffordshire.

THE BOOK OF
FOOTBALL
QUOTATIONS
NINTH EDITION

PHIL SHAW

EBURY
PRESS

5 7 9 10 8 6

Published in 2014 by Ebury Press, an imprint of Ebury Publishing
A Random House Group company

The Random House Group Limited Reg. No. 954009

Addresses for companies within the Random House Group can be found at
www.randomhouse.co.uk

A CIP catalogue record for this book is available from the British Library

The Random House Group Limited supports the Forest Stewardship Council® (FSC®),
the leading international forest-certification organisation. Our books carrying the
FSC label are printed on FSC®-certified paper. FSC is the only forest-certification
scheme supported by the leading environmental organisations, including Greenpeace.
Our paper procurement policy can be found at www.randomhouse.co.uk/environment

Designed and set by seagulls.net

Printed and bound by Clays Ltd, Elcograf S.p.A

ISBN 9780091959678

To buy books by your favourite authors and register for offers visit
www.randomhouse.co.uk

CONTENTS

INTRODUCTION

Dour Yorkshiremen. Efficient Germans. Samba-style Brazilians. Tight-fisted or fiery Scots. To these stereotypes, trotted out daily in the media and in the 'real world', can be added The Thick Footballer.

It has long been widely accepted that the game's main practitioners, especially the players, are brainless, monosyllabic morons. There was once a TV sketch, in *Monty Python's Flying Circus* I believe, in which a player that may have been loosely based on George Best (whose self-destructive streak actually belied his brightness) answered questions put to him with 'I'm opening a boutique, Brian.'

Little has changed, it seems. Early in 2014 the televised charity event *Sport Relief* featured a spoof of *Celebrity Mastermind* in which three Premier League players in full playing kit – Michael Dawson, Scott Parker and Jack Wilshere – went head to head. It was undoubtedly funny as they epic-failed on a succession of scripted stupid answers to risibly simple questions, especially when, as quizmaster David Walliams announced a three-way tie on zero points, Dawson exclaimed: 'Yessss – joint top!' However, the humour worked principally because it fed into the misconception that footballers are poorly endowed when it comes to grey matter.

Such episodes remind me of a radio interview I did in the course of publicising the first edition of *The Book of Football Quotations*, in 1984. My interrogator, a plummy BBC veteran, was incredulous that anyone should have attempted what myself and my co-compiler, Peter Ball, had done. Having clearly not taken a moment to study the erudition and wit on display within its pages, he wondered aloud how we had contrived to make such a sturdy volume out of 'sick as a parrot' and 'over the moon' utterances.

While it was never our mission to rectify the sweeping generalisation about the intelligence of football folk, it has, over the course of seven previous editions, been a pleasing by-product. There are, of course, many footballers whose brains are to be found only in their feet, which in turn are often in their mouths. But to suggest it is a defining personality trait of an entire profession betrays ignorance bordering on snobbery and is not borne out by my experiences as a sports journalist over the past 35 years.

But why has the notion arisen? One reason is that players and managers are frequently interviewed within seconds or minutes of finishing a match, when their adrenalin is still pumping furiously. Microphones are thrust in their faces and they are asked 'how it felt' to score the winner or to lose in the last minute. The question invites, nay demands, a stock answer, but if the response starts with 'obviously', whose fault is that?

That's why, incidentally, *The Book of Football Quotations* initially tended to resist pressure from various publishers, not to mention reviewers, to include more Colemanballs – the slips of the tongue that have been such a source of merriment to readers of *Private Eye*. This dour Yorkie's take on this used to be that sneering at other people's mistakes under pressure was not particularly amusing. I have since been persuaded, not least by one of the great gaffemasters, Bobby Gould, that it is fine provided it produces an image or wordplay that is funny in its own right (such as Mark Lawrenson declaring: 'Newcastle are besotted by injuries'). Gould didn't object to his Unwinesque mauling of the language causing mirth. Why should I?

Another factor that has led to the perception of footballers being capable only of inanities is the sheer ridiculousness of trying to capture the essence of the sport in words. The wonderfully unpredictable nature of football means that participants and watchers (among whom I include the media, however dispassionate they may strive to be) are often plunged into the depths of despair or propelled to great emotional heights in the space of seconds.

How to articulate and encapsulate such extremes is a task with which the most exceptional wordsmiths, men and women of the chattering classes, can struggle, even with the comparative luxury of an hour to go before deadline. Yet we expect a member of the clattering classes, or a manager whose job may have been on the line, to come up with bons mots.

In the circumstances, there is something brilliantly succinct and all-encompassing about a reply like Alex Ferguson's to the TV interviewer who collared him immediately after Manchester United turned defeat into victory in the Champions League final of 1999 with two implausibly late goals: 'Football,' he said, shaking his head and breaking into a grin. 'Bloody hell.'

Footballers do not, it is true, tend to be well educated, often having devoted themselves to the sport at the expense of academic learning before they reach puberty. Their intelligence develops in a different way from ordinary mortals, but it is there nonetheless, expressed in the humour of the dressing room, which is often scalpel-sharp and savagely witty, rather than in correct syntax or grammar. An interview with an experienced pro with a fund of anecdotes can be as entertaining as seeing a top comedian. And managers may tell you they will let their players do the talking but cannot help filling your notebook or tape.

The book was originally Peter Ball's idea. Peter, who was then my sports editor at *Time Out* and later worked for *The Guardian*, *The Observer*, *The*

Times and Dublin's *Sunday Tribune*, would literally surround himself with massive piles of newspapers and magazines. He particularly liked *Sports Illustrated*'s 'They Said It' section, which was the inspiration for the first-ever 'Quotes of the Week' column which I started in *The Independent* in 1986.

Every December, Peter and I trawled through this newsprint mountain and produced a 'Quotes of the Year' spread. A common feature nowadays, it had previously been found solely in *The Guardian*, where my late colleague Frank Keating could claim to be the father of a cottage industry.

Peter was as keen on the polished prose he found in football literature (which is often lazily or snootily dismissed as 'not as good as cricket's', despite the evidence to the contrary produced by Brian Glanville, John Moynihan, David Lacey, Paul Hayward, Henry Winter et al) as the off-the-cuff quips by the Shanklys, Dochertys, Cloughs or Atkinsons in the pre-Ferguson and pre-Mourinho era. Anything that made 'Bally' smile or snarl, whether a bizarre verbal flight or a cold, hard put-down, would make the cut.

My more anal approach to quote-collecting, which betrayed my past incarnation as a GLC clerk and librarian, entailed clipping them throughout the year instead of the annual needle-in-haystack search. We shared equal billing in what became a solo venture after Peter died of leukaemia in 1997.

The book was launched at a time when football was in decline, yet reviewers, from *The Sun* to *The Field*, were almost all positive or enthusiastic. It endured during the 'boom' years leading up to the millennium. Now, although 'bust' is always lurking like a ticket tout outside a big match, talking a good game is a more apt expression than ever. Speaking to the press (dailies, evenings, Sundays, local), and TV (satellite and terrestrial), and radio (local, national and commercial), and websites, and so on, is acknowledged as part of the job, be it the player, manager, chairman, groundsman, tea lady, supporters' representative or referee. With the advent of social media – Twitter rears its head in this edition for the first time – there has never been so much source material to choose from.

My role is to scan the myriad press interviews, homing in on anything in inverted commas. Programme columns, letters pages and the burgeoning number of books offer rich pickings, as do press conferences, commentaries and what we still call 'terrace' humour. I also look for anything pithy said about the game by pop singers, soap actors and film stars, politicians, cricketers or vicars. Having collected great carrier-bagfuls of cuttings (my typically low-tech idea of a database), the task then is to seek out quotations that will have a life beyond the week in which they appear and to juxtapose them with remarks that provide a different, perhaps ironic twist.

My preference is for the punchy one-liner that makes me chuckle or think. Profane or profound, hilarious or humbug, the best quotations have a certain rhythm to them (it did not surprise me when a football bard approached me recently about the possibility of doing a *Two Ronnies*-style routine at various literary and poetry festivals, which would draw heavily on the book).

I am invariably asked which is my favourite, but that could be any one of a couple of dozen from down the decades, depending on my mood on the day in question. I have phases where neat, finely honed epigrams seem better than anything, and others where I prefer the stream of semi-consciousness (cf. the aforementioned Mr Gould).

This book tries to cover all bases – I believe it will prove equally useful as a reference work or something to peruse while seated in the smallest room in the house – and is updated here to include everything from Jose Mourinho's endlessly provocative broadsides and Brendan Rodgers' often David Brent-like statements to the Beckhams' adventures in a faraway Galaxy plus the emergence of characters such as Mario Balotelli, Zlatan Ibrahimovic, Luis Suarez and Joey Barton, whose every throwaway comment is now newsworthy.

This, the ninth edition, combines the classics with around 2,000 new entries of comparable quality. TV scriptwriters would kill for a line like Paul Jewell's when the then Wigan Athletic manager was asked at what point he stopped fretting over relegation and started dreaming of Europe: 'After about 10 pints.'

But the book was never just about the humour of the game. There's eloquence, too, as Derek Dougan proved after serving as a pall-bearer at George Best's funeral. 'He carried us for so long. It was an honour to carry him,' said Best's former Northern Ireland team-mate, his words gaining poignancy from his own subsequent death. And there are classics of contempt; witness Sir Alex Ferguson insisting, in vain as it turned out, that he 'would not sell Real Madrid a virus, let alone Cristiano Ronaldo'.

If pushed to nominate the quotes that always make me smile, I think of three in particular. Curiously, two are by Joe Royle, who is not especially renowned as a wisecracker. Returning as a media pundit to Manchester City, where he had been manager, he was asked by the commentator for his view of the wild-child Italian striker that Roberto Mancini had signed. 'Balotelli's like Marmite – you either love him or hate him,' he replied. 'Me, I'm in between.'

Two decades earlier when Royle was manager of Oldham, his player Paul Warhurst was sent off. As we hacks clamoured for Joe's view, which we hoped would be suitably outraged, he declared, without missing a beat: 'The ref says it was for foul and abusive language, but the lad swears blind he never said anything.'

I despised Margaret Thatcher's politics, and her passing has scarcely softened my opinion, but I thank her profusely for her reply when, attending the Ipswich–Arsenal FA Cup final of 1978 as Leader of the Opposition, she was asked who her man of the match was. Not realising that there had been a programme change which meant David Geddis had played instead of Trevor Whymark, she opined with that regal authority we came to know so well: 'I thought the Ipswich number 10, Whymark, played particularly well.'

Even then, you see, the Iron Lady only had eyes for No. 10. But please, don't quote me on that.

① PLAYERS: PRESENT

EMMANUEL ADEBAYOR

I have more important issues than [Arsenal fans' hostility to him].
I was in a bus where people were shooting and I had people dying in my hands.
ADEBAYOR, Tottenham, Togo and former Arsenal striker, 2011; the Togo team coach had been attacked by gunmen

Thierry Henry came to Arsenal and he left. Cesc Fabregas came to Arsenal and he left. Why not Adebayor? I am not obliged to die at Arsenal.
ADEBAYOR, 2011

Leaving a club is the easiest thing for me to do. Especially when the club wants you out. I will just leave, as I have proved. Arsenal wanted me out. I left the club. Manchester City wanted me out. I left the club... I know everywhere I go I have the door open because I am a great footballer and a great person.
ADEBAYOR, 2011

SERGIO AGUERO

I wish I could tell you how I did it but I can't.
AGUERO, Manchester City and Argentina striker, on the stoppage-time goal v Queens Park Rangers that won the Premier League title, 2012

Sergio is a photocopy of Romario, they are the same player. He's going to be fantastic for us.
ROBERTO MANCINI, City manager, on paying Atletico Madrid £38m for Aguero, 2011; Romario was a prolific scorer for Brazil

ANDERSON

I no speak England very very good mate.

ANDERSON, Brazilian midfielder with Manchester United in an interview with MUTV, 2010

NICOLAS ANELKA

Nicolas Anelka has all my support. I consider him a brother in humanity, someone who is very courageous and for whom I have very much respect and admiration. Anelka is a descendant of slaves and if he wants to remark on this history he has the right to. We're all very proud of him doing so.
DIEUDONNE M'BALA M'BALA, French comedian, 2014; Anelka had celebrated his first goal for West Bromwich Albion with the allegedly anti-semitic 'quenelle' salute popularised by the comic

[Anelka] knew full well what he was doing when he did the 'quenelle' before the cameras, and what it meant. He may be a provocateur but he's not an imbecile. He has a real political conscience.
FREDERIC VEZARD, *editor of French sports newspaper* L'Equipe, *2014*

He has played for nearly every club in the world. It would be amazing to know how much he's moved for. He is, himself, a bank.
ARSENE WENGER, *who gave Anelka his English debut at Arsenal, 2008*

I'd compare myself to Zinedine Zidane – a humble guy who just happened to be the best.
ANELKA, 2008

I wasn't surprised Nic wanted to take Chelsea's offer. We were only paying him two dead frogs and a conker.
GARY MEGSON, *Bolton manager, 2008*

He didn't deal with the transfer business as well as he should but he was badly advised. As the boss [Arsene Wenger] said: 'He's not bad, he's just young.'
LEE DIXON, *Arsenal defender, on Anelka's exit from Highbury, 1999*

[David] Dein bought me for £500,000 and sold me for 44 times as much, so he has made a huge profit. And he still tried to block

things. This man thinks only about money.
ANELKA, 1999

I'm no longer part of Arsenal. To hell with the English people.
ANELKA, 1999

I think he's confused. He lives in a world of his own and he'll have to get out of it.
VICENTE DEL BOSQUE *as Anelka's stay at Real Madrid turned sour, 2000*

We used to have romantic nights in, watching films – with his agent. We only ever went out to Tesco. It was embarrassing – I'd get dressed up for a lovely night out and end up at the seafood counter.
BETH MOUTREY, *Anelka's ex-girlfriend, 2003*

GARETH BALE

The grass on that wing will never grow back again.
MARCA, *Spanish newspaper, on Bale's run down the left flank from his own half to score Real Madrid's late winner v Barcelona, Copa del Rey final, 2014; the headlines hailed 'Usain Bale' and 'Gareth Bolt'*

The best Premier League player? Gareth Bale, a force of nature.
PABLO ZABALETA, Manchester City and Argentina defender, on the then Tottenham and Wales player, 2013

The fee was nothing to do with me, it's between Tottenham and Real Madrid. I'd have come here for a penny.

BALE after his £85.3m world-record transfer was completed, 2013

Eighty-five million pounds is a huge amount of money. I think it's just a commercial stunt. For Real Madrid to take a British player, it's probably for sponsor-related reasons.
ARRIGO SACCHI, former Real Madrid director of football and ex-Italy coach, 2013

If we sell him, we've had it haven't we? There's not a weakness in his make-up. He can head the ball, he's as strong as an ox, he can run, dribble and shoot.
HARRY REDKNAPP, Tottenham manager, 2011

One reason he's improved so much is he's stopped messing about with his barnet.
REDKNAPP, 2010

We were at Heathrow once after a Wales Under-21 game and I said: 'Gareth, if you don't get a full cap while you're a teenager, I'm out of work because that's my job.'
BRIAN FLYNN, FA of Wales coach, 2013; Bale became Wales' youngest-ever full cap aged 16

Gaz is up there with [Cristiano] Ronaldo and [Lionel] Messi in terms of ability. Some of the things he does would make Ronaldo blush.
MICHAEL DAWSON, Tottenham defender, before his team-mate's move to Spain, 2013

He made me feel an inch tall. Took me to pieces.
MICAH RICHARDS, Manchester City and England defender, 2012

I don't go out, so I don't get attention from girls. They're not going to have posters of me on their walls. I know people my age like to go clubbing but it doesn't interest me much. I just like chilling indoors, watching DVDs or going for a meal.
BALE, 2010

MARIO BALOTELLI

Balotelli is like Marmite, you either love him or hate him. Me, I'm in between.
JOE ROYLE, former Manchester City manager, on the club's Italian striker, 2012

Why always me?
SLOGAN on a T-shirt worn beneath his City top and revealed after he scored v Manchester United, 2011

I like Balotelli. He's someone who can damage himself, the team and his opponent. He can score the winning goal then set fire to the hotel.
GORAN IVANISEVIC, retired Croatian tennis player, 2011

I don't speak to him every day. If I did I would need a psychiatrist.
ROBERTO MANCINI, City manager and fellow Italian, 2012

If you played with me 10 years ago, I give to you every day maybe one punch in your head.
MANCINI to Balotelli, 2012

When I decide to score, I score. I think I am a genius. I believe I am more intelligent than the average person. If you find another guy like me, I'll buy you dinner. The talent God gave me is beautiful, magnificent, but it's difficult to deal with because people are always ready to judge you. Only a few people have such talent, so only a few people should be able to judge what I'm doing.
BALOTELLI, 2012

I don't celebrate [after scoring] because I'm only doing my job. When a postman delivers letters does he celebrate?
BALOTELLI, as above

I used to only think of myself before, but after the red card against Arsenal I understood how important it is to worry about your team-mates. I can't leave them down to 10 men.
BALOTELLI, as above

[Manager] Roberto [Mancini] said: 'You're an idiot and I don't know why I bought you.' I hate people who say: 'Oh Mario, you played well' and then say to others: 'Mario was shit.' Roberto has never lied to me.
BALOTELLI after being sent off playing for City in Ukraine, 2010

I could write a 200-page book about my two years with Mario Balotelli at Inter. It wouldn't be a drama, but a comedy.
JOSE MOURINHO, Real Madrid and former Internazionale coach, 2012

Against Kazan in the Champions League I had all my strikers injured. I was really in trouble and Mario was the only one. Mario got a yellow card in the 42nd minute, so when I got to the dressing-room at half-time I spent about 14 minutes of the 15 available speaking only to Mario. I said: 'Mario, I cannot change you, I have no strikers on the bench, so don't touch anybody and play only with the ball. If we lose the ball, no reaction. If someone provokes you, no reaction. If the referee makes a mistake, no reaction.' What happened next? The 46th minute – red card.
MOURINHO, 2012

If someone throws a banana at me in the street, I will go to prison because I will kill him. Racism is unacceptable to me, I cannot bear it. I hope there will not be a problem at the Euros because if it does happen I would straight away leave the pitch and go home.
BALOTELLI on the threat of racism in Ukraine and Poland, European Championship finals, 2012

They didn't get angry because I was booked for taking my shirt off, but they saw my physique and got jealous.
BALOTELLI after scoring twice in Italy's semi-final win v Germany, European Championship finals, 2012

People say I should be a tutor to Mario Balotelli? Well, in that case we're in big trouble! Who is going to look after me, then?
ANTONIO CASSANO, fellow Italy striker, European Championship finals, 2012

Balotelli is just selfish. Against Germany he did two good things but in the end I saw a player who was just waiting to celebrate. Balotelli does not play for the team, only for himself. He is an egotist, who thinks the world revolves around him. Guys like Balotelli deserve lots of slaps rather than pats on the shoulder.
PAOLO DI CANIO, Italian manager of Swindon Town, 2012

REPORTER: What will you miss about England?
BALOTELLI: Nothing. Apart from the football.
REPORTER: What didn't you like?
BALOTELLI: Everything: the food, the weather, the press.
EXCHANGE when Balotelli was unveiled as an AC Milan player, 2013

I didn't sign Balotelli as a political statement but because he scored

two goals against Germany and made them cry.
SILVIO BERLUSCONI, AC Milan owner and ex-Prime Minister of Italy, 2013

Balotelli would have been carrying the bags of players such as Marco Van Basten, George Weah and Andriy Shevchenko in my day. He does not understand what it means to wear the Milan shirt. People like Marcel Desailly, Paolo Maldini and Franco Baresi would have slapped him for showing up late.
ZVONIMIR BOBAN, former Milan and Croatia player, 2013

Balotelli is an imbecile, an idiot, or at best a spoiled child full of money who lives in a world where it is difficult to distinguish good from evil.
ROSARIA CAPACCHIONE, Italian senator, after Balotelli appeared to distance himself from an anti-Mafia campaign, 2013

Balotelli's got a bit of a glass jaw, metaphorically speaking of course.
ADRIAN CHILES, ITV presenter, 2011

PHIL BARDSLEY

It's disgusting for me even to see the image for the club. It's not about going out with your friend and getting back at two or three in the morning, which is late. You can close one eye. But not full of alcohol and walking like this.
PAOLO DI CANIO, Sunderland manager, after the Scotland defender was pictured on his back in a casino, plastered with £50 notes, 2013; Bardsley denied being drunk

Always I give a second chance to the people. He is not a kid; he has a family at home. I'm not here to be a priest.
DI CANIO, as above

ROSS BARKLEY

Ross Barkley goes past players when they're not even there.
JAMIE REDKNAPP, Sky, on the Everton midfielder, 2014

JOEY BARTON

Depending on who you listen to … I'm a footballer, ex-con, ranting anti-celebrity, 'football's philosopher king', loving dad and violent thug all rolled into one.
INTRODUCTION to Barton's website, 2014

You need someone to grab people by the throat – in a nice way – and get them going.
NEIL WARNOCK, Queens Park Rangers manager, on signing Barton from Newcastle, 2011

Sitting eating sushi in the city, incredibly chilled out reading Nietzsche.
TWEET by Barton after he joined QPR, 2011

I was Labour until the Gordon Brown and Tony Blair debacle. Brown is a talentless idiot who I can't believe was running the country. I don't think the working class should be running the country and that's coming from me. I am working class. I don't like Ed Miliband either. He's a dickhead. His voice is so strange. It's like a Monty Python scene where you see the other MPs sniggering behind his back.
BARTON, 2011

Where I'm from, if you couldn't defend yourself you'd have your trainers nicked. If I went home crying that someone had hit me with their fists, I'd be told to pick up a stick, get back out and sort it.
BARTON on his upbringing in Huyton, 2011

My reputation will always precede me to the day I die. For some people, that probably can't be quickly enough.
BARTON as a Newcastle player, 2009

I thought his bum cheeks looked very pert. Nice and tight, no cellulite. If anyone's offended by that they should go and see a doctor.
IAN HOLLOWAY, Plymouth manager, after Manchester City midfielder Barton bared his backside following a game at Everton, 2006

CRAIG BELLAMY

There's no loyalty in football any more.
BELLAMY at Manchester City before joining his ninth club, Cardiff, on loan, 2010

I want to become one of the greatest managers that has ever lived. Why not?
BELLAMY, 2013

He says he's a Red but they all say that when they sign, don't they?
STEVEN GERRARD, Liverpool captain, after Bellamy's arrival, 2006

Has no one learned the lesson about signing him? If only [Liverpool manager] Rafa Benitez

had rung me, I'd have told him exactly what he was like.
ALAN SHEARER, former Newcastle team-mate, on reports that the Tyneside club might re-sign Bellamy, 2007

NICKLAS BENDTNER

I've wanted to play in pink boots since I was little. The only way anyone can top me now is to wear diamond-encrusted boots.
BENDTNER, Arsenal and Denmark striker, 2008

DIMITAR BERBATOV

I don't have the same hair, but I'll try to show the best of myself.
BERBATOV, Bulgarian striker, after transferring from Fulham to Monaco, 2014

Stay calm and pass me the ball.
SLOGAN on a T-shirt worn by Berbatov with Fulham, 2012

Lots of people tell me that I look like [actor Andy Garcia]. He has actually influenced my choice of hairstyle and I have even studied the way he smokes so I can hold my cigarette in the same way.
BERBATOV on his 'double' during his spell with Manchester United, 2009

If the ball were a woman she'd be spending all night with Berbatov.
IAN HOLLOWAY, Blackpool manager, 2009

ARTUR BORUC

He is not a bad lad. If it had said 'God bless Myra Hindley' I might have had a problem.
GORDON STRACHAN, Celtic manager, after his Polish goalkeeper incensed Rangers fans with a T-shirt saying 'God Bless the Pope', 2008

WES BROWN

The boy is the best natural defender in the country, but he's had two cruciates and a broken ankle. Everyone at the club is praying he gets a break.
SIR ALEX FERGUSON on the Manchester United and England defender, 2009

GIANLUIGI BUFFON

I say that for a sportsman, after the age of 30 you become like a dog – each year is worth seven.
BUFFON, Juventus and Italy goalkeeper, aged 35, 2013

I don't watch penalties in my hotel room. I watch naughty videos.
BUFFON 24 hours before Italy beat England in a shoot-out, European Championship finals, 2012

ANDY CARROLL

It's handy to look up and see we have that big lump up front.
JACK COLLISON, *West Ham team-mate, 2014*

I'm disappointed [that Italy beat England at Euro 2012]. You might find this hard to understand but I do feel more for England in football. And I care a lot about Andy Carroll. He's a very good-looking man.
NANCY DELL'OLIO, Italian ex-partner of Sven-Goran Eriksson, on the England striker, 2012

Hopefully Andy has only tweeted his hamstring.
SAM ALLARDYCE, West Ham manager, 2012

PETR CECH

I played my first rock festival during the summer. I was far more nervous than for any match I've ever played in.
CECH, Chelsea and Czech Republic goalkeeper, on his role as drummer with the Prague band Eddie Stoilow, 2013

LUKE CHADWICK

I remember coming on in a Champions League quarter-final against Bayern Munich. That was a nerve-wracking, incredible experience. But Tuesday is the biggest one now.
CHADWICK, former Manchester United midfielder, on achieving his 'lifetime ambition' of playing for Cambridge United (while on loan from MK Dons), 2014

The missus buys me the Cambridge kit every Christmas or my birthday. I've had it the past 10 to 15 years, so to wear one in a proper game was a great feeling.
CHADWICK, as above

PAPISS CISSE

He gets so upset when he misses a chance in training. Sometimes you will see him arguing with himself for five minutes about how he missed it.
TIM KRUL, Newcastle goalkeeper, on the club's Senegalese striker, 2012

TOM CLEVERLEY

I've been in the England set-up with Tom since the Under-21s, and he loves ketchup. He even has it on Sunday dinners. When we were told we're not allowed ketchup in the senior set-up I could see the devastation on his face.
KYLE WALKER Tottenham defender, on the Manchester United midfielder, 2012

ASHLEY COLE

I am what I am!!! Winnerrr!!!!
Hahahahahahah, 11 to me 0 for
you!!!
*COLE in a tweet directed at Arsenal fans
after helping Chelsea win the Champions
League, his 11th trophy since leaving the
north London club, 2012*

Hahahahaa, well done #fa I lied did
I, #BUNCHOFTWATS.
*COLE in a tweet about the FA finding
his colleague with club and country John
Terry guilty of racially abusing QPR's
Anton Ferdinand, 2012; Cole, a witness
in Terry's defence, later apologised*

Germaine Greer said that Cheryl
Cole isn't a feminist, as a healthy
girl is a fat-bottomed creature.
What nonsense. Cheryl does have a
big arse – he's called Ashley.
*AL MURRAY, comedian, on the BBC
TV show* Mock the Week, *2009*

Ashley Cole is getting a lot of stick,
but you'd expect that when you're
playing away from home.
*STEVE WILSON, BBC TV
commentator, on Portsmouth v Chelsea
after press reports that Cole was cheating
on his wife, 2008*

I wouldn't play for Arsenal again
even for £200,000 a week.
*COLE after the then Arsenal defender
was found to have had illegal talks with
Chelsea, 2005; six weeks later he re-signed
for Arsenal for a reported £70,000 a week*

When I heard the figure of £55k
I nearly swerved off the road.
I yelled down the phone: 'He's
taking the piss, Jonathan [Barnett,
Cole's agent].' I was so incensed, I
was trembling with anger.
*COLE on how he heard Arsenal would
not meet his demand for a wage of
£60,000 a week, from the book* My
Defence, *2006*

People think I'm a greedy pig. But
it's nothing like that. I am genuine.
I want to win things and play for the
club I'm at. It's never been about
money. For me it's about respect.
*COLE on being dubbed 'Cashley' by
Arsenal fans after joining Chelsea, 2006*

CARLTON COLE

One of his great attributes is that
he doesn't think too much.
*ROB GREEN, West Ham goalkeeper, on
his striker club-mate, 2009*

JOE COLE

I can only play for teams that
I'm passionate about and I think
that's what went wrong for me at
Liverpool. I didn't feel a connection
with the club or place that I had at
West Ham and Chelsea.
*COLE, England midfielder, during his
second spell at West Ham, 2013*

The older players all love him. When we took him to Newcastle before he broke into the side, they started singing his name as he boarded the coach.
HARRY REDKNAPP, West Ham manager, 1998

THIBAUT COURTOIS

He even saves the ones that are going wide.
ANDER HERRERA, Athletic Bilbao midfielder, on the Belgian goalkeeper loaned to Atletico Madrid from Chelsea, 2014

PETER CROUCH

What would I have been if I hadn't become a footballer? A virgin.
CROUCH, then playing for Liverpool, interviewed on Sky's Soccer AM show, 2007

Your bird's too fit for you.
SONG by Southampton fans when Crouch played for Stoke, 2014; Crouch is married to the model Abbey Clancy

He's had a lovely career for the talent he's got.
DAVID PLEAT, media summariser, 2011

I've thought about [going on Twitter] many a time, but there's a lot of people that I try to avoid in this life and they seem to be on there as well.
CROUCH as a Stoke player, 2013

Crouch has such a great touch he could bring down a shot put.

CLIVE TYLDESLEY, ITV commentator, at Liverpool v Toulouse, Champions League, 2007

A basketball player.
ARSENE WENGER, Arsenal manager, 2006

If you say you do not like Crouch that means you do not know a lot about football.
RAFAEL BENITEZ, Liverpool manager, 2005

NIGEL DE JONG

I know Nigel as a sweet guy. He doesn't want to injure anyone but to win every match. Thanks to Nigel we reached the World Cup final. And now I hear people calling him a criminal. What nonsense.
MARK VAN BOMMEL after a chest-high foul by his Netherlands team-mate, World Cup final, 2010

KEVIN DOYLE

I love Doyle. As a player, not as a man. I love women, without doubt.
GIOVANNI TRAPATTONI, Republic of Ireland manager, on Wolves' Irish striker, 2013

If anyone's seen a better centre-forward display then I'd like to see it on DVD, VHS, 8-track or Cathay Pacific.
MICK McCARTHY, Wolves manager, 2010

DIDIER DROGBA

I used to have two Drogba jerseys, one to sleep in and another for when I played in the streets with my friends. I had a poster of Didier on the ceiling above my bed. I always wore the same shoes as him. When I met Didier for the first time I was thinking: 'Wow, is he talking to me?'
ROMELU LUKAKU, Anderlecht striker, prior to joining his idol at Chelsea, 2011

Drogba's just a big lovable lump. Graham Norton seemed to get inside him last night.
CLIVE TYLDESLEY, ITV commentator, 2012

A fighter – the kind of player you could go to every war with.
JOSE MOURINHO, Chelsea manager, 2006

Drogba – the strength of a bull but the pain threshold of a lamb.

TYLDESLEY on the Ivorian striker's tendency to go to ground, 2005

Every time I got the ball I looked up and their goal seemed really far away, like it was on the M25.
DROGBA after scoring the winner for Chelsea v Barcelona, Champions League semi-final first leg, 2012

Drogba's quick and strong as an ox. I'd have said: 'Look, Didier, me old pal, don't fall over. Knock 'em over. You and me will get 80 goals a season.'
JIMMY GREAVES, former Chelsea and England forward, 2010

SAMUEL ETO'O

[Eto'o] can't write a text message or use a laptop. This isn't a lack of knowledge, it's just that he's not interested. All he thinks about is football.
OTTO PFISTER, former Cameroon coach, as the Cameroonian striker joined Chelsea, 2013

CESC FABREGAS

For every bad game I have, 10 good ones are wiped out.
FABREGAS , Barcelona and Spain midfielder, during a run of poor form, 2013

Cesc, seriously, it's minute 65 and you still haven't started running?
EDI TIBAU, Spain hockey player, tweeting during Barcelona's defeat by Bayern Munich, Champions League semi-finals, 2013

We even watched him in training. How did I do that? With a hat and moustache.

ARSENE WENGER on Arsenal's then-teenaged prodigy from Spain, 2004

RADAMEL FALCAO

My father always told me to play with my heart – and to play up front because forwards make the most money.
FALCAO, Atletico Madrid and Colombia striker, 2012; in 2013 he joined Monaco on a reported annual salary of £11.5m

MAROUANE FELLAINI

Not been great, has he? For a central midfielder at Manchester United, for £27m, I'm expecting a few goals at least. I'd be expecting a lot more, to be honest with you.
PAUL SCHOLES, Sky TV summariser and former United midfielder, on his old club's Belgian signing from Everton, 2014

RIO FERDINAND

Rio thinks he's Snoop the dog.
PAT CRERAND, ex-Manchester United player, after Ferdinand rapped at United's Premier League championship victory parade, 2013

So if u shorten words to get what u want in within 140 characters it makes u a twit?
FERDINAND tweeting on being branded the footballer with the 'most basic vocabulary', 2013

When I hear about a defender who is good on the ball, I think: 'Oh Christ.'

JACK CHARLTON, ex-England defender, when Ferdinand left West Ham for Leeds, 2000

I just can't get my head round the idea that someone has a five-year contract, and after 18 months he thinks: 'Well, that was very nice of you, thanks very much, but I want to move on.'
TERRY VENABLES, Leeds manager, before Ferdinand joined Manchester United for £29.1m, 2002

It was wicked meeting Nelson Mandela.
FERDINAND with the England squad in South Africa, 2003

I found him to be an incredible professional. If you asked me to name five players as role models, he'd be among them.
CARLOS QUEIROZ, Real Madrid and former Manchester United coach, after Ferdinand missed a drug test, 2003

Having known Rio very well, I'm sure he's not a drug-taker. But he is a forgetful lad. If he'd been caught doing drugs, I'd have said give him three years.
HARRY REDKNAPP, Portsmouth and former West Ham manager, 2003

Rio has fantastic ball skills. This, of course, is fine by us. As is the sight of his sexy, sweaty body every Saturday afternoon.
ATTITUDE, gay magazine, naming the England defender as one of its top 'fantasy' players, 1999

DIEGO FORLAN

As a boy, whenever I was with my dad, people would say: 'Look, there's Forlan's son.' That made me feel proud. Three generations of my family have been crowned South American champions with Uruguay. I don't think there's another like it in the world – it's gone down in history.
FORLAN, former Manchester United striker, whose father Pablo and grandfather Juan Carlos Corazzo also played for Uruguay, 2013

One Sally Gunnell, there's only one Sally Gunnell.
SONG by Manchester City fans as Forlan prepared to come on for United, 2004

BEN FOSTER

I enjoy playing, but when I get home I just want to switch off, chill out. I can't be bothered watching football, I don't even like talking about it. The main thing in my life is my family and my kids. I've just had builders round my house wanting to talk about football all the time, and, honestly, it does my head in.
BEN FOSTER, Birmingham and England goalkeeper, 2011

Not so long ago he was working in the kitchen as a chef, so he has the hunger.
AIDY BOOTHROYD, Watford manager on his on-loan goalkeeper, 2006

STEVEN GERRARD

I had a letter off them [Manchester United] wanting to sign me on a seven-year deal when I was 13. Sir Alex [Ferguson] tried to sign me in early 2002–03; he tried to sign me again to play for United. I obviously refused, so I can't really take it to heart. But I'm a bit gutted because I'm a big fan of his.
GERRARD after Ferguson said he was 'not a top, top player', 2013

107 caps isn't bad for someone who isn't 'a top, top player', is it?
GERRARD, 2013

[Ferguson] is probably one of the very few – if not the only one – who does not believe Steve is a top, top player. He may not have won the title but that is more because of the teams he's been in.
BRENDAN RODGERS, Liverpool manager, 2013

Gerrard has good skills, unlike normal English players.
ZLATAN IBRAHIMOVIC, Sweden striker, before Gerrard's 600th Liverpool appearance, 2012

It was so weird. Liverpool were 3–0 down at half-time, just like we were all those years ago and Steven psyched the boys up just like he did this time. We went on to win 4–3.
STEVEN MONAGHAN, teacher and coach when Gerrard led Cardinal Heenan Catholic High School to a cup final victory at 11, after the Champions League final, 2005

When I ran towards The Kop I could almost hear them saying: 'Who's this skinny little twat?'
GERRARD remembering his 1998 debut as an 18-year-old substitute, 2008

We were having breakfast at the training ground when news came that he was staying, and I spat my cornflakes out all over the table.
JAMIE CARRAGHER, Liverpool team-mate, after Gerrard ended speculation about a move to Real Madrid or Chelsea by re-signing for the club, 2005

I told him: 'Widen your horizons, leave your provincial town and come to Leeds.' I said I could only offer a grand a week and all the Yorkshire pudding he could eat. Sadly, he chose money above fame. He will never know the thrill of playing at Yeovil, Darlington and Wycombe.
KEN BATES, Leeds chairman, on meeting Gerrard in a London restaurant, 2009

RYAN GIGGS

Having a great career doesn't mean you're a great player.
ROY KEANE, former Manchester United captain, after omitting Giggs from his 'best United XI' in the ITV documentary Keane and Vieira: Best of Enemies, *2013*

I'm going to have to see what he's been eating and copy everything he's doing. He must have been very lucky with his genetics.
RIO FERDINAND, United team-mate, on Giggs at 40, 2013

I went to watch him train [as a teenager]. He was stick-thin but like nothing I had ever seen. I remember thinking: 'If that is what it takes to be a player for Man United, I may as well pack in now.'
PHIL NEVILLE, United coach and ex-player, in the documentary film Class of 92, *2013*

Viv [Anderson] was shouting: 'You can't play him, he's far too small.' Ryan gets the ball and – boom boom boom – he's gone round three of them. Viv's chasing him, can hardly breathe and he's going: 'Who the hell is that?'
SIR ALEX FERGUSON recalling the teenaged Giggs, 2013

He's an incredible human being. It's as simple as that.
FERGUSON before Giggs's 1,000th senior appearance, 2013

The most precious, skill-based player I've ever had.
FERGUSON, 2013

How I would love to adorn my team-sheet with the words 'Sir Ryan Giggs'.
FERGUSON, 2010

He's been 20 years at Old Trafford and in probably 18 of those he's been involved in championship races. It's almost like having a bath for him, a relaxing experience.
GARY NEVILLE, former United colleague, 2012

From the first time I interviewed him, he had an unwavering gaze and held your eye. For a young footballer, interviews can be unnerving but there was something intent about the way he fixed you with those dark eyes.
DAVID MEEK, former Manchester Evening News *reporter, on Giggs's 40th birthday, 2013*

I remember when I first saw him. He was 13 and he just floated over the ground like a cocker spaniel chasing a piece of silver paper in the wind.
FERGUSON, 1997

When Ryan was 13 he was the only one I felt was a certainty to make it. I remember saying to Bobby Charlton: 'You must come and see this kid.'
FERGUSON before Giggs, 33, captained Manchester United in the FA Cup final, 2007

I admire his pace and skills. I'd only look that fast if you stuck me in the 1958 FA Cup final.
RICK HOLDEN, Manchester City winger, 1993

Whatever happened to that Ryan Wilson you used to rave about?

GEORGE GRAHAM, Arsenal manager to Ferguson, 1995; Giggs's father is called Danny Wilson

The next deal will take Giggs beyond 40 and, to put it into context, if George Best had had the same kind of longevity he would have played for Ron Atkinson in the 1985 FA Cup final and, best of all, still been at the club when (Sir Alex) Ferguson took over the following year.
DANIEL TAYLOR, chief football writer, The Guardian, *2013*

He's just a dirty dog. He has no morals. It was one thing having an affair with Imogen [Thomas], but this is said to be with his brother's wife, for God's sake. I could almost understand if it was someone else, another footballer's wife – then so what? But not with his own sister-in-law. And it went on for such a

long time. It's horrendous.
JOANNA WILSON, Giggs's aunt, after claims he had an eight-year affair with his sister-in-law, 2011

I could never see myself on Twitter. If you're going to get some stick, it's going to affect you.
GIGGS, 2013

OLIVIER GIROUD

I've got a tattoo on my right arm from a Psalm in Latin [*Dominus regit me et nihil mihi deerit* – The Lord's my shepherd; I shall not want]. I'm a believer. I don't cross myself before games, but I do say a little prayer.
GIROUD, Arsenal and France striker, 2012

I apologise to my wife, family and friends and my manager, team-mates and Arsenal fans. I now have to fight for my family and for my club and obtain their forgiveness. Nothing else matters at the moment.
GIROUD after admitting that a tabloid story alleging a 'hotel romp' with a model the night before a Premier League game – which he originally denied – contained some truth, 2014

ROB GREEN

REPORTER: How can Rob Green get over a mistake like that?

TIM HOWARD (USA goalkeeper): A lot of alcohol.
EXCHANGE after the England goalkeeper's error gifted the Americans a goal, World Cup finals, 2010

JOE HART

Joe Hart made a few mistakes around Christmas time and got crucified for them.
JOE CORRIGAN, former Manchester City and England goalkeeper, 2013

Hart looked very confident with himself, so I thought we had to bring him down a peg or two.
ANDREA PIRLO, Italy playmaker, after beating the City and England goalkeeper with a penalty chipped down the centre of goal in the shoot-out win v England, European Championship finals, 2012

Joe Hart is there to be shot at.
DAVE BEASANT, former England goalkeeper, 2013

EDEN HAZARD

Hazard's only crime is he hasn't kicked him hard enough.
JOEY BARTON, Queens Park Rangers midfielder, on Twitter after Chelsea's Belgian midfielder Hazard kicked a 17-year-old ball-boy who lay on the ball to waste time during a Capital One Cup semi-final v Swansea, 2013

To me it was a lot of money. He's a good player, but £34m? [Manchester United] placed a value on him that was well below what they were talking about.
SIR ALEX FERGUSON after Chelsea bought Hazard from Lille, 2012

THIERRY HENRY

Henry plays like he's a Brazilian.
ROBERTO CARLOS, Real Madrid and Brazil defender, 2004

I have to kick a ball around the home. Even in the narrow corridor at my house, I'm always trying to dribble past my friends. I once broke a glass but one breakage in five years isn't bad.
HENRY, 2003

Stubborn, committed, honest – maybe a bit too much. Arrogant? Maybe, I don't know. Sometimes, when you are honest with people, they say you're a bit up yourself.
HENRY describing himself, 2004

I've never thought of myself as a star. The word disturbs me.
HENRY after his Barcelona debut, 2007

GRANT HOLT

The lads have nicknamed him Horse but I'm not going into details.
BRYAN GUNN, Norwich manager, on signing the striker from Shrewsbury, 2009

TIM HOWARD

I think I've gained most of my strength from the beard.
HOWARD, Everton and United States goalkeeper, on the secret behind saving an Aston Villa penalty, 2013

ZLATAN IBRAHIMOVIC

REPORTER: How did it feel to score such a great goal with your weaker foot?
IBRAHIMOVIC: I don't have a weaker foot.
EXCHANGE after the Swede's goal for PSG v Bayer Leverkusen, 2014

For me it was probably the last attempt to reach the World Cup with the national team. One thing for sure, a World Cup without me is nothing to watch.
IBRAHIMOVIC, Paris St-Germain and Sweden striker, after defeat by Portugal in a World Cup play-off, 2013

I don't give a shit who wins it now. I'm going on holiday.
IBRAHIMOVIC after Sweden's exit from the European Championship finals, 2012

After a perfectly normal challenge Ibra turned to me and provoked me. He made a joke about my moustache, saying: 'That really is terrible.' I responded by saying he should think about his nose.
SACHA KLJESTAN, Anderlecht player, 2013

You're just a shit Andy Carroll.
SONG by England fans to Ibrahimovic before the striker's four-goal demolition of Roy Hodgson's side, 2012

That's the way it is with the English: if you score against them you're a good player, if you don't, you're not. I remember Lionel Messi before the 2009 Champions League final. Then he scored against Manchester United and suddenly he was the best player in the world. Maybe now they'll say something like that about me.
IBRAHIMOVIC, 2012

Good grief, he's the most overrated player on the planet.
MARTIN O'NEILL, shortly to become Aston Villa manager, as a BBC TV pundit, World Cup finals, 2006

I wasn't hungry, I was very hungry. I stole many bikes. I also stole cars. That was how we got by. We did those things on adrenalin, motivation. I came from Rosengard. In Sweden it's considered a ghetto, but for me it was paradise.
IBRAHIMOVIC, 2013

ANDRES INIESTA

Andres doesn't dye his hair, doesn't wear ear-rings and hasn't got tattoos. That may make him unattractive to the media, but he's the best.
PEP GUARDIOLA, Barcelona coach, on the Spain midfielder, 2009

ANDY JOHNSON

You only need to breathe on Andy for him to go down.
NEIL WARNOCK, former Sheffield United manager, in Made In Sheffield, *2007*

KAKA

We made an offer to Milan for Kaka and it was turned down. We offered them Stoke-on-Trent.
TONY PULIS, Stoke City manager, 2009

I belong to Jesus
SLOGAN on the Brazilian's undershirt after he helped Milan beat Liverpool, Champions League final, 2007

ROBBIE KEANE

Well, family-tree aficionados will be aware that Robbie and I share the same Irish blood; his late grandfather [Thomas Nolan] being my own father's cousin. In filial terms the Irish blood, English heart genetic between Robbie and I is evident – his chin is my chin, my chin is his. Robbie was raised on Captains Road (as was my mother) in Crumlin (Dublin), before he was shipped out to Tallaght. He is a gentleman of the highest caliber (or, if you must, calibre), and to watch him on the pitch – pacing like a lion, as weightless as an astronaut – is pure therapy. Robbie, the pleasure, the privilege is mine.
MORRISSEY, singer-songwriter, after watching the Republic of Ireland striker play for LA Galaxy, 2013

PADDY KENNY

Paddy was in the wrong place at the wrong time. Judging by the photos he was also with someone hungrier than him.
NEIL WARNOCK, Sheffield United manager, after his goalkeeper's eyebrow was bitten off in a fight at Ziggy's Curry House in Halifax, 2007

VINCENT KOMPANY

[Winning the Premier League] is an incredible feeling, up there with the best feelings I've ever experienced. To be politically correct I have to say up there with the birth of my daughter and my wedding.
KOMPANY, Manchester City and Belgium captain, on the club's first championship in 44 years, 2012

Struggling to remember what happened. Woke up with a medal around my neck. Been told the party was deeecent! Memo to myself: Next time you're champion, drink less, dance more.
KOMPANY tweeting about City's championship party, 2012

RICKIE LAMBERT

I couldn't get a club anywhere, I was training at Macclesfield without a contract and I had no money so I had to earn some by working in a factory. It was a beetroot factory, screwing lids on jars. I don't even like beetroot.
LAMBERT, Southampton and soon-to-be England striker, on his early career after being freed by Blackpool, 2013

FRANK LAMPARD

I would love to get to the stage where I can actually write the whole book myself.
LAMPARD, Chelsea and England midfielder, on the publication of his first children's book, Frankie vs The Pirate Pillagers, 2013

There are very few midfielders today who can play 130 Premiership matches in a row. But there are freaks and that's freakish.
SIR ALEX FERGUSON, Manchester United manager, on Lampard's 'amazing statistic', 2005

I told my players Frank Lampard has got 17 goals from midfield this season, but they just said: 'Perhaps that's why he's on 150 grand a week.'
HARRY REDKNAPP, Portsmouth manager, 2007

DAVID LUIZ

It was like he was being controlled by a 10-year-old on a PlayStation.
GARY NEVILLE, Sky TV pundit, on the Chelsea and Brazil defender, 2011

Gary Neville say bad, other people say good. When he say this, [he] don't respect me. The stats show I am up there among the best.
LUIZ, 2011

ROMELU LUKAKU

So, Romelu Lukaku, you speak six languages. Which ones? Obviously, there's Belgian.
PAT MURPHY, Radio 5Live reporter, interviewing the then West Bromwich Albion and Belgium striker, 2013

I go to school three or four days a week. The rest I do at home. I'm doing a two-year High School diploma in tourism and public relations. I want to prove to other people that I have something in my mind and intellectual qualities, not just the ability to play football.
LUKAKU, then an 18-year-old striker with Brussels club Anderlecht, 2011

FLORENT MALOUDA

You're powerless to do anything sitting in the stands. You've got fleas in your pants.
MALOUDA, Chelsea and France midfielder, on being left out of the national side, 2009

JUAN MATA

I'm really happy you're here but a bit sad too. Now I'm only the second best left-footer here.
RYAN GIGGS welcoming Mata to Manchester United after the Spaniard's switch from Chelsea, 2014

GARY MEDEL

For my own sake, it's a good job that I chose football. If not, perhaps I'd be stealing or drug-trafficking.
MEDEL, Chile international who later joined Cardiff, 2010

PER MERTESACKER

He looks like he's pulling an old fridge when he runs.

MARK LAWRENSON, BBC pundit, on Arsenal's German defender, 2013

The Germans do well economically and we respect that. They are the only ones that make money in Europe. That's why we've chosen a German.
ARSENE WENGER on why Mertesacker was deputed to collect fines from Arsenal players for breaches of club discipline, 2013

LIONEL MESSI

[Messi] isn't handsome, but he has an interesting gaze and is very charismatic. The only reason I'd give up politics would be if he asked me to marry him.
RACHIDA DATI, French Member of the European Parliament, 2013

I'm sorry for those that want to sit on his throne, but this lad is the best.
PEP GUARDIOLA, Barcelona coach, after the Argentinian striker broke Barcelona's all-time scoring record at the age of 24, 2012

Messi wins the ball playing as the false No. 9. If you put him at left-back, he would be just as good. He's the best defender in the world.
GUARDIOLA, Bayern Munich coach, 2013

Messi is the only player better in real life than on PlayStation. With his goals, work, assists, playing football like one does in the playground, he is the number one.
MUNDO DEPORTIVO, *Barcelona-based sports newspaper, 2012*

It's as if someone controls him from the stands, like a video game. I have never seen a human run with the ball at that speed.
MIKEL ARTETA, Everton midfielder, 2011

Every time [Messi] grabs the ball and accelerates I see Maradona. We must protect him. I'd personally put him in a drawer of my bedside table.
JUAN SEBASTIAN VERON, former Argentina midfielder, 2011

I am more worried about being a good person than being the best football player in the world. When all this is over, what are you left with?
MESSI, Barcelona and Argentina striker, 2012

More than anything, I love playing football. And it's been like that since I was very young. It's not something that feels like a job. It still feels like fun, like it did when I was a very small boy.
MESSI, 2010

You know where Messi was at this time last year? He was being eliminated in the Copa America, in his own country. I think that's worse, no?
CRISTIANO RONALDO on Denmark fans' chant of 'Messi! Messi!' during the game v Portugal, 2012

PEPE: Every time I mark you, you shit yourself.
MESSI: Every time you mark me, I score.
EXCHANGE between Real Madrid's Pepe and Messi in the 'Clasico' as reported in The Independent, *2014; Messi scored a hat-trick*

We always have problems with each other. You know what bothers me so? That tone with which he always says, 'negro, negro'. I understand that 'negro' is very common in South America, but we cannot stand it.
ROYSTON DRENTHE, black Dutch midfielder with Real Madrid, 2012

On TV he looks very quick but in life he is quicker than he is on TV. Sometimes you watch it and say: 'Yes, that was good but the defender can do more.' But when you're live, on the pitch, he is so, so quick. There really is nothing you can do.
FABRICIO COLOCCINI, Newcastle defender, who played with Messi for Argentina and against him in Spanish football, 2012

Messi is unique, the best player in the history of the sport. He has been touched by a magic wand.
JAVIER MASCHERANO, Argentina team-mate, 2012

When Leo Messi approaches you, you have to make the sign of the cross and pray everything will be all right.
THIAGO SILVA, AC Milan defender, 2012

To be this close to him, playing against him, we felt like we were in a movie.

VACLAV PILAR, Viktoria Plzen (Czech Republic) winger, 2011

You might say we've got no out-and-out attacking player, but Luke Freeman and Lionel Messi are a similar type of player and you wouldn't accuse Barcelona of playing without an attacking threat.
GRAHAM WESTLEY, Stevenage manager, after a 0–0 draw v Tranmere, 2013

How do you say 'cheating' in Catalan? Can Messi be suspended for acting? Barcelona is a cultural city with many great theatres and this boy has learned play-acting very well.
JOSE MOURINHO, Chelsea manager, after facing Barcelona, 2006

I owe Barcelona everything because they paid for my growth-hormone treatment.

MESSI, 2007; he was below average weight and height on arrival in Catalonia

ANNE ROBINSON: The Barcelona footballer who won the Ballon d'Or in 2010 for the world's best player is Lionel who?
CONTESTANT: Richie.
EXCHANGE on The Weakest Link, 2011

RAVEL MORRISON

I would pay to watch him train, let alone play in a match. He was taking the mick out of everyone on the pitch when he was about 14.
RIO FERDINAND, Manchester United and England defender, on the United striker who went on to join West Ham and Queens Park Rangers, 2013

VICTOR MOSES

You don't see many players like him. Charles N'Zogbia is one, [Lionel] Messi is another.
ROBERTO MARTINEZ, Wigan manager, on the club's former Crystal Palace winger, 2012

SAMIR NASRI

I'd like to give him a punch, because a player like him should play like this always.
ROBERTO MANCINI, Manchester City manager, lamenting the inconsistency of City's France midfielder after his outstanding display v Newcastle, 2013

I've not had a good season, I know it, and I'm the first to be self-critical. But I think the coach still doesn't handle English very well and sometimes uses expressions that aren't really suitable.
NASRI on Mancini's remarks, 2013

I think he goes missing in big games for City – and he's the only one. He doesn't put a shift in. I played against Nasri three or four years ago at the Emirates – he pulled my pants down for 60 minutes and I got subbed because he absolutely battered me. This is a player you'll see when the 'olés' are coming out, but not when the going gets tough.
GARY NEVILLE, Sky pundit and ex-Manchester United defender, 2012

NEYMAR

Now everyone's talking about Messi, and he's a star. But [to be the best] he must first become better than Neymar. At the moment Messi is just more experienced.
PELE on his latest successor in Brazil's attack, 2012

Neymar reminds me of Mane [Garrincha]. I see him emerging with the same tricks, the same dribbles. Not to the extent of Mane, because I've never seen anybody give the people as much happiness as he did. But Neymar is producing beautiful, happy, gracious football. It's football art, and he has it mastered.
ELZA SOARES, Brazilian samba singer and ex-wife of two-time World Cup winner Garrincha, on the soon-to-be Barcelona striker, 2012

Neymar is the Justin Bieber of football. Brilliant on the old YouTube. Cat piss in reality. Stop going on about goals in Brazil Lge as well. I once scored 77 in 1 season in the Rainhill and Byrne u14 league and that's a stronger comp.

JOEY BARTON, Queens Park Rangers midfielder, on Twitter, 2013

JOHN O'SHEA

I nut-megged Luis Figo

SLOGAN on T-shirt sent to O'Shea by a Manchester United fan after the defender played the ball through the Real Madrid star's legs, 2003

MESUT OZIL

I would have loved to have played with him. It seems like he's playing on his own in his garden.

THIERRY HENRY, former Arsenal striker, on the club's new £42m Germany midfielder, 2013

Ozil is a bit better at dribbling than Zidane was. They have a similar form of technical ease and similar humility. Ozil also has a special quality: he always takes the right decision quickly.

ARSENE WENGER, Arsenal manager, 2013

On one hand he has a German mentality as evidenced by his discipline, his respect, his willingness to learn and the way he works with his team-mates. But he also possesses, through his Turkish mentality, creativity, dynamism, and technique.

JOSE MOURINHO, Real Madrid coach, when Ozil played for the Spanish club, 2011

They make fun of [Ozil], saying: 'Look, your father's coming' or 'Mister, your son's here'. Others say things like 'Your son's much more handsome than Ozil and you'd never have a son as ugly as Mesut.'

MOURINHO on the 'affectionate' taunts of Real players after Ozil described him as a 'father figure', 2011

GERARD PIQUE

I was 13, 14. [Barcelona coach Louis] Van Gaal was coming over for a meal, and he was the Barca manager for God's sake! I thought to myself: 'In three or four years I'd like to play for them,' and I wanted to impress him. But he brushed me aside and I fell over. I felt devastated. I didn't say a damn word for the rest of the meal.

PIQUE, Barcelona and Spain defender whose grandfather was a former Barcelona director, 2013

ANDREA PIRLO

Pirlo has the face of an angel, but he is a son of a bitch! He's always making jokes, always breaking the rules. One time when I was eating at the training ground, I had the bright idea of leaving my phone on the table. He sent a text message from it to [vice-president Adriano] Galliani and [director of sport Ariedo] Braida offering them my sister.
GENNARO GATTUSO, former Milan and Italy team-mate, 2013

I lifted my eyes to the heavens and asked for help because if God exists, there's no way he's French. I took a long, intense breath. That breath was mine, but it could have been the manual worker who struggles to make it to the end of the month, the rich businessman who is a bit of a shit, the teacher, the student... the well-to-do Milanese signora, the hooker on the street corner. In that moment, I was all of them.
PIRLO on taking the first penalty in the shoot-out that decided the 2006 World Cup final, France v Italy, in I Think Therefore I Play, *2014*

Why, for the life of me, hasn't Pirlo played in England? Is he just homophobic? Is he Italian through and through and doesn't want to leave?
PHIL BROWN, former Hull manager, working as a media pundit, 2012

LOIC REMY

Remy looked like he might be getting over that groin strain. He showed a few flashes.
HARRY REDKNAPP, Queens Park Rangers manager, on the France striker, 2013

MICAH RICHARDS

I'm getting to that age where I'm not 18 any more.
RICHARDS, 26-year-old Manchester City and England defender, 2013

ARJEN ROBBEN

I would never wear leggings like Robben. I'm never cold. I'm hot-blooded – my wife says so. We always sleep spooning.
LOUIS VAN GAAL, Bayern Munich coach, on the Dutch winger's habit of wearing leggings in winter, 2011

ROBINHO

I did a joke about [Brazil striker] Robinho and he laughed. I thought 'oh, that's nice'. I met him afterwards and he didn't speak a word of English, so I said to his interpreter: 'How come he laughed

at that joke?' And he said: 'He just heard his name, so he was being polite.'
JASON MANFORD, comedian and Manchester City fan, on doing a show for the club's players, 2010

PAUL ROBINSON

I thought: 'That's a sweet connection, I never even felt it touch my foot.' Then I looked round and it's in the back of the net.

ROBINSON, England goalkeeper, on missing his kick to concede an own goal by Gary Neville v Croatia, 2006

RONALDINHO

Ronaldinho does incredible things in training. One day they'll come off in a match and the stadium will collapse.
LUIS GARCIA, Liverpool player and former Barcelona colleague, 2004

Ronaldinho is the kind of player who makes kids dream. They're not going to walk around with [Marcel] Desailly or [Didier] Deschamps on their shirts, are they?
ERIC CANTONA, 2005

CRISTIANO RONALDO

People boo me because I'm rich, good-looking and a great player.
RONALDO at Real Madrid, 2013

As a boy he would get angry and cry easily if other boys didn't pass him the ball, or because they did not play as he wanted. They called him cry-baby.
DOLORES AVEIRO, Ronaldo's mother, 2013

If I could, I'd vote for myself. I am what I am, and I'm happy with that. Being too humble isn't good. In Portugal we say that too much humility is vanity.
RONALDO on the Ballon d'Or, the award for the World Footballer of the Year, which he won, 2013

The only bad thing about Ronaldo's life is [Lionel] Messi. But for him, he would have been the best player in the world for five years in a row now.
LUIZ FELIPE SCOLARI, Brazil and former Portugal coach, 2012

He always begins the game like he hasn't played football for three days.

ARSENE WENGER, Arsenal manager, 2012

He'd have loads of little sayings. 'Manchester, it's raining all the time,' he used to say, but he loved being here, though he knew he was on a journey and he knew it was going to take him somewhere else.
MIKE CLEGG, former Manchester United power-development coach, 2014

Hunger will lead a fox out of the forest. But will he have the desire to take the tournament by the scruff of the neck? A strutting peacock or a striding colossus?
JONATHAN PEARCE, BBC TV commentator, on Ronaldo, European Championship finals, 2012

He's six-foot something, fit as a flea, good-looking…he's got to have something wrong with him. Hopefully he's hung like a hamster. That would make us all feel better. Having said that, my missus has got a pet hamster at home and his cock's massive.
IAN HOLLOWAY, Leicester manager, 2009

I bet [Ronaldo] he wouldn't get 17 League goals and I'm going to have to change my bet with him. If he gets to 15 I can change it – I'm allowed to do that because I'm the manager. I'm going to make it 150 now.
SIR ALEX FERGUSON, 2006

For me the sight of the red London buses is what my first thoughts of England were. My nieces and nephews would love to play on one, so I'm going to buy one for them.
RONALDO, 2009

Ronaldo very rarely never gets a cross in.
MARK LAWRENSON, BBC TV summariser, 2012

There have been a few players described as the new George Best over the years, but this is the first time it's been a compliment to me.
GEORGE BEST, 2004

When they get back to Man United's training ground, I wouldn't be surprised if Wayne Rooney doesn't stick one on him.
ALAN SHEARER, BBC TV pundit, on Ronaldo's apparent role in Rooney's dismissal playing for England v Portugal, World Cup finals, 2006

Maybe it's a difficult childhood, no education.
JOSE MOURINHO, Chelsea manager, alleging a lack of maturity in his compatriot, 2007

It's really below the belt to bring class into it. Ronaldo has principles, which is why he hasn't responded. Other people are educated but have no principles.
SIR ALEX FERGUSON defends his player, 2007

Cristiano is the only one with a personal mirror in the dressing room. He spends hours doing his hair and putting on his gel.

PATRICE EVRA, United team-mate, 2007

WAYNE ROONEY

Every now and then, when I tried to explain tactics, things didn't work out. Maybe it's because Rooney doesn't speak English.
He doesn't understand English. I think Rooney understands only Scottish. That's because he plays well only in Manchester, where Sir Alex Ferguson speaks Scottish.
FABIO CAPELLO, former England manager, 2012

When we signed him at 18, everyone said: 'What will he be like at 21?' Now he's 21, people are saying: 'What will he be like at 25?' It was always destined to be that way.
SIR ALEX FERGUSON, 2006

I think the people who are calling him thick have got a certain element of thickness about them.
FRANK LAMPARD, England team-mate, 2010

Now I have someone to look after and I just want to be with Kai and Coleen as much as possible. Becoming a dad means you have to be a role model for your son and be someone he can look up to.
ROONEY, when his first son was six months old, 2010

Just to confirm to all my followers I have had a hair transplant. I was going bald at 25, why not?
ROONEY on Twitter, 2011

A boy from Croxteth should not use hair product.
JAMIE CARRAGHER, ITV pundit and Liverpool defender, on the Rooney 'rug', 2012

I don't want Rooney to leave these shores but if he does, I think he'll go abroad.
IAN WRIGHT, former Arsenal and England striker, 2012

I got on stage and said: 'I don't know if you know this, Wayne, but the only reason I've agreed to play this fucking gig tonight is if you change your nationality to Welsh and you sign for Leeds. So until you sign this contract here, I'm not playing a fucking note.' He got me a glass of wine and reminded me how much I was being paid. I thought 'fair dos' and just got on with the bloody show.
KELLY JONES, Stereophonics singer, on playing at the reception after Rooney married Coleen McLoughlin, 2008.

I had two obsessions [as a child] – football and Ninja Turtles... We copied [the Ninja moves] off the TV until we got them perfect and if anybody else wanted to be Raphael I used to sit on them until they gave in. I rated Raphael up there alongside Alan Shearer.
ROONEY quoted in England's Hero *by Sue Evison, 2004*

I asked their manager, Big Neville: 'Who's the little fella?' He looked at me and groaned: 'We've only just signed him. Leave him alone.' I said: 'Leave him alone? You must be joking.'
BOB PENDLETON, Everton scout, on how he spotted Rooney playing for Copplehouse Juniors in the Walton & Kirkdale Junior League, 2003

I came home and said to my dad: 'Are we Irish?' 'How do I know?' he replied.
ROONEY in My Story So Far, *2006*

We have to look after Wayne and that includes every Evertonian. If you see him out in the street, send him home. Sir Alex Ferguson used to offer £100 to anyone telling him where his young stars were. I might do the same.
DAVID MOYES, Everton manager, 2002

I suspect he hasn't had many positive experiences with older male figures. I want him to turn 30 and be able to say to himself: 'David Moyes was all right for me.'
MOYES, 2003

One of the last street footballers, part of a dying breed.
MOYES, 2003

My old mate Colin Harvey, who coaches the kids at Everton, is not one to go overboard. He described Kenny Dalglish as 'all right', but Rooney as 'a good player'.
PETER REID, Leeds United caretaker manager, 2003

If [Rooney] thinks he's got pressure now, things are going to get 10 times worse.
GEORGE BEST, 2003

After that incredible first goal [for Everton] against Arsenal, when Arsene Wenger was talking to the world's media about his special talent, Wayne was already out on his BMX bike, meeting his mates outside the local chip shop. He even ended up kicking a ball against a wall with them.
PAUL STRETFORD, Rooney's agent, 2003

It's hard for a Scotsman to say, but I was supporting England. And when Wayne nearly scored, I jumped out of my seat.
DAVID MOYES after Rooney's full debut for England v Turkey, 2003

Wayne's the antithesis of Beckham. He'll never wear a sarong out in Liverpool, for example.

DAVE BARRACLOUGH, designer of Rooney's clothing line, 2004

He's incredible – I don't remember anyone making such an impact on a tournament since Pele in 1958.
SVEN-GORAN ERIKSSON, Rooney's manager with England, at the European Championship finals, 2004

When I scored my first goal for England, I was so excited I didn't know what to do or where to run. David [Beckham] just pointed and said: 'Well, the England fans are that way, mate.'
ROONEY, 2004

I sat next to Rebekah Wade [editor of *The Sun*] at a party for Max Clifford's birthday and we were discussing Hillsborough. She didn't know much about it, and why should she? Wayne Rooney at 18 ought to know more because there isn't a footballing kid of 18 in Liverpool that doesn't know exactly what happened at Hillsborough.
DEREK HATTON, broadcaster, Everton fan and former Liverpool councillor, after Rooney sold his 'story' to The Sun, *2004*

Once a Blue, Always a Blue
SLOGAN on T-shirt worn by Rooney beneath his Everton top after scoring in the FA Youth Cup final, 2002

Once a Blue, Always a Red
SLOGAN on T-shirts on sale outside Old Trafford, 2007

DAVID SILVA

David is the one who makes us play better. He's the one who has everything.
PABLO ZABALETA, Manchester City colleague, on the Spain midfielder, 2014

THOMAS SORENSEN

I'm just as good as Peter Schmeichel, but I'm more modest by nature.
SORENSEN, Sunderland and Denmark goalkeeper, 2000

DANIEL STURRIDGE

He has said he wants to play football for a big club. The stage is set for him. There will be no excuses for him.
STEVEN GERRARD, Liverpool and England captain, after the widely travelled striker moved to Anfield, 2013

When you're a kid you dream of playing until your mum calls you in and you can't play any longer. People think I chased the money because I have played for big clubs in [Manchester] City and Chelsea. I always chased the opportunity to play.
STURRIDGE, Liverpool and England striker, 2014

LUIS SUAREZ

I have sacrificed so much to be where I am and fought so hard for it. I can't conceive of anyone wasting even five minutes in a game. I can't bear the idea of not trying to make the most of every single second. There are only three million people in Uruguay but there is such hunger for glory: you'll do anything to make it, you have that extra desire to run, to suffer. I can't explain our success but I think that's a reason.
SUAREZ, Liverpool and Uruguay striker, 2012

You have to have balls to do what Luis did. He followed his principles. We live in a democracy, and if you don't want to greet someone you don't do it, and less so if that person has made you experience some bad moments.
DIEGO LUGANO, Uruguay captain, on Suarez's refusal to shake hands with Patrice Evra after he was ruled to have racially abused the Manchester United player, 2012

It's a huge honour to wear No. 7 at Liverpool. I think about the legends: Dalglish, Keegan and that Australian guy.
SUAREZ, 2011

[Suarez] bit someone. It happens. I'm sure he'll make amends with this guy. I made amends with Evander [Holyfield] and we got on with our lives.

MIKE TYSON, former world heavyweight boxing champion, after Suarez bit Chelsea's Branislav Ivanovic, 2013

There is no precedent for what Suarez did, other than he's done it before.

DANNY MILLS, Radio 5Live analyst, 2013

You can never be called a great player when your behaviour is like that. Our idea is to help the perception of Luis Suarez from a world-class player to a truly great one.

BRENDAN RODGERS, Liverpool manager, after Suarez bit Ivanovic, 2013

At least Suarez showed some energy and appetite.

JAMIE REDKNAPP, Sky analyst and ex-Liverpool player, after the biting incident, 2013

I made my own views clear just as a dad watching the game. I've got a seven-year-old son who just loves watching football and when players behave like this it just sets the most appalling example to young people in our country.

DAVID CAMERON MP, Conservative Prime Minister, on Suarez's subsequent 10-game ban, 2013

I would give my soul every time I step on the pitch [for Real Madrid]. I have done this with Uruguay, Ajax and Liverpool. I always walk off the pitch having given everything. A player always aspires to be at the top of their profession and Madrid is at the top for any footballer.

SUAREZ on Real Madrid's reported interest, 2013

Maybe it's because I don't speak English or something.

SUAREZ pondering why Liverpool's young players do not ask him for advice, 2012

In the way he likes playing football, he sometimes has the mentality of a child.

HENK VELDMATE, coach to Dutch club Groningen in 2006 when they signed Suarez from Uruguayan football, 2013

Managing against him last year [with Swansea] he was one of the players I thought: 'You need to be careful of this little bugger.'

BRENDAN RODGERS on Suarez, 2012

ADEL TAARABT

Being a Muslim has had a big impact on my career. We don't drink alcohol or smoke, so essentially we've become healthier, more professional footballers because of our lifestyle. Before every game, I perform salat [prayer]. Without it, I just don't feel confident. I make sure I pray after a match, too – to give thanks for the stamina and strength God graced me with.
TAARABT, Queens Park Rangers and Morocco midfielder, 2010

JOHN TERRY

Improbable, implausible and contrived.
FA VERDICT on the Chelsea and England captain's defence against allegations that he racially abused Queens Park Rangers' Anton Ferdinand, 2012

Three vile words muttered by Terry at Loftus Road ultimately removed Fabio Capello from the England manager's job; inflicted much distress on the Ferdinand family; brought a £45,000 fine for Rio Ferdinand for his endorsement of a 'choc ice' tweet aimed at Chelsea's left-back; removed Terry from the England reckoning and shed yet more light on the fantasy world of Ashley Cole.
PAUL HAYWARD, Daily Telegraph chief sports writer, 2012

How can you call me a cunt? You shagged your team-mate's missus. You're the cunt.
ANTON FERDINAND to Terry during the QPR v Chelsea match, 2012

If someone calls you a cunt that's fine, but if somebody puts your colour into it, it takes it to another level. It's very hurtful.
ANTON FERDINAND in court for the trial, 2012

My mum dated a guy from Liverpool for a while. The Liverpool fans made up a song that my mum 'loves Scouse cock'.
TERRY in court, on the abuse players routinely receive, 2012

Thanks football, you set the entire country back a decade. 'Black c*nt' now officially ok to say.
JOHN AMAECHI, black former NBA basketball player, tweeting after Terry was found not guilty in court, 2012

Say no more about the UK justice system then. May as well go behave how we want, people. May as well go rob a bank and when I get caught just say it was only banter and they started it by calling me names.
CAMERON JEROME, black Stoke City striker, on Twitter after the Terry trial verdict, 2012

The way Terry played against Germany, if I was Terry, I wouldn't be able to go back to my country.
MARTIN DEMICHELIS, Bayern

Munich and Argentina defender, World Cup finals, 2010

We've lost hundreds of soldiers [in Iraq], 100,000 people have been killed and nobody in this country gives a toss. Yet John Terry sleeps with some bird and everyone's up in arms.
JIMMY GREAVES, former England striker, after Terry allegedly slept with the partner of club-mate Wayne Bridge, 2010

I made a speech before the game at Middlesbrough in the dressing-room and afterwards John Terry said: 'Now you are a man.' If John Terry says I am now a man then I am a man.
JOHN OBI MIKEL, Chelsea and Nigeria midfielder, 2008

Gary Cahill asked me: 'Did you mean it?' I definitely meaned it.
TERRY, 2014

OSCAR: What was your favourite toy when you were little?
JOHN TERRY: Ooh... It's quite embarrassing actually. I had a little teddy bear called Gordon the Gopher. I took him to bed with me 'cos he was my favourite.

EXCHANGE in an interview between Terry and a five-year-old boy in the Guardian Weekend *magazine.*

CARLOS TEVEZ

Carlitos is amazing. He does what he wants with the Arabs. He tells them 'I want to go to Buenos Aires' and they say 'No, stay here now, we'll give you more money.' Then he gets more money!
DIEGO MARADONA, Argentina coach, on Tevez's relationship with Manchester City's Abu Dhabi-based owners, 2010

I never saw [Tevez] as volatile. I can't think of one incident where there were flashpoints with Carlos. That's not to say it wouldn't have happened. Actually, I take that back because it would never have happened on my watch.
MARK HUGHES, ex-Manchester City manager, after Tevez allegedly refused to warm up at Bayern Munich, 2011

mcfc statement re no chips at halftime v Newcastle: 'The chips were put in the fryers but refused to warm up.'
IAN CHEESEMAN, BBC Radio Manchester commentator, tweeting after City announced 'no chips on sale in the concourse' at a game soon after the Munich incident, 2011

He's a mercenary. You can't really back him. Sure, I'm a hoodlum, I've got into scrapes – but Tevez is someone who in the last six months has gone on strike, gone off to Argentina to play golf, tried to get himself sacked. If that's not the epitome of what's wrong with modern players, I don't know what is.
JOEY BARTON, Queens Park Rangers and former City midfielder, 2012

Carlos Tevez's English should be better that what it is.

GRAHAM TAYLOR, Radio 5Live summariser, 2010

FERNANDO TORRES

Romanticism is over in football.
TORRES, Spain striker, on leaving Liverpool for Chelsea, 2011

Loyalty in football has changed. Players kiss the badge but the reality is that you do as well as you can and then you move on. You can't get too attached to any club.
TORRES, 2011

In my time at Liverpool there were games where I would not be playing well or I would be doing nothing, but every time I touched the ball I scored. It's such a strange feeling because physically I'm feeling better than ever, but I'm not finding the chances. Even when I do, I cannot score.
TORRES after three goals in 34 games in a year for Chelsea, 2012

Torres scored three but otherwise I kept him pretty quiet.
MICHAEL DUBERRY, Reading defender, after defeat by Liverpool, 2008

YAYA TOURE

I asked him who Chelsea were worried about and he said three words: Yaya Toure.
ANDY GRAY, TV summariser and radio presenter, on the Manchester City and Ivory Coast midfielder, 2014

It counts against Yaya being from the Cotes d'Ivoire. If he were Brazilian or Argentinian everyone would be talking about him. Everyone.
SAMIR NASRI, City team-mate and France midfielder, 2014

ROBIN VAN PERSIE

Arsenal are part of my life. They've been great to me. We didn't agree on the future – that's life. When I have to make tough decisions in my life, I listen to the little boy inside me. That little boy was screaming:

'Manchester United'. Manchester United breathes football. This club is the perfect match for me.
VAN PERSIE, United and Netherlands striker, 2012

Robin was 29 and impatient. Of course it's strange because for me he's an Arsenal man.
ARSENE WENGER, Van Persie's former manager at Arsenal, on the Dutchman's defection, 2013

His great quality is that in a fraction of a second he understands where to go. You can talk and talk and talk but a defender has to read that at the same time. His speed in analysing the little pockets around the box is exceptional. [We] know him well from playing against him in training, but in a game it's a question of timing. Will you read it as quickly as he does?
WENGER before the Dutchman scored United's winner v Arsenal inside three minutes, 2012

When Robin was a child we had this eclipse and I took him out of his bed late at night and said: 'Come on, I've got to show you something.' We went outside and stood on the bridge and you could see the shadow of the earth slowly move over the moon. And then he realised we were standing on a huge ball. That fascinated him. Even the world was a ball.
BOB VAN PERSIE, artist and Robin's father, 2013

I don't see things the way my parents do. They can look at a tree and see something amazing, whereas I just see a tree.
VAN PERSIE on his bohemian upbringing, 2009

Van Persie is the right player for Asenal. He can open a can of worms.

PAUL MERSON, Sky pundit and ex-Arsenal player, 2009

NEMANJA VIDIC

Vida has that mentality of the proper, really authentic defender. Watch him in training, and he'll batter Louis Saha and then pick him up, as if to say: 'This is my job, this is what I do.' I'll be yelling from the touchline: 'Watch the tackling, watch the tackling,' and Vidic will shout: 'Sorry boss.' But he's not sorry at all – he just loves defending.
SIR ALEX FERGUSON after signing the Serbia defender for Manchester United, 2006

Q: What's the strangest aspect of English culture you've noticed?
A: Driving on the left and tea with milk.
VIDIC, 2007

THEO WALCOTT

I've been consistent in patches this season.

WALCOTT, *Arsenal and England striker, 2012*

You've been shite, son, in your daft pink boots.
RICHARD KEYS, Sky anchor man, discussing Walcott when he thought the microphone was switched off, 2010

I played so badly that even my parents booed me off when I was substituted.
WALCOTT on playing for England Under-21s, 2009

I didn't watch the England–Argentina match in 1998. I can't remember why not. It may have been past my bedtime.
WALCOTT, 17-year-old Arsenal striker, on being named in England's World Cup squad, 2006

JON WALTERS

Walters is begging them to let him take it but they won't let him.
PAUL MERSON, Sky Soccer Saturday panellist, when Chelsea were awarded a penalty after Stoke striker Walters had

scored two own goals to put him on a hat-trick, 2013

DANNY WELBECK

The shot was sweet, into the top corner. When the ball went in, that feeling...if that feeling was a drug, I would be dead!
WELBECK, Manchester United striker, on his first goal for the club, 2012

JACK WILSHERE

For me if you're English you're English and you play for England. The only people who should play for England are English people. If you live in England for five years it doesn't make you English. If I went to Spain and lived there for five years I'm not going to play for Spain.
WILSHERE, Arsenal and England midfielder, after reports that Belgian-born Adnan Januzaj, of Manchester United, might qualify for England, 2013

I think @JackWilshere will make a damn fine pundit when he's out of long socks.
TWEET by Gary Lineker, Match of the Day presenter, 2013

I completely disagree with [Wilshere's] behaviour. When you are a footballer you are an example, and you don't do what damages your health. You can damage your health at home. You can drink at

home but nobody sees it, but when you do it in public, you damage your reputation as well
ARSENE WENGER, Arsenal manager, after Wilshere was pictured smoking outside a nightclub, 2013

But for the record...I don't smoke.
TWEET by Wilshere, 2013

He is focused and determined but also very young. I don't think he even shaves yet.
WENGER after Wilshere's debut, aged 16, 2008

REPORTER: Why did you take Wilshere off?
ARSENE WENGER: It was 9.25, past his bedtime.
EXCHANGE, 2008

Kieron Dyer has retired from football. He will now be sold to Arsenal as spare parts for Jack Wilshere.
TWEET by betting firm Paddy Power after former England player Dyer retired following an injury-ravaged career, 2013

HARRY WILSON

My wife's over the moon. I retired immediately. I told my manager that if Harry plays I won't be coming back. Not bad for a daft bet. He used to chase the ball around the front room on his hands and knees even before he could walk. That's what gave me the idea.
PETER EDWARDS, 62-year-old electrical contractor, after winning £125,000 on a £50 bet at odds of 2,500–1 in 2000 that three-year-old grandson Harry Wilson would play for Wales, 2013; Wilson, 16, a Liverpool winger, played as substitute v Belgium

SHAUN WRIGHT-PHILLIPS

I'll have to turbo-charge my Zimmer frame.
DAVID EYRES, 41-year-old Oldham midfielder, on the prospect of facing Wright-Phillips in an FA Cup tie v Manchester City, 2005

XAVI

I'm not strong, nor fast, nor skilful. I'm a player from the street. Without my team-mates, without space, I am nothing.
XAVI, Barcelona and Spain midfielder, 2012

[Former Barcelona coach Frank] Rijkaard did not believe in me. He wanted our game to be based on a superior physical level. He believed it was the only way to be at the same level as the top clubs in Europe. Four or five years ago, I was deemed terrible and useless. I was Barca's cancer. A player 1.70m tall was simply worthless.
XAVI, 2012

ASHLEY YOUNG

I don't like to use the word 'dropped'. He just fell outside the 23.
ROY HODGSON, England manager, on omitting the Manchester United attacker from his squad, 2013

2

PLAYERS: PAST

TONY ADAMS

I was never too aware of his problems with booze, but he was still a hell of a player when he had them.
ALAN SHEARER, Newcastle opponent and England colleague, 1998

For Tony to admit he is an alcoholic took an awful lot of bottle.
IAN WRIGHT, Arsenal and England team-mate, 1996

The greatest Arsenal man of all time. As a player, he goes beyond Liam Brady, Alex James, Joe Mercer or Frank McLintock. I don't think anyone has represented the club from the age of 17 to 35 and sustained all the injuries he's had, while half the time fighting for his own soul. Only those close to him knew how bad it was.
BOB WILSON, goalkeeper with Arsenal's 1971 Double-winning side and club goalkeeping coach, after Adams led them to League and FA Cup success, 2002

CRISTIAN CHIVU

In every stadium people shout things at me like 'you gypsy, go and become a builder', but I don't take any offence.
CHIVU, Romania international, on playing in Italy with with Internazionale, 2008

SAM ALLARDYCE

Sam was a ball-playing defender. If he wasn't with the ball, he was playing with your balls.
DAVE BASSETT, TV pundit and former manager, 2006

DAVID ARMSTRONG

Four hours after playing for England against World Cup finalists West Germany in front of 68,000 at Wembley, I was attempting to clean a sheepdog's diarrhoea from a shagpile carpet at my home.
ARMSTRONG, former Middlesbrough, Southampton and England midfielder, in the first paragraph of his autobiography The Bald Facts, *2013*

JEFF ASTLE

Jeff had this window- and office-cleaning business. His slogan was: 'We never miss a corner.'
FRANK SKINNER, comedian and West Bromwich Albion fan, after the death of Astle, who was renowned for his heading, 2003

ALAN BALL

As I was running towards the German goal, Alan Ball was shouting: 'Hursty, Hursty, give me the ball!' I said to myself: 'Sod you, Bally. I'm on a hat-trick.'
SIR GEOFF HURST recalling England's 1966 triumph, 1999

Jim Baxter drove him mad calling him Jimmy Clitheroe but Bally couldn't get near enough to him to do anything about it.
BILLY BREMNER, former Scotland captain, recalling his country's 1967 defeat of world champions England, 1992; Clitheroe was a high-voiced comic actor

I didn't need telling when I hadn't played as well as I'd have liked, but my dad told me all the same. I also didn't need him to tell me when I'd played well. And he never did.
BALL on the influence of his late father, Alan Ball Snr, 2005

GORDON BANKS

I enjoyed it so much, I'd go through everything again. The only thing I wish I'd done better was drive more carefully.
BANKS, former Leicester, Stoke and England goalkeeper, whose top-class career was ended by the loss of sight in one eye after a 1972 car crash, 2008

At that moment I hated Gordon Banks more than any man in soccer. But when I cooled down I had to applaud him with my heart for the greatest save I had ever seen.
PELE after Banks saved his header, Brazil v England, World Cup finals, 1970

JOHN BARNES

The best Liverpool player I've seen – and that's saying something.
JAN MOLBY, former team-mate of the England winger, 2011

Coming from Jamaica, I am blessed with rhythm.
BARNES in The Autobiography, *1999*

Revenge does not feature in my psyche. The black community loves how Ian Wright reacts, the way he flings out a fist or mouths off... I'm different.
BARNES, as above

GABRIEL BATISTUTA

Batistuta was a snob. He was Argentinian but he acted really posh. One day at training we were queuing at the bar, he arrived and pushed in front of me. We were both getting a cafe macchiato. So I stuck a finger up my nose and stirred his drink with it, like it was a spoon.
ANTONIO CASSANO, former Roma team-mate, 2008

DAVID BATTY

Batty would probably get himself booked playing Handel's *Largo*.
DAVID LACEY *reporting in* The Guardian *on a Charity Shield match between Leeds and Liverpool in which Batty was cautioned, 1992*

Batty and Le Saux there, arguing over who has the sillier name.

RORY BREMNER *as Des Lynam on his Channel 4 show, after the two Blackburn players traded punches in Moscow, 1995*

JIM BAXTER

He was a magician on the park. He could have put a size-five football in an egg cup.
SIR ALEX FERGUSON *on the late Rangers and Scotland midfielder, 2006*

PETER BEARDSLEY

The bottom line is that Beardsley comes from God.
ANDY ROXBURGH, *Scotland manager, after Beardsley's winner for England, 1988*

Christ, he looks like a thin Ann Widdecombe.
NICKY CLARKE, *hairstylist, 2001*

FRANZ BECKENBAUER

Tell the Kraut to get his ass up front. We don't pay a million for a guy to hang around on defense.
NEW YORK COSMOS *executive on the former West Germany captain's deep-lying role, 1977*

DAVID BECKHAM

[Beckham] never attained the level where you would say: that is an absolute top player.
SIR ALEX FERGUSON, *former Manchester United manager, in* My Autobiography, *2013*

You can go down a list of footballers since the Premier League and David Beckham probably wouldn't be in the first 1,000.
CHRIS WADDLE, *media pundit and former England winger, describing Beckham as 'good but not great' after his last game for Paris St-Germain, 2013*

And then of course his life changed when he married the girl from the Spice Girls. His focus changed. He got drawn into that celebrity status.
FERGUSON *in a radio interview on American Public Service Broadcasting, 2013*

I don't think I've been too critical on David. How can I argue with how he has turned out as a human being? He is an icon to kids and a very wealthy guy. I never had an issue with him.
FERGUSON *on suggestions that he had been harsh on Beckham in his book, 2013*

If there's one thing I could change, it would be winning something with England. I'm proud of the amount of times I've played for England [115] and proud that I've captained my country, but I'd give up a lot to have won a trophy.
BECKHAM *after retiring as a player, 2013*

That regimented schedule of getting up in the morning, training, coming home, seeing the kids. I miss that, miss being around the lads. And game days. Nothing can replace that.
BECKHAM, *as above*

Half-jokingly, I asked him if he wanted to move back to England and come play for us. David said that it sounded interesting, which was typical of David... But Victoria looked at me as if I was mad. 'Sven,' she said, 'could you see me in Leicester?' David laughed and said: 'When we lived in Madrid, it wasn't posh enough for my wife.'
SVEN-GORAN ERIKSSON, *former England manager, recalling his time at Leicester City in* Sven: My Story, *2013*

One episode that might have turned Posh off Leicester is her appearance at the BBC's One Big Sunday music festival at Victoria Park, Leicester, in September 2001. The *Mercury* reported at the time: 'The boos and jeers from the audience as she performed "Not Such An Innocent Girl" soon gave the Leicester verdict... She was also pelted with fruit and veg.'
REPORT *in the* Leicester Mercury, *2011*

It was Milan and Prada or Sunderland and Primark.

STEVE BRUCE, *Sunderland manager, after reports that he hoped to beat AC Milan to the signing of Beckham, 2010*

I read lots of footballers' books before taking this on, and they were all bad, and dripping with sentimentality. Beckham's was stuffed with stupidities. When I met Zlatan for the first time in 2010, I told him I didn't want to use Beckham's book as a model. He cut me short and asked: 'First things first: who the hell is Beckham?'
DAVID LAGERCRANTZ, *ghostwriter to Paris St-Germain and Sweden striker Zlatan Ibrahimovic, 2013; Beckham and Ibrahimovic became team-mates at PSG*

Beckham is no rocket surgeon.
PADDY O'CONNELL, BBC Radio 4 presenter, 2011

My new tattoo is Jesus being carried by three cherubs. Obviously the cherubs are my boys, so my thought of it is that at some point they are going to need to look after me and that's what they're doing in the picture. It means a lot.
BECKHAM, 2011

You know who really gives kids a bad name? Posh and Becks.

STEWART FRANCIS, comedian, in his Edinburgh Festival show, 2012

Becks dumps Posh!
HEADLINE on Leeds United website after Jermaine Beckford scored twice against Peterborough, 2009

I enjoy his fashion more than his football.
ANDRE AYEW, Marseille and Ghana player, 2013

I must admit I have a dressing-room curiosity over Beckham. I want to see if he's as equipped as he is in the underwear adverts.
MARCO BORRIELLO, AC Milan striker, during Beckham's loan spell in Italy, 2008

In his interviews, Beckham manages to sit on the fence very well and keeps both ears on the ground.
BRIAN KERR, former Republic of Ireland manager, 2013

When they picked teams at school, I was always the last chosen. I used to get booted everywhere because I was really little. I didn't have many friends really.
BECKHAM, 2002

He is making his mark on the school sportswise and never shows any sign of this going to his head – congratulations, David.
EXTRACT from 11-year-old Beckham's school report, 1986

My wife picked me out of a football-sticker album and I chose her from a music video off the television.
BECKHAM in the book My Side, *2003*

I was with David that fateful night he first saw the Spice Girls on telly and said: 'See that girl who can't dance or sing, I'm going to marry her.'
GARY NEVILLE, best man at Beckham's wedding, 2003

Beckham's silly little, smart little kick at his Argentinian opponent was what is wrong with the national character. This Gaultier-saronged, Posh-Spiced, Cooled Britannia, look-at-me, what-a-lad,

loadsamoney, sex-and-shopping, fame-schooled, daytime-TV, over-coiffed twerp did not, of course, mean any harm.
DAILY TELEGRAPH *leader article after Beckham's sending-off v Argentina, World Cup finals, 1998*

I think the majority of people in Britain dislike me.
BECKHAM, *interviewed by Alan Hansen on the TV documentary* The Football Millionaires, *1999*

Nobody should ever underestimate David Beckham. The lad has balls. At times I have disagreed with decisions he has taken off the field but he has a stubbornness that cannot be broken, and he will make up his own mind, whatever Alex Ferguson might think.
ALEX FERGUSON *in his first autobiography, 1999*

I'm not married to David Beckham. I'm not even engaged to him.
SVEN-GORAN ERIKSSON *on his close relationship with England's captain, 2006*

People say you get married and spend the rest of your life in the kitchen, but my life is not like that. I'm not very domesticated – I don't even know how to turn on the washing machine and I have no intention of ever bloody learning. David does all that.
VICTORIA BECKHAM, *David's pop-star wife, 1999*

We don't really have many rows. We're quite childlike.
VICTORIA, 1999

They are precisely the kind of people one would dread having as neighbours. They have lots of money but no class and no idea how to behave.
DAME BARBARA CARTLAND *on hearing the Beckhams planned to move near her, 1999*

The face of an angel and the bum of a Greek god. Rumour has it that his tackle is enough to not only take your breath away but possibly do you serious damage.
ATTITUDE, *gay magazine, naming Beckham top of its 'fantasy' players, 1999*

I'm partial to a bit of Beckham... I prefer him with his cropped hair – it makes him a little more rough and ready.
BOY GEORGE, *gay pop singer and DJ, 2000*

Whether it's men or women who fancy you, it's nice to be liked.
BECKHAM *in* OK! *magazine on going to gay bars with his wife, 2000*

He walks around the kitchen going: 'I'm a gay icon, I'm a gay icon.' When I try to say 'So am I' he just goes: 'But they love me more.'
VICTORIA, 2000

Beckham can't kick with his left foot. He can't head a ball, can't tackle and doesn't score many goals. Apart from that, he's all right.
GEORGE BEST, 2000

He's a really intelligent person. He's really deep, which I like.
VICTORIA, 2000

Posh Spice needs publicity desperately for her career. It is her oxygen. But for Beckham it is cyanide.
JOHN GILES, ex-Leeds and Manchester United midfielder, in his Daily Express *column, 2000*

David is an animal in bed. Some woman asked me in an interview: 'Are you so thin because you shag all day?' And I said: 'Actually, yes.'
VICTORIA, 2000

I've read it, cover to cover. It's got some nice pictures.

VICTORIA on a biography of her husband, 2000

This is what I do when I'm bored – new tattoos, new cars, new watches.
BECKHAM, 2000

Football is such a male environment, but the fact that he is so prepared to be involved with his baby [Brooklyn] really matters to all the young men who want to be affectionate to theirs but have had no role models.
PROFESSOR ANTHONY CLARE, psychiatrist, 2000

Football has become a religion and to be up to date we have to share the feelings of millions of people who admire this man.
CHAN THEERAPUNYO, Buddhist monk, after unveiling a gold statue of Beckham in a Thai temple, 2000

Do you fancy me or something?
BECKHAM to a male reporter who asked about his 'Mohawk' haircut, 2001

David Beckham will not be asked to take a turn in the black chair on *Mastermind,* but I doubt whether I'd be wanted there either. David's not thick, just a normal guy having to put up with a lot of shit thrown at him by people who don't even know his personality.
JAAP STAM, Manchester United colleague, in the book Head To Head, *before his sudden transfer to Lazio, 2001*

[Beckham] has an almost Garbo-like frozen facial perfection.
JULIE BURCHILL in the book Burchill on Beckham, *2001*

A man who has done nothing. Anyone can wear clothes but not quite as badly as him. He looks embarrassed about every single thing he puts on. His hairdos start out as some radical idea but end up as a horrific compromise, usually around the back.
JOHN LYDON, aka Johnny Rotten of the Sex Pistols, 2002

He's extremely good-looking, isn't he? And so noble. I think he's wonderful, especially when you consider what a brat he used to be.
DORIS LESSING, 83-year-old novelist, 2002

They are Mr and Mrs Everyday who suddenly got famous.
DAVID FURNISH, Elton John's partner, 2002

He's very good-looking and very rich, he's a fantastic footballer with an attractive wife and a lovely child. He has what everyone wants, which is why everyone hates him.
ROBBIE WILLIAMS, pop singer, 2002

He represents something for every woman – father, husband, footballer, icon. In a word he's the ultimate hero.
MARIE O'RIORDAN, editor of Marie Claire, *on her decision to make Beckham the first man to appear on its cover, 2002*

Normally when you swap shirts they are soaked in sweat, but Beckham's smelt only of perfume. Either he protects himself against BO or he sweats cologne.
RONALDO, Brazil striker, after the World Cup quarter-final win v England, 2002

It's not easy when someone pulls your ponytail.
BECKHAM on being provoked on the pitch, 2003

At least his hair is OK.
DAVID JAMES, England goalkeeper, after Beckham, sporting a 'corn-braid' style, sustained a hand injury v South Africa, 2003

The Blackest White Man in Britain
HEADLINE in Time *magazine on Beckham's braids and penchant for 'bling' fashions, 2003*

The gaffer had had enough. I'd grown up as a person and he didn't seem to like what I'd become. Now it looked like he'd seen enough of me as a player as well.
BECKHAM on being relegated to United's bench, in the book My Side, *2003*

The trouble is that he is a pony without a trick.
BRIAN CLOUGH, 2003

What do you buy David Beckham? He's the guy who has everything, so I might just stick myself in a box with a bow on it and leap out naked. He did ask for a briefcase to keep his laptop in. He's very intelligent when it comes to computers – much more so than me.
VICTORIA, before Christmas, 2003

I'm not the world's best talker, not at least until I know someone well.

BECKHAM in the book My Side, *2003*

Beckham should guide Posh in the direction of a singing coach because she's nowhere near as good at her job as he is at his.
BRIAN CLOUGH, 2003

The ladies think he's a nice-looking young man. From what I've seen, though, he has always lived perfectly.
SVEN-GORAN ERIKSSON, England manager, 2003

The way I and my family have been treated is an absolute disgrace because at the end of the day I'm a nice person and a loving husband and father.
BECKHAM complaining of press reports alleging affairs with Rebecca Loos and Sarah Marbeck, 2004

As far as the tabloids are concerned, David Beckham is the new Princess Diana. This was the biggest kiss-and-tell ever.
MAX CLIFFORD, publicist, on Loos' claims, 2004

I will not let that tart ruin my marriage.

VICTORIA on Loos, 2004

Sleeping with David was a momentous day for me, not just a one-night stand. This is probably the most famous father, family man and husband in the world and he changed my life. When we made love David told me: 'I know what we're doing is wrong, but I can't help it.' I looked down and there was David Beckham kissing my breasts! David Beckham!
SARAH MARBECK alleging a sexual liaison (denied by Beckham) during United's 2001 tour of Singapore, 2004

Me and David have always been very compatible. We're going to get old together. We have a laugh. We got into bed together the other night, he put on the TV, and what's

he watching? *Ground Force.* I said to him: 'But I heard you're really into porn.'
VICTORIA on her husband's alleged adultery, 2004

Much as it pains a feminist such as myself, Beckham has been grotesquely, massively, pussy-whipped by his talentless ambition-hound of a wife.
JULIE BURCHILL, journalist, in The Guardian, *2004*

[Beckham] has managed single-handedly to change male behaviour globally, and for the better.
DR ANDREW PARKER, Warwick University sociology lecturer, in One David Beckham: Celebrity, Masculinity and the SocNo*, a research paper, 2002*

Beckham seems to scare the pants off macho men because he shows he's hurt when he feels it.
JENNI MURRAY, presenter of BBC Radio 4's Woman's Hour, *after the 'flying boot' incident, 2003*

Beckham is more of a pop star than a footballer.

PELE, 2003

I can totally understand the way the manager thought. When you're a footballer, traditionally all you're meant to think about is football, but I need other things outside of football as well. This is me. This is the way I am.
BECKHAM on whether the 'distractions' of fashion and global branding accounted for Ferguson's change of opinion on him, 2003

Throughout the Far East the adoration extended to him is a heady brew of sexual longing and a need for a blond messiah.
WILL SELF, author and journalist, on Beckham's promotional trip to Japan, 2003

We need to sign players the coach wants, not ones who appear in *Hello!* magazine.
ARTUR BALDASANO, candidate for the Real Madrid presidency, 2004

David wanted to come from the theatre of dreams to the team of dreams.
FLORENTINO PEREZ, president of Real Madrid, 2003

I'm so glad there will now be two good-looking guys at Real. I've felt so lonely in such an ugly team.
ROBERTO CARLOS, Brazilian defender, 2003

At the age of 28, to be known as Sir David Beckham is some achievement.
ROBERTO CARLOS after Beckham was made an OBE, 2003

I'm really happy to receive the OBE and it's a great honour. The Queen said it was great for her to be giving me the award, and it's an honour to be with Her Majesty, obviously. I'm very honoured to be given this honour.
BECKHAM at Buckingham Palace, 2003

People love me because of football. To me, merchandising is an extra and derives from the fact that I'm a footballer. It doesn't interfere with my football.
BECKHAM at Real, 2003

[As a player] he may not be the perfect lover, but he's an ideal husband. He pushes the Hoover around, cooks up romantic dinners and never falls asleep on you.
JUANMA TRUEBA, Spanish journalist, in AS newspaper, on Beckham's strong start in La Liga, 2003

The only footballer in the world that doesn't need to beat a man to play well.

HUGO GATTI, Madrid-based journalist and former Argentina goalkeeper, 2003

Beckham has a special hinge in his ankle which lets him place the ball wherever he wants.

ROBERTO PALOMAR, Spanish journalist, in Marca newspaper, 2003

I don't know what it is about David Beckham and kicking.
SERENA WILLIAMS, American tennis player at Wimbledon, after Beckham's second penalty miss of the European finals, 2004

His passing was so accurate, as if he had a hand instead of a foot. We do miss him, despite what some may think.
MIKAEL SILVESTRE, Manchester United defender, 2004

Why do people criticise his intelligence when he can do miraculous things with a ball?
SHANIA TWAIN, American country-pop singer, 2003

He's the most famous athlete in the world (except in the USA)
HEADLINE on a profile of Beckham in USA Today, 2003

I think of my horse, Tamarillo, as David Beckham. He's obsessed with his looks and would love a diamond earring.
WILLIAM FOX-PITT, British Olympic showjumper, 2004

Sir David Beckham? You're having a laugh. He's just a good footballer with a famous bird.
IAN HOLLOWAY, Plymouth manager, on reports that Beckham might be knighted, 2006

[Victoria] is very thin. I leaned forward to kiss her but there is so little of her, I almost missed.
DAVID CAMERON MP, leader of the Conservative Party, on meeting Mrs Beckham at a pre-World Cup party, 2006

He [Steve McClaren] just said he had other ideas and wanted to move on. He said: 'You're one of the casualties.' There was no shouting, no crying. Not on the phone to the manager anyway.
BECKHAM on being dropped by England after the World Cup, 2006

The best part for me was the [singing of the US] national anthem. I got goose bumps. I love LA. It's a great place to live.
BECKHAM after playing against LA Galaxy for Real Madrid two years before agreeing to join them, 2005

Beckham is not joining the Los Angeles Galaxy as an athlete, but as an advertising campaign. His job here is not to win, but to give his sport one last chance to work in the biggest place where it doesn't. His success will be defined not by corner-kicks, but by converts.
BILL PLASCHKE, sports writer, in the LA Times, *2007*

People [in LA] probably think we'll win my first game 10–0. But I'm not a player who'll run past six men or score four goals. My game is about working hard and being a team player.
BECKHAM, 2007

The Senate announced today that they've doubled the reward for information that could lead to the capture of Osama Bin Laden to $50m. Sounds a lot until you realise that we here in LA have paid $250m for David Beckham.
JAY LENO, American satirist and broadcaster, on The Tonight Show, *2007*

Everything he does is about challenging convention. David's childhood dreams all started young, and he's managed to realise most of them. That's because he's always heading somewhere, with a vision. And Miami is his vision now. He gets to promote the sport he so loves in a country he loves.
SIMON FULLER, British entertainment mogul and co-backer of Beckham's prospective Miami soccer club, 2014

For me, I'm a Manchester United guy – that's it, that's why I could never play for any other club in England.
BECKHAM *when asked why he was investing in Miami rather than a British club, 2014*

COLIN BELL

He didn't seem to grasp his own freakish strength. I said to him: 'You're a great header of the ball, you have a terrific shot, and you're the best, most powerful runner in the business. Every time you walk off the pitch unable to say you were streets ahead of the other 21 players, you have failed.'
MALCOLM ALLISON, *Bell's coach at Manchester City, 1968*

DENNIS BERGKAMP

If he thinks he's going to set the world alight he can forget it. When the fog, ice and cold arrive, he won't want to know.
ALAN SUGAR, *Tottenham chairman, after Bergkamp's £7.25m move to Arsenal, 1995*

Intelligence and class. There's always a brain behind what he does, and his technique allows him to do what he sees and decides to do.
ARSENE WENGER, *Arsenal manager, summing up the Dutch striker on his retirement, 2006*

Dennis is such a nice man, such a tremendous gentleman with such a lovely family. It's going to be very hard for me to kick him.
TONY ADAMS *before England v Netherlands, European Championship finals, 1996*

If he were in *Star Trek*, he'd be the best player in whatever solar system he was in.
IAN WRIGHT, *Arsenal team-mate, 1997*

GEORGE BEST

I'm not decrying Lionel Messi and others, but George was the pick for me. He did it in an era when defenders could kick you and you had to play on bad pitches. David Beckham would have struggled to get a game then.
MIKE SUMMERBEE, *Manchester City and England winger (at whose wedding Best was best man), 2012*

George Best was the best player I ever attempted to kick.
RON HARRIS, *former Chelsea defender, 2014*

When I die, they won't remember who I dated, the fights and the car crashes because they're not important. They will remember the football.
BEST *shortly before his death, 2005*

Unquestionably the greatest player of all time.
SIR ALEX FERGUSON, *2002*

There are times when you want to wring his neck. He hangs on to the ball when other players have found better positions. Then out of the blue he does something which wins the match. Then you know you're in the presence of someone special.
PAT CRERAND, Manchester United team-mate, 1970

Best makes a greater appeal to the senses than the other two [Stanley Matthews and Tom Finney]. His movements are quicker, lighter, more balletic... And with it all, there is his utter disregard for physical danger... He has ice in his veins, warmth in his heart, and timing and balance in his feet.
DANNY BLANCHFLOWER, former Northern Ireland captain, in David Meek's book Anatomy of a Football Star: George Best, *1970*

PARKINSON: What was the nearest to kick-off that you made love? BEST: Er… I think it was half-time actually.

EXCHANGE on Michael Parkinson's BBC TV chat show, 1980s

I don't drink every day but when I do it's usually for four or five days on the trot. I've got a drink problem.
BEST, 1979

Well, I suppose that's the knighthood fucked.

BEST at Southwark Crown Court, waiting to be sentenced after being found guilty of assaulting a policeman, 1984

We had our problems with the wee feller, but I prefer to remember his genius.
SIR MATT BUSBY, the United manager who gave 17-year-old Best his debut, 1988

If you'd given me a choice between beating four defenders and smashing in a goal from 30 yards or going to bed with Miss World, it would have been difficult. Luckily, I had both. It's just that you do one of those things in front of 50,000 people.
BEST, 1991

I always had a reputation for going missing – Miss England, Miss United Kingdom, Miss World...
BEST, 1992

I spent a lot of my money on booze, birds and fast cars. The rest I squandered.

BEST, 1992

It's a pleasure for me to be standing up here. It's a pleasure to be standing up.
BEST, accepting the Footballer of the Century award, 1999

It was typical of me to be finishing a long and distinguished drinking career just as the government is planning to open pubs 24 hours a day.
BEST trying to give up alcohol, 2001

In her youth the Queen was quite a stunner. Who knows what might have happened if I'd met her in Tramp in my heyday.
BEST during the Queen's Golden Jubilee celebrations, 2002

I celebrated my 56th birthday with a banana and honey milkshake. A new liver would have been a nice present.
BEST, 2002

He's a totally different person now. The lovely side was always there, which is why I married him. It's just that I've got it all the time now.
ALEX BEST, Best's wife, before his liver-transplant operation, 2002

I love the simple life and being on my own. The only thing I want out of our marriage is our dogs.
BEST on splitting with Alex, 2003

Now I truly believe he wanted to be caught with another woman so he had the excuse to leave me and continue his love affair with the bottle. Alcohol is the only thing he's ever really loved.
ALEX BEST on estrangement from George, 2003

George once turned down trifle because it had sherry in it. I trusted he had sent his demons packing, but whenever the going is good George grows restless.
MICHAEL PARKINSON, writer, broadcaster and friend of Best's, 2003

George shouldn't be criticised for going back on the booze. Alcoholism is a disease and he should have our sympathy.
BRIAN CLOUGH, who also had a liver transplant, 2003

Our talking point this morning is George Best, his liver transplant and the booze culture in football. Don't forget – the best caller wins a crate of John Smith's bitter.
ALAN BRAZIL, Talk Radio chat-show host and former Manchester United striker, 2002

In 1969 I gave up alcohol and women. It was the worst 20 minutes of my life.
BEST, 2003

The only thing I have in common with George Best is that we come from the same place, played for the same club and were discovered by the same man.
NORMAN WHITESIDE, former United and Northern Ireland forward, 2003

One of the few fellas I know that does *The Times* crossword.
PAT CRERAND, former United team-mate, 2004

People seem to believe I have a death wish. Sometimes I think they sit around hoping that I'll die. I bet the obituary is already written.
BEST, 2003

People always say I shouldn't be burning the candle at both ends. Maybe because they haven't got a big enough candle.
BEST, 2003

Years later I asked him to stand in front of me so I could see his face. He wondered why and I told him: 'Because for years all I saw was your arse disappearing down the touchline.'
GRAHAM WILLIAMS, the West Bromwich Albion full-back who faced the 17-year-old debutant Best, 2005

It's very sad that he has gone. The good thing is that he lived 100 years in his 59 years.
BARRY McGUIGAN, former world champion boxer and fellow Northern Irishman, 2005

Shevchenko £50m. Ronaldinho £80m. George Best priceless.
MESSAGE on a card attached to a floral tribute, 2005

He carried us for so long. It was an honour to carry him.
DEREK DOUGAN, Northern Ireland team-mate and a pall-bearer at Best's funeral, 2005

GARRY BIRTLES

People used to say that if I'd shot John Lennon, he'd still be alive today.
BIRTLES, former England striker, on his long goalless run at Manchester United, 2004

DANNY BLANCHFLOWER

In a poor side Danny is an expensive luxury. That's why I dropped him when we had a poor team. But in a good side as Spurs are now he is a wonderful asset through his unorthodox approach and marvellous ball skill.
BILL NICHOLSON, Tottenham's Double-winning manager, on his captain in Julian Holland's book Spurs – The Double, *1961*

TONY BOOK

The old man lifts the trophy – it's becoming quite a habit.
BARRY DAVIES, TV commentator, when Manchester City captain Book, then 35, collected the European Cup-Winners' Cup, 1970

Tony was a bricklayer as well as playing hundreds of games for Bath City before joining us in his thirties. No wonder he played with such enthusiasm.
MIKE SUMMERBEE, former City and England winger, 2012

STAN BOWLES

I was invited to appear on the *Kilroy* show. The subject was gambling addicts, though I'm not sure what it had to do with me. I declined and spent the day at Sandown Races.
BOWLES, 2003

BILLY BREMNER

If every manager in Britain were given his choice of any one player to add to his team, some, no doubt, would toy with the idea of Best; but the realists, to a man, would have Bremner.
JOHN ARLOTT, Guardian writer, hailing Bremner as 'the best footballer in the four countries', 1970

10st of Barbed Wire
HEADLINE on Sunday Times profile, 1970

TREVOR BROOKING

Floats like a butterfly and stings like one, too.
BRIAN CLOUGH, Nottingham Forest manager, before Brooking headed West Ham's winner in the FA Cup final v Arsenal, 1980

STEVE BULL

REPORTER: If you were holding a dream dinner party, who would you invite?
BULL: Muhammad Ali, if he was alive.
INTERVIEW, 2009

People say his first touch isn't good, but he usually scores with his second.
GRAHAM TURNER, Wolves manager, 1988

CRAIG BURLEY

Q: Most embarrassing moment?
A: Trying to follow Craig Burley's instructions on the park when he didn't have his teeth in, and getting it hopelessly wrong.
MALKY MACKAY, Norwich defender, on his former Celtic colleague, 2001

TERRY BUTCHER

I haven't had the chance to kick a Celtic player for many years.
TERRY BUTCHER, former Rangers captain, on playing in the Old Firm Veterans' Challenge, 2001

ERIC CALDOW

I was the only British player to play 450 games and never get a red or yellow card. That could even be a world record for a defender. Speed is all I had. No one could run past me. I couldn't tackle a fish supper.
CALDOW, 73-year-old ex-Rangers and Scotland defender, on being inducted to Scottish FA Hall of Fame, 2007

SOL CAMPBELL

I believe if I was white, I would have been England captain for more than 10 years – it's as simple as that… I've asked myself many times why I wasn't. I keep coming up with the same answer. It was the colour of my skin.
SOL CAMPBELL, former Tottenham, Arsenal and England defender, in The Authorised Biography *by Simon Astaire, 2014*

I'm sorry about the situation with me going and I'm sorry how it happened. I'm not going to apologise for the move [Spurs to Arsenal] because I was very successful. I'm sorry about the hurt it inflicted on them.
CAMPBELL, 2014

Sol is a tortured soul.
KELLY HOPPEN, interior designer and ex-girlfriend, when Campbell went AWOL after being substituted by Arsenal, 2006

Big Sol never says a word. When we play Spurs and I have a go at him, it's like talking to the deaf and dumb.
IAN WRIGHT, Arsenal and England striker, 1998

ERIC CANTONA

He was a quiet man, Eric Cantona, but he was a man of few words.
DAVID BECKHAM, former Manchester United colleague, 2013

It's not easy when you quit football. I should know because sometimes I feel I quit too young. I loved the game but no longer had the passion to go to bed early, not to go out with friends, not to drink.
CANTONA, 2003

1966 was a great year for English football. Eric was born.
NIKE advertising slogan, 1994

Just as I can bring happiness to people with my spontaneity, my instinctiveness, so there are always going to be dark shadows, black stains.
CANTONA, 1994

I just yelled: 'Off you go, Cantona – it's an early shower for you.'
MATTHEW SIMMONS, Crystal Palace fan, explaining what he had said to provoke Cantona's 'kung-fu' assault, 1995

Pressure is no excuse. I would take any amount of personal abuse for £10,000 a week [Cantona's reputed salary].
SIR STANLEY MATTHEWS after the Selhurst Park incident, 1995

I'd have cut his balls off.

BRIAN CLOUGH after Cantona's fracas at Crystal Palace, 1995

My initial feeling was to let him go. I couldn't imagine his playing for the club again... My wife Cath said: 'You can't let him off. Never let it be said that you put winning the championship above doing the right thing.'
ALEX FERGUSON, in his diary A Year in the Life, *1995*

I told him: 'Eric, you can't go to court like that' [in a shirt unbuttoned to his chest]. He says: 'I am Cantona. I can go as I want.' So he got into the dock and he got 14 days in prison. I thought: 'Oh my God, it must be the shirt.'
PAUL INCE, former United team-mate, recalling the 1995 incident, 2004

I'd give all the champagne I've ever drunk to have played alongside him in a big European match at Old Trafford.
GEORGE BEST, 1997

He gave interviews on art, philosophy and politics. A natural room-mate for David Batty, I thought immediately.
HOWARD WILKINSON, Leeds manager, in Managing to Succeed: My Life in Football Management, *with David Walker, 1992*

Eric likes to do what he likes, when he likes, because he likes it – and then fuck off. We'd all want a bit of that.
WILKINSON after offloading the Frenchman to Manchester United, 1993

For my next film role I would love to play a psychopath or an unpleasant person.
CANTONA, who had become an actor, 2000

JAMIE CARRAGHER

We all dream of a team of Carraghers.

SONG by Liverpool supporters celebrating the long-serving defender, 2000s

Carra doesn't like me to fist him before the games, so I give him a high-five instead.
PEPE REINA, Liverpool and Spain goalkeeper, on the TV programme Soccer AM, *2011*

Carragher is 10 times a better defender than I could ever be. If we look at the Liverpool greats over the years, he's up there with the best.
ALAN HANSEN, former Liverpool captain, 2005

JOHN CHARLES

John always looked like a Greek god. He could have been a boxer, a rugby player. He could have been anything.
TERRY MEDWIN, former Wales team-mate, after Charles's death, 2004

John was never interested in money. He thought you lived on fresh air.
GLENDA CHARLES, his second wife, 2002

If you had 22 players of John's character on the pitch, you wouldn't need a referee, only a timekeeper.
CLIVE THOMAS, former international referee and fellow Welshman, after Charles's death, 2004

BOBBY CHARLTON

He always possessed an elemental quality; jinking, changing feet and direction, turning gracefully on the ball or accelerating through a gap surrendered by a confused enemy.
GEOFFREY GREEN, The Times *football correspondent, 1969*

Trumpets sound
Doves take flight
Lisa Stansfield sings
And Bobby Charlton's haircut
forms the five Olympic rings
HOVIS PRESLEY, Bolton poet, on Manchester's bid to stage the Olympics, from the anthology Poetic Off Licence, *2005*

The fact that they accused Bobby Charlton of sheltering me while I 'stole' a bracelet proves I'm innocent. Bobby has never done a dishonest thing in his life.
BOBBY MOORE, England captain and colleague, after the 'jewel theft' incident in Bogota, 1970

Bobby deserves to keep the record. He was a much better player than me and scored far better goals.
GARY LINEKER on retiring from international football one goal short of Charlton's England record, 1992

I sent my son to one of his schools of excellence and he came back bald.
GEORGE BEST, former Manchester United team-mate, on TV's Mrs Merton Show, *1996*

It's the most famous quote in football.
ALEX FERGUSON after Manchester United paid Newcastle £7m for Cole, 1995

BRIAN CLOUGH

I got one or two goals a season, give or take the odd 30.
CLOUGH aged 69 on TV documentary Local Heroes, *2004*

The only thing I enjoyed during my six years at Middlesbrough was scoring goals. From Saturday to Saturday I was very unhappy. My ability was never utilised, by me or the management. Only goals kept me sane. That was my only pleasure.
CLOUGH, 1973

GEORGE COHEN

We used to say of George Cohen: 'He's hit more photographers than Frank Sinatra.' Usually he would hit his cross into the crowd, or into the photographers.
BOBBY ROBSON, former Fulham team-mate, in his book Time on the Grass, *1982*

ANDY COLE

It always amazes me when people say: 'All he can do is score goals.'

STAN COLLYMORE

He had everything Thierry Henry has got and more.
JOHN GREGORY, Collymore's former manager at Aston Villa, 2004

I'm no angel but I think I'm more misunderstood than anything else. I think I'm a pretty interesting bloke.
COLLYMORE, then with Liverpool, 1997

Some days he could climb Everest, others he can't even climb out of bed.
JOHN GREGORY, Aston Villa manager, on his striker's clinical depression, 1999

I find it difficult to understand how someone in Stan's position, with the talent and money he has, is stressed. I wonder how a 29-year-old at Rochdale, in the last three months of his contract, with a wife and three kids, copes with stress.
GREGORY, 1999

At the end of the day I haven't killed anybody. A million players have done it [letting off a fire-extinguisher in a hotel lobby] and a million more will do it in the future.

COLLYMORE *on hitting the headlines following a prank on a Spanish break with his new club, Leicester, 2000*

I went looking for extreme forms of gratification to replicate the buzz I'd had as a footballer.

COLLYMORE *on why he went 'dogging', 2006*

EDDIE COLMAN

When he waggled his hips he made the stanchions in the grandstand sway.

HARRY GREGG, *Manchester United goalkeeper, on the colleague nicknamed 'Snakehips' who perished in the Munich disaster, 1958*

CHARLIE COOKE

When he sold you a dummy you had to pay to get back in the ground.

JIM BAXTER, *Scotland team-mate, on the Chelsea winger, 1976*

JIM CRAIG

When Billy McNeill [Celtic's captain in 1967] was recovering from a heart operation, I called to see how he was and his eight-year-old grandson James picked up the phone. He asked who I was and when I told him he snapped back: 'You're the guy that gave away the penalty in Lisbon.'

CRAIG, *a member of Celtic's European Cup-winning side of 1967, 2003*

JOHAN CRUYFF

There are two types of footballers, the legends and the mortals. My father is a legend and I am a mortal. The legends like my father; they come, they do and they remain. I am part of the vast majority of mortals; we come, we do and we die.

JORDI CRUYFF, *son of Johan and a former Netherlands and Manchester United player, 2013*

[He is] Pythagoras in boots. Few have been able to exert, both physically and mentally, such mesmeric control on a match from one penalty area to another.

DAVID MILLER, *football journalist, on the Ajax and Netherlands attacker, 1960s*

KENNY DALGLISH

Is he better in midfield or up front?
Och, just let him on the park.
JOCK STEIN, *Dalglish's former Celtic
manager, 1977*

When he scored...he had a better
smile than Clark Gable. Beautiful
teeth, arms wide, that's how he
celebrated. He wasn't that big but
he had a huge arse. It came down
below his knees, and that's where
he got his strength from.
BRIAN CLOUGH, *former managerial
adversary, 1995*

The best player this club has signed this century.

JOHN SMITH, *Liverpool chairman, 1986*

I'm going to rip off your head and
shit in the hole.
VINNIE JONES, *Wimbledon midfielder,
to Dalglish before a Liverpool v
Wimbledon match, 1987*

DIXIE DEAN

He belongs in the company of the
supremely great, like Shakespeare,
Rembrandt and Beethoven.
BILL SHANKLY *honouring the
legendary Everton centre-forward at*

*a dinner hours before Dean died at the
Mersey derby, 1980*

RORY DELAP

He plays the ball better with his
hands than with his foot – it's
fantastic!
LUIZ FELIPE SCOLARI, *Chelsea
manager, on the Stoke and Republic of
Ireland midfielder with a long throw, 2008*

In football you need to have
everything in your cake mix to make
the cake taste right. One little bit
of ingredient that [Stoke manager]
Tony Pulis uses in his cake gets
talked about all the time is Rory's
throw. Call that cinnamon and he's
got a cinnamon-flavoured cake.
IAN HOLLOWAY, *Blackpool manager,
2009*

PAOLO DI CANIO

When I scored that goal to knock
out Manchester United it was like
having sex with Madonna.
DI CANIO *remembering his 2001
winner in the FA Cup for West Ham at
Manchester United, 2012*

He's a smashing professional and
a leader. He's like Bobby Moore in
that respect, though he wouldn't
have made it into Bobby's drinking
school.
HARRY REDKNAPP, *West Ham
manager, 2000*

There would have to be a bubonic plague for me to pick Di Canio.
GIOVANNI TRAPATTONI, Italy coach, 2000

What fascinates me – and this is probably where Mussolini and I are very different – is the way he was able to go against his morals to achieve his goals.
DI CANIO on his admiration for the late Italian fascist leader, 2000

The salute gives legitimacy to fascism, a murderous and tyrannical ideology. I take my hat off to Di Canio the footballer but Di Canio the fascist is a disgrace.
ENZO FOSCHI, Italian centre-left politician, after Di Canio made a fascist salute after scoring for Lazio, 2005

JULIAN DICKS

I met [Glenn Hoddle's assistant] John Gorman during an end-of-season tour in Spain. We were all drinking in a bar and John and I bumped into each other. We had a chat and he told me I'd never play for England unless I grew my hair. I told him to fuck off.
JULIAN DICKS, shaven-headed West Ham full-back of the 1990s, 2012

ALFREDO DI STEFANO

One of the greatest, if not the greatest footballer I had ever seen. At that time [the 1950s] we had forwards and defenders doing separate jobs, but he did everything.
MATT BUSBY, Manchester United manager, on the Real Madrid centre-forward, in Motson and Rowlinson, The European Cup 1955–80, 1980

TOMMY DOCHERTY

I once told Tommy that if we had five Bill Shanklys and five Tommy Dochertys, plus a goalkeeper, we'd beat the world. Tommy said: 'If there were five Bill Shanklys and five Tommy Dochertys, we wouldn't need a goalkeeper.'
BILL SHANKLY reminisces about his successor in the Preston team, quoted in John Keith's Shanks For The Memory, 1998

DUNCAN EDWARDS

His talent, his energy, his unselfconscious fun and enjoyment of the chase, his ability to make everything seem possible, all this added up to a volcano of excitement that gripped the crowds and the game wherever he played... Certain it is that Duncan Edwards, had he survived, would have captained England to the World Cup in 1966.
GEOFFREY GREEN, The Times football correspondent, in Soccer in the Fifties, 1974

Duncan was the only player that made me feel inferior.

SIR BOBBY CHARLTON, former Manchester United team-mate, 2006

EUSEBIO

Today it's easier. I scored 41 times for Portugal in 60 games, but I never played against Liechtenstein and Azerbaijan.
EUSEBIO, former Benfica and Portugal striker, when asked about Cristiano Ronaldo overtaking him as the national team's second-highest scorer, 2013

Eusebio received a cut over his left eye when he collided with Szentmihalyi and he spent the rest of the game wearing a bandage round his head. This had the look of an outsize coronet, an apt comparison perhaps because there was something regal about everything Eusebio did.
ERIC TODD, Guardian football writer, on Portugal v Hungary, World Cup finals, 1966

Everyone remembers the day he left the field in tears, crying for Portugal. Today, Eusebio's tears are ours.
ANIBAL CAVACO SILVA, Portugal's president, marks Eusebio's death by

recalling his crying after the nation's loss to England in the 1966 World Cup semi-finals, 2014

Coming up, a tribute to the immortal Eusebio. Of course, if he was immortal we wouldn't be doing this tribute.
DANNY KELLY, talkSPORT radio presenter, 2014

ALEX FERGUSON

I scored 45 goals in 51 games for Dunfermline one season [1965–66]. Modesty forbids me broadcasting it, of course, but I may have mentioned it to [Ruud] Van Nistelrooy and [Ole Gunnar] Solskjaer. They're fed up of listening to me, in fact.
FERGUSON, by now Sir Alex, recalling his playing days, 2004

LUIS FIGO

Which player would I pay to watch? I like what is beautiful. I would pay to see Figo, not Beckham. Even if they are both effective, I take more pleasure from watching the first.
THIERRY HENRY, Arsenal and France striker, 2003

You could put Figo in a phone booth with 11 opponents and he would find his way to the door. He'd beat them all and dribble his way out.
CARLOS QUEIROZ, Real Madrid coach, 2003

TOM FINNEY

When I watch Lionel Messi play for Barcelona, I close my eyes and I can see Tom. Messi is the Tom Finney of today. Just like Finney, Messi is always getting fouled, but doesn't complain and just gets up and gets on with the game.
JIMMY ARMFIELD, media pundit, former manager and ex-England defender, on Sir Tom's death, 2014

Finney was a more difficult opponent than Stanley Matthews. You knew how Stanley wanted to beat you, and what he would do if he did. With Tom, you never had that luxury. He could beat you in more ways.
SAMMY COX, Scotland full-back, 2005

We would all be effing and blinding in the dressing-room but we would stop the second Tom walked in. Every one of us. It was an effort but we did it because we knew the great man would be offended.
TOMMY DOCHERTY, former Preston colleague, 2009

Tommy was grizzly strong and could run for a week. I'd have played him in an overcoat. There'd have been four men marking him at the kick-in. When I told people in Scotland that England were coming up with a winger better than Stanley Matthews, they laughed at me. They weren't bloody laughing when Big Georgie Young was running all over Hampden looking for Tommy Finney.
BILL SHANKLY recalls his former Preston team-mate, 1972

ROBBIE FOWLER

When you come from a council estate in Liverpool, how you come across is important. You don't want to be seen as a biff – some busy bollocks like Gary Neville, or someone who has sold his soul like [David] Beckham.
FOWLER, Liverpool and England striker, on his Toxteth roots, 2005

Robbie taught me a new phrase because he said he was 'over the moon' to be back and I'd never heard that before.
RAFAEL BENITEZ, Spanish manager of Liverpool, after re-signing Fowler, 2006

WILLIAM GALLAS

William Gallas has been all over the back pages like an incontinent newsagent.
JAMES RICHARDSON, *Setanta Sports presenter, on the then Arsenal and France defender, 2008*

I'm sorry – I don't follow football.
GALLAS *after highlighting the threat of Milan's Antonio Cassano and then being told he was ineligible for the Champions League match at Tottenham, 2011*

GARRINCHA

The one man above all others to turn pumpkins into coaches and mice into men.
GEOFFREY GREEN, The Times *football correspondent, on Brazil's outstanding winger, World Cup finals, 1958*

PAUL GASCOIGNE

I didn't ask to be an alcoholic. It's just like asking someone why he's a diabetic. I wish I wasn't but I am.
GASCOIGNE, *former Tottenham, Lazio and England midfielder, in the ITV documentary* Being Paul Gascoigne, *2013*

I hope I don't die through it, because I won't get any sympathy because, well, he was warned.
GASCOIGNE, *as above*

Are we not enough? I feel like we're not enough for him. It makes you think does he not care about us? Because if he did he would think about our feelings.
BIANCA GASCOIGNE, *Gascoigne's daughter, as above*

I was walking up the street and some guy comes up and looked shocked, and he went 'Gazza?' I said 'yeah' and he went: 'Oh! It's in the paper that you're dead. There's just been a newsflash.' I went: 'Oh, am I? Ah well never mind.'
GASCOIGNE, *2011*

Police were called to a report of a man allegedly being drunk and disorderly at Stevenage railway station at 10:30pm on Thursday 4 July. Officers attended the location and arrested a 46-year-old male on suspicion of common assault and being drunk and disorderly.
STATEMENT *by Hertfordshire Police after Gascoigne was arrested, 2013*

I took Gaddafi's two sons out and got them lamped. I also signed this thing in his compound. I think it was a bomb.
GASCOIGNE *after a trip to Libya before the fall of Colonel Gaddafi, 2012*

Looking back, I don't think too many people had Gazza's best interests at heart. We let him down – everyone from the president downwards.
JANE NOTTAGE, *Gascoigne's personal*

assistant when he played in Italy for Lazio, 2012

I left clubs at the wrong time. I shouldn't have left Tottenham, I shouldn't have left Rangers when I did and then I should have stayed at Everton when David Moyes took over, instead of leaving when Walter Smith left. Who knows what might have happened to me if I could have worked with David Moyes? I might still be there now.
GASCOIGNE, 2009

The season after the [1990] World Cup, with Tottenham. Everything went right. It was a magical time. On the pitch, I could do no wrong.
GASCOIGNE, 2009

[Gascoigne] wasted the gifts he was blessed with and doesn't have an excuse.
BRIAN CLOUGH in Cloughie: Walking On Water, *2002*

He is accused of being arrogant, unable to cope with the press and a boozer. Sounds like he's got a chance to me.
GEORGE BEST, 1988

He can be a loony with a fast mouth. He's either going to be one of the greats or finish up at 40 bitter about wasting such talent.
JOHN BAILEY, former Newcastle colleague, 1988

Literally the most famous and probably the most popular person in Britain today.
TERRY WOGAN, introducing Gascoigne on his TV chat show, 1990

I'm no poof, that's for sure.
GASCOIGNE on Wogan, *1990*

A dog of war with the face of a child.
GIANNI AGNELLI, Juventus owner, admiring Gascoigne during England's World Cup run, 1990

Coping with the language shouldn't prove a problem. I can't even speak English yet.
GASCOIGNE after agreeing to move to Lazio, 1991

He wears a No. 10 jersey. I thought it was his position, but it turns out to be his IQ.
GEORGE BEST, 1993

He's an intelligent boy who likes people to think he's stupid. He doesn't have a bad bone in his body but he does some stupid, ridiculous things. That's what makes him so interesting.
ALLY McCOIST, Rangers colleague, 1996

ANNE ROBINSON: In the equation E=MC², devised by Einstein, what does the letter E stand for?
GASCOIGNE: Er... elephant?
EXCHANGE on the BBC TV quiz programme The Weakest Link: Sporting Heroes' Special, *2010*

They [the schoolboys] asked me things like: 'How big are Gazza's balls?'
VINNIE JONES after addressing the boys of Eton College, 1996

Gazza is no longer a fat, drunken imbecile. He is, in fact, a football genius.
EDITORIAL in the Daily Mirror *headed 'Mr Paul Gascoigne: An Apology' after his solo goal v Scotland, 1996*

He's a fantastic player when he isn't drunk.

BRIAN LAUDRUP, Rangers team-mate, 1997

Once you've played in the same side as Gazza, you fall in love with him because of the sort of person and player he is.
DAVID BECKHAM, England colleague, 1998

He was charming, he was funny... Literally, he was an angel.
SHERYL GASCOIGNE, ex-wife, on when she first met him, 1999

I knew managing him would have been no joy ride, but the hazards that went with the talent would never have put me off.
SIR ALEX FERGUSON recalling a thwarted bid to sign Gazza, 1999

Is there anything I'd like to change? Oh yes. I'd like to change the family's bank account numbers and that tackle I did [on Nottingham Forest's Gary Charles] at Wembley in the 1991 FA Cup final.
GASCOIGNE in TV interview by ex-Rangers colleague Ally McCoist, 1999

People think Paul and I have a father-and-son relationship. Well, I've got two sons and I have never felt like hitting them, but I have certainly felt like smacking him.
WALTER SMITH, his manager at Everton and Rangers, 2000

There's a little man in my head saying: 'Have a drink, have a drink.' You cannot get him out of your head, especially when there's only you and him.
GASCOIGNE after returning from China where he coached Gansu, 2003

There's been suicide thoughts, I don't mind admitting that. I don't want any sympathy. I honestly thought I couldn't live without a drink.
GASCOIGNE, 2004

I have been spat at and hit on planes loads of times, but nobody

said a word because it was First Class and it was Paul.
SHERYL GASCOIGNE, ex-wife, calling his autobiography 'a catalogue of half-truths', 2004

I thought he [Glenn Hoddle] said: 'Do you want to visit a brewery?'

GASCOIGNE on why he jumped at the chance to visit faith healer Eileen Drewery, quoted in his autobiography, 2004

I've got the full set of problems. It's not just the booze, it's the panic attacks, bipolar disorder, the purging – it's everything I have to deal with every day. For me to be alive it proves there really is a God.
GASCOIGNE, 2005

JOHN GILES

I thought he was miles better than [Billy] Bremner. A better passer, shrewder, more devious and harder when he wanted to be.
STEVE PERRYMAN, Tottenham captain, in A Man For All Seasons, *1985*

[Giles] could grab hold of a match, tuck it in his back pocket, and carry it around with him. He didn't

need to find space; it was as if space found him.
BRIAN CLOUGH, on the midfielder he inherited from Don Revie at Leeds, from Cloughie: Walking On Water, *2002*

DAVID GINOLA

Men will love his skills and women his looks. He could end up being popular enough to replace Robbie Williams in Take That.
CHRIS WADDLE, former England midfielder, 1995

I'm told he ran up the tunnel and dived into the bath.

JOE ROYLE, Everton manager, alleging Ginola went to ground too easily, 1995

JIMMY GLASS

Some go on to fame and fortune and some go on to driving a cab and living a normal life like me. It's quite difficult to understand your place in life from being this guy who'll never be forgotten to being the guy worrying about your next bill.
GLASS, taxi driver and former goalkeeper, whose stoppage-time goal while on loan to Carlisle in 1999 saved them from relegation to non-league football, 2013

ANDY GORAM

When is Andy Goram going to piss off and stop annoying us with his bloody wonder saves? Yours in victimisation.
LETTER to the Celtic fanzine Not the View, *1997*

ANDY GRAY

You're from Drumchapel, laddie. What do you know about prawn cocktails? You'll have soup like the rest of us.
JOCK STEIN, Scotland manager, to Aston Villa striker Gray after he tried to order from the menu on a trip abroad, 1979

EDDIE GRAY

When he plays on snow, he doesn't leave any footprints.

DON REVIE on the Leeds and Scotland midfielder, 1970

JIMMY GREAVES

Jimmy Greaves would walk past four defenders, send the goalie one way, roll the ball into the opposite corner and walk away as if to say 'What am I here for?', then have a fag at half-time.
HARRY REDKNAPP, Portsmouth manager, on the former Tottenham and England inside-forward, 2008

They were taking questions from the audience and a bloke asked Jimmy: 'Would you have got more goals if you hadn't been so lazy?' I jumped up and wagged my finger. I said: 'Now just hold on. That man is the best striker I ever played with. He scored five at Preston and five against Wolves. You don't do that if you're lazy.' Everyone applauded.
FRANK BLUNSTONE, former Chelsea and England winger, on seeing his former team-mate Greaves in a theatre show, 2009

Me and George Best are collaborating on a book about our lives in the 1970s, so if anyone can tell us where we were, we'd be very grateful.
GREAVES, a recovering alcoholic, on the BBC TV panel show They Think It's All Over, *1995*

Jimmy Greaves was controversially left out of the 1966 World Cup final winning team. And if he ever finds out, he'll be gutted.
NICK HANCOCK, host, They Think It's All Over, *1995*

JIMMY GREENHOFF

Our partnership was better than the one I had with Ossie (Chelsea's

Peter Osgood), who was more of an individualist and didn't need anybody else. Jimmy's touch, even on muddy pitches, was unbelievable. How could [Don] Revie have let him go from Leeds? Because he wouldn't kick anyone. He didn't get a single cap, which beggars belief when Carlton Palmer has played for England.

ALAN HUDSON, Stoke City and England midfielder, on his link with the striker, 2011

BRUCE GROBBELAAR

I'd rather have Grobbelaar trying to throw a game than Dave Beasant trying to win one.

CALLER to 606 radio phone-in after the former Liverpool goalkeeper's arrest on match-fixing charges, 1994

RUUD GULLIT

Watching Ruud was like watching an 18-year-old play in a game for 12-year-olds.

GLENN HODDLE, Chelsea manager, on the Dutch midfielder's English debut, 1995

ALAN HANSEN

A good skipper, but he could have been a really great one if he had been a bit more extrovert.

BOB PAISLEY, former Liverpool manager, 1989

JOHN HARTSON

With my ability I'd have played for a top foreign side or Manchester United or Liverpool if I'd gone through my career a stone and a half lighter... But there's plenty of slim, fit footballers who'd swap for my 50 caps, 200 goals and £20m of transfers.

HARTSON at West Bromwich Albion, 2006

Before our five-a-side in training one day, John yelled: 'Let's have Wales v The Rest.' Someone shouted: 'But you're the only Welshman here.' He said: 'Yeah, me against you fucking lot.' That's him.

TERRY WESTLEY, Hartson's former manager at Luton, 1997

TERRY HENNESSEY

Dear Terry, Sorry to hear about you having to retire from the game. The same thing happened to my sister. Mind you, she wasn't in the game, she was on it.

ERIC MORECAMBE, comedian and Luton director, in a letter to Derby and Wales defender Hennessey, 1973

JIMMY HILL

If he can find a ground where he scored a league goal, I'll meet him there.

BRIAN CLOUGH replying to Hill's challenge to debate, 1979

GLENN HODDLE

Hoddle a luxury? It's the bad players who are a luxury.

DANNY BLANCHFLOWER, predecessor in Tottenham's midfield, 1981

I hear Glenn has found God. That must have been one hell of a pass.
JASPER CARROTT, comedian, 1988

ALAN HUDSON

People ask me if we went out socialising. We socialised on the pitch.
JIMMY GREENHOFF, Stoke City striker of the 1970s, on his 'telepathic' understanding with the hard-drinking England midfielder, 2011

MARK HUGHES

A warrior you could trust with your life.

ALEX FERGUSON in the David Meek and Mark Hughes book, Hughesie: The Red Dragon, *1994*

ROGER HUNT

One morning Bob Paisley said to me: 'The boss wants to see you.' I thought it would be a pat on the back because I was scoring goals and thought I was doing OK. Instead, [Bill Shankly] said: 'Middlesbrough have put in a bid for you. What do you think?'
HUNT, World Cup-winning England striker, on the beginning of the end of his 11-year Liverpool career, 2013; he joined Bolton in 1969

Yes, he misses a few. But he gets in the right places to miss them.
BILL SHANKLY, the England forward's manager at Liverpool, 1966

NORMAN HUNTER

Norman bites yer legs
BANNER by Leeds fans honouring the hard-tackling defender, 1972

GEOFF HURST

Q: In your heart of hearts would you like to see another player score a World Cup final hat-trick?
A: No. That hat-trick and the win itself have transformed my life.
HURST in an interview with The Independent, *2006*

I wanted to play for England and score three goals in the World Cup final like Geoff Hurst in 1966. I

used to pray for that every night.
That's why I no longer believe in
God. He let me down.
*HUGH GRANT, screen actor and
Fulham fan, 2002*

DAVID ICKE

David Icke says he is here to save
the world. Well, he saved bugger
all when he played in goal for
Coventry.
JASPER CARROTT, comedian, 1992

PAUL INCE

When a player is at his peak, he
feels as if he can climb Everest in his
slippers. That's what he was like.
*ALEX FERGUSON, Ince's manager at
Manchester United, 1997*

After Bobby Moore, I'm probably
the greatest player to come out of
West Ham, which is to their credit.
INCE, 2001

FILIPPO INZAGHI

That lad must have been born offside.

*SIR ALEX FERGUSON on Italian
striker Inzaghi after a Manchester
United v Milan game, 2010*

DAVID JAMES

It's not nice going into the
supermarket and the woman at the
till is thinking: 'Dodgy keeper.'
*JAMES, then playing erratically in goal
for Liverpool, 1997*

MAURICE JOHNSTON

I didn't do it [sign the Catholic
Johnston for the traditionally
Protestant Rangers] to be a
revolutionary. I did it because he
was a bloody good player.
*GRAEME SOUNESS, Blackburn and
former Rangers manager, 2002*

JIMMY JOHNSTONE

Bless him. What would he be
earning today? What's Beckham on?
Double it.
*TERRY COOPER, former opponent
with Leeds and England, pondering the
terminally ill ex-Celtic and Scotland
winger's worth in the modern game, in
the documentary film* Lord of the Wing,
2004

Just as well you've no' got a touch
like [Celtic defender] Bobo Balde
or you'd go straight through that
window.
*GORDON STRACHAN, Celtic
manager, to Johnstone as he controlled
his wheelchair with his left foot because of
motor neurone disease, 2006*

VINNIE JONES

There's nothing to come back to here. To me, England is past its sell-by date. It's not the country I grew up in. It's a European country now. If someone blindfolded you and put you on a plane in LA, and you landed at Heathrow and they took it off, you wouldn't have a clue where you were.
JONES, former Wales captain and now an actor in Los Angeles, 2013

My best feature is my skin. When I played, my mate John Fashanu said: 'Jonesy, you've got to moisturise – you'll thank me when you're older.' So I've been moisturising for 20 years and it's paid off. When I have a shave, my skin is very soft.
JONES, as above

I've had about 80 stitches in my head and faces from football and bar incidents, so I have a lot of scars. I don't think I look intimidating, but I'm sure other people have their opinions.
JONES, as above

I've been trying to be a footballer and that isn't me. I got a bit carried away with the *Wogan* show and all that.
JONES, 1990

Vinnie admits he threw a piece of toast at Gary Lineker. What he didn't say was that it was still in the toaster.
TONY BANKS MP, Labour, on Radio 4's News Quiz, *1997*

ROY KEANE

He is my favourite enemy... I loved every aspect of his game.
PATRICK VIEIRA, former Arsenal and Manchester City adversary, in the ITV documentary Keane and Vieira: Best of Enemies, *2013*

Many times I went out to hurt a player because that was my job.

KEANE, as above

Stuff like that [Sir Alex Ferguson praising Keane's performance against Juventus in the 1999 Champions League semi-final] kind of insults me. That was my job.
KEANE, as above

The manager accused me of trying to manage Manchester United behind his back. What I did do was manage the dressing-room. That was my job.
KEANE, as above

A lot of my preparation was about fear; of losing, of letting my neighbourhood down, my family down. Fear played a big part in my sporting career.
KEANE, as above

I shed a few tears in my car outside the training ground. For about two minutes.
KEANE on his exit from United eight years earlier, 2013

Roy will be the hardest to replace. Forget the playing part, it's the spiritual and emotional thing he gives you. In his will to win, he's an absolute beast of a man.
SIR ALEX FERGUSON, 2005

Young Keane shouldn't screw up his privileged position at Old Trafford for the sake of a few thousand extra quid he might make abroad. It's tempting – 60 grand a week after tax, and a four-year contract. But I reckon that on top of what he has got already, he'd have to live until he's 634 to spend that lot.
BRIAN CLOUGH, who had brought Keane to England by signing him for Nottingham Forest from Cobh Ramblers, 1999

If I was in management now and had the money to take my pick of any player, anywhere, if I could have the best at Arsenal, Leeds, Chelsea or Real Madrid, I'd take Keane.
BRIAN CLOUGH, 1999

If that is not a sending-off offence, what is? What do we need to see, a leg with blood dripping off the stump?
PETER WILLIS, president of the Referees' Association, after Keane was sent off in the Charity Shield, 2000

I'm a great admirer of Roy Keane. He has been there, done it and still wants to do it. I don't like Manchester United but to be mentioned in the same breath as him is great.
STEVEN GERRARD, Liverpool midfielder, 2000

As if cutting [Alf-Inge] Haaland in half wasn't bad enough, Keane then swoops over him like Dracula. All he needed was the black cloak.
BRIAN CLOUGH after Keane was sent off in the Manchester derby, 2001

I'm sick and tired of hearing commentators telling us how much running Keane does in a match, how he covers every blade of grass. He's entitled to be fresher than most because he has so much time off – eight red cards and that long injury lay-off, which was his fault, incidentally, and not Alf-Inge Haaland's. He's had more than enough rest through the suspensions alone. He's had more holidays than Judith Chalmers.
CLOUGH, 2001

I'll have to see whether any of Keane's studs are still in there.
ALF-INGE HAALAND, Manchester City midfielder, before a scan on his knee, 2002

On the field [Keane] is a major asset. Off it he's quite unassuming, an ordinary lad. He'll say 'What are you all doing tonight?' and he'll come to the pictures or whatever. What you see on the pitch is a usually extravagant character but he's not like that off it.
MICK McCARTHY, Republic of Ireland manager, before leaving for the World Cup finals, 2002

As he waded in with one expletive after another, I asked myself if this was my captain. Was this a man who could serve Ireland as a role model for our children? The answer was no.
McCARTHY after banishing Keane from the squad in Japan, 2002

Roy Keane has no manners. There's never any reason not to be polite, even with people you don't like.
GEORGE BEST, former Manchester United player, after the falling out between Keane and McCarthy, 2002

Oh, I'd have sent him home all right, but I'd have shot him first.
BRIAN CLOUGH after Keane's expulsion by McCarthy, 2002

I've made mistakes. I was naive and probably drank too much.
KEANE in his autobiography, 2002

I'm surprised he did a book in the first place. He'd be the first to give someone stick in the dressing room if they had done something similar.
DENIS IRWIN, former United and Ireland colleague, now with Wolves, 2002

I only ever hit Roy the once. He got up so I couldn't have hit him that hard.
BRIAN CLOUGH, 2003

A lot of people think I'm a traitor. I can't worry about that. I believe I've given good service. All I'd ask is to be judged on what I did on the pitch in my 58 matches for Ireland, not on what I said in an interview.
KEANE after quitting international football, 2003

Alex Ferguson is Manchester United. His mentality is in the team and Roy Keane is an expression of this. Keane is Ferguson as a player.
CLAUDIO RANIERI, Chelsea manager, 2003

KEVIN KEEGAN

He's not only blossomed into a player but he can talk as well. I think maybe he'll get one of those jobs on television. Or perhaps he'll be Prime Minister. Who knows?
BILL SHANKLY, the manager who took Keegan to Liverpool from Scunthorpe, 1975

To call Keegan a superstar is stretching a point. As a player he's not fit to lace my boots.

GEORGE BEST, 1982

Keegan isn't fit to lace Best's drinks.
JOHN ROBERTS, football writer, in the Daily Mail, 1982

LEDLEY KING

Ledley was amazing. He couldn't train because of his knee problems but he'd still be unbelievable on a Saturday. You'd never see him making last-ditch tackles and diving in – the classic defender tackles – like a John Terry. Because he always read it so well, he was already in the right place at the right time. And he didn't know if he was left- or right-footed because he was so comfortable on both. We'd ask him and he'd say: 'I don't know.'
JERMAIN DEFOE, Toronto FC and England striker, on former Tottenham team-mate King, 2014

JURGEN KLINSMANN

Jurgen Klinsmann scored into a goal as wide and inviting as a tunnel painted on to a mountain by Wile E. Coyote to halt the Roadrunner.
MIKE DOWNEY, Los Angeles Times columnist, on the opening game of the World Cup finals, Germany v Bolivia, 1994

Me, dive? Never. I always go straight for goal.
KLINSMANN rebutting charges of diving, World Cup finals, 1994

I was watching Germany and got up to make a cup of tea. I bumped into the telly and Klinsmann fell over.
FRANK SKINNER, comedian, 1994

PAUL LAKE

[Manchester City] have certainly come on a bit since my day. And yet – and this is not me coming on all arrogant – I still think I could get in that team. Fans have suggested one or two past City players who would have got into today's side. I've been included on that list and I'm proud of that. There are players who cost £30m and there's me with my semi-detached in Stockport.
LAKE, City utility player of the 1980s–90s before his career was ruined by injury, 2011

HENRIK LARSSON

He has improved so much as a player, maybe because he has cut off his dreadlocks. He is more aerodynamic.

WIM JANSEN, Celtic manager, 2001

Before a game, I always tell myself that it will hurt and it should hurt. I know I am bloody strong, stronger than them. Even if it hurts, it is going to hurt them even more.
LARSSON, Celtic and Sweden striker, 2003

MICHAEL LAUDRUP

When Michael plays like a dream, a magical illusion, determined to show his new team his extreme abilities, no one in the world comes anywhere near his level.
JOHAN CRUYFF, Laudrup's former coach at Barcelona, on the Dane's display in 1994 when Real Madrid beat Barca 5–0, in Christian Mohr Boisen, Laudrup: A Football Dynasty, 2008

Had he been born in a poor ghetto in Brazil or Argentina with the ball his only way out of poverty he would today be recognised as the game's biggest genius ever. He had all the abilities but lacked the ghetto instinct that could have driven him there.
CRUYFF, 2008

DENIS LAW

Denis Law could dance on eggshells.
BILL SHANKLY, former Liverpool manager, on the forward he signed for Huddersfield as a teenager, 1970s

Denis didn't look like a footballer. He was very skinny and wore patched-up National Health glasses. I really thought he'd just delivered the milk.
KEVIN McHALE, the teenaged Law's wing partner at Huddersfield in the 1950s, recalling their first meeting, 2013

Denis was in the class of Alfredo Di Stefano because he could do everything, organise a side and score goals... Matt Busby knew how important he was – when Denis was doubtful [due to injury] the boss would practically be on his hands and knees hoping he would play.
HARRY GREGG, Manchester United goalkeeper, in the Motson-Rowlinson book The European Cup 1955–80, 1980

MARK LAWRENSON

I'm 18, I'm playing in the old Third Division with Preston; I thought I'm never going to be good enough to play for England.
LAWRENSON, BBC TV pundit, on why he became 'Irish' for international purposes, 2012

JENS LEHMANN

Lehmann belongs in *The Muppet Show*, on the couch or in a mental institution.
TIM WEISE, Werder Bremen goalkeeper, on criticism from ex-Arsenal keeper turned TV pundit, 2010

I have to accept that there are people who don't have a clue about football.

LEHMANN, Arsenal goalkeeper, on critics who argued he was the team's weak link, 2004

GRAEME LE SAUX

I've been slaughtered for reading *The Guardian*. In most walks of life, that would be respected, differences valued. I took stick from the lads and often it was upsetting. But I stuck it out when I had plenty of opportunities to fit in with the sheep.
LE SAUX, Blackburn and England defender, 1995

I got plenty of comments from other players about being a faggot or a queer. Robbie Savage seemed to get a particular thrill out of it.
GRAEME LE SAUX, who is heterosexual, in Left Field: A Footballer Apart, *2008*

MATTHEW LE TISSIER

You're never sure you want him playing for you, but you're sure you don't want him playing against you.
DARIO GRADI, Crewe manager, on the Southampton midfielder, 1995

The one thing I'd like to rid myself of is the word 'but'. You know: 'He's a great player, but...' or 'So much skill, but...'
LE TISSIER, 1997

GARY LINEKER

My record, averaging a goal every two games, sounds good, but that's only one goal every three hours. Most of the time I'm frustrated, pissed off, waiting for the right ball.
LINEKER, England striker, 1992

He had no feel for the game, no passion, and that's why, now that he has retired, he's best keeping out of football.
VINNIE JONES, former opponent, 1994

Too good to be true.
ALEX FERGUSON, Manchester United manager, 1996

PETER LORIMER

It's quite irritating to me that, having apparently been able to hit a football 300 yards, I can't do the same to a golf ball.
LORIMER, former Leeds and Scotland player renowned for his shooting power, 2013

DAVE MACKAY

My toughest opponent? No contest. Dave Mackay was a true leader who could drive others on and make them play. He could finish and he defended like his life depended on it. He was good enough to play for Celtic.
BERTIE AULD, former Celtic and Scotland midfielder, recalling his Tottenham compatriot, 2011

DIEGO MARADONA

I think I'm the best player ever. Why compare me to Pele? My mother says I'm stronger and that he used to play with players who didn't even move on the pitch. I don't like comparisons with Pele because of the stupid things he says. He keeps on saying stupid stuff when he takes the wrong pills.
MARADONA, 2013

I am a symbol of peace in the world. I have always expressed fairness in my football and that is what I'd like to see in every single match.
MARADONA, 2012

World Cup 2010: Maradona makes plea for fair play
HEADLINE on the BBC sports website, 2010

At the time I called it the Hand of God. Bollocks! It was the Hand of Diego!

MARADONA on his controversial goal for Argentina v England at the 1986 World Cup finals, 2005

A little bit the hand of God, a little the head of Diego.
MARADONA describing his 'volleyball' goal against England in the World Cup, 1986

Pele had nearly everything. Maradona has everything. He works harder, does more and is more skilful. Trouble is he'll be remembered for another reason – he bends the rules to suit himself.
SIR ALF RAMSEY after Maradona's 'Hand of God' goal, 1986

The best one-footed player since Puskas.
SIR STANLEY MATTHEWS, 1986

FIFA cut off my legs just when I had the chance to prove to my daughters that I could play with 20-year-olds.
MARADONA leaving the World Cup finals after failing a drugs test, 1994

I was, I am and I always will be a drug addict. A person who gets involved in drugs has to fight it every day.
MARADONA signing up to an Argentinian government anti-drugs campaign, 1996

For me, he was the perfect footballer. Pele was a better team player, but I believe Maradona was better than anyone who has played football on this planet.
GLENN HODDLE, England manager, 1998

If Jesus stumbled, then why shouldn't I as well?
MARADONA on his Argentinian TV chat show The Night of 10, *recalling his descent into drugs and obesity, 2005*

As far as we know, corpses can't speak.

MARADONA calling a Buenos Aires radio station after reports of his death, 2007

MARCO MATERAZZI

We shook hands and I said: 'Sorry for what happened. Now it's finished.' From man to man, there's nothing better. He said: 'No, don't worry. No problem.'
MATERAZZI, newly retired Italy defender, on meeting Zinedine Zidane five years after the former France captain was sent off for butting him in the World Cup final, 2011

STANLEY MATTHEWS

George Best and David Beckham rolled into one.
KENNETH WOLSTENHOLME, former TV commentator, on Matthews' death, 2000

If I had to get 'stuck in' to get through a game I'm afraid my career would have ended long ago.
MATTHEWS, then 45, in The Stanley Matthews Story, *1960*

Last night I had the strangest dream
I've never had before
Stan Matthews on the wing for
   Stoke
At the age of 84.
SONG on a Keele University students'
rag record, 1964

You usually knew how he'd beat you, but you couldn't do anything about it.

DANNY BLANCHFLOWER, former
Tottenham captain, 1970

Stan used to put the ball on my
centre parting. They don't do that
any more.
TOMMY LAWTON, former England
centre-forward, 1985

His name is symbolic of the beauty
of the game, his fame timeless. A
magical player, of the people, for
the people.
INSCRIPTION on a statue of Matthews
in Hanley, his birthplace, 1987

I'm not a scientist. I'm not a poet.
I'm not a writer. But of course I am
very honoured.
MATTHEWS accepting an honorary
degree from Keele University, 1987

I'm no hero. Doctors and nurses
are heroes. Surgeons, people like
that. We had a real hero born right
here in Stoke-on-Trent: Reginald
Mitchell, who designed the Spitfire.
He saved Britain. Now that's what
I call a hero.
SIR STAN, 1995

He never criticised the modern
game, never said that the players
weren't as good as in his day.
PETER COATES, Stoke City director, 2000

BENNI McCARTHY

He has an unfortunate addiction
to sugars. He can't carry that extra
weight, it's like expecting him to
play with two big bags of Tate
& Lyle strapped to his hips.
SAM ALLARDYCE, Blackburn
manager, on his club's former striker,
2010

ALLY McCOIST

He's handsome, he's rich, he's
funny and he's happy. My envy
knows no bounds.
BILLY CONNOLLY, comedian, in the
foreword to Ally McCoist: My Story, 1992

I met Michael Jackson backstage at
the Tokyo Dome in '93, but to be
honest, meeting Ally McCoist was a
bigger buzz.
ALAN McGEE, Creation Records label
owner, 1995

JOHN McGOVERN

I never got close to Brian Clough at all. I didn't want to. I thought: 'He's the boss.' And I've got a cupboard full of medals that prove it's the right way to go about doing the job.
McGOVERN, Clough's two-time European Cup-winning captain at Nottingham Forest, 2012; the Scottish midfielder also served Clough at Hartlepools, Derby and Leeds

Clough told me: 'Stand up straight, get your shoulders back and get your hair cut. You look like a girl.' I cycled home and told my mum: 'I'm not going back there – the bogey man has arrived.'
McGOVERN recalling his first meeting with his future mentor in 1965 as a teenaged trialist with Hartlepools United, 2012

PAUL McGRATH

One of the all-time greats – someone to compare with Bobby Moore.

JACK CHARLTON, McGrath's Republic of Ireland manager and former defensive partner to Moore with England, 1995

BILLY McNEILL

Billy sets a high standard of conduct for all of us, and this is the main reason why you do not see any long-haired wonders walking through the doors at Celtic Park... Professional football is our business. We feel we do not have to look like a crowd of discotheque drop-outs to attract attention.
BOBBY MURDOCH, Celtic and Scotland colleague, in All The Way With Celtic, *1970*

PAUL MERSON

Three million for a player is hardly anything. I had three million once.
MERSON, studio pundit on Sky's Soccer Saturday, *2009*

My addictions are always there, waiting for me. They're doing press-ups outside my door.
MERSON, Aston Villa midfielder, on his fight against alcoholism, gambling addiction and drug abuse, 1999

BOBBY MOORE

We're going to win the World Cup, and this man (pointing at Moore) is the reason why. He can already see in his mind's eye a picture of himself holding up the trophy.
RON GREENWOOD, West Ham and future England manager, in training with the London club, 1965

He was on a par with [Franz] Beckenbauer. He wasn't just cool, he was refrigerated.
TERRY VENABLES, Moore's contemporary and fellow England player, 2008

The slowest player I ever played with, without question, but no one ever ran him.
JACK CHARLTON, Moore's defensive partner in England's World Cup-winning side, 2006

There should be a law against him. He knows what's happening 20 minutes before anyone else.
JOCK STEIN, Celtic manager, 1969

Someone would come and kick a lump out of him, and he'd play as though he hadn't noticed. But 10 minutes later, whoof! He had a great 'golden boy' image, Moore. But he was hard.
GEOFF HURST, former West Ham and England colleague, in Brian James's Journey to Wembley, 1977

Bobby would never take a liberty, let alone a bracelet.
JIMMY GREAVES, friend and ex-England team-mate, after Moore's arrest for alleged theft of jewellery in Bogota, 1970

FABRICE MUAMBA

The only thing I remember about the game is running back and falling. I felt very dizzy while I was moving back. It was a strange sensation, like I was running inside someone else's body. Then I fell. My head hit the ground twice and I lost consciousness. I didn't feel anything. I was dead. That happened on the Saturday and I didn't wake up until Monday. I've never watched the video because I'm not yet ready. Now I intend to enjoy life.
MUAMBA, former Bolton and England U-21 midfielder, who suffered a heart attack and stopped breathing for an hour while playing in an FA Cup tie v Tottenham, 2012

Did we lose?
MUAMBA to friends and family on waking from his coma

When they were trying to resuscitate him the whole stadium went quiet. You could sense the Spurs fans were shocked. Then the Bolton fans began to sing his name. And then the Spurs supporters. I nearly broke down. I'm not a person who cries that much but it sent a real tingle down my spine.
NIGEL REO-COKER, Bolton captain

I'm a deeply faithful man, a religious man, and I believe there's something more than just playing the game. There's somebody who looks after us.
SEPP BLATTER, FIFA president, after Muamba regained consciousness

If I was ever going to use the term miraculous it could be here.
DR ANDREW DEANER, the cardiologist who ran from the crowd to attend to Muamba

GARY NEVILLE

As captain, I would organise the team nights out – and I used to plan meticulously. 'We'll go there at 2pm, leave at 4, eat at 5…' The lads used to say: 'Let's go with the flow, shall we? Maybe we'll leave the pub at 5.23pm rather than 5pm.' But that's just the way I am.
NEVILLE, former Manchester United captain, 2013

Being a robot devoid of passion and spirit is obviously the way forward for the modern footballer.

NEVILLE on being fined for celebrating a United goal in front of Liverpool fans, 2006

If he was an inch taller he'd be the best centre-half in Britain. His father is 6ft 2in – I'd check the milkman.
ALEX FERGUSON on his 5ft 11in defender, 1996

PHIL NEVILLE

I've never been so certain about anything in my life. I want to be a coach. Or a manager. I'm not sure which.
NEVILLE, Everton captain, 2009

CHARLIE NICHOLAS

It was like buying a Van Gogh and sticking it away in a bank vault.
BRIAN CLOUGH on Nicholas's spell in Arsenal Reserves, 1987

People reckoned I spent all my time in Stringfellow's but I never went there that much. I preferred Tramp.
CHARLIE NICHOLAS on his spell with Arsenal, 1995

MARTIN O'NEILL

O'NEILL: Why am I playing for the second team?
BRIAN CLOUGH: Because you're too good for the thirds.
EXCHANGE between Nottingham Forest player and manager circa 1980, recalled by O'Neill, 2004

PETER OSGOOD

I am a pagan god.

FIRST SENTENCE of the former Chelsea, Southampton and England striker's autobiography, 2002

MICHAEL OWEN

An emotion that lives with me is a sense of 'what might have been' had injuries not robbed me of my most lethal weapon – speed. Many of my highlights were early on in my career and I can only wonder what more I would have achieved had my body been able to withstand the demands that I was making of it. I was almost too quick.

OWEN, former England, Liverpool, Manchester United and Real Madrid striker, announcing retirement, 2013

It's ironic, but the people who gave me flak for building up Manor House [the Cheshire stables where Owen breeds racehorses], who told me I'd taken my eye off the ball, are probably the same people who will be depressed in later life because they didn't plan ahead.

OWEN, as above

I'm not sure whether he's a natural goal-scorer.

GLENN HODDLE, England manager, 1998

He showed the sureness of a surgeon in every movement, the high-speed precision of a computer in every touch and the ambition of a thief in the final shot.

JORGE VALDANO, former Real Madrid and Argentina striker, after Owen scored for England v Argentina, World Cup finals, 1998

I'm not a tights wearer. Maybe in my own household but not on the pitch.

OWEN after declining to wear leggings when playing for Real Madrid in freezing Kiev, 2004

OWEN: I've worked my nuts off to get back. INTERVIEWER: How are you feeling now? OWEN: My groin's a bit sore.

EXCHANGE in TV interview when Owen returned to Newcastle's side after injury, 2007

STUART PEARCE

I went to have a look at him playing for Wealdstone on a stinking night at Yeovil. After eight minutes he put in a thundering tackle and the Yeovil winger landed in my wife's lap. I said to her: 'That's it. I've seen enough. We're going home.'
BOBBY GOULD recalling how he signed Pearce for Coventry, 1991

Two days after a hamstring strain that would have kept anyone else out for a fortnight, on a freezing day when we were all training in bobble hats and gloves, he emerged, running out of the mist, wearing nothing but a pair of underpants and a towel wrapped round his head. That's why they call him Psycho.
KEVIN KEEGAN, Manchester City manager, after Pearce's last playing season ended in promotion to the Premiership, 2002

PELE

When I turn 100, I want all my friends there [in Rio de Janeiro's Maracana Stadium] with me. If I'm well physically, I'll even play for ten minutes. But it has to be in the Maracana.
PELE, 2012

Today the players blow a kiss to the camera and it appears all over the world. In my day we had to play in every country to be known. The only reason I'm not famous on the moon is because I didn't play there.
PELE, as above

I go much faster
Than those who run
Without thinking.
POEM by Pele, from My Life and the Beautiful Game, *1977*

I score more than a thousand goals in my life, but the one I don't score they remember.

PELE recalling the save by Gordon Banks that kept out his header, Brazil v England, 1970 World Cup finals, 2008

Football is like music, where there is Beethoven and the rest. In football, there is Pele and the rest.
PELE on the decision by FIFA, football's world governing body, to split a player-of-the-century award between himself and Diego Maradona, 2001

Pele knows nothing about the game. He's done nothing as a coach and his analysis is always wrong. If you want to win a title, do the opposite of what Pele says.
LUIZ FELIPE SCOLARI, Brazil coach, on winning the World Cup after criticism by Pele, 2002

Nowadays a player given a yellow card is scared to get sent off. In my day you didn't have this. That's why if I was playing today I wouldn't have scored 1,200 goals, I would have scored 2,400 – double the amount – because there is better protection.
PELE, 2003

Pele is the John Lennon of football. He's still the benchmark.

NOEL GALLAGHER, member of Oasis and Manchester City fan, 2006

Pele is well known for the shit he talks. Nobody should take him seriously. I don't want to end up a bitter old man like him who talks only bollocks.
RONALDO, Brazil striker, after Pele criticised him, 2006

MARTIN PETERS

Martin Peters is a player 10 years ahead of his time.
ALF RAMSEY, England manager, 1968

He's the one who's 10 years ahead of his time so we've got to wait for him to come good.
MALCOLM ALLISON, Manchester City

manager and TV World Cup panellist, 1970

ROBERT PIRES

Does he do it on purpose? Only God will be able to decide.
ARSENE WENGER, Arsenal manager, after Portsmouth accused Pires of diving to win a penalty, 2003

Sometimes when you play against these types of players, it's as if they have it in their contracts that you're not allowed to tackle them.
PHIL NEVILLE, Everton defender, after the Frenchman accused him of trying to injure him, 2005

MICHEL PLATINI

I bought him for the price of a piece of bread. But the bread came liberally spread in pate de foie gras.
GIANNI AGNELLI, Juventus owner, on signing the French international, 2002

ROBERT PROSINECKI

This man was on another planet. He went to Barnsley one night and I've never seen a performance like it. When I took him off with four minutes left, 14,000 people stood up, clapping him. He was that good. Good players can play anywhere. If they can't play at

Barnsley then they're not top players.

HARRY REDKNAPP, Queens Park Rangers manager, on managing the former Real Madrid and Croatia midfielder at Portsmouth, 2013

TONY PULIS

Bread and butter player. A booter. Takes no prisoners. Ball-winner though never sees much of the ball. Tony's motto was 'They don't limp fast'.

JOHN RUDGE, Stoke City director of football, in a tongue-in-cheek 'scouting report' of the Stoke manager when he was a 1970s playing colleague at Bristol Rovers, 2008

FERENC PUSKAS

His shooting was unbelievable and his left foot was like a hand. He could do anything with it. In the showers he would even juggle with the soap.

FRANCISCO GENTO, Real Madrid colleague, in Motson and Rowlinson, The European Cup 1955–80, *1980*

He had a seventh sense for football. Offer him 1,000 solutions and he'd pick the 1,001st.

NANDOR HIDEGKUTI, team-mate in the great Hungary side of the 1950s, at Puskas's 70th birthday party, 1997

NIALL QUINN

Anyone who uses the word 'quintessentially' during a half-time talk is talking crap.

MICK McCARTHY, Republic of Ireland manager, after Quinn made a suggestion during an international match, 1998

LUCAS RADEBE

What are you doing here? [To aides]: This is my hero. I call him 'Big Tree'.

NELSON MANDELA, former president of South Africa, after meeting Radebe at a civic reception in Leeds (when he thought he was in Liverpool), 2001

I love the club, place, the vibe. But when I leave I have to be able to walk.

RADEBE after serious injuries forced his retirement at Leeds, 2005

FABRIZIO RAVANELLI

I started the shirt-lifting thing and I'm still the best at it.

RAVANELLI struggling with colloquialisms at Derby, 2002

CYRILLE REGIS

I know Cyrille has found God. Now I want him to find the devil.
RON ATKINSON, Aston Villa manager, 1992

JOHN ROBERTSON

Manny Kalz? We've got a little fat guy who'll turn him inside out.
BRIAN CLOUGH on his Scotland winger before Nottingham Forest v Cologne, European Cup semi-final, 1979

BRYAN ROBSON

[Alex Ferguson] had me in the office and said: 'I know you can run for fun even after you've had a drink, but I'd sooner you cut the drinking down and you'd be able to run even further and for longer.' I had no problem with that. Paul McGrath did, and didn't change at all. That's why he went.
BRYAN ROBSON, former Manchester United and England captain, on Ferguson's retirement, 2013

Some said his bravery bordered on stupidity, but without that courage he would have been just another good player.
BOBBY ROBSON, former England manager, in Against All Odds, 1990

ROMARIO

I never acted professionally. I was never an athlete. I did not sleep properly. I did not eat like a sportsman. I was always late to training. I didn't put in the effort in training sessions every day. But I still scored 1,002 goals. If I had not gone out so much, I would have scored 2,000 goals. But 1,000 is still good, right?
ROMARIO, former Brazil striker, 2012

RONALDO

I want to go down in the history of world football. I want to mark an era, to be a different player, to score special goals. Just to be a good player is not enough.
RONALDO, Brazil striker, before becoming the top scorer in the World Cup finals, 2002

IAN RUSH

Painful to watch, but beautiful.

DAVID PLEAT, Luton manager, after Rush scored five for Liverpool against his team, 1983

If I was really unhappy I would rather go home and play for Flint Town United.
RUSH, struggling to settle in Italy with Juventus, 1988

Sometimes I think people don't realise that Wales exists as a country. Pele has picked Gary Lineker in his list of the 125 greatest living footballers. Having played with Lineker and Ian Rush, I can tell you Rushie was twice the player.
NEVILLE SOUTHALL, former Everton and Wales goalkeeper, 2004

ROBBIE SAVAGE

I love football, that's what people don't realise. They just see the hair and the teeth, and the tan and the big house, and the car and the model wife, and the Dolce & Gabbana clothes and the houses all over the world.
SAVAGE during his final season as a player, with Derby, 2010

My new yellow Ferrari broke down on the M42. I ended up on the side of the motorway with everyone driving past giving me 'V' and 'wanker' signs, even old men and women.
SAVAGE, 2009

Robbie Savage was put on his arse by our James Harper and Robbie said: 'I've been earning £40,000 a week for a decade, what have you earned?' It took James three weeks to get over it.
GRAHAM MURTY, Reading captain, 2008

Here's one for Mr and Mrs Robbie Savage. You do know he's gay?
ROBBIE WILLIAMS, pop singer, during a concert attended by the midfielder, 2006

PETER SCHMEICHEL

Schmeichel was towering over me and the other players were covering their eyes. I was looking up and thinking: 'If he does hit me, I'm dead.'
SIR ALEX FERGUSON, the Dane's former manager, recalling a dressing-room clash, 2006

Peter returns, but the operation has not worked because he still won't admit it when he has made a mistake.

BRIAN McCLAIR, Manchester United colleague, in his diary in Manchester United Magazine, *1995*

His sheer presence frightens opponents. In one match recently, Spurs hit the bar twice and I'm sure it was because they were trying to avoid him.
RUUD GULLIT, Chelsea player-manager, 1997

PAUL SCHOLES

Around Europe people ask me to name the best player I've worked with. I say Paul Scholes because he could do absolutely everything. Apart from tackle.
STEVE McCLAREN, former England manager and ex-Manchester United coach, 2013

[Scholes] was always unbelievably talented. Quiet. And dirty. When he got his tackle right, it was a great tackle. But when he got it wrong, he could kill someone.
DAVID BECKHAM, former United and England colleague, in the documentary film Class of 92, *2013*

If it's desperation bringing back the best midfield player in Britain over the past 20 years then I think we can accept that.
SIR ALEX FERGUSON, Manchester United manager, after Manchester City official Patrick Vieira said Scholes' decision to reverse his retirement was a sign of 'weakness', 2012

I'm sure if he was 6ft 2in, he'd be the best player in the world.
RAY WILKINS, Millwall coach and ex-United player, on the 'wonderful, world-class' Scholes before the FA Cup final, 2004

[Scholes and Wayne Rooney] batter the ball in training. Gary Neville was having a piss one day, 45 yards away by a fence. Scholes whacked him right in the arse.
SIR ALEX FERGUSON, 2004

Scholes is nasty and I like that in him. You need that if you play in the centre of the park.
ROY KEANE, Sunderland manager, working as a TV summariser, 2006

Scholes is getting to his feet, but very gingerly.
DAVID PLEAT, media pundit, 2006

DAVID SEAMAN

Q: Why is Nayim the most virile player in Europe?
A: Because he can lob Seaman from 50 yards.
JOKE by Tottenham fans after the ex-Spurs player Nayim scored from long range to clinch the Cup-Winners' Cup for Zaragoza against Arsenal, 1995

After the Nayim goal in Paris, people thought it was funny to totter backwards like I did that night and pretend to watch a ball dipping over their heads.
SEAMAN, 1997

That David Seaman is a handsome young man but he spends too much time looking in his mirror rather than at the ball. You can't keep goal with hair like that.
BRIAN CLOUGH on the England keeper's ponytail, 2000

David Seaman looked a broken man afterwards. I told him: 'If you go on thinking about that goal, you'll break yourself down. You must stop it. It's over. You saved us in Germany and in other games here, so you shouldn't think about it any more.'
SVEN-GORAN ERIKSSON after Seaman let a long-range free-kick drift over him for Brazil's winner v England, World Cup finals, 2002

I haven't seen [Ronaldinho's] winner yet. It's not that I'm avoiding it, just that my little girl has been watching Teletubbies all the time.
SEAMAN after arriving home from England's exit, 2002

A great ability of Seaman's, one I lacked, was his knack of calming people. I've always thought it a travesty that people talk of 'the famous Arsenal back four'. It should be 'the famous back five'.
PETER SCHMEICHEL, Seaman's

predecessor in Manchester City's goal, on his sudden retirement, 2004

ALAN SHEARER

I have a lot of respect for Shearer. He is the forward I dreaded meeting in the Premier League. Shearer would always fight for anything and everything. He was never into theatrics like [Liverpool striker] Luis Suarez. Suarez always thinks the football pitch is a swimming pool.
MARCEL DESAILLY, former Chelsea and France defender, 2013

In terms of bringing charisma to the club, Eric [Cantona] had an impact Shearer could never have matched. Yet in the long term, Shearer could have won us the European Cup. I think he was the missing ingredient for us in Europe.
SIR ALEX FERGUSON, Manchester United manager, on being spurned by the young Shearer, 2003

I remember Ray Harford when he was Blackburn manager telling me how Bill Nicholson, the great Spurs manager, walked his daughter down the aisle in floods of tears on her wedding day. He found himself asking: 'Where have all the years gone?' He had missed seeing her grow up because of his involvement in football. I don't want that to happen to me.
SHEARER announcing his international retirement, 2000

The truth was that Alan's game really had fallen away. I sat him down and we had long, intense chats. I told him bluntly he had stopped doing the things that made him a genuine great. Some people told me Newcastle expected him to do too much, but I told them – and Alan – he wasn't doing half enough.
BOBBY ROBSON, Newcastle manager, 2000

TEDDY SHERINGHAM

When he played for me at Nottingham Forest he was the slowest player in the squad – perhaps due to all those nightclubs he kept telling me he didn't frequent.
BRIAN CLOUGH after Sheringham was named Footballer of the Year, 2001

TOMMY SMITH

Tommy Smith wasn't born. He was quarried.
BILL SHANKLY, Liverpool manager, 1967

With 11 Tommy Smiths you would not only win the European Cup, you would fancy your chances against the whole Russian Army.
MARTIN BUCHAN, Manchester United captain, 1977

OLE GUNNAR SOLSKJAER

He's the best substitute in the world. If I ever feel guilty about the teams I pick, it invariably centres round him because he really deserves better. But the fact is that he's better than anyone at the club as a sub. He can come on and find the flow easily.
ALEX FERGUSON after the Norwegian scored four for Manchester United in an 18-minute cameo at Nottingham Forest, 1999

GRAEME SOUNESS

If he was a chocolate drop, he'd eat himself.
ARCHIE GEMMILL, Scotland team-mate, 1978

He's the nastiest, most ruthless man in soccer. Don Revie's bunch of assassins at Leeds were bad enough, but there is a streak in Souness that puts him top of the list.
FRANK WORTHINGTON, widely travelled striker, 1984

GARETH SOUTHGATE

I've only taken one penalty before, for Crystal Palace at Ipswich when it was 2–2 in the 89th minute. I hit the post and we went down that year. But I think I would be far more comfortable now than I was then.
SOUTHGATE, England defender, tempts fate before his decisive miss in the shoot-out v Germany, European Championship semi-final, 1996

I'm sure that people will always say: 'He's the idiot who missed that penalty.'
SOUTHGATE, 1997

GARY SPEED

I'm going to miss his childlike laugh. I'll forget the goals but I'll never forget that laugh.
GORDON STRACHAN on the apparent suicide of Wales manager Gary Speed, his former Leeds team-mate, 2011

Go on Gary Speed lad. Get one yourself son.
BANNER in the Leeds end at Nottingham Forest soon after Speed's death, 2011; the wording came from a radio commentary before his 1990 goal v Sheffield United

NOBBY STILES

Andy Lochhead was streaking towards goal when Nobby clipped him from behind. Out came my book and Stiles, full of apologies, pleaded: 'It's the floodlights, ref. They shine in my contact lenses and I can't see a thing.' As I was writing, Nobby leaned over and said: 'You spell it with an "I" not a "Y".'
PAT PARTRIDGE, Football League referee, in Oh, Ref!, *1979*

GORDON STRACHAN

There are true legends in the Hall of Fame. I was a half-decent player who had good team-mates. I'm quite annoyed with myself because, in the acceptance speech, I forgot to mention these guys.
STRACHAN, former Scotland midfielder, on being inducted to the Scottish FA Hall of Fame, 2007

A lot of the time he was playing from memory – but my God, what a memory.
RON ATKINSON, Manchester United manager, on Strachan's comeback after injury, 1985

He can destroy at once the big tough guys in the dressing room with one lash of his coruscating tongue. That's why he earned the nickname 'King Tongue'.
HOWARD WILKINSON, Leeds manager, in Managing to Succeed: My Life in Football Management, *1992*

MICKEY THOMAS

I don't mind Roy Keane making £60,000 a week. I was making the same when I was playing. The only difference is that I was printing my own.
THOMAS, former Manchester United midfielder with a conviction for counterfeiting currency, 2002

BERT TRAUTMANN

Non-City fans see his heroics as incredible, beyond the call of duty. But Bert had been diving at forwards' feet for 10 years without getting hurt. He didn't bother trying to force attackers wide. He just plunged in, head first, five or six times a game. It wasn't surprising that he dived in; the surprise was that he took a knock.
FRED EYRE, former Manchester City apprentice, lifelong fan and broadcaster, recalling after Trautmann's death how City's German goalkeeper played on in the 1956 FA Cup final after breaking his neck, 2013

MARCO VAN BASTEN

Marco played football like a ballerina, like Rudolf Nureyev with a colossal body, but eventually his ankle wouldn't stand the strain.
RENE MARTI, Swiss surgeon who treated Van Basten before his retirement, 1995

RUUD VAN NISTELROOY

You get the impression that if United won 5–0 and Van Nistelrooy didn't score, he would sulk on the way home. That's why he is where he is.
GARETH SOUTHGATE, Middlesbrough and England defender, on the Dutch striker, 2004

Even when he farts he seems to score.

ALESSANDRO DEL PIERO, Juventus striker, on his Manchester United counterpart, 2003

In years to come, we could well be unveiling a statue of him at Old Trafford. That's how good he is.
SIR ALEX FERGUSON, 2003

You see Thierry Henry and it's beautiful. You see me and it's not classic.
VAN NISTELROOY, 2004

TERRY VENABLES

A clever, cocky player – arrogant, but then he was good.

MICK PEJIC, ex-Stoke and England defender, 1989

PATRICK VIEIRA

By not getting drawn into a life of crime, I've already won. After going through all that drama with my dad, my mum was already really happy that I went down the sporting route.
PATRICK VIEIRA, Manchester City reserves' manager and former Arsenal and France captain, 2013

Vieira was bragging about all the things he'd done in Senegal. I said to him: 'If you're so fucking worried about Senegal, why didn't you play for them?'
ROY KEANE recalling a tunnel fracas before an Arsenal v Manchester United game, 2006

There are players who have no interest in playing the game properly. They are just trying to upset Patrick. There are

certain managers who encourage this.
ARSENE WENGER, Vieira's manager at Arsenal, after he was sent off for the second time in three days, 2000

Patrick would love to have come here last year, but they wouldn't let him. Players always want to play for a bigger club.
SIR ALEX FERGUSON, Manchester United manager, 2002

BERTI VOGTS

A team of 11 Berti Vogtses would be unbeatable.
KEVIN KEEGAN after playing for England against the West Germany defender, 1975

PAUL WARHURST

The lad was sent off for foul and abusive language but he swears blind he didn't say a word.

JOE ROYLE, Oldham manager, after Warhurst's dismissal v Notts County, 1990

NEIL WARNOCK

I was very quick but brainless. At Rotherham they used to shout 'Open the gate!' when I was going down the wings. I got my brains as a player when I was about 31, but by then my legs had gone. I was like Ronaldinho, only without the skill.
NEIL WARNOCK, Sheffield United manager, 2006

TARIBO WEST

Probably the weirdest guy I've ever met. We were playing at Pride Park and Taribo shouted something at me. I said something back and thought that was the end of it. But in the dressing-room at half-time he practically pinned me against the wall and said: 'You are not welcome in my church.' In his world that was the worst he could say to me.
CHRIS RIGGOTT, former Derby defender, on the Nigerian centre-back, an evangelical Christian who ran his own church in Milan, 2010

RAY WILKINS

He played the game in the Liverpool fashion and I could never understand why he was criticised for that.
TREVOR BROOKING, former England midfielder, in his book 100 Great British Footballers, *1988.*

BERT WILLIAMS

Ninety years old, that's fantastic. If I can get even halfway there I'd be happy.
STEVE BULL on his fellow former Wolves and England player, goalkeeper Williams – a month before Bull's 45th birthday, 2010

DENNIS WISE

Whatever player he's up against, he tries to wind them up. If he fouls you he normally picks you up, but the referee doesn't see what he picks you up by.
RYAN GIGGS, Manchester United opponent, 2000

Ninety-five per cent of my language problems are the fault of that stupid little midget.
GIANFRANCO ZOLA on his former Chelsea team-mate, 2003

FRANK WORTHINGTON

The way he is losing his hair he'll be the first bald guy ever to do impressions of Elvis Presley.
GRAEME SOUNESS, Scotland midfielder, 1984

IAN WRIGHT

On his first day at Palace he told me he wanted to play for England,

a bold statement for someone who had just walked in off a building site.
STEVE COPPELL, Crystal Palace manager, 1993

I just wish the record was going to someone else. I don't have a very high opinion of Ian Wright.
JOAN BASTIN, widow of Cliff Bastin, before Wright broke his all-time Arsenal scoring record, 1997

RON YEATS

He's a colossus. Come outside and I'll give you a walk round him.

BILL SHANKLY, Liverpool manager, to reporters after signing the 6ft 2in, 14-stone centre-half, 1961

TONY YEBOAH

The third goal was in the net in the time it takes a snowflake to melt on a hot stove.
HOWARD WILKINSON, Leeds manager, on the Ghanaian's hat-trick v Ipswich, 1995

DWIGHT YORKE

If that lad makes a First Division footballer, my name is Mao Tse Tung.
TOMMY DOCHERTY, former manager, on the Aston Villa and future Manchester United striker, 1991

I think he's an idiot… It's a shame I'm having his kid really.

JORDAN, model aka Katie Price, accusing Yorke of treating her 'like dirt' during her pregnancy with their child, 2002

ZINEDINE ZIDANE

Why do you want to sign this Zidane when we've got Tim Sherwood?
JACK WALKER, Blackburn Rovers owner, in a remark reputedly made to manager Kenny Dalglish, 1992

He was very sad for everything that happened, but this is life. He is a human being.
ALAIN MIGLIACCIO, Zidane's agent, after the France captain was sent off for butting Italy's Marco Materazzi in the World Cup final, 2006

What [Marco Materazzi] said was very personal. He insulted my mother, my sister, my whole family, and he did it not once, twice, but three times. I'd rather have been punched in the face than hear those insults. The third time it was too much. I'm a man first and foremost.
ZIDANE on why he assaulted Italy's Materazzi in the World Cup final, 2006

I did not call Zidane a terrorist. I'm ignorant; I don't even know what the word means. It was an insult like you hear dozens of times. I certainly didn't mention Zidane's mother – for me, a mother is sacred.
MARCO MATERAZZI, Italy defender, on what he said to provoke Zidane into butting him, 2006

You are a virtuoso, a genius of world football. You are also a man of heart, commitment, conviction. That's why France admires and loves you.
JACQUES CHIRAC, President of France, to Zidane before the final, 2006

Sometimes you just want to stop playing just to watch him.
CHRISTOPHE DUGARRY, France colleague, 2000

My father was my inspiration. He taught us that an immigrant must work twice as hard as anybody else; that he must never give up.
ZIDANE, whose Algerian father was a warehouseman in Marseilles, 2004

They say an unmade bed is art. But what Zidane does, that's art.
GORDON STRACHAN, former Scotland captain, working as a TV summariser, European Championship finals, 2004

Zidane plays as if he has silk gloves on each foot.
ALFREDO DI STEFANO, Real Madrid predecessor, 2005

GIANFRANCO ZOLA

The moment I turned up for training and saw Zola, I knew it was time to go.
JOHN SPENCER, Scotland striker, on the Italian's impact at Chelsea, 1997

③

CLUBS

ABERDEEN

I could see the Real Madrid players looking across at us and some of them were laughing, as if to say: 'Look at this bunch here.'
ALEX McLEISH, former Aberdeen defender, recalling the tunnel scene before the 1983 European Cup-Winners' Cup final, won by the Scottish club, 2013

If a cup had to go flying then it had to go flying. It certainly worked.
WILLIE MILLER, McLeish's former centre-back partner, remembering Alex Ferguson's managerial methods at Aberdeen, on the 30th anniversary of their European success, 2013

I had a baseball bat. I would sometimes go into the boot room with a baseball bat and let fly at a few of them.
ARCHIE KNOX, Ferguson's assistant, 2013

I grew up thinking that's what normal dressing-rooms were like.
ERIC BLACK, striker in Ferguson's Aberdeen side, 2013

I don't think we should sell the skin before we kill the bear.
EBBE SKOVDAHL, Danish manager of Aberdeen, counselling against assuming a top-six spot was secure, 2002

AJAX

We are the best! And not just the best from Amsterdam, but also the best from Rotterdam. And Eindhoven. And Europe. And the world.
LOUIS VAN GAAL, Ajax coach, after winning the Intercontinental Cup, 1995

ARSENAL

The Invincibles – I don't like saying that bloody word, but they were pretty strong at the time.
ROY KEANE, former Manchester United captain, on Arsenal's unbeaten championship-winning side of 2004 in the ITV documentary Keane and Vieira: Best of Enemies, *2013*

Hatred. I can't think of any other word when I was going into battle with Arsenal.

KEANE, as above

In 2006 we reached the Champions League final. Can you say we failed that season? I don't think so. We beat Real Madrid with [Zinedine] Zidane, but nobody speaks about

it. It's like we have done nothing. Why? Because at the end of the season you don't parade with the trophy.
ARSENE WENGER, Arsenal manager, as the club's run without silverware approached eight years, 2014

England is bankrupt. Europe is bankrupt. But still everyone keeps on spending. Arsenal are not bankrupt. That's because we spend in a sensible way.
WENGER, 2012

The type of player they had, the likes of [Patrick] Vieira, [Emmanuel] Petit, [Thierry] Henry, Tony Adams and Steve Bould, have been replaced by a different type now. It's a younger player, a different kind altogether. But [Wenger] is still trying to do the same things – to entertain and play their football their way.
SIR ALEX FERGUSON, Manchester United manager, 2012

We worked our socks off [in pre-season] and at the end of the trip [Arsene] Wenger said we could all go out. We went straight to the pub and the French lads went to the coffee shop. I'll always remember Steve Bould going to the bar and ordering 35 pints for five of us. After we left we spotted all the French lads in the coffee shop, sitting around smoking. I thought: 'How are we going to win the league this year? We're all drunk and they're all smoking.' We ended up winning the Double.
RAY PARLOUR, former Arsenal midfielder, on the 1997–98 side, 2013

Arsenal stole Tottenham's clothes and haven't given them back yet.
JIMMY GREAVES, former Tottenham and England forward, on Arsenal's 'purist' values under Wenger, 2010

An embarrassment of titches.
DESCRIPTION of Arsenal's allegedly small and unphysical team by a poster on a fans' online message board, 2010

Arsenal will be in my blood as well as my heart. I said I was going to be a Gunner for life and I didn't lie because when you are a Gunner you will always be a Gunner.
THIERRY HENRY, France striker, on leaving Arsenal for Barcelona, 2007

One–nil to the Arsenal, and that's how we like it.
GEORGE ALLISON, Arsenal manager, playing himself in the crime-thriller film The Arsenal Stadium Mystery, *1939*

Only people who will not spend big money on transfers need apply.
ADVERTISEMENT for post of Arsenal secretary-manager in Athletic News, *1925; Herbert Chapman got the job*

Bill Shankly didn't really give Arsenal any credit. He said: 'They're nothing to beat, these Cockneys from London.'
PETER THOMPSON, *former Liverpool winger, on his manager's team talk before Arsenal won the FA Cup in 1971 to complete their first Double, in David Tossell's* Seventy-One Guns, *2002*

I didn't want to play another 300 games with mediocre players and be up against it. I wanted the ball to be up the opposing end so I could get my cigars out at the back.
TONY ADAMS, *Arsenal captain, on the importance of bringing in Dennis Bergkamp and others, 1995*

At some clubs success is accidental. At Arsenal it is compulsory.

ARSENE WENGER, *manager, on his first Premiership and FA Cup Double, 1998*

When Arsenal aren't doing well in a game they turn it into a battle to try to make the opposition lose their concentration...The number of fights involving Arsenal is more than Wimbledon in their heyday.
ALEX FERGUSON, *Manchester United manager, 1999*

We give people what they like to see – pace, commitment, attacking football – and sometimes if we go overboard, I'm sorry.
WENGER *on his team's red-card tally, 2002*

We should not have reacted like we did. But I find the sensitivity of this country very selective. Suddenly the whole of England is so shocked, as if there's never any violence in your society.
WENGER *after Arsenal incurred FA charges following the 'Battle of Old Trafford', 2003*

You [the media] have the right to say Arsenal are a dirty team and should have been fined £700,000. But you will never, ever find anyone in my club that I told to go out and kick someone to win the game. If you find him, introduce him to me and I will face him.
WENGER *after the FA punished several Arsenal players following the United game, 2003*

I have read that Arsenal did a deal [with the FA] and I think that was the suspicion throughout the country. They've been doing deals for years. We hope we win titles without anybody's help.
SIR ALEX FERGUSON *claiming the punishments for Arsenal were not strong enough, 2003*

Even if you hang us, it is not enough for some people. They want

us hung twice, and in Hyde Park, in front of the whole country.
WENGER responding to Ferguson, 2003

What Arsenal players did [at Old Trafford] last season was the worst thing I've seen in this sport. They're a mob – they get away with murder.
FERGUSON during the build-up to Arsenal's visit to United, 2004

That's what children do, throw food. That's not fighting. We were real men. We'd have chinned them.
GEORGE BEST after Arsenal players allegedly threw pizza at Ferguson, 2004

If you look at our red cards, it's mostly a case of provocation. You can say that winding someone up is clever but you'll never convince me it's fair. Unfortunately it has worked for 52 players.
WENGER after Arsenal passed the half-century for dismissals under him, 2003

It's amazing how a team can go from the most boring to the most exciting in the league. This is the closest I have seen to the Dutch concept of Total Football. They can all play one-touch stuff, and if you have that throughout your side, it's unstoppable.
DENNIS BERGKAMP, Arsenal's former Netherlands striker, after Premiership title success, 2004

Arsenal caress a football the way I dreamed of caressing Marilyn Monroe.
BRIAN CLOUGH, 2004

Arsenal are nothing short of incredible. They could have been nearly as good as us.
CLOUGH after Arsenal beat Nottingham Forest's 42-match unbeaten record, 2004

They're the worst losers of all time. They don't know how to lose. Maybe it's just Manchester United. They don't lose many games to other teams.
SIR ALEX FERGUSON, 2005

When you work on the training ground every day, you don't notice where they're from. I don't even know where I'm from.
WENGER after Arsenal's XI and substitutes contained no British players, 2005

It's an English club but not an English success. It's probably a greater reflection of youngsters from France and elsewhere in Europe...none of the players is home-grown.
GORDON TAYLOR, Professional Footballers' Association chief executive, after Arsenal beat Real Madrid, Champions League, 2006

For me, Arsenal is a football training centre. You watch the match, you enjoy it, but are you going to win a title afterwards?
PATRICE EVRA, Manchester United defender, on another trophy-free year at the Emirates, 2010

ASTON VILLA

Big clubs do get the decisions
[from referees]. I'm not moaning
about that – I just want to make
Aston Villa a big club so we get
them too.
*MARTIN O'NEILL, Villa manager,
2007*

REPORTER: Doug Ellis has had
10 managers at Villa since you've
been at United.
FERGUSON: That averages out at
a year and a half per manager. You'll
never get continuity like that.
*EXCHANGE at Sir Alex Ferguson's
press briefing before Manchester United v
Villa, 2003*

There's an aura about this club, a
sense of history and tradition. Even
the name is beautifully symmetrical,
with five letters in each word.
JOHN GREGORY, Villa manager, 1998

We were wimpish. And wanky,
like that character says on *Men
Behaving Badly*. Have you seen
that?
*GREGORY to the media after Villa's
Worthington Cup semi-final loss to
Leicester, 2000*

I want to thank the mothers of
these players we have at Atletico
Madrid because they gave birth to
them with balls this big.
*DIEGO SIMEONE, Atletico coach, after
his team reached the Champions League
final by winning at Chelsea, 2014*

BARCELONA

Mes que un club
(More than a club).
BARCELONA club motto

I'd love to have gone to Barcelona
at one time. Ideology and
philosophy, the whole place is
fantastic.
*SIR ALEX FERGUSON, Manchester
United manager, 2010*

What makes daily life interesting
is that we try to transform it to
something that is close to art. And
football is like that. When I watch
Barcelona, it is art.
*ARSENE WENGER, Arsenal manager,
2009*

If Barcelona didn't exist we would
have to invent them.
*FLORENTINO PEREZ, Real Madrid
president, 2013*

When you go back [for a second
spell], you realise what Barca really
is. It's not just about winning
trophies, it's a model. Recently we
played Rayo Vallecano and won
4–0, but people weren't happy
because they had slightly more
possession than us. That's why
this club is so special. No one plays
quite like Barca. In England there's
a lack of control but people don't
want it any other way.
*CESC FABREGAS, Barcelona, Spain
and former Arsenal midfielder, 2013*

There's so much pressure here that it's not always good for young players. When everything's going well this is the best club in the world, but when they go badly you hardly leave the house.
FABREGAS, *as above*

Great teams always have a Plan B. Look at Barcelona. Their Plan B is to stick to Plan A.

JOHN GILES, *Irish TV pundit, 2013*

It's very simple: Barca are the best team in history. Not even the Milan team I played in achieved their results. Their strength is that they are professionals. They live for football, that's what motivates them, not celebrity status. [Ruud] Gullit was a super player, but also a celebrity. Xavi is a super player, but he likes being with his family. [Lionel] Messi and [Andres] Iniesta are the same. Perhaps the only one who enjoys being the centre of attention is [Gerard] Pique. To the others, all that interests them is their job as a footballer.
MARCO VAN BASTEN, *former Ajax, Milan and Netherlands striker, 2012*

The way Barcelona play is a pleasure for everybody who likes football, because the technical qualities are the highest standard and every little child can try to do them. It's not like somebody runs 100 yards in nine seconds [and] if you can't do it, you don't count. You always count because you can always get better. If you want to play basketball you've got to be two metres; otherwise you can't play. Here, everyone can play and develop. That's the nicest thing about football.
JOHAN CRUYFF, *adviser to Barcelona and former club captain and coach, 2013*

If, over the past four years, Barcelona were the first team I saw playing when I was four years of age – this serenity of football, they win 5–0, 6–0 – I would have played tennis. It is not my sport. I don't like winning with 80 per cent of possession. Sorry, that is not enough for me.
JURGEN KLOPP, *Borussia Dortmund coach, 2013*

This is football. The best doesn't always win. You can't play beautifully against Barca, they're the best team in the world.
FERNANDO TORRES, *Chelsea and Spain striker, after the London team put Barcelona out of the Champions League, 2012*

I think what we're doing at the moment is the closest thing to art. Our team works in the spirit of the great musicians and great ballets.
JOAN LAPORTA, Barcelona president, 2009

Barca won the World Cup. It's just that they were wearing the wrong shirts.

LAPORTA after Spain won the World Cup, 2010

[Cristiano] Ronaldo is not the second best player in the world. He's 12th best. The first 11 are Barcelona players.
SANDRO ROSELL, Barcelona president, 2012

Barcelona play football to die of.
MICK QUINN, talkSPORT radio pundit, 2010

The true philosophy is to educate players and bring them through. I don't think [Sandro] Rosell understands the club.
JOHAN CRUYFF, former Barcelona coach, 2012; Rosell resigned in 2014 amid investigations into Barca's £47m signing of Brazil striker Neymar

When I arrived at Barcelona I had bought a white suit to look handsome. Unfortunately, everybody was looking strangely at me. I'd forgotten white is the colour of Real Madrid! At the end of the first day, the club's president told me: 'That, never again!' The next day I threw the suit in the bin.
LUDOVIC GIULY, former Barcelona and France player, 2013

Here at Barca we keep our feet on the ground. So we don't turn up for training sessions in Ferraris and Porsches.
PEP GUARDIOLA, Barcelona coach, to Zlatan Ibrahimovic, quoted in I Am Zlatan Ibrahimovic, *2013*

Barcelona is the best club in the world but a dreadful place to be. They never let you forget you're a South American and a spot on the face of humanity.
DIEGO MARADONA, ex-Barcelona player, 2001

BARNET

Barnet has been a big part of my life. I took a second mortgage to save them. I gave them my testimonial money. I got arrested driving the tractor on Christmas Day to flatten the pitch, and when I told the policeman I was the manager, he said: 'Oh yeah, and I'm George Best.'
BARRY FRY after leaving the Barnet manager's job for Southend, 1993

BARNSLEY

I have watched Barnsley and it is clear they are not Real Madrid.
ROBERTO MANCINI, Manchester City manager, before his team's 5–0 win, FA Cup, 2013

BAYERN MUNICH

After some games this season I haven't needed a shower.

MANUEL NEUER, Bayern and Germany goalkeeper, as the European and German champions enjoyed a long winning run, 2013

I've been at Bayern for six years. It's always good here, I'm happy, and I have fun. For me, it's more important than the national team.
FRANCK RIBERY, France midfielder with Bayern, 2012

No one demands that Dortmund be the champions. But at Bayern you have to be champions. That's a huge difference.
OLIVER KAHN, former Bayern and Germany goalkeeper, 2011

Who has the best defence? Bayern! Who has the best attack? Bayern! And that's why we're champions. And not just in Munich. Also in Gelsenkirchen, also in Bremen and in Hamburg! We are the best of Germany. And perhaps soon of Europe!
LOUIS VAN GAAL, Dutch coach to Bayern, 2010

BIRMINGHAM CITY

The team played the long-ball game, practically bypassing midfield. To get into the game you had to linger at the back with the defenders to get hold of the ball, which more often than not flew right past me. The day before a game [manager Alex McLeish] would come onto the pitch and show us what to do: 'You stand here, the goalkeeper will give you the ball here, kick it as far as you can and don't pass to anyone nearby. And we all run.'
ALEXANDER HLEB, Belarus international midfielder, on his 2010–11 spell with Birmingham, 2012

We're not at the level of The Beatles yet. We're still a work in progress. Maybe at the Hamburg stage.
ALEX McLEISH, Birmingham manager, after derby defeat by Aston Villa, 2009

Q: What attracted you to
Birmingham City?
A: Nothing. I was told by my boss
[David Sullivan] to come here.
KARREN BRADY, managing director,
in interview with King's Heath Concorde
FC fanzine, 1993

BLACKBURN ROVERS

Luckily I have my wife and two kids. If I was left alone in Blackburn, I'd have hung myself already.

GAEL GIVET, French defender with
Blackburn, 2013

The directors of the club are in
dialect with the protesters.
STEVE KEAN, Blackburn manager, on
demonstrations against him, 2012

Eriksson obviously fancied the
sunshine more than the cobbled
streets and flat caps.
TONY PARKES, regular Blackburn
caretaker-manager, after Sven-Goran
Eriksson rejected Rovers to remain in
Italy, 1997

During the afternoon it rained only
in Blackburn's stadium. Our kit
man saw it. There must be a micro-
climate here.
JOSE MOURINHO, Chelsea manager,
2005

It's obviously not our dream to
have to go to Blackburn. It's
hardly the most fantastic place
touristically.
ARSENE WENGER as Arsenal faced
an FA Cup replay at Ewood Park, 2007

All hail, ye gallant Rover lads!
Etonians thought you were but
        cads
They've found at football game
        their dads
By meeting Blackburn Rovers.
SONG by Blackburn supporters before the
FA Cup final, 1882; Old Etonians won
1–0

BLACKPOOL

Blackpool getting promotion to the
Premier League is like reaching the
moon without a rocket or a space
helmet.
BRETT ORMEROD, veteran Blackpool
striker, 2010

We've bitten off more than we
can chew but we'll chew as fast as
we can.
IAN HOLLOWAY, Blackpool manager,
on their travails in the Premier League,
2010

I may be in a Skoda garage rather than a Mercedes, but some old bangers don't half polish up great.
HOLLOWAY after a 6–0 thrashing at Arsenal, 2010

Blackpool's plan is to almost sort of try and outscore the other team.
TONY COTTEE, Sky summariser, 2010

Blackpool are flying by the skin of their pants.
DAVID MOYES, Everton manager, 2011

The fat lady has finished singing and unfortunately I don't like her tune. That's it in football. You're famous for two seconds in football and then you're gone.
HOLLOWAY after Blackpool's relegation from the top flight, 2011

BOLTON WANDERERS

I have a dream to play in England. I prefer Bolton Wanderers and Chelsea.
STOPPILA SUNZU, defender in the Zambia side that won the African Cup of Nations, 2012; in 2014 he joined Sochaux in France

BURNLEY

We have to get this monkey off our back. It has grown from a chimp to an orangutan to a mountain gorilla.
CLARKE CARLISLE, Burnley defender, on the club's poor away form, 2010

[Libyan dictator] Colonel Gadaffi was keen to invest in the club in the 1990s because when he grew up Burnley were a big club and he had become a fan. I thought when I heard it 'imagine that – the BNP [British National Party] on the council and Gadaffi at the football club. That's an eclectic mix for any town.'
BRENDAN FLOOD, Burnley owner, 2009

They have the potential to be a sleeping giant.

CHRIS WADDLE on becoming player-manager, 1997

CARDIFF CITY

Cardiff City = Bluebirds, played in blue for yonks, synonymous with capital city club side... Red + dragon = synonymous with Wales as a country. Makes no sense whatsoever...throwing away decades of hard work growing a fanbase in Cardiff who eat sleep and eat BLUE!
JAMIE ROBERTS, Cardiff-supporting rugby union player, when the club's Asian owners changed their traditional colours, 2012

When I first came to Cardiff we used to train in what we called Dogshit Park.
DAVE JONES, Cardiff manager, 2008

The only way you can see Cardiff is as another Barcelona. Yes, Barcelona is a football club, but it is also something that brings all the Catalan people together. Except Cardiff is more.
SAM HAMMAM, club owner, 2002

CELTIC

Henrik [Larsson] was good enough to play for any team in Europe, but after playing at Celtic it is easy to understand why he chose to stay there for so long. No player would ever want to leave playing for those fans.
ZLATAN IBRAHIMOVIC, Paris St-Germain striker and Larsson's fellow Swede, 2013

Celtic make a song and dance about everything, don't they? Paranoid FC.
KENNY SHIELS, Kilmarnock manager, after Celtic counterpart Neil Lennon criticised the absence of his players on the Scottish PFA player-of-the-year shortlist, 2013

I liked the evening we beat Barcelona and when we did the same to Manchester United. I like any moment when we've had victories at Celtic Park, especially over teams wearing blue.
DERMOT DESMOND, Celtic majority shareholder, on the highlights of his 20 years at the club, 2014

At Celtic you're a draw away from a crisis.

PAUL LAMBERT, Norwich manager and former Celtic midfielder, in the DVD The Official History of Celtic, 2009

Time was when the budget at Celtic was the fourth or fifth biggest in British football. Nowadays we're finding we can't compete for wages with the likes of Hull City.
GORDON STRACHAN, Celtic manager, 2009

We don't just want to win the European Cup. We want to do it playing good football, to make neutrals glad we won it, pleased to remember how we did it.
JOCK STEIN, Celtic manager, before the victory v Inter Milan in Lisbon, 1967

I can still remember it exactly as it was. And they can't take that feeling away from you. It was the most wonderfullest feeling in my life. I'll never ever, ever, ever forget it.
JIMMY JOHNSTONE, Celtic winger in the 1967 final, in the documentary film Lord of the Wing, *2004*

Winning the European Cup might have been for Scotland but it definitely wasn't for Britain. It was for Celtic.
BILLY McNEILL, captain of the 1967 'Lisbon Lions', 1995

There's nothing worse than sitting in the dressing room at Celtic Park after a defeat, not a word being said, listening to them going mental next door.
ALLY McCOIST, Rangers striker, 1994

CHARLTON ATHLETIC

Strange how a ground can catch hold of you. I came past The Valley tonight and found myself staring at it. All those memories! We had to go back, didn't we?
ROGER ALWEN, Charlton chairman, announcing their return 'home', 1989

CHELSEA

My accountant could manage Chelsea to fourth or fifth place.
GIANLUCA VIALLI, former Chelsea manager, on the funding by billionaire Russian owner Roman Abramovich, 2014

We are becoming a big club in every aspect. In the beginning we needed cups, silverware to help us become a big club. Now we are a big, mature club. This decision [to sell Juan Mata to Manchester United] was made by a group of people all with different perspectives but one common interest: what is best for Chelsea?
JOSE MOURINHO, Chelsea manager, arguing that selling a high-class player to rivals showed the strength of his club, 2014

It's time for a big party with the cup with the big ears.
ROBERTO DI MATTEO, acting Chelsea manager, after guiding the club to their first Champions League final success, 2012

At Chelsea a sacking is just like another day at the office.

ANDRE VILLAS-BOAS, Tottenham manager, on the dismissal of his successor at Chelsea, Roberto Di Matteo, 2012

The game was crazy. Bayern Munich scored on about 80 minutes, and with the last corner – our only one – Didier [Drogba] scored. After my penalty was saved I still believed in Petr Cech. He was like an angel and saved the important ones. It was an explosion of feelings when Didier scored that [trophy-winning] penalty. It was destiny.
JUAN MATA, Chelsea and Spain midfielder, after the Champions League triumph, 2012

Chelsea have got to be more cynical in their finishing.
GIANFRANCO ZOLA, ex-Chelsea player, working as a TV summariser, Champions League final, 2012

It's impossible to match Chelsea's spending power – unless we find oil at Highbury.
ARSENE WENGER, Arsenal manager, as Abramovich financed massive spending at Stamford Bridge, 2005

Chelsea are the most unusual of clubs. They have never done what every other club was doing at the same time as every other club was doing it.
RALPH FINN, author, A History of Chelsea FC, 1969

I hate Chelsea. They stand for everything I hate in football, with their showbiz supporters. They come out looking more like the [dance troupe] Young Generation than a football team.
TERRY COLLIER, played by James Bolam, in the TV sit-com Whatever Happened to the Likely Lads? by Dick Clement and Ian La Frenais, 1974

Obviously there's a language barrier. The majority of the lads speak Italian, but there's a few who don't.
DENNIS WISE, Chelsea captain, 2000

When the first overseas players came we produced this book of Cockney rhyming slang. Luca [Vialli] and Ruud [Gullit] were fascinated and took it home to study. One day we were in a team meeting and Ruud suddenly said: 'I am a grave-digger...and a very rich one.'
WISE, 2000

We're a Continental team playing in English football.
COLIN HUTCHINSON, Chelsea managing director, 2000

Chelsea are the Foreign Legion. They may play in the English league but they are no longer an English club. Sometimes there is not one Englishman in the team. I don't like it at all. I can't understand how the fans accept that.
JOHAN CRUYFF, Dutchman and former Barcelona player and coach, 2000

Chelsea is a very nice, beautiful, great club, but something is missing. Only small things need to be done to make this a top, top, top European club. It is a top club, but not a top, top, top club.
JIMMY FLOYD HASSELBAINK, Chelsea striker, 2002

Chelsea are a financially doped club. They have enhancement of performances because their financial resources are unlimited. It's not healthy for the market. If they see Steven Gerrard or Rio Ferdinand, they say: 'How much are you on? We'll offer you twice as much.'
ARSENE WENGER, 2005

Frankly, I'm amazed this could have happened in a hotel in the centre of London. They seem to think they are above everything.
WENGER on Chelsea's 'tapping up' of Arsenal's Ashley Cole, 2005

Chelsea now welcome black supporters, employ black stewards and have the most diverse team in the Premiership. If you'd told me that was going to happen when I played at Stamford Bridge in 1987, I'd have called you a liar.
GARTH CROOKS, BBC TV football reporter and former Tottenham player, 2005

I guess when you've invested £500m it's a fantastic season to win the League Cup.

RICK PARRY, Liverpool chief executive, after they beat Chelsea to reach the Champions League final, 2007

It looks like there's one rule in football that it is forbidden to give a penalty against Manchester United and another to give none in favour of Chelsea.
JOSE MOURINHO, 2007

Chelsea will never be as big a club as Man United. United have a history and charisma that can't be bought.
BRYAN ROBSON, former United captain, 2007

Liverpool fans can continue to chant 'No history' at us, but we continue to make it.

MOURINHO, 2007

There were two buses parked today, never mind one.
BRENDAN RODGERS, Liverpool manager, alleging Mourinho deployed a six-man defence in Chelsea's win at Anfield, 2014

COVENTRY CITY

I won't go to Northampton because I class that team as Northampton reserves. It's not a Coventry team if they're not playing in Coventry. At my age [78] I realise I may never get to see them again.
RONNIE FARMER, former wing-half who played for Coventry in all four divisions, 2014; the Sky Blues staged home fixtures at Northampton, 34 miles away, because of a dispute over use of the Ricoh Arena

Will we have to change 'being sent to Coventry' to 'being sent to Northampton'?
POSTING on a Guardian *message board, 2013*

If the *Titanic* had been painted sky blue it would never have sunk.
BRYAN RICHARDSON, Coventry chairman, after another escape from relegation from the top flight, 1997

CRYSTAL PALACE

In extra time I thought both teams had settled for a replay. I was panicking then because I hadn't re-booked our hotel for midweek.
STEVE COPPELL, Palace manager, after the 4–3 victory over Liverpool in the FA Cup semi-final, 1990

It's like one of those fairytales where you see a beautiful castle but when you get inside you discover years of decay. The princess, which is the players, is asleep. I'm trying to wake her but it takes more than one kiss.
ALAN SMITH, Palace manager, 2000

I always thought Palace were a bit flighty, bit flash, lacking in substance – a legacy of Terry Venables and Malcolm Allison. In human form we were the *Fast Show* character – a little bit tasty, a little bit 'whoooar', a little bit 'wayyy'.
SIMON JORDAN, Palace chairman, 2005

DAGENHAM & REDBRIDGE

Whatever happened to Dagenham and Redgrave?
ALAN BRAZIL, talkSPORT presenter, 2013

No offence to ginger people but I'd play in a ginger wig if it meant me playing for this club.
PAUL BENSON, Dagenham & Redbridge striker, after playing wearing a mask to protect a broken nose, 2010

DERBY COUNTY

The league championship trophy seemed to spend a lot of time at our house. Dad would take it and show the neighbours. It went up and down Ferrers Way, Allestree! And the dustbin men didn't miss out. They would nip in for a drink on a regular basis on their round and they got to see the trophy.
NIGEL CLOUGH, Derby manager, remembering his father's 1972 title success with the club, 2012

Whichever teams win the league championship in the next 20 years, and I hope teams like Rochdale and Halifax will be among them, none of them will have as hard a job as we had. We did it with 12 players. Those London bums can't explain it.
BRIAN CLOUGH, Derby manager, 1972

EVERTON

I'd have broken every bone in my body for every club I played for, but I would have died for Everton.
DAVE HICKSON, who played centre-forward in the 1950s for Everton and Liverpool, 2013

We played to our capabilities. That's what this team is capable of.
PHIL NEVILLE, Everton captain, 2010

I want people to look back and say it was a golden period; to create a legacy. We've built slowly and there will be a moment in time soon when we win something. We're getting much closer to doing it.
DAVID MOYES, eight years into his 12-year, trophy-less reign as Everton manager, 2009

I've always believed that the folk on the streets of Liverpool support Everton. That's why this is the People's Club.
DAVID MOYES on joining Everton from Preston as manager, 2002

When you play against the smaller clubs at Anfield you know the game will be narrow.
RAFAEL BENITEZ, Liverpool manager, after a derby draw, 2007

PRINCESS MARGARET: But Mr Labone, where is Everton?
BRIAN LABONE: In Liverpool, Ma'am.

PRINCESS MARGARET: Of course, we had your first team here last year.
BILL SHANKLY, Liverpool manager, story of FA Cup final, 1966

If anyone ever mentions the Everton 'School of Soccer Science' to me again, well, I'm sorry, I just don't see it.
ROY EVANS, Liverpool manager, after bruising derby draw, 1995

I was told I was going to be the first of many big-money signings. Someone was telling fibs.
JOHN COLLINS, Everton midfielder, 1999

I soon got out of the habit of studying the top end of the league table.

WALTER SMITH, Everton manager, on the difference with his previous club, Rangers, 1999

I went on to play for other clubs, and though I always wanted to win, losing never really seemed to hurt any more.
KEVIN RATCLIFFE, Everton captain of the 1980s, in Becky Tallentire's book Still Talking Blue, 2002

FULHAM

Fulham have been slowly sinking to the bottom very, very quickly.
MARK LAWRENSON, BBC pundit, 2004

We've got a long-term plan for this club and apart from the results it's going well.

ERNIE CLAY, Fulham chairman, 1980

REPORTER: Are funds available for new signings?
IAN BRANFOOT: Oh, yes. About £2.54.
EXCHANGE at the Fulham manager's post-match press conference in the pre-Fayed era, 1994

I am going to make Fulham the Manchester United of the South.
MOHAMED AL FAYED, Harrods owner, on buying the then third-tier club, 1997

When I joined Fulham, in '97, we didn't even have enough bloody kit. I couldn't get my shorts on for my debut. They were all too small, so we had to snip the sides with scissors. That's how far away we were from being a proper Premier League club.
CHRIS COLEMAN, Real Sociedad coach and former Fulham player and manager, 2007

GRIMSBY TOWN

It's a hard place to come for a southern team. You can dress well and have all the nice watches in the world, but that won't buy you a result at Grimsby.
ALAN SMITH, Crystal Palace manager, at Grimsby, 2000

HARTLEPOOL UNITED

Since Hartlepool last scored you could have watched all three *Godfather* movies, waded through every technicolour moment of *Gone With the Wind*, and still had time to settle down to a two-hour episode of *Inspector Morse*.
HARTLEPOOL MAIL on the club's record-breaking run without a goal, 1993

HEART OF MIDLOTHIAN

I wanted to kill some of the people in my dressing-room at half-time, but then I have to go to jail and we don't get a point.
CSABA LASZLO, Hungarian manager of Hearts, after they came from 2–0 down to draw at Rangers, 2009

We have the chances with Andy Driver. I don't like to name names but this is the difference with the player who plays in the Champions League: he comes, he scores, he takes his Ferrari and goes and looks for the nice girls. We get in our Skodas and Citroens and go home from Falkirk with one point.
LASZLO, 2009

If you see that your team plays this shit like we did in the first half, you can just run out of the stadium and say 'it's Mother's Day tomorrow' and forget about football.
LASZLO, as above

[Vladimir] Romanov used to be a Soviet naval commander. He thinks he can run Heart of Midlothian as a Soviet submarine.
GEORGE FOULKES, former Hearts chairman, on Lithuanian owner Vladimir Romanov, 2006

We feared the worst. We got it.
REPORT on the club website after Hearts lost 5–0 at Celtic, 2007

HULL CITY

[Manager Steve Bruce] said: 'You're not going to be here for life. Work hard for us, and you can go for a slot at a bigger club.'
YANNICK SAGBO, Ivory Coast striker, after joining Hull, 2013

I did not know of them. I know nothing. Maybe with my satellite navigation I could find it. I would have no idea where it is on the map, though.
OBAFEMI MARTINS, Nigerian striker with Newcastle, 2009

JUVENTUS

People ask whether I like to see a Juve victory or the better team win. I'm lucky – the two often coincide.
GIANNI AGNELLI, Juventus owner, 2001

LEEDS UNITED

The players pissed me off because they didn't fight for the club. They made the fans feel ashamed. For what they did, I would kick their asses one by one. They are guilty. They were without pride and should be ashamed of themselves. They are chickens.
MASSIMO CELLINO, Italian businessman and prospective majority shareholder in Leeds, after a 5–1 home defeat by Bolton, 2014; he became club owner two months later

We have to focus on the St Johnstone's Paint Trophy game now.
DENNIS WISE, Leeds manager, 2007

Ridsdale – you started this
nightmare
Bates – you were the nightmare
Mr Cellino – please wake us from
this nightmare
We need you!!!
Leeds United – England's True
Sleeping Giant
*BANNER displayed by Leeds fans at
Burnley before Cellino's attempt to buy
the club was initially blocked by the
Football League, 2014*

[Leeds United] remind me of a
young Pamela Anderson – in great
shape, with superb assets and a
great future ahead.
*DAVID HAIGH, chief executive of GFH
Capital, who had bought the club from
Ken Bates, 2012*

Having 30 Premier League
footballers in a city, buying dinner
and gifts, is like have 30 small
businesses.
*ADAM PEARSON, former Leeds
commercial director, on why the city and
club needed top-flight football, 2013*

As a proud Yorkshireman, I'll be
among the first to offer Leeds my
commiserations. Well, I will as soon
as I stop laughing.
*NEIL WARNOCK, future Leeds
manager then with Sheffield United,
after the club dropped into the third tier,
2007*

I didn't like the Leeds dressing-
room before games [in the Don
Revie era]. Some guys would turn

psycho, others would be physically
sick and the goalie Gary Sprake
got himself in a terrible state – his
eyes actually started blinking on
the Tuesday. Then there was Don
with all his superstitions: lucky
mohair suit with the arse falling
out, twice round his lucky lamp-
post, a final comb of the hair in
the mirror.
*PETER LORIMER, Leeds' all-time
record goalscorer, interviewed in* The
Scotsman, *2013*

Our attitude was – an eye for an eyelash.

*JOHN GILES, Leeds midfielder of the
1960s and '70s, on Don Revie's side,* A
Football Man: The Autobiography,
2010

In a really tight match one day
against Chelsea at Elland Road,
down near one of the corner flags,
and with our backs to the referee,
I caught [Eddie McCreadie] with
a late tackle. 'What the hell was
that for?' I told him it was for
doing my ligaments at Stamford
Bridge in 1964. McCreadie looked
bewildered. It was 1972.
GILES, as above

You heard what? That I said
Palermo in Sicily was meant to be
the Mafia headquarters, but
I reckoned it was the Leeds

dressing-room? I said that? Well it's possible.
BRIAN CLOUGH, *Leeds manager for 44 days seven years earlier, interviewed in* Shoot! *magazine, 1980*

I didn't used to be frightened on the football pitch. But I was always relieved to get off in one piece, particularly during those mid- and late 1960s when the likes of Leeds United were kicking anything that moved.
JIMMY GREAVES, *former Tottenham striker, in* This One's On Me, *1979*

Leeds [under Don Revie] would try to win by fair means or foul... They were too good to do things like that and should have won more than they did. They were a magnificent side, a team made in heaven.
FRANK McLINTOCK, *former Arsenal captain, in David Tossell's book* Seventy-One Guns, *2002*

There's a stereotype that goes with a lot of clubs. Spurs are called stylish, West Ham is the academy, Arsenal are resilient. But Leeds are always seen as cynical and intimidating. It becomes a tired cliché.
HOWARD WILKINSON, *Leeds manager, 1991*

The first day I went down for lunch, there was so much smoked salmon, steaks, king prawns, seven-inch-long langoustines, I asked

[manager] David O'Leary and [assistant manager] Eddie Gray who was getting married.
GREG ABBOTT, *Carlisle United manager, recalls working for Leeds United's youth academy, 2012*

Q: Which team's results do you look for first?
A: Leeds United, Leeds Reserves, Leeds youth team, Leeds Permanent Building Society pub team, Leeds & Holbeck pub team, Leeds ice hockey team, East Leeds chess under-19s, South Leeds over-19 poker team, anyone with Leeds in their name. And Middlesbrough.
JONATHAN WOODGATE, *Teesside-born Leeds defender, in magazine questionnaire, 1999*

People hate Manchester United because they are so successful. People will hate us in a few years because we shall be winning everything.
WOODGATE, *1999*

Those Leeds guys are simply out of this world. The energy just rushes through them. And their fans are just as aggressive as the team.
ROBERT PIRES, *Arsenal and France midfielder, 2002*

He wants to play for a bigger and better club.
PINA ZAHAVI, *Rio Ferdinand's agent, on the Leeds captain's desire to move to Manchester United, 2002*

We've got to work twice as hard as other clubs to get some good news. I've never known another club that so many people have such a negative image of, for reasons that are difficult to put a finger on.
PETER RIDSDALE, Leeds chairman, on employing the PR consultant Max Clifford, 2002

It wasn't me that ran up a debt of £40m, £50m, £60m or £80m. I didn't force [Leeds] to sign one player. I nominated players and the club sorted out the wages.
DAVID O'LEARY, sacked as Leeds manager in 2002, after resurfacing at Aston Villa, 2003

They reacted like a gambler on a losing streak in a Las Vegas casino. They went out and gambled more. It was a triumph of vanity over sanity. The whole future of the club has been put in jeopardy to fund a dash for glory.
DR BILL GERRARD, sports finance specialist, on Leeds' mounting debts and failure to reach the Champions League, 2003

Post-war Iraq is being better run than Leeds

HEADLINE in the News of the World, 2003

I've never known a club like it. If it can go wrong, it will go wrong.

KEVIN BLACKWELL, manager, after ex-Leeds player Jody Morris's late equaliser for Millwall, 2004

You wonder how someone could have come up with a plan straight out of *Blackadder*. You can see Baldrick: 'I've got a cunning plan that'll take us further into debt.'
BLACKWELL on the Ridsdale era, 2005

Right now we're at the bottom of our cycle but Leeds United are still one of the big six clubs. The small clubs can have their day in the sun but eventually they go back where they came from. Leeds will always be a big club.
KEN BATES, Leeds chairman, on taking the club into administration after relegation to the third tier, 2007

LEICESTER CITY

One day before a game [owner] Vichai [Srivaddhanaprabha] came knocking on my door. His son was with him and five yellow-clad Buddhist monks. The monks wrote something on my desk and gave me a

piece of paper to stick in my pocket. Vichai was convinced that we would win after that. But we didn't and I never saw those monks again.
SVEN-GORAN ERIKSSON recalling his turbulent reign as Leicester manager in Sven: My Story, *2013*

Wouldn't it be great to go to a club that's boring, where nothing happens?
MICKY ADAMS, resigning as Leicester manager after a spell in which the club went into administration, were promoted and relegated and endured the La Manga sex scandal, 2004

LEYTON ORIENT

We have already had a few phone calls but to clear things up Beckham's last game is against FC Lorient, not us.
ORIENT website statement, 2013

Drugs? Who needs 'em? Just come to Leyton Orient. In celebration, we're going to drink from the elixir of life, here at Brisbane Road, centre of the universe.
BARRY HEARN, Orient chairman, after his team reached the Third Division play-off final (which they lost), 2001

LIVERPOOL

If you don't revel in this pressure and tension, you're at the wrong football club.

STEVEN GERRARD, Liverpool captain, on being involved in the Premier League title race, 2014

Do you know what it is like to play for Liverpool? I've suffered at Liverpool, but when I think of what it represents to play for this club, and the love my daughter has – she sings the hymn – the hairs on the back of my neck stand up when I play at Anfield.
LUIS SUAREZ, Liverpool and Uruguay striker, 2013

It was United's ground, mostly their fans, but it was our ball.
BRENDAN RODGERS, Liverpool manager, on the club's 3–0 win at Manchester United, 2014

Defeats wearing an England shirt never hurt me in the same way as losing with my club.
JAMIE CARRAGHER, Liverpool and England defender, in Carra: My Autobiography, *2009*

When I went to Liverpool I must admit it was more of a culture shock than coming to France.
JOE COLE, London-born England midfielder, on his year's loan from Liverpool to Lille, 2012

When I signed for Liverpool, the guy interviewing me said: 'You've joined the biggest club in the country' and reeled off the trophies they'd won. I just said: 'Yeah, if you put it like that, I suppose you're right,' and Liverpool used that as the headline to the interview... But obviously they're not the biggest club in the country any more. How do you judge how big a club are? Nottingham Forest won the European Cup twice but they're not a bigger club than Chelsea.
COLE after leaving Liverpool for a second spell with West Ham, 2013

We've got a lot more expensive failures on our list than good players that we've brought in for next to nothing.
ROY HODGSON, Liverpool manager, on his inheritance from Rafael Benitez, 2010

When Roger Hunt won the World Cup with England he came back to Liverpool and the boss [Bill Shankly] said to him: 'Well done, but now we've got more important things to think about.'
IAN ST JOHN, Liverpool and Scotland forward, 2009

They say we're predictable. Well, Joe Louis was predictable. He'd knock his man down to the floor. Goodbye!
BILL SHANKLY, Liverpool manager, 1965

If you've got three Scots in your team you've got a chance of winning something. Any more and you've got trouble.
SHANKLY, 1967

Yes, there are two great teams on Merseyside. Liverpool and Liverpool Reserves.

SHANKLY, 1965

I want to build a team that's invincible, so they'll have to send a team from Mars to beat us.
SHANKLY, 1971

Liverpool are the most uncomplicated side in the world. They all drive forward when they've got the ball, and they all get behind it when they haven't.
JOE MERCER, former Manchester City manager, 1973

My idea was to build Liverpool into a bastion of invincibility. Napoleon had that idea. He wanted to conquer the bloody world. I wanted Liverpool to be untouchable, to build the club up and up until everyone would have to submit.
SHANKLY, a year after he retired, 1975

Mind you, I've been here during the bad times too. One year we came second.

BOB PAISLEY, Shankly's successor, 1979

A lot of teams beat us, do a lap of honour and don't stop running. They live too long on one good result. I remember Jimmy Adamson crowing after Burnley beat us that his players were in a different league. At the end of the season they were.
PAISLEY, 1979

We do things together. I'd walk into the toughest dockside pub in the world with this lot. Because you know that if things got tough, nobody would 'bottle' it and scoot off.
EMLYN HUGHES, Liverpool captain, in Brian James's Journey to Wembley, *1977*

As we all knew would happen when Ian Rush went abroad, Liverpool have fallen to pieces.
TED CROKER, FA secretary, as Kenny Dalglish's side advanced to the league title, 1988

I thought there might be eight goals but I never expected we'd get four of them.
DAVE LANCASTER, Chesterfield player, after 4–4 draw at Anfield during Liverpool's decline, 1992

We're an old-fashioned football club, not a quoted plc, and we don't pay dividends to shareholders. We are here for one reason: to win trophies.
PETER ROBINSON, Liverpool chief executive, 1996

We were playing for history tonight. For immortality. What these players have achieved is unique.
GERARD HOULLIER, Liverpool manager, after his side beat Alaves of Spain 5–4 to win the UEFA Cup and complete a Treble, 2001

People say we're not pretty to watch but I'll tell you something: winning's pretty.
HOULLIER, 2002

I was only a kid the last time Liverpool won the league. In fact I think I was still an Everton fan.
MICHAEL OWEN, Liverpool striker, 2002

Liverpool–Manchester United games are fantastic. It doesn't matter if you were playing tiddlywinks, it would be really competitive.
SIR ALEX FERGUSON, 2003

I can't stand Liverpool. I can't stand Liverpool people. I can't stand anything to do with them.
GARY NEVILLE, Manchester United defender, 1999

You have to realise that, even by British standards, Liverpool are unique. You are not playing for yourself. You're playing for an ideal.
CRAIG JOHNSTON, former Liverpool player, 2003

It wasn't just the best comeback in a European Cup final; it wasn't just the best comeback I've seen in football; it was the best comeback I've seen in sport anywhere in the world.
HANSEN on the recovery from 3–0 down to beat Milan on penalties in the Champions League final, 2005

I've made Liverpool my English team. I remember that amazing night in Istanbul at half-time. They were losing, but they kept singing. They showed that football is truly a beautiful game.
DIEGO MARADONA, 2005

Football is made up of subjective feeling, and in that Anfield is unbeatable. Put a shit hanging from a stick in the middle of a passionate, crazy stadium and some people will tell you it's a work of art. It's not – it's a shit hanging from a stick.
JORGE VALDANO, sporting director of

Real Madrid, alleging a lack of style in Liverpool, 2007

Two finals in three years – not bad for a little club.
STEVEN GERRARD, Liverpool captain, after winning a Champions League semi-final against Chelsea, whose manager Jose Mourinho had called them 'a little club', 2007

LOS ANGELES GALAXY

The Galaxy are looked on as the jewel in the crown of Major League Soccer. All this leads to the race to become the first MLS super-club, an American team to compete with Real Madrid and Manchester United.
ALEXI LALAS, Galaxy president, after signing David Beckham, 2007

We have a good name but we need a more legendary, traditional look. We decided it was time we started thinking how we create a world brand. David Beckham will obviously help enormously with that.
TIM LEIWEKE, president of the Galaxy's parent company, on plans to change the club's colours and crest, 2007

MANCHESTER CITY

They brought on someone who cost more than our stadium.
BRENDAN RODGERS, Swansea manager, on City's £38m signing Sergio Aguero, 2012

Kun [Sergio Aguero] is doing really well in England and so is [Manuel] Pellegrini. That doesn't surprise me. But if you had told me 10 years ago that one of the best managers in the world and one of the best coaches in the world would be doing well at Manchester City, that would have surprised me.
DIEGO FORLAN, Uruguay and former Manchester United striker, 2014; Forlan had played with Aguero at Atletico Madrid and under Pellegrini for Villarreal

City in the next five or 10 years can be the top club in the world.
ROBERTO MANCINI, City manager, on why striker Mario Balotelli was making 'a big mistake' in leaving, 2013

The best team on the planet,
TIM SHERWOOD Tottenham manager, after City added a 5–1 away win over Spurs to a 6–0 home win, 2014

I didn't realise until about five years ago that Manchester had two teams. Of course United have been one of the most famous and successful clubs in Europe for many years – but I thought they were the only one.
DANI ALVES, Barcelona defender, 2014

In attack City are a fur coat made from pure Siberian mink. But defensively, the knickers come straight from Primark.
TIM RICH, football writer, on City's sixth-round FA Cup defeat to Wigan, The Independent, 2014

Manchester City are built on sand and I don't mean that because their owners are from the Arab countries.
KEVIN KEEGAN, media pundit and former City manager, 2013

There's Eastlands in the distance, Manchester City's ground. Or should I say Middle Eastlands.
DAVID LLOYD, Sky cricket summariser, at a Test Match at Old Trafford, 2009

Miracles do happen in Manchester. The difference was this one was on our side of the road.
VINCENT KOMPANY, City's Belgian captain, after they dramatically beat Manchester United to the Premier League championship, 2012

The fact that an Englishman has an Argentinian as an idol is something very rare. I keep watching the goal I scored against QPR and every time that I do, I get more emotional. I have no intention of joining another club. My plan is to stay here because City can measure up with Real Madrid, Barcelona and the likes. I am convinced City will be at their level.
SERGIO AGUERO, Argentinian striker, after scoring the stoppage-time goal that gave City the Premier League title ahead of Manchester United, 2012

It's very difficult to compliment City. But we're not stupid. They won it.
SIR BOBBY CHARLTON, United director and former player, 2012

It'll take them a century to get to our level of history.
SIR ALEX FERGUSON, United manager, 2012

City have had 21 penalties in the past year, haven't they? If we were to get that many there would be an inquiry in the House of Commons.
FERGUSON before United played City, 2012

We have laid the first brick. Now we can build a house.

KOMPANY after FA Cup success ended City's 35 years without a trophy, 2011

It's a different game when you can buy players and pay them £250,000 a week. To be honest you would have a chance [of winning the Premier League]. I'd fancy you to manage them. You'd win it.
HARRY REDKNAPP, Tottenham manager, to journalists before claiming his net spend was below £18.5m compared with Mancini's £190.5m at City, 2012

I never took to it. There was something about the place I didn't like.
RYAN GIGGS, who attended City's School of Excellence before joining United, 2010

Comedy has always been at the heart of what this club is all about.
GARY COOK, City's chief executive, defending the 'Welcome To Manchester' billboard City erected after signing Carlos Tevez from United, 2009

It's City, isn't it? They're a small club with a small mentality. All they can talk about is Manchester United; they can't get away from it. That arrogance will be rewarded. It is a go at us. They think taking Carlos Tevez away from Manchester United is a triumph. It's poor stuff.
SIR ALEX FERGUSON on the Tevez transfer and billboard, 2009

It's been unusual for us to accept that City are top dogs in terms of media attention but sometimes you have a noisy neighbour and you have to live with it. You can't do anything about them if they keep on making noise but what you can do, as we showed today, is get on with your life, put your television on and turn it up a bit louder.
FERGUSON after a stoppage-time goal gave United a 4–3 win over City, 2009

There was way too much pressure. It came from everyone: the club, the fans. I think too much pressure just hurts the team.
CARLOS TEVEZ, Argentinian striker, on leaving City for Juventus, 2013

Manchester [City] had two attackers who – and I exaggerate

a bit – sat in their deckchairs on the halfway line when we were in possession.
THOMAS MULLER, Bayern Munich player, Champions League, 2013

If there was a cup for cock-ups, you wouldn't be able to move in City's trophy-room.
FRANCIS LEE, former City player and chairman, 1990s

A Thai chairman and a Swedish manager. It could only happen at Manchester City.
GRAHAM TAYLOR, former England manager, in his Daily Telegraph *column after former Thailand Prime Minister Thaksin Shinawatra recruited Sven-Goran Eriksson following his takeover of City, 2007*

Check out the details about Manchester's second-largest club.
BLURB on the dustcover of Manchester City FC: An A to Z, *by Dean Hayes, 1995*

1976 was a strange year for English football – City won a trophy

SLOGAN on T-shirts sold outside Old Trafford, 1995

Watching City is probably the best laxative you can have.
PHIL NEAL, City caretaker-manager, after they lost a 2–0 lead before beating Bradford City, 1996

May I wish Joe Royle well in a task equivalent to nailing jelly to a ceiling.
LETTER to the Manchester Evening News *'Pink' after Royle became manager, 1998*

The worse City play, the better the crowds are. It's as though the fans feel the team needs them. The other factor is that we are not United. Their fans are the most horrible in the world, as everybody knows.
DAVE WALLACE, editor of Manchester City fanzine King of the Kippax, *1999*

To score four goals when you are playing like pigs in labour is fantastic.
JOE ROYLE, City manager, after a 4–1 win at Blackburn took them into the Premiership, 2000

They're my old club and I hate to speak badly of them, but they are crap.
RODNEY MARSH as City went straight back down, 2001

Manchester City are a springboard for me... I'm ready to play for a big club again and have no preference.
NICOLAS ANELKA, City striker and former Real Madrid and Arsenal player, 2004

We can't keep gambling on players who have scored six goals in the Pontins League or in Belgium.
JOEY BARTON, City midfielder, 2007

MANCHESTER UNITED

I think all young boys want to play for Manchester United.

DAVID MOYES, United manager, after Adnan Januzaj, 18, broke into the first team, 2013

People want us to fail because we've won the League so many times. Everyone hates the best clubs.
PHIL JONES, United defender, on their stuttering start under David Moyes' management, 2013

I've not looked at the league table for ages, but it's because you don't want to. It's embarrassing. You don't want to see where we are.
RIO FERDINAND when Manchester United occupied seventh place with three Premier League games remaining, 2014

Unless they wanted to sell me there was no way I would ever ask to leave. Why would you leave somewhere that you live, somewhere that you love and which is one of the best clubs in the world?
PAUL SCHOLES on retiring as a player and temporarily joining United's coaching staff, 2013

You can't think that Manchester United could have only one cycle of players as good as that [the class of 1992]. We'll always keep chasing the dream. We will get a bunch like that again. We have to.
SIR ALEX FERGUSON, United manager, 2011

History's there to be broken.
MIKE PHELAN, United assistant manager, on the club's record-breaking 19th league title, 2011

When you are with a top side and have had more money than anyone for years, then you can keep winning and you can keep talking. But when you play against another top side in Europe, it's always more difficult. Should United have done more in Europe? I don't know.
RAFAEL BENITEZ, interim Chelsea manager, on United's Champions League record under Ferguson, 2013

We are a football club. We are not a business. The way I describe it to staff is: 'We are a 135-year-old club and that's what you have to remember. A club with a capital C: Club.'
ED WOODWARD, United chief executive, 2013

Maybe they will get some joy from it and realise how important we are to England instead of treating us like shit.
FERGUSON on the FA after United had eight players named in the England squad, 2011

I remember Alex Ferguson telling me when I first signed: 'You won't believe what it's like to play for Man United.' And I was like, 'Yeah, yeah, yeah.' But he was right.
TEDDY SHERINGHAM, West Ham and former Manchester United striker, 2006

The road back may be long and hard, but with the memory of those who died at Munich, of their stirring achievements and wonderful sportsmanship ever with us, Manchester United will rise again.
H.P. HARDMAN, chairman, in a message headed 'United will go on' on the cover of the first match programme after the tragedy, 1958

[United] stand for something more than any other person, any player, any supporter. They are as was once written in the club programme of 1937 – the soul of a sporting organisation which goes on from year to year, making history all the time. They remain a club with a rich vein of character and faith. Because of that they have no fear of the morrow.
GEOFFREY GREEN, former Times *football writer, in* There's Only One United, *1978*

It's the only stadium in the world I've ever been in that's absolutely buzzing with atmosphere when it's empty and there isn't a soul inside. It's almost like a cathedral.
TOMMY DOCHERTY, former United manager, in Call the Doc, *1982*

This team makes you suffer. I deserve a million pounds a year for doing this job.
ALEX FERGUSON after drawn FA Cup final v Crystal Palace, 1990

ICI is a world-class business. There's no way it would want to buy a second-class football team.
CITY ANALYST quoted in the Sunday Times *on rumours that ICI wanted to buy United, 1990*

I had to get rid of this idea that Manchester United were a drinking club, rather than a football club.
FERGUSON on his problems with Paul McGrath and Norman Whiteside, in Six Years at United, *1992*

I value truth, honesty, respect for one another, compassion and understanding. I have found these qualities in Manchester United.
ERIC CANTONA in La Philosophie de Cantona, *1995*

This has been a love story...
The love of the club is the most important weapon in the world. I just couldn't leave.
CANTONA on his decision to stay with United, 1995

A Manchester United player has to want the ball, have the courage to want it. He's a player with imagination, someone who sees the bigger picture.
FERGUSON, 1995

I get to my feet when Chelsea fans sing: 'Stand up if you hate Man U.' But though I hate them, I have to admire them too.
KEN BATES, Chelsea chairman, 1997

We are the most loved club – and the most hated.

GARY NEVILLE, United defender, 1997

There is a terrible amount of jealousy towards this club. I don't know why.
FERGUSON, 1997

The Kings of Perseverance
HEADLINE in the Catalan newspaper La Vanguardia *after United's two late goals in Barcelona beat Bayern Munich in the Champions League final, 1999*

At the end of this game, the European Cup will be only six feet away from you and you'll not even be able to touch it if we lose. And for many of you that will be the closest you will ever get. Don't you dare come back in here without giving your all.
FERGUSON in his half-time team-talk during the Champions League final, 1999

In a Cairo taxi the four words of English my driver knew were 'Thatcher', 'Blair' and 'Manchester United'.
STEPHEN BYERS MP, Labour, Trade and Industry Secretary, 1999

We would love to have a [Luis] Figo, [Zinedine] Zidane or Rivaldo at United, but we realise those sort of players are never really going to come here. Some people think it's sad, with us being the richest club in the world, but clubs have their policies and you have to respect that.
ROY KEANE, United captain, 2000

This team never lose games – they just run out of time occasionally.

STEVE McCLAREN, United coach, 2000

The nation was warming to us during the build-up to last season's Champions League final. But the warmth was only ever going to be temporary. It's the British culture of being quick to put down people at the top. We are a soft target.
FERGUSON, 2000

You have to put all the criticism down to jealousy. United have produced more people who've played for their country, more world-class players and more who've won European Footballer of the Year than any other club in the country, so we must be doing something right.
FERGUSON after United suffered a poor run, 2000

United have got into Europe thanks to the FA Cup. Where are they going? Brazil? I hope they get bloody diarrhoea.
BRIAN CLOUGH, former Nottingham Forest manager, on United's decision to play in the new World Club Cup rather than defend the FA Cup, 1999

Everyone knows that for us to get awarded a penalty we need a certificate from the Pope and a personal letter from the Queen.
FERGUSON after Leeds were awarded a spot-kick v United, 2001

To get a penalty at Old Trafford, Jaap Stam needs to take a machine gun and riddle you full of bullets.
PAOLO DI CANIO, West Ham striker, 2001

[The club] thought merchandising was more important than the team and players. When the business is more important than the football, I don't care. I just gave up. I don't want to be treated like a pair of socks, a shirt, like shit. I'm not shit.
ERIC CANTONA, recalling why he had suddenly retired five years earlier, 2002

When I pull on a Manchester United shirt I still get a buzz that is impossible to describe.
DAVID BECKHAM, 2002

Everyone thinks he has the prettiest wife at home.
ARSENE WENGER, Arsenal manager, after Ferguson claimed United had been 'the best team in the country since Christmas' at the height of their tussle for the title, 2002

You see all the faces on the wall – George Best, Denis Law, Bobby Charlton – and you just want to be part of it.
RIO FERDINAND after his £29.1m switch from Leeds, 2002

United see themselves as an international, multi-national club, not a provincial-city club. We are a globally visioned brand. We're not about England, but about the world. Nationality doesn't matter.
RICHARD KURT, deputy editor of United fanzine Red Issue, *2003*

Manchester United is a perfect vehicle for all the ambitious people in football to have a go at. If someone wants to make a name for themselves, this club provides a perfect target.
FERGUSON after the FA's chief executive, Mark Palios, backed the banning of Rio Ferdinand for missing a drug test, 2003

Manchester United believe they are above the law and have the right to bully refs.
JEFF WINTER, ex-Premiership referee, in Who's the Bastard in the Black?, *2006*

During 90 minutes of football I want United to die.
STEVEN GERRARD, Liverpool captain, 2006

MIDDLESBROUGH

Our long-term aim is to make Middlesbrough synonymous with a good team rather than cooling towers and chemical plants. We're well on our way, even though Ruud Gullit had never heard of us when we contacted him last summer.
STEVE GIBSON, Middlesbrough chairman, 1995

Bryan Robson has certainly brought in the big names. But it is like going into a nightclub and getting off with a big blonde. The lads will say: 'Phwoar!' But can you keep her?
BERNIE SLAVEN, former Boro player, as Robson made some exotic signings, 1998

AC MILAN

When people think of Italy, after the Mafia and pizza, they think of AC Milan.
SILVIO BERLUSCONI, Milan president, 1997

We sat like a bunch of half-wits in the dressing-room... we were bloodthirsty zombies faced with an unseen problem – the blood was ours and they had drunk every last drop. We couldn't speak. We couldn't move. They had mentally destroyed us. Insomnia, rage, depression, a sense of nothingness. We'd invented a new disease with multiple symptoms: Istanbul syndrome.
ANDREA PIRLO recalling how Milan's 3-0 lead over Liverpool in the 2005 Champions League final turned into defeat on penalties, I Think Therefore I Play, *2014*

My Milan team was brilliant because it was full of great professionals who wanted to be together and have fun.
ARRIGO SACCHI, coach to Milan's 1989 and '90 European Cup-winning sides, 2010

At five in the morning, we were all drunk in the hotel, completely snookered on English beer. We went out and started playing football on the hotel golf course, tearing up the green. We were the masters of all Europe, and so, for that one magical night, we were the masters of Manchester as well.
CARLO ANCELOTTI, Chelsea manager, on Milan's win v Juventus at Old Trafford in the 2003 Champions League final, Beautiful Games of an Ordinary Genius, *2010*

MILLWALL

REPORTER: Someone was stabbed at West Ham–Millwall.
ALLARDYCE: That nearly happened to me at Millwall once; and I was playing for them.
EXCHANGE after a match involving Blackburn, where Sam Allardyce was manager, 2009

I met a pal who'd lost track of me and asked what I was doing. I said I was player-manager of Millwall. His wife immediately said: 'How embarrassing.'
MICK McCARTHY, 1995

Personally, I thrive on a hostile environment. Maybe it's because I played for Millwall.
KASEY KELLER, United States goalkeeper, anticipating a rough reception in Costa Rica, 1997

We have played for some of the great clubs in Europe, but we regard this as the pinnacle of our careers.
SERGEI YURAN, Russian striker, on an unhappy, short-lived spell with Millwall with Vassili Kulkov, 1996

MILTON KEYNES DONS

I'm not proud of the way this club came into being, but it wasn't the big Norwegian billionaire owners who moved [Wimbledon FC] to Milton Keynes. It was an administrator who said: 'I'm going to liquidate the club tomorrow unless you come up with the money to keep it going.' The only way I could do that was to move it here.
PETE WINKELMAN, MK Dons chairman, when club first met AFC Wimbledon, FA Cup, 2012

When AFC Wimbledon started, I wished them all the success in the world. But as the internet has developed, the lies, the half-truths they constantly put out against us, my sympathy has largely disappeared. What surprises me is why they can't move on. Think about it: the move to Milton Keynes has been a triumph but AFC have done really well, too. So everyone should be celebrating this.
RYAN RAY, MK Dons season-ticket holder and former Wimbledon FC fan, 2012

NEW YORK COSMOS

The Cosmos were 30 years ahead of their time. We had 13 nationalities in the dressing-room in 1979. The big Premier League clubs' squads are like that now, but we were the first truly global, cosmopolitan club.
DENNIS TUEART, Cosmos and England 'wide striker', 2012

The Cosmos have a great past…a mixture of football and art, a rock 'n' roll club. New York and me are a perfect match. The plan is to win trophies but also to build. The model is Barcelona under Cruyff. This is not a job but a passion.
ERIC CANTONA, director of soccer with the re-formed Cosmos, 2011

NEWCASTLE UNITED

It is the city, this football club. It's 24/7 when you are part of it. The Newcastle shirt is a heavy shirt to wear, as we've seen over the years, certainly over my time here. There have been very good players that have struggled at this club with the responsibility of wearing it. That is what it can do to you. But it's an amazing club to play for – if you can handle it.
STEVE HARPER, Newcastle goalkeeper, after his final game in 20 years at the club, 2013

I'll resist the urge to write a book, though I think I'd sell more copies than J.K. Rowling. It's a basket case of a club: Newcastle are either top of the mountain or bottom of the trenches. There's no middle ground.
HARPER, 2009

A wee club in the north-east.
SIR ALEX FERGUSON, Manchester United manager, after a heated exchange with Newcastle manager Alan Pardew, 2012

Among the criticism there were also messages from people who feel they have been let down by the club and that it has not matched their own ambitions for success.
FERGUSON on the response to his 'wee club' comment, 2013

We dealt with everything they threw at us, apart from the three goals we conceded.
STEVE TAYLOR, Newcastle defender, on defeat at Chelsea, 2014

I'm horrified by [pay-day loan company] Wonga cynically trying to buy respectability by linking

their name with Newcastle United.
I hate the damage this deal is doing
to people's lives, people who can
least afford to get into debt. I hate
this as an image for this club and
feel we could play a much more
positive civic role.
NICK FORBES, *leader of Newcastle city
council, on Newcastle's shirt-sponsorship
deal, 2013*

Don't worry about all the
bad publicity over the Wonga
sponsorship, lads. Just go out on
that pitch and give it 4,120 per cent.
TEAM TALK *by Alan Pardew,
Newcastle manager, as imagined by an
internet joke, 2012*

When I talk about our Geordie
core and my hopes for a Geordie
dynasty, people say: 'Does it
matter? Does where somebody
comes from really affect their
job?' I tell them it does make a
difference. I believe Geordies in
key posts at this club give you
a potentially vital extra one per
cent that non-Geordies don't.
Geordies have extra passion and
understanding. We are always going
to be superior.
FREDDY SHEPHERD, *Newcastle
chairman, 2003*

Newcastle have been very unlucky
with injuries this season. The
players keep recovering.
LEN SHACKLETON, *journalist and
former Newcastle and Sunderland player,
1965*

I've heard of players selling
dummies, but this club keeps
buying them.
SHACKLETON, 1976

Newcastle have the potential to
allow me to pick up the phone and
say to someone like Alex Ferguson:
'I want to buy your best.' I believe
that day will come.
JIM SMITH, *Newcastle manager, 1988*

Tell Alex [Ferguson] we're coming
to get him.
KEVIN KEEGAN, *Newcastle manager,
after winning promotion, 1993*

We're like the Basques. We are
fighting for a nation, the Geordie
nation. Football is tribalism and
we're the Mohicans.
SIR JOHN HALL, *Newcastle chairman,
1995*

It's madness – Newcastle are £40m
in debt yet they are the darlings of
the City.
ALAN SUGAR, *Tottenham chairman,
1997*

People talk about Newcastle as
a 'sleeping giant'. They last won
the championship in 1927 and
the FA Cup in 1955. They already
make Rip Van Winkle look like a
catnapper.
HUGH McILVANNEY, Sunday Times
writer, 1999

NEWPORT COUNTY

And they were lucky to get nil.
LEN SHACKLETON *on his six-goal Newcastle debut, a 13–0 win v Newport,* in Clown Prince of Soccer, *1955*

NORWICH CITY

Norwich were very, very less than average.

PHIL THOMPSON, *studio analyst on* Sky TV's Soccer Saturday, *2012*

I'd love Norwich to become famous for its football club again, and not just for Delia Smith and Alan Partridge.
NIGEL WORTHINGTON, *Norwich manager, 2002*

The last 10 years has been one long story of learning how to cope with disappointment.
DELIA SMITH, *celebrity chef, on being a Norwich City director, 2002*

NOTTINGHAM FOREST

We were very disappointed in the dressing-room after the first European Cup final win. It was as if we had lost. We wanted to put on a show. By the standards Cloughie set, we fell short.

JOHN McGOVERN, *Brian Clough's Forest captain, remembering the 1979 victory over Malmo, 2012*

Nottingham Forest will never know how lucky they were, that day they asked me to get on with the job of rebuilding their run-down club. They didn't just need a new manager – the bloody place was so dead it needed a kiss of life.
BRIAN CLOUGH *on his 18-year reign* in Clough: The Autobiography, *1994*

We won two European Cups yet we never practised a free kick. 'Just give it to Robbo' [John Robertson] was the cry.
MARTIN O'NEILL, *Forest player under Clough,* in Clough: The Autobiography, *1994*

The only person certain of boarding the bus to Wembley for the Littlewoods Cup final is Albert Kershore, and he'll be driving it.
CLOUGH *keeping his players on their toes, 1990*

I've got a young team. Acne is a bigger problem than injuries.
CLOUGH, *1992*

The evil slime from across the River Trent.
DAVID McVAY, *journalist and former Notts County player, in his memoir* Steak...Diana Ross, *2003*

NOTTS COUNTY

I started to have doubts when they
came and told me the milk bill has
not been paid.
SVEN-GORAN ERIKSSON, former
Notts director of football, on how he
realised there were broken financial
promises, 2011

We're like Lady Di. She's not the
Queen yet. She's not even married.
But like us, she's nicely placed.
JIMMY SIRREL, Notts manager,
chasing promotion as royal wedding fever
spread, 1981

Most people who can remember when County were a great club are dead.

JACK DUNNETT, Notts chairman, 1983

PARIS SAINT-GERMAIN

When somebody's paying £35m for
a 19-year-old boy, you have to say
the game's gone mad.
SIR ALEX FERGUSON after PSG
signed Lucas Moura from Brazilian
football following substantial Qatari
investment in the French club, 2012

We all need to be mindful that at
PSG now, a draw is the same as a
defeat.
NENE, Brazilian winger, on the raised
expectations for the club, 2012

No one says it, but Paris Saint-
Germain are an Italian club who
play in France. I've only had one
experience of this very Italian
dug-out, last season. At 0–0, they
were very angry with the referee at
half-time. There's a big difference
between the personalities you see
on TV, who all look very nice, and
what I've seen in the corridors.
FREDERIC ANTONETTI, Corsican
coach of Rennes, 2012; PSG's coach was
Carlo Ancelotti

PARTICK THISTLE

For years I thought their name was
Partick Thistle Nil.
BILLY CONNOLLY, comedian, 1988

PORT VALE

We looked like the last turkey on
the shelf on Christmas Eve.
MICKY ADAMS, Vale manager, after a
pre-Christmas defeat at MK Dons, 2013

My team look like a woman who has
a big fur coat on, but underneath
she's got no knickers on.
ADAMS after losing to Notts County,
2009

The reason Samantha Fox is so big in Eastern Europe and the Third World is that they are neglected in terms of the range of talent prepared to visit them. So even a small star becomes big once they arrive. In football terms, she has been playing Port Vale instead of Arsenal.
MAX CLIFFORD, public relations consultant, 1992

PORTSMOUTH

So Portsmouth have won the FA Cup. I don't want to alarm you, but the last time that happened World War Two broke out.
GARY LINEKER, BBC TV presenter, after Pompey beat Cardiff City to win the trophy they had last lifted in 1939, 2008

I remember saying to the lads: 'This is what we get paid to do.' Then I remembered we were not being paid.

MICHAEL APPLETON, Portsmouth manager, as the club's financial problems mounted, 2012

Losing a staff member like Tug, the training ground manager, is detrimental to the team. Yes, he's also a nice bloke and we have the odd chat about environmental issues but I don't want him back for chats, I just want him there so that when the bogs get blocked up he can sort it out. Without Tug around those kind of problems are going to cause friction to the team as well as a stink.
DAVID JAMES, Portsmouth and England goalkeeper, after the club entered administration 2010

Paolo Maldini can say he has done it all now.
PETER CROUCH, Portsmouth and England striker, on AC Milan's Uefa Cup visit to Fratton Park, 2008

Winning the FA Cup, playing Milan – I wouldn't give it up for the world, but ultimately it was to our detriment. Even I lost track of who actually owned the club at one point.
ANDY AWFORD, Portsmouth caretaker manager and ex-player and coach, 2014; the club were near the foot of League Two after three relegations, two periods in administration and owners from Russia, Lithuania and Hong Kong

QUEENS PARK RANGERS

Joe Royle texted to say keeping us up would be like – was it turning fish into something, or water into

wine, or feeding the 5,000? I've never read the Bible but I think he meant it would be a miracle.
HARRY REDKNAPP on becoming manager, 2012. QPR were relegated

Over the years, QPR have been a bit of a flitty, farty, we-like-a-Fancy-Dan-footballer club.
IAN HOLLOWAY, QPR manager, 2003

We were like the Dog and Duck in the first half and Real Madrid in the second.
HOLLOWAY after a draw v Hull, 2005

I thought QPR were a Scottish club, but I said to myself: 'Why not, if it's good for them and me?'
STEPHANE MBIA, Cameroonian defender, after signing from Marseille, 2012

It's easier to stick to 'sir' or 'gaffer' on the training ground than try to remember their names.

MIKELE LEIGERTWOOD, QPR and Antigua & Barbuda midfielder, on managerial changes at the club, 2010

RANGERS

For every five pounds Celtic spend, we will spend 10.
DAVID MURRAY, Rangers chairman, 2000

That would be bad luck – to have the worst Rangers team in history and the worst chief executive in history at the same time.
ALLY McCOIST, Rangers manager, after defeat at Forfar, 2013; Charles Green, having labelled the team 'the worst in Rangers' history', had said McCoist had to win a trophy

Without Rangers there is social unrest and a big problem for Scottish society. They have a huge fanbase and to contemplate the situation where those fans don't have a team to support, and are effectively left without a game to follow, could lead to all sorts of issues. There are thousands of Rangers fans whose fathers, parents and grandfathers have been Rangers fans. If Rangers weren't to exist that could have real dire consequences.
STEWART REGAN, chief executive of the Scottish FA, when Rangers became insolvent and entered administration before relaunching as a new company in the Third Division, 2012

This is my club, the same as it is for thousands of Rangers supporters. We don't do walking away.
McCOIST as Rangers' crisis deepened, 2012

I'll play for Rangers for as long as I can, then spend the rest of my life being depressed.
McCOIST, when he was a striker at the club, quoted in former team-mate Ian Redford's autobiography Raindrops Keep Falling On My Head, *2013*

Forget about playing in Europe – we might not even be playing in Glasgow.
CHARLES GREEN, would-be owner of Rangers, when the financially stricken club were placed in liquidation, 2012

The Scottish Premier League threw us out. They then stole our money that was due for last year and are pursuing us to strip titles. It's like coming home, finding your wife in bed with the milkman, asking for a divorce and then a week later asking: 'Can you forgive me? We'll make up.'
GREEN, Rangers chief executive, 2012

There isn't anyone round the board at Ibrox who knows anything about football and that includes me. My knowledge you could carry in a mouse's handkerchief.
GREEN, as above

Rangers are
all right, but they still haven't invented blue grass.
JOCK STEIN, Celtic manager, 1960s

Rangers like the big, strong, powerful fellows, with a bit of strength and solidity in the tackle, rather than the frivolous, quick-moving stylists like Jimmy Johnstone, small, tiptoe-through-the-tulips type of players who excite people.
WILLIE WADDELL, Rangers manager, 1972

Playing Rangers tonight was like trying to carry a ton weight up the down escalator. You wonder how Scotland could ever lose a football match.
HOWARD WILKINSON, Leeds manager, after his team's European Cup defeat by the Scottish champions, 1992

How many Scots have they got at Ibrox now? They're rushing out buying Englishmen, Italians and Chileans when every other kid in Scotland dreams of pulling on the blue jersey.
RON DIXON, former Dundee chairman, 1998

It isn't about balance sheets. Rangers is a world brand where everything follows from what happens on the park.
DAVID MURRAY, Rangers chairman, 1998

READING

This lot would kick the board over at Monopoly.
GRAEME MURTY, Reading captain, after a 33-game unbeaten run took them into the Premiership, 2006

REAL MADRID

They sign the best players, but not the best players needed in a certain position. It's no good having an orchestra with the 10 best guitarists if I don't have a pianist. Real Madrid have the best guitarists, but if I ask them to play the piano they won't be able to do it so well. [President Florentino Pérez] sold players I considered important. We didn't win the Champions League because we didn't have a squad properly structured to be able to win it.
MANUEL PELLEGRINI, Malaga and former Real coach, on the policy of signing 'Galacticos', 2012

Rafa would have preferred to play for Real Madrid rather than become a tennis player.

TONI NADAL, uncle and coach to Rafael Nadal, 2012

To be honest I was terribly pleased I wasn't playing. I saw [Alfredo] Di Stefano and these others, and I thought: 'These people just aren't human. It's not the sort of game I've been taught.'
BOBBY CHARLTON quoted in Motson and Rowlinson's The European Cup 1955–80, on watching Real play Manchester United, 1957

They could dish out the hard stuff, too, especially [Jose] Santamaria. People gloat about them and say they never kicked anybody. Well, they certainly kicked me.
JOHN CHARLES, Juventus's Welsh centre-forward, in Motson and Rowlinson, as above

The most educated person at Real Madrid is the woman who cleans the toilets.
JOAN GASPART, Barcelona vice-president, 1997

You can never have too many stars.
JORGE VALDANO, sporting director of Real, 2003

Real have turned themselves from a football club into a circus. I've never seen a chimps' tea party like it.
ULI HOENESS, Bayern Munich director and former player, after Real made Beckham their latest galactico, 2003

If this is a five-star club that stays in five-star hotels, why would they want a two-star coach?
VICENTE DEL BOSQUE, Real coach, on rejecting a contract offer, 2003

Real's movement and touch meant it was like facing the Harlem Globetrotters at times. They were passing it about and we couldn't get near them.
GARY NEVILLE, *Manchester United defender, 2003*

We're like a big blockbuster movie. Like *Men in Black*, or in our case, *Men in White*. We have a great story to tell, a great production and the biggest box-office stars.
JOSE ANGEL SANCHEZ, *Real's director of marketing, in John Carlin's* White Angels: Beckham, Real Madrid and the New Football, *2004*

The pressure [of having to win] does not oppress the great players. When we buy players, the responsibility that goes with pulling on a Real Madrid shirt is one of the most important things to consider. A great footballer sleeps equally well with or without pressure.
JORGE VALDANO, *sporting director of Real, 2003*

Protesting in front of the referee is a sign of weakness. Insults never achieve anything. Real Madrid never complain.
ENTRY *in Real's* Little Blue Book, *issued by the club to players, 2004*

In my time in Madrid I've had six managers, four presidents and we've signed 20 players. In a successful club you need stability, and we haven't had that.

DAVID BECKHAM *shortly before leaving Spain for Los Angeles, 2007*

SHEFFIELD UNITED

Sheffield Eagles [rugby league team] play the ball on the ground more than Sheffield United.
JONATHAN FOSTER *reporting on a United match in* The Independent, *1990*

When I was a lad and we played Wednesday, they wore blue and white stripes and we'd wear red and white stripes. Now they wear all sorts of stuff, like a fashion parade. Where have our stripes gone this season? Blades' strip looks like it was designed by Julian Clary when he had a migraine.
SEAN BEAN, *actor and United fan, 1996*

I remember the day when this club sold Brian Deane and Jan Aage Fjortoft. It was like when President Kennedy was shot – that's how deeply I felt.
NEIL WARNOCK, *lifelong fan, on taking over as manager, 1999*

SHEFFIELD WEDNESDAY

The big-city team with the small-town mentality.
HOWARD WILKINSON, *Leeds and former Wednesday manager, 1991*

There are Wednesday players with more money than the club, which can't be right.
GARY MEGSON, Sheffield-based West Bromwich Albion manager, on his favourite club's financial difficulties, 2002

SOUTHAMPTON

We don't want to be judged by the young, handsome players that we have. We want to be judged in the same manner, being judged by the same rigour, in the same way all other clubs are.
MAURICIO POCHETTINO, Southampton manager, alleging refereeing decisions went against them v Everton, 2013

STOKE CITY

I wouldn't sign for any other club. I don't see why I can't go on a season or two. I still get butterflies before a match – when I play at the Victoria Ground again, there will be a swarm inside me.
STANLEY MATTHEWS on rejoining Stoke from Blackpool, aged 46, 1961

[Manager Tony Pulis] would say: 'Look at this lot, they don't want us in the Premier League.' I remember when we used to play Arsenal, you could almost sense them thinking: 'What the hell are you doing on the same pitch as me?' As a group, we loved that.
DANNY HIGGINBOTHAM, former Stoke defender, 2014

You can't lose against Stoke if you aspire to be the next champions.

SANTI CAZORLA, Arsenal midfielder, 2014

I would hate to play against us.
HIGGINBOTHAM on Pulis's emphasis on making Stoke hard to beat, 2010

They bully you. I admire their style, but it's almost like a rugby team.
MARTIN JOL, Fulham manager, after 1–0 loss at Stoke, 2012

One-nil to the rugby team.
SONG by Stoke fans mocking Arsenal manager Arsene Wenger, 2014; they also sang the England rugby union anthem 'Swing Low Sweet Chariot'

We're talking about a team that has respect, who've got integrity and honour – who get on with the game.
GARY NEVILLE, Sky pundit and ex-Manchester United and England defender, 2012

We've got the jolly green giants coming to play against us. The biggest team in Europe. Michael [Owen] is not allowed to play unless he brings ladders.
SIR ALEX FERGUSON awaiting Stoke's visit to Manchester United, 2012

Don't even think of Stoke City and Manchester United in the same breath.
PULIS, 2008

Secret pictures, gained by our intrepid Albion reporters, have unearthed Stoke's secrets. They train with cannons, rescued from local medieval ruins. Footballs are loaded into them and fired into the distance for [Mamady] Sidibe to head and [Ricardo] Fuller to chase.
REPORT on Stoke's victory over West Bromwich Albion in the Albion programme, 2007

SUNDERLAND

After Sunderland came through against Manchester United to reach the [Capital One Cup] final, the only thing that would make my life easier would be if there had been a 'flu epidemic on their coach back from Old Trafford, a two-hour contraflow and it had been 120–118 on penalties.
ANDY THORN, Kidderminster Harriers manager, as the non-leaguers prepared to face Sunderland in the FA Cup four days after the Premier League team won a shoot-out to reach Wembley, 2014

Everything that did go wrong could go wrong.
STEVE BRUCE, Sunderland manager, after a 5–1 derby loss at Newcastle, 2010

I'd rather go and collect stamps than stick on that shirt.
STEVEN TAYLOR, Newcastle defender, when asked if he would ever consider playing for Sunderland, 2012

I remember talking to [Sir Alex Ferguson] when we got off the bus here before a game. He said, 'Sunderland is a bloody big club.' That stuck with me.
ROY KEANE, Sunderland manager, 2007

First, Margaret Thatcher does her best to destroy the town. Now Ben Thatcher viciously elbows our best crosser of the ball to destroy the Sunderland team at Wimbledon. Just what have they got against us?
LETTER to the Sunderland Echo, 2000

SWANSEA CITY

Some people tell me Swansea are the enemy. Swansea? For Pete's sake. There's nothing wrong with Swansea. But is that the extent of our ambition? Swansea will never be a big club and if they are honest about themselves they will say so. If Swansea fans are Welsh and want

to see top-class football in Wales, they should recognise that Cardiff are the only Welsh club with a cat's chance in hell of making it.
SAM HAMMAM, Cardiff City owner, when Swansea were in the fourth tier and Cardiff in the third, 2000

After their keeper was sent off I heard one of their players say to another: 'They'll score eight or nine.' I said: 'Don't worry. We will keep the ball.' It's respect.
MICHU, Swansea's Spanish striker, after they beat Bradford City 5–0 in the Carling Cup final, 2013; the League Two club were reduced to 10 men when Swansea led 3–0

It really doesn't matter if we finish 10th or 14th. Who will remember if we have 43 or 48 points? It's overall – how did they play? If you asked the people on the street in Swansea, 'What do you prefer, 10th and changing the style of play or 14th and remain the same style?' the answer is obvious.
MICHAEL LAUDRUP, former Denmark, Real Madrid and Barcelona player, on becoming Swansea manager, 2012

TOTTENHAM HOTSPUR

We sold Elvis and bought the Beatles.
ERIK THORSTVEDT, former Tottenham and Norway goalkeeper, on manager Andre Villas-Boas using the

world-record fee of £85.3m received for Gareth Bale to make signings, 2013

Erik Thorstvedt said Spurs had sold Elvis and bought the Beatles; but a Norwegian would.
JEFF STELLING, Sky Soccer Saturday anchor, 2013

They are all internationals, but it's like fixing a washing machine with someone else's tool bag. Sometimes you might not have the right bit.
TIM SHERWOOD, Tottenham manager, on the seven players Villas-Boas bought with the Bale fee, 2014

With all their guns flying, Tottenham would be a real threat.
GLENN HODDLE, Sky TV pundit and former Spurs manager and player, 2012

Than the famous Spurs there is probably no more famous club in the whole of England. Did they not recover the Association Cup for the south? Did they not play pretty and effective football? Are they not scrupulously fair? Are they not perfectly managed?
WILLIAM PICKFORD and ALFRED GIBSON, authors, Association Football and the Men Who Made It, 1906

We have no desire just to be a football club. That is not the basis for success.
PAUL BOBROFF, chairman of Tottenham Hotspur plc, 1983

The cold and damp dressing room is our secret weapon for Spurs. Not forgetting their lukewarm pot of tea at half-time.
PHIL SPROSON, Port Vale defender, before the Third Division side faced Spurs in the FA Cup, 1988

Spurs were like West Ham used to be, all fancy flicks and sweet sherry.
SPROSON after scoring for Vale in their victory over Spurs, 1988

When Ilie Dumitrescu asked me when Spurs last won the championship, I couldn't answer him. That shouldn't be the case for a club this big.
OSVALDO ARDILES, Spurs manager, 1995

I don't think Spurs would ever sign a superstar like [Jurgen] Klinsmann or [Dennis] Bergkamp again. Those guys are floaters. They'll go anywhere, play for anyone who pays them the most.
ALAN SUGAR, Spurs chairman, after Arsenal paid £7.25m for Bergkamp, 1995

I want a consistent team, not a flash one. When I was at Highbury, the message from White Hart Lane used to be 'let Arsenal win things with boring football, we'd rather play entertainingly and lose'. But to me that was just a psychological crutch. I want my team to be exciting, and to win week in, week out. I'm working on it.
GEORGE GRAHAM, Spurs manager, 2000

We're good enough to survive in the Premiership and maybe have a good cup run or even earn a UEFA Cup spot if things go really well. But we are never going to win the championship.
SHERWOOD, then a Spurs midfielder, on the 'harsh reality' of under-investment, 2002

It might sound strange to say it, but Tottenham are an important club.
ROBERTO MANCINI, Lazio coach, on being linked with Spurs' managerial vacancy, 2004

As we say in Portugal, they brought the bus and left it in front of the goal.
JOSE MOURINHO, Chelsea manager, after Spurs drew 0–0 at Stamford Bridge, 2004

WATFORD

Blimey, the ground looks a bit different to Watford. Where's the dog track?
LUTHER BLISSETT after exchanging Vicarage Road for Milan's San Siro stadium, 1983

If it was a war, it would be America against San Marino. In boxing it would be Muhammad Ali against Jimmy Krankie.
AIDY BOOTHROYD, Watford manager, before facing Manchester United, 2007

WEST BROMWICH ALBION

That's typical of this club. For an extra £10,000 they could have got John Snow.
JEFF ASTLE, West Bromwich Albion striker, after they bought goalkeeper Jim Cumbes, a fast bowler with Lancashire, 1969

They've made some signings, but it's like putting lipstick on a pig. It's still a pig.

RODNEY MARSH, Sky pundit and former England player, as Albion prepared for the Premiership, 2002

We haven't got his type of player at the club, someone who can pass and score goals.
GARY MEGSON, Albion manager, on signing Jason Koumas from Tranmere, 2002

WEST HAM UNITED

This is football from the 19th century. The only [other] thing I could bring was a Black and Decker [tool] to destroy the wall.
JOSE MOURINHO, Chelsea manager, after West Ham drew 0–0 at Stamford Bridge, 2014

We're West Ham United, we play on the floor.
SONG by West Ham fans concerned about the team's more direct style under Sam Allardyce, 2012; Allardyce responded by saying 'I'm sick of all that rubbish'

[West Ham] should revert to playing British football instead of all this European tarting about. Crush, kill, destroy. And wear tight shorts. I think we should phone up Julian Dicks and get him back because, if we did go down, at least he'd kick the shit out of everyone. Proper geezer.
RAY WINSTONE, actor and West Ham fan, 2010

I'm only 27 but I look 60. This club has made my hair turn grey.
DAVID GOLD, 76-year-old co-owner, after West Ham won promotion, 2012

Even when we had Moore, Hurst and Peters, West Ham's average finish was about 17th. Which shows how crap the other eight of us were.
HARRY REDKNAPP, former player and manager at the club, 2001

The crowds at West Ham haven't been rewarded by results, but they keep turning up because they see good football. Other clubs will suffer from the old bugbear that results count more than anything. This has been the ruination of English soccer.
RON GREENWOOD, England and former West Ham manager, 1977

All that 'happy losers' stuff is a load of cobblers. I hate losing.
BILLY BONDS, West Ham manager, on claims that the club put style above winning, 1991

West Ham's performance was obscene in terms of the effort they put into the match.

ALEX FERGUSON, Manchester United manager, on a 1–0 defeat which damaged their championship prospects, in Six Years at United, 1992

I want the West Ham fans to know that we are going to win something before I finish my career here. Otherwise I'll kill myself.
PAOLO DI CANIO, West Ham's Italian striker, 2001

WIGAN ATHLETIC

CALLUM McMANAMAN: I always believed we'd win it.
REPORTER: How does it feel?
McMANAMAN: I can't believe it.
EXCHANGE on ITV after Wigan won the FA Cup with McManaman named man of the match, 2013

[Chairman Dave Whelan] told me the first day: in 10 years we're going to have a new stadium and we'll be in the Premier League. The most amazing thing is that I believed him.
ROBERTO MARTINEZ, Wigan manager, before the FA Cup final victory v Manchester City, 2013; Wigan were in the fourth tier when Martinez arrived from Spain as a player in 1995

AFC WIMBLEDON

AFC Wimbledon in the League! Talk about the ashes rising from the flames.
STAN COLLYMORE, talkSPORT radio summariser, when the club formed by fans after Wimbledon moved to Milton Keynes completed a nine-year rise from the Combined Counties League, 2011

AFC Wimbledon have shown just what can happen when people don't just sit on the sidelines, but choose to get involved and really pull together – a great example of the Big Society.
DAVID CAMERON MP, Conservative Prime Minister, 2012

Businessmen tried to take our club away from us so we decided to form our own. We'd like to pass them on the way up as they slip towards extinction. For the good of football, it's important they fail miserably.

KRIS STEWART, chairman of AFC Wimbledon, set up after Wimbledon pursued their intention to relocate from London to Milton Keynes, 2002

WIMBLEDON

The borstal of football.

DAVE BASSETT, Wimbledon manager, 1987

The only hooligans here are the players.

BASSETT after fans invaded the pitch when the Dons won promotion to the First Division, 1986

It was just welly, welly, welly. The ball must've been screaming for mercy.

RON YEATS, Liverpool scout, after watching Wimbledon, 1988

Wimbledon are killing the dreams that made football the world's greatest game.

TERRY VENABLES, Tottenham manager, 1988

There is one London club that have got it right. Whatever you think of Wimbledon's style of play, you can't argue with their results.

BOB PAISLEY, former Liverpool manager, 1988

Wimbledon will take to Wembley. Once you've tried to get a decent bath at Hartlepool, you can handle anything.

WALLY DOWNES, ex-Wimbledon stalwart, before the FA Cup final, 1988

The Crazy Gang have beaten the Culture Club!

JOHN MOTSON, BBC TV commentator, as Liverpool were beaten, 1988

For us to compete in the Premiership with our finances is like going into a nuclear war with bows and arrows.

JOE KINNEAR, Wimbledon manager, 1997

It's the young players I feel sorry for, like Joe McAnuff. He'd be bringing the house down if there was a house to bring down.

NEIL SHIPPERLEY, Wimbledon captain, as defections to AFC Wimbledon saw crowds fall below 2,500 in the First Division, 2002

The best way to watch Wimbledon is on Ceefax.
GARY LINEKER, TV pundit, 1993

WOLVERHAMPTON WANDERERS

This club is an environment where, if we lose or draw, it's not good enough. It's a win-or-nothing thing. We call it Wolfism.
DAVE JONES, Wolves manager, on the expectations surrounding the club, 2003

Hail Wolves 'Champions of the World' Now
HEADLINE in the Daily Mail *after Stan Cullis's team beat Hungarian side Honved in a floodlit friendly before the launch of the European Cup, 1954*

Wolves' success does Mr [Stan] Cullis great credit, but it has also done much harm to the game in England because so many lesser managers have attempted to ape the Wolves-Cullis technique. Artistry with the ball is not all-important with Wolverhampton Wanderers.
JIMMY McILROY, Burnley midfielder, criticising Wolves' long-ball style in Right Inside Soccer, *1960*

Bring back the fifties!
CHANT by Wolves fans during protest against Graham Taylor's management, 1995

There are only four clubs I'd have considered leaving Leicester for – Manchester United, Newcastle, Rangers and Wolves. This is the last of the sleeping giants.
MARK McGHEE, Wolves manager, 1995

When I came here I found a lot of people living in the past, and I upset them by telling them so. Billy Wright won't win me promotion. And how is Steve Bull going to help me? Let's put all the great names in a museum, treasure the memories and move on.
DAVE JONES, Wolves manager, striving to lead the club to the Premiership, 2002

4
COUNTRIES

AMERICAN SAMOA

Their players weren't allowed to
swap shirts with us at the end.
I think they got theirs from a
supermarket when they first arrived
in Australia.
ARCHIE THOMPSON, Australia
striker, after scoring 13 goals in a world-
record 31–0 defeat of the Samoans, 2001

ANDORRA

Andorra? Well, it's just a little
island in the mid-Atlantic.
BOBBY GOULD, talkSPORT radio
pundit, 2011

ARGENTINA

We have the best player in the
world and we're also playing on the
patio beside our house. The only
problem is that that house is owned
by the five-time world champions.
ALEX SABELLA, Argentina coach and
former Leeds and Sheffield United player,
before the World Cup finals in Brazil,
2014

We should not have played in the
1982 World Cup. A lot of kids died
in the Malvinas and as the captain,
I should have done something to
stop us going on the pitch.
DANIEL PASSARELLA, former
Argentina captain, recalling the effect
of the Falkands War shortly before their
defence of the World Cup, 2001

Malvinas 2 England 1! We blasted
the English pirates with Maradona
and a little hand. He who robs a
thief has a thousand years of pardon.
CRONICA newspaper of Buenos Aires,
1986; Malvinas is the Argentinian name
for the Falkland Islands

It seems a pity so much Argentinian
talent is wasted. Our best football
will come against the right type of
opposition – a team who come to
play football, and not act as animals.
ALF RAMSEY, England manager, after
his side won a foul-strewn World Cup
quarter-final, 1966

There haven't been so many
headbands and leather necklaces
on TV since the Allman Brothers
played The Old Grey Whistle Test.
WHEN SATURDAY COMES
magazine describes a 'hairy' Argentinian
substitutes' bench against England,
World Cup finals, 2002

AUSTRALIA

Sheilas, Wogs and Poofters
TITLE of the autobiography of former
Australia captain Johnny Warren, 2003;
Warren said it summed up how other
sports in Australia perceived football

If we'd lost I'd already got my
excuse worked out – that it took 22
of you to beat us.
FRANK FARINA, Australia manager,
after the Socceroos beat an England side
that featured 11 substitutes, 2003

BELGIUM

I'm nobody. I'm nothing at all. Like everyone else, I will die one day and finish up in a wooden box. I'm just happy to see that the national team is riding a new, positive wave. It's especially fun for a squad that has struggled for 10 years.

MARC WILMOTS, Belgium coach, on their resurgent fortunes, 2013

BRAZIL

If I were playing [against Spain's World Cup-winning side of 2010], we would win, no doubt. The 1970 side set the standard by which others are measured. These comparisons will always be there, but you cannot compare them individually. But the 1970 team had better players than Spain, who have only two or three great players.

PELE, 2012

I would never pay for a ticket to watch this Brazilian team. Where has the Brazil team we all know disappeared to in this World Cup? Where is the Brazilian magic?

JOHAN CRUYFF, former Netherlands captain and Barcelona coach, World Cup finals, 2010

Brazil just aren't that Brazilian any more. Like Harlem Globetrotters just travelling round for the dough.

JOEY BARTON, Queens Park Rangers midfielder, tweeting after Brazil's draw v Russia at Chelsea, 2013

A player who conjugates a verb in the first person singular cannot be part of this Brazilian squad. He has to conjugate the verb in the first person plural. We. We want to conquer. We are going to conquer. Using the word 'I' when you're in a group makes things complicated.

VANDERLEI LUXEMBURGO, Brazil coach, 1999

We have the most important football on the planet.

LUIZ INACIO LULA DA SILVA, president of Brazil, on why his country should host the 2014 World Cup, 2007

It's an absolute myth to say we are individualists. We play a collective game, as disciplined as anybody else.

TOSTAO, member of Brazil's celebrated 1970 World Cup-winning team, 2006

Brazil played in shoes which could only be likened to Grecian slippers. We cannot laugh even about that. After all, they won the World Cup in them [in 1958].

TOM FINNEY, England winger, in Finney on Football, 1958

We have nothing to learn from these people.

ALF RAMSEY, England manager, after defeat by Brazil, World Cup finals, 1970

Our football is like our inflation:
100 per cent
HEADLINE in Jornal da Tarde *after
Brazil beat England, 1981*

It feels like the magic has gone. It's
as if we've been cursed.
RIVALDO, *Brazil playmaker, after
World Cup qualifying defeat by
Paraguay, less than two years before he
helped his country regain the trophy, 2000*

There's no beautiful game any
more. You are not going to see the
Brazil of 1958, '62 or '70. This is
2001.
LUIZ FELIPE SCOLARI, *Brazil coach,
2001*

They are better than us, which is
the difference.
SVEN-GORAN ERIKSSON, *England
manager, after Brazil beat his side in the
World Cup quarter-finals, 2002*

We prepare for a game much more
than people think. They think we
run out on the pitch, all laughter
and joy and then it's goal, goal,
goal.
RONALDINHO *before the World Cup
finals, 2006*

It's through football that our
people feel avenged. It's like a
message saying: 'We may be First
World in other things, but we're
better at this.'
TOSTAO, *member of Brazil's 1970
team, 2007*

CAMEROON

We didn't underestimate them.
They were a lot better than we
thought.
BOBBY ROBSON, *England manager,
after a 3–2 win v Cameroon, World Cup
finals, 1990*

CONGO

I love playing for Congo. When
you arrive at the airport and
then to the arrivals hall, people
physically pick you up and carry
you to the waiting car, dancing and
singing.
CHRIS SAMBA, *France-born Blackburn
and Congo defender, to Fifa.com, 2011*

CZECH REPUBLIC

This is not the best Czech Republic
side in the world.
JASON CUNDY, *talkSPORT radio
pundit, 2011*

People ask what is the secret recipe
of our success. Recipes are for cakes
and pies.
KAREL BRUCKNER, *Czech coach,
2004*

DENMARK

I have told Chancellor Kohl that it
is absolutely not on for the Danes
to want to leave the European

Community and be European champions at the same time.
BERTI VOGTS, Germany manager, after Denmark beat his team to win the European Championship, 1992

ENGLAND

England's only important victory in a major tournament was based, as we all know, on a referee's mistake.
LARS WALLRODT, football correspondent of Germany's Die Welt *newspaper, 2010*

England can sometimes be quite painful to watch, and I know from some of the [Tottenham] players that it is not an enjoyable experience for them, either.
HARRY REDKNAPP, Queens Park Rangers and former Tottenham manager, 2013

We have to reduce our expectations of England and we have the players to do it.

STEVE McCLAREN, former England manager, 2011

We're like 11 bulldogs who'll never give up and basically die on the pitch.
ASHLEY COLE, England defender, European Championship finals, 2012

Great memories #Italia90 and so, so close. Gazza's tears, Bobby Robson, Platt's volley, Cameroon pens and bloody Germans! #haveawordwithhim
GARY LINEKER tweeting as England reached the last eight, European Championship finals, 2012

As usual they are going through a familiar sequence of events in England. They all expected a first-round elimination, but now they're through to the next round they're already talking about a semi-final against Germany, as if Italy were Luxembourg.
GABRIELE MARCOTTI, London correspondent of Il Corriere dello Sport, *before England played Italy in the quarter-finals of the European Championship, 2008; Italy won on penalties*

A grey bird alighted on the Algerian goal, appreciating it to be a place of sanctuary, having clearly checked on [Wayne] Rooney's recent form and being familiar with [Emile] Heskey's work. The ultimate ignominy for England was that the bird actually changed ends at half-time.
HENRY WINTER, Daily Telegraph football correspondent, on England's display v Algeria, World Cup finals, 2010

I do not like saying this but the truth is I was so bored watching the England game the other night that I went on eBay to buy a table.
IAN HOLLOWAY, Blackpool manager, in his Independent on Sunday column, 2010

Thank heaven The Few didn't defend as badly as England's footballers did in Bloemfontein yesterday, otherwise we'd all be speaking German.
RICHARD LITTLEJOHN, Daily Mail columnist, after England's 4–1 defeat by Germany, World Cup finals, 2010

England are the New York Mets. Massively, ridiculously overrated by their media, always involved in some sort of comic downfall, insane injuries, woeful management. A car crash waiting to happen, at which stage the local media go berserk.
BOSTON GLOBE verdict before the World Cup finals, 2006

The World Cup wasn't won [in 1966] on the playing fields of England. It was won on the streets.
SIR BOBBY CHARLTON, member of the class of '66, 1995

It never crossed our minds that we could lose. No, no never. It didn't come into it.
BOBBY MOORE, captain of the '66 side, in Ian Ridley, Season in the Cold, 1992

You've beaten them once. Now go out and bloody beat them again.

ALF RAMSEY to the England players before extra time, World Cup final, 1966

As we came round the corner from the 18th green, a crowd of members were at the clubhouse window, cheering and waiting to tell me that England had won the World Cup. It was the blackest day of my life.
DENIS LAW, former Scotland international, 1979

The English team had some outstanding players. Men like [Gordon] Banks and Bobby Moore, and Cooper and Bobby and Jack Charlton. They can play on any Brazilian team at any time, and that is no light compliment.
PELE after Brazil's defeat of England during the World Cup finals, 1970, from My Life and the Beautiful Game

England can't always win 6–0. Bobby Charlton has retired.

DAVE BASSETT, Sheffield United manager, after a 0–0 draw, 1995

I can't say England are shite because they beat us in the [Euro 2000] play-offs, and that would make us even shittier.
ALLY McCOIST, former Scotland striker, 2000

Portugal play football as I like to see it played. As a neutral it was fantastic. Unfortunately I'm not a neutral.
KEVIN KEEGAN, England manager, after Portugal beat his team, Euro 2000

All the European teams who have gone out have played too defensively, as if they were scared. I thought England were the worst.
GUUS HIDDINK, South Korea's Dutch coach, after his team went a stage further than England to the World Cup semi-finals, 2002

It was obvious England were overawed by Brazil, Brazil with 10 players, men against boys. You could see England's body language at the end. 'We've done OK, haven't we? Got to the quarter-finals.' England should expect to be in the semi-finals or final every time. Come on, lads, wake up!
ROY KEANE, former Republic of Ireland captain, 2002; he also claimed 'the priority' for some England players was to swap shirts with a Brazilian

I wouldn't watch a whole England game but I see the highlights.
KEANE, 2003

It would have been great to win 1–0. But 0–0 seems even better because it shows character to get such a result.
DAVID BECKHAM after England's goalless draw in Turkey, 2003

When the St George flag was burned the lads got a look at it and were fuming.
JOHN TERRY, England defender, after Macedonia fans set light to the England flag in Skopje, 2003

We're not as good as we think we are. Me and the other players constantly claimed we could win the World Cup. It was stupid.
STEVEN GERRARD after England's failure in Germany, 2006

Nobody in Europe likes England. England invented the sport but has never made any impact on world football.
JACK WARNER, Trinidadian vice-president of FIFA, on why England should not be awarded the 2018 World Cup, 2007

We went around Germany blowing our own trumpet and returned home mute with embarrassment.
GERRARD in his autobiography, 2007

'We got beat in the quarter-finals. I played like shit. Here's my book.'
JOEY BARTON, Manchester City midfielder, on what England's World Cup squad might say, 2006

FAROE ISLANDS

We're a small country and it's strange that he wants to put us down even more. Ibra tells us we're 'a bunch of fishermen' and yes we are – it's a part of our culture. We finish work at four and then go training in the evening. I can't understand why he behaves like that to us.
SIMUN SAMUELSEN, Faroe Islands striker, alleging that Sweden's Zlatan Ibrahimovic 'belittled' their players, 2013

FRANCE

Ultra-liberalism applied to football is why the French team lost.
MARINE LE PEN, leader of the ultra-right National Front, after France's 2–0 first-leg defeat by Ukraine in a World Cup play-off, 2013; France won the second leg 3–0

These players, from some of the biggest clubs in Europe, have distinguished themselves by a lack of humility, an immaturity and an inability to represent their country and millions of supporters.
JOEL MULLER, head of the French coaches' association, after France's failure at the European Championship finals, 2012

It's a good thing France came home. One more week and they would have eaten each other. It's best to avoid cannibalism.
ERIC CANTONA, former France

player, after Les Bleus' ill-starred campaign in South Africa, World Cup finals, 2010*

Half the team are foreigners who don't even know the words to the Marseillaise.
JEAN-MARIE LE PEN, Marine Le Pen's father and then leader of the National Front, on the France team at the European Championship finals, 1996

Me, sing to satisfy Le Pen? I don't think so.
MARCEL DESAILLY, black France defender, 1996

A tricolour orgasm!
HEADLINE in France Soir after France's World Cup triumph, 1998

The French team has been my life and has led me to do things I shouldn't have. It has been my mistress – a beautiful mistress.
LAURENT BLANC retiring from the national side after the triumph at Euro 2000

Long live France – not the one he wants, but the real one! [Jean-Marie] Le Pen is not aware that there are black, blond and brown French people. He doesn't know his history.
LILIAN THURAM, France defender, on criticism of the composition of the

squad by the leader of the far-right National Front, 2006

The France team all tested positive for being assholes.
LANCE ARMSTRONG, former Tour de France winner, after France lost to Italy in the World Cup final, 2006

GERMANY

Football is a simple game where 22 men chase a ball for 90 minutes and at the end, the Germans win.
GARY LINEKER, England striker, on West Germany's victory over England in a penalty shoot-out, World Cup finals, 1990

Football is a simple game where 22 men kick a ball about for 90 minutes and at the end, the Germans lose a four-goal lead.
TWEET by Lineker, now anchoring BBC TV football coverage, after Germany drew 4–4 with Sweden, 2012

Q: What do you admire most about Germany? A: Their results.

TERRY VENABLES, England coach, after the Germans beat them on penalties, European Championship finals, 1996

The reason we Germans are so good at penalties is that we have had to rebuild our country twice.
JURGEN KLINSMANN, Germany captain, in a TV documentary, On the Spot: The 12-yard Club, *1999*

What is Germany? It is a country that likes to attack – unfortunately twice in the wrong way in the past century.
KLINSMANN, 2010

The 5–1 defeat by England was like the explosion of a nuclear bomb. The scars will last for life.
OLIVER KAHN, Germany goalkeeper on that fateful night in Munich, 2001

You have to, you know, to some degree, er, admire the Germans.

SIR BOBBY ROBSON, ITV pundit, leads the grudging praise for Germany's feat in reaching the World Cup final, 2002

Diving fucking cheats.
CHRISTIAN DAILLY, Scotland defender, after Germany's 2–1 win featured a contentious penalty, 2003

GIBRALTAR

We're getting dropped in the middle of the ocean with a massive tidal wave coming our way. What we have to do now is work even harder to swim towards the tidal wave and not away from it.
ALLEN BULA, Gibraltar manager, on the rock's impending debut in competitive internationals, 2014

GREECE

I was delighted Greece won Euro 2004 because they played as a team, not individually. The so-called great nations – that idea makes me laugh, really – didn't produce, despite their talent. Good on the Greeks. The team with the fewest egos won, and that's always nice.
ROY KEANE, Manchester United captain, 2004

HUNGARY

I was in my kit, hanging around the corridor, when I saw the England inside-right Ernie Taylor, who wasn't very tall. I popped back in the dressing room and said to the others: 'We're going to be all right – they've got someone even smaller than me.'
FERENC PUSKAS on playing in Hungary's 6–3 defeat of England at Wembley 50 years earlier, 2003

The 1954 Hungarian soccer masters did not go into the record books as the champions of the world. But they went into my personal memory file, and that of millions of other football lovers, as the finest team ever to sort out successfully the intricacies of the wonderful game.
TOM FINNEY, Preston and England forward, in Finney on Football, 1958

IRAQ

It was frightening to play for Iraq because every mistake you made put you in prison. The sentence depended on the mistake: for a defensive error, two or three days; for missing a penalty, maybe three weeks.
SAITH HUSSEIN, Iraq striker, on when the national side was run by Saddam Hussein's son Uday, 2003

ITALY

We've done nothing yet. There's no use in going to Rome and not seeing the Pope.
ANDREA PIRLO, Italy playmaker, after semi-final victory v Germany, European Championship finals, 2012; Italy lost to Spain in the final

Four years ago we were hailed as champions, today we are playing like billy goats.
GENNARO GATTUSO, Italy midfielder, as the holders went out of the

World Cup without winning a match, 2010

The Eyeties don't have it.
PAUL INCE, South African TV summariser, on Italy, World Cup finals, 2010

We've shown that we're not criminals but great footballers.

ALESSANDRO DEL PIERO, Italy striker, as they reached the World Cup final while his club, Juventus, were embroiled in a financial scandal, 2006

On the pitch the Italians looked no different to us. It was like playing Bournemouth on a wet Saturday.
JASON McATEER, Republic of Ireland midfielder, after beating Italy in the World Cup, 1994

The Italians still don't know how to lose. Mussolini was the same when he told the players not to return from France without the World Cup in 1938.
BYRON MORENO, Ecuadorian referee, after Italy complained they were cheated by him when South Korea knocked them out of the World Cup, 2002

LIBERIA

The worst team to feature a European Footballer of the Year since George Best turned out for Dunstable Town.
ANDY LYONS, editor of When Saturday Comes magazine, on George Weah and his national team's failure at the African Nations Cup, 1996

NETHERLANDS

Sadly, they played very dirty. This ugly, vulgar, hard, hermetic, hardly eye-catching, hardly football style... If with this they got satisfaction, fine, but they lost.
JOHAN CRUYFF, former Netherlands, Ajax and Barcelona player and coach, after his country were beaten by Spain in the World Cup final, 2012

Holland started as if they meant to go on.
LEE DIXON, BBC TV pundit, European Championship finals, 2012

The Dutch think innovatively, creatively and abstractly about space in their football because for centuries they have had to think innovatively about space in every other area of their lives.
DAVID WINNER, author, in Brilliant Orange: The Neurotic Genius of Dutch Football, 2000

It's time we let go of these pathetic egos. We don't need a psychologist with the Dutch team, we are grown-up men. The ones who have a problem with other players or the manager should tell them face to face. That's the only psychology we need. We have to stop living on little islands.
WESLEY SNEIJDER, Netherlands midfielder, after three defeats at the European Championship finals, 2012

During the European Championship finals we went out every night until two or three in the morning. The problem with Italians is that they don't like to go out after playing.
RUUD GULLIT, Dutch captain, after they became European champions, 1988

NEW ZEALAND

We beat a team that is no more than a group of buddies who were rejected because they couldn't play rugby well, and they had no choice but to switch to soccer.
HUGO SANCHEZ, former Mexico and Real Madrid striker, on his country's victory over the All Whites in the play-off to reach the World Cup finals, 2013

NORTHERN IRELAND

He plays sort of international football with Northern Ireland.
PHIL THOMPSON, Sky Soccer Saturday summariser, on Manchester United's Jonny Evans, 2010

Our tactic is to equalise before the others have scored.
DANNY BLANCHFLOWER, Northern Ireland captain, World Cup finals, 1958

We're the Wycombe or Wimbledon of international football. We're ranked 124th in the world and there are countries above us who you wouldn't even know played the game.
LAWRIE SANCHEZ, ex-Wycombe manager and Wimbledon player, on becoming Northern Ireland manager, 2004

I didn't shake the hand of their manager [Sanchez] because I just wanted to get down the tunnel away from it all. I needed to get to the changing room and wash my face because I felt dirty. After watching that I had to wash it all away.
CARLOS ALBERTO, Azerbaijan manager, after a 0–0 draw with 'negative' Northern Ireland, 2004

NORWAY

The Norwegian team's eating habits surprised me, especially mixing jam with smoked fish and even bananas and mackerel.
GEORGES-MARIE DUFFARD, manager of the Norway squad's hotel, World Cup finals, 1998

PORTUGAL

Portugal have a national team called Cristiano Ronaldo and a group of players who run after him.
CARLOS QUEIROZ, former Portugal coach, 2012

REPUBLIC OF IRELAND

Ireland don't have the players they used to – the O'Learys, the Stapletons, the Bradys.
DAVID O'LEARY, former Ireland defender, 2009

I told them when you lose, conceding one goal or six goals or three goals, it's the same.
GIOVANNI TRAPATTONI, the Republic's Italian manager, after Germany's 6–1 win, 2012

The Irish force an unattractive game on the opposition. No team has managed to escape this contagious crap.
AHMED EL-MOKADEM, Egyptian FA official, after 0–0 draw v the Republic, World Cup finals, 1990

Look at the Irish. They sing their national anthem and none of them know the words. Jack [Charlton] sings, and all he knows is 'Cushy Butterfield' and 'Blaydon Races'. But look at the pride they have in those green shirts.
LAWRIE McMENEMY, England assistant manager, calling for Graham Taylor's team to sing 'God Save The Queen' before games, 1991

As the first bars ring out, I notice the TV camera start to zoom in. Should I move my lips and sing the two or three lines that I know?
ANDY TOWNSEND, Republic captain, on an Anglo-Irishman's problems with the Irish anthem, in Andy's Game, *1994*

Italy turn up in Armani suits looking the dog's bollocks and we arrive in bright green blazers and dodgy brogues.
PHIL BABB, Republic defender, at the World Cup finals, 1994

We're from Ireland, not the bloody Gobi desert.
JACK CHARLTON before the Republic played in intense heat at Orland, World Cup finals, 1994

Ireland are a team of impertinents and battlers led by Roy Keane.

CAMEROON TRIBUNE, state-run newspaper, on the eve of the country's World Cup clash with the Irish, who had sent home Keane in disgrace more than a week earlier, 2002

We're the team that doesn't study the opposition, that takes supporters on the team coach, is not really bothered, that likes a pint and the craic. And yet here we are in the last 16 of the World Cup again. If that scenario were true, we must be the greatest group of guys who ever played the game.
MICK McCARTHY, *Republic of Ireland manager, on the team's media image, 2002*

RUSSIA

God doesn't get involved in these things, he is totally fair. He's not with Spain or anyone else, although Russia is of course atheist.
LUIS ARAGONES, *Spain coach, before the semi-final v Russia, which Spain won before going on to win the final, European Championship finals, 2008*

SCOTLAND

Some of the Scotland players need to look themselves in the face.
ALAN BRAZIL, *talkSPORT presenter and former Scotland striker, 2012*

I can't remember having a quieter night at any time in my career, either for Chelsea or the national team. It would have been a travesty if we'd only drawn.
PETR CECH, *Czech Republic goalkeeper, after a 1–0 win over Scotland,*

whose manager Craig Levein played a 4–6–0 formation, 2010

A good team with strong English character.
RUUD GULLIT, *Netherlands midfielder, before match v Scotland, 1992*

Our qualifying campaign was a successful failure.
KENNY MILLER, *Scotland striker, after the team beat France away yet missed out on the European Championship finals, 2008*

I never hide away from the fact that when Scotland got knocked out of World Cups in the past, like in 1982 and 1986 and 1990, we cheered the roof off, the England team did.
TERRY BUTCHER, *Scotland assistant manager and former England captain, 2008*

Playing for Scotland is fantastic. You look at your dark blue shirt and the wee lion looks up at you and says: 'Get out there after those English bastards!'
BILL SHANKLY, *Scotland player of the 1930s, quoted in John Keith,* Shanks for the Memory, *1998*

I warned it would take a great team to beat us. Let's give them their due.
ALF RAMSEY *after Scotland became the first team to beat his newly crowned world champions, 1967*

If patriotism is silly, then OK, we're silly. When we go on to the field for Scotland, we're ready to give blood. Of course, we'd like a lot of money, but even without it we'll play till we drop.
DAVID HAY, Scotland player, at World Cup finals, 1974

If you keep saying, 'We'll win it, we'll win it, we'll win it,' eventually they believe you.
ALLY MacLEOD, Scotland manager, before the team's ill-fated World Cup, 1978

I am proud of my team for beating the best side in Europe. I want to congratulate Scotland for the team they presented to us.
MARCUS CALDERON, Peru manager, after they beat MacLeod's Scots 3–1, World Cup finals, 1978

It riles me to think of all the great players Scotland have had over the years and yet they haven't won anything. It's criminal that there hasn't been a really successful Scotland team.
BILL SHANKLY after his country's World Cup exit, 1978

We've been playing for an hour and it has just occurred to me that we're drawing 0–0 with a mountain top.
IAN ARCHER, Radio Scotland summariser, during San Marino v Scotland match, 1993; the Scots won 2–0

Bagpipes, warpaint and claymores won't win us games in the European Championship or World Cup.
CRAIG BROWN, Scotland manager, 1994

Scotsman's desire to struggle is as if sucked in almost from mother's milk.
GUNTIS INDRIKSONS, Latvian FA president, in the programme for the meeting of their countries, 1996

They'll be home before the postcards.
TOMMY DOCHERTY, former Scotland manager, before his country's first-round exit, World Cup finals, 1998

Unless we batter sides we are on a hiding. The way international football is going that won't happen very often. Yet if we don't play well and win, we're rubbish, and if we play well and don't win, we're rubbish.
CHRISTIAN DAILLY, Scotland defender, 2000

I remember when every great English club had two or three Scots in the team. Where the talent has gone, I don't know. But when I go home to Sauchie, the park I played in as a kid – jackets down, 25-a-side – is empty now.
ALAN HANSEN, former Scotland defender, after a draw with the Faroe Islands, 2002

We Scots don't mind laughing at ourselves. But it's getting to the stage where other people are laughing at us.
GORDON STRACHAN, former Scotland player and future national manager, on the team's decline, 2004

SENEGAL

Their teamwork is a good model for Christian-Muslim co-existence.
FIDES, Vatican missionary service news agency, World Cup finals, as Senegal reached the quarter-finals of the World Cup, 2002

SPAIN

Spain have had an unbelievable amount of sex, er, success.
ALAN SHEARER, BBC TV pundit, after Spain beat Italy to retain the European Championship, 2012

Spain's play is like love without the sex. It lacks a bit of spice.
BIXENTE LIZARAZU, defender in the France team that won the 1998 World Cup and 2000 European Championship, 2012

If I don't reach the final with you lot, it means I'm a crap coach and I've organised a crap team.
LUIS ARAGONES, Spain coach, to his players before the win v Russia en route to victory in the final, European Championship finals, 2008

Spain may be winning but it's not the beautiful game any more! It's boring.
BORIS BECKER, German former tennis player, tweeting as world champions Spain won the European Championship, 2012

The 2008 Euros were so important because they showed that you could win that way [using a passing game] with a group of players who weren't physically imposing in any way. If anything, we're the opposite.
ANDRES INIESTA, Barcelona and Spain midfielder, after World Cup success, 2012

A match between the current Spain and Oranje [Netherlands] from '74? Spain would really struggle, and I think we'd win. We had power in defence, a strong midfield, and a fantastic attack. Plus Johan Cruyff. Spain would have it all with a player like Cruyff.
GERRIE MUHREN, former Ajax and Netherlands player, after Spain added a second European Championship to the 2010 World Cup triumph, 2012

I was excited by the Brazil team of 1970, but I have to say Spain are making me feel a similar way, though with more continuity. Brazil 1970 were just Brazil 1970, but Spain were European champions, then world champions, then again in Europe, and I think that they should get credit for giving continuity to

a team that has a coach with a defined style which their opponents cannot figure out.
JORGE VALDANO, Argentinian former Real Madrid player and general manager, on the new world champions, 2012

I have never seen a team play with such precision at such pace. Spain are even better than Pele's Brazil.
GIOVANNI TRAPATTONI, veteran Republic of Ireland coach, 2013

REPORTER: What went wrong?
VICENTE: We're Spain. What do you expect?
PLAYER press conference after Spain's defeat by Portugal, European Championship finals, 2004

SWEDEN

The operation went well but the patient died.
ERIK HAMREN, Sweden manager, after a 3–2 loss to England ensured their exit from the European Championship finals, 2012

TAHITI

Nine of the squad are unemployed. We have delivery boys, a truck driver, some are PE teachers, some accountants. And we also have a player – Teheivarii Ludivion – who wakes every day at 4:30 in the morning and climbs mountains all day long. He'll climb anything – coconut trees, all kinds of things – and then comes training.
EDDY ETAETA, Tahiti coach, on the squad he took to the Confederations Cup in Brazil, where they lost 10–0 to Spain and 8–0 to Uruguay, 2013

TURKEY

Their players were shouting: 'Wait till you come to Turkey.' Even their kit man was running his fingers across his throat.
GARETH SOUTHGATE, England defender, after a fracas between England and Turkey players at Sunderland, 2003

UNITED STATES OF AMERICA

The US finally came up with an exit strategy. Unfortunately it's for the World Cup.
JAY LENO presenting The Tonight Show *on American TV three years after the US-led invasion of Iraq, 2006*

If we lived in another country we would be asking for political asylum. Since we're American we'll stay in New York and nobody will recognise us.
TAB RAMOS, US midfielder, after 5–1 defeat in the World Cup by Czechoslovakia, 1990

It's easy for the US team. Everyone in their country is interested in baseball and American football. So they're not playing under any pressure. My mother, my grandmother and my great-grandmother could play in a team like that.
RICARDO LA VOLPE, Mexico coach, after defeat by the Americans, 2005

URUGUAY

We won the first World Cup and are also the smallest country to have won the World Cup. Can you imagine Wales or Scotland winning the World Cup?
DIEGO FORLAN, Uruguay and former Manchester United striker, interviewed in FourFourTwo *magazine, 2010*

Other countries have their history. Uruguay has its football.
ONDINA VIERA, Uruguay coach, 1966

WALES

Everyone goes on about Wales's 'golden generation'. It's nonsense. They will be the 'golden generation' only when we qualify [for a major finals]. Until we do, they're not. It's just an added pressure on the likes of Gareth Bale and Aaron Ramsey.
CHRIS COLEMAN, Wales manager, 2014

I want Wales to win at bowls, darts, everything. We're a small country. We don't need any divisions. That's why I hate this football-rugby thing. I played rugby for Clwyd Schools and thought I was all right playing centre. Then we came down to play Mid-Glamorgan Schools and got beat 78-0 by lads who had beards.
GARY SPEED, Wales manager, 2011

They gave us a difficult game, for five or six minutes.
GUUS HIDDINK, Netherlands manager, after a 7–1 win v Wales, 1996

MRS MERTON: Is it your ambition to play in a World Cup final?
VINNIE JONES: I play for Wales.
EXCHANGE on TV's Mrs Merton Show, *1997*

I actually want Wales to lose every game so that [manager] Bobby Gould might be sacked. We're the Man City of international football. We rank 98th in the world, below the Congo Republic.
NICKY WIRE of the Welsh rock group the Manic Street Preachers, 1998

The smaller the nation, like Wales, the more patriotic you seem to be. I don't like the showy nationalism – a tattoo, wrapping yourself in the flag. The way to show your fervour and commitment is to go and support and play for your team.
GARY SPEED, then Wales captain, 2003

⑤

MANAGERS

MICKY ADAMS

When you start winning you become a bit sexy, don't you? Maybe I'm getting my sexy image back.

ADAMS, Port Vale manager, 2014

TONY ADAMS

I've done the lower leagues and it's a different style of managing. No disrespect but I don't want to be Swansea boss, either. They probably don't want me. Aston Villa? What's the point? What can you do with them? So it's the Arsenal or nothing and I'm not ready for that.

ADAMS, former Arsenal captain and ex-Portsmouth manager, 2012

He's disappeared to Azerbaijan, or somewhere ridiculous in the world.

HARRY REDKNAPP, Tottenham manager, on Adams, 2011

I've set aside everything I learned from Arsene Wenger. It's a complete waste of time at this level [the Second Division]. They just can't take a lot of information on board.

ADAMS on his role at Wycombe, 2003

NIGEL ADKINS

Who needs Mourinho, we've got our physio.

SONG by Scunthorpe fans after Adkins was promoted from physio to manager and led the club to the League One title, 2007

DICK ADVOCAAT

I always take my notebook into the toilet with me to sketch out some match situations.

ADVOCAAT, Rangers coach, 2000

SAM ALLARDYCE

I think what he does is a model for other managers around the world – it's a perfect model for all the kids as well. As for the style of football, even Barcelona are now copying his style.

RAFAEL BENITEZ, Liverpool manager, in sarcastic mode after facing Allardyce's Blackburn, 2010

It's my birthday tomorrow so obviously that was an early Christmas present from the lads.

ALLARDYCE, Blackburn manager, after a derby victory v Burnley, 2009

He's a big man so he must need a big ticker to keep him going. But it will take a lot to knock over that old elephant.
RYAN NELSEN, Blackburn captain, after Allardyce had heart surgery, 2009

If my name were Alardicci people would probably think I was the best thing since sliced bread.
ALLARDYCE claiming foreign managers received more recognition than their British counterparts, 2003

I don't want to comment on who or what might take over my job at Newcastle.
ALLARDYCE after his short-lived spell as manager at St James' Park, 2008

I can't help the way I look. I suppose some people still think of me as a big, ugly centre-half who doesn't know about the game's finer points.
ALLARDYCE on his hopes of becoming England manager, 2006

MALCOLM ALLISON

Malcolm changed football by making us train like athletes. He was way ahead of his time in that respect, He was one of the lads but he knew how to crack the whip and we all respected him. My wife always said: 'You love Malcolm Allison more than you love me.'
MIKE SUMMERBEE, Manchester City and England winger, on the death of the former City coach and manager, 2010

Jose [Mourinho] worked with Malcolm at Vitoria Setubal and I can see Malcolm in him in 90 per cent of the things he does. Malcolm was a luminary and a visionary.
ROGER SPRY, Uefa fitness and conditioning coach, 2010

On the coach back from London, Allison asked where Francis Lee was. 'He's hiding in case you give him a right-hander for missing that penalty,' said Rodney Marsh. Allison was in pensive mood. 'I never tear them off a strip when they've lost. I've done it before and it's led to bad feelings that take too long to heal.' He became absorbed in his cigar. 'This game is like being in love. You've got to suffer to enjoy it.'
TONY PAWSON, author, on the aftermath of a defeat at Crystal Palace during Allison's first reign as Manchester City manager, in The Football Managers, *1973*

CARLO ANCELOTTI

Many coaches have won it [the Champions League] more than once but there's only one club that was leading 3–0 in the final that managed to lose.
JOSE MOURINHO, Internazionale coach, 2009; Ancelotti was then in charge of Milan, who had led Liverpool 3–0 in the 2005 final but lost on penalties

The first thing Ancelotti said to me after his arrival was that I owe him a European Cup.
XABI ALONSO, Real Madrid and former Liverpool midfielder, on the 2005 final, 2013

My ass is earthquake-proof.

ANCELOTTI, Real Madrid coach, on how fear of the sack has receded down the years, Financial Times *interview, 2013*

Ancelotti will be a breath of fresh air at Real Madrid. They have great players but just need to play like a teeam. He'll make that happen. He has played and coached at the very top, so he knows full well what goes on in the dressing-room.
JOHAN CRUYFF, former Barcelona coach, 2013

I have a lot of power. Here I can decide: training at six in the morning! Training 11 in the night! But my style is not to impose. I would like to convince the players of what they are doing.
ANCELOTTI, Real Madrid coach, on eschewing 'authoritarian' management, 2014

If I had been the owner Ancelotti would have stayed, but I'm not.
ANCELOTTI reflecting on his spell with Chelsea, 2012

I couldn't smoke before the match, but afterwards, oh yes!
ANCELOTTI after victory over Hull City on his debut as Chelsea manager, 2009

As a bloke, he's a really funny guy, always joke-telling. I have to translate, unfortunately, if he wants to crack into something quite humorous. But he tells the players jokes and seems to enjoy their company.
RAY WILKINS, Ancelotti's No 2 at Chelsea, 2009

I don't see differences between Ancelotti the player and Ancelotti the coach... he has balance and wisdom.
ROBERTO MANCINI, Manchester City manager, on his then Chelsea counterpart, 2010

OSSIE ARDILES

I'll never compromise my ideals, whichever division I'm in. I tell the boys to try to play like Pele.
ARDILES, Swindon manager, 1990

JIMMY ARMFIELD

He would sit in a comfy chair in his office, cardigan and slippers on, smoking a pipe. Once he dropped me and I went to ask him why. He said: 'Brian, I didn't drop you. I just picked someone else.'

BRIAN FLYNN, Leeds midfielder in the 1970s under Armfield, 2013

RON ATKINSON

You're from *The Only Way Is Essex*. So where are you from?
ATKINSON, former manager and broadcaster, on meeting TOWIE star Mario Falcone on Celebrity Big Brother, 2013

You're welcome to my home phone number, gentlemen. But please remember not to ring me during *The Sweeney*.
ATKINSON on taking over as manager at Manchester United, 1981

The only relaxed boss is Big Ron. He had me drinking pink champagne – before the match.
HARRY REDKNAPP, West Ham manager, 1995

Half an hour? You could shoot *Ben-Hur* in half an hour. You've got 15 seconds.
ATKINSON to photographer who asked for 30 minutes with him, 1984

I've had to swap my Merc for a BMW, I'm down to my last 37 suits and I'm drinking non-vintage champagne.
ATKINSON on life after his sacking by United, 1987

He has never slagged off United or criticised anyone here since he left, and he could have made a few bob doing so.
ALEX FERGUSON, Atkinson's successor at Old Trafford, 1991

I'm still the best five-a-side player in the club. Mind you, that's probably why we're in the position we're in.

ATKINSON at 56, when his Coventry side propped up the Premiership, 1995

His teams were always gifted and played some lovely football... But his legacy at Manchester United was a pool of older players. Ron always liked to buy the finished article whereas I've always preferred to watch young talent grow.
FERGUSON, 1996

Have you seen that scene in the film *Kes*, where Brian Glover thinks he's Bobby Charlton? Ron's like that. He thinks he's the best five-a-side player in the club.
LIAM DAISH, Coventry defender, 1997

The champagne-and-jewellery image has stuck with me, but it has been perpetuated by people who don't know me. When I was burgled the thieves were gutted not to find my place bulging with gold watches and trinkets.
ATKINSON on retiring as a manager at 60, 1999

I met Mick Jagger when I played for Oxford United and the Rolling Stones did a concert there. Little did I know he'd be as famous as me one day.
ATKINSON, 2003

My favourite politician was Margaret Thatcher. She was a bugger but she would have made the best football manager.
ATKINSON, 1999

They could have been yellow, purple with two heads so long as they could play and they were good lads – which they were.
ATKINSON recalling the black trio of Brendan Batson, Laurie Cunningham and Cyrille Regis during his first spell as West Bromwich Albion manager, 2004

[Desailly] is what is known in some schools as a fucking thick lazy nigger.
ATKINSON after a Monaco v Chelsea match when he thought the microphone was off, 2004

I must have had rocks for brains.
ATKINSON on losing his ITV contract because of the Desailly comment, 2004

What he said was unambiguous, non-negotiable and hugely offensive.
PIARA POWAR, director of Kick it Out, a campaign against racism in football, 2004

I was totally out of order. I've worked longer and harder with black players than anybody.
ATKINSON, 2004

'Lazy nigger.' That's like a plantation vibe. What really gets me is that in his interviews about this he says he took off his microphone and headphones before he said it. Does that make it any better?
IAN WRIGHT, former England striker, on Atkinson's off-guard remark, 2004

You should be made to clean Rio Ferdinand's boots for 10 weeks.
DARCUS HOWE, black broadcaster, to Atkinson on the TV documentary What Ron Said, *2004*

We played at Everton in the early 1990s – when you were allowed two subs – and of the 13 players on each side, eight of ours [Aston Villa] were black and Everton didn't have one. And how many black players did Blackburn have when Jack Walker was there? Now that's what I call racism.
ATKINSON, 2004

It's the language of the football field – they do swear. In that context, you wouldn't think words like 'nigger' were particularly insulting; it would be funny. Without wishing to insult any black men, it's us having fun. What about people who make jokes about my long chin?

JIMMY HILL, broadcaster and ex-player and manager, after Atkinson's sacking by ITV, 2004

Big Ron remains a good friend and being called racist was a terrible representation of the man. In my time at Coventry, he treated me with utmost respect. Big Ron doesn't mean any harm to anyone. Well, apart from one time, when he hit Steve Ogrizovic in the face with a fish during a club trip.

PETER NDLOVU, black Zimbabwean former striker, 2008

DAVE BASSETT

I can still see 'Harry' screaming: 'You're just a bunch of clowns and amateurs, and that's why you'll never reach the top.' Twenty minutes later, the van chugged to a halt on the M4. He had forgotten to fill it up with petrol.

WALLY DOWNES, who had been a Wimbledon player in the Fourth Division under Bassett, 1988

It's going to be my epitaph, isn't it? Deep in the shit, where he started.

BASSETT, facing relegation with Nottingham Forest, 1997

One thousand games in purgatory, eh?

SIR ALEX FERGUSON presenting Bassett with an award for 1,000 matches as a manager, 2002

RAFAEL BENITEZ

I think he's very concerned about his CV. He refers to it quite a lot.

SIR ALEX FERGUSON on Benitez when the Spaniard was interim manager of Chelsea, 2013

I think he was an angry man. He must have been disturbed for some reason. I think you have to cut through the venom of it and hopefully he'll reflect and understand what he said was absolutely ridiculous.

FERGUSON on Benitez's 'fact' rant during his Liverpool reign, 2009.

Chelsea gave me the title of interim manager, which is a massive mistake. I am the manager. The fans are not helping us. But at the end of the season I will leave; they won't have to worry about me.

BENITEZ on the negative reaction of many fans to his sojourn at Stamford Bridge, 2013

If Chelsea are naive and pure then I'm Little Red Riding Hood.

BENITEZ, Liverpool manager, after Jose Mourinho said his team were 'naive, pure and clean', 2007

I never got on with Rafa Benitez. He even made me remove the photographs of my happiest moments with Jose Mourinho and Marcello Lippi from my locker.
MARCO MATERAZZI, former Internazionale defender, on Benitez's six-month tenure at Internazionale, 2012

So I'm a liar? He's thin then.
MATERAZZI after Benitez denied his claims, 2012

REPORTER: Is winning the Champions League the greatest accomplishment in your life?
BENITEZ: In football, yes. But I have two daughters and a wife.
EXCHANGE at press conference after Liverpool lifted the European Cup, 2005

Friends ask me whether Rafa's cold attitude pisses me off, but it doesn't. My aim is still to get a 'well done' off him before I retire. But then, if he gives me a 'well done' I might need a long lie down.

STEVEN GERRARD on the Spaniard's businesslike manner, in the Liverpool captain's autobiography, 2007

JOHN BOND

John Bond gave me my first acting lesson – how to break forward from defence and then, when you lose the ball and get stranded, how to look completely innocent as the other team close in on your goal. The lessons I learnt in the Hammers' academy certainly served me well.
DAVID ESSEX, actor, singer and former West Ham apprentice, in his autobiography A Charmed Life, *2002*

CRAIG BROWN

Kevin [Keegan] and I have 63 international caps between us. He has 63 of them.
CRAIG BROWN, Scotland manager, before the countries' Euro 2000 play-off, 1999

My job is my holiday. I travel all the time and see the world in this business. I take my holidays at home in Ayr.
BROWN on the Scotland managership, 1997

My brother Bob has three degrees from universities, my other brother Jock is an MA from Cambridge and I'm a BA from the Open University. As a player I was the

one the manager would turn to last and say: 'Right, son, nothing clever from you this week.'
BROWN, 1995

PHIL BROWN

The antics of an angry manager aren't particularly what I want to be remembered for. Don't wash your dirty clothes in public is a golden rule, isn't it? But Manchester City's third goal that day was scored by a guy [Robinho] who cost £32m, more than my whole squad.
BROWN, Southend manager, recalling his 2008 half-time team-talk on the pitch to Hull players who trailed City 4–0, 2014

I've been asked to do [the finger-wagging team-talk] a million times – at wedding parties, stag weekends, race meetings and airport lounges where suddenly everyone hits the floor and I have 30 grown men asking me to give them a rollicking.
BROWN, as above

STEVE BRUCE

How long did it take for you to realise your tactics were rubbish?
NEIL WARNOCK, BT Sport summariser, to Bruce after his Hull team's FA Cup semi-final win v Sheffield United, 2014; the Premier League side trailed their League One opponents at half-time before winning 5-3

In the immortal words of Steve Bruce, you've just got to grin and bank it.
RON ATKINSON, former manager of numerous clubs, on Channel 5's Celebrity Big Brother, *2013*

No disrespect to the country. It's a wonderful place, the... Where's he gone again?
BRUCE, Sunderland manager, after striker Asamoah Gyan's move to the United Arab Emirates, 2011

I must thank God for this success. Credit also goes to Steve Bruce.
ZAKI, Egypt striker when Bruce was Wigan manager, 2008

The biggest mistake I made was believing that a great footballer would make a great manager.
BARRY RUBERRY, Huddersfield chairman, after the former Manchester United captain's departure, 2001

Among those who rang me was Sir Alex Ferguson, who said you couldn't damage a face like mine.
BRUCE, Birmingham manager, after his face was scarred in a scuffle with car thieves, 2004

MATT BUSBY

When I arrived, Matt was still in the manager's office and workmen were constructing a new small office for the new manager – me – down the corridor. The alarm bells started ringing. Matt wasn't manager any more, but he was still going to keep the office.
FRANK O'FARRELL on replacing Busby's successor Wilf McGuinness in 1971 as United manager, 2011

Matt was very charming and patient. I never saw him lose his head, even if we had lost heavily. And there was great freedom for players to play. But a lot of [ex-] players talk up his man-management skills and I honestly thought they were poor. He wasn't great on the tactical side either. I don't remember us ever being out on the training ground early on a Monday, putting right a technical or tactical flaw. It was 'OK , lads, we'll start again on Wednesday.'
JOHN GILES, Manchester United player under Busby before his 1963 transfer to Leeds, 2011

You would go in [to Busby's office] fighting and full of demands. And he would give you nothing at all. He might even take a tenner off your wages. And you would come out thinking: 'What a great guy.' I remember going in there once, absolutely livid. And 10 minutes later I came out, no better off, walking on air.
EAMON DUNPHY, former United reserve, in Only a Game?, *1976*

His greatest achievement was to create the illusion of beauty in a craft wretchedly deformed from the beginning.
DUNPHY, in A Strange Kind of Glory, *1991*

Matt was the eternal optimist. In 1968 he still hoped Glenn Miller was just missing.
PAT CRERAND, former Manchester United player under Busby, 1997

He has held his magnetism right through five decades. I remember in Rotterdam for the final of the Cup-Winners' Cup, a lot of fans were gathered at the main entrance chanting the names of players like 'Hughesy' as they went in. Suddenly Sir Matt arrived and the wild cheering turned to respectful applause. It was quite touching, just like the Pope arriving.
ALEX FERGUSON in Six Years at United, *1992*

It would have been Sir Matt Busby's 90th birthday today. All I know is that someone was doing an awful lot of kicking up there.
FERGUSON after Manchester United's last-gasp victory over Bayern Munich in the Champions League final, 1999

FABIO CAPELLO

It is a little surprising that the motherland of football has ignored a sacrosanct law or belief that the national team manager should be from the same country as the players.
SEPP BLATTER, Swiss president of FIFA, football's world governing body, on Capello becoming England manager, 2008

I bet an Englishman won't get that [Capello's reported £6m-a-year salary]. I can't get to grips with [foreign England managers]. I never have. Internationally it's like what went on in wars – you can't trade generals, you have to go for your own. I'd rather lose with one of our own people.
TERRY VENABLES, former England manager, 2012

I think Capello's coming into a fantastic situation where the game is at its lowest. England are at their lowest and the only way is up.
STEVE McCLAREN, Capello's predecessor as England manager, 2008

The Germans were better than us. Then, at 4–1, we needed a goal and we took off [Jermain] Defoe and sent on [Emile] Heskey!
HARRY REDKNAPP, Tottenham manager, criticises England's Italian manager after the defeat by Germany, World Cup finals, 2010

To keep criticising the manager is crazy. Capello is a brilliant manager; the players have to look at themselves. They get away with murder.
ROY KEANE, former Republic of Ireland captain, after Germany's rout of England, 2010

I have a contract and I refused a lot of opportunities to be the manager of important clubs because I want to stay here. I like this job. I like to be the England manager.
CAPELLO after England's World Cup debacle, 2010

One minute they're talking about [Fabio] Capello as world-class, now they need a fortnight to decide if he is the man for them after all. What are they waiting for – to see what's in the newspapers?
GARY NEVILLE, former England defender, as the Football Association considered whether to let Capello stay, 2010; Capello survived

We had a terrible World Cup. He was responsible for that and he should have gone then. I don't see what we've gained under his term as manager.
PETER COATES, Stoke City chairman and member of the FA's international committee, 2012

I didn't run away, I left because there was a misunderstanding. I felt great but sometimes you decide to leave.
CAPELLO explains his departure from the England post, 2012

REPORTER: What does Her Majesty think of your leaving? CAPELLO: The Queen is above it all.

EXCHANGE on Italian TV, 2012

Wayne [Rooney] should keep his nose out of it. He didn't do enough on the pitch when Capello was manager. Capello is a strong character and obviously thought his authority was questioned with John Terry losing the captaincy. You've got to admire him. He stuck to his guns. They went over his head, taking the captaincy off Terry. Obviously they've asked him to apologise and he's gone.
ROY KEANE after Rooney tweeted in favour of Harry Redknapp succeeding Capello, 2012

JOURNALIST: Was the Capello era an expensive mistake?
DAVID BERNSTEIN: It was certainly expensive, no one can argue anything other than that, but it wasn't a mistake.
EXCHANGE at press conference held by FA chairman Bernstein, 2012

I understand Fabio Capello wrote a letter to the bus workers, praising them for the extra workers they put on for the strike. I had a lot of time for Fab until then, but he actually supported strike-breakers so he's not one of my favourites no more. I shall remind the Italian trade union movement when I meet them of what he done.
BOB CROW, RMT union leader, after his members took industrial action when England played Andorra at Wembley, 2009

My story last week about Fabio Capello was illustrated with a picture, not of the new England manager but of Irish builder Michael McElinney, a professional Capello lookalike. Apologies to Mr Capello and congratulations to Mr McElinney – a remarkably small number of readers spotted the difference.
CORRECTION in the Homes & Property supplement of London's Evening Standard, 2008

HARRY CATTERICK

Towards the end, when he wasn't well, he said to me: 'Everton won't pay me off. They're waiting for me to die.' It's a hard business is football.
HOWARD KENDALL, Catterick's captain and later managerial successor at Everton, 2013

You quickened your pace when you saw him. I spent six years as his captain but couldn't tell you what he was like as a bloke. The people he employed, his coaching staff, didn't like him. We players were terrified of him. His great skill was identifying players and balancing his team.
KENDALL, 2013

HERBERT CHAPMAN

Chapman borrowed the idea of the five-year plan from Joseph Stalin, and it worked, albeit with more humanity.
PATRICK BARCLAY, journalist and biographer of the great 1930s Arsenal manager, 2014

The only goal he talked about was the one we gave away.
ARSENAL PLAYER after their 7–1 away win over Wolves in 1932, quoted in Barclay, The Life & Times of Herbert Chapman, *2013*

Confidence! It is the greatest asset a man can possess. Seventy-five per cent of players have not the courage to attempt things which are well within their scope, and there's no doubt that spectators are largely responsible for this.
CHAPMAN, Arsenal manager, 1931

JACK CHARLTON

I won't die at a match. I might die being dragged down the River Tweed by a giant salmon, but a football match, no.
CHARLTON, Republic of Ireland manager, 1988

Jack makes out he is not really interested in football, and tells the world he's going fishing. But we know what he's thinking about when he's fishing. Football.
JOHAN CRUYFF, Barcelona coach, 1990

Jack is not always right, but he is never wrong.
JOHN GILES, former Republic of Ireland manager and ex-Leeds colleague, 1991

One of his cardinals introduced us, saying: 'This is Mr Charlton.' He said: 'Ah yes, the boss.'
CHARLTON after meeting the Pope with the Irish squad, World Cup finals, 1990

BRIAN CLOUGH

I wouldn't say I was the best manager in the business. But I was in the top one.
CLOUGH, looking back at his career, 2002

INTERVIEWER: Who was the best manager you played for?
ROY KEANE: Without a doubt, Brian Clough.
INTERVIEWER: Not Sir Alex [Ferguson].
KEANE: You asked me the question. I answered you.
EXCHANGE in the ITV documentary Keane and Vieira: Best of Enemies, *2013*

I don't think *The Damned Utd* was very fair to Brian. Some of the guys were unhappy that they were portrayed as having got him the sack from Leeds, but really, we did.
PETER LORIMER, former Leeds United and Scotland player, on Clough's reign at Elland Road and its depiction in the David Peace novel, 2013

There's something about football that movie makers have never been able to grasp. They don't seem to be able get across the idea that Brian Clough hated Leeds for all sorts of reasons mainly to do with the football we played. So they invent this little scene in which Don Revie shunned Clough before a cup match.
JOHN GILES, Leeds player under Revie and Clough, on the film The Damned United *in* A Football Man: My Autobiography, *2011*

In the Seventies, Saturday-night TV consisted of [impressionist] Mike Yarwood, Michael Parkinson's chat show and Match of the Day. Brian Clough would have been at home in all three.
MICHAEL SHEEN, actor, on playing Clough in The Damned United, *2009*

I wanted to give my grandchildren a bit more time than I gave my children.
CLOUGH in retirement, 2001

He was a genius. What he achieved at Derby and Forest was incredible. He was also unique in his approach to discipline, and over the years I've come to appreciate that he was right.
GILES, interviewed in Backpass *magazine, 2011*

If he had stayed at ICI he would probably have ended up running the company with the same principles he had in football.
NIGEL CLOUGH, Brian's son and then Burton Albion manager, 2009; Clough Snr joined the petrochemical company as a messenger aged 15

I haven't regretted [leaving management] until I listen to some bloody rubbish on TV and think 'I'm going to throw my cap into the ring and come back.'
CLOUGH, aged 66, 2001

Manager of England? Too late. I'm too old.
CLOUGH, aged 44, in Shoot! *magazine, 1980*

He gave by far the best interview of all the candidates – confident,

passionate, full of common sense and above all patriotic. If Ron Greenwood hadn't been around, he'd have clinched it.
PETER SWALES, former FA international committee chairman, on Clough's 1977 application to manage England, 1995

They didn't want an England manager who was prepared to call the Italians cheating bastards. They failed to understand that I would have curbed my language and revelled in the relief from the day-to-day grind of club management.
CLOUGH, 1995

The fact that he was never England manager was a travesty. It was our loss – the public. We missed out because the people at FA were frightened of him.
GEOFFREY BOYCOTT, Clough's friend and a former Yorkshire and England cricketer, 2004

Success? Tell me the date when my obituary is going to appear and I'll tell you whether I've been a success or not. If I get to 60 I shall have done pretty well.
CLOUGH when Brighton manager, 1973

I'm a socialist and have been since I was 20. Possibly I'm more socialist now than ever. You've only got to open your eyes to find reinforcement for your beliefs.
CLOUGH at Forest, 1980

Of course I'm a champagne socialist. But the difference between me and a Tory is that he keeps his money while I share mine about a bit.
CLOUGH, 2002

He's a kind of Rolls-Royce communist.

MALCOLM ALLISON, rival manager with Crystal Palace and Manchester City, 1973

I think conceit and arrogance are part of a man's make-up. Perhaps I've got too much.
CLOUGH at Derby, 1970

MUHAMMAD ALI: I heard all the way in Indonesia that this fella talks too much. They say he's another Muhammad Ali. There's just one Muhammad Ali. I'm the talker. Now Clough, I've had enough. Stop it.
BRIAN MOORE (presenter): Are you going to stop it?
BRIAN CLOUGH (pundit): No. I want to fight him!
EXCHANGE on ITV's Sunday football highlights show The Big Match, *1973*

He's worse than the rain in Manchester. At least God stops that occasionally.
BILL SHANKLY, former managerial adversary with Liverpool, on Clough's pronouncements, 1979

You stop Brian Clough talking, you might as well cut off his right arm.
PETER TAYLOR, assistant to Clough at Derby, 1972

Clough and [Peter] Taylor used to crack me up. They were like Morecambe and Wise. It was a real bad-cop, good-cop routine, and it worked perfectly.
KENNY BURNS, Forest defender under the late managerial duo, 2004

Outside of family life there is nothing better than winning European Cups.
CLOUGH, Nottingham Forest manager, 1980

I want the [Leeds] job because they're a top club, if not the top club... I'm going to incorporate a little bit of me into their machine. Now I can't do better than win the League because [Don] Revie won it last year, but I can perhaps win it a little bit better with luck.
CLOUGH, interviewed by Yorkshire TV on starting work at League champions Leeds, 1974

I don't think it will take [the Leeds players] long to realise that I am a

very, very, very honest man. I think they will have realised that already.
CLOUGH, 1974

I could have made it work if I'd had time.
CLOUGH, sacked by Leeds after 44 days, in a TV interview with David Frost, 1974

One of my sons is studying German – in case they try another invasion!
CLOUGH, 1980

I hope you were as delighted as I was last week when Nelson Mandela was freed from a South African jail. But what I hadn't bargained for was that his release was going to cut across the start of our Littlewoods Cup final.
CLOUGH, Nottingham Forest programme column, 1990

If the BBC ran a Crap Decision of the Month competition on *Match of the Day*, I'd walk it.
CLOUGH as Forest headed for relegation, 1993

I played under Bill Shankly and Bob Paisley, and Clough is a better manager than either of them. As a manager there's no limit to my respect for him, but as a man he's not my cup of tea. I once told him I'd never be caught standing at a bar having a drink with him. He said the feeling was mutual.
LARRY LLOYD, former Liverpool and Forest defender, 1991

Clough went to Charlie [George] and said: 'When I say play centre-forward, laddie, you play centre-forward.' Charlie turned to him and said: 'Fuck off you northern tosser.' That was on the Saturday. He was gone on the Monday.
STAN BOWLES, former Forest and England midfielder, recalling George's loan spell from Southampton, 2009

My wife says 'OBE' stands for Old Big 'Ead.
CLOUGH, 1991

Like all the great dictators, from de Gaulle to Thatcher, he stayed on a little too long.
GAZZETTA DELLO SPORT,
Italian sports newspaper, after Clough's retirement, 1993

I'm ill-tempered, rude and wondering what's for tea, same as ever.

CLOUGH on what he was like at 4.45pm on Saturdays after retirement, 1994

There was talk of a testimonial match, of a stand being named after me, but there was nothing, not even a toilet. They could have had a Brian Clough Bog.
CLOUGH alleging lack of recognition

for his 17 years' service to Nottingham Forest, 1997; two years later Forest named a stand after him

He's the best manager of all time in my book because of what he's done and where he did it.
RON ATKINSON, one of Clough's successors at Forest, 1995

When this young man says, 'Grandad, you did not get many academic qualifications,' I get out my medals. They are my O and A levels.
CLOUGH on the Master of Arts degree bestowed on him by Nottingham University, 1999

Brian Clough provided ample proof that he was one of British football's greatest managers. That he was almost certainly its rudest is perhaps another distinction he is proud to claim. He is welcome to it.
SIR ALEX FERGUSON in Managing My Life, *his first autobiography, 1999*

One day my grandson turned to me and said: 'You're not having a drink, Grandad, are you?' I knew something had to be done. Sometimes when I went to bed, instead of counting sheep, I'd count the drinks I'd had. If I'd had six, I'd call it five. I'd kid myself about the numbers, like all drinkers do.
CLOUGH admitting to problems with alcohol, 2003

I know most people will say that instead of walking on water I should have taken more of it with my drinks. They are absolutely right.
CLOUGH, 2003

Don't send me flowers when I'm dead. If you like me, send them while I'm alive.
CLOUGH, 2003

As someone who worked with him for 16 years and appreciated, even at 16, that I was working for a genius, it would be nice if the genius recovered.
JOHN McGOVERN, former Derby and Forest captain, after Clough had a liver transplant, 2003

To put everybody's mind at rest, I'd like to stress that they didn't give me George Best's old liver.

CLOUGH after a transplant brought him 'back from death's door', 2003

He was a disciplinarian and perhaps one of the sad facts was that he couldn't discipline himself.

GEOFFREY BOYCOTT on his late friend's drinking, 2004

Our loss for the second time.
MESSAGE on a Leeds shirt hung in memorial display at Forest's ground after Clough's death, 2004

We thought he was indestructible.
GARRY BIRTLES, former Forest striker, 2004

NIGEL CLOUGH

I managed to take the kids to school this morning, and I still got to Sainsbury's as well this afternoon.
NIGEL CLOUGH after his first day as manager of Derby County, 2009

Dad would probably have said: 'Don't be so stupid!' I don't know, but I hope it would have been a positive response. I just wish he was around for a bit of advice.
NIGEL CLOUGH when asked what his father, a former Derby manager, would have thought of him managing the club, 2009

He's not as bright as me, despite his A levels... Everybody likes him, so there's obviously something wrong.
BRIAN CLOUGH, father of the then Burton Albion manager, 2003

I'm fed up with hearing people say what a nice, fine lad he is. He

doesn't get that from me. You have to be prepared to be unpopular and tell people things they don't want to hear. Would he be able to look someone in the eye and tell him he wasn't playing in a European Cup final? I had to tell Martin O'Neill and Archie Gemmill. O'Neill couldn't look at me for a week and little Archie still hasn't.
BRIAN CLOUGH, 2003

CHRIS COLEMAN

He has the look of a celebrity chef about him.
ARTICLE about the then Fulham manager in the Charlton programme, 2005

STEVE COPPELL

It's a nice feeling which I liken to when I got my O-level results or when I passed my driving test. I just felt 'I've worked hard and done well'.
COPPELL, Reading manager, on winning promotion to the Premiership, 2006

OWEN COYLE

I understand why they would chant Judas at me, but if we're going to get biblical, then maybe it should be Moses, because we led them from the wilderness.

COYLE, Bolton Wanderers manager, on receiving a hostile reception from fans at his previous club Burnley, 2010

JOHAN CRUYFF

I only decided to become a manager when I was told I couldn't.
CRUYFF, former Barcelona and Ajax coach, recalls being informed by the Dutch FA that he lacked the necessary qualifications, 2004

STAN CULLIS

I can learn more from 10 minutes with Stanley than from hours with the so-called coaching geniuses of the game. He's a true gentleman. But I bet he was a right bugger to work with.
BRIAN CLOUGH on the manager who delivered three League titles, two FA Cups and European football to Wolves, 1985

[The announcement] has knocked me sick of human nature. How could people do such a thing after you giving them your life's blood? What more success can they get than what you've given them? What loyalty have they shown you after the loyalty you have given them in every way?
MATT BUSBY, Manchester United manager, in a letter to Cullis after he was sacked by Wolves, 1964

KENNY DALGLISH

I spoke to him just before he was getting on his flight and asked: 'Is it Kenny now or gaffer?' He said: 'It's Kenny now.'
JAMIE CARRAGHER, Liverpool and England defender, the morning after Dalglish's second stint as Liverpool manager ended in his dismissal, 2012

Kenny has reinstored the belief.
JOHN ALDRIDGE, media pundit and ex-Liverpool team-mate of Dalglish, 2010

I did not conduct myself in a way befitting of a Liverpool manager during that interview and I'd like to apologise for that.
DALGLISH after telling a TV interviewer he was 'out of order' for suggesting Liverpool's Luis Suarez had snubbed a handshake by Manchester United's Patrice Evra, 2012

We had a lovely dinner with Kenny, his wife Marina and son Paul. I understood about half of what he said and just nodded when I couldn't understand.
TOM WERNER, Liverpool's American chairman, after Dalglish returned to Anfield as manager, 2010

With Kenny it's like he still thinks he's a player. He's still trying to get a game on the training ground.
STEVEN GERRARD, Liverpool captain, 2012; Dalglish was approaching his 61st birthday

Dalglish and Liverpool go together like herring and potatoes.
INTERVIEWEE on the BBC Alba programme View from the Sofa about Dalglish's visit to a cancer hospice on the Isle of Lewis, 2012

Would Kenny have signed for Blackburn when he was a player? I know what he'd have done if United and Blackburn had both come in for him.
ALEX FERGUSON after Alan Shearer spurned Manchester United in favour of Dalglish's Blackburn on leaving Southampton, 1992

I have no hesitation in saying he was one of the great players of all time, but I can't speak of him in the same terms as a manager. That's not a criticism, but he didn't begin the job at the grass roots, start with a Second or Third Division club or build a side from scratch. So there are some doubts.
HOWARD KENDALL, Everton manager, after Dalglish resigned at Liverpool, 1991

He's incredibly intense about football. He's the only person I've ever seen come off during a match who is still playing every ball. Normally when players are substituted, you'll see them in the dug-out, winding down. Kenny still kicks and heads everything.
ALAN HANSEN, friend and former Liverpool colleague, 1992

I've always felt there's a scriptwriter up on a cloud somewhere penning Kenny's life story.
GORDON STRACHAN on Dalglish's championship success with Blackburn, 1995

The pressure on match days is making my head explode. I can't go on.
DALGLISH on quitting Anfield, 1991

Is Kenny Dalglish a big girl's blouse?

JEREMY PAXMAN, presenter of BBC2's Newsnight programme, introducing a feature about managers, 1998

I love Kenny... Very easy to talk to, very hard to understand.
GARY SPEED, Wales manager and one-time Dalglish signing for Newcastle, 2011

BILLY DAVIES

Will I invite him in for a drink after the game? Absolutely, before or after, probably not during.
STEVE McCLAREN, Derby manager, on his first tussle with Nottingham Forest and former Derby manager Davies, 2014; Davies was sacked by Forest after a 5–0 defeat

Me and him [Sir Alex Ferguson] both come from Govan. We both like picking up chewing gum from the street and eating it.
DAVIES, Derby manager, on his Glasgow roots, 2007

PAOLO DI CANIO

Many times since we took over the club Paolo Di Canio has approached [West Ham co-owners] David Sullivan and David Gold about being the manager. I think they considered him briefly – something I never did – but dismissed him on the basis that football and fascism do not mix.
KARREN BRADY, West Ham vice-chairman, after Di Canio was named Sunderland manager, 2013

I know other Romans came 2,000 years ago. They conquered the north-east and were here for 100 years. Maybe after two months it will be 'Di Canio f*** off, bye-bye Paolo'. It can happen but I'm sure it won't.
DI CANIO on arriving at Sunderland, 2013; he was sacked after 13 games

Me walk away? What? Never. I always believe that I am the best manager in the world. Why should I have to walk out? I have been working 24 hours a day. The players have to adapt to me, to one person. I cannot be a fake Di Canio.
DI CANIO after the defeat by West Bromwich Albion which preceded his sacking by Sunderland, 2013

Often I refer to it as management by hand grenade. Paolo would chuck a hand grenade and I would do the repair work at the end, like the Red Cross.
NICK WATKINS, former Swindon Town chief executive, 2013

Paolo Di Canio managed with a bar of iron.
PAUL MERSON, Sky pundit, 2013

Before Christmas I went to Stonehenge for the winter solstice. I waited until 4am before going there to see the sunrise. It was raining and I didn't see anything, so I left and went straight to training.
DI CANIO, Swindon manager, 2013

I can improve my players maybe 25 per cent, but I am not God. I am one of the best managers, but I am not God.

DI CANIO at Swindon, 2012

Some say my ego is as big as an elephant. They're wrong. It's 10,000 times bigger than that. As big as the world.
DI CANIO shortly before becoming Sunderland manager, 2013

TOMMY DOCHERTY

No one will ever equal Sir Matt Busby's achievements and influence at Old Trafford, but I'd like to go down as someone who did nearly as much.
DOCHERTY after leading Manchester United to promotion, 1974

I have been punished for falling in love. What I have done has nothing at all to do with my track record as a manager.
DOCHERTY after his sacking by United because of an affair with the wife of the club physio, 1977

All this talk about Tommy Docherty not being fit to run a football club is rubbish. That's exactly what he's fit for.
CLIVE JAMES, TV critic, 1979

They offered me a handshake of £10,000 to settle amicably. I told them they would have to be a lot more amicable than that.
DOCHERTY on being dismissed by Preston, 1981

They sacked me as nicely as they could – one of the nicest sackings I've had.
DOCHERTY on leaving Preston, 1981

There's no excitement. Tommy's just been sacked again, that's all.

MARY BROWN, Docherty's partner, to door-stepping journalists after the Preston sacking, 1981

Tommy Docherty criticising Charlie Nicholas is like Bernard Manning telling Jimmy Tarbuck to clean up his act.
GORDON TAYLOR, players' union leader, after Docherty spoke of Nicholas's 'indiscipline', 1984

His interests are limited... At home he never read anything in the newspapers but the sports pages. His knowledge of what goes on outside football is so restricted that he couldn't understand why he kept getting into trouble for parking on double yellow lines. He thought they were a new form of street decoration.
CATHERINE LOCKLEY, Docherty's daughter by his first wife, 1981

RAYMOND DOMENECH

I'm not superstitious. It brings bad luck.
DOMENECH, France manager, 2009

DUNGA

Calling me a donkey doesn't offend me because they're one of the hardest-working animals.
DUNGA, former Brazil coach and captain, after supporters of the Brazilian team he coached, Internacional, chanted 'donkeys' at them, 2013

SEAN DYCHE

There are a couple of brain cells in there, more than you might expect of a 6ft 1in ginger skinhead.
DYCHE, Burnley and former Watford manager, on himself, 2014

SVEN-GORAN ERIKSSON

Sven-Goran Eriksson tinkers with the Ivories.

PETER DRURY, ITV commentator, as the Ivory Coast coach and former England manager made a substitution, World Cup finals, 2010

I didn't take it for the money or even for the weather. I took it because it's a great challenge.
ERIKSSON, a Swede, on becoming England's first foreign manager, 2000

Q: Do you know who the Leicester goalkeeper is?
A: No.
Q: Do you know who the Sunderland left-back is?
A: No. But when I come here I will know everything.
ERIKSSON on his first meeting with the English press, 2000

I've read the book about all the other England managers [*The Second Most Important Job in the Country*]. They were more or less killed, all of them. Why should I be different?
ERIKSSON, 2001

England's humiliation knows no end. In their trendy eagerness to appoint a designer foreigner did the FA pause for so much as a moment to consider the depth of this insult to our national pride. We sell our birthright down the fjord to a nation of seven million skiers and hammer-throwers who spend half their year living in total darkness.
EDITORIAL in the Daily Mail, *2000*

It [Eriksson's appointment] is a betrayal of our heritage and coaching structure. Terry Venables isn't considered because the FA has laid down criteria which maybe even the Archbishop of Canterbury wouldn't meet.
GORDON TAYLOR, players' union leader, 2001

I'm nervous about meeting so many new people. It's like when you go out with a woman for the first time – you're bound to wonder how it will end up.
ERIKSSON before his first game with England, v Spain, 2001

If he should need any acclimatising, I'm here waiting on his call.

ULRIKA JONSSON, fellow Swede, when Eriksson became England manager – more than a year before their affair, 2001

They were actually at it, naked in the middle of the day. I don't know who got the bigger shock, them or me.
MICHELLE SMITH, Ulrika Jonsson's nanny, claiming her employer had 'sex sessions' with the England manager, 2002

I had never known such keenness in a man.
JONSSON, 2002

My son having a romance with a weather-girl? I spoke to him this week and he talked as always about the weather, but not a weather-girl.
ULLA ERIKSSON, the England manager's mother, 2002

I don't know if we ate much. But Nancy had not come over for the food.

ERIKSSON on the start of his relationship with Italian lawyer Nancy Dell'Olio, in Sven: My Story, *2013*

I used to tell [Nancy] that she wouldn't have been as interested in me had I been a plumber. She didn't like that.
ERIKSSON, as above

The Gulf War was a cakewalk compared with Eriksson's love life.
PAUL NEWMAN, FA head of communications and former BBC war correspondent, 2002

We needed Winston Churchill and we got Iain Duncan Smith.
ENGLAND DEFENDER, anonymously alleging Eriksson gave an 'uninspiring' half-time talk during the World Cup defeat by Brazil, 2002

When I want to tease Sven I say, 'Your language sounds like the noise made by some animals in the forest.' It's not musical. It's like speaking in the language of a telegram or text message. Very regimented, very Swedish.
NANCY DELL'OLIO, 2004

I couldn't believe what was happening to me. He was a master in the art of love-making. He did not use a condom. There was no contraception. He was not concerned about me getting pregnant.
FARIA ALAM, former FA secretary, on her affair with Eriksson, 2004

Sven is a very giving man in the area of passion.
FARIA ALAM, 2006

The man's like a wet fish. He's got as much passion as a tadpole.
IAN WRIGHT, former England striker and father of England's Shaun Wright-Phillips, 2005.

Sven would have been a nice easy choice for them in terms of nothing really happens. He doesn't change anything. He sails along. Nobody falls out with him.
SIR ALEX FERGUSON on reports that Manchester United had considered Eriksson in the event of his retiring, 2003

If you lose 2–0 to the United States, that is not exactly your decision. Whether to unzip your trousers – now that is your decision.
GRAHAM TAYLOR, former England manager, 2004

In Sweden we don't discuss our private lives. We have other things to talk about.
TORD GRIP, Eriksson's assistant with England, 2004

If Sven had won Euro 2004, he could have slept with the guard dog and got away with it.
DAVID MELLOR, former Conservative minister and self-confessed adulterer, 2004

I know Sven has a roving eye. He is like a seagull and can wrap his wings around people.
DAVID DAVIES, executive director of the FA, during industrial tribunal at which Eriksson's former lover Faria Alam alleged unfair dismissal by the FA, 2005

At the start of the second half against Portugal, I said to my grandson Stephen: 'Eriksson hasn't got the guts to substitute Beckham. He's the only candidate, he's out on his feet...' But he bottled it. Beckham's hurt feelings wouldn't have bothered me.
BRIAN CLOUGH on watching the European Championship finals on TV, 2004

If you want someone shouting, you will have to change the coach. I will never do it.
ERIKSSON, 2003

INTERVIEWER: How would you like to leave the England job?
ERIKSSON: Alive.
INTERVIEW on television before the World Cup finals, 2006

The 5–1 victory over Germany in 2001 apart, I settle down to watch every England game at 8pm. An hour and a half later my watch says 8.15.
JIMMY GREAVES, former England striker, on Eriksson's England in his autobiography, 2004

Sven has spent most of his time in this country chasing skirt. What's he done for English football? Sweet Faria Alam.
EDITORIAL in The Sun, after England's World Cup exit, 2006

Did I really do so badly with England?
ERIKSSON, by now Manchester City manager, to a reporter who suggested he had been unsuccessful in his previous job, 2007

The English people are still very nice to me. They still want my autograph.
ERIKSSON at City, 2007

STEVE EVANS

I've never heard his name. I don't have anything to say to a person who is one of a million people talking about me in the world, so I'm happy for him if he has one

line in the national newspaper. I've played in front of Mafia people. I've laughed in the face of 70,000 Man United fans when I scored. So you could imagine what it would be like if I was worried by the words of him.
PAOLO DI CANIO, Swindon Town manager, after the then Crawley Town manager talked of the 'Di Canio circus', 2011

JOE FAGAN

Joe was right up there with [Bill] Shankly and [Bob] Paisley. There was nobody during my time at Liverpool who was more influential.
ALAN HANSEN, former Liverpool captain, on the manager who led the club to a Treble of championship, League Cup and European Cup in his first season, 2011

ALEX FERGUSON

I'm a phenomenon.
FERGUSON on his first 25 years as Manchester United manager, 2012

You can never beat Alex Ferguson and when you do you come off second best.
STEVE McCLAREN, former United coach under Ferguson, 2013

The most important thing in my job is control. The minute they

[players] threaten your control, you have to get rid of them.
FERGUSON on what he told Prime Minister Tony Blair, in My Autobiography, *2013*

The two words the manager spoke to me about, a number of times, were control and power. That was how he worked. I think we can still see that now, even though he's not a manager – I don't think that will ever leave him. There's a massive ego involved in that you have power and control over people – and you try to have it even when you are not working with them.
ROY KEANE, Ferguson's former captain at United, on criticism of him in the newly retired manager's autobiography, 2013

In my opinion he doesn't know the meaning of the word loyalty. It doesn't bother me too much what he has to say about me, but I find it very strange to constantly criticise players who brought him a lot of success.
KEANE responding to Ferguson, 2013

Nothing surprises me with that man.
KEANE on whether he felt 'let down' by Ferguson, 2013

It's not about settling scores. It's about explaining decisions.
FERGUSON on why he criticised Keane, Beckham, Benitez et al in his autobiography, 2013

Sir Alex is going to be such a big, big, big hole to replace.

STEVE BRUCE, Hull City manager and ex-United captain, after Ferguson announced his retirement, 2013

He's like a seat in the stadium, the grass on the pitch. He is a part of United.
ROBERTO MANCINI, Manchester City manager, 2013

[Ferguson] is the epitome of the mantra 'Survive, Win, Succeed'. In private, with those he trusted, he was the very best sort of friend you could ever wish for.
HOWARD WILKINSON, League Managers' Association chairman and former Leeds manager, 2013

[Ferguson] was more Brownite than Blairite – I cannot imagine what attracted him to the ruthlessly single-minded, control-freak Scot.
SIMON KELNER, i newspaper columnist, 2013

Everyone loves Alex Ferguson and he's a great, great manager, but he couldn't put on a coaching session to save his life. I've spoken to people about it – he can barely lay out cones.
JOEY BARTON, Queens Park Rangers midfielder, 2013

I loved working with Sir Alex. We got on really well and today he is my friend. As far as I'm concerned, he's the best coach in the world
CRISTIANO RONALDO after leaving United for Real Madrid, 2009

I was always underpaid until [United chief executive] David Gill took charge... To be told you are doing a fine job is all very well as far as it goes, but there has to be monetary recognition.
FERGUSON, My Autobiography, 2013

There's nothing wrong with losing your temper for the right reasons and those were the right reasons. I mirrored what every person in that ground felt. Knowing the damage it was going to do to my players, I think I did the right thing.
FERGUSON after his berating of the fourth official when Nani was sent off v Real Madrid, Champions League, 2013

I never understood a word Alex Ferguson was saying. One day I walked into the dressing-room and he was staring at me. He motioned at me to cut my hair, so I did so later that day. In training next day he didn't recognise me. I went past him several times and he didn't have a clue who I was.
BEBE, Portuguese striker, after being loaned by United to Rio Ave in his home country, 2013

We always looked forward to playing Aston Villa to hear him

mangle Ugo Ehiogu's name. 'Make sure you pick up Ehugu, Ehogy, whatever his name is.'
GARY NEVILLE, former United captain, 2011

As soon as he sees you as a threat, your relationship with him changes. After the game he's great if he's won but a little different if he's been beaten. It'll be the ref's fault or the fault of one of his players.
MARK HUGHES, Fulham manager and ex-United player under Ferguson, 2011

Fergie was doing an interview where he made it clear he felt we hadn't won it so much as United had lost it. I was watching in Lee Chapman's living-room, waiting to be interviewed. I shouted: 'There he goes again, gracious as ever.' Denis Law came on in my earpiece and said: 'You do know he can hear you?' It's only now, 20 years later, that Fergie's speaking to me.
GARY McALLISTER, midfielder in Leeds' 1992 title-winning side, 2012

If I said Sir Alex was the best [manager ever], that light fitting might come down and hit me on the head.
NIGEL CLOUGH, Derby manager and son of Brian Clough, 2009

I hear people talk about [Ferguson] leaving. Why would we ever want somebody so good to step down? We should be talking about the greatness and embracing what he has achieved.
DAVID MOYES, Everton manager and Ferguson's eventual successor, before his club's FA Cup semi-final v Manchester United, 2009

They gave us four minutes [of stoppage time]. That's an insult to the game. It denies you a proper chance to win a football match.
FERGUSON after defeat at home to Tottenham, 2012.

It's getting tickly now – squeaky-bum time, I call it.

FERGUSON during the title run-in with Arsenal, 2003; United finished top

My greatest challenge was knocking Liverpool right off their fucking perch. And you can print that.
FERGUSON to the press, 2002

The FA have approached chief executive David Gill today to speak to me [about becoming England manager]. So I said I would make the decision on April 1st. It's a good idea – I could relegate them.
FERGUSON, 2012

People get carried away and use superlatives such as 'fantastic', 'wonderful'. I just minimise it to 'well done'. I think they're two fantastic words.
FERGUSON, post-retirement, in a radio interview on American Public Service Broadcasting, 2013

Sir Alex gets under people's skin because he actually says what he feels.
IAN HOLLOWAY, Blackpool manager, 2010

I don't understand it [Twitter]. How do you find the time to do that? There's a million things you can do in your life without that. Get yourself down to the library and read a book. Seriously.
FERGUSON, 2010

It was our worst-ever day. It's the worst result in my history, ever. Even as a player I don't think I ever lost 6–1.
FERGUSON after United crashed at home to Manchester City, 2011

I think the fact that Sir Alex Ferguson rested Howard Webb had a lot to do with the result. But if Carlsberg did weekends, it was one of the best.
NOEL GALLAGHER, City-supporting musician, after the 6–1 win at Old Trafford, 2011

It seems Ferguson is the president of England. Each time he speaks badly about a player, and he has said the worst about me, I never asked him to apologise. But if somebody makes a joke about him, you must apologise to him. But I don't apologise. There's no relationship at all between me and Ferguson.
CARLOS TEVEZ, Argentinian former United striker, after waving an 'RIP Fergie' placard during City's title celebrations, 2012

[Ferguson] has brought football of butterfly beauty to Old Trafford. He bought Eric Cantona, the rebel with a cause. He nurtured the Golden Generation. He discovered Ole Gunnar Solskjaer, the baby-faced assassin. He signed Wayne Rooney, the assassin-faced baby. He has brought trophies, glory, prestige and the kind of happiness, over twenty years, that United supporters once only dreamed of.
DANIEL TAYLOR, Guardian football writer, in the introduction to his book This Is the One, 2007

You might as well talk to my [baby] daughter. You'll get more sense out of her.

KENNY DALGLISH, Liverpool player-manager, to a reporter interviewing Ferguson after a bitter Liverpool v Manchester United match, 1988

I don't think I ever saw Alex smile. Even when United had won 4–0 he would still have a go at someone for not defending properly or for missing a chance.
NEIL WEBB, Nottingham Forest and former United midfielder, 1993

He did at Aberdeen what he's still doing at United. He gave us a persecution complex about Celtic and Rangers, the Scottish FA and the Glasgow media; the whole West of Scotland thing. He reckoned they were all against us, and it worked a treat.
MARK McGHEE, Leicester manager and ex-Aberdeen striker, 1995

I can meet ministers and monarchs and my children are not much impressed. But when we met Alex Ferguson they realised there was some point.
TONY BLAIR MP, Labour party leader, 1995

ALEX FERGUSON: Five hours' sleep is all I need.
INTERVIEWER: Like Margaret Thatcher.
FERGUSON: Don't associate me with that woman.
EXCHANGE during a press interview, 1995

In the early days we named him The Hairdryer because he would come right up to your face and scream at you.
GARY PALLISTER, Manchester United defender, 1997

He's very understanding when it comes to fellow managers. Unless you beat him.
FRANK CLARK, Manchester City manager, who had got the better of Ferguson with Nottingham Forest, 1997

If there is an apology, it must be coming by horseback.
ARSENE WENGER, Arsenal manager, after Ferguson said he had apologised for the publication of off-record comments about Arsenal 'turning games into battles', 1999

A knighthood? He should get a sainthood.

RICHARD WILSON, aka Victor Meldrew, after United won the European Cup, 1999

Some people said you can't be a great manager until you've won the European Cup. I don't think like that, but it was good to put that one to bed.
FERGUSON, 2005

Apparently I'm allowed to hang my washing on Glasgow Green, which is an interesting one. And if I ever get arrested in the city, I'm entitled to my own cell, which could come in handy at some point.
FERGUSON on being made a freeman of his native Glasgow, 1999

This is the toughest, meanest and most cussed competitor I've met in the whole of my football life. To be any use to him, you have to win.
STEVE BRUCE, Ferguson's former captain, 2000

When I see Alex, I'm always civil, but there's no exchange of Christmas cards. His book should have been a celebration of his achievements, something positive, but he chose to use it as something else. He had a different agenda.
GORDON STRACHAN, another of Ferguson's former captains, on the United manager's criticism of him in his first autobiography, 2000

I look upon him as a father figure, just like all the young players do who have grown up under his guidance. Maybe you're afraid of him at times but the main thing is we all have great respect for him.
DAVID BECKHAM, 2000

Sometimes I wish I'd turned 60 that night in Barcelona. That could have been the final day of my career.
FERGUSON recalling the 1999 Champions League triumph, 2001

He doesn't seem to have any problem spotting an opponent offside. He can see his watch all right when he wants to check the amount of injury time. How long before fans around the country see a foul by United and set up the chant: 'Fergie didn't see it'?
BRIAN CLOUGH, after Ferguson claimed not to have seen the foul which led to Roy Keane being sent off v Manchester City, 2001

I was worrying about what I was going to do at three o'clock on Saturday afternoons. I just couldn't see myself riding off into the sunset just yet.
FERGUSON after reversing his decision to retire, 2002

Retirement is for young people – they can do something else.
FERGUSON approaching his 69th birthday, 2010

My father retired on his 65th birthday and a year later he was dead. The worst thing you can do is put your slippers on. People say: 'I've worked for 45 years. I have the right to rest.' Not at all. One has a duty to keep active and in good shape.
FERGUSON, 2011

Sir Alex is irreplaceable. I wondered whether I could work with anyone else.
DAVID BECKHAM after Ferguson changed his mind about retiring, 2002

When I had played 15 first-team games, I knocked on the gaffer's door, went in and told him I thought I deserved a club car like the other guys were getting. He just looked at me for a moment before shouting: 'Club car? Club car? Club bike, more like.' I've never been in there since.
RYAN GIGGS, 2002

His weakness is that he doesn't think he has any.

ARSENE WENGER, Arsenal manager, 2002

He's the best sports psychologist in the world. He tests people when they are younger and weeds out the weak-minded. You can be technically and physically OK, but if you're weak-minded you can go. That's his philosophy.
GORDON STRACHAN, Southampton manager and former player under Ferguson, 2003

The manager is a very intimidating person to talk to and to confront. Until two years ago when you walked into his office, your lip started to quiver and your mouth went dry. Maybe [Ferguson] saw he didn't have that effect on me any more.
DAVID BECKHAM after leaving United for Real Madrid, 2003

This was a man I really respected. He gave me the opportunity to become the player I am by playing for United. He still hasn't spoken to me except briefly at a funeral... I just expected a bit more respect when I had been at the club for that many years.
BECKHAM, 2003

Without being unkind, we wouldn't try to sign a 61-year-old.
KEN BATES, Chelsea chairman, after reports that his club approached Ferguson, 2003

Football is an emotional game. Sometimes people making comments at the end of a game become mental.
JOSE MOURINHO, Porto coach, after Ferguson defended Roy Keane following his dismissal for stamping on goalkeeper Vitor Baia, 2004

If I tried it a million times I couldn't do it again. If I could, I'd still be playing.
FERGUSON denying he kicked a boot deliberately into David Beckham's face in the dressing room after a match v Arsenal, 2003

He's a work alcoholic.

GERARD HOULLIER, Liverpool manager, 2003

He does what he wants. I will never answer questions any more about this man.
ARSENE WENGER, *Arsenal manager, on his differences with Ferguson, 2004*

What were you like when you were 19? I was trying to start a workers' revolution in Glasgow. My mother thought I was a communist.
FERGUSON *after Wayne Rooney was substituted in a volatile display for England v Spain, 2004*

A great manager, but not, in my opinion, a great man.
TOMMY DOCHERTY, *former United manager, 2005*

Fergie is driven by anger. It's like petrol to him.
GORDON STRACHAN, 2005

Whatever he does, and maybe he has upset a few people, he'll always do what he thinks is best for the club.
ROY KEANE, *Sunderland manager, 2006*

My wife cringes every time someone calls me Sir Alex or calls her Lady Cathy. She says to me: 'I don't know why you accepted it in the first place.'
FERGUSON, 2009

In honour of Sir Alex Ferguson we're proud to introduce #NandosFergieTime – all our Manchester Nandos will be open five minutes later tonight.
TWEET *by Nandos, fast-food restaurant chain, 2013*

Of course I can remember my first game. We bloody lost 2–0. I said to myself: 'Oh Christ almighty, I've picked a job all right.' Luckily I was able to get back to Aberdeen that night.
FERGUSON *recalling his 1986 debut as United manager at Oxford, 2011*

[Ferguson] went through the team and said: 'Right, up front, Frank and Nigel. OK lads?' Bryan Robson said: 'Nigel? Who's Nigel?' Fergie points at me and goes: 'Him. Nigel Davenport.' He'd confused me with the actor from *Howards' Way.*
PETER DAVENPORT, *former United and England striker, on Ferguson's first match, 2011*

DARREN FERGUSON

I can't change my name, can I?
DARREN FERGUSON *on the pressures of being Alex Ferguson's son after becoming player-manager of Peterborough, 2007*

BARRY FRY

His management style seems to be based on the chaos theory.
MARK McGHEE, *Wolves manager, as Fry managed nearby Birmingham, 1996*

Someone said you could write Barry's knowledge of tactics on a stamp. You'd need to fold the stamp in half.
STEVE CLARIDGE, Birmingham striker, 1997

These days I no longer run down the touchline when we score. I just waddle a bit.
FRY, by now Peterborough manager, 2000; he had suffered two heart attacks

PAUL GASCOIGNE

OK, I had a double brandy before the game, but it used to be four bottles of whisky.

GASCOIGNE after drinking was cited as a reason for his sacking by Kettering, 2005

One minute I was manager of a football club. The next I was banged up in a police cell with just a bed and a potty.
GASCOIGNE recalling the day he lost his job, 2006

RYAN GIGGS

Ryan could definitely be a manager because he is so wise and players invariably respect him.
SIR ALEX FERGUSON, My Autobiography, *2013*

It's good to know I can turn to the manager if I ever need him.
GIGGS, interim United manager, calling Ferguson 'the manager' ten months after the Scot's retirement, 2014

Every time you pull on the red shirt you give everything you've got. Otherwise you're coming off.
GIGGS before his first match as 'caretaker' successor to David Moyes, 2014

His speech before the team went on the pitch against Norwich was spine-tingling in a way I have only experienced from Sir Alex.
ANDERS LINDEGAARD, Manchester United substitute goalkeeper, on Giggs's managerial debut, 2014

BOBBY GOULD

He'd make a great double-glazing salesman. We had a meeting and by the end we thought: 'When's he going to sell us a new car?'
NEVILLE SOUTHALL, Wales goalkeeper, after Gould became national manager, 1995

I resigned as Coventry manager in the gents' toilet at QPR. This time I sorted out the terms of my departure in the dope-test room in Bologna.
GOULD, quitting as Wales manager after 4–0 defeat v Italy, 1999

GEORGE GRAHAM

George Graham's regime was like living in Iraq under Saddam [Hussein]. He was disgusting. You would turn up for training and he would call [one player] into his 'room', though it wasn't a room because everyone could hear what he was saying. Then he would say: 'I've sold you to Leeds.' So the player replies: 'I don't want to join Leeds.' Graham then says: 'Well, you just have to pack your bag and leave.' What a swine. I have never seen a guy like that [player]. Tears running down his cheeks. He'd been at Arsenal since he was 16.
ANDERS LIMPAR, Swedish winger who won the League, FA Cup and League Cup under Graham in the 1990s, 2012

I remember George. He was a bit of a poseur at first, a bit lazy when he played up front, the last one you could imagine going into management. Different now. He has poseurs for breakfast.
FRANK McLINTOCK, captain of the 1971 Arsenal 'Double' side, on Graham's methods as manager at Highbury, 1992

If ever there was a player I felt definitely would not have what it took to be a manager it was George Graham. Running a nightclub? Yes. A football club? Absolutely not.
DON HOWE, Arsenal coach during Graham's 1970s playing days, 1999

I admit I'm single-minded. I think all of the great football managers have been single-minded.
GRAHAM on the Arsenal players' nicknames for him – 'Ayatollah' and 'Gadaffi', 1991

Mr Graham did not act in the best interests of the club.
STATEMENT by Arsenal announcing their manager's dismissal, 1995; the Premier League found him guilty of accepting a 'bung' from an agent

The meeting with [agent Rune Hauge] was all very normal but the money came as a shock. I thought: 'Jesus, what a Christmas present. Fantastic...' The ridiculous thing is it wouldn't have changed my life. I was on a good salary, but greed got the better of me. I'm as weak as the next man when it comes to temptation.
GRAHAM after being sacked by Arsenal, 1995

He loved a 1–0 win, he really did.
STEVE BOULD, Arsenal defender, 1997

In six months he said just two words to me: 'You're fired.'
TOMAS BROLIN, Leeds' Swedish international, 1997

I came back last season with blond hair, and I think that did his head in.
LEE SHARPE, Leeds midfielder, 1999

At least all the aggravation will keep me slim.
GRAHAM on encountering fan hostility at Tottenham because of his Arsenal background, 1999

He's a gutless coward who will not stand up and admit he has made mistakes. Like Spurs fans, I got mugged into believing that this Adonis of the football world was the be-all and end-all in management skill and tactics.
ALAN SUGAR, former Tottenham chairman, on the last manager he appointed, 2001

With George, everything was predicated on winning. If they weren't winning anything there was absolutely nothing to watch.
NICK HORNBY, writer and Arsenal fan, in Jasper Rees's book Wenger: The Making of a Manager, *2003*

AVRAM GRANT

I am not the Special One. I'm the Normal One. But my wife says I am special.
GRANT, Jose Mourinho's successor as Chelsea manager, 2008

The key to Chelsea is [owner Roman] Abramovich. The only

difference I see between Mourinho and Grant is in their press conference. I watched them at Everton and they were playing the same as they always did.
RAFAEL BENITEZ, Liverpool manager, 2008

RON GREENWOOD

There's only one thing better than getting an interview with Ron Greenwood. That's not getting one.
TONY FRANCIS, ITN reporter, on the England manager, 1981

JOHN GREGORY

He handled the pressure brilliantly during our poor spell, except when he smashed the physio's bag across Goodison Park.
GARETH SOUTHGATE, Aston Villa captain, 2000

PEP GUARDIOLA

Guardiola is the Steve Jobs of football: experimental, brave, a lover of beauty, and innovative. He is an important reference point in the footballing world, and rightly so. Barca have turned their football into a culture.
JORGE VALDANO, former Real Madrid player and general manager, after the Catalan's resignation, 2012

I've been a coach for 12 years and I'll be annoyed in June when I don't have any matches as I'll miss training and playing, playing and training. But everyone is the way they are and you have to respect and accept that and hope they really do find enjoyment because the most important thing in life is to enjoy it. If for [Guardiola] that means withdrawing from football for a while, so be it and I send him a hug.
JOSE MOURINHO, Real Madrid coach, 2012

Four years is an eternity at Barcelona. I'm the coach with the third-most games in the club's history, which tells you how difficult it is here.
GUARDIOLA after quitting Barcelona, 2012

What do I do when we're doing badly at half-time? I tell the players a joke.
GUARDIOLA at Barca, 2012

Pep is incredible. When they signed him I said: 'Madre mia, we're going to be flying.' I swear it. He's hard-working. He's a perfectionist. He demands so much from himself. And that pressure that he puts on himself is contagious.
XAVI, Barcelona and Spain midfielder, 2011

Johan Cruyff was building the dream team and it would have been exciting to be part of that. Barcelona ended up promoting from within, and the place earmarked for me went to a kid called Pep Guardiola. I wonder what happened to him?
JAN MOLBY, former Liverpool and Denmark midfielder, remembering a proposed transfer to Barcelona in 1990 that fell through, 2011

RUUD GULLIT

I was just as disappointed as Mandela.
GULLIT after a meeting with South African president Nelson Mandela had to be cancelled, 1997

If you're a playboy and you're not there, you can't win the FA Cup and be second in the Premier League. That's impossible.
GULLIT answering Chelsea's reasons for sacking him, 1998

GLENN HODDLE

He's got a very, very tough persona, despite the fact that they used to call him Glenda.
PETER SHREEVES, Hoddle's assistant at Chelsea and his former manager at Tottenham, 1996

You won't be surprised to know that I have some faith in astrologers and particularly what the stars predict for Scorpios.
HODDLE, by now England manager, 1998

You and I have been given two hands, two legs and a half-decent brain. Some people have not been born like that for a reason.
HODDLE, arguing in The Times *interview which brought him down that people born disabled were being punished for sins in a previous life, 1999*

Hoddle's attitude betrays a disabled mind. It seems he has no compassion, no allowance for weakness.
IAN DURY, handicapped singer and actor, 1999

Had he stuck to football rather than theology he would have been playing on a better pitch.
RAY STIRLING, Hoddle's former father-in-law, 1999

At the end of the Argentina game I found myself asking the same question again and again: 'Why am I here?'

HODDLE, England manager, World Cup finals, 1998

My biggest mistake of the World Cup was not taking Eileen Drewery.
HODDLE, as the controversy over his faith healer continued after England's exit from the World Cup, 1998

If promotion with Swindon and keeping Chelsea in 11th place qualifies a man to lead England in a campaign against the Germans and the Argentinians and the French, a bloke who can make a paper aeroplane is qualified to pilot a jumbo jet.
BRIAN CLOUGH in Cloughie: Walking On Water, *2002*

We didn't get on. I couldn't warm to the man. He was very egotistical and incredibly arrogant. I think it annoyed him that people compared me to him. He probably thought I was deeply inferior.
MATT LE TISSIER, former England player, on Hoddle's time as Southampton manager, 2002

Because of his pride, he wanted to be the best player in training every day – at 46 years of age. I don't think you can see the whole picture when you're out there training with the guys. Can you imagine Arsene Wenger playing with Thierry Henry and the rest?
DAVID PLEAT, acting Tottenham manager, on his predecessor, 2003

ROY HODGSON

Oh why, Oh why, Oh Woy? – FA have done another 'Cloughie'... snubbed Redknapp, the people's choice, for a 'Yes' man in a blazer.
DAILY MIRROR *headline ridiculing Hodgson's minor speech impediment on his appointment as England manager, 2012*

Hodgson was immediately faced with headlines mocking an occasional failure to roll his Rs. Like it matters. Alf Ramsey's misplaced aspirates made him sound like Eliza Doolittle, Ron Greenwood was apt to say 'revelant' when he meant relevant and Bobby Robson warned his players to stay out of the sun because of the dangers of 'ultra-ray violets'. Yet each left the England team in a better state than he found it.
DAVID LACEY, *football journalist,* The Guardian, *2012*

A broadsheet man in a tabloid world.
HENRY WINTER, Daily Telegraph *football correspondent, on Hodgson taking the England job, 2012*

I wouldn't trust the FA to show me a good manager if their lives depended on it. How would they know? What clubs have they ever run? Who do they speak to who really knows the game?
HARRY REDKNAPP, *former favourite to become England manager, in* Always Managing: My Autobiography, *2013*

[The FA] made a good choice. Roy's an excellent manager and nobody disputes that. Looking at it he was better equipped and better qualified, maybe at international level, than I was. I don't want to dispute that. He's a very well-qualified guy.
REDKNAPP *a few days later*

I'd have to be living on another planet to believe I was the fans' choice.
HODGSON *after the FA selected him ahead of Redknapp, 2012*

Roy Hodgson is an Italian Englishman.
ROBERTO MANCINI, *Manchester City manager and former Italy player, before Hodgson's England played Italy, European Championship finals, 2012; Hodgson had coached Internazionale and Udinese*

Hodgson mispronounced my name. He called me 'Pirla' (dickhead), perhaps understanding my true nature more than other managers.
ANDREA PIRLO, *who played under Hodgson for Inter Milan, in his autobiography* I Think Therefore I Play, *2014*

There is a great quote from Henry Kissinger, which I became aware of from reading [Joseph] Heller's *Good As Gold.* He said: 'Every great

achievement was a dream before it became a reality.'
ROY HODGSON, England manager and avid reader, 2012

Turns out Roy Hodgson likes John Updike and Philip Roth. This does endear him to me, tho' I'm not sure they can work together in midfield.
DAVID BADDIEL, comedian and Chelsea supporter, on Twitter, 2012

REPORTER: And does Roy Hodgson throw tea cups?
STEVEN REID: Yes, and a table if he has to. He's got that in his locker.
RADIO INTERVIEW with Reid, a defender under Hodgson at West Bromwich Albion, 2012

One could say what we have done is beyond our dreams. But you'd have to be a dreamer in the first place to get beyond your dreams and I've never been a dreamer.
HODGSON, Fulham manager, ahead of Europa League tie v Juventus, 2010

[Fulham striker] Andy Johnson was literally banjoed out of the game by a player who made no attempt to win the ball.
HODGSON, 2009

Allow me to grieve for the result in a dignified way and get out of here before I say something that makes me look like an idiot.
HODGSON to the media after defeat for Fulham by Sunderland, 2008

Q: Who would play you in a film of your life?
A: A hypothetical question, of course. There won't be one. If I had to choose someone, I'd say Hugh Grant. He's about the only actor I've met who has taken any proper interest in football, being a big Fulham supporter. He'd be far too good-looking to play me in any film, mind you.
HODGSON in a Daily Mail *questionnaire, 2012*

The best advice I've taken is from American basketball coach Bobby Knight. He said: 'Most people have the will to win. Few people have the will to prepare to win.' That's important in professional sport. We talk about winners as if there's a group of people who are happy to be losers. It's a nonsense. It's a question of how much you are prepared to put in.
HODGSON, West Bromwich Albion manager, 2012

Last night I saw a quote from Benjamin Disraeli when he became Prime Minster: 'I have achieved my goal and climbed to the top of the greasy pole.' That is really what we do. That is how I feel. Coming to Liverpool for me was a pinnacle; to some extent it was a reward for the work I had put in, a recognition of my competence.
HODGSON on becoming Liverpool manager, 2010

Manager of the Year seems a long time ago, doesn't it?

HODGSON *before his demise at Liverpool, 2010*

What do you mean 'do your methods translate'? They've translated from Halmstad to Malmo to Orebro to Neuchatel Xamax to the Swiss national team. So I find the question insulting. To suggest that, because I've moved from one club to another, that the methods which have stood me in good stead for 35 years and made me one of the most respected coaches in Europe suddenly don't work, is very hard to believe.
HODGSON *facing press questioning after poor results for Liverpool, 2010*

My lasting memory of him is that he always had a runny nose.
DAVE MOGG, *Bath City goalkeeper, after Hodgson, once his manager at Bristol City, took charge of Inter Milan, 1995*

I've gone sideways, backwards and upwards again. If you were to do a graph of my career it would look like a Kandinsky painting.
HODGSON, *Fulham manager, 2010*

IAN HOLLOWAY

I read about the Battle of Agincourt – it's amazing. All my life I have been outnumbered. I don't feel I have ever had the chance to be with all the horses or with the numbers like some managers have.
HOLLOWAY, *Millwall manager, 2014*

People said I'd lost the dressing room but I know where it is, down the corridor on the left.
HOLLOWAY, *Crystal Palace manager, after play-off semi-final victory over Brighton, 2013*

I'm trying to talk in a way people don't think is funny. I'm fed up with that. I'm not a comedian. I'm a football manager.
HOLLOWAY, *2013*

In the papers this morning: 'Police closing in on Ian Holloway.' Sorry, it's 'Palace closing in on Ian Holloway.'
ALAN BRAZIL, *talkSPORT radio presenter, 2012*

The worst thing was reading back what the referee and the linesman wrote. I actually said it and it's not very good. My mum would have washed my mouth out with soap, like she did when I was little, although I could eat a bar of soap and swear like a trooper, so I don't know what she was trying to achieve.
HOLLOWAY *after incurring a touchline ban for criticising a referee, 2013*

I'd say I was over-competitive and I get over-zealous, over-angry and over-determined. You can make anger a friend of yours, when it isn't; it's an enemy. You have to be calm. I've always wished I was more like Bjorn Borg's temperament. He was my hero growing up. I was more like John McEnroe.
HOLLOWAY, 2013

You can ask my wife what time I finish and what time I start. She'll tell you. Last night it was half past 12, watching clips.
HOLLOWAY, as above

I laid out these 22 teddy bears in the hotel we went to before the Derby game. It was hard work to get all the bears to sit up but I put them in two groups of 11, with the names of our starting line-up next to one group and the names of the team I expected Derby to play next to the other.
HOLLOWAY, Blackpool manager, 2009

I love Blackpool. We're very similar – we both look better in the dark.
HOLLOWAY, as above

I believe totally in what I'm doing and once people speak to me, they do too. I could sell snow to the Eskimos.
HOLLOWAY, as above

If I had a Scottish accent I might have had a chance at a better job with my CV. Unfortunately I'm this ooh-aah person and that isn't really the fashion. I can't remember anyone from Bristol being like Jock Stein or Sir Alex Ferguson. I wish I was related to William Wallace because did that bloke deal with some injustice. Would you like your wife to be taken off and shafted by an English laird on her wedding night?
HOLLOWAY, Leicester manager, 2007

I was never tempted to become a punk. I was always as smooth as a cashmere codpiece.

HOLLOWAY, as above

If that was a penalty I'll call myself Alec McJockstrap and put a kilt on.
HOLLOWAY after Leicester conceded a penalty v Ipswich, 2007

I'd have put my house, its contents, my entire wardrobe, my under-garments, my socks and my shoes on him scoring. How he didn't, I've no idea.
HOLLOWAY on a miss by Leicester's Iain Hume, 2007

I was a bit worried no one was going to turn up at my book signing. I was relieved to see some people there. I thought about sitting outside Northern Rock because there would be a queue there.
HOLLOWAY, *Plymouth manager, on the publication of his autobiography,* Ollie, *2007*

I was given some decent values from my mum and dad in our council house, and one of them was honesty and trust and loyalty. And I forgot to do all that at Plymouth. I left them. And I made the biggest mistake of my life.
HOLLOWAY, *Blackpool manager, 2010*

I'm so unlucky that if I fell in a wheelbarrow of boobs I'd come out sucking my thumb.
HOLLOWAY, *Queens Park Rangers manager, after a defeat, 2004*

There was a spell in the second half when I took my heart off my sleeve and put it in my mouth.
HOLLOWAY *after QPR won at Coventry, 2004*

We threw everything at them – the kitchen sink, the golf clubs, emptied the garage. It wasn't enough but at least my garage is tidy now.
HOLLOWAY, *now manager of Plymouth, after FA Cup defeat by Watford, 2007*

GERARD HOULLIER

Hand on heart, I think it's best if he doesn't come back.
ALAN BRAZIL, *talkSPORT radio presenter, after Houllier stood down as Aston Villa manager because of heart problems, 2011*

I have never spoken to him and never will. I could have killed him from hate, not for what he did to me but because he made the people I love cry.
DAVID GINOLA, *recalling how Houllier called him 'a criminal' for a mistake which cost France a place in the 1994 World Cup finals, 1998*

They are two-faced and treat people like dirt.
PAUL INCE, *former England captain, on Houllier and his No. 2, Phil Thompson, after leaving Liverpool for Middlesbrough, 1999*

I wasn't disappointed with his comments because I know the man.
HOULLIER *responding to Ince, 1999*

I have been described as a French revolutionary with a guillotine, but

I prefer to convince people rather than dictate to them.
HOULLIER after leading Liverpool to a Cup Treble, 2001

There are those who say maybe I should forget about football. Maybe I should forget about breathing. As Arnold Schwarzenegger said: 'I'll be back.'
HOULLIER during his recovery from heart surgery, 2002

I've changed my routine since the heart surgery. I get in to work at 8.30am instead of 8.00.

HOULLIER on resuming his duties, 2002

He's a very intelligent, rounded person, capable of dealing with different nationalities, finance and sports medicine. He fits exactly the profile of a top modern manager. He's also very modest. It's like Mrs Thatcher said: 'To be powerful is like being a lady; if you have to tell people you are, then you aren't.'
ANDY ROXBURGH, UEFA coaching official and ex-Scotland manager, 2002

MARK HUGHES

Nobody here thought Mark Hughes would become a manager, not in a million years.
SIR ALEX FERGUSON, Hughes' former manager at Manchester United, 2009

I personally hope Mark Hughes follows me again and destroys another team of mine.
NEIL WARNOCK on leaving Leeds United, 2013; Hughes had succeeded him at Queens Park Rangers

This was one of those occasions where Neil engaged his mouth before his brain.
HUGHES, Stoke City manager, 2013

Is it true you used to play for Barcelona? That's not Barcelona football.
CESC FABREGAS, Arsenal and Spain midfielder, to Hughes after Blackburn's defensive display in a 0–0 draw at the Emirates Stadium, 2007

KENNY JACKETT

I want to apologise to Chelsea Football Club. I usurped their announcement of the return of the Special One by announcing the arrival of Wolverhampton Wanderers' 'Special One', Kenny Jackett, as head coach.
JEZ MOXEY, Wolves chief executive, as Jackett joined from Millwall, 2013

PAUL JEWELL

REPORTER: When do you stop thinking about relegation and start thinking about Europe?
JEWELL: After about 10 pints.
JEWELL, Wigan manager, in an interview with Sky Sports as Wigan hit the Premiership's top six, 2005

REPORTER: Do you have a Churchillian speech up your sleeve for games like this?
JEWELL: I'll just say what I usually say: 'Get out there and win the fucking game, you cunts!'
JEWELL to a journalist before the game which decided whether Wigan or Sheffield United would stay up, 2007

MARTIN JOL

Can you imagine how the players would react if I turned up one day and said: 'I'd like you to meet Cock and Dick'?
JOL, Tottenham's Dutch manager, on why he does not employ his brothers, 2005

I was nervous towards the end. My heart rate was 189. Almost a heart attack.
JOL after Tottenham's victory over Chelsea, 2006

DAVE JONES

People in football and outside have been fantastic. I don't have to decorate my kitchen because it is covered in cards.
JONES on returning to management with Wolves after clearing his name of sex crimes in court, 2001

ROY KEANE

I am the bad cop and he is the bad, bad cop.
MARTIN O'NEILL on being named Republic of Ireland manager with Keane as his assistant, 2013

He's won fuck all.
GIOVANNI TRAPATTONI, O'Neill's predecessor as Ireland manager, in a mumbled response to criticism by Keane after the 4–0 loss to Spain, European Championship finals, 2012

Maybe I will get chance to give my views to [the] FA, but last time they had a murder lawyer against me, so it could be a hard case to win.
KEANE, Sunderland manager, facing an FA misconduct charge, 2008

Backsides and opinions, we've all got them, but it's not always a good idea to air them in public.
MICK McCARTHY, Wolves manager, with whom Keane feuded before the 2002 World Cup, on his

former player's departure from
Sunderland, 2008

INTERVIEWER: Do you think
Roy Keane will make a good
manager one day?
NIALL QUINN: No, I don't
think so.
EXCHANGE on television, 2005;
Quinn, who had sided with Mick
McCarthy against Keane, was the
Sunderland chairman who appointed
Keane as manager

REPORTER: Great players don't
always make great managers.
KEANE: That's all right because I
was never a great player.
EXCHANGE at a Sunderland press
conference, 2006

I don't see Sunderland as a
stepping stone to something
bigger. That would be an insult
to this club. I don't sit at home
every night thinking that one day
I'd like to manage Manchester
United.
KEANE after leading Sunderland to
promotion to the Premiership, 2007

If you're going to give everything
and push it to the limit, Roy
Keane's the manager for you. The
players love him, and I just wish I
had worked with him when I was
playing. I wish I had bought into
his way of thinking earlier.
NIALL QUINN on the eve of Sunderland's
return to the Premiership, 2007

KEVIN KEEGAN

I've got the passion, but no idea
of tactics. I'd be like a black Kevin
Keegan.
IAN WRIGHT, broadcaster and former
Arsenal and England striker, 2006

I tell you honestly, I would love it
if we beat them. Love it!
KEEGAN, Newcastle manager, in an
emotional tirade after Alex Ferguson said
teams tried harder against Manchester
United than title rivals Newcastle, 1997

God on the Tyne
HEADLINE in FHM magazine on
Keegan interview, 1993

If Kevin Keegan fell into the Tyne,
he'd come up with a salmon in his
mouth.
JACK CHARLTON, one of Keegan's
Newcastle predecessors, 1995

People are saying that Kevin leaving is like the Queen dying, but it's worse than that.

JOHN REGAN, secretary of Newcastle
Independent Supporters' Association,
after Keegan's resignation, 1997

He wasn't tactically aware. He just had a charisma and used it to hide the deficiencies.
MALCOLM MACDONALD, former Newcastle striker, after Keegan left, 1997

When Kevin broke into the squad he used to sit on my knee when we travelled away. I would pretend to be a ventriloquist and he would let me bounce him up and down on my knee.
TOM TAYLOR, journalist and father of ex-England manager Graham, recalling when Keegan started his career at Scunthorpe, 1999

I'm glad it is not Ukraine because I'm not your man for a 0–0 in Kiev.
KEEGAN after England drew Scotland in the play-offs for Euro 2000, 1999

I don't sit down with boards and start painting pictures all over the place, it is not my style and I think the FA knew that when they appointed me. They saw a different style of management where we get people to play by getting into their minds and improve them that way.
KEEGAN after England qualified for Euro 2000 despite a home defeat by Scotland in the play-offs, 1999

He is feeding on rocket fuel. He's perfect to work with.
WATT NICOLL, Scottish 'guru of self-motivation', after Keegan asked him to help inspire the England squad, 1999

A lot of my time is taken up with thinking adventurously.

KEEGAN before Euro 2000

Kevin has a lot of strengths but standing up to failure isn't one of them.
NOEL WHITE, FA international committee chairman, responding to Keegan's claim that he would resign if England did not win Euro 2000 [they did not]

I've told the players that that's me finished. I just feel I fall a little short of what is required in this job. I sat there in the first half and could see things weren't right but I couldn't find it in myself to solve the problem. In my heart of hearts, I'm not up to the job.
KEEGAN on resigning as England coach after defeat by Germany at Wembley, 2000

Some parts of the job I did very well, but not the key part of getting players to win football matches.
KEEGAN, 2000

If Kevin is anything like I was, his first difficulty, the first problem to overcome, will be coming out of the house and facing people.
GRAHAM TAYLOR, one of Keegan's predecessors with England, 2000

We defended really well. That's very unlike my team. I must do something about that.
KEEGAN after City's 1–0 win over Chelsea, 2004

HOWARD KENDALL

30,000 stay-at-home fans can't be wrong. Bring back attractive, winning football. Kendall out!
SLOGAN on Everton Action Group banner, December 1985; in May, Kendall's team won the FA Cup; the following season they were champions

JOE KINNEAR

I'm out at the moment, but should you be the chairman of Barcelona, AC Milan or Real Madrid, I'll get straight back to you. The rest can wait.
KINNEAR'S answerphone message, 1995

NEIL LENNON

I've had to put up with a bit of crap here and there but as long as the security people tell you that you're not in imminent danger, you just get on with things.
LENNON, Celtic manager, on personal threats against him, 2012

[Other managers] are seen as a breath of fresh air for calling things as they see them, whereas I'm perceived as the enfant terrible or the thug on the touchline.
LENNON 2012

FELIX MAGATH

I knew Felix would pop up again somewhere, but not in Germany. His only chance would be abroad, where they don't know him well. For him it's natural to squeeze a player's body to its final drop, like a lemon... I'd never want to treat human beings like he does. He should ask himself why all the players at clubs where he worked throw a massive party when he leaves. Even when he was successful, they still had a blast once he was out the door.
ULI HOENESS, Bayern Munich president, after the coach he sacked at Bayern was named Fulham manager, 2014

ROBERTO MANCINI

Genius.
MANCINI, Italian manager of Manchester City, on an Italian TV show where guests have to describe themselves in one word, 2012

Mancini is lucky. He has an owner [Sheikh Mansour] who speaks little and asks only: 'What do you need?'
MARIO BALOTELLI, City and Italy striker, 2010

Mancini has done a good job, but I don't think there are many coaches in the world who would be given the opportunity to say: 'I'll throw away Adebayor and someone will buy me Edin Dzeko, I'll throw away Carlos Tevez and someone will buy me Sergio Aguero, I'll throw away Craig Bellamy and someone will buy me Mario Balotelli.'
KIA JOORABCHIAN, Tevez's agent, 2012

JOURNALIST: Do you know how many managers City have had in your 25 years with United?
SIR ALEX FERGUSON: Fourteen, but I wish it was 15.
EXCHANGE as City and United vied for the Premier League title which City eventually won, 2012

I said Roberto is cut from the same cloth as Sir Alex, and people thought I was being a balloon. But the top managers handle themselves in a certain way, and we've seen over the past two years that Roberto has what it takes to make the big decisions. He knows how to handle top players and big personalities. They don't frighten him. Tactically he's very good at setting the team up and changing things during a game. If things aren't right he will pick up on it straight away.
BRIAN KIDD, City coach and former assistant to Ferguson at United, 2012

Mancini's got that Italian style, the old joie de vivre.
PERRY GROVES, Radio 5Live pundit, 2010

As a person everybody loved Mancini when he was a player. But with referees? Oh, he was awful. He couldn't control himself.
SVEN-GORAN ERIKSSON, Leicester manager and coach to Sampdoria when Mancini played for the Genoa club, 2011

The scarf is cool. I want one. Mancini is certainly cooler than that Taggart from across the road – he's a good manager but he looks like a dustbin man.
LIAM GALLAGHER, rock singer and City fan, after Mancini took to wearing a 1950s-style club scarf, 2010; the nickname 'Taggart' was applied to Sir Alex Ferguson by City supporters

Mancini is just such a cool dude. He always wears good trousers that go exactly with his shoes, for a start.
JOHNNY MARR, City-supporting guitarist and singer, 2013

In terms of human qualities, Mancini is already 2km ahead of [Jose] Mourinho – wait, make that 10km.

MARIO BALOTELLI, who served Mourinho at Internazionale, 2011

[Mancini] treated me like a dog.
CARLOS TEVEZ, the Argentina striker Mancini signed from Manchester United, 2012

I never treated him badly. Maybe it is the opposite and I treated him too well.
MANCINI on Tevez, 2012

[Mancini] hates injured players. He will be like: 'No, they should be out training. It's not as bad.'
WAYNE BRIDGE, City and England defender, 2012

When I told [Mancini] my knee was hurting, he tried to tell me it wasn't.
CRAIG BELLAMY, Wales striker, after leaving City for Liverpool, 2011

For some English managers, whether they've won or lost, once the game's over it's finished. For me, it's not finished. For 24 hours if we lose the only thing in my head is: 'Did I make mistakes? What could I have done differently? Why did we lose?' I'll get a few hours' sleep, but not much.
MANCINI in his final months as City manager, 2013

I live for football. It's impossible for me to accept defeat.
MANCINI, as above

I like being a manager. I like being angry every day.
MANCINI, as above

[Managing England] can happen if they want to win. And if I win the World Cup with England I want to be knighted.
MANCINI, 2013

DIEGO MARADONA

My girlfriend would tell you that she wakes up every night to find me writing down players' names.
MARADONA, Argentina coach, before the World Cup finals, 2010

If we win the World Cup, I'll run naked round the obelisk in Buenos Aires.
MARADONA, 2010

I say this: the player who scores our winning goal in the final is free to enter me from behind.
MARADONA, 2010

This is the hardest thing I have had to go through since the day I retired from playing. It was like a smack in the face from Muhammad Ali.
MARADONA after Argentina's 4–0 loss to Germany, World Cup finals, 2010

ROBERTO MARTINEZ

He was football-mad. I'd be watching *EastEnders* in our hotel room and he'd stick on a bloody Ukrainian Second Division game.
LEON BRITTON, Swansea City midfielder, on rooming with the Everton and ex-Wigan manager as Swansea team-mates, 2013

If you don't give him a chance, what chance has he got?
PAUL MERSON, Sky pundit, on Martinez's initial problems finding a win as Everton manager, 2013

Our draws have been more like victories without goals.

MARTINEZ during the same period at Everton, 2013

We now have a manager who wants to win games.
KEVIN SHEEDY, Everton youth coach and former player, in a pointed comparison between Martinez and the club's former manager David Moyes, 2014

BERTIE MEE

Bertie would be perfect in today's game. All this stuff about foreign coaching is nonsense. What the majority of managers do now is hire a coach, discuss tactics and let them get on with it. That is what he did 30 years ago.
GEORGE GRAHAM, Arsenal player in Mee's Double-winning side and later manager at Highbury, in David Tossell's Seventy-One Guns, *2002*

PEPE MEL

The first word I learned in English here was 'fucking'. Fucking this, fucking that.
MEL, Spanish manager of West Bromwich Albion, 2014

JOE MERCER

Look, son, imagine this huge pot of money. Franny [Lee] has had a bit, Colin [Bell] has dipped in and of course Malcolm [Allison] has had a dollop. In fact, all the lads have had a bit. So there's none left for you.
JOE MERCER, Manchester City manager of the 1960s, to a player seeking a pay rise, quoted in Fred Eyre's Another Breath of Fred Eyre, *1982*

PAUL MERSON

After what I've gone through – life-threatening problems – managing a football club feels like an absolute pleasure.
MERSON on taking the reins at Walsall, 2004

JOSE MOURINHO

Any coach can come into my office, plug a memory stick into my computer and download my training schedules and ideas, but they can't download my DNA.
MOURINHO, 2014

At the moment, football is full of philosophers, people who understand much more than me.
MOURINHO in a tongue-in-cheek riposte to critics of Chelsea's 'negative' approach at Liverpool, 2014

If [Arsene Wenger] is right and I am afraid of failure it is because I didn't fail many times.
MOURINHO, Chelsea manager, responding to his Arsenal counterpart, 2014

Mourinho would love to beat Wenger on his 1,000th birthday.
MARK LAWRENSON, BBC pundit, before Chelsea routed Arsenal 6–0 in the Frenchman's 1,000th match, 2014

Jose Mourinho is living, swaggering proof that when you fall in love with yourself there is every chance it will prove a life-long romance.
JAMES LAWTON, chief sports writer, The Independent, *on Mourinho's return to Chelsea, 2013*

Mourinho is a coach who focuses only on results. He says he is 'The Special One' because he won this and that in so many countries, but I don't like the way his teams play. Who remembers the Inter side who were champions of Europe? He has not left a legacy, unlike [Johan] Cruyff. [Roberto] Di Matteo was the same. He won the Champions League, but that team didn't play football at all.
XAVI, Barcelona and Spain midfielder, after Mourinho's return to Chelsea, 2014

In this [press] room he is the fucking boss. I don't want for a moment to compete with him for that. Off the pitch he is the winner, but this is a game of football.
PEP GUARDIOLA, Barcelona coach, on Mourinho's use of media conferences, before Barcelona v Real Madrid, 2011

Mourinho is the best coach in the world. He is not God, but he almost is.

EDEN HAZARD, Chelsea and Belgium midfielder, 2013

I am the Happy One.
MOURINHO on rejoining Chelsea after leaving Real Madrid, 2013

There I can be happy rather than have to pretend that I am happy.
MOURINHO to the media on plans to celebrate his 51st birthday at a family dinner, 2014

I am not out of a bottle. I am a special one.

MOURINHO at his introductory press conference at Chelsea, 2004

I'm the Special One. He's not taking that away from me.
PAUL GASCOIGNE, 2005

Like me or not, I am the only one who has won the world's three most important leagues [in England, Italy and Spain]. So maybe instead of 'The Special One', people should start calling me 'The Only One'.
MOURINHO, 2012

[Mourinho] could not manage to do anything as a footballer, but now he has something to be proud of. Yes, he is 'The Only One', but he's mostly the only one in the world crazy enough to say such a thing about themselves. He's so crazy he should be put in a straightjacket.
JOHAN CRUYFF, former Barcelona coach, 2012

What kind of coach wins the Champions League twice and does not fly home on the same 'plane as his players? You would think he'd want to celebrate with his players, enjoy the moment. Not him. He's thinking of himself.
CARLES VILARRUBI, Barcelona vice-president, 2013

Mourinho says he and I are the same? I will have to revise my behaviour then.
PEP GUARDIOLA, Barcelona coach, during Mourinho's spell at Real Madrid, 2011

Just because you wear a cashmere sweater that does not make you a gentleman. He is a rude man with no education.
FRANZ BECKENBAUER, Bayern Munich honorary president and former West Germany coach and captain, 2011

Mourinho can't deal with losing. He is simply not compatible with it. After a loss it's very difficult to work with him the following day.
RICARDO CARVALHO, Monaco and former Real Madrid and Chelsea defender, 2013

I will not mention the name of that person. He's not worth it.
CRISTIANO RONALDO, Real Madrid winger, after Mourinho said he was 'not the real Ronaldo', 2013

[Mourinho] can't take it because we've out-tactic-ed him, outwitted him. He just can't cope. He can say what he wants. I don't give a shite.
SAM ALLARDYCE, West Ham manager, after his Chelsea counterpart accused West Ham of '19th-century football', 2014

I say thanks to God for giving me a season with him at Inter. We both

understand that we were born to win together.
SAMUEL ETO'O, *Cameroon and former Internazionale striker, reunited with Mourinho at Chelsea, 2013*

He dragged things out of me that no other coach had done before. When I was playing under him, I was feeling like a terminator. I was so confident in my game. From being a cat I felt like a lion.
ZLATAN IBRAHIMOVIC, *Paris St-Germain and Sweden striker, who served Mourinho at Inter, 2013*

I understand perfectly why Alex [Ferguson] is still in the job, and I think I will be the same. I love football so much, I love coaching so much. I will still be very young when I become 50. Fifty is a number which I believe sometimes has a psychological negative impact on many people because they realise the world spins very, very fast and our lives are very, very short. It's a number that makes me think and look back but also look forward too.
MOURINHO, *Real Madrid coach, aged 49, 2012; Ferguson was then 70*

I'm such a happy person because what I have done so far I think is amazing. But I feel stronger than ever and I believe I'm still at the beginning of my professional life.
MOURINHO, *2012*

Charles [Saatchi] dreamt I had an affair with Steve Coppell. I told him: 'Thanks a lot. You might have made it Mourinho.'
NIGELLA LAWSON, *TV chef, 2008*

I miss English football and English football misses me.

MOURINHO, *Internazionale coach, 2010*

He's also modest and shy. He's an ambitious man, like me, and always wants to win. He loves the game, like me, but now he's better than me.
LOUIS VAN GAAL, *Netherlands manager who made Mourinho his assistant at Barcelona, 2014*

How can my love for Italy have finished if I never had any love for it?
MOURINHO, *2010*

I sent my Christmas wishes to [Mourinho], but he didn't answer. He's the world's best coach, but as a man he still has to learn manners and respect.
MARIO BALOTELLI, *Manchester City striker who played for Mourinho at Inter, 2011*

It was like a husband cheating on his wife. He cares for her but doesn't have the courage to admit to it – he climbed out the window.
MASSIMO MORATTI, Internazionale owner, on Mourinho's defection to Real Madrid, 2010

It is my fault [that my record at Real Madrid appears modest]. I have won so, so, so much that it is hard to live up to those expectations. Eighteen coaches in 21 years reached five Champions League semi-finals. Meanwhile, the rubbish Mourinho got to three in three years.
MOURINHO near the end of a three-year reign at Real that produced one La Liga title and two Copa del Rey successes, 2013

Of all the coaches awarded three years to work at [Real] Madrid, he has the worst record in terms of trophies won.
DIEGO TORRES, El Pais columnist, 2013

Of course he has been a failure. What I really don't like, and what many Real supporters don't like, is the way he has behaved. We have a part of our hymn which says: 'When we lose, we shake hands.' We don't poke fingers in eyes, which is what he did to [Barcelona coach] Tito Vilanova.
RAMON CALDERON, Real president, on Mourinho's departure, 2013

Welcome to Porto... From here each practice, each game, each minute of your social life must centre on the aim of being champions. First-teamer will be a meaningless term. I need all of you. You need each other. We are a team.
MOURINHO in a letter to Porto's players on taking over, 2002

I understand why he [Sir Alex Ferguson] was a bit emotional. You would be sad if your team got clearly dominated by one built on 10 per cent of your budget.
MOURINHO after Porto's 2–1 win over Manchester United in the Champions League, 2004

If I want a quiet, easy job, I would stay with Porto. There is a beautiful blue chair, we were league champions, won the UEFA Cup and Champions League. There was God, and after God, me.
MOURINHO in his first week in charge of Chelsea, 2004

The Great Communicator, He Who Knows, the Lord of the Press Conference, the Immense Provocateur, the Special Coach.
CARLO ANCELOTTI, Chelsea manager, describing Mourinho in his autobiography Beautiful Games of an Ordinary Genius, *2010*

We have top players and – sorry if I am arrogant – we have a top manager.
MOURINHO on why he expected success at Stamford Bridge, 2004

I like the look of Mourinho. There's a bit of the young Clough about him. For a start, he's good-looking, and like me he doesn't believe in the star system. He's consumed with team spirit and discipline.
BRIAN CLOUGH shortly before his death, 2004

When he talked his mind, [Brian] Clough was funny. Mourinho, for all his colourful opinions, is never funny. And we all know how hard it is to like a man who seems to lack a sense of humour.
ALAN HANSEN, TV pundit and ex-Liverpool captain, 2004

People think the reason I went to Chelsea was financial. I'm not a hypocrite – I don't say that the money isn't important for my family. But the reason I went there was to work under pressure.
MOURINHO, 2005

That coat's from Matalan.

SONG by Manchester City fans as Mourinho patrolled the technical area in an overcoat, 2005

People like Mourinho are the enemy of football.
VOLKER ROTH, chairman of UEFA referees' committee, after Swedish referee Anders Frisk quit the game following accusations by Mourinho and threats against him, 2005

Sometimes, if you give success to stupid people, it makes them more stupid, not more intelligent.
ARSENE WENGER, Arsenal manager, after Mourinho accused him of a 'voyeur'-like interest in Chelsea, 2005

REPORTER: Do you believe in God?
MOURINHO: I think more important is love. Love is what matters.
EXCHANGE during interview, 2005

Maybe I'm not such a good manager. And maybe the players are not such good players.
MOURINHO after Chelsea's home draw v Fulham, 2006

The Paris Hilton of Premiership managers: spoilt, petulant, vain and lapdog-owning.
SIMON MILLS, style journalist, 2006

Mourinho's the funniest thing to come out of London since Del Boy and Rodney.
JAMIE CARRAGHER, Liverpool defender, on the Chelsea manager's sniping at Liverpool before the clubs' Champions League semi-final, 2007

It was a beautiful and rich period of my career. I want to thank all Chelsea supporters for what I believe is a never-ending love story.
MOURINHO after suddenly leaving Stamford Bridge by mutual consent, 2007

Maybe when I turn 60 and have been managing in the same league for 20 years and have the respect of everybody I will have the power to speak to people and make them tremble a bit.
MOURINHO, 2005

TONY MOWBRAY

I'm not wearing Mr Wenger glasses. I really didn't get a good view of the incident.
MOWBRAY, West Bromwich Albion manager, 2008

PRESS STEWARD: Ladies and gentlemen, the West Brom manager.
MOWBRAY: You don't know my name, do you?
STEWARD: No.
EXCHANGE after a Burnley v Albion FA Cup tie, 2009

DAVID MOYES

The Chosen One
SLOGAN on a banner which hung in the Streford End and carried a portrait of Moyes, 2013

Moyes was the Badly Chosen One
HEADLINE on a Manchester Evening News article on Moyes' sacking by Manchester United which argued Sir Alex Ferguson 'got it wrong' when he nominated his successor, 2014

All I can do is do what David Moyes has done before. Even Sir Alex has testing times and it is no different for David Moyes. I needed it to be the David Moyes era now and I had to take David Moyes' era and David Moyes' time so that meant me taking some of my own people.
MOYES after succeeding Sir Alex Ferguson at United, 2013

Sitting in [Sir Alex's old] chair for the first time felt odd. I did it myself with nobody looking. I thought I'd have to see how it felt in case anyone thought I looked stupid.
MOYES in his new office, 2013

Feel sorry for Moyes. He inherited a dynasty in decline. Fergie [Sir Alex Ferguson] is there again. Lurking in the shadows like the Grim Reaper. I've got a feeling David Moyes gets the bullet and [Ferguson] emerges to save the day. What was the point of him retiring? He's at every game. Go on holiday. Play golf. Spend time with your family. Or friends.
JOEY BARTON, Queens Park Rangers midfielder, as Moyes struggled at United, 2014

[The results] have hurt more because I joined United with big expectations myself – that I'm coming to the winning football club. I'm disappointed with myself.
MOYES, 2014

[Moyes] must accept that he does not have the same intimidating presence as his predecessor had.
GRAHAM POLL, *former Premier League and World Cup referee, 2014*

Punt the ball up to [Marouane] Fellaini. Great viewing.
KEVIN SHEEDY, *Everton youth coach under Moyes, tweeting sarcastically about the United manager's tactics in the 3–0 home loss to Liverpool, 2014*

I have not changed my mind about him one bit. He is absolutely awesome. But he is not the kind of guy you can just drop into a situation and expect him to grasp it all instantly.
MICHAEL FINNIGAN, *performance psychologist under Moyes at Everton and Preston, as United's patchy form persisted, 2014*

I've never been able to get my hands fully around the top teams and grab them and grasp them and pull them back into us, but there have been times when I've touched them.
MOYES *on the 10th anniversary of his appointment as Everton manager, 2012*

[Moyes] is like the bloody Rain Man...[with an] almost supernatural ability to read, understand, analyse and recount every single passage of play while he is in the dug-out.
MICK RATHBONE, *former Everton physio under Moyes, in his autobiography* The Smell of Football, *2011*

If you ask him who the Chancellor of the Exchequer is, he probably won't be able to tell you. But ask him who gave the free-kick away that led to Aston Villa's equaliser at Villa Park six years previously and he will get it in an instant.
RATHBONE, *as above*

I think David Moyes is the greatest manager in the world bar none and he's my best friend in football and I'd do anything for him.
BILL KENWRIGHT, *Everton chairman, 2009*

It would have been interesting to have seen the man [Sir Alex Ferguson] working and be around him. I'd probably have enjoyed it, but if I'd gone to United I may not have had the opportunity to manage Everton.
MOYES, *Everton manager, on the possibility that he might have become No. 2 at United when he was manager of Preston, 2009*

David always called me 'chairman', which was his approach. And we never spoke after a game. We always made time for reflection first.
BRYAN GRAY, *Preston chairman in 1999 when Moyes became manager, 2013*

When he realised I was getting so much of the limelight, I felt he resented it.
WAYNE ROONEY *on his former Everton manager in* My Story So Far, *2006*

I'd have gone almost anywhere just to get away from David Moyes. He appeared overbearing.

ROONEY, as above

MICK McCARTHY

Some people are frustrated with that result? Some people can fuck off.
McCARTHY, Ipswich manager, to the media after a 1–1 draw at Leeds, 2014

In the first half I didn't see the second half coming.
McCARTHY, Wolves manager, after what proved his last game in charge, a 5–1 home defeat by neighbouring West Bromwich Albion, 2012

The ref gave Arsenal a goal and as I turned around I saw this big furry microphone so I laid into it. I kicked it and it spun away like a boomerang before landing 20 yards away. Then the Sky touchline reporter came up to me and said: 'So, Mick, you must be disappointed.'
McCARTHY, Millwall manager, 1995

You were a crap player, you're a crap manager. The only reason I have any dealings with you is that somehow you are manager of my country and you're not even Irish, you English cunt. You can stick it up your bollocks.
ROY KEANE, Republic of Ireland captain, to McCarthy during a team meeting which led to Keane being sent home from Japan on the eve of the World Cup finals, 2002

The other lads will be asking Jason McAteer: 'What's he like? Is he all right? Has he got a sense of humour? What's his training and coaching like? Is he a big-nosed miserable sod?'
McCARTHY at Sunderland, 2003

It wasn't just a monkey on my back, it was Planet of the Apes.
McCARTHY after Sunderland gained their first Premiership victory in nearly three years, 2005

STEVE McCLAREN

It was difficult in the beginning, in the middle and at the end.
McCLAREN recalling his England career during his brief reign at Nottingham Forest, 2011

A Wally with a Brolly
HEADLINE in the Daily Mail *after McClaren held an umbrella while watching England lose to Croatia, 2007*

Just look at the results Steve McClaren hasn't produced.
BOBBY GOULD, former Wales manager, in his role as a talkSPORT radio pundit, 2007

The matsch againscht Arshenal isch big newsch in the Englisch media.
McCLAREN, coach to Twente Enschede in the Netherlands, puts on a Dutch accent in a TV interview, 2008

Steve's first game as United coach was an 8–1 win at Nottingham Forest. I told him afterwards: 'We're looking for some improvement.'
SIR ALEX FERGUSON on the new England coach's spell with Manchester United, 2006

Steve's lucky. He's the luckiest guy I've ever worked with. Some have it, others don't, but he has it all right.
JIM SMITH, Oxford manager, on his former assistant at Derby, 2006

Every defeat hurts. You might think it doesn't, but you ask the family. You ask the dog.
McCLAREN, Middlesbrough manager, 2006

I wouldn't say I'm a counter-attacking coach. I'm a find-a-way-to-win coach.
McCLAREN before his first game in charge of England, 2006

Only in England could a man with such limited abilities be made into the national coach. The ever-smiling McClaren is without doubt the most two-faced, false person I've had the misfortune to meet in football.
MASSIMO MACCARONE, former McClaren player at Middlesbrough, 2007

They'll have to drag me kicking and screaming out of Soho Square.
McCLAREN on calls for his head after poor early results as England manager, 2007

ALLY McCOIST

McCoist is a prick, game against Stenny should be midweek? Why, so we are fucked after working all day whilst your boys can lie and get a massage for three days before checking their £5k a week wages are in? Away and fuck off #Embarrassing.
TWEET by part-time Stenhousemuir striker John Gemmell on the Rangers manager's complaints about their crowded fixture schedule, 2014

MARK McGHEE

He's fat, he's round, he's taken Leicester down.
SONG by Reading fans aimed at their former manager, 1995

He's covering his backside in a way that takes the biscuit.
GRAHAM TAYLOR after being criticised by McGhee, his successor at Wolves, 1997

ALEX McLEISH

Sometimes the gap between a genius and an idiot is wafer-thin. I've seen both sides of it.
McLEISH looking back on his unpopular reign and sacking at Aston Villa, 2013

Having finally stayed up, I went to see Villa's chief executive [Paul Faulkner] and said: 'I'll have a report on your desk tomorrow morning outlining exactly what we need for next season.' He just looked back at me with a pair of big puppy eyes and I thought: 'Right, I'll go and clear my desk instead.'
McLEISH, 2013

Master of Paris
HEADLINE in the Scottish Sun after McLeish's Scotland side won in France, 2007

ALLY MacLEOD

Q: What will you do if you win the World Cup?
A: Retain it.
EXCHANGE between reporter and Scotland manager MacLeod before the ill-fated World Cup campaign in Argentina, 1978

With a bit of luck in the World Cup I might have been knighted. Now it looks as though I might be beheaded.
MacLEOD, 1978

When you talk as much as he does none of it can mean very much.
RON GREENWOOD, England manager, 1978

BILL NICHOLSON

Bill was as important to Spurs as Matt Busby was to United or Bill Shankly was to Liverpool. I think the establishment made a mistake – Sir Bill Nicholson would have sounded perfect.
TERRY DYSON, winger in Nicholson's Double-winning side of 1960–61 at Tottenham, interviewed in Backpass magazine 2013

He was such a part of the club that he even lived next door to White Hart Lane. Imagine that happening today.
DYSON, as above

Bill managed from the bottom up to the boardroom. Took all the training and did the training

schedules. He was even involved in the upkeep of the ground. Bill was so hands-on we used to say he could be changing a light bulb in a toilet.
CLIFF JONES, Welsh winger in Nicholson's all-conquering team, 2009

I did not enjoy dancing around, waving trophies in the air. I'm sure he [Nicholson] didn't like it either. His comments regarding success were always cold... I was embarrassed by the boasting around us but I escaped it with humour. He gruffed his way out of it. Our satisfaction was in doing the job.
DANNY BLANCHFLOWER, Nicholson's Double-winning captain, 1961

DAVID O'LEARY

We're not fickle – we just don't like you
BANNER by Aston Villa fans after O'Leary, then Villa's manager, described the club's supporters as 'fickle', 2006

David O'Leary was one of those players we all looked up to. We'd go to him for advice as a senior pro and he was always willing to help. I must admit, though, when Frank McLintock said George Graham was the last player he expected to go into management, I thought the same about O'Leary.
IAN WRIGHT, former Arsenal team-mate, 1999

I was a bit of an arsehole during my last year at Leeds. I became too opinionated about things that had no relevance to myself. I started playing a media game, spinning and counter-spinning. Too bleedin' quote-happy.
O'LEARY reflecting on his final season before being sacked by Leeds United, 2004

MARTIN O'NEILL

A charlatan is a manager who spends £40m to be a top 10 club and then sees the club sink into the relegation zone.
PAOLO DI CANIO, Sunderland manager, on his predecessor O'Neill, who had reportedly called him 'a managerial charlatan', 2013

[O'Neill] makes me look like Mother Teresa.

ROY KEANE after becoming assistant manager when O'Neill took charge of the Republic of Ireland team, 2013

He's upset, I'm upset. I hope he comes in for a glass of wine, but I'm told he's gone so it looks like I'm drinking on my own.
ALAN PARDEW, Newcastle manager, to the media after the derby v Sunderland, 2012

Martin O'Neill looks like a man who's got nits and worms at the same time.
MARK LAWRENSON, BBC TV pundit, on the then Aston Villa manager's animated touchline behaviour, 2008

Anyone who can do anything in Leicester but make a jumper has got to be a genius.
BRIAN CLOUGH, O'Neill's former manager at Nottingham Forest, 2001

I looked upon O'Neill as a bit of a smart-arse.
BRIAN CLOUGH in Clough: The Autobiography, *1994*

Martin runs up and down the touchline quicker and more often than his No. 2, John Robertson, used to during his playing days at Nottingham Forest.
RON ATKINSON, television pundit and former manager, 2000

I'm not even liked in my own household, so I'll be fine.
O'NEILL on the prospect of abuse from Rangers' fans after becoming Celtic manager, 2000

I will calm down when I retire or die.

O'NEILL on his manic touchline style, 2002

If there was one player I clashed with more than any other during my time in management, it was Martin O'Neill. Management gave him the platform on which he can display his intelligence. He had an opinion on almost anything and was never slow to express it.
BRIAN CLOUGH, O'Neill's manager at Forest, in Clough: The Autobiography, *1994*

If the players are looking for a sign from me, I'm sorry but I'll be in the toilet somewhere.
O'NEILL, Celtic manager, before his team faced Porto in the UEFA Cup final, 2003

It's not my job to keep everyone happy. I'm not a social worker.
O'NEILL at Celtic, 2003

I'd dearly love to have played lead guitar with Jethro Tull. That would have done me. I saw Tull playing Birmingham Odeon in 1974 and they had a fellow called Jeffrey Hammond-Hammond who made Pete Townshend look 90.
O'NEILL, 2004

If Brian Clough, who had an ego the size of 15 houses, had the humility to go for an interview for the job, the rest of us mortals should be able to subject ourselves to that.
O'NEILL on his unsuccessful bid to become England manager, 2006

During 90 minutes I can show my passion for 10, but with Martin it is 90. He shouts at everything and complains about everything.
JOSE MOURINHO, Chelsea manager, after drawing v O'Neill's Aston Villa, 2006

BOB PAISLEY

Other people have earned more money than me in football, but no one has enjoyed it as much as me.
PAISLEY, Liverpool manager, 1982

Bill Shankly was the excitable one and Bob Paisley the calming influence. I can still hear Paisley chipping in when Shankly was in full flow and Shanks saying: 'Oh, is that right, Bob?' I believe it was the same at Manchester City when Malcolm Allison and Joe Mercer worked together.
PHIL CHISNALL, the last player to transfer directly between Manchester United and Liverpool when he moved in 1964, on Paisley as No. 2 to Shankly, 2013

His great strength was that he knew something about everything... He could watch a game, even on television, and forecast that a player was going to have an injury, and invariably he would be right.
KENNY DALGLISH, former Liverpool player under Paisley, in Manager of the Millennium, *by John Keith, 1998*

His smile was as wide as Stockton High Street. He had the nicest face in football.

BRIAN CLOUGH, former managerial adversary, on Paisley's death, 1996

He has broken this silly myth that nice guys don't win anything. He's one of the nicest you could meet in any industry or walk of life.
CLOUGH, 1978

ALAN PARDEW

I'm ageing by the day.
PARDEW, Newcastle manager, during a poor sequence of results, 2014

[Pardew] is the worst at haranguing referees. He shoves them and makes a joke of it. How he can criticise me is unbelievable. He forgets the help I gave him, by the way.
SIR ALEX FERGUSON after Pardew complained that the Scot had encroached on the pitch and sought to influence the referee during Manchester United's 4–3 win v Newcastle, 2012

STUART PEARCE

He has done nothing as a manager.
His work with the England Under-
21s last summer was dreadful, and
I genuinely don't know how he
has the nerve to put himself in the
frame for the job.
*JOHN ALDRIDGE, former Liverpool
and Republic of Ireland striker, on
Pearce's credentials to become England
manager after Fabio Capello's exit, 2012*

When people ask if I find certain
places intimidating I say, 'Behave
yourself.' The more intimidation,
the more it means to win. I
remember going to Derby with
Forest and they were spitting on
me and chucking coins when I took
throw-ins. And that was just the
old ladies. I loved it.
*PEARCE, Manchester City manager,
before the derby at Old Trafford, 2005*

My daughter told me Beenie the
horse wanted to sit next to me by
the drinks holder on the touchline.
It's difficult to tell a seven-year-old:
'This is the Premiership, I'm known
as Psycho and I'm a hard man.'
*PEARCE with a cuddly toy on the
touchline after City beat West Ham, 2006*

I was probably the first of the
footballing night-watchmen. I got
sent in to bat through the night
until some money was available.
*PEARCE, England Under-21 coach,
after being succeeded at Manchester City
by Sven-Goran Eriksson, 2007*

MANUEL PELLEGRINI

Sheikh Mansour went to Spain in a
Lamborghini.
Brought us back a manager,
Manuel Pellegrini.
*SONG by Manchester City fans to the
tune of 'Hooray, Hooray, It's a Holiday',
2014*

Pellegrini understood his players.
He'd say: 'Be calm tomorrow.
Don't be anxious.' Simple,
soothing and yet effective words,
like hearing a doctor say that you'll
be OK. Because I trusted him, I
believed him.
*DIEGO FORLAN, Uruguayan former
Manchester United striker, who played
under Manchester City's Chilean
manager Pellegrini at the Spanish club
Villarreal, 2014*

I asked Pellegrini why they call him
'The Engineer'? He told me about
his life as an engineer in Santiago,
and he explained that working on
buildings in an earthquake area was
another challenge in a tough job.
He was proud he had worked on
two buildings which had survived
'quakes. There was no chance of him
leaving anything he did to chance,
either as an engineer or a coach.
FORLAN, as above

For the individual well-being in
this profession, it is better to be
alone, and that's hard to maintain
for 12 years abroad [in Argentina
and Europe]. A lot of big coaches

from Argentina have managed only two or three years in Europe. I could have brought my family with me, but my wife would have had to give up an important job, my son leave medical school and my other children come out of college. I don't think I have the moral authority to do that.
PELLEGRINI on why his family continued to live in Chile while he managed City, 2013

Second place is just the first of those who finish last. If Madrid were to fire me, I wouldn't go to Malaga. I'd go to a top-level team in Italy or England.
JOSE MOURINHO, Real Madrid coach, after Malaga coach Pellegrini defended his record of taking Real to the runners-up spot in La Liga, 2010

DAVID PLATT

The Nottingham Playhouse hosted a *David Platt in Conversation* evening on 13 September. I kid you not. Forest could make a fortune flogging the tape to insomniacs.
LETTER to the Daily Express *about the then Forest manager, 2000*

DAVID PLEAT

David Pleat should have managed England, no question. He was way ahead of his time. He was the first to play one up front with Clive

Allen at Tottenham, although with Chris Waddle, Glenn Hoddle and Nico Claesen behind him, it certainly wasn't negative.
BRIAN HORTON, Pleat's former Luton Town captain, 2012

Pleat chews gum, constantly and aggressively, as if he had a personal grudge against it.
MARTIN KELNER, sport-on-TV columnist, The Guardian, *2003*

GUS POYET

If we go down I'll hide somewhere in the middle of Asia. If we stay up you will see me in every single newspaper on a beach somewhere famous.
POYET, Uruguayan manager of Sunderland, 2014

TONY PULIS

We signed Peter Crouch without anyone knowing. That took almost four days of non-stop conversations between us and Tottenham and Peter. If other clubs had found out, they would have been attracted and might have signed him before us.
PULIS, Stoke City manager, successfully arguing to magistrates why he could not use a chauffeur, 2012; he thus avoided a speeding ban despite being clocked at 96mph in a 60mph zone with a licence already on 15 points

I'm amazed to find those countries are in Europe.

PULIS, Stoke City manager, after the Europa League draw sent Stoke to Turkey, Ukraine and Israel, 2011

He wears the club shop, he wears the club shop, Tony Pulis, he wears the club shop.
SONG by Manchester City fans at Stoke, 2012; Pulis always wore a Stoke tracksuit, trainers and baseball cap

The most evil and despicable person I have ever worked with.
PAUL SCALLY, Gillingham chairman, 2011

ALF RAMSEY

When the chairman of Ipswich came to congratulate him on the [1961–62 League] title at a reserve game, Ramsey is said to have stared coldly and said: 'D'you mind? I'm working.'
DAVID GOLDBLATT, author, in The Ball Is Round: A Global History of Football, 2007

He's the most patriotic man I've ever met.
GEOFF HURST, Ramsey's World Cup-winning centre-forward, 1966

I suppose I'll have to get used to being addressed as 'Sir', but if a player gets formal on the field I will clobber him.
RAMSEY on being knighted, 1967

REPORTER: Welcome to Scotland.
ALF RAMSEY: You must be fucking joking.
EXCHANGE at Prestwick Airport when Ramsey arrived with England, 1968

He is more careful of his aspirates than his answers.

ARTHUR HOPCRAFT, author, The Football Men, 1968; Ramsey had received elocution lessons

Alf was never one for small talk when he was with England parties [as a player]; football was his one subject of conversation. He was always a pepper-and-salt man, working out moves and formations with the cruets on the table.
JACKIE MILBURN, former England team-mate, 1968

We talked Alf into letting us have a bit of sun [by the hotel pool]. He blew a whistle and we all lay down. Ten minutes later he blew it again and we all turned over.
JACK CHARLTON, former England defender, on the 1970 World Cup finals in Mexico, in Jeff Dawson, Back Home, 2001

CLAUDIO RANIERI

I am a lovely man as long as everyone does what I say.
RANIERI on becoming Chelsea manager, 2000

I could say: 'What has he ever won?' But I won't.
JOSE MOURINHO, who succeeded Ranieri after his sacking, 2004

I created the Chelsea miracle from nothing and my achievement convinced [Roman] Abramovich to buy the club.
RANIERI before leaving Parma to coach Juventus, 2007

HARRY REDKNAPP

I'm a fantastic football manager. I'm not a hard-headed businessman.
REDKNAPP in Southwark Crown Court answering tax-evasion charges, 2012

Ask my solicitor if he's ever come across anyone as bad, business-wise.
REDKNAPP, as above

I write like a two-year-old and I can't spell. I can't work a computer. I don't even know what an email is. I've never sent a fax or a text message. I'm the most disorganised person in the world – I can't even fill in the team-sheet.
REDKNAPP, as above

By his own admission under-fire Spurs boss Harry Redknapp writes like a two-year-old. So who writed his weekly *Sun* column then?
LETTER to The Guardian when Redknapp was on trial, 2012

I'd rather give you a hundred grand than nick a few quid off you. We are givers not takers.
REDKNAPP in court, 2012

You find yourself being questioned by a man who is probably 100 times better educated than I am. He's a clever man. He's probably gone to Eton. I'm standing there uneducated really and I have to try to stand your corner.
REDKNAPP on being prosecuted, 2012

Milan [Mandaric, co-defendant] had been very strong all the way through the trial and he suddenly said to me: 'What do you think?' You don't know, do you? You have 12 people that are going to decide to finish your life, basically. It's not a feeling you would wish on anybody.
REDKNAPP on being acquitted, 2012

I talk to everybody. But I've found that you can be as nice as you want with people, but then the day comes and you will be shafted just as badly. That's a fact of life.
REDKNAPP on how he might become 'less open' after his trial, 2012

I'm not really one for being careful about every word I say. If you're going to sit down and keep talking a load of cobblers, what's the point? *REDKNAPP, 2012*

We want an Englishman, full of passion and commitment for our country. I'm telling you, we've had enough of these foreigners. They ain't got no passion, they ain't got no commitment, all they want is money. Let's get Harry in, there's only one bloke, forget about anybody else, Harry Redknapp is our man.
BARRY FRY, Peterborough director of football and former manager, after Fabio Capello vacated the England post, 2012

I feel really bad for Harry, especially as my biggest success in football turned out so unlucky for him. He deserved Champions League football. That's why I'm still shell-shocked by what's happened. I have some mates who are Spurs fans and they're desperately disappointed. They remember how they were rock-bottom when Harry came in. All of a sudden, they're playing in the Champions League and competing at the top. He certainly didn't deserve to lose his job.
FRANK LAMPARD, Chelsea midfielder, after his Uncle Harry's sacking by Tottenham, 2012; Chelsea, by winning the Champions League final, took fourth-placed Spurs' place in the Champions League

With Harry, two plus two always makes five, not three. Harry sees the whole picture.
MILAN MANDARIC, Redknapp's former chairman at Portsmouth and co-defendant on tax-evasion charges of which they were cleared, 2012

I called Harry. I said: 'I've just seen Steve Stone on the beach in Dubai.' Harry said: 'He's getting uptight, I need him to be fresh.' And in the game, against Manchester United, who scored the only goal, who was man of the match? Steve Stone. This is why the players love Harry.
MANDARIC recalling his shock in 1994 on finding a Portsmouth player sunbathing in the Middle East, 2012

I've found myself on some days leaving home at three in the morning. Then I'm outside the training ground at five but they don't open up until seven. I'm just sitting there, listening to the radio.
REDKNAPP, Tottenham manager, 2011

[Redknapp] thinks he's like Alex Ferguson, but there's a difference. In all his long career he's won only one trophy. He doesn't seem to know what he's saying. He's a bit confused. It could be age.

JOSE BOSINGWA, Portuguese former QPR defender, responding to claims in Redknapp's autobiography that he was 'unprofessional', 2013

I told my chairman that David O'Leary spent £18m to buy Rio Ferdinand from us and Leeds have given [O'Leary] £5.5m in share options, whereas I bring in £18m and all I get is a bacon sandwich.

REDKNAPP, West Ham manager, 2000

The Del Boy comparisons piss me off. I'm not like him at all. I've been married 35 years and this is my third football club in 20-odd years. I'm not a ducker and diver. I may be a Cockney, but that doesn't mean I fit some silly stereotype.

REDKNAPP, Portsmouth manager, 2003

I'll be mightily relieved when this transfer window closes. Morning, noon and night over the past few weeks it has been non-stop phone calls. I took the missus out for a meal. I was outside the restaurant for a good hour and a half negotiating with three other parties.

REDKNAPP, 2004

I don't get involved in transfers in any way, shape or form.

REDKNAPP after Portsmouth owner Milan Mandaric called him 'a wheeler dealer', 2004

DON REVIE

If something happened on a Saturday, however small, Don would put it right on the Monday. He would say who should have been where, who was in the wrong position. Don was the only person I ever came across in football who could do that without video replays.

JOHN GILES, Leeds and Republic of Ireland midfielder, on the club's late manager, 2011

The boss said to me: 'If you screw the nut and do what we tell you, then you could play for England.' I did and he was correct. He was a good man.

JACK CHARLTON, Leeds and England centre-half, on Revie's role in his becoming a World Cup winner, 2011

DAVID FROST: Why don't you want me to ask why you don't like him?
BRIAN CLOUGH: Because I can't tell you. It's impossible. We'd get closed down, David.

EXCHANGE when Clough, recently sacked from his job as Revie's successor at Leeds, appeared on Frost's TV show, 1974

I'm loath to mention him. He's a very talented man and his record is unsurpassable. I don't happen to like him. And I don't like the way he goes about football either.

CLOUGH, as above

I'm not one to envy people. I haven't been jealous of many people. But I do feel envy when this particular man has got this particular job.
CLOUGH on Revie's new role as England manager, 1974

Don Revie's appointment as England manager was a classic example of poacher turning gamekeeper.

ALAN HARDAKER, former Football League secretary, in Hardaker of the League, *1977*

If he had one chink in his armour it was that he probably paid teams more respect than they deserved. He should have just told us certain points and then told us to go out and beat them. Just left it to us.
NORMAN HUNTER, ex-Leeds defender, in An Alternative History of Leeds United, *1991*

As soon as it dawned on me that we were short of players who combined skill and commitment,

I should have forgotten all about trying to play more controlled, attractive football and settled for a real bastard of a team.
REVIE after resigning as England manager, 1977

Don Revie was the cleverest of all of us [England managers]. He walked out before they threw him out.
SVEN-GORAN ERIKSSON, 2003

BOBBY ROBSON

I can't describe how much he meant to me. I've just been crying for three hours. Bobby was like my second dad and I was like a son to him.
PAUL GASCOIGNE, who played for England under Robson, on his former manager's death, 2009

I'm fed up with him pointing to his grey hair and saying the England job has aged him 10 years. If he doesn't like it, why doesn't he go back to his orchard in Suffolk.
BRIAN CLOUGH, 1983

If the pressure had frightened me, I'd have kept my quality of life at Ipswich. I'd have kept driving my Jag six miles to work every day and got drunk with the chairman every Saturday night.
ROBSON on calls for his resignation after England's failure at the European Championship finals, 1988

The Spencer Tracy of football.

CORRIERE DELLO SPORT, *Italian newspaper, 1999*

I intend to be at St James' Park as long as my brain, heart and legs all work...simultaneously.
ROBSON, 1999

Football is my life, my obsession, my hobby, my theatre.
ROBSON, 2003

BRYAN ROBSON

He's the only man I've ever known who could drink 16 pints and still play the next day.
PAUL GASCOIGNE on his admiration for Robson, who later became his manager at Middlesbrough, 1997

BRENDAN RODGERS

I told him: 'I want England to play like you play. Pass the ball, play and play and play.'
HARRY REDKNAPP on approaching Rodgers, then Swansea City manager, to be his No. 2 if he landed the England job, in Always Managing: The Autobiography, *2013*

He makes you go on the pitch feeling like a million dollars.

STEVEN GERRARD, Liverpool captain, 2014

Brendan Rodgers has been singing the praises of Suarez and Sturridge: The SS.
ALAN BRAZIL, talkSPORT presenter, 2013

When we lost at Stoke last season, I got home on Boxing Day night and family and guests were all around the house. I went straight upstairs to my room and didn't come out.
RODGERS, Liverpool manager, 2014

I think there's three players who will let us down this year – the cause, the fight, everything – and I have written them down already in these three envelopes. Make sure you are not in one of the envelopes.
RODGERS addressing the Liverpool squad in the Channel 5 documentary Being: Liverpool, *2012*

There never were any names.
RODGERS claiming the 'envelopes' was a psychological ploy, 2013

I've always said that you can live without water for so many days, but you can't live a second without hope.
RODGERS, 2013

You can't turn an ocean liner around like you can a speedboat.
JOHN W. HENRY, Liverpool principal owner, on the task facing Rodgers on his arrival from Swansea City, 2012

I started coaching for one reason and that was to make a difference for people, not just as footballers but as human beings.
RODGERS in his first media conference as Liverpool manager, 2012

I use a quote with the players, *per aspera ad astra*, which is Latin for 'through adversity to the stars'.
RODGERS in Being: Liverpool, *2012*

I will leave no stone unturned in my quest, and that quest will be relentless.

RODGERS at Liverpool, 2012

I always say a squad is like a good meal – I'm not a great cook but a good meal takes a wee bit of time, but also to offer a good meal you need good ingredients.
RODGERS, as above

I believe a young player will run through a barbed-wire fence for you. An older player looks for a hole in the fence.
RODGERS, as above

You train dogs. I like to educate players.
RODGERS, as above

I promise I'll fight for my life and for the people in this city. We might not be ready for the title now but the process begins today.
RODGERS, as above

My biggest mentor is myself because I've had to study, so that's been my biggest influence.

RODGERS, Swansea City manager, 2011

I was brought up in a traditional 4–4–2, kick the ball up the pitch, but when I was a youth international with Northern Ireland we would play France, Spain and Switzerland and we would chase the ball. I wanted to play in their teams. I liked the ideology. I educated myself by studying, watching and learning.
RODGERS, as above

I used to help Dad paint and decorate to earn pocket money. He installed in me the value of a hard day's work. He believes that leads to success in whatever you do, and he's right. He'd work from dawn

to dusk to ensure his young family had everything. I think you can see his philosophies in my team.
RODGERS, Watford manager, 2008

DEAN SAUNDERS

I have got self-belief. If you said to me: 'Do you want to open the batting for England? They're playing down the road,' I'd say: 'Go on then, give me a bat.' Then I'd get to the bottom step and see the fast bowler marking his run-up and realise I can't do that. But my first reaction is: 'I'll give it a go.'
SAUNDERS, Wolves manager, 2013

LUIZ FELIPE SCOLARI

I will go down as the Brazil coach that lost to Honduras. It's horrible.
SCOLARI after Brazil's defeat in Copa America, 2001; the following year he led Brazil to World Cup triumph

I'm going home to give my wife a big hug, because I doubt if I can manage anything else.
SCOLARI, Portugal coach, after a 'draining' victory over Spain, European Championship finals, 2004

BILL SHANKLY

Mr Shankly is a man with a reputation for living football.
EDITORIAL in the Huddersfield Town

programme welcoming the new assistant manager, 1955

I'm going to a place where they live, eat, sleep and drink football.
SHANKLY on leaving Huddersfield for Liverpool, 1959

I go to Liverpool's home games and as I walk through the Shankly Gates and see the crowds, I think: 'He started all this.'
IAN CALLAGHAN, former Liverpool and England winger, on the 50th anniversary of Shankly's arrival at Anfield, 2009

Football's not a matter of life or death. It's much more important than that.
SHANKLY, Liverpool manager, 1964

Shankly famously said: 'Football's not a matter of life and death, it's more important than that,' though it was said with a smile on a TV chat show. He knew there was more to life than football. At the same time it dominated his life.
JOHN KEITH, former Daily Express *football writer and Shankly confidant, 2009*

He built the great Liverpool team on Scousers and Jocks.
IAN ST JOHN, Liverpool and Scotland forward, 2009

The only religion he'd tolerate at Liverpool was football.
ST JOHN, 2009

We were playing Anderlecht and Shanks never had a good word for them beforehand. Afterwards he came in and told us: 'You've just beaten one of the best sides in Europe.'
ST JOHN, 2009

After we thrashed Newcastle, Shanks asked me, 'Have you got eyes in the back of your head?' I said no. He said, 'Well you just tried to back-heel the ball into their goal. I don't want fancy-dan stuff at this club.'
CHRIS LAWLER, former Liverpool and England defender, 2009

Shanks used to tell us: 'If you're going to get married, do it when you're 55, and make sure you marry a cook.'
GORDON LOW, Huddersfield defender during Shankly's managerial reign, 2013

My scout told me this lad had football in his blood. I said: 'Aye, but it hasn't reached his legs yet.'
SHANKLY, 1967

I'm a people's man, a player's man. You could call me a humanist.
SHANKLY, 1970

I don't drop players, I make changes.

SHANKLY, 1973

If a player isn't interfering with play or seeking to gain an advantage, what the hell is he doing on the pitch?
SHANKLY on the offside rule, 1967

I've been so wedded to Liverpool that I've taken Nessie [his wife] out only twice in 40 years. It's time she saw more of my old ugly mug.
SHANKLY on his retirement, 1974

I left because I was satisfied. I had proved a point. I was manager of a big club. If I'd wanted to buy a player there were no arguments about it. All the arguments were won.
SHANKLY on why he retired unexpectedly, 1975

Retirement is like having a coat in a wardrobe for years, which you decide you don't want and give to a friend. When he's worn it for a week you want it back.
SHANKLY, 1975

Last thing every night Bill takes the dog out for a walk on the Everton training pitch. The poor animal is not allowed back in until he's done his business.
NESSIE SHANKLY, 1983

I'm glad he's not here now. He would have been devastated.
NESSIE, now a widow, as Liverpool struggled, 1993

I believe Shankly died of a broken heart after he stopped managing

Liverpool and saw them go on to even greater success without him. Giving your whole life to a football club is a sad mistake.
JOHN GILES, *former Republic of Ireland manager, 1984*

I was managed by the best sports psychologist the world has ever seen. Bill Shankly made us feel we were superhuman.
RAY CLEMENCE, *former Liverpool goalkeeper, 2002*

Shankly – He Made The People Happy
INSCRIPTION *on a bronze statue of Shankly at Anfield, 1990s*

ANN ROBINSON: The American author of travel books such as *Notes from a Small Island* and *A Walk in the Woods* is Bill...?
CONTESTANT: Shankly.
EXCHANGE *on the BBC TV quiz show* The Weakest Link, *2011*

BOB SHANKLY

Bob was a stickler for the first-team photo. You had to be immaculately groomed or you didn't get on. He'd say: 'Christ, Craig, just you stand at the end of the back row. A pair of scissors will soon get rid of you.'
CRAIG BROWN, *former Scotland manager, on his manager, brother of Bill Shankly, as a 1960s Dundee player, 2008*

TIM SHERWOOD

The best players – Steven Gerrard, Paul Scholes – hurt when they lose. Kenny [Dalglish] used to say to me: 'You show me a good loser and I'll show you a loser.' People say Arsene [Wenger] is a poor loser. I am a poor loser.
SHERWOOD, *Tottenham manager and former Blackburn captain under Dalglish's management, 2014*

They are men. I'm a manager, not a babysitter.

SHERWOOD *after criticising the Spurs players' 'lack of bravery and commitment' in a 4–0 defeat at Chelsea, 2014*

RUSSELL SLADE

The hairs stood up on the back of my neck. He really is inspirational. I've done a few pep talks to fighters, snooker players and darts players and that was Shankly. I began to understand how he's put together this team spirit because you could cut the atmosphere with a knife. It was a beautiful moment in sport.
BARRY HEARN, *Leyton Orient chairman, after hearing manager Slade's team talk before Orient beat Colchester, 2013*

WALTER SMITH

It always gets back to the same question for me. Could a former electrician from Carmyle win the European Cup?
SMITH as Rangers failed honourably, 1993

I didn't know Walter personally. But I knew he must be Scottish because I used to see him carrying big discount cases of lager back from the supermarket.
PAUL GASCOIGNE on his first acquaintance with his future Rangers manager in Florida, 1995

OLE GUNNAR SOLSKJAER

Back in Norway, when we've been watching [Manchester] United games, I've nudged the kids and said: 'They are still singing about your dad.'
SOLSKJAER, newly appointed Cardiff City manager and ex-United striker, on taking the Welsh club to Old Trafford, 2014

GRAEME SOUNESS

If I was in Alex Ferguson's company, I would tell him first that Manchester United never knocked Liverpool off their fucking perch, as he put it. That's nonsense. Graeme Souness did that.
JAMIE CARRAGHER, Liverpool defender who played under Souness, 2010

He has gone behind my back right in front of my face.
CRAIG BELLAMY, Newcastle striker, on his feud with Souness, 2004

If I get a hostile reception from the Celtic support, I'll take that as a great compliment. If I had gone to Rangers and not done well, there would be no big deal about going back. In my five years at Rangers we won the championship four times. If I get lots of stick, I'll be chuffed to bits.
SOUNESS before taking Blackburn to Celtic for a UEFA Cup tie, 2002

I had to remind my players that I've had open-heart surgery and there's no way I can have that every week.
SOUNESS after a 4–3 win for his new team, Newcastle, over Manchester City, 2005

JOCK STEIN

With four games to go, Jock Stein says: 'Rangers can only throw it away.' And we did!
SIR ALEX FERGUSON, Stein's No. 2 with Scotland in the 1980s, on recalling the late Celtic manager's use of psychology, 2012

The papers say I'm Celtic's first Protestant manager. I prefer to say 25 per cent of our managers have been Protestant.
STEIN, the fourth manager in Celtic's history, 1960s

He understood how to work the press to his and Celtic's advantage. He was probably the first to do that. I remember Jock telling reporters he had two 15-year-olds he wanted to sign. He said one was a Catholic, one a Protestant, and he was going to sign the Protestant first. They asked why. He said: 'Because I know Rangers won't sign the Catholic.'
BERTIE AULD, Celtic midfielder in 1967 when Stein led the Glasgow club to the European Cup, 2011

He had no time for all that religious nonsense. He loved football. He couldn't understand all the rubbish about Catholics and Protestants supporting different teams.
JESSIE McNEILL, Stein's sister, in Michael Grant and Rob Robertson, The Management, 2010

John hated smoking. He said if you were meant to smoke you would have a chimney coming out of the top of your head.
JESSIE McNEILL, as above

John, you're immortal.
BILL SHANKLY, Liverpool manager, to Stein in the Celtic dressing room after the European Cup final triumph over Inter Milan, 1967

The Hibs players were talking about how Stein didn't raise his voice much in the dressing-room. John Parke, who went on to Sunderland, said: 'Aye, but he's got a diarrhoea stare.' I asked what he meant and he said: 'When he fixes you with a look, you shit yourself.'
MICK CULLERTON, former Hibernian youth player, 2010

GORDON STRACHAN

All this 'breathe in and stabilise' stuff – the instructor never told us to breathe out again, so for two minutes I was holding my breath. I nearly killed myself.
STRACHAN on taking up pilates after leaving Middlesbrough, 2010

I know how people see me, but all my life I've been a victim of self-doubt. There have been many times when I have felt despondent, when I think I'm useless. I felt it many times as a player and I've often experienced it as a manager.
STRACHAN shortly before leaving Coventry, 2001

REPORTER: Welcome to Southampton. Do you think you're the right man to turn things around? STRACHAN: No. I was asked whether I thought I was the right man and I said: 'No, I think they should have got George Graham because I'm useless.'
EXCHANGE at a press conference on Strachan's arrival at St Mary's Stadium, 2001

REPORTER: Bang goes your unbeaten run. Can you take it?
STRACHAN: No, I'm just going to crumble like a wreck. I'll go home, become an alcoholic and maybe jump off a bridge.
EXCHANGE at a press conference, 2002

REPORTER: Gordon, you must be delighted with that result.
STRACHAN: Spot on. You can read me like a book.
EXCHANGE after a Southampton victory, 2002

REPORTER: What was your impression of Leeds? STRACHAN: I don't do impressions.

EXCHANGE after a draw at his old club, 2003

REPORTER: What areas did you think Middlesbrough were superior in?
STRACHAN: That big grassy one out there for a start.
EXCHANGE after a Southampton defeat, 2003

Sometimes I have to turn the telly over when I'm watching Gordon going berserk on the touchline. I'm worried that he might have an aneurysm and burst a blood vessel.
MARK McGHEE, Brighton manager and later his assistant when Strachan became Scotland manager, 2003

When I'm dead, it will be inscribed on my headstone: 'This isn't as bad as that night in Bratislava.'
STRACHAN, by now manager of Celtic, after a 5–0 Champions League defeat by Slovakian side Artmedia Bratislava in his first game, 2005

People don't understand a manager wanting to spend more time with his wife and family. Do I wait until people are screaming at me, my wife is going off her head and I'm a nervous wreck? I love football, but it's not an obsession.
STRACHAN still 'between jobs', 2004

I've never taken drugs but I wonder if it's a bit like this.

STRACHAN on winning at Kilmarnock to clinch the Scottish title with Celtic, 2007

GRAHAM TAYLOR

My advice to the next England manager? Don't lose matches.
TAYLOR on leaving the job, 1993

It was nearly my finest hour, but life is made up of so-nearlies.
TAYLOR after his England side surrendered a 2–0 lead to draw with the Netherlands, 1993

Napoleon wanted his generals to be lucky. I don't think he would have wanted me.
TAYLOR after England failed to reach the World Cup finals, 1993

I can live with a newspaper putting a turnip on my head, except that it encourages people to treat me like shit.
TAYLOR, former England manager, on why he no longer attended England matches at Wembley, 1998

You can call me a turnip, but don't ever call me Gordon.
TAYLOR after being incorrectly addressed before Turkey v England match, 2003

Q: Tell us something about yourself that would surprise people.
A: Member of the Royal Shakespeare Company and enjoy all forms of theatre.
TAYLOR interviewed in the Football Foundation magazine Onside, 2013

PETER TAYLOR (1928–90)

I'm not equipped to manage successfully without him. I'm the shop front, he is the goods at the back.
BRIAN CLOUGH, Derby manager, when he and Taylor still worked together, 1973

We pass each other on the A52 going to work on most days of the week. But if his car broke down and I saw him thumbing a lift, I wouldn't pick him up. I'd run him over.
CLOUGH, by now managing Nottingham Forest while Taylor was in charge at Derby, after their falling-out, 1983

PETER TAYLOR (b. 1953)

He's very experienced. He's done his time. He's managed Dover Athletic.
JOHN GREGORY, Aston Villa manager, on Taylor's appointment as caretaker-manager of England, 2000

I was sitting there during the game thinking to myself: 'I can't believe this – I am manager of England.'
TAYLOR, Leicester manager and England caretaker-manager v Italy, 2000

JOHN TOSHACK

There's more chance of me flying Concorde to the moon blindfolded than there is of him taking Wales to the South African World Cup.
ROBBIE SAVAGE, Blackburn and former Wales midfielder, 2007

REPORTER: Did you realise it's Wales' worst home defeat in 98 years?
TOSHACK: I didn't, but I've broken records all my life, so that's another one.
EXCHANGE after Wales' 5–1 defeat by Slovakia, 2006

LOUIS VAN GAAL

Congratulations on signing the best coach in the world.
VAN GAAL to an Ajax director on his appointment as coach, 1991

I achieved more with Ajax in six years than Barcelona has in one hundred years.
VAN GAAL on becoming coach to Barcelona, 1997

Van Gaal deserved what happened to him at Barcelona. He had many bad things to say about me, and for that nonsense, God punished him.
RONALDO, Real Madrid, Brazil and former Barcelona striker, 2003

Louis Van Gaal has nothing more to learn.
VAN GAAL, Netherlands coach, 2001

Van Gaal was a pompous arse. He wanted to be a dictator, without a hint of a gleam in his eye. He was one of those in the club who referred to the players as numbers.
ZLATAN IBRAHIMOVIC, Swedish striker, who played under Van Gaal for Ajax, in his autobiography, 2013

I have the body of a god. Lederhosen suits me. But I also have a belly.
VAN GAAL, Bayern Munich coach, before the club's annual trip to the city's Oktoberfest, 2010

The Bavarian attitude to life suits me perfectly. Why? Bayern's motto is 'Mia san mia' – 'We are who we are'. And I am who I am: confident, arrogant, dominant, honest, hard-working and innovative.
VAN GAAL at Bayern, 2011

Van Gaal's failure is clearly in his attitude. If that mentality is customary, you have to have success. If it fails, you lose your friends.
KARL-HEINZ RUMMENIGGE, Bayern Munich ex-player and official, 2011

In my career I've found players are fascinated by my philosophy. It's an attacking, technical and tactical philosophy.
VAN GAAL, interviewed by Fifa, 2013

As a human being he is top; he has heart. But in football he is right and you are wrong. You can discuss it for hours and hours but he will never admit you are right.
ROGER VAN GOOL, 1970s team-mate of Van Gaal's at Royal Antwerp, 2014

If a journalist writes 90 per cent good and 10 per cent bad about Louis [Van Gaal], it's the 10 per cent that he'll talk about.
VAN GOOL on Van Gaal's 'over-sensitive' side, 2014

TERRY VENABLES

Terry made everybody, including the players, feel better about themselves.
DAVID DAVIES on leaving the post of executive director of the Football Association, 2006

When I arrived in the summer, one of my predecessors told the Spanish press that Meester Terry would be gone by Christmas, but he forgot to say which year.
VENABLES, Barcelona coach, 1984

A lot of people seem to think I'm just a slippery Cockney boy with a few jokes. It's taken one of the biggest clubs in the world to

acknowledge what I can really do: coach.
VENABLES on his initial success with Barcelona, 1985

I can still go out as long as it's after midnight, I'm wearing dark glasses and it's a dimly lit restaurant.
VENABLES as Barca suffered the bad run that led to his sacking, 1987

Tottenham without Terry is like Westminster without Big Ben.

PAUL GASCOIGNE reacting to Venables' sacking by Alan Sugar, 1993

I must be the only person who actually gets less publicity by becoming manager of England.
VENABLES, newly appointed England manager, on controversy over his business dealings, 1994

Terry gave us an extra dimension in [Euro] 96. We had always had good technique – I'll argue that endlessly because I've played with enough top players to recognise it. We've just been a little bit slow up top. We were all heart and no brains but Terry started putting that right.
TONY ADAMS, Arsenal and England defender, 1999

ANDRE VILLAS-BOAS

I'm like a maestro from the Boston Philharmonic whose biggest breakthrough as a leader was realising that he didn't make any sound himself; the players did.
VILLAS-BOAS, Tottenham and former Chelsea manager, 2013; he was sacked later in the year

My passions are outside football. I'm not one of those people who's obsessed with the game. I have a couple of bikes from the (Paris-) Dakar rally. I have a bit of a crazy head and I go into the mountains with the big rocks and almost kill myself. It's my escape.
VILLAS-BOAS, Chelsea manager, on his love of off-road motorcycles, 2011

Who is the muppet coaching Chelsea??? AVB??? Hmmm!! 25yrs for Ferguson, hopefully not even 6 months for this AVB geezer!
KEVIN PIETERSEN, Chelsea-supporting England cricketer, on Twitter, 2011

Would Burnley players have ever understood what he wanted if he'd told them to 'solidificate'?
PAUL FLETCHER, former Burnley chief executive and ex-player, recalling that in 2010 Villas-Boas had been a candidate for their manager's job, 2012

With Mourinho they either loved him or hated him, but with AVB it's the other way.
DARREN GOUGH, talkSPORT presenter and former England cricketer, 2013

BERTI VOGTS

If people saw me walking on water you can be sure someone would say: 'Look at that Berti Vogts, he can't even swim.'
VOGTS, Germany coach, on mounting criticism of his style, 1996

What's his name? Vorti Begts? I don't like Germans. They shot my dad.
BRIAN CLOUGH, 2003

Get stuck into the fucking Germans.
VOGTS to the Scotland team before a World Cup qualifier between the countries, 2003

The subtleties of our language were maybe a little beyond him.
JOHN McBETH, Scottish FA president, after the 'mutual' parting with Vogts, 2004

TONY WADDINGTON

A lot of managers go in for that stuff about football being more important than life or death. Tony knew that was rubbish. No one could have loved football more than him, but he always told us to enjoy ourselves too.

ALAN HUDSON, Stoke City and England midfielder, on Stoke's long-serving manager of the 1960s and '70s, 2009

NEIL WARNOCK

I think Paul [Lambert] was embarrassed when he accepted it, to be honest. There was only one Manager of the Year in my eyes.

WARNOCK, Queens Park Rangers manager, after the Championship award went to Norwich's Lambert despite QPR winning the title, 2011

I'm not a communicator by tweet, I'm afraid, so I was always going to be the last to know.

WARNOCK on his sacking by QPR, 2012

Twitter cost him his job???? I can think of a million other things! #shutitwarnock

TWEET by Joey Barton, QPR midfielder and Warnock signing, 2012

Lost his job and the guy is blaming everyone but himself. Embarrasing, time to look in the mirror mate.

BARTON, as above

If people think it's funny to call me Colin Wanker, so be it. I'm all for anything that makes people laugh. And I've certainly been called a lot worse.

WARNOCK, Sheffield United manager, 2006

Neil Warnock was a chiropodist? He can sort out my back then.

IAN ABRAHAMS, talkSPORT reporter, 2013

After the game, we're walking off the pitch. We've just won 2–1. The ref's given us a goal that was blatantly offside, so I'm absolutely elated. Neil Warnock, the Sheffield United manager, is going ballistic. Anyhow, I am shouting at Neil, as we walk off: 'I always supported you. But now I see I was wrong. Everybody else in football is right. You are a twat.'

IAN HOLLOWAY, Queens Park Rangers manager, 2005

Look at the state of Neil Warnock. His head was coming off and quite rightly so.

HOLLOWAY after Warnock's Crystal Palace side were refused a penalty, 2009

When I'm doing an in-growing toenail operation, I find my patient talking to me and I'm not listening. At the end I say: 'I'm very sorry, Mrs Kirk, I was away – I was just picking the side for Saturday.'
WARNOCK, Scarborough manager and chiropodist, 1987

I'd love to manage Wednesday. I'd buy so many tosspots – their current squad would do – and fuck 'em up so badly. Then I'd retire to Cornwall and spend the rest of my life laughing my fucking head off.
WARNOCK, Sheffield United manager, 2002; he later claimed he had been taken 'out of context' and denied including the current squad in his remarks

ARSENE WENGER

Eight years without a piece of silverware, that's failure. He is a specialist in failure.
JOSE MOURINHO, Chelsea manager, 2014

I am on earth to try to win games.
WENGER, Arsenal manager, 2012

I was a complete unknown, and there was no history of foreign managers succeeding in England.

I changed a few habits, which isn't easy in a team where the average age is 30. At the first match the players were chanting: 'We want our Mars bars.'
WENGER reflecting on his arrival in 1996 before his 1,000th match in charge of Arsenal, 2014

Then in the afternoon we would come out and there would be footballs all over the pitch! 'What? Footballs!' It was unheard of, a football session on the first day back in pre-season training.
NIGEL WINTERBURN, Arsenal defender, on Wenger's first pre-season with the club 17 years earlier, 2014

He is really something. I love him. He is Sir Arsene Wenger. But he likes having the ball, playing football, passes. It's like an orchestra, but it is a silent song. I like heavy metal more. I always want it loud. I love Arsenal's style, but I cannot coach it because I am a different guy. If you watch me during the game I celebrate when we press the ball and it goes out.
JURGEN KLOPP, Borussia Dortmund coach, 2013

I played with him for six years. I've met him a few times. The more I get to know him the less I know him. I haven't a clue how that man thinks, how he works. He's difficult to fathom.
TONY ADAMS, former Arsenal captain under Wenger, 2013

I don't think we need foreign managers running the national sides. I've got nothing against foreign managers, they are very nice people. Apart from Arsene Wenger.
TONY PULIS, Stoke City's Welsh manager, 2010

Arsene Wenger did a brilliant job, but the cupboard has been dry for seven years.
MICK QUINN, talkSPORT radio pundit, 2012

Arsene Wenger doesn't give his players pacific roles.

MARTIN KEOWN, Radio 5Live analyst and ex-Arsenal player, 2011

[Wenger's] strength was he bought players who had not made the grade, like Thierry Henry, who was a winger at Juventus. [And] nobody really knew [Patrick] Vieira or [Emmanuel] Petit. He polished them up and made them international players and won everything. He's trying to do the same with players people don't really know in this country and it's not working as well.
GEORGE GRAHAM, one of Wenger's predecessors at Arsenal, after the club's 8–2 humiliation at Manchester United, 2011

No disrespect to Arsene, but George Graham's coaching ability, defensive structure and technical ability, for me, is far better. Arsene was a magnificent physiologist and psychologist, a lovely man.
TONY ADAMS, former Arsenal captain, 2011

The perception that I am resistant to spending is unfair. Why should I resist?
WENGER after Arsenal did not pay a fee for a player during the close season, 2013

I am supposed to take the bullets and absorb them. Like a bear. A polar bear.
WENGER on fans' criticism, 2011

Arsene Wenger is a genius but he just doesn't like getting beaten.
STEVE BRUCE, Sunderland manager, after his team's late equaliser v Arsenal, 2010

He cultivates this image of the wise man, but he's less polished in reality. When it comes to transfers he always wants to be cleverer, slyer, than you are.
JEAN-LOUIS TRIAUD, Bordeaux president, 2010

I think Arsene's a great manager. The trouble is that if you ever make a valid point about him and the club, it's like criticising the Pope. Everybody gets up in arms.
FRANK McLINTOCK, 1971 Arsenal Double-winning captain, 2009

We know that Arsene Wenger likes the look of [Andrei] Arshavin, but I like the look of Angelina Jolie. It doesn't mean you get what you want.
DENNIS LACHTER, agent of the then Zenit St Petersburg player, 2009

My secret is adapting to the country I'm in. Here I eat roast beef and Yorkshire pudding.
WENGER, 2009

When Bruce Rioch was sacked, one of the papers had three or four names. It was Venables, Cruyff and then at the end, Arsene Wenger. I remember thinking as a fan: 'I bet it's fucking Arsene Wenger... Trust Arsenal to appoint the one you haven't heard of.'
NICK HORNBY, author, journalist and Arsenal fan, in Jasper Rees's Wenger: The Making of a Legend, 2003

I've got to play for a Frenchman? You have to be joking.

TONY ADAMS, Arsenal captain, recalling his reaction to Wenger's arrival, 1997

He arrived unnoticed at the training ground. A meeting was called, the players filed in and in front of us stood this tall, slightly built man who gave no impression whatsoever of being a football manager.
LEE DIXON, Arsenal and England defender, on Wenger's first day, in Rees's book, 2003

He has put me on grilled fish, grilled broccoli, grilled everything. Yuk!
IAN WRIGHT, Arsenal striker, on Wenger's dietary regime, 1997

Mr Wenger's a very clever man, but I have to say that what he said is crap.
PETER REID, Sunderland manager, after his Arsenal counterpart claimed an opponent had helped get Patrick Vieira sent off, 2000

Arsene Wenger disappoints me when he is reluctant to give credit to Manchester United for what we have achieved. And I don't think his carping has made a good impression on other managers in the Premiership.
SIR ALEX FERGUSON, 2000

Arsene Wenger is somebody I'd like to get to know better. People who do know him tell me he is a good man but I don't suppose I'll ever find out for myself. He seems to pull down the shutters when you meet him and he never has a drink with you after the game.
FERGUSON quoted in Jasper Rees's Wenger: The Making of a Legend, 2003

Wenger has an English mind but also a German mind, which is very disciplined.

GLENN HODDLE, *a Monaco player under Wenger, in Myles Palmer's book* The Professor, *2001*

The Arsene brand of football is based on five things: power, pace, skill, technique and, in capital letters, YOUTH. He looks for perfection in those areas... In his time at Arsenal, only one player has achieved his ideal – Thierry Henry, although Dennis Bergkamp, Patrick Vieira, Robert Pires and Sol Campbell have come close.
BOB WILSON, *former Arsenal goalkeeper and coach, 2004*

The biggest bollocking I got in six years of playing for Arsene was when we lost a game and he came in and said: 'I cannot stand for this. This is not acceptable.'
TONY ADAMS, *former Arsenal captain, 2003*

To not apologise to another manager for the behaviour of the players is unthinkable. It's a disgrace. But I don't expect him to ever apologise.
SIR ALEX FERGUSON *on his feud with Wenger, 2004*

I like to read a book or talk to my wife or daughter, for an hour or so. But to have a whole day without thinking about football – that is impossible.
WENGER, *2003*

You live in a marginal world as a manager. I know three places in London: my house, Highbury and the training ground [in Hertfordshire].
WENGER, *2003*

There are some guys who, when they're at home, have this big telescope to see what happens in other families. He must be one of them. Being a voyeur is a sickness.
JOSE MOURINHO, *in his first spell as Chelsea manager, alleging Wenger was obsessed with his club, 2005*

Mr Wenger and I were engaged in a previous life. We had a romance when I was Joan of Arc and he was the Dauphine [*sic*] of France. He was the same man we know him to be today. Highly intelligent but very stubborn.
STEPHANY COHEN, *self-proclaimed 'god of all aliens', interviewed in the* Bromley Shopper *newspaper, 2014*

HOWARD WILKINSON

There are bigger heads than mine in this division – Howard Wilkinson springs to mind.
BRIAN CLOUGH, *1991; he later apologised for the remark*

He disliked personalities who had a rapport with the fans.
ERIC CANTONA in Cantona: My Story, *1994*

At the end of Wilkinson's team talks we'd be thinking: 'Eh?'
DAVID BATTY, England midfielder, on Leeds' former manager, 1999

I saw Ron Greenwood break out in sores, Bobby Robson go grey and poor Graham Taylor double up in anguish and stick his head so far between his legs that it nearly disappeared up his backside. If I was single, with no kids, it'd be no problem. But I've a wife and three children and I've seen how this job can affect your family. It won't happen to mine.

WILKINSON, Leeds manager, after Graham Taylor's exit, 1994; Wilkinson later took on the job as 'caretaker' on two occasions

WALTER WINTERBOTTOM

Just because I play for England, he thinks I understand peripheral vision and positive running.
JIMMY GREAVES, Chelsea striker, on the then England manager, 1960

I'm as bad a judge of strikers as Walter Winterbottom – he gave me only two caps.
BRIAN CLOUGH, Nottingham Forest manager, 1988

6

MANAGING

I've sat in the hot seat and felt its hotness.
BOBBY GOULD, talkSPORT radio pundit and former Wales manager, 2009

The problem with being a manager is it's like trying to build an aircraft while it is flying.
BRENDAN RODGERS, Swansea City manager, 2012

I remember working with Sam [Allardyce] at Newcastle and he said: 'I f***ing hate match-days.' I know where he's coming from. The nerves. The emotion. Getting the preparation right. That build-up to the game is horrible. This job is love-hate. It motivates me but also brings the worst out of me. It's like being a masochist.
NIGEL PEARSON, Leicester manager, 2014

To manage a club with common sense used to be fine. But football has changed. Since the arrival of people with big money, the Premier League has changed.
RAFAEL BENITEZ, Chelsea interim manager, 2013

[A club's board] must discuss the qualities of the manager they are going to offer the job to, must look at his CV, his character, the philosophy he has. Now, if that is the way they have gone about giving the man the job, why don't they persevere with it? So then maybe it goes for a year, then they

change, and then they go through the same procedure again. It seems to me so stupid.
SIR ALEX FERGUSON, 2014

To be England manager you must win every game, not do anything in your private life and hopefully not earn too much money. They are the only qualities you need and if you have those you're perfect.
SVEN-GORAN ERIKSSON, former England manager, 2008

You can't really win as England manager. Unless you win.

GARY NEVILLE, Sky pundit and former England defender, 2011

As a manager you accept that you need a double skin: a rhino's and an elephant's, just to survive in the job.
SAM ALLARDYCE, West Ham manager, 2012

I had a nice time over Christmas. I watched *EastEnders*. Blimey, that makes my job look easy.
MICK McCARTHY, Wolves manager, 2010

The chap who protects me is a seventh dan in karate, but he's not big or butch. He knows how to

handle himself. It's a bit strange having him around, but there are some good things too. He's bloody interesting to talk to, for a start.
STEVE KEAN, Blackburn manager, on the 'minder' who protected him from dissenting fans, 2012

There's huge sways back and forth in terms of emotion and how the ebb and flow of the game affects you, in terms of the desire, you have to see fair play and make sure you're competing. It's human nature that your emotions can get the better of you on occasion – and managers aren't immune to that.
MARK HUGHES, Stoke City manager, after being 'sent off' during match v Newcastle, 2013

As a manager at any level, when things are going wrong it's with you every minute of the day. You go home and your wife will be talking but you are not listening. You are thinking: 'Do I pick him, or him?' You'll watch TV but you aren't really watching; you're doing it to be sociable. Inside you are thinking: 'How do I leave a top player out?'
NEIL WARNOCK, former Sheffield United and Leeds manager, in his Independent *column, 2014*

Managers are the people in the game with more pressure on their shoulders. They have the most difficult job in the game, plus the referees. If, on isolated occasions managers, they lose their emotional

control and have a certain behaviour that cannot be accepted by the authorities, in this case by the refs, we should be punished – but in a way where people don't feel the managers are strange or weird or impolite people, or people without control.
JOSE MOURINHO, Chelsea manager, 2013

The reason we're sat in a TV studio (as pundits) is because we look at football management as being an absolute world of madness where the average manager gets sacked every 12 months.
GARY NEVILLE, Sky summariser and ex-Manchester United captain, as reports emerged of David Moyes' dismissal by United, 2014

Real players like a manager who's tough. Or can be tough. They like a manager to be a man.

SIR ALEX FERGUSON in My Autobiography, *2013*

A proper manager can deal with different personalities.
ZLATAN IBRAHIMOVIC, Paris St-Germain and Sweden striker, 2013

The manager and chief scout must be in unicism with each other.
BOBBY GOULD, talkSPORT radio pundit and former Wales manager, 2008

With your club it is a love story that you have to expect will last for ever and also accept that you could leave tomorrow.
ARSENE WENGER, Arsenal manager, 2006

I can't get inside my players' heads. One minute they're saving your life, the next they're breaking into your house and robbing your telly.
JOHN COLEMAN, Accrington Stanley manager, after defeat by Farnborough, 2004

We lost a bad third goal because of an individual error by the goalkeeper, but I'm not going to point the finger of blame at anyone for that.
JOHN HUGHES, Falkirk manager, 2009

The boys' performance today was so good I've run out of expletives to describe it.

MICKY MELLON, Fleetwood Town manager, 2011

We jump up and down like fucking lunatics for 90 minutes, but it doesn't have any effect.
PAUL JEWELL, Wigan manager, 2007

If you don't know what's going on, start waving your arms about as if you do.
GORDON STRACHAN, Southampton manager, on how to be seen as a bona fide manager, 2003

Ranting and raving gets you nowhere in football. If you want to be heard, speak quietly.
BOB PAISLEY, Liverpool manager, 1982

I don't think I'm big-mouthed enough to be a manager.
ROBERT PIRES, Arsenal and France midfielder, 2004

I had so much trouble sleeping that for a while I was addicted to Night Nurse. When I told [my wife] Sandra she thought I was talking about some bird in suspenders.
HARRY REDKNAPP, Portsmouth manager, during a run of defeats, 2008

[Scotland manager] George Burley will be at the sponsor event at the Urban Brasserie, not the Urban Brassiere as previously advised.
ROB SHORTHOUSE, Scottish FA head of communications, 2009

I love football and all the build-up to a game, but I absolutely hate match days. I wake with a knot in

my stomach and it never goes away until the final whistle.
SAM ALLARDYCE, Bolton manager, 2002

If it weren't for Saturdays, managing would be the best job in the world. You get that horrible feeling in your guts and your head is going round.
RONNIE MOORE, Oldham manager, 2006

I work in the most intense job where my day starts at 6am and finishes very late. The advantages are that I'm well paid and love what I do. But your highs are never as high as your lows are low. After a defeat or bad performance I feel physically ill.
GARY MEGSON, West Bromwich Albion manager, 2004

Ninety minutes before a match, there's not much a manager can do. You can't talk to players, so you sit drinking tea.
SVEN-GORAN ERIKSSON, England manager, 2006

I'll celebrate with a green tea and a chocolate biscuit.

ROY KEANE, Sunderland manager, after victory v Tottenham, 2007

In my line of work, if you win, you continue. If you don't, you're out. I must build something special this year. If I don't, I'm a dead man walking.
CLAUDIO RANIERI, Chelsea manager, 2003

Football managers are like a parachutist. At times it doesn't open and you splatter on the ground. Here, it is an umbrella. You understand, Mary Poppins?
RANIERI under growing pressure at Chelsea, 2004

A manager can't give players what they haven't got. The job is to make them find what they need inside themselves.
DAVID BECKHAM in his book My Side, *2003*

A lot of players think they'll go into management and stay friends with everybody, but you have to make unpleasant decisions that will hurt people. If you don't like that, don't go into football management.
GEORGE GRAHAM, former manager, 2002

I have mates who did become teachers and I know that I couldn't have done it. It's ridiculously hard – far harder than what I do.
STEVE COPPELL, Reading manager, 2006

Sometimes I'm still at work at three in the afternoon.

PAUL MERSON on being caretaker player-manager at Walsall, 2004

People say you have to take your coaching badges to be a manager. I don't agree. When I went to Newcastle my only qualification was 1,000 rounds of golf in Spain, but it didn't do me any harm.
KEVIN KEEGAN, 2007

I never wanted to be a manager; I wanted to be a coach. But to have the power of coaching you've got to be the manager because the manager tells you how to coach. So the only reason I'm a manager is to be a coach.
GORDON STRACHAN at Southampton, 2003

The glory moment is when you sign the contract. From then on the situation deteriorates.
CARLOS QUEIROZ on becoming coach to Real Madrid, 2003

My brother always said you would have to be mad to be a manager. What other job is there where your livelihood depends on 11 daft lads?

FRANCIS LEE, Manchester City chairman, 1996

In my office I often regret the fact that players do not sit in chairs fitted with a lie-detector and an ejector seat.
GORDON STRACHAN, Southampton manager, 2002

I left out a couple of my foreigners the other week and they started talking in 'foreign'. I knew they were saying: 'Blah, blah, blah, le bastard manager, fucking useless bastard.'
HARRY REDKNAPP, Portsmouth manager, 2004

Some managers in England are fat and drink beer. How can players respect that, and not drink and stay fit?
ERIC CANTONA, 2003

Management is the only job in the world where everyone knows better. I would never tell a plumber, a lawyer or a journalist how to do his job but they all know better than me every Saturday.
JOE ROYLE, Manchester City manager, 2001

Who wants to be out of management? Nobody. We all want to be there, winning and losing, reading in the papers that we don't know anything about football.
SVEN-GORAN ERIKSSON, England manager, 2001

Having one year without football [after the England job] has been the most stressful time, far worse than sitting on any bench. After one month off it is awful to wake up in the morning not knowing what to do.
ERIKSSON on returning to management at Manchester City, 2007

The face of the manager is a mirror to the health of the team.
ARSENE WENGER, Arsenal manager, 2002

Football management these days is like nuclear war. No winners, just survivors.
TOMMY DOCHERTY, 1992

I don't know how people last in this game [management] until they're 60.

BRIAN CLOUGH, Derby County manager, 1972; he retired in 1993 aged 58

If you're a painter you don't get rich until you're dead. The same happens with managers. You're never appreciated until you're gone. Then people say, 'he was ok.' Just like Picasso.
SIR BOBBY ROBSON, former England manager, 2008

We all end up yesterday's men in this business. You're very quickly forgotten.
JOCK STEIN, former Celtic manager, in Archie Macpherson, The Great Derbies: Blue and Green, *1989*

As a manager it's a case of have suitcase, will travel. And I certainly don't want to travel with my trousers down.
IAN HOLLOWAY, Plymouth manager, 2006

One minute you're God, the next you're something the dog left behind.
KIM HOLLOWAY, wife of Ian, on the insecurity of management, 2004

When you're a football manager you don't have fitted carpets.
JOHN BARNWELL, Walsall manager, shortly before his sacking, 1990

There aren't many managers who truly believe they can stay at one club long enough to qualify for a gold watch.
GORDON STRACHAN shortly before quitting as Southampton manager, 2003

I wouldn't go to a club that changes manager every six months. I'm not a fan of upheaval in football. Big clubs tend to win trophies only when they have stability. Spending money is one thing; building a team is another.
ARSENE WENGER as Arsenal closed in on the Premiership title, 2004

My son is a surgeon and makes life-and-death decisions every day. Yet I think of my job as the most important imaginable.
DAVID PLEAT, Sheffield Wednesday manager, 1997

Managing is a seven-day-a-week, almost 24-hour-a-day job. There's no rest or escape but I'm hooked on it.
BARRY FRY, Peterborough manager, 1999

I'm not a politician, a social worker or clergyman. I'm a provider of distraction, and fans want to go home happy to whatever bores the arse off them during the week.
HOWARD WILKINSON, Leeds manager, 1994

You have to have a bit of everything these days: coach, social worker, the lot. If Claire Rayner knew soccer, she'd be a great manager.
MICK McCARTHY, Millwall manager, 1995

Every dressing room should have a poster that says: 'There is more to life than just football and football management.'
GERRY FRANCIS, Bristol Rovers manager, 1988

There are too many silly, unrealistic demands on a manager, and they can take the pleasure out of this job. He's a very influential person so he can expect a certain

amount of criticism and blame. But you can't expect one man to be responsible for everything.
GRAHAM TAYLOR, Watford manager, 1999

Being a manager means responsibility. It's an awful, thankless task most of the time. The only thing you get is that adrenalin rush you had as a player.
GARY LINEKER when his ex-Everton team-mate and fellow TV presenter Andy Gray was reputedly offered the Everton job, 1997

I still miss playing. Management offers only second-hand thrills.
JOE ROYLE, Everton manager, 1997

My guts are eating my insides again and I haven't felt that since I was a player.
STEVE WIGLEY, acting manager of Southampton after Gordon Strachan's departure, 2004

Playing was great. Managing was unrewarding and stupid.

GEOFF HURST, former England World Cup player and ex-Chelsea manager, 1991

You think you're working hard when you're a player but you really just have to look after yourself, physically and mentally. As a manager you can multiply all that by 14, which tells you how much tougher it is.
CRAIG LEVEIN, Cowdenbeath manager and former Scotland defender, 1999

In the public's mind, players win games and managers lose them.
BRYAN ROBSON, Middlesbrough player-manager, 1995

A manager is responsible for 10 per cent of wins and 90 per cent of defeats. That's how it works.
DIDIER DESCHAMPS, Monaco manager, after Chelsea's Champions League defeat by his team was blamed on Claudio Ranieri, 2004

Many people think a coach accounts for around 80 per cent of a team's results, but I'd say it's more like 15 per cent.
SERGIO CRAGNOTTI, Lazio president, after Sven-Goran Eriksson's departure, 2000

Did I put something of myself into the team? When we were playing well, yes. When we were playing shite, no.
FRANK BURROWS, caretaker-manager of West Bromwich Albion, 2004

The nice aspect of football captaincy is that the manager gets the blame if things go wrong.

GARY LINEKER, former Leicestershire schools cricket captain, on being named England football captain, 1990

Managers get too much credit when things go well and too much blame when they go badly.
GRAHAM TAYLOR, England manager, 1994

As a coach you have a squad of 24. You can only pick 11, so you have 13 enemies straight away. And you can multiply that by four – they all have wives, parents, kids.
JOHN TOSHACK, Wales manager, 2007

A manager's aggravation is self-made. All he has to do is keep 11 players happy – the 11 in the reserves. The first team are happy because they're in the first team.
RODNEY MARSH, Manchester City striker, 1972

As a manager you've got 30 or 40 players and staff to look after, and every one of the players' problems is your own because you're relying on them. I'd know if my centre-back's little boy had a problem, but my own wife and kids I knew nothing about. Your own life and family end up 50th best.
CHRIS NICHOLL, former Southampton and Walsall manager, 2003

I'd booked a holiday with my wife and three children. I don't see them that much. I'm absolutely obsessed with them, and they're the only thing I'm in football for, apart from loving the game a little bit. The fact that I'd taken them away, I didn't care whether Leeds, Liverpool or England came up, I was going to finish my holiday.
BRIAN CLOUGH, between jobs, on why he went away immediately after becoming Leeds manager, 1974

I had a pile of books by my bed and I turned to my wife one night and said: 'I could die tomorrow and not know any of these, but I could tell you the name of every centre-forward in the bottom two divisions.' You think it's the most important thing, but in the whole scheme of life it isn't.
FRANK BARLOW, caretaker-manager of Nottingham Forest, 2006

It takes an enormous amount of energy to manage or coach properly. It's not only a matter of technique and tactics, but you have to move deep into the soul of your squad.
MARCO VAN BASTEN, former Netherlands striker and soon-to-be manager, 2003

I hate to work with a big squad. It's like a big box of oranges and one goes rotten. A month later, you have to throw the lot in the bin.
JOSE MOURINHO, Chelsea manager, 2004

I think if you can't do anything else you end up as a manager. It's a last resort.
NIGEL CLOUGH, Burton Albion manager, in the ITV documentary about his father, Clough, *2009.*

There isn't another industry in the world where the employees still call the manager 'Boss' or 'Gaffer'. It's a throwback to the days of the Victorian mill-owners.
JON HOLMES, players' agent, in Colin Malam, Gary Lineker: Strikingly Different, *1992*

In this business you've got to be a dictator or you haven't a chance.
BRIAN CLOUGH at Hartlepools, 1965

The real key to management is to inject character into a club, not just the players. Jock Stein, Bill Shankly, Brian Clough – they dominated the whole place.
GEORGE GRAHAM, former Arsenal, Leeds and Tottenham manager, 2002

Football is in my blood, but do I want to put myself in a world where I rely on players, get sacked after six games and not see my two children grow up?
GARETH SOUTHGATE, Middlesbrough captain, 2003; Southgate became Boro manager in 2006

When you're building a team, you're looking for good players, not blokes to marry your daughters.
DAVE BASSETT, Sheffield United manager, after buying Vinnie Jones, 1990

My youngest daughter gets married on Saturday, which is more important to me than either job.
GRAHAM TAYLOR, Aston Villa and soon-to-be England manager, 1990

One thing I have learned about management is that you don't fall in love with players.
TAYLOR, by now England manager, 1992

To me there's no point in having confrontation for the sake of it. Look at Ruud Gullit. Can you tell me that he was a shrewd manager in what he did to Rob Lee, who was captain of Newcastle and Alan

Shearer's best mate? Why make problems for yourself?
HARRY REDKNAPP, West Ham manager, 2000

I've told my players never to believe what I say about them in the papers.

GRAHAM TAYLOR, Aston Villa manager, 1988

I'm like a dad to my players, mixing small tellings-off with a lot of love.
GORDON STRACHAN, Coventry manager, 1999

Q: Who is your closest friend at the club?
A: I am the manager. I have no friends.
STRACHAN in a Coventry programme Q & A, 1999

Q: Best mates at the club?
A: Managers have very few.
JOHN RUDGE, Port Vale manager, in a programme Q & A, 1993

I love football, but management is the loneliest job in the world. You sometimes think it is you against the world.
DICK ADVOCAAT, Netherlands manager, 2004

As a manager you're like a prostitute – you depend on other people for your living.
STEVE COPPELL, Crystal Palace manager, after a controversial refereeing decision in his club's FA Cup defeat by Hartlepool, 1993

Being a football manager is a thankless, hopeless task. It's a dreadful job and most of them can be seen on the brink of madness or deep depression.
GARY LINEKER on why he went into the media rather than management, 1999

My wife says: 'If you're going to get ill, get wet pyjamas in the night, then pack it in.'
DAVID PLEAT, Sheffield Wednesday manager, 1997

There are grounds where you know you'll get covered in spittle and you wear your old clothes.
DAVE BASSETT, Sheffield United manager, after Wolves' Graham Taylor was abused at Bramall Lane, 1995

Losing is like experiencing a death in the family. For a while there is no comfort in anything.
JOHN GREGORY, Aston Villa manager, 1999

I always enjoy the summer. You can't lose any matches.
ROY EVANS, Liverpool manager, 1997

It's like being in the middle of an oven.
BOB PEARSON, Millwall manager, after stepping from the post of chief scout into a long run of defeats, 1990

It was like being in the dentist's chair for six hours.

HOWARD WILKINSON, Leeds manager, after a tense match v Leicester, 1990

I feel raped.
RAY GRAYDON, Walsall manager, after a 4–1 defeat by Crewe, 1999

No one, unless they manage a team, can know how I feel. No one, not an assistant manager, a player, anyone. They haven't a clue.
GORDON STRACHAN, Coventry manager, after a home defeat v Middlesbrough, 2000

The world looks a totally different place after you've won. I can even enjoy watching Blind Date.
STRACHAN at Coventry, 1996

If you're obsessed with winning and you don't do it, you end up a lunatic.
STRACHAN at Coventry, 1998

When you win you feel 25 years old. When you lose you feel more like 105.
GORDON LEE, Leicester manager, after a 5–2 defeat v Swindon, 1991

You wait a lifetime for a feeling like tonight.
ALEX FERGUSON after Manchester United's first title success in 26 years, 1993

It's the best day since I got married.
FERGUSON after winning at Sheffield United, 1992

I think my team are trying to kill me.

JOE ROYLE, Oldham manager, after a successful fight to stay in the Premiership, 1993

If it meant getting three points on Saturday I would shoot my grandmother. Not nastily. I would just hurt her.
BRIAN CLOUGH at the foot of the Premier League with Nottingham Forest, 1992

If I became a manager the first thing I'd do is buy a bottle of Grecian 2000.
CHRIS WADDLE, former England player, 1997

Welcome to the Grey Hair Club.
KEVIN KEEGAN in a message to John Aldridge when he became player-manager of Tranmere, 1996

The plan is to get out of management while I've still got all my marbles and all my hair.
JOE ROYLE, Manchester City manager, 2000

We really go through it on the bench. When we were 2–1 up and Cambridge got a couple of late corners, the others were all laughing at me because I was curled up in a ball in the corner of the dug-out saying: 'I hate this job.'
BRIAN LITTLE, Leicester manager, 1993

I love football but I positively hate being a manager.
LOU MACARI, West Ham manager, 1989

If you don't get uptight, you're either a saint or you don't care. And there aren't many who don't care.
DON HOWE, England coach, before suffering a heart attack, 1988

I loved everything about the job – even the chants of 'Sit down Pinocchio.'
PHIL THOMPSON, former assistant manager to Gerard Houllier at Liverpool, 2004

How can anybody call this work? People in the game don't realise how lucky they are. You drive to the ground, play a few five-a-sides, then have lunch. It's wonderful, enjoyable fun.
RON ATKINSON, Aston Villa manager, 1993

No crowd, no money – sometimes I ask myself why I do the job.
JOE KINNEAR, Wimbledon manager, 1997

It's getting to the point where I'm ready to swear.
RAY GRAYDON, Walsall manager, after defeat at Charlton, 1999

I'm convinced a big-name manager will actually top himself soon.
PROFESSOR TOM CANNON, stress expert, 1997

I was there the night Jock [Stein] died in Cardiff, and I know where Bobby [Robson] is coming from, but I want to go when I'm in bed with my beautiful young wife.
GRAEME SOUNESS, Blackburn manager, after Robson talked of the possibility of a manager dying from stress, 2001

It doesn't matter whether you're successful, moderate and hopeless, whether it's Peterborough United and Manchester United, the pressure follows you around like a monkey on your back.
BARRY FRY, Peterborough manager, 1999

You are under pressure in war zones, not in football.
ARTHUR COX, Derby manager, 1993

The biggest pressure is to have no pressure.

ARSENE WENGER, Arsenal manager, 2006

Stress is when you have no money and are living on the street, or lying in hospital fighting for your life. Stress is being bottom of the league. This is pure joy.
RUUD GULLIT on life as Chelsea player-manager, 1997

Pressure to me is being homeless or unemployed. This isn't pressure, it's pleasure.
ANDY ROXBURGH, Scotland coach, after losing 17 players from his squad to face Germany, 1993

Pressure goes with the job, whether you're spending £3m or £30,000.
PHIL NEAL, Bolton manager and former Liverpool team-mate of Kenny Dalglish's, 1991

Five grand a week? That's my kind of pressure.
LOU MACARI, Birmingham manager, after Dalglish's shock departure from Liverpool, 1991

I happen to like the aggravation that goes with football management. It seems to suit my needs.
GRAEME SOUNESS on succeeding Dalglish at Anfield, 1991

My cardiologist tells me that for some people, what I do would represent pressure. For others, pressure is going home and sitting in front of *Coronation Street* with your slippers on. I would find that very stressful.
SOUNESS, by now Blackburn manager, 2001

I've learned how to relieve managerial stress. When the ball gets into your last third, avert your eyes. Turn to your physio, ask for chewing gum, have a few words about the match. Anything. It stops the tension building up. You might miss a goal, but someone will always tell you how it happened.
BILLY BINGHAM, Northern Ireland manager, 1992

I close my eyes every time the ball comes near our penalty area.

JOHN TOSHACK, Real Madrid coach, on his erratic goalkeeper Albano Bizzarri, 1999

You want to try sitting in the dug-out when it's your arse in the bacon-slicer.
MICK McCARTHY, Republic of Ireland manager, on being told by a reporter that he 'looked tense' during a World Cup game v Saudi Arabia, 2002

Some do it by smoking hash, others by making love or racing a rally car. We managers experience extremes all the time. You can find yourself at the highest point or the lowest ebb in the same week.
ARSENE WENGER, Arsenal manager, 2002

I can feel when I'm ready to lose it. Then I get my things and go home. I read a book for an hour or watch TV and come back a different man. It's what I call experience.
WENGER, 2002

I always thought managers were more involved. But when it comes down to it, I just sit there and watch like everyone else.
KEVIN KEEGAN in his early days at Newcastle, 1993

We've lost seven games 1–0 and drawn another seven 0–0. If we'd drawn the 1–0 games we lost, we'd have another seven points. If the seven draws had been 1–0 to us, we'd have 28 points more and we'd be third in the Premiership instead of going down.
ALAN SMITH, Crystal Palace manager, wrestling with arithmetic while sliding towards relegation, 1995

As I mulled it over on the bus, reliving every kick, I could hear the players laughing and playing cards. They soon forget, but it's a seven-day punishment for managers.
ANDY KING, Mansfield manager, 1994

As manager, it's your head on the block. You have to make cold-blooded decisions and if you can't, you shouldn't be in the job. To be honest, I found it difficult to be a bastard.
TERRY BUTCHER, former Coventry and Sunderland manager, 1994

I've heard it said that you can't be a football manager and tell the truth. Well, I'm going to have a go at it.
LIAM BRADY, newly appointed Celtic manager, 1991

When I was appointed manager of Stoke, the first phone call I received was from Joe Mercer, then with Aston Villa, offering congratulations. He told me: 'My advice is never to trust anyone in the game, and when I put down the phone don't trust me either.'
TONY WADDINGTON, former Stoke manager, 1990

Lots of times managers have to be cheats and conmen. We are the biggest hypocrites. We cheat. The only way to survive is by cheating.
TOMMY DOCHERTY, manager of numerous clubs, 1979

There are two types of people who succeed in coaching: the conman and confidence trickster, or the intelligent man who builds your confidence and belief. I'm the conman.
MALCOLM ALLISON on becoming chief coach to Bristol Rovers aged 65, 1992

You hope and you pretend that you know what you're doing.

KEVIN KEEGAN, newly appointed Newcastle manager, 1992

The buying and selling of players sounds rather like a slave market. Moreover, the payment of large transfer fees can be the refuge of the incompetent manager.
SIR NORMAN CHESTER, chairman of committee examining English football's problems, 1968

The power managers, like Brian Clough, Alex Ferguson and, up to a point, myself are beginning to drift out of the game. Alex can take negotiations about 85 per cent of the way, but there are very few like him. Things have changed.
GEORGE GRAHAM, Tottenham manager, 2000

There are no bungs in football. With my so-called reputation, I would be the one they approached. I deal with most managers, most clubs and I've never been asked for or offered a bung. Fact.
ERIC HALL, players' agent, 1995

When Leeds sacked me, all my worries about pensions and bringing up three kids were gone, and I became a better manager.
BRIAN CLOUGH on his £90,000 'golden handshake' from Leeds 16 years earlier, 1990

When [the sack] arrives, I won't cry. I will enjoy my family, then the next week, or month, I'll get another club. Remember, the richest managers are those that are sacked the most.
JOSE MOURINHO, Chelsea manager, 2004

You've never really been a manager until you've been sacked.
BRIAN HORTON on replacing Peter Reid as manager of Manchester City, 1993

There are only two certainties in this life. People die and football managers get the sack.
EOIN HAND, Limerick and Republic of Ireland manager, 1980

There's only two types of manager. Those who have been sacked and those who will be sacked in the future.

HOWARD WILKINSON, Leeds manager, 1995

Every manager gets sacked, but it's better to be sacked by Real Madrid than any other club.
JOHN TOSHACK, on becoming Real's coach for a second (short-lived) spell, 1999

Ninety-nine per cent of managers that lose their jobs deserve it.

MARK McGHEE, Wolves manager, 1996

I told the chairman that if he ever wants to sack me, all he has to do is take me into town, buy me a meal, a few pints and a cigar, and I'll piss off.
MICK McCARTHY, Millwall manager, 1995

The manager picks the team but invariably it's the punters who pick the manager.
ALAN BALL alleging a 'get-rid-of-the-manager' syndrome after leaving Manchester City, 1996

Managers are like fish. After a while, they start to smell.
GIOVANNI TRAPATTONI, Fiorentina coach, confirming his departure, 2000

A manager can smell the end of his time. The whole club reeks of an imminent sacking. Not that they actually say: 'You're bloody fired!' It's all innuendo and muttering – 'Things aren't going well, are they?' But you know they're after your blood, and if truth were told you've already had your bag packed for weeks.
ROY SPROSON, former Port Vale manager, 1988

I stood up and was counted.

ROGER HYND on being sacked as Motherwell manager, 1978

How ironic that I should have been sacked on the anniversary of the Coventry blitz. When the chairman phoned me, I felt like my house had been bombed.
JOHN SILLETT on his dismissal by Coventry, 1991

King Louis XVI had his head cut off in the French Revolution. It's the same for managers.
JEAN TIGANA, Fulham manager, pondering possible dismissal during a long run without a win, 2002

You just have to wait for someone to suffer the same misfortune as you. It's the only job where you can study the vacancies on Teletext as they happen.
GRAHAM TURNER, Hereford United manager, 1995

When the TV people asked whether I'd play a football manager in a play, I asked how long it would take. They told me 'about 10 days', and I said: 'That's about par for the course.'
TOMMY DOCHERTY, 1989

It's me in the electric chair now.
BOBBY COLLINS on succeeding Norman Hunter as Barnsley manager, 1984

I had to go. Towards the end I felt like a turkey waiting for Christmas.
FRANK CLARK, after leaving the Nottingham Forest manager's job, 1996

Remember that film A Bridge Too Far? Well, I probably came a game too far.
GERRY FRANCIS leaving the QPR manager's job after a 5–0 defeat by Wimbledon, 2001

Football is about now, it's about your contract... We're in the age of instant solutions and the job of being manager is set in that context. You could argue, given the demands today, that you don't want to be at a club more than three years.
HOWARD WILKINSON, former Leeds manager, 1999

You have to be a masochist to be an international manager.
ARSENE WENGER, 1998

The England job should be the best in the world but it's become a horrible job. To think of my children getting hammered in the school playground because their dad is England manager. Perhaps we should be looking for a guy who's divorced with no kids.
GLENN HODDLE, then Chelsea player-manager, 1994; within two years he was in charge of England

I wouldn't take the England job for a big gold clock.
STEVE COPPELL, former Crystal Palace manager, 1993

The only way I'd be interested in the England job is as player-manager.

RON ATKINSON, Aston Villa manager, 1993

As England manager you know that you're probably the most hated man in the country, apart from the Chancellor [of the Exchequer].
OSSIE ARDILES, Tottenham manager, ruling himself out of the running, 1993

Even the Pope would think twice about taking the England job.
ROY HODGSON, Switzerland manager, 1993

The England manager has to fight the system and fight the press from day one.
HOWARD WILKINSON, Leeds manager, 1993

There's no difference between coaching England and coaching Newbury Town. The reason is that they're all blokes. There are England blokes, Manchester United blokes, Arsenal blokes and Newbury blokes. You are coaching men, human beings.
DON HOWE, who worked with both the England squad and his local Isthmian League part-timers, 1994

I'm the man for the job. I can revive our World Cup hopes. I couldn't do a worse job, could I?
SCREAMING LORD SUTCH, leader of the Monster Raving Loony Party, on why he should succeed Graham Taylor as England manager, 1994

Football managers are treated like the proverbial football. Unfortunately, instead of being passed around, they get a real good kicking.
GRAHAM TAYLOR on leaving Watford (of his own volition), 2001

Managers are treated as public property, as if we do not have feelings or families. People feel we can cope and are impervious to hurt.
MARK McGHEE, Wolves manager, 1997

After a few years, managing in England is like working for the weather forecast office. You know when a storm is coming.
ARSENE WENGER, Arsenal manager, 1999

One person who thinks it is ridiculous that I earn so much money from football is my grandmother. She never understood you get so much from kicking a ball. So every time I go to see her she gives me £5 or £10.
SVEN-GORAN ERIKSSON, England manager, 2002

Just because a coach comes from overseas, it doesn't mean he's a tactical genius.
TONY ADAMS, former England captain, cautioning against expecting too much from Eriksson, World Cup finals, 2002

We get carried away with coaching and coaches. I have my coaching badges but they came out of a cornflakes packet.
HARRY REDKNAPP, West Ham manager, 2001

Coaching is for kids. If a player can't pass and trap the ball by the time he's in the team, he shouldn't be there in the first place. At Derby I told Roy McFarland to go out and get his bloody hair cut. Now that's coaching at the top level.
BRIAN CLOUGH after retiring as Nottingham Forest manager, 1994

Fulham Football Club seek a Manager/ Genius.
NEWSPAPER advert, 1991

Charisma comes from results, and not vice versa.
CRAIG BROWN, Scotland manager, 1996

It would've taken a brave man not to wear brown pants after comparing our team-sheet with theirs.
NEIL WARNOCK, Notts County manager, after playing Arsenal, 1991

I always say I'll get over it when I grow up, but there are no signs of it happening yet. I still find it impossible to drive past any sort of match. I've got to stop and watch it.
CRAIG BROWN, Scotland Under-21 manager, 1988

The greatest thing about being a manager is when you're out on the training pitch with your players. No phones, agents, media or directors, just you and a group of players committed to improving themselves.
GRAHAM TAYLOR, Watford manager, 1999

Great teams don't need managers. Brazil won the World Cup in 1970 playing exhilarating football, with a manager they'd had for three weeks. What influence can a man have who has only been with them that length of time? What about Real Madrid at their greatest? You can't even remember who the manager was.
DANNY BLANCHFLOWER, former Tottenham captain, in his Sunday Express *column, 1972*

The Monday after we won at West Brom in the FA Cup I received 193 calls from assorted media and well-wishers. I even got a call from my first wife's parents, which surprised me seeing as they hadn't bothered to ring in the 15 years since our divorce.
GEOFF CHAPPLE, manager of non-league Woking, 1992

It may sound selfish but I want to dedicate this triumph to my dog, who died two years ago.

CARLOS BIANCHI, Boca Juniors coach, after his team won the Treble in Argentina, 2001

You could have Mickey Mouse in charge of the team on Saturday. You could stick a bucket out there with a mop in it or a snowman with a carrot for a nose. It wouldn't matter because no one needs motivating for a match like this.
IAN ATKINS, Carlisle manager, before the Third Division club's FA Cup tie v Arsenal, 2001

I've come from caviar to fish 'n' chips. At Spurs you can buy daft. At Leicester I have to buy sensibly.
DAVID PLEAT, Leicester manager, 1987

I haven't seen the lad but he comes highly recommended by my greengrocer.
BRIAN CLOUGH on signing Nigel Jemson from Preston, 1988

The easiest team for a manager to pick is the Hindsight XI.
CRAIG BROWN, Scotland manager, 1998

The last manager who led this club to the FA Cup semi-finals [Archie Macauley in 1959] ended up as a traffic warden in Brighton.
DAVE STRINGER, Norwich manager, on reaching the last four, 1989

I'm going to go out and get lambasted on wine.
MARTIN O'NEILL, Leicester manager, after his team won the Coca-Cola Cup, 1997

We will worry about the final later.
Now is the time for wine and
cigarettes!
*KLAUS TOPPMOLLER, Bayer
Leverkusen coach, after his team
reached the Champions League final at
Manchester United's expense, 2002*

Funny how other managers always
want to swap one of their reserves
for your best player.
*MURDO MacLEOD, Partick Thistle
manager, on exchange deals, 1996*

7

THE GAME

[Football is] a kinetic sculpture or abstract light show. Quadrilaterals, round balls and the shifting lines of force and energy made by the players' movements.
A.S. BYATT, novelist, in an article for The Observer, *2008*

Football is an art more central to our culture than anything the Arts Council deigns to recognise.
GERMAINE GREER, feminist academic, journalist and broadcaster, 1996

Football isn't something you plan in advance. Football just happens.
ZLATAN IBRAHIMOVIC, Paris St-Germain and Sweden striker, in his autobiography, 2013

Football is like chess, but without the dice.
LUKAS PODOLSKI, Cologne and Germany striker, 2010

Football's not just physical, it's menthol too.
PHIL BROWN, Southend manager and radio pundit, 2013

Football is like a drug which is difficult to give up.
SIR ALEX FERGUSON, 2008

Football is the most important of the less important things in the world.
CARLO ANCELOTTI, former Milan coach, on why he was not 'angry' at their defeat after leading Liverpool 3-0 in the 2005 Champions League final, 2013

Football takes up all of our time, but it's still a relatively minor subject in terms of world importance.
ROY HODGSON, West Bromwich Albion manager, 2012

Football is not a fair game. It's made up by good things, beautiful things, moments of great skill – and mistakes.
MANUEL PELLEGRINI, Manchester City manager, 2014

Football is a game of mistakes.
JOHAN CRUYFF, former Netherlands captain and Barcelona coach, 2013

Football connects people in a way that's hard to describe. This is its true beauty and power.
BENOIT ASSOU-EKOTTO, Tottenham and Cameroon defender, on the worldwide support for heart-attack victim Fabrice Muamba, 2012

Football's not a sport populated by honest people. It's a business and no one is friends.
FERNANDO TORRES, Spain striker, after his £50m transfer from Liverpool to Chelsea, 2011

Football is a sport which has become so commercial. It may be thought by some to have lost its way.
LORD JUSTICE LEONARD summing up after the trial of Tottenham manager Harry Redknapp on tax-evasion charges, 2012

Football has to work hard to put a smile on people's faces and not just be so focused on money.
GORDON TAYLOR, chief executive of the Professional Footballers' Association, 2013

Football has a social responsibility for bringing people together in a world where there are tensions, whether economic, racial, religious, political.
TAYLOR, as above

Football sometimes appears to cocoon itself from the real world.
TOM FLANAGAN, head of employment law at the law firm Irwin Mitchell, after the John Terry trial, 2012

Football is so uncool. When I was growing up it was dangerous and it wasn't corporate.
NICK HORNBY, author, screenwriter and Arsenal obsessive, on the 'Nike-isation' of the game, 2009

Football's a difficult business and aren't the players prima donnas? They fall down and roll around.
QUEEN ELIZABETH II while knighting Premier League chairman David Richards, 2006

Football is nothing compared to life. For me, pressure is bird flu.
JOSE MOURINHO, Chelsea manager, 2006

Football is like the world. It's a bit crazy.

MOURINHO, 2007

Football is never drama. Football is always passion and pleasure.
MOURINHO, Inter Milan coach, 2009

Football is important, but life is important too.
MAXIME BOSSIS, France player, after defeat by West Germany, World Cup semi-final, 1986

Football is like Hollywood – never stand on anyone on the way up because you're going to have to wave at them on the way back down.
CLARKE CARLISLE, Burnley defender, 2010

Football at a professional level is an interval between real life and real life.
TONY AGANA, Sheffield United striker, 1990

Football is like a beast. It can overtake your whole life so you forget who you are and who your family are.
IAN HOLLOWAY, Plymouth Argyle manager, 2007

Football has a habit of destroying your confidence in human beings.
KEVIN BLACKWELL, Luton manager, reflecting on his sacking by Leeds, 2007

Football is the one international language.
NANCY DELL'OLIO, Sven-Goran Eriksson's partner, 2003

Football is a game – the language it don't matter as long as you run your bollocks off.
DANNY BERGARA, Stockport's Uruguayan-born, Spanish-speaking manager, 1991

Football is a bitch goddess.
BILL KENWRIGHT, Everton chairman, 2005

Football. Bloody hell.

ALEX FERGUSON to TV interviewer moments after Manchester United had won the European Cup with two last-gasp goals v Bayern Munich, 1999

Football is about what happens in the two penalty areas. Everything else is propaganda.
GORDON STRACHAN, Southampton manager, 2003

Football is an excuse to feel good about something.
JORGE VALDANO, sporting director of Real Madrid, 2003

Football is a great healer.
RIO FERDINAND, England defender, after a strike by England players was averted and they drew with Turkey to qualify for the European Championship finals, 2003

Football is loved by everyone, everywhere, because it has no definitive truth.
MICHEL PLATINI, former France captain and manager, 1998

Football is a battle, a small war. You can't expect 22 players to behave like Sunday-school boys. You have to remember they are human.
SVEN-GORAN ERIKSSON, England manager, 2002

Football became popular because it was considered an art, but now too many pitches are becoming battlefields.
SOCRATES, Brazil captain, 1981

Football is war and I have to kill and not be killed.
LUIZ FELIPE SCOLARI, Brazilian coach of Portugal, 2006

Football's like war. When the chips are down, you need fighters.
IAN BRANFOOT, Southampton manager, 1991

Football doesn't matter a damn. It used to be a game, now it's a war.
ANTHONY BEAUMONT-DARK MP, Conservative, 1991

Football is war without bloodshed.

SHIMON PERES, Prime Minister of Israel, 2005

Football is not just a simple game. It is also a weapon of the revolution.
CHE GUEVARA, Argentinian revolutionary, 1960s

Football is the biggest thing that's happened in creation, bigger than any 'ism' you can name.
ALAN BROWN, Sunderland manager, 1968

Football turns stupid people into thugs and bright people into bores.
CHARLES SPENCER, Daily Telegraph theatre critic, 2003

Football is ball, pitch, opponent and mentality, that's football.
GIOVANNI TRAPATTONI, Italian manager of the Republic of Ireland, 2010

Football is concrete. We are not a theatre, La Scala or Madison Square Garden – it's football.
TRAPATTONI, as above

Football is a damn sight more important than arty-farty people pushing themselves around the Royal Opera House.
TERRY DICKS MP, Conservative, 1990

Football is the opera of the people.
STAFFORD HEGINBOTHAM, Bradford City chairman, 1985

Football as popular culture is a space of intertextuality.
RICHARD HAYNES, author, The Football Imagination: The Rise of Fanzine Culture, *1996*

Football is not family entertainment.
CILLA BLACK, TV presenter, after ITV replaced her Blind Date *show with* The Premiership, *2001*

Football is a game and people have to be cunning.
RIVALDO, Brazil midfielder, after admitting he feigned injury to get an opponent sent off in a World Cup match v Turkey, 2002

Football's a rat race and the rats are winning.
TOMMY DOCHERTY, 1982

Football is a much more cynical game all round than cricket.
PHIL NEALE, Lincoln defender and Worcestershire cricketer, 1982

Football is self-expression within an organised framework.
ROGER LEMERRE, France coach, 1999

Football is a fertility festival. Eleven sperm trying to get into the egg. I feel sorry for the goalkeeper.
BJORK, Icelandic singer, 1995

Football is a permanent orgasm.
CLAUDE LE ROY, Cameroon coach, 1998

Football is only for healthy people.
VLATKO MARKOVIC, Croatia FA president, on why he was against having a gay player in the national team, 2010

Football is a pantomime of pain and disappointment.

NICK HANCOCK, Stoke City supporter and TV celebrity, 1999

Football and cookery are the two most important subjects in the country.
DELIA SMITH, television chef, after becoming a Norwich City director, 1997

Football has become the religion of the 20th century... Its fervour, enthusiasm, battle cries, violence and flags have replaced the wars of yesteryear.
EDITORIAL in the French newspaper Le Figaro – by its literary critic, 1998

Football is like a flower. When you attack, the flower is open and in bloom. Defend and the flower closes.
TOMMY SODERBERG, Sweden coach, 2000

Football's like dope. You try to take a few months away, but it keeps pulling you back.
LEO BEENHAKKER, Dutch coach of Trinidad & Tobago, 2006

Football is a state of mind and when the mind is healthy, the performances follow.
RONALDINHO, Brazil and Barcelona striker, 2004

Football is a simple game made complicated by people who should know better.
BILL SHANKLY, Liverpool manager, 1968

What would we do without football, for God's sake?

SIR BOBBY CHARLTON, 2006

Football is a simple game. The hard part is making it look simple.
RON GREENWOOD, England manager, 1978

Football is a beautiful box of surprises, and the reason is that the ball is round. The day they make the ball square, the Germans or Japanese will dominate everything because they're good at maths.
TONINHO CEREZO, former Brazil player, 2004

Football is not mathematics. In this game two plus two almost never makes four. Sometimes it's three, other times five.
LEO BEENHAKKER, Dutch coach of Trinidad & Tobago, 2006

Footballers are the modern-day gladiators.
GIORGIO ARMANI on being named official couturier to the England team, 2003

There is absolutely no question that the world turns around a spinning ball.
EDUARDO GALEANO, Uruguayan poet, journalist and football fan, 1995

The beauty of football is that win, lose or draw, you can't relax.
ROY KEANE, Sunderland manager, 2007

We wrote the governance of the game. We wrote the rules, designed the pitches and everything else. Fifty years later some guy came along and said you're liars and they actually stole it. It was called FIFA. Fifty years later, another gang came along, called UEFA, and stole a bit more.
DAVE RICHARDS, chairman of the Premier League and FA board member, 2012; he later called the remarks 'light-hearted'

We've been brainwashed by this Premier League, that it's the best league in the world. Nonsense. It's the best brand, but we've seen with the English teams struggling [in the Champions League] that these teams are falling behind the top teams in Europe.
ROY KEANE, ITV analyst, 2014

The Champions League is the crème de la crème. This is where the trend is made, in the Champions League. The way they play this year in the Champions League, you will see it in the World Cup in the summer. The systems, the approaches: it is the best of the best.
JURGEN KLINSMANN, United States coach and former Germany striker, 2014

It's the entertainment industry, for heaven's sake, not life or death.

MATT LE TISSIER after retiring as a Southampton player, on the 'strain' of playing for 'heavy-handed' managers, 2002

Football has gone global. If you'd told me 30 years ago that Brazilians would be playing in Moscow, I'd have said you were crazy. Now it's the reality.
FRANZ BECKENBAUER, former West Germany captain and coach, 2007

Football is fashionable. Political parties jockey to enlist football men to their cause; celebrities and glamorous women speak openly about their love for football; and literary critics pepper their erudition with references to 'the beautiful game'.
JOHN WILLIAMS, lecturer at the Sir Norman Chester Institute for Football Research, Leicester University, 1998

The story of rugby and football is the story of two nations – not of rich and poor, or privileged or unprivileged, but of two approaches to life. Rugby represents much of what is best about our society, football much of what is worst.
EDITORIAL in the Daily Mail after England won rugby union's World Cup, 2003

We invented the game and let everybody play it and we haven't seen a penny in royalties. It makes you sick.
JOHN CLEESE, comic actor and member of Monty Python, 2006

Football is bankrupt without the TV deals. If the banks ever withdrew, you would see a bigger collapse than Black Monday.
SIR JOHN HALL, Newcastle chairman, 1995

Premier League football is a multi-million-pound industry with the aroma of a blocked toilet and the principles of a knocking shop.
MICHAEL PARKINSON, Daily Telegraph column, 2003

The reason the transfer market exists is to provide a means of shifting dodgy money around a bent game.
PARKINSON, 2003

The riskiest thing you can do in football is not take any risks.
PEP GUARDIOLA, Barcelona coach, 2010

The football Spain and Barcelona play is not a science, and it's not the only kind of football there is. Counter-attacking football, for instance, has just as much merit. Different styles make this such a wonderful sport.
ANDRES INIESTA, Barca and Spain midfielder, 2012

To be attacking, to try to take control of the game, to take responsibility, to be attractive. There are small differences, of course, depending on what players you have, but there is a footballing concept and a concept of spectacle that is non-negotiable.
MANUEL PELLEGRINI, Chilean coach of the Spanish club Malaga, 2011

English football must change. We do not know how to play football. We just boot the ball up the pitch and it gets us nowhere. We don't

have the kids coached the same way – the right way – from a young age. As a result we have a senior team that's greatly under-achieving. Look at the so-called 'golden generation' of Gerrard, Lampard, Terry, Rooney and Ashley Cole. Man for man, there wasn't a country on Earth that could match that on paper. But together they never produced because we just hoofed the ball forwards and hoped for the best. In international football, you can't just hit and hope because you give the ball away. It's all about possession, retaining the ball, controlling the game.
HARRY REDKNAPP, Queens Park Rangers manager, 2013

In English football you are called Prof if you have two GCSEs. No wonder we are outwitted on the pitch.

BORIS JOHNSON MP, Conservative, 2007

Here in Scotland, you have football, you have the pubs, the church and after that comes the family. First is football.
CSABA LASZLO, Hungarian manager of Hearts, 2010

The great fallacy is that the game is first and foremost about winning. It's nothing of the kind. The game is about glory. It's about doing things in style, with a flourish, about going out and beating the other lot, not waiting for them to die of boredom.
DANNY BLANCHFLOWER, former Tottenham captain, in Hunter Davies's book The Glory Game, *1972*

See the boy Rudyard Kipling, who said it wasn't whether you won or lost but how you played the game that mattered, well, he obviously never played football. Winning is the only thing that matters.
ANDY GORAM, Rangers and Scotland goalkeeper, confusing Kipling with American writer Grantland Rice, 1996

Playing is the biggest thing there is. It's such a great life. I would urge anyone to cherish every moment. Life is better now, but in a different way. I have more time with my family. There's not as much travelling. But nothing can replicate the thrill of making a great save at an away ground, or hearing your own fans cheering you, or the atmosphere when you score or win a big game.
EDWIN VAN DER SAR, former Manchester United and Netherlands goalkeeper, on retirement, 2012

Winning all the time is not necessarily good for the team.
JOHN TOSHACK, Real Madrid coach, 1999

The fair play gave me goose pimples. Everyone respected each other. It was beautiful.
SEPP BLATTER, FIFA general secretary, after West Germany v England, World Cup semi-final, 1990

It takes time for a player to understand that, in [Liverpool's] way of working, the most courageous players are the ones who take the ball 20 yards from their own goal – not the guys at the top end of the field.
BRENDAN RODGERS, Liverpool manager, 2013

When you've got the ball 65 to 70 per cent of the time, it's a football death for the other team. We're not at that stage yet, but that's what we will get to. It's death by football. You just suck the life out of them.
RODGERS, 2012

My template for everything is organisation. With the ball you have to know the movement patterns, the rotation, the fluidity and positioning of the team. When we have the football everybody's a player. If you are better than your opponent with the ball you have a 79 per cent chance of winning the game.
RODGERS, as above

I saw Arsenal v Spurs. The pace of the game was incredible. An hour later I watched a Dutch game, and there is no point. It was so slow. A lot of things are happening in English football – openings, the high pace – and that is beauty too.
DENNIS BERGKAMP, Ajax assistant manager and ex-Arsenal and Netherlands striker, 2013

It's true that foreigners brought the culture [of diving] to England. It doesn't make me feel bad because I was always against it. I always fight against it. It's not just a European problem – it happens elsewhere in the world.
JOSE MOURINHO, Chelsea manager, 2014

Everything is beautiful in English football. The stadiums are beautiful, the atmosphere beautiful, the cops on horseback beautiful. And the crowds respect you.
ERIC CANTONA on making an early impact at Leeds, 1992

The most beautiful game is winning matches.
GLENN HODDLE, Chelsea manager, 1995

I would rather play ugly football and win than play beautifully and lose.
MARIO ZAGALLO, Brazil coach, 1997

I told them I'd like them to win ugly and they certainly won ugly

today. That was the ugliest thing I've seen since the ugly sisters fell out of the ugly tree.
TERRY BUTCHER, Motherwell manager, 2005

The worst thing you can do as a professional footballer is to be in the hotel after the game with a coffee or a beer and to realise you could have done more.
DANI ALVES, Barcelona and Brazil defender, on losing, 2012

What other way would you approach a game? Must-lose? Must-draw?

ROY KEANE, Sunderland manager, 2008

People complain about the results-first culture, but there's no way you can beat your opponent by playing worse than them.
ARRIGO SACCHI, former AC Milan and Real Madrid coach, 2012

Thank you for letting me play in your beautiful football.
ERIC CANTONA accepting the PFA Player of the Year award, 1994

It was beautifully done. It was wrong but it was necessary.
JACK CHARLTON, former England defender, commenting as a TV pundit on a 'professional foul' in a Barcelona v Dusseldorf game, 1979

When you're winning, you want to be playing every day. When you've had bad results, you start to feel tired.
GRAEME SOUNESS, Blackburn manager, 2002

The one thing you can guarantee in football is disappointment. If you expect it, it's not so hard to take when it comes along.
SOUNESS, 2004

You feel so good, so comfortable, so powerful when you win. If you don't win, it's terrible.
MARCEL DESAILLY, Chelsea and France defender, 2000

It's the greatest game in the world. It is also the most frustrating, exasperating, infuriating, desolating game. But there is nothing else.
KEN BATES, Chelsea chairman, 1995

In football you can be close to being in hell then rise to heaven just like that.
JENS LEHMANN, Arsenal goalkeeper, after his penalty save at Villarreal put his team in the Champions League final, 2006

There is a God up there. I love Margaret Thatcher, Ken Livingstone and everybody. It's not Rwanda, it's not Bosnia and it's not Ethiopia. It's crazy, it's wonderful. It's football.
MICHAEL KNIGHTON, Carlisle chairman, after his club avoided relegation from the league on the season's final day, 2000

Great players are always the same. If you ring them and ask them to play a game with friends, will they say yes? If they love the game, they'll play, even if they're on holiday.
ARSENE WENGER, 2003

What the fuck is art? A picture of a bottle of sour milk lying next to a smelly old jumper? What the fuck is that all about? And look at opera. To me it's a load of shit. But people love it. I'd say football is art. When I watched France v Holland at Euro 2000, I was orgasmic.
JOHN GREGORY, Aston Villa manager, in Loaded interview, 2000

We've all heard that Einstein is a genius but few of us are in a position to judge. Football is one of the few areas of life where, even if you're untutored, you can go to a ground, see George Best beat three men and you can realise: 'I have seen a genius.'
SIMON KUPER, writer on world football, 1999

No player, manager, director or fan who understands football, either through his intellect or his nerve-ends, ever repeats that piece of nonsense: 'After all, it's only a game.' It has not been a game for 80 years; not since the working-classes saw in it an escape route out of drudgery and claimed it as their own.
ARTHUR HOPCRAFT, author, The Football Man, *1968*

Even if George Orwell's Big Brother is ruling us in 1984, people will still be talking about football.
NEIL FRANKLIN, Stoke and England defender, in Soccer at Home and Abroad, *1956*

Football in Britain could not be in a sorrier state. Sport is dying. The future lies in culture, spirituality and religion.
ROBERT MAXWELL, millionaire publisher and chairman of various clubs, 1990

People are always kicking, old or young. Even an unborn child is kicking.

SEPP BLATTER, general secretary of football's world-governing body, FIFA, 1990

Twenty-two grown men chasing a piece of leather round a field.
BERNARD LEVIN, English journalist, describing English football in the New York Times *after the Hillsborough disaster, 1989*

I jolly well hoped that they would keep hold of me so I would never have to hear about the blasted game again.
TERRY WAITE, former hostage in Lebanon, on his dislike of football, 1999

The culture of the 1990s can be summed up by *Neighbours* and football.

SPIKE MILLIGAN, comedian, 1999

Sport is an unfailing cause of ill will, and if the visit of Moscow Dynamo had any effect at all on Anglo-Soviet relations, it could only be to make them worse.
GEORGE ORWELL, in the socialist Tribune *newspaper, 1945*

If this is what soccer is to become, let it die.
EDITORIAL in L'Equipe, *French sports paper, after 39 spectators died following trouble at the European Cup final, 1985*

If somebody is celebrating it means we still have much to learn.
GIORGIO CARDETTI, Mayor of Turin, after Juventus beat Liverpool in the European Cup final, 1985

All that I know most surely about morality and the obligations of man, I owe to football.
ALBERT CAMUS, French philosopher, novelist and goalkeeper for Oran of Algeria, 1957

I believe that sport is on the highest possible plane…as something above real life.
DAVE SEXTON, Manchester United manager, 1980

There were plenty of fellas [in the 1950s] who would kick your bollocks off. The difference between then and now is that they would shake your hand at the end and help you look for them.
NAT LOFTHOUSE, former Bolton and England centre-forward, 1986

I'm so old I can even remember the days when tackling was allowed in this sport.

PETER REID, Leeds manager, 2003

I would kick my own brother if necessary. That's what being a professional is all about.
STEVE McMAHON, Liverpool and England midfielder, 1988

It's the first time that we've had to replace divots in the players.
RON ATKINSON, Manchester United manager, after a European match against a rugged Valencia side, 1982

Nobody ever won a tackle with a smile on his face.
BRUCE RIOCH, Bolton manager, 1994

Men like me were never a danger anyway. It wasn't that we were desperately late, just a little slower in getting there.
CHRIS KAMARA, Sun columnist and former midfield hard man, 1999

In open play I don't think I would use gamesmanship, but if someone went through with just the goalkeeper to beat and I could catch him by bringing him down, I would bring him down. If I didn't, I'd feel I'd let my team-mates and my fans down.
BRYAN ROBSON, Manchester United and England captain, in David Hemery, The Pursuit of Sporting Excellence, 1986

Football is made for cunning people. It's not true that you are disloyal to the sport if you feign injury or tug a shirt or do something else to win the game, which is the purpose of football. Cheating the referee is not a sin if it helps your team to win. I play against cheating forwards every week.
PAOLO MONTERO, Juventus and Uruguay defender, 2003

Sometimes you feel that someone is tugging your shirt and you take a quick look at where the linesman is and then you hit the opponent on the hands or in the stomach. Sometimes you get in front of the defender and pull his shorts. If you get hold of 'the package', you pull a bit harder.
HENRIK LARSSON, Celtic and Sweden striker, 2004

I've played my last match, scored my last goal and elbowed my last opponent.
MARTIN DAHLIN, Swedish international striker, announcing his retirement, 1999

When I called my midfield the 'Dogs of War', it was done half-jokingly. But the game has changed: the playmaker who stands on the ball and sprays it everywhere after

five pints and a cigar in the pub simply doesn't exist any more.
JOE ROYLE, Everton manager, 1995

At Liverpool you'd read an interview in the programme with a lad from the youth team. They'd ask: age, heroes, strong points, etc. He'd reply: 'Shooting and tackling'. I can't get into my head that football development would educate tackling as a quality, something to learn, to teach, a characteristic of your play. How can that be a way of seeing the game? Tackling is a [last] resort, and you will need it, but it isn't a quality to aspire to.
XABI ALONSO, Real Madrid, Spain and former Liverpool midfielder, 2011

Brazil don't expect Zico to tackle back. It might be worth England taking a chance on a midfield player whose principal asset is not his lungs.
PETER SHREEVES, Tottenham coach, in defence of Glenn Hoddle, 1982

Tackling is better than sex.
PAUL INCE, England midfielder, 1998

The only thing I miss about football is that feeling you get in the 10 seconds after you've scored, when you completely lose your head. I wouldn't say it's better than sex, but it's a close call.
LEE CHAPMAN, former striker with 10 clubs, 1999

[Ruud] Van Nistelrooy told me that goals are like ketchup. Sometimes, as much as you try, they don't come out and then they come all of a sudden.
GONZALO HIGUAIN, Real Madrid and Argentina striker, 2010

For me, the ball is a diamond. If you have something that precious you don't get rid of it, you offer it.
GLENN HODDLE on signing for Monaco, 1988

People keep on about stars and flair. As far as I'm concerned you find stars in the sky and flair at the bottom of your trousers.
GORDON LEE, Everton manager, 1974

His problem was that they kept passing the ball to his wrong feet.

LEN SHACKLETON, former England player, recalling an unidentified team-mate, 1955

It took me 16 years to realise that football is a passing game and not a dribbling game.
JIMMY HILL, television presenter and ex-Fulham forward, 1974

[Sven-Goran] Eriksson goes on about pace but nothing and nobody can run faster than the ball.
LUIZ FELIPE SCOLARI, Brazil coach, after his team beat England, World Cup finals, 2002

Our game is being crippled by the lawmakers. Those out-of-touch people who think players should not be allowed to tackle or talk for the period of 90 minutes.
IAN WRIGHT, former England striker, after a weekend of 15 red cards in the English league, 1999

I start from the principle that the more you shout at each other [during a match], the better you play.
FABIEN BARTHEZ, Monaco and France goalkeeper, 2000

Attack and be damned.
DAVID PLEAT, Luton manager, 1982

All-out attack mixed with caution.
JIM McLAUGHLIN, Shamrock Rovers manager, on his tactics for a European Cup game, 1985

There's no rule to say a game can't finish 9–9.
GRAHAM TAYLOR, Watford manager, after 7–3 defeat at Nottingham Forest, 1982

It only takes a second to score a goal.
BRIAN CLOUGH, Nottingham Forest manager, 1984

If you're in the penalty area and you're not sure what to do, stick it in the net and we can discuss the options afterwards.
BILL SHANKLY, Liverpool manager, 1960s

If ye dinnae score, ye dinnae win.
JIMMY SIRREL, Notts County manager, 1983

The best team always wins. The rest is only gossip.
SIRREL, 1985

Strikers are very much like postmen. They have to get in and get out as quick as they can before the dog starts to have a go.
IAN HOLLOWAY, Queens Park Rangers manager, 2005

Strikers win you games, but defenders win you championships.
JOHN GREGORY, Aston Villa manager, 1998

The secret of winning championships? Good players working hard.
GEORGE GRAHAM after managing Arsenal to the title, 1991

In England the captaincy is of massive importance. But who

is captain and leader shouldn't guarantee you a place in any team.
ARSENE WENGER, Arsenal manager, 2013

If you don't start belting that ball out of our penalty area, I'll get some big ignorant lad who can do the job better.
BRIAN CLOUGH to defenders Colin Todd, Roy McFarland and David Nish after Birmingham v Derby game, 1973

No footballer of talent should play in the back four.
MALCOLM ALLISON, manager with various clubs, 1975

It's a lot easier to rip the picture up than to paint it. I've spent my career ripping the picture up. I can kick the ball high into the stand and people say: 'Oh, great defending.'
RICHARD GOUGH, Everton captain, 1999

A goalkeeper is a goalkeeper because he can't play football.
RUUD GULLIT, 1997

I'm looking for a goalkeeper with three legs.

BOBBY ROBSON after Newcastle goalkeeper Shay Given was twice nutmegged by Marcus Bent of Ipswich, 2002

I'd be the ruination of the game if I got my way. All I want to see is goalies keeping clean sheets. And that's not what the fans want, is it?
ALAN HODGKINSON, former England keeper and Scotland goalkeeping coach, 1996

The goalkeeper is the jewel in the crown and getting at him should be almost impossible. The biggest sin in football is to make him do any work.
GEORGE GRAHAM, Leeds manager, 1997

The penalty is the one thing goalkeepers don't fear, because they can't lose. If it is scored, no one blames him. If he saves it, he's a hero.
DAVE SEXTON, Queens Park Rangers manager, on the Wim Wenders film The Goalkeeper's Fear of the Penalty, *1975*

A penalty is a cowardly way to score.
PELE, whose 1,000th goal came from the penalty spot, 1966

I know only one way to take penalties: to score them.
ERIC CANTONA in La Philosophie de Cantona, *1995*

I asked the players who wanted to take a penalty and there was an awful smell coming from some of them.
MICK McCARTHY, Millwall manager, after victory in a shoot-out, 1995

It is not possible to play football with your pants full.
ERNST DOKUPIL, Rapid Vienna coach, after defeat by Manchester United, 1996

Any player not inspired by that atmosphere should go off and play golf with his grandmother.
CLEMENS WESTERHOF, Nigeria coach, in Boston during the World Cup finals, 1994

Angels don't win you anything except a place in heaven. Football teams need one or two vagabonds.
BILLY McNEILL, Manchester City manager, 1983

If you threaten certain spiv players, you must carry it out and not let them get away with it. A football team only has 11 players. It just needs one bad 'un to affect the rest. In ICI, with thousands and thousands of people, you can afford to carry scoundrels. Not in a football team.
BRIAN CLOUGH, Brighton manager, 1973

It would be great if we could put a load of kennels alongside the training pitch to put the players in afterwards. Luxury kennels, take them out, feed them at 9am, train them at 10, get them back out after lunch and then back in the kennels and keep them there.
DAVID O'LEARY, Aston Villa manager, pondering ways to control errant players, 2004

Players today look after themselves far more than I ever did. I used to do what all young men do when they've got the hormones raging. It was a mental thing. If you can get your head strong, you can achieve anything.
GRAEME SOUNESS, Blackburn manager, 2002

Players are a strange breed. If everything is going smoothly they are happy to take the plaudits and rewards which come with success. But once results start going wrong they look for an excuse or someone to blame.
RON ATKINSON, TV summariser and former manager, 1999

They're squeezing the entertainment out of football now. Footballers with no character and referees behaving like Nazis. Fucking basketball on grass now, innit?
VINNIE JONES, by now a film actor, 1999

You ought to get a bunch of clowns if you just want entertainment.

ALAN DURBAN, Stoke City manager, answering critics of his team's negative display at Arsenal, 1980

Over the past 10 years a myth has grown up that football should in some way strive to be entertaining. Sport is not entertainment. It's an activity for the benefit of the participants. If you run away from that fact, you risk having the wrong pipers calling the tune.
HOWARD WILKINSON, Leeds manager, 1990

The game almost broke the health of a highly intelligent man like Joe Mercer. It cut George Best off at adolescence. It has the power to destroy because it releases unnatural forces. It creates an unreal atmosphere of excitement and it deals in elation and despair and it bestows these emotions at least once a week.
MALCOLM ALLISON, manager, in Colours Of My Life, *1975*

When the Queen came to the Bahamas, I told her – and football is not her favourite pastime – 'Ma'am, you must realise that people live for this game.'
SIR JACK HAYWARD, Bahamas-based owner of Wolves, 1994

Acting is the easiest thing in the world. You just do it and do it until you get it right. It's not like being a footballer, where you ruin everyone's week if you get it wrong.
GARY LINEKER, 1999

I'm sure Sunday-morning players get more pleasure than professionals.
JIMMY PEARCE, Tottenham winger, in Hunter Davies's The Glory Game, *1972*

I love football but I do not like the professional version.
GARETH SOUTHGATE, Middlesbrough and England defender, in Woody and Nord: A Football Friendship, *co-written with Andy Woodman, 2003*

I never say I'm going to play football. It's work.
MIKE ENGLAND, Tottenham and Wales player, in The Glory Game, *1972*

If we train three times a week, that's five or six hours a week out of 168 hours. So if the players can't work hard for those five or six hours, they shouldn't be playing football. It's about being ready to work for what, compared to normal working people, is a very short period.
NIGEL CLOUGH, Derby County manager, 2010

We looked bright all week in training, but the problem with football is that Saturday always comes along.
KEITH BURKINSHAW, Tottenham manager, 1983

I asked the manager for a ball to train with. He couldn't have been more horrified if I'd asked for a transfer. He told me they never used a ball at Barnsley. The theory was that if we didn't see it all week, we'd be hungry for it on Saturday. I told him that come Saturday, I probably wouldn't recognise it.
DANNY BLANCHFLOWER, former Tottenham captain, recalling his first English club, 1961

I am grateful to my father for all the coaching he did not give me.

FERENC PUSKAS, Hungary captain, 1961

Everywhere I go there are coaches. Schoolmasters telling young boys not to do this and that and generally scaring the life out of the poor little devils. Junior clubs playing with sweepers and one and a half men up front, no wingers, four across the middle. They are frightened to death of losing, even at their tender age, and it makes me cry.
ALEC STOCK, former manager with several clubs, in A Little Thing Called Pride, *1982*

I'm uncoachable, it's true. That's because I know more than the stupid coaches.
GIORGIO CHINAGLIA, New York Cosmos striker, 1979

I don't think the average English fan knows much about coaching. I don't believe we are a coaching nation.
DARIO GRADI, Crewe Alexandra manager, 1999

You have to coach the players' minds...get them to understand the need for sacrifice.
ALEX FERGUSON, Manchester United manager, 1999

You just cannot tell star players how they must play and what they must do when they are on the field in an international match. You must let them play their natural game... I have noticed that in recent years these pre-match instructions have become more and more long-winded while the ability of the players has dwindled.
STANLEY MATTHEWS in The Stanley Matthews Story, *1960*

I've given him carte blanche, as Ron Greenwood used to say, though I didn't use that phrase in the dressing room. Told him to go where he likes.
GEOFF HURST, Telford player-manager and former England striker, in Brian James's Journey to Wembley, *1977*

If the tacticians ever reached perfection, the result would be a 0–0 draw, and there would be no one there to see it.
PAT CRERAND, Manchester United and Scotland midfielder, 1970

Some of the jargon is frightening. They talk of 'getting round the back' and sound like burglars. They say, 'You must make more positive runs' or 'You're too negative,' which sounds as if you're filling the team with electricians.
BOB PAISLEY, Liverpool manager, 1980

Another feature of England training is 'mime practice'. As you jog round you go through all the motions without the ball that you do when you have the ball. You trap, pass, volley, head for goal, head clear and weight imaginary passes. All that is missing is the ball.
PHIL NEAL, Liverpool and England defender, in Attack from the Back, *1981*

I'm very keen on a maxim by the American football coach Vince Lombardi: the only place where winning comes before work is in the dictionary.
HOWARD WILKINSON, FA technical director, 2000

My football philosophy is never to overplay it. The best advice I ever heard was from [former Chelsea captain] Ray Wilkins: simplicity is genius.
JOHN TERRY, Chelsea and England defender, 2006

The world's best 11 players wouldn't make a team. You must have blend.
LEN SHACKLETON, former England player, in Clown Prince of Soccer, *1955*

You can't have stars in winning teams – only great players.
LUIZ FELIPE SCOLARI, Portugal and former Brazil coach, 2004

Players don't win trophies. Teams win trophies.

JOSE MOURINHO, Chelsea manager, 2005

Everybody likes each other. It's not like we're all friends, but it's a good team. You can have 11 enemies in a team and still win.
SANDER WESTERVELD, Netherlands goalkeeper, at Euro 2000

Team spirit is an illusion that you glimpse only when you win.
STEVE ARCHIBALD, Barcelona and Scotland striker, 1985

It's amazing what can be achieved when no one minds who gets the credit.
HOWARD WILKINSON, Sheffield Wednesday manager, on the value of teamwork, 1982

Team individualism is what you want. It might sound daft, but there's a lot of sense in it.
DAVID JAMES, England goalkeeper and student of sports psychology, 2004

If I had wanted to be an individual I would have taken up tennis.
RUUD GULLIT after the Netherlands' European Championship triumph, 1988

But you cannot have enjoyed it. There were so many mistakes, so much unprofessional play.
SIR ALF RAMSEY, England manager, to a journalist enthusing over a five-goal match between Stoke and Liverpool, quoted in The Football Managers, *1973*

The pitch was playable. I've been in football over 25 years and it has become a game for poofters.
JOHN BURRIDGE, veteran Manchester City goalkeeper, after his match was postponed, 1995

Could I point out that the gay Stonewall FC's third XI played a West End League fixture on a Somme-like afternoon in Regent's Park on Sunday, thereby challenging [Burridge's] theory that sexual orientation has any connection with getting muddy knees.
LETTER to The Independent, *1995*

I always thought golf was a poof's game. Now I prefer it to football.
JULIAN DICKS, West Ham defender, 1998

It's hard to be passionate twice a week.

GEORGE GRAHAM, Arsenal manager, on the physical demands of the English game, 1992

Hump it, bump it, whack. That may be a recipe for a good sex life, but it won't win us the World Cup.
KEN BATES, Chelsea chairman, after England's failure to qualify for the World Cup under Graham Taylor, 1993

Make it simple, make it accurate, make it quick.
ARTHUR ROWE, manager of Tottenham's push-and-run side of the 1950s, on his football philosophy, 1975

Since I've been in football there has been a basic question to face. Are you pretty or are you efficient? It's as if you have to choose. It makes me happy this season that we've won games but people have enjoyed watching us. It's dangerous for football when people become convinced you must play boringly to win.
ARSENE WENGER as Arsenal moved towards a complete unbeaten Premiership season, 2004

Speed has become everything, not just the physical speed of players, but the speed of moving the ball

and speed of thought. This is absolutely what Arsenal are about. The counter-attack has become the key factor.
ANDY ROXBURGH, UEFA technical director and ex-Scotland manager, 2004

What I look for in a young player is game intelligence, speed (not purely physical speed but speed of reaction and speed with the ball) and technique. But even if they just have attitude and technique, you can build on that. What makes you saddest of all is to see talent but no desire to achieve something.
WENGER, 2003

The speed of the game is the big difference from my playing days. When a team-mate passed to me, I had the time to control the ball, look, make a decision and pass it. Now you have to make that decision before the ball reaches your feet. Otherwise it's too late because players are fitter and faster and teams have improved tactically.
CARLO ANCELOTTI, Chelsea manager, 2010

Left-wing football is about creativity, attack and pleasure, and about out-scoring the opposition. Right-wing football is negative, cautious and result-oriented.
CESAR LUIS MENOTTI, left-wing former coach of Argentina, 1985

What counts, winning or putting on a show? Success remains in the record books. Having fun passes with time.
FABIO CAPELLO, Juventus coach, 2006

The good player keeps playing even without the ball. All the time he is placing himself so that when the ball comes to him he is able to make good use of it. We improved the English saying of 'Kick and run' to 'Pass accurately and move into a good position'.
FERENC PUSKAS, Hungary player, on his country's 6–3 win v England at Wembley, 1953

A football team is like a piano. You need eight men to carry it and three to play the damn thing.
BILL SHANKLY, Liverpool manager, 1968

Running is for animals. You need a brain and a ball for football.
LOUIS VAN GAAL, Dutch coach of Bayern Munich, 2010

People who talk of short passes and on-the-ground moves as the essence of good football do not help the progress of football in Britain.
STAN CULLIS, Wolves manager, defending his 'scientific kick-and-rush football' in All for the Wolves, 1960

Our failure has not been because we have played the British way, but because we haven't. Football should be open, honest, clean, passionate. Part of a nation's culture, its heritage. And the English way is with passion, commitment.
GRAHAM TAYLOR, manager of 'long-ball' exponents Watford, after England's World Cup exit, 1982

Possession and patience are myths. It's anathema to people in the game to say this, but goals come from mistakes, not from possession.
TAYLOR as Watford established themselves in the top division, 1982

I can't watch the long-ball teams like Wimbledon, Watford and Sheffield Wednesday. Football wasn't meant to be run by two linesmen and air-traffic control.
TOMMY DOCHERTY, 1988

People who talk about sophisticated football don't know what they're talking about. To me, the more shots you can get, the more times you threaten the opposition keeper, the better chance you have of winning. Is that any different at international level than on a Sunday park? I happen to believe that it's not.
GRAHAM TAYLOR, by now England manager, 1991

Because I'm a British centre-forward they expect me to be heading the ball all the time.

IAN RUSH, Welsh striker, during his season with Juventus, 1987

A pass rising a yard above the ground should be a foul. A player receiving a pass has two feet and only one head.
WILLIE READ, St Mirren manager, 1959

Balloon ball. The percentage game. Route one. It has crept into the First Division. We get asked to loan youngsters to these teams. We don't do it. They come back with bad habits, big legs and good eyesight.
RON ATKINSON, Manchester United manager, on the long-ball game, 1984

If God had meant football to be played in the air, he'd have put grass in the sky.
BRIAN CLOUGH, Nottingham Forest manager, 1992

If current trends continue, it'll be a game of 6ft 10in defenders heading the ball back and forth with 6ft 11in forwards.
JOHN CARTWRIGHT, former director of the FA National School, on his fears over the prevalence of the long-ball game, 1992

When I had him at Derby, Stefano Eranio could stop the ball dead with his toe. One game, at half-time, he said to our big, ugly centre-half Spencer Prior: 'Spencer, why you always put ball in stand? No players in stand.'
JIM SMITH, Oxford manager, 2006

My philosophy is to play in their half of the pitch. Get the ball in behind them. Get the buggers turning, turning. When you've done that enough times, holes will open up, and one of our fellas, whoever's nearest, gets to the ball first. And then all the rest pile in.

JACK CHARLTON, *Republic of Ireland manager, 1988*

We don't favour a passing game [at Crewe] because of any moral principles, but because it's the best way to play. If bashing the ball were the best way, we'd do it.

DARIO GRADI, *Crewe Alexandra manager, 1999*

The first time I came to England, I said to myself: 'Without a doubt, football was created here!'

ARSENE WENGER, *Arsenal's French manager, 2002*

Sometimes now, when I watch the continental matches on TV, I'm a bit bored. I'm thinking: 'Where's the intensity?'

WENGER, *1998*

England are a nation of warriors. If I go to Liverpool and someone puts the ball into the area, and [Jamie] Carragher hammers it out of play, then the fans applaud. In Camp Nou you would never be applauded for that. It's a different culture that values different things. Here, if they see you are afraid when in possession, you get whistled. It's the world in reverse.

XAVI, *Barcelona and Spain midfielder, 2012*

Fighting football, not serenity football, that is what I like. What we call in German 'English' football – rainy day, heavy pitch, 5–5, everybody dirty in the face and goes home and cannot play for weeks after.

JURGEN KLOPP, *Borussia Dortmund coach, 2013*

In England you have to die on the pitch, go home exhausted.

GIUSEPPE SANNINO, *Italian manager of Watford, 2014*

I've never seen so much violence on the pitch as in England. Before certain matches, I'm scared an opponent might harm me.

FRANK LEBOEUF, *Chelsea's French defender, 1999*

I spent five years playing non-league football for Wealdstone. If Frank [Leboeuf] thinks the Premiership is hard, he should see what goes on there. Referees had to protect me from the wingers I was marking.
STUART PEARCE, *England defender, 1999*

It's a bit of a nancy game now. And if Leboeuf isn't too happy, he should go home. Anyway, spitting is the vilest thing in the world, and the Vieira lad and some other foreigners have brought that with them.
TOMMY SMITH, *former Liverpool defender, 1999*

Why is it that so many foreign players are queuing up to come here if our football has so many faults? I don't hear Gianfranco Zola complaining about the English game.
GORDON TAYLOR, *players' union leader, responding to Leboeuf, 2000*

I'm committing wicked fouls that would have horrified me six months ago. That's how you have to play in England... Going for a high ball I use my elbow or I'm dead.
THIERRY HENRY, *Arsenal and France striker, 2000*

Guys like 'Chopper' Harris, Nobby Stiles, Tommy Smith, Jack Charlton and Norman Hunter would be sent off every week these days. It would be a doddle for me playing today.
GEORGE BEST *on his 50th birthday, 1996*

I once described English football as the working man's ballet. It's more like a clog dance now.
TONY WADDINGTON, *former Stoke manager, 1991*

English football's just like rugby. All the balls go flying through the air or you're kicked into the stand.
RICHARD WITSCHGE, *Dutch midfielder, recalling a loan spell with Blackburn, 1996*

I think of myself as one of the old guard. When I started playing you could kick owt that moved.
DAVID BATTY, *Leeds midfielder, 2000*

English football is all about running, fighting war for 90 minutes non-stop.
TONY YEBOAH, *former Leeds striker, happy to be back in German football, 1999*

English football is hard work. You have to run all the time.

NWANKWO KANU, *Arsenal's Nigerian striker, 1999*

A great pianist doesn't run around the piano or do push-ups with his fingertips. To be great, he plays the piano. To be a great footballer is not about running, doing press-ups or physical work. The best way to become a great player is to play football.
JOSE MOURINHO, Chelsea manager, 2005

I love the speed of the game here [in England]. Playing from goal to goal, keeping the momentum going at all times. There's beauty in the game here. The spontaneity is beautiful.
ERIC CANTONA, from La Philosophie de Cantona, *1995*

In the English league you can't play at less than 100 per cent. I've had to change my mentality since joining Arsenal to become more aggressive. The English game makes that inevitable.
ROBERT PIRES, Arsenal and France midfielder, 2002

The average Englishman is a very limited player.

GLENN HODDLE, England midfielder, on moving from Tottenham to Monaco, 1987

The English prejudice against educated footballers has not only led to yobbery off the pitch but to a certain mental weakness on the pitch. The England players had plenty of heart. What they lacked was the ability to think; they were out-thought by their opponents.
EDITORIAL headlined 'Why can't we pass?' in The Spectator, *after Euro 2000*

The attitude in England is that tricks are OK if they work. If they don't you're a wanker. It doesn't seem to have sunk in that if you never try you'll never succeed.
DUNCAN McKENZIE, maverick striker, 1976

The English are plagued by industrial football, yet the potential remains enormous.
MILJAN MILJANIC, Real Madrid manager, on the congested schedule of England's top clubs, 1976

England will never win World Cups. We simply don't have enough people who believe in playing football.
ALEX FERGUSON, Manchester United manager, 1995

Football is like a car. You've got five gears, but the trouble with English teams is that they drive in fourth and fifth all the time... When they crash in Europe they say it's bad luck. It isn't – it's bad driving.
RUUD GULLIT on joining Chelsea after playing in Italy and the Netherlands, 1995

When English clubs play in Europe, their opponents know what is coming: the long ball into the penalty area, which gets nowhere; the next ball, which the opposition win; and the counter-attack, which the English cannot deal with.
ANTONIO PACHECO, Portugal player, 1995

I love watching English football but I used to love playing against English teams. They always gave you the ball back if you lost it. Still do.
JOHAN CRUYFF, former Ajax, Barcelona and Netherlands captain, 1998

I don't want people in Spain to regard me as an English footballer in the traditional sense, an idiot with lots of money who boots long balls upfield.
STEVE McMANAMAN, Real Madrid midfielder, 2001

I love English football, even though it strikes me sometimes as a crazy game. Where are the best playmakers? Not in England.
MICHEL PLATINI, former France captain and vice-president of the French FA, 2002

English football is based on physicality. To be honest, I don't like it much. It's certainly different. It's interesting. Like a rollercoaster.
FRANCESCO TOTTI, Roma and Italy player, 2007

You must take care of your own football culture. English football is world-famous, but the result of all the foreigners in the Premiership is that the national team is second-class.
JOHAN CRUYFF, former Barcelona coach, after England's failure at Euro 2000

I love English football, but the tactics haven't changed in the past 20 years – 4–4–2 and a flat back four pushing up as far as possible makes it easier for strikers to shine than in Europe.
MICHEL PLATINI, former France captain, 2002

You can play 10 at the back or 10 up front. There is no 'best way'. To defend well isn't easy, nor is to attack well. What matters is the result.
DIEGO SIMEONE, Atletico Madrid coach, 2014

Dennis Bergkamp told me the Dutch always thought of the English as strong but stupid.
TONY ADAMS, Arsenal and England defender, 1997

The most important space on the pitch is between the ears.
ADRIAN BOOTHROYD, Watford manager, 2006

I admire the English mentality because they are so strong, so hard-working. But we have talent.

SVEN-GORAN ERIKSSON, then coach of Portugal's Benfica, after his side knocked Arsenal out of the European Cup, 1991

English and British players still kick the ball while continental players prefer to pass it. And while British players want to crack the ball at goal, today's really top players want to pass it into the net.
CRAIG BROWN, Scotland manager, after watching Euro 2000

I've been infected by the English football virus. I'd miss that anywhere I went.
ARSENE WENGER, Arsenal manager, on signing a new contract, 2004

The reason we haven't signed any English players is that there aren't enough good ones about, as the European Championship showed.
KEN BATES, Chelsea chairman, 2000

The British don't like fancy dans or fanny merchants, as they used to call them, but different players give 100 per cent in different ways.
JOHN BARNES, former England midfielder, 2000

Passion is the most overworked word and excuse in English football. Control is the key to winning. Fire in the bellies is all very well but you need ice in the head too.
BILL BESWICK, sports psychologist, 1999

There are too many hammer-throwers in the Scottish League. I sign a world-class player and have him put out of action after a game and a bit. This league is too tough.
GRAEME SOUNESS, Rangers manager, after injury to Oleg Kuznetsov, 1990

I got a shock when I first saw a Scottish League match on TV. The keeper was basically elbowed off the ball at a corner-kick, but the goal was given. It was a wake-up call.
FABIEN BARTHEZ, Manchester United's French keeper, 2000

In Scotland the mentality is not to pass the ball in midfield. It goes directly to the attack, which makes it difficult for midfielders like me.
JUNINHO, Brazilian midfielder, shortly before leaving Celtic, 2005

I would hate to play that kind of football. The pleasure of playing that would be zero. As a player you want to enjoy the game. I don't think the players enjoy it there. It's no fun playing with 10 men behind the ball. I wouldn't pay to watch Liverpool, but I would to watch Arsenal or Manchester United.
FRANK DE BOER, Barcelona player, on Liverpool's 0–0 draw in the Nou Camp in 2001 before the sides were again goalless there in the Champions League, 2002

The leagues I like are Spain, England and Holland, where most teams try to play football. Italy is horrible. If you put a camera above an Italian stadium you just see this line of activity across midfield. Incredible! It's just fighting in the midfield and expecting to score goals from free kicks. It's in the culture – the Italians have always played for results.
FRANK DE BOER, 2002

We are all footballers and as such we should be able to perform competently in all positions.
ALFREDO DI STEFANO, Real Madrid striker, anticipating 'total football', 1961

In Europe you have more time to use the ball, to turn around. In England they are on top of you as soon as you get the ball. That pressure, that obsession with contact, makes life hard for me. But it's the downfall of English teams in Europe because they leave space that European players know how to use.
LUIS GARCIA, Liverpool and Spain striker, 2007

In Spain, all 22 players make the sign of the cross as they enter the pitch. If it worked, it would always be a draw.
JOHAN CRUYFF, former Barcelona player, 2006

A 0–0 draw in Italy is crap. A 0–0 draw in England can be really interesting.
IAN WRIGHT, Arsenal and England striker, 1995

When a game goes to 2–0 in Italy you tend to think the losing side will accept it won't happen for them. That never happens in England. We don't have that way of thinking.
SIR ALEX FERGUSON, 2006

Italian League football was rubbish – totally defensive. Games were either no score or 1–0... When we had lost a couple of matches, we began to feel the attitude of the directors. It was as though we had lost a war. With a reaction like that, players don't want to be adventurous.
DENIS LAW, Scottish international, on his spell with Torino, An Autobiography, *1979*

The Premiership took a page out of American football and now have Saturday Showdowns and Super Sundays... This is high-calibre marketing, taking an inferior product and improving it through packaging.
ALEXI LALAS, president of the Major League Soccer club Los Angeles Galaxy, 2007

In England our league is considered second class, but I honestly believe if you took a helicopter, grabbed a bunch of MLS players and took them to the perceived best league in the world, they wouldn't miss a beat and the fans wouldn't notice any drop in quality.
LALAS, 2007

Goodbye soccer, hello football!
SLOGAN aimed at Mexicans to games at Los Angeles-based Major League Soccer club CD Chivas, 2006

In England, soccer is a grey game played by grey people on grey days.
RODNEY MARSH, former England player, to a Florida TV audience at the peak of the North American Soccer League's popularity, 1979

America is the land of opportunity for soccer.

RON NEWMAN, English coach of NASL club Fort Lauderdale Strikers, 1978

America is an elephants' graveyard.
GIANNI RIVERA, Italian international forward, rejecting an offer from an NASL club, 1978

If the US becomes enthralled by soccer it will be when every back street and stretch of urban waste ground has its teams of kids playing their makeshift matches, the players claiming the temporary identity of the world's stars... Environments like that produce those stars. Football is an inner compulsion. It cannot be settled on a people like instant coffee.
ARTHUR HOPCRAFT, author, The Football Man, *1968*

To say that American soccer is the football of the future is ludicrous. You've got to see football in the black townships of South Africa or in Rio de Janeiro before you can talk about the future of football. Who can name five top American players?
JACK TAYLOR, English World Cup referee, 1978

Soccer is a game in which everyone does a lot of running around... Mostly, 21 guys stand around and one guy does a tap dance with the ball. It's about as exciting as *Tristan and Isolde.*
JIM MURRAY, sportswriter, Louisville Courier Journal, *1967*

Those Stoker guys are so cocky. They make me mad saying our game [baseball] is dull. Boy, if ours is dull, theirs is even duller. Those nuts. Running around in shorts, chasing a big ball like a bunch of schoolboys.
JOE AZCUE, Cleveland Indians baseball coach, 1967; Cleveland Stokers were Stoke City, guesting in the US city for the summer

In this bloody country, Americans think that any guy who runs around in shorts kicking a ball instead of catching it has to be a Commie or a fairy.
CLIVE TOYE, English general manager of New York Cosmos, 1970

Biathlon. Luge. Soccer. Three of a kind.
THE PLAINS DEALER *newspaper, Ohio, on the prospect of the US staging the World Cup finals, 1990*

Get ready. The first 0-0 tie might be only hours away.
MIKE LOPRESTI, USA Today sports writer, before the opening game of the World Cup finals, 1994

I expect to see people walking down the streets of every major city now, kicking balls when they should be going to work.
BILL CLINTON, US President, in his message to the American squad before the finals, 1994

They're going to bring this thing to the US in 1994 and charge people money to watch it? Listen, if this thing were a Broadway show it would have closed after one night.
FRANK DEPFORD, editor-columnist of US-based The National, *on the World Cup final, 1990*

Soccer is cruel, fate is relentless and the most coveted championship in the world hinged on the caprice of a leather boot striking a leather ball on a chalk spot 12 yards from goal.
REPORT in Los Angeles Times *after goalless World Cup final was settled on penalties, 1994*

If I could live for a thousand years I'd now set aside a decade for soccer. Before this World Cup, I'd have given it the same time slot in eternity as auto racing: maybe a week.
THOMAS BOSWELL, sportswriter and baseball aficionado, Washington Post, *1994*

Soccer will never take over from baseball. Baseball is the only chance we blacks get to wave a bat at a white man without starting a riot.

EDDIE MURPHY, actor, during the US World Cup, 1994

For us Americans the bottom line is to win a championship.

So we invent baseball and call ourselves world champions. We invent [gridiron] football and do the same. But they're not world champions, just the best team in the US in that professional sport. Only soccer has a true world championship. Our challenge is magnified thousands of times. Our situation is so much more difficult and complicated. This is the real one.
BRUCE ARENA, US coach, World Cup finals, 2002

The FA Cup final is better than the Oscars because it's honest.
VINNIE JONES, footballer turned actor, at the Hollywood awards ceremony, 2000

Our football comes from the heart, theirs comes from the mind.
PELE on the difference between South American and European football, 1970

These are players – men who play with their heads and their hearts.
FERENC PUSKAS, Real Madrid player, 1961

Lots of footballers don't have a high IQ to start with, so it would be difficult to gauge the effects of heading the ball too much.
JOHN COLQUHOUN, former Scotland striker, on research which claimed that heading led to brain damage, 1995

What is the world coming to when you get a red card and fined two weeks' wages for calling a grown man a wanker? It's an adults' game, so what's wrong with a bit of industrial language in the workplace?
PAUL GASCOIGNE after being sent off for Middlesbrough v Chelsea, 2000

Everyone knows I am looking for a striker but I hope that makes the players say: 'I'll show that bastard that I can do it.'
EBBE SKOVDAHL, Aberdeen manager, 2001

These days you spend £2m before you realise the player can't even trap a ball.
GRAHAM TAYLOR, back as Watford manager, 2000

When I was at Bournemouth I kicked a tray of cups up in the air. One hit Luther Blissett on the head. He flicked it on and it went all over my suit hanging behind him. Another time, at West Ham, I threw a plate of sandwiches at Don Hutchison. He sat there, still arguing with me, with cheese and tomato running down his face. You can't do that any more, especially with all the foreigners. They'd go home.
HARRY REDKNAPP, West Ham manager, 1999

Let us not forget that the place of truth for an athlete is, and always will be, the stadium.
ERIC CANTONA, from La Philosophie de Cantona, 1995

The hardest part is what you find to replace football, because there isn't anything.
KEVIN KEEGAN, 'chief operating officer' at Fulham, 1998

Sometimes, driving home from a game, you do wonder if you're getting a bit old. But I always remember what Kenny Dalglish once told me: 'Never forget that football made you feel knackered when you were 17.'
GORDON STRACHAN, Leeds and Scotland midfielder, in An Autobiography, 1992

I'm frightened to stop because there can be no life as enjoyable as this.
STRACHAN on a footballer's life at 35, 1992

I've still got what every old footballer misses – the banter of the dressing room. It's vicious. If you're a sensitive peach in this business, you're buggered.
ALAN BIRCHENALL, former player, on his PR role with Leicester City, 2004

Let nobody tell you that life begins at 40. Death begins at 40. You get fat, your hair falls out and you get arthritis... Now I'm just trying to grow old as gracefully as I'm able to.
MIKE CHANNON, racehorse trainer and former England striker, 2004

They shoot horses, don't they? A lot of players would prefer to be shot once their career was over.
JIMMY GREAVES, former England striker, 2003

8

THE LIFESTYLE

I played in the streets with my friends, bare-footed... I never had the chance to say to my mother or father: 'I want these boots.' It's different in Europe. They have it easier. I saw that already in Holland. Kids of 17 or 18 years old were given cars already. Audis. Big cars. In Uruguay you don't have that. That can be an advantage: you don't give everything on the pitch if you have it all.
LUIS SUAREZ, Liverpool, Uruguay and and former Ajax striker, 2012

The whole problem with football players is they really take themselves seriously. We kick a ball around and we earn 100,000, 200,000 or even 300,000 euros a week. We don't improve the world. It's not like we invented hot water.
BENOIT ASSOU-EKOTTO, Tottenham and Cameroon defender, 2010

God gave me this life and I'm enjoying it...but I'm trying not to be the typical player, who people will judge and assume is stupid, worried about his cars and his looks. The way I see football, there is loads of fake. For me, real life will start when I stop playing football.
SEBASTIEN BASSONG, Norwich and Cameroon defender, 2014

Are we overpaid compared to the public service people, the army that serves our country? I'd say definitely. But we don't get paid as much as athletes from a lot of other sports – the golfers, tennis players, basketball players, the baseball stars. They get paid ridiculous money compared to what we get paid.
RIO FERDINAND, Manchester United and England defender, 2013

I remember [Portsmouth] getting beaten at Bolton last year and looking at our bench. Two of them were asleep with hats pulled down and blankets over them. I said: 'I'm sorry to drag you up here. I know it's fucking cold and you could be at home having a cup of tea with the missus. It's hard for 30 grand a week to watch a game.'
HARRY REDKNAPP, Tottenham manager, 2009

In my years, we played with our feet and head, connected to the heart. We laughed, we rejoiced and wept. Now there are many players with too much money, it is polluting the sport.
DIEGO MARADONA on his time in Italy with Napoli, 2012

Zlatan [Ibrahimovic] likes to point out [during a match] how much money he earns. He's also on a level that everyone else can only dream of – he's among the best three players in the world. He should be very happy. Why is he so angry? Why does he need to trash-talk? Why does he need to behave the way he did?
SIMUN SAMUELSEN, Faroe Islands striker, after defeat by Sweden, 2013

If you pay them the wages they'll come. We all kid ourselves: 'I've wanted to play for Tottenham since I was two. I had pictures of Jimmy Greaves on my wall.' It's a load of bull. Here's £80,000 a week. Lovely jubbly.

HARRY REDKNAPP, Tottenham manager, 2011

Football has become like Hollywood and the players are like film stars. They have to recognise the responsibility they have. Football was traditionally a working-class sport, with fans walking into grounds with players. It has completely changed.

TONY PULIS, Stoke City manager, 2013

Dressing-room culture has changed to the extent where if [a manager] criticises a player, he will happily say: 'OK, I have three years left on my contract, so you can either sell me or I will sit here for three years.'

ANDY COLE, former Manchester United and England striker, 2014

I'm never quite sure how far to go in praise of a young player. Next thing you'll see him driving a Mercedes or wearing his socks over his knees, or he'll have four earrings and a Walt Disney hat.

PAUL LAMBERT, Norwich City manager, 2009

My first FA Cup game was Runcorn away in 1995 [as a Wigan player] and we went in a bus. It was full of alcohol. It was an eye-opener. It used to be a case of train hard and party hard, but you can't do that any more.

ROBERTO MARTINEZ, Wigan Athletic manager, before his team beat Manchester City to win the FA Cup, 2013

I was shocked whenever I went to the players' Christmas party because you don't expect to go out and not have a meal.

MARTINEZ, who is Spanish, 2010

Before, when the players said: 'I've been out and drunk seven beers,' the masseurs participated. They wouldn't say: 'It's not good. It's wrong.'

PAOLO DI CANIO, Sunderland manager, 2013

From now on if someone comes inside with a mobile phone, even in their bag, I'll throw it in the North Sea. They're banned.

DI CANIO, as above

Twitter is talking to a bunch of Herberts you don't know. It's beyond belief that you have to go on a page or whatever and tell people you're having a cup of tea.
TONY PULIS, Stoke manager, on players tweeting, 2012

Just had tattoo added to. look like an idiot now with my cling film arm!
ELLIOTT BENNETT, Norwich City winger, on Twitter, 2012

I always spray perfume on my shirt before we play. The other guys are happy with it because they know I smell good when we celebrate. And also when we change shirts after matches, mine smells good even when it needs to be washed.
FLORENT MALOUDA, Chelsea and France midfielder, 2010

REPORTER: Does anyone ever buy the £21,000 watches advertised in there?
SHERWOOD: I've never seen watches that cheap in there.
EXCHANGE in a Guardian Q & A with Tim Sherwood, former Tottenham and Blackburn player, who was promoting Icon, a magazine aimed at high-earning footballers, 2008

We were driving back from Birmingham when Kieron [Dyer] suddenly shouted: 'Stop the bus! I've left my diamond earring in the dressing room.' Can you imagine in my playing days a player telling Bill Shankly: 'Stop the bus, Bill, I've left me earring in the dressing room.'
SIR BOBBY ROBSON, Newcastle manager, 2003

We want football players, not fashion models. Last year Kevin-Prince Boateng had more hairstyles than goals.

JOSE MOURINHO, Chelsea manager, 2013

Playing the role of the weird old eccentric works well for me. When everyone else is getting their new clothes cut up, they tend to think my gear is going to be awful and don't even bother with me.
MATT JACKSON, 33-year-old Wigan Athletic defender, on avoiding the attention of dressing-room pranksters, 2007

Rio [Ferdinand] has shown what can be done by setting up his own business in fashion. My dream? Well, I'd love to have my own range of suits sold in Marks and Spencer.
JERMAINE JENAS, Tottenham and England midfielder, 2010

He came with long hair and a big bone in his ear... Typical young guy who thinks about silly things.
PAOLO DI CANIO, Swindon Town manager, on striker Miles Storey, 2012

He dressed in a costume consisting of empty bottles of Jagermeister and cans of Red Bull strapped to his chest in an attempted comedy play on the popular 'jager bomb' drink. Although he fully accepts in hindsight it was an ill-thought-out and insensitive decision, absolutely no harm was intended whatsoever and he apologises for any offence caused.
STATEMENT by Chris Smalling's management company after the Manchester United and England defender attended a fancy dress party apparently dressed as a 'suicide bomber', 2014

They are cocooned by parents, they need to be seen with their tattoos and earrings. Some even cry in the dressing room.
SIR ALEX FERGUSON on young players, 2010

I'm obsessive about trainers. I've got about 300 pairs. I'm a real sneaker-head. I don't buy designer ones. Mine are old-school. I've got them upstairs in my garage... I'm on eBay all the time.
BEN FOSTER, West Bromwich Albion and England goalkeeper, 2013

Back in my time, and I sound old now, it was black and white boots and that was it. Now you've got snoods, people wearing headphones when they're doing interviews, which I find disrespectful, pink boots, green boots.
PAUL INCE, Notts County manager and former England captain, 2011

There are magazines, letters, pictures, clothes, creams, everything, he cannot open the door. If he did it would make a bigger mess.
FERNANDO TORRES on his Chelsea and Spain colleague Juan Mata, 2012

Some of us like our afternoon snoozes.

JOE HART, Manchester City and England goalkeeper, when asked how the players passed the time when not training, 2012

It doesn't make it any easier to run your heart out when you've just woken up in a five-star hotel. Too much comfort makes you comfortable.
JURGEN KLOPP, Borussia Dortmund coach, 2012

In football there are players who mature at 18, some at 25 and others at 30. In fact, some never mature at all.
ALESSANDRO DIAMANTI, 29-year-old Italy and former West Ham striker, 2012

Most footballers are knobs.

JOEY BARTON, *Newcastle midfielder, on Radio 4's* Today *programme, 2010*

Q: How many wives have you had?
A: That's easy. Two. More difficult is how many women I've had a child with. It's eight by six or seven mothers.
Q: Six or seven?
A: I don't know. A Mexican, a Hungarian, Brazilians. Four plus two…six.

ROBERTO CARLOS, *former Real Madrid and Brazil defender, interviewed in Italy's* Gazzetta dello Sport, *2014*

REPORTER: Your first goal for a while?
ROSENIOR: Yeah, I've had two kids since my last one.

EXCHANGE *after Hull City defender Liam Rosenior scored v West Bromwich Albion, 2014*

When I first told her I was a footballer, she said: 'Yes, but what do you do for a living?'

CHRISTIAN KAREMBEU, *former France midfielder, on his wife Adriana Sklenarikova, the former Wonderbra model, 2005*

I read this piece by the car man, Jeremy Clarkson, saying a footballer goes out in the morning, gets in his Aston Martin, forgets to take a drugs test, takes coke, has a drink, then shags a bird. And that was 'a day in the life of a footballer'. But a lot of players are decent fellas.

FRANK LAMPARD, *Chelsea and England midfielder, 2003*

Footballers like to think they are boss drinkers, boss gamblers and boss shaggers.

MICK QUINN, *former striker with several English clubs, in his autobiography* Who Ate All The Pies, *2003*

If you retire at 35 you can live wherever you bloody well like: London, Monaco, whatever. Any half-decent footballer will be a multi-millionaire.

ROY KEANE, *Sunderland manager, claiming some transfer targets snubbed Wearside in favour of cities with better shopping for their wives, 2007*

Do the players think they're in the shop window? You only have to see the look on their faces when they hear Roman Abramovich is in the stadium.

ALAN CURBISHLEY, *Charlton manager, at the European Championship finals, 2004*

People say I'm cocky because I have two cars and a diamond watch. But that means 90 per cent of footballers are cocky. We're in a fortunate position and we can afford these things.
KIERON DYER, Newcastle and England midfielder, 2004

Footballers are the new pop stars. Who cares about a pop singer drinking lots and taking drugs. People want to read about footballers now.
MICKEY THOMAS, former Wales midfielder, 2003

Hero worship has gone through the roof and footballers have replaced rock stars in popularity. But footballers can't start behaving like rock stars. Many musicians die at a young age because of their lifestyle. Football is going the same way.
TERRY VENABLES, former England manager, 2003

I advise players to surround themselves with people who don't idolise them. If we commit traffic offences we should pay the fines. And at the restaurant we should wait our turn like others.
JOSE MOURINHO, Chelsea manager, 2006

The perception of footballers has changed a lot since I played. There used to be celebrity, showbiz and football. Now it's all one thing.

KEVIN KEEGAN, England manager, 2000

I detest politicians saying that footballers should be role models. If anyone should be, it's the politicians.
GRAHAM TAYLOR, Aston Villa manager, 2003

There will never, ever be a better time to be a footballer than now.

ALAN SHEARER, England captain, 1999

If you become a big star today, the mass media is marking you, man to man, 24 hours a day. Boys of 18 or 19 could get away with taking a wrong step 20 years ago. Now it's on the front page of *The Sun* or *Bild*. We don't want front pages, we want back pages.
SVEN-GORAN ERIKSSON, England manager, 2005

There's a word you don't hear around footballers' dressing rooms any more – mortgage.
NIALL QUINN, former Sunderland striker, on the handsome salaries of top players, 2002

This rain is relentless, my stream is running faster than I have ever seen.
MICHAEL OWEN tweet, 2012

No monetary bullshit. No media bollocks. Just pure, old school, mortgages and livelihoods on the line, balls-out football. I feel that training in the lower leagues will give me a reality check and maybe help me become a better person; a little more humility will serve me well.
JOEY BARTON, Queens Park Rangers midfielder, training with Fleetwood Town ahead of a loan move that was eventually cancelled, 2012

When you're chatting in the dressing room, the last thing you talk about is football.
HERNAN CRESPO, Chelsea and Argentina striker, 2004

I've become cynical about my profession. Players abuse their position, signing long contracts and then not bothering to play, happy sitting in the reserves. Clubs employ staff for years and then sack them. Football has become a business rather than a sport and a passion.
GARETH SOUTHGATE, Middlesbrough and England defender, 2003

There are lots of players who will kiss your club's badge one week and the badge of another club the next.

ALAN CURBISHLEY, Charlton manager, on reluctantly selling Scott Parker to Chelsea, 2003

Sir – I was delighted to read that 50 per cent of GPs now earn an annual salary which is less than Rio Ferdinand's weekly wage. I am sure society has its values right.
LETTER to the Daily Telegraph, 2005

I don't think the salaries can ever be good for the game. You think to yourself: 'How has it come to this?'

SIR ALEX FERGUSON, Ferdinand's manager at Manchester United, 2004

I worry about the ones who have got a lot of money and are expected to stay at the top and how much you can keep the hunger in them. It's an unconscious thing. I signed a new contract and the first thing I thought after I'd put my name on that line was: 'I'm comfortable now.'
FERGUSON, 2003

Players' attitudes have changed because of money. Getting vast amounts takes away the hunger,

that little edge. Players of today say, 'I go out and play with the same desire,' but it can't be that way when the comfort zone comes so quickly and easily.
ALAN BALL, former England World Cup-winner, 2006

[The big salaries] distort the way you look at life. When someone would value going out for a meal, perhaps buying a car, you've bought your car at 19. It's very dangerous. There's no discipline.
TONY FINNIGAN, players' agent and ex-player, 2003

They're on £20,000 to £30,000 a week, and they're not earning it. It makes you resentful. I've reached the stage where I don't like footballers.
DAVID SULLIVAN, co-owner of Birmingham City, 2006

It's crazy.
If you want to win, you have to pay up to £100,000 a week to a player who can hardly read or write.
MOHAMED AL FAYED, Fulham chairman, 2007

Semi-educated, foul-mouthed players on £100,000 a week hold clubs to ransom until they get, say, £120,000.
SEPP BLATTER, president of football's world governing body, FIFA, 2005

I find it bizarre that the head of an organisation which has built its wealth on the backs of players is having a go at these players.
GORDON TAYLOR, chief executive of the players' union, the PFA, replying to Blatter, 2005

I don't feel any guilt about anything I earn. It's life. Businessmen earn 100,000 times more than us.
MARCEL DESAILLY, Chelsea and France defender, 2003

I never think about the money. I have never, ever gone on the pitch thinking: 'I have to win to get the bonus.' I don't care about the bonus, just about the game.
THIERRY HENRY, Arsenal and France striker, 2003

Money is important. Why shouldn't players make as much as they can?

LUIS FIGO, Internazionale and Portugal midfielder, 2005

What's a £1,500 fine for a Premiership footballer? Nothing.
BRIGITTE CHAUDHRY of the road-safety campaign Roadpeace, after Leeds' Seth Johnson was fined £1,500 for driving at 135mph with two-and-a-half times the permitted amount of alcohol in his blood, 2003

I have a little girl and I hope she never comes home with a professional footballer. Even the car insurance for footballers is expensive because the companies know they drive under the influence of alcohol.
GEORGE BOATENG, Middlesbrough's Dutch midfielder, 2003

I understand Lazio are in a difficult position financially, but I cannot go to the supermarket and buy groceries for my family with shares.
JAAP STAM, Dutch defender, on his club's 'laughable' request for him to take a pay cut from £45,000 a week to £21,000 plus shares, 2003

The game's full of young, rich, spoilt thugs. A lot of footballers haven't the moral fortitude to say: 'Stick your money, I'd rather be myself.'

MARK BOSNICH, former cocaine addict and ex-Premiership goalkeeper, 2005

I get paid on the last Thursday of the month and from there my mam looks after it... I don't go round flashing the cash. That's not me. I came here for ridiculous money. It's not my fault, it's the job I'm in. I didn't ask for the game to be like this. I play because I love the game. That, and the fact that it's the only thing I'm good at.
DAMIEN DUFF, £17m Chelsea winger, 2003

Between the ages of 14 and 20 I knew I was getting paid the same as the guy next to me. At 18, we all signed the same contract until we were 22. That breeds a spirit of 'We're all in this together.' Imagine if you're on £1,000 a week at 16 – it would breed a feeling of 'I want to play for the first team but don't need to.' I didn't want that kind of money before I'd played in the first team.
GARY NEVILLE, Manchester United and England defender, 2003

I don't hold with those who say they would play for England for nothing. I'd play for Northern Ireland for nothing if they let everybody in for nothing. If they are collecting a £50,000 gate, playing for hope and glory has nothing to do with the facts.
DANNY BLANCHFLOWER, Tottenham captain, in The Encyclopaedia of Football, *1960*

Johnny Haynes is a top entertainer and will be paid as one from now on. I will give him £100 a week to play for Fulham.
TOMMY TRINDER, Fulham chairman and comedian, making Haynes the English game's first £100-a-week player, 1961

Italian players wonder how on earth players like Haynes live on such a salary! If anyone suggested that the Italians should play a whole season and bank only £5,000, plus another £90 or so in expenses, there would be a nationwide strike.
JOHN CHARLES, Juventus and Wales player, in The Gentle Giant, *1962*

You always want hungry players, but the country is getting richer and that's already been bad for boxing. I can also see it harming football.
BILL SHANKLY, Liverpool manager, 1968

The permissive society has given us young footballers totally concerned with what they can get rather than what they ought to be giving.
BERTIE MEE, Arsenal manager, 1974

I don't begrudge the special players a penny. In fact, in 1960 I predicted in *Charles Buchan's Football Monthly* that there would be an elite league paying footballers what they're worth. But these big wages should go only to the players who really

are worth it and there's not that many. There are a few around the Premier League but there are a lot more ordinary players getting £60,000-70,000-80,000 a week who wouldn't have got into any of my Preston teams.
TOM FINNEY, former Preston North End and England winger, 2009

People say the wages are too high, but it's a short career.
SIR STANLEY MATTHEWS, whose own playing career lasted 40 years, 1987

You can't blame the players for taking advantage. If you can get £40,000 a week, you'll take it. That's human nature.
ALAN HANSEN, TV pundit and former Liverpool captain, 1999

My first contract was bigger than my father, an electrician, had ever earned in his life. So I realise how it is. Then again it would be crazy to say: 'No, I don't want it.' It's just how it is in football. Everybody makes money. Why shouldn't we? A lot of people are there to watch.
DENNIS BERGKAMP, Arsenal striker, 1999

Society finds it hard to accept men from the lower classes, where most footballers are recruited, being paid salaries that would normally be out of bounds to them.
LETTER to The Times *amid criticism of the top Premiership players' wages, 2002*

A successful football career used to be about winning things. Now it's about how much money you end up with.
GRAEME SOUNESS, Liverpool manager, 1993

Too many players these days judge themselves by how good their car is and by the size of their house, rather than by the medals they've won. I see players who are rich after five years in the game but have never got close to winning anything. I can see people retiring at 25 in the future.
PAUL MERSON, Aston Villa and England midfielder, 2000

I wince at players who cheat and foul, who abuse referees and who think only about winning and the money it will bring.
TONY BLAIR MP, Labour, on the modern game, 1995

Some of the players think: 'I've got a million in the bank. Why work harder?'

RAY HARFORD, Blackburn manager, on the champions' poor start to the season, 1995

Look on the bright side if your [sic] not getting played take the L out and get payed.
RYAN HALL, Leeds United winger, tweeting on being out of the side, 2014; the comment led to his departure from the club

They are just guys who get paid ridiculous amounts of money for not doing very much.
JADE JOHNSON, international long-jumper, on modern footballers, 2002

It's weird, isn't it? I remember when a hundred quid seemed like loads of money.
JONATHAN WOODGATE, Leeds defender, after his club paid £18m for Rio Ferdinand, 2000

It will be a story about how young men can earn £20,000 a week and virtually own whole cities, yet somehow think that they're bullet-proof.
ALLEN JEWHURST, Granada TV producer, planning a drama-documentary on the case that led to the trial of Leeds' Lee Bowyer and Jonathan Woodgate, 2002

Rolex watches, garages full of flashy cars and mansions, set up for life, forgot about the game, lost the hunger that got you the watches, cars and mansions.
ROY KEANE, Manchester United captain, reacting to their Champions League semi-final defeat by Bayer Leverkusen, 2002

Even the young players are so polite. At [Manchester] City they're not like that. They're coming in with £10,000 watches on their wrists and walking around as if they've played 200 Premier League games.
STEPHEN IRELAND, Republic of Ireland midfielder, on joining Villa from City, 2010

Some players are cocky gits. You see them out and about, giving it large but they haven't done anything in the game to justify it.
KEANE, 2000

If you're a top player, you have a fucking great big ego that follows you round everywhere. Sometimes it gets in the way, though you must have it.
GRAEME SOUNESS, Blackburn manager, 2004

There's a great American saying: 'Why bother to get out of bed when you're wearing silk pyjamas?' I think it applies to some young players. A lot earn huge amounts before they're the finished article and undoubtedly find it hard to motivate themselves.
STEVE COPPELL, Crystal Palace manager and former players' union chairman, 1999

Some players would still be world-class if you paid them £20 a week. But for others it's now all about how much you can earn. I don't begrudge them the big salaries, but how can you say that someone on £30,000 a week does a better job than a nurse or a policeman, who have to risk their lives for £14,000 a year?
NEVILLE SOUTHALL, former Everton and Wales goalkeeper, 1999

Whenever we take our young players away they have to dress in shirt and tie. They have to learn how to eat properly in restaurants and how to make speeches of thanks to the opposition. We don't produce greedy, money-grabbing bastards.
KIT CARSONS, director of Peterborough United's youth academy, 1999

Money brings bad habits. The players live too easily.
JAVIER CLEMENTE, Marseille coach, 2001

Money cannot buy you happiness.
YAKUBU, Nigeria and former Premier League striker, after signing a £5m-per-year, three-year contract with Chinese club Guangzhou, 2012

Being a footballer has its advantages. Earning £40,000 to £80,000 a month deserves some sacrifice. Guys in the street work hard for eight hours a day. Players put in only one hour a day and two on Saturday.
BERNARD TAPIE, Marseille director of sport, 2001

Money is not a criterion for some people. There are multi-millionaires who still get up at 6am to get going about their business. They are winners. For players it doesn't matter what bonus they are on, playing is the meat and drink and winning is the bonus. It's the winning that gives them the kicks.
ALEX FERGUSON, Manchester United manager, 1995

What makes big players is their love of the game. Money should not control the game. It alienates fans. If tomorrow there was no money in football, I would still love it.
ARSENE WENGER, Arsenal manager, on losing Nicolas Anelka to Real Madrid for 'non-footballing reasons', 1999

I wouldn't give up football even if I won the £18m jackpot on the National Lottery. I love this job and I would even pay to play.
DEAN HOLDSWORTH, Bolton striker, 1995

People will say I've got a screw loose, but perhaps I'm in the 0.1 per cent of footballers who don't give a toss about unlimited money.
MATTHEW LE TISSIER on why he had stayed loyal to Southampton, 1995

I took a pay cut to come here. As long as the fridge is full, I'm happy.
GORDON STRACHAN on joining Coventry as player-coach from Leeds, 1995

I've given up this year. I've decided to bin it off. I've signed my three-year deal and I thought I'd leave it this year, sit back, have a few cans and a few cigarettes and chill with the kids.
GRANT HOLT, Norwich City striker, responding sarcastically to being asked by a reporter if he had 'lost his hunger' after signing a three-year contract, 2012

The money I make, I give it all to my mother. I don't even know where it goes.

CHRISTIAN VIERI, Inter Milan striker, after Vatican criticism of players' wages, 1999

You go into a shop and it's just Armani this and that, and you buy it. Clothes you don't even need. I spent a grand once. Bit of a waste.
GARY KELLY, Leeds and Republic of Ireland defender, 1995

I earn more than all you wankers put together.
CARLTON PALMER, Leeds midfielder, to police after he was arrested during a night out in the city, 1997

I was nearly a soccer brat, but the more I earned the louder my conscience became.

NIALL QUINN, Sunderland striker, on giving the proceeds of his testimonial match to charity, 2002

They are rich, they've got everything, but there must be something else. Something you cannot buy: honour, morals and inner desire.
GUNTER NETZER, former Germany midfielder, after his country's exit from Euro 2000

You can make a player fitter by giving him a pay rise. It may sound daft, but he works harder and he's happier at home.
LOU MACARI, Swindon manager, 1986

I cannot feed my child on glory.
PAOLO ROSSI, Italy striker, during pay dispute with Juventus, 1982

Two months ago [after he helped Italy win the World Cup] Rossi was over the moon. Now he is asking for it.
JUVENTUS OFFICIAL, 1982

It's almost theft taking money after a performance like that. I'll be using the winter break to make the players' lives as miserable as possible.
CRAIG LEVEIN, Hearts manager, after defeat at Aberdeen, 2001

We are meant to be these hard-headed, money-obsessed professionals but we are still little boys at heart. Just ask our wives.
ROB LEE, Newcastle midfielder, before playing in the FA Cup final, 1998

Three cheers for FIFA [football transfers to be scrapped, 1 September]. At last the likes of Keane and Beckham will be able to receive the rewards they deserve, rather than struggling on today's paltry sums.
LETTER to The Guardian, 2000

Footballers are well paid and have a fantastic lifestyle. They get up every morning and go to training grounds and work a couple of hours a day. Any player who moans should have to work a month down the pits in a real job.
RON ATKINSON, TV summariser, former player and manager, on BBC TV's Room 101, 2003

When a manager rests players because they've played two games in six days, I laugh my cock off.

RICKY HATTON, IBF world welterweight boxing champion and Manchester City fan, 2005

Every day is Christmas for a footballer, doing a job they love for huge amounts of money in most cases. A quiet Christmas, preparing for the next match, is a small price to pay for the privilege of playing for a living.
GORDON STRACHAN, Southampton manager, on the 'small sacrifices' players make over the festive season, 2003

Footballers, particularly those like me who are lucky enough to play for one of the more glamorous clubs, have a great life. You feel that nothing can touch you. You feel somehow totally protected. Then something happens to let you know that you are just as vulnerable as everyone else.
DENNIS WISE, then a Chelsea player, in his autobiography, 2000

The image of the footballer as a glamorous, show-business type, surrounded by pretty girls and flash cars, is firmly implanted in most people's minds. I know him more accurately as the deeply insecure family man or the tearful, failed apprentice.
EAMON DUNPHY, Republic of Ireland player, 1973

Take away Match of the Day and all the hangers-on and it's all very empty and lonely being a footballer.
RODNEY MARSH, England striker, 1971

Footballers are the most vulnerable people. They exude confidence but inside they are so lacking in it. They know they can lose form or be injured. The profession is so insecure you wouldn't believe it.
GORDON TAYLOR, chief executive of the players' union, the PFA, 2003

Of course it would help [the public perception of footballers] if they were choirboys and gave all their money to charity. Life doesn't work like that.
GORDON TAYLOR, 2003

Footballers are only interested in drinking, clothes and the size of their willies.
KARREN BRADY, Birmingham City managing director, 1994

Today you have prima donnas and they are highly paid. Their intelligence, across the board, is a lot higher than in my day. Comic Cuts was the typical newspaper of the dressing room then whereas now it's the serious papers. We actually got complaints that there was only one public phone in the changing rooms because they wanted to ring their stockbrokers after training.
DOUG ELLIS, Aston Villa chairman, 2000

[Footballers are] scum. Total scum. They don't know what honesty or loyalty are. All they're interested in is themselves.
SIR ALAN SUGAR, former Tottenham owner, 2005

I like a bit of rough – footballers, roofers, blokes who get banged up.
DANNIELLA WESTBROOK,
EastEnders *actress, 1996*

I hope that 2003 brings me a fantastic, intelligent and kind man. Not a footballer.

VANESSA KELLY, Australian model, dismissing reports of romance with the Italy striker Christian Vieri, 2003

You just don't get professional players climbing trees.
MIKE FORD, Oxford City manager, after his goalkeeper Victor Francoz suffered a serious cut when falling from a tree while rescuing a cat, 2014

I prefer footballers not to be too good or clever at other things. It means they concentrate on football.
BILL NICHOLSON, Tottenham manager, 1973

I wouldn't quote Kipling to the lads. They'd probably think I was talking about cakes.
ROB KELLY, Leicester manager, 2006

Politics is my specialist subject. Let me tell you, not all footballers are thick, no matter what the press would have you believe.
PAT CRERAND, former Manchester United midfielder, 2004

When you're away with a team, everyone has their way of filling in the time. Mine is a book, a movie or replying to my mail. But you still get bored. In 2002 I stayed in hotels for 260 days. It was the most horrible thing. For me, travel creates the most stress of anything I do in my job. By comparison, the playing is relaxation.
JENS LEHMANN, Arsenal's German goalkeeper, 2004

The glut of football books is a sorry reflection of our current cultural life. The status of footballers and the money they earn is appalling. They may not even be writing these books. Most are ghosted. They are simply selling their names and lifestyle.
FAY WELDON, novelist, 2005

Further to your recent letter I am sorry that we cannot help you with your search for academic footballers. In fact, two of the back four cannot read.
JOE ROYLE, Oldham manager, replying to a journalist researching a feature on footballers with degrees, 1987

Without being rude, footballers are not the best talkers in the world.
JIMMY HILL, former player, chairman and TV pundit, 1998

What they say about soccer players being ignorant is rubbish. I spoke to a couple yesterday and they were quite intelligent.

RACQUEL WELCH, American actress, after a visit to Chelsea match, 1973

We're paid to play football, not to think.

PAUL BASTOCK, Boston United goalkeeper, when asked whether he thought an FA inquiry into the running of the club had affected their start in league football, 2002

Excuse me, but there are footballers who think.

SOL CAMPBELL, Arsenal and England defender, rebutting the stereotype of the 'thick' footballer during a press interview, 2002

There are only two things you can be certain of with footballers. One, they'll let you down. Two, you don't know when they'll let you down. They are flawed characters.

SECRETARY of a Premiership club, quoted anonymously in the press, 2000

I never wanted to be a coach because I have a low opinion of players. Footballers are the most obnoxious, ignorant and selfish people.

EDWIN STEIN, Birmingham coach, 1993

Professionalism in rugby union implies a soccer-style mentality; training in the morning and reading comics in the afternoon.

ED GRIFFITHS, chief executive of the South African Rugby Union, 1995

Footballers couldn't run a fish-and-chip shop.

BOB LORD, Burnley chairman, 1961

I would not hang a dog on the word of an ex-professional footballer.

ALAN HARDAKER, Football League secretary, 1961

I can remember the day when, as a goalkeeper playing for Reading against Millwall at The Den in 1951, I collected ninepence in old pennies which had bounced off my skull. We needed the money in those days.

LETTER to the Daily Telegraph *after coin-throwing incidents at matches, 2002*

My role, when I wasn't working the lathe, was that of general dogsbody and butt of jokes. Once I was told to go and fetch a bucket of steam. Another time it was a left-handed screwdriver. Being young and naive I actually went looking for them.

NORMAN HUNTER, former Leeds and England defender, recalling his first job in an engineering works, in his autobiography Biting Talk, *2004*

I walked to work when I was captain of West Brom [before the abolition of the maximum wage in 1961]. I didn't have a car and at that stage I never looked like getting one either.
SIR BOBBY ROBSON, Newcastle and former England manager, 2004

If Mr Football Fan went to many a car park when the players are rolling up for training he would probably be unable to restrain himself from a muttered 'Cor blimey'. For he'd see a fair number of the 'slaves' turning up for their daily stint in nice, shiny cars. At my own club, for instance, many of the lads have cars. I have myself, I'll admit.
RONNIE CLAYTON, Blackburn and England player, in A Slave to Soccer, *1960*

Some folks tell me we professional players are soccer slaves. Well, if this is slavery, give me a life sentence.
BOBBY CHARLTON a year before the lifting of the maximum wage, 1960

You're a slave if you work with no contract and aren't paid. Some players join Manchester United, kiss the shirt and next day say they want to go to Barcelona.
PELE on Cristiano Ronaldo's claim that United treated him 'like a modern-day slave' by resisting Real Madrid's overtures, 2008

None of the players can change a tyre. One asked Albert the kit man to look at his car as he thought he had a nail stuck in a tyre. Albert asked where the key was to loosen the locking wheel nuts. He was confronted by a bemused-looking footballer who told him: 'If it's a problem I'll just phone the garage and get them to swap the car for a new one.'
BRIAN McCLAIR, Manchester United youth coach and former player, 2004

Parking is a disaster for me. I usually have to park a mile away from the place I need.
ANDREI ARSHAVIN, Arsenal and Russia striker, 2010

Mickey [Thomas] gave you everything on the pitch, but there was no real discipline. He even managed to write off a club car in a car wash.
HOWARD KENDALL, former Everton manager, on the Welsh winger's 'hyper' antics, 2013

These stories about Manchester United players with six cars worry me. I fear some young players are losing touch with reality. Because there is so much money in the game, it's only right that we get our proper share, but I'd like to see young players on big, five-year contracts being paid that money over a 10- or even 15-year period, so they didn't have so much in their pocket.
NIALL QUINN, Sunderland and Republic of Ireland striker, 2000

Motivating players isn't easy when their first signing-on fee pays off the mortgage. There is great consolation in not playing and going home in a Porsche. In my day the car park was all Vivas and Cortinas.
JOE ROYLE, *Manchester City manager, 2001*

We had to win to get a £2 bonus, yet now there are three players in the City side getting £230,000 a week.
BERT TRAUTMANN, *City goalkeeper of the 1950s, 2011*

Dwight [Yorke] is getting £100,000 for this book but it couldn't be further down his priorities. His Ferrari cost twice as much, so why bother?
HUNTER DAVIES, *journalist, on collaborating on Yorke's autobiography, 2000*

We're going to burn your Ferraris.

CHANT *by Real Madrid fans after their 5–1 defeat by Zaragoza, 1999*

The Bosman ruling has ensured that players have much more power. Look at the car park: it used to be the directors who drove fancy motors, now it's the players.
GEORGE GRAHAM, *Tottenham manager, 2000*

Q: What car do you drive? A: Two Mercs and a Porsche.

ADE AKINBIYI, *Crystal Palace striker, in a programme questionnaire, 2002*

Maybe it's difficult to motivate players if they earn 40 grand a week, have three Mercs and mistresses everywhere.
JOE KINNEAR, *Wimbledon manager, 1997*

Things were so much easier when I earned 100pound a week on wts #stress
JAMIE O'HARA, *Wolves midfielder, who was reportedly paid £35,000 a week and was married to former Miss Great Britain Danielle Lloyd, 2012*

Players are a club's best assets, so they must be dealt with grandly. We are not looking for a bargain but for a great player, and he deserves everything his rank and industry can get.
DON RAIMUNDO SAPORTA, *vice-president of Real Madrid, 1961*

It's not the likes of me who have pushed transfer fees and wages sky high but the clubs competing for our services.
TREVOR FRANCIS, *England striker, before his move into Italian football, 1982*

As a player you're nothing more than a piece of meat. We're nothing more than cattle. I had a conversation with Roy Keane about it and he agreed. He said: 'They sold you like a cow.' The fact is he [Alex Ferguson] sold me behind my back. I don't know anything about it. He fired me because he had problems about his own reputation.
JAAP STAM on his surprising transfer from Manchester United to Lazio, 2001

As a footballer you can be happily playing away, your children can be doing well at school and your wife settled. But if the manager wants rid of you he can make life very difficult until you agree to go.
MARK McGHEE, Wolves manager, 1995

Where else in the world do you get the scuzzy standards British football has? The players have too much time on their hands and they're surrounded by sycophants.
MARK BORKOWSKI, celebrity publicist and Chelsea fan, on the John Terry/Anton Ferdinand case, 2010

I moved to Manchester and stayed at [agent Paul] Stretford's house. He made me part of the family. I thought it was a generous gesture. I later found out he'd been deducting rent from my earnings.
ANDY COLE, former United and City striker, 2010

A lot of players think they need them agents but that's not the case. They need good advice from a solicitor or an accountant, not people taking hundreds of thousands off them.
GARY NEVILLE, Manchester United captain, 2007

I sometimes say to footballers' agents: 'The difference between you and me is that if there were no more money in football tomorrow, I'd still be here, but not you.'
ARSENE WENGER, Arsenal manager, 2003

A footballer's ability is in his feet and his head. They are not used to doing deals. Agents do that on their behalf and you would expect them to be remunerated. Anyone who does not see that is not in the real world.
DAVID GILL, chief executive of Manchester United, after 2003 figures revealed the club paid £5m to agents, 2004

No football-club owner in his right mind would willingly invite an average agent into his academy, any more than a brothel owner would let a syphilitic nutter into his brothel.
SIMON JORDAN, Crystal Palace chairman, 2005

Agents are nasty scum. They are evil and divisive and pointless. They survive only because the rest of the sport is so corrupt and because leading football people employ their sons in the job.
JORDAN on the 'bullshit world' of football, 2004

Take away corruptible managers and officials, and you take away the problem [of 'bungs']. And that's far easier a concept to get your head around than the proposed alternative – FIFA weeding through every agent worldwide, choosing the churchgoing ones and culling the rest.
JORDAN, 2006

I can't argue with people seeing us as the scum of the earth.

COLIN GORDON, agent, 2006

Greed and blackmail drive the game now. Players and agents run football, not managers and chairmen. Half the time I'm not dealing with players but with millionaires.
DAVE BASSETT, Nottingham Forest manager, 1998

The fees some of them take for spending a few hours on the phone! Don't forget that money goes out of football and doesn't come back.
JOE ROYLE, Ipswich manager, 2003

The money coming into the game is incredible. But it's just the prune-

juice effect – it comes in and goes out straight away. Agents run the sport.
ALAN SUGAR, Tottenham chairman, 1997

It used to be the wives who affected players, now it's agents.
BOBBY GOULD, Wimbledon manager, 1988

Agents do nothing for the good of football. I'd like to see them lined up against a wall and machine-gunned… Some accountants and solicitors with them.
GRAHAM TAYLOR, Watford manager, 1983

I wouldn't cross the road to talk to an agent, let alone go to Manchester.
GRAHAM KELLY, FA chief executive, declining an invitation to a meeting attended by agents, 1992

We have to deal with these people [agents], but Bill Shankly wouldn't have done.
BRIAN CLOUGH, 1991

What do I think of agents? Dogs, worms, vermin.
JOE KINNEAR, Wimbledon manager, 1995

There's always a tendency for players to under-price themselves. No one likes to say: 'I'm worth this or that.' It's better if someone else does the talking for you and leaves you to do the playing.
RAY WILKINS, former England captain, 1993

Manchester United were bad payers in the 1970s. They had the mentality that people would play for them for nothing. People moan about agents but I wish they had been around in my day.
STUART PEARSON, former United and England striker, 1995

A lot of players are dominated by their agents. You get agents who do their groceries, do their travel, polish their boots.
MARK HUGHES, Fulham manager, 2011

Agents are disliked by managers and directors but this is because they give players power – through the simple device of letting them know the going rate. No one I know, in any job anywhere, wants to earn less than the going rate. Footballers are no different.
ROB LEE, Newcastle and England midfielder, 1998

I am trained in economics, I have the ability to run a company and I don't see why I shouldn't put these gifts at the service of my brother. But the football scene is crawling with sharks and profiteers, and my diplomas did not prepare me for facing them.
DIDIER ANELKA, Nicolas's brother, on acting as his agent, 1999

Most agents wouldn't know a ball from a banana.
JOHN LAMBIE, Partick Thistle manager, 2002

It is turning into a spivs' market place.

JIM SMITH, Derby manager, 2000

Q: Who's your favourite player?
A: I can't say. I don't know anything about football.
ERIC HALL, self-styled 'monster' agent, interviewed in Total Football *magazine, 1995*

Don't know much about the game, don't even like it much. What's that got to do with it? My business is selling people. Makes no difference what they do.
HALL, 1990

I now believe in Father Christmas, I really do. I owe him [Jean-Marc Bosman] a monster Christmas present.
HALL after the European Union's highest court ruled the game's transfer system illegal, 1995

I have no morals when it comes to dealing with my clients. I would deal with the Devil to get the best deal for them.
HALL, 1989

If there was a really star name who was represented by the Devil, there would still be a queue of clubs wishing to negotiate with him.
ATHOLE STILL, players' agent, 1999

When people ask my wife what I do, she tells them I'm a Kwik-Fit fitter rather than admit I'm an agent.

JON HOLMES, players' agent, 1996

You think I want to get together with other agents? I wouldn't have most of them in my garden.
HOLMES, 2006

I realised how sinister it had become when I was manager of Peterborough and I tried to sign a lad who had played one league game. He told me to talk to his agent. There are 2,000 professionals in England, but only 20 need an agent.
MARK LAWRENSON on his stint as an 'alternative agent', backed by the players' union, 1991

Every player needs an agent because whatever their status, they are in no position to negotiate contracts. As for signing up young players I see nothing wrong in that. I also handle showbiz people and often

take on groups before they have made a record.
ERIC HALL responding to Lawrenson, 1991

I don't want my players playing for England because when they come back, all they want is big wages, sponsored cars, a big house, Page Three birds, ecstasy and cocaine. I'm happy they don't know about all that lark.
DAVE BASSETT, Sheffield United manager, 1990

Once I went training with £4,500 in my pocket and then ran out of petrol on the way home because I'd spent it all betting on horses. I had to hitch a lift.
STEVE CLARIDGE, Leicester City striker, on being a serial gambler, 1996

What can footballers do? They can't drink, can't smoke, can't take drugs. They have to have something to do. Some people can have a bet and walk away and then there are others, like me, who have to keep on chasing, chasing and chasing.
PAUL MERSON, gambling addict and former England player, 2003

If players are earning £50,000 a week, they're not going to bet in fivers.
JAMIE REDKNAPP, former England midfielder, on reports of a gambling epidemic among top players, 2006

When you're a millionaire, winning a few quid on a horse means nothing.

HARRY REDKNAPP, Portsmouth manager, on his players' lack of interest in racing, 2004

I've won and lost tens of thousands. It's like a drug. You start on cigarettes and end up on heroin. I started on £10 or £20 a race, finished up on many thousands. You can't go back.
STEVE CLARIDGE, widely travelled striker and gambling addict, 2003

With me, the gambling was a serious problem. With him, if you're talking £40,000 over two years with the wages he's earning, it's pocket money. He has probably got more cash in his ashtray than that.
CLARIDGE after reports of Michael Owen's gambling, 2003

I had an understanding with the bookies where they added a nought to whatever I put on. My missus thought I was phoning up with £250 bets when it was really £2,500. People laugh, but it's an illness.
JOHN HARTSON, West Brom striker, 2006

They [gambling addicts] lose their self-respect and before they know it they are nicking money out of their kids' savings to have a bet.
TONY ADAMS, former England captain and recovering alcoholic, 2003

It's nobody's business how much I've lost because it's my money. I've earned it and can do whatever I want with it. Doctors, lawyers and newspaper publishers go to casinos, so what's the problem?
JIMMY FLOYD HASSELBAINK, Chelsea striker, on reports that he had lost £1.1m on gambling, 2003

Loads of footballers have horses they like to socialise with.

MICK QUINN, talkSPORT pundit and former striker, 2011

From the first time I kicked a ball as a pro 19 years ago, I began to learn what the game was all about. It's about the drunken parties that go on for days. The orgies, the birds and the fabulous money. Football is just a distraction: you're so fit that you can carry on all the high living in secret and still play at the highest level.
PETER STOREY, former Arsenal and England player, 'telling all' in a tabloid, 1980

I don't want them going out having Christmas parties. What chance have you got? The press will be waiting, someone will be taking pictures of them. Somebody can just have their eyes closed and it looks like they are boozed. You don't need it.
HARRY REDKNAPP, *Tottenham manager, 2011*

Shunsuke [Nakamura] told me not to touch alcohol and chips, but I tried them one night and I won't be doing that again. I didn't feel too well.
KOKI MIZUNO, *Celtic and Japan player, 2009*

Everywhere you go in football, you're offered booze.
BRIAN CLOUGH *on the roots of his problems with alcohol, 2003*

They were on a lager diet.
RON ATKINSON *describing the European Cup-winning sides of Nottingham Forest and Liverpool 25 years earlier, 2003*

The team that drinks together wins together.

RICHARD GOUGH, *Rangers captain, on how a group 'binge' helped with bonding, 1995*

I used to go to the Alva Supporters' Club function every year. I'd go after a Saturday game, stay all day Sunday and get home at some point on the Monday. We called it the equestrian because it was a three-day event.
ANDY GORAM, *former Rangers goalkeeper under Gough's captaincy, 2005*

It just goes to show that cricketers can be as stupid as footballers.
GRAHAM TAYLOR, *former England manager, after England all-rounder Andrew Flintoff was drunk on a pedalo at the cricket World Cup, 2007*

When I first went out for a night with some English players, they couldn't believe I didn't drink. Coke? They said it like they had never heard of such a thing. 'Go on. Go on,' they said. 'Have a drink. What's wrong with you?'
MARIO MELCHIOT, *Chelsea's Dutch defender, 2004*

There's only one drug at Bayern and that's beer... After a night of cards and lager I used to spread the empties around the hotel corridor so it wouldn't give the impression there was an alcoholic in my room.
STEFFEN EFFENBERG, *former Germany midfielder, in his memoir* I've Shown Everything, *2003*

Even after a skinful, I don't have a hangover and can still be up with the others [in training].

BRYAN ROBSON, *former England captain, on reports that he was a heavy drinker, 1990*

The legendary drinkers at a club are usually the best trainers. They go out and get into an unathletic state, but come the next training day, they put in more effort than the non-drinkers because they feel they have to.
JOHN COLQUHOUN, *Hearts striker, 1996*

Quite a few of them [footballers] can knock back a pint or two, but none are alcoholics.
JIMMY HILL, *then a Fulham player, in his book* Striking for Soccer, *1961*

Of course I'm against Sunday soccer. It'll spoil my Saturday nights.

JOHN RITCHIE, *Stoke City player, as his club prepared to play in one of the first-ever Sunday matches, 1974*

The need for a couple of beers and small talk after a hard match is part of my way of life. But do not be misled, this is only applicable after a hard match and certainly only a once-a-week event.
GEORGE KIRBY, *Walsall and former Everton, Sheffield Wednesday and Coventry striker, in a programme column about his 'philosophy', 1966*

It was a totally different culture [in the 1960s and '70s]; big lapels, kipper ties. You had a good time until Wednesday, Friday lunchtime you were back to being reasonable and Saturday night you were out. But Saturday afternoon you really wanted to be on that team-sheet.
MIKE CHANNON, *racehorse trainer and former England striker, 2004*

The young players of today drink a lot more than in my teenage-to-early-twenties period. We used to be pint sinkers but now the orders are more likely to be Bacardi and Cokes or gin and tonics. I have seen them pay out for a single round what I used to earn in a week at Chelsea.
JIMMY GREAVES, *recovering alcoholic and former England striker, in* This One's On Me, *1979*

When I was a young player, if I ever went into a pub or restaurant and my manager came in, I'd sneak out the back door. Nowadays a player would probably come up and ask me if I wanted a drink.
PAUL JEWELL, *Bradford City manager, on the modern player's lack of fear of their manager, 2000*

All the great players I've ever known have enjoyed a good drink.
JIM BAXTER, *former Scotland midfielder, 1993*

The players can get out of their brains every night as long as they're man of the match on Saturday.

JOHN GREGORY, *Aston Villa manager, 1999*

There are one or two players around who'd like it renamed the Vodka and Coca-Cola Cup.
RON ATKINSON, *Aston Villa manager, 1994*

When he first arrived all he could say was 'yes', 'no' and 'morning'. A week later he'd added, 'thank you' and 'a Budweiser, please'.
JIM DUFFY, *Dundee manager, on Czech defender Dusan Vrto, 2003*

Now it's a gallon or two of cold lager, a day to recover and back to the building site at seven o'clock on Monday morning.
CHRIS BRINDLEY, *part-timer with non-league Kidderminster, after an FA Cup win at Birmingham, 1994*

Some of the younger players think lager makes you invisible.
CRAIG BROWN, *Scotland manager, 1999*

I have always been against players drinking and I'm always thinking of ways of getting a team that doesn't drink.
ALEX FERGUSON, *Manchester United manager, 1997*

I don't understand why a player must drink after a game. Maybe one drink is OK but three, four, five, six...drinking until they're drunk. That is no good.
ROBERTO MANCINI, *Manchester City manager, 2010*

I won't stand for booze. One player who joined the club said: 'I may as well tell you, I like a drink.' I found out he was taking others along... Instead of one lager they had three. Three becomes four and it escalates. I had to get rid of him.
LOU MACARI, *Swindon manager, 1986*

One drink was too many and after that, a thousand wasn't enough. If I was happy, I'd be down the pub. If I was sad, I'd be down the pub.
CLARKE CARLISLE, *Queens Park Rangers defender and recovering alcoholic, 2003*

Football is an industry where you don't want to show any weakness. Only the strongest survive. Even if you're not feeling good, you put on a front so that people think you are.
CARLISLE, *2003*

If I had my time again, I wouldn't do anything different. Except that knowing what I do now, I'd never open a pub.
GERD MULLER, former West Germany striker, on his alcoholism, 1991

Alcohol controls me. It's a disease and has nothing to do with me personally. I never go a day without thinking about drinking.
GEORGE BEST, 1990

If I go into a bar and have a lager shandy, word goes back that I'm knocking back bottles of champagne. By the time it gets to the papers or my manager at Arsenal, it's me lying in the gutter.
CHARLIE NICHOLAS, Arsenal and Scotland striker, 1984

Scottish players booze, smoke and eat whatever comes to hand.

JEAN LUC WETZEL, French agent, 2000

One reason [why Portuguese clubs are doing better than English teams in Europe] is that they don't bloody drink. There are no 12-pints-a-night men here. They go straight home to their families and behave like responsible adults.
BOBBY ROBSON, Porto coach, 1995

Alcohol isn't part of the lifestyle for Italian players. They work on the principle that your body's a machine. When you drain that machine, the one thing you don't fill it with is alcohol.
GRAEME SOUNESS, Liverpool manager and ex-Sampdoria player, 1991

In France if you say the players can have a drink, they have two. Here they have double figures.
GERARD HOULLIER, Liverpool manager and former French FA technical director, 1999

I compare top players to racing cars. Drinking alcohol is as silly as putting diesel in a racing car.
HOULLIER, 2000

If left to their own devices the players would have two weeks in Tenerife, another two in Cyprus and two more in the pub.
DAVID SULLIVAN, joint owner of Birmingham City, on allegations that the club's pre-season training was too gruelling, 1995

[Fabien] Barthez sat in my office smoking during the second half. He comes off for ill health and puts a fag in his mouth. Is that not ironic? It's a no-smoking area, too.
GORDON STRACHAN, Southampton manager, after the Manchester United goalkeeper was substituted, 2003

The Italians smoke, yet they're world-class. They even nip into the toilets at half-time for a crafty fag.

PAUL GASCOIGNE, 1998

Drink lots of beer and smoke loads of fags.
GERRY TAGGART, Leicester and Northern Ireland player, when asked for his advice to aspiring players, 2001

The beers are for laughing and the fags for opening up the lungs.
STEVE DAVEY, postman and striker with Harrogate Railway Athletic, detailing his habits during the club's FA Cup run, 2003

Liverpool won the FA Cup a few years ago with a team of 11 foreigners, including Scots, Welsh and Irish. Now we have Spanish, French and Italians. They speak better English, are more civilised and know how to use a knife and fork.
KEN BATES, Chelsea chairman, on the influx of players from abroad, 2000

They've got to stop going in betting shops, going out boozing and eating McDonald's and start living how a young professional should. If not, they're going to get their P45.
DAVE ALLEN, Sheffield Wednesday director, on the club's young players, 2002

In the 1960s and '70s football gave you an education in life. We were the post-war generation. Nobody came out of a centrally heated house. In my first season I went to the Royal in Southampton for our pre-match meal and the waitress asked how I'd like my steak cooked. I hadn't a clue – my mum cooked for me.
MIKE CHANNON, racehorse trainer and former England striker, 2004

Of course I miss Manchester; it felt like I left a family back there. I especially miss the apple crumble and custard they served at Carrington after training.
CRISTIANO RONALDO, Real Madrid and former Manchester United striker, 2012

[Alex Ferguson] would come into a pre-match meal and say: 'Get that salt off the table, I don't want any of that butter there, get margarine. And no sugar in your tea or coffee.' We couldn't believe it.
BRYAN ROBSON, former Manchester United and England midfielder, 2013

We had a teetotal right-back called Stuart Kennedy who brought

in books about the diets of Ivan Lendl and Martina Navratilova. That's when we started good eating habits. That team invented pasta.
ALEX McLEISH, Birmingham manager, on the Alex Ferguson era at Aberdeen, 2011

We've got sports scientists who insist it's important for the lads to eat after games to refuel, even if it's 2am. I used to refuel after [playing for] West Ham until 3.30 in the morning in a different way – but then I'm old school.
HARRY REDKNAPP, Tottenham manager, 2009

We need to have lectures about why we can't have things like mayonnaise, ketchup and Coke every day.
PAOLO DI CANIO, Sunderland manager, on his strict dietary regime, 2013

Doping in English football is restricted to lager and baked beans with sausages. After that the players take to the field, belching and farting.
DI CANIO, playing for Lazio in Italy, 2005

People cook up some unbelievable stuff for breakfast over here. As for eating baked beans at breakfast time, they can trigger off a violent reaction in anybody not used to them.
HERITA ILUNGA, West Ham's Congo international defender, 2010

When you go to the supermarket and you see the cheese designed in a triangle shape and you move it, it's sexy.
ASAMOAH GYAN, Sunderland and Ghana striker, on life in England, 2011

[In Los Angeles] a bottle of Ribena is $14. But I get my Walkers crisps delivered once a month. I have a box of Roast Chicken, a box of Salt and Vinegar and a box of Monster Munch.
VINNIE JONES, Hollywood-based actor and former Wales captain, 2013

The Beckhams clearly prefer McDonald's to cassoulet.

CANAL PLUS NEWS, France, after David Beckham turned down a move to Paris St-Germain, 2012

Sometimes you go into Nando's and you want to tuck into the chicken wings with your fingers but you know someone's watching you, so you don't. I'm thinking: 'If these chicken wings were at home they would get demolished.' But I have to use a knife and fork. You end up saying: 'Could I get a bag to take these home, please?'
DANNY WELBECK, Manchester United and England striker, 2012

We were encouraged to open ourselves to the Japanese cuisine on offer, but having been away from home so long I could have died for a McDonald's.
DANNY MILLS, England defender, at the end of the team's World Cup run, 2002

Obviously we're not in the army but there have to be rules in place. They include not being late for training, not leaving your training kit on the floor...living your life properly, eating like an athlete, not going away from here into McDonald's. Looking at her, I don't think [Olympic gold medal winner] Jessica Ennis stops off at McDonald's on the way home.
DEAN SAUNDERS on being appointed Wolves manager, 2012

Before every game I usually go to Burger King or McDonald's – very good for the hamstring.
PATRICE EVRA, Manchester United and France defender, 2009

We eat a lot of McDonald's, where you have Ronald McDonald. So we chose the name Ronald.
RONALDO, Brazil striker, on his new-born son, 2000

The odd hamburger doesn't do you any harm but you can't live on them.
MATTHEW LE TISSIER on losing weight after his actress girlfriend, Emily Symons, encouraged him to eat more healthily, 2000

A friend had a burger van in Glasgow and he encouraged me to work behind the bar because it meant I had to communicate with people ordering food. I was determined to learn English. Some of the customers used to stare, thinking: 'That looks like Stiliyan Petrov, but it can't be.'
STILIYAN PETROV, Aston Villa and Bulgaria midfielder, on taking on an unusual extra job after signing for Celtic, 2006

I haven't got used to English life. The food is truly disastrous and it rains all the time.

PATRICE EVRA, Manchester United and France defender, 2006

I always found Lee Bowyer a cheery lad, especially when I brought him up some pie and mash from London.
TERRY VENABLES, Leeds manager, 2003

We have this traditional kind of food in England called pie and mash. It's a meat pie and mashed potato. I think it's disgusting but David loves it.
VICTORIA BECKHAM to the Japanese press, 2003

I've raised the white flag with the English food, and when I refused a beer my team-mates looked at me as if I were an alien.
ROLANDO BIANCHI, Italian striker with Manchester City, 2007

I define myself as an Epicurean. I take great pleasure in eating. I'm a salad specialist and I do a good gratin dauphinois at home. And a little tiramisu I learned from Granny Giroud.
OLIVIER GIROUD, Arsenal and France striker, on French TV's MasterChef, *2013*

If I go to a restaurant I'm thinking: 'He knows what I'm eating.' Will I order chips or not?
STEVEN TAYLOR, Newcastle defender, on the club's interim manager Alan Shearer, 2009

Early on, one of the guys posed me a question – 'Ereyergoinfersumscran?' I later understood that this was a polite invitation to go to lunch.
BRAD FRIEDEL, Aston Villa and United States goalkeeper, recalls language difficulties during his spell with Liverpool, 2009

When we found out that the club's owners wanted us to do a chicken advert for Venky's, we didn't really know what to think. I had to pretend to love it, but the truth is, one bite and my stomach was in knots.
MICHEL SALGADO, Blackburn and Spain defender, 2011; Venky's, an Indian chicken meat-processing firm, owned Blackburn

The thing I miss most about London is bread and butter pudding.
THIERRY HENRY on leaving Arsenal for Barcelona, 2008

The surgeon had cut right across the width of my armpit and removed the whole of my top rib. When the lads were out having a Chinese meal, they'd think it funny to send me pictures on their mobiles of spare ribs.
GARY CAHILL, Bolton defender, after having a blood clot removed from his arm, 2010

I have never known a group of people like footballers for eating. A huge evening meal is digested and forgotten by 9.30pm. Then they still want endless rounds of sandwiches.
ALEC STOCK, former manager, in A Little Thing Called Pride, *1982*

'A bit crude when eating' states the report of an Arsenal scout, referring to a well-known international in whom Arsenal were interested... Personal background sometimes damns a player who has the necessary football qualifications.
BERNARD JOY, journalist and ex-Arsenal player, in Forward, Arsenal, *1952*

Once I saw John Charles shift two steak pies, a heaped plate of potatoes and vegetables, two helpings of apple tart and literally gallons of tea.
ROY PAUL, Manchester City and Wales player, in A Red Dragon of Wales, *1956*

Chelsea were a sausage, egg and chips club before the foreign players arrived. That's what we had to eat before training. Andy Townsend, Vinnie Jones, Tony Cascarino and me went to the cafe for a slosh-up before training. I have even had it before games.
DENNIS WISE, Chelsea midfielder, 2000

The diet in Britain is really dreadful. The whole day you drink tea and coffee with milk and cakes. If you had a fantasy world of what you shouldn't eat in sport, it's what you eat here.
ARSENE WENGER, Arsenal manager, 1997

The players go on to the training pitch clutching cups of coffee. Apparently they are given bacon sandwiches with all kinds of colourful sauces. That would be unthinkable in France.
MIKAEL SILVESTRE, Manchester United defender, 1999

My only problem seems to be with Italian breakfasts. No matter how much money you've got, you can't seem to get any Rice Krispies.
LUTHER BLISSETT after transfer from Watford to Milan, 1983

My team-mates at Chelsea have very funny ways of celebrating. In France, when it's your birthday, they buy you champagne and cake. Here they just shove your face in the mud. Very strange.
FRANK LEBOEUF, Chelsea defender, 1999

They go and eat free scampi after a game while I go home with indigestion from watching them play like that and I'm up all night because I can't sleep.
ULI HOENESS, Bayern Munich commercial manager and ex-player, after defeat by lowly St Pauli, 2000

Q: Are you romantic?
A: I'm great at romantic meals. I can only make beans on toast and Pot Noodles, so I buy a takeaway, pile up some dirty pans and serve it up so it looks like I've cooked it.
MATT JANSEN, Blackburn striker, in a newspaper questionnaire, 2001

When I was an apprentice there was this lad who really fancied himself with the girls. We were on this tour in Ireland and he went up to this girl, gave her 10 pence and said: 'Ring your mum, tell her you're not coming home tonight.' And it worked actually! But I've never used it myself.
RYAN GIGGS, Manchester United and Wales winger, interviewed in FourFourTwo *magazine, 2002*

I haven't got a clue about the exact number of women I had – four or five maybe. But I regret it deeply.
KIERON DYER, Newcastle midfielder, on tabloid claims about his holiday in Ayia Napa, 2000

flow... If a girl comes up to you and says 'I want to do this to you', if you turned it down there must be something wrong with you.
NIGEL REO-COKER, Wimbledon midfielder, on the sex life of wealthy young players, 2003

If a footballer presents himself as a family man and goes and has sex with a prostitute, should he gag her?

NICKY CAMPBELL, Radio 5Live presenter, 2011

I'm like 90 per cent of footballers. When we meet a woman, we're thinking: 'Are they just after me for the money?'

SOL CAMPBELL, England defender, 2003

If you're a footballer in England, girls come to you. If you're an ordinary person, you have to go to girls. That's the difference. It's so easy for the players, and the girls just say: 'Let's go, we'll have sex, no problem.' There was no chat, which was strange.
LARS LEESE, ex-Barnsley goalkeeper from Germany, 2004

Women will come to you and start leaving the signs, talking dirty and everything. So obviously a young footballer would just go with the

Players are no worse now than they were 30 years ago. It's getting to a stage where players will have to carry a contract in their pockets for girls to sign, saying that they consent to sex and won't go running to the papers.
PETER LORIMER, Leeds player in the 1970s, recalling how he and seven Scotland team-mates had sex with a woman during the World Cup finals, 2005

I told the players these opportunities may never come again, so they should get out there and do it for their wives, girlfriends – or both for that matter.
PAUL JEWELL, *Wigan manager, after beating Arsenal in the Carling Cup semi-final, 2006*

How does your girlfriend or wife feel about your travelling away from home with all these beautiful American women about?
AMERICAN JOURNALIST to *Manchester United players at press conference on their US tour, 2003*

[In the 1960s] you could take a girl out for a meal, with champagne, for a fiver. All she brought with her was 10 bob in case she didn't like you and needed a taxi home.
MIKE SUMMERBEE, *former Manchester City and England winger, recalling his days as George Best's close friend, in a* Backpass *magazine interview, 2012*

I'm just a normal boy of 19. I like going out with my mates and having a meal and a few drinks. Of course I get propositioned sometimes, and it's nice. My mates love it – they get all the cast-offs.
MARK BURCHILL, *Celtic striker, 1999*

Maybe my players have a rampant sex life when they stay at home on Friday nights.
TERRY BURTON, *Wimbledon manager, on his team's poor home form, 2001*

Of course a player can have sexual intercourse before a match and play a blinder. But if he did for six months he'd be a decrepit old man. It takes the strength from the body.
BILL SHANKLY, *Liverpool manager, 1971*

After having sex the night before a match I lose all feelings in my feet. I'm totally empty. I can't control the ball. Instead I watch erotic movies the night before. That doesn't affect my power.
FREDRIK LJUNGBERG, *Sweden and Arsenal midfielder, 2000*

It's not the sex that tires out young players. It's staying up all night looking for it.

CLEMENS WESTERHOF, *Dutch coach to Nigeria, 1994*

We don't want them to be monks. We want them to be football players because monks don't play football at this level.
BOBBY ROBSON, *Newcastle manager, after some of his players visited nightclubs until the early hours, 2002*

I have been reborn because of my faith. I'm an evangelical now. I have not had sex for two years now. There's nothing going on down there. Really.
NICOLA LEGROTTAGLIE, Juventus defender, 2008

FOWLER: I know someone who had a wank two hours before a game and went out and scored a hat-trick.
McMANAMAN: I know him. He captains his country. But I think the no-sex thing is a load of shite really.
INTERVIEW with Robbie Fowler and Steve McManaman in Loaded *magazine, 1995*

Sex before a match? The boys can do as they please. But it's not possible at half-time.

BERTI VOGTS, Germany coach, World Cup finals, 1998

This is supposed to make us world champions. Of what? Masturbation?
LUIS PEREIRA, Brazil player, on his country's policy of no women in their camp, World Cup finals, 1974

I don't think sex could ever be as rewarding as winning the World Cup. It's not that sex isn't great, just that this tournament comes around only every four years and sex is a lot more regular than that.
RONALDO, Brazil striker, immediately after his goals won the World Cup for Brazil, 2002

Q: What's more satisfying, scoring a hat-trick or having great sex?
A: The missus might be reading this, so I'd better say the sex.
KEVIN PHILLIPS, Sunderland striker, in Loaded *magazine interview, 1999*

If it was a straight choice between having sex and scoring a goal, I'd go for the goal every time. I've got all my life to have sex.
ANDY GRAY, Sky TV summariser and ex-Scotland striker, 1995

Gazza said that scoring was better than an orgasm. Lee Chapman reckoned it wasn't as good. I'll go with Pele – he thought it was about the same.
RYAN GIGGS, Manchester United winger, 1994

Footballers come pretty high up the list now in terms of shagability. Rock stars must still be first, but then it's footballers, then actors, firemen, insurance brokers, then TV quiz show hosts.
ANGUS DEAYTON, host of the TV quiz Have I Got News For You, *1997*

Dwight [Yorke] and Fabien [Barthez] could definitely do with some extra coaching from Angus [Deayton].
CAROLINE MARTIN, kiss-and-sell 'vice girl', claiming sexual liaisons with the TV personality as well as with the two Manchester United players, 2002

Let the players show their athletic torsos. We can't understand how the voluntary showing of a gorgeous male chest can be objectionable.
MOTION to the German parliament by two female Green MPs after Cristiano Ronaldo was booked in Euro 2004 for removing his shirt when celebrating a goal, 2004

The average English footballer could not tell the difference between an attractive woman and a corner flag.

WALTER ZENGA, Italy goalkeeper, responding to Wimbledon manager Bobby Gould's quip that his players wanted the phone numbers of the Italian players' wives while the Azzurri were away at the World Cup, 1990

Trying to explain it to you would be impossible. It would be like you trying to explain childbirth to me.
GORDON STRACHAN, Celtic manager, to radio reporter Michelle Evans (who was childless) when she asked his view on defeat by St Mirren, 2009

When I was with Norwich my wife Dawn had a baby and we called her Darby. A month later I joined Derby. The Norwich lads told me they were all trying for babies and were going to name them Lazio or Barcelona.
ASHLEY WARD, Derby striker, 1996

I named our new baby Lionel because I'm a massive fan of the best player in history. My wife wasn't keen, but I convinced her. I'm in love with Messi on a footballing level.
ANTONIO CASSANO, Italy striker, 2013

There have been a lot of rumours about players sleeping with each other's wives. But it's not true. We're all pulling together.
FABIEN WILNIS, Dutch defender with Ipswich Town, 2001

Bill Shankly had a thing about players not having sex the night before a game. He used to tell us: 'And don't forget to put your boxing gloves on before you go to bed.'
PHIL CHISNALL, 1960s Liverpool player, 2013

When I won the Player of the Year award in 2004 we had a gala dinner and [Fulham owner Mohamed Al Fayed] called me up to get the prize. He took a couple of pills out of his pocket, told me it was Viagra and said: 'You should have a good night.'
LUIS BOA MORTE, former Fulham striker, 2013

In Madrid it was easy because I lived in a hotel. The bell boy's job was to bring me three pastries after sex. He would hand me the pastries, I would hand him the girl, and he'd return her into the night. Sex plus pastries – could it be any better?
ANTONIO CASSANO, Sampdoria, Italy and former Real Madrid striker, in his book Dico Tutto, *2009*

What harm is there in players having sex during the World Cup? My son Stefano was conceived during the 1994 tournament when I spent a day off in San Francisco with my wife.
BRANCO, former Brazil defender, 2010

Sex in the camp relieves tension. It should only be ruled out with a team-mate's wife.
BRANCO, as above

The players can have sex with their wives and girlfriends during the finals. They're not Martians. But it shouldn't be at 2am with champagne and cigars.
DONATO VALLANI, Argentina team doctor, World Cup finals, 2010

Of course the players can have sex with their wives and girlfriends during the tournament. But the women must do all the work.
DIEGO MARADONA, Argentina coach, World Cup finals, 2010

Marriage helps footballers. It settles them down and you know where they are.

SIR ALEX FERGUSON when Manchester United's Wayne Rooney married Coleen McLoughlin, 2008

Most people say that, after marriage, they don't like jumping into bed with their partner because there is no desire. But my wife is the person I love and it was worth waiting. A lot of people were shocked with me, but I am an evangelical Christian and I believe in those values. I think people need to prevent themselves from having sex before marriage.
KAKA, AC Milan and Brazil player, on why he remained a virgin until the age of 23 when he was married, 2008

With the luck we've been having, one of our players must be bonking a witch.
KEN BROWN, Norwich manager, 1987

The young lads [at Leeds] mock me because if you phone me I'm always at home at night. If you want a long career you've got to learn to like a quiet life.
NIGEL MARTYN, Leeds and England goalkeeper, 2000

Don [Revie] liked players to have a stable home life. He wanted us all married off so that we would be at home at night watching TV, not out on the town. He used to get on to me because I was a single lad.
MIKE O'GRADY, Leeds and England winger of the 1960s, 2009

I tend to buy family men. With a married player you generally know he is at home of an evening, watching *Coronation Street.*
BRUCE RIOCH, Arsenal manager, 1995

Being a father has changed everything for me. I would advise young players to find the right girl as quickly as possible because it gets harder and harder to find the right one when you're older. I've got three children now and players with families are way more likely to be responsible and not go out partying until the early hours.
LOUIS SAHA, Tottenham and France striker, 2012

Abel Hernandez is a really strong player who could remain in Serie B with us, but he has to visit fewer bars and find the right wife.
MAURIZIO ZAMPARINI, president of the Sicilian club Palermo, 2013

Q: Girl groupies?
A: Last year I got more Valentine's cards off blokes than girls. They write love poems. It's scary.
MATT JANSEN, Blackburn striker, in newspaper questionnaire, 2001

I'd say that more than 25 per cent of football is gay. It's got to be higher than average. It's a very physical, closed world, a man's world, and you form deep bonds with people you hardly know.
JUSTIN FASHANU, homosexual striker who was then with Torquay and later committed suicide, 1992

I would not encourage any gay professional footballer to come out. I would fear that he would end up like Justin Fashanu.
PHILIPP LAHM, Bayern Munich and Germany defender and captain, in his autobiography, 2011

Football is an amazing sport. But it is also a brutal sport that picks people up and slams them on their heads. Adding the gay aspect doesn't make a great cocktail.
ROBBIE ROGERS, United States international and ex-Leeds winger, on coming out as gay, 2013

Would I want to do interviews every day, where people are asking: 'So you're taking showers with guys – how's that?' If you're playing well it will be reported as: 'The gay footballer is playing well.' And if you have a bad game it'll be:

'Aw, that gay dude. He's struggling because he's gay.'
ROGERS on why he had decided to retire as a player, 2013; he resumed his career with Los Angeles Galaxy

[The coaches] are not homophobic but they'll say: 'Don't pass the ball like a fag.' That's when you look at them and think: 'Fuck you. What are you talking about? Does it make a difference, if you're gay or straight, as to how you pass the ball?' I guess they say it because they think it's funny. There's the stereotype of a gay man being soft and flamboyant.
ROGERS, as above

Sometimes I'd feel bad [for team-mates who used homophobic 'banter']. Sometimes I would laugh because it was kinda funny. And sometimes it got malicious. It's that pack mentality, they're trying to get a laugh and be the top guy. But it's brutal. It's like high school again – on steroids.
ROGERS, as above

Gay footballers don't exist officially.

THOMAS HITZLSPERGER, retired former Aston Villa, West Ham, Everton and Germany midfielder, on coming out, 2014

People think in professional football you have to be strong, powerful. They think being gay means you aren't that – you're the opposite, you're soft, you don't like to tackle, you're very weak. I was nicknamed 'Der Hammer' because I have a powerful left foot, I'm a strong guy. So that's a contradiction. Why do people think being gay also means you're weak? I think I proved the opposite.
HITZLSPERGER, as above

God created Adam and Eve, not Adam and Yves.
ALEX, Paris St-Germain, Brazil and former Chelsea defender, on the Canal-Plus documentary The Jesus Football Club Show, *2014*

Sad times when people have to wait till they retire from their chosen profession before they feel other people will judge them solely on who the human being is... But it's understandable when brainwashed religious zealots still believe in a fictional book written over 2,000 years ago. To be a religious extremist you must first be extremely dumb in my opinion. Alex from PSG confirms my theory with his comments.
JOEY BARTON, Queens Park Rangers midfielder, reacting to Hitzlsperger's 'courageous' announcement, 2014

I am against divorce and abortion. I'm not really for homosexuality.
CEARA, Brazilian defender with Paris St-Germain, on The Jesus Football Club Show, *2014*

Football is toxic and not just for gay people – it's toxic for Asians who want to play the game, for women who want to be executives, for black people who want to do anything but play. It's toxic in many different ways, but football doesn't see itself like that.
JOHN AMAECHI, the first National Basketball Association player to come out as homosexual, 2014

Are there any gays in the [Italy] dressing-room? I hope not. If I say what I really think there will be chaos.
ANTONIO CASSANO, Italy striker, European Championship finals, 2012

Our defence was a wall of real men facing Valencia's homosexuals.
ALEJANDRO LAGO, Uruguayan defender with the Norwegian team Rosenberg Trondheim, Champions League, 2008

Football's Coming Homo

SLOGAN of the International Gay & Lesbian Football Association to publicise the 2008 Gay World Cup, 2007

In the Bible it does state that homosexuality is detestable unto the Lord.
MICHAEL JOHNSON, former Derby and Birmingham defender, on BBC TV's The Big Questions *programme, 2012*

I don't have a girlfriend for the moment but I'm a heterosexual. These rumours are completely false. I've watched only two musicals during my entire spell in London, *Mamma Mia* and *Saturday Night Fever.*
FREDDIE LJUNGBERG, Arsenal and Sweden player, on speculation that he was gay, 2000

One night we went out in Bangkok and there were transsexuals everywhere. Everybody fancied them because they were absolutely gorgeous. They'd be playing with your cock under the table and it was like living in a different world.
MEL STERLAND, former England defender, on touring with Sheffield Wednesday in his autobiography Boozing, Betting & Brawling, *2008*

I was made to stand on a chair and sing Lulu's 'Shout' to the lads as part of the initiation. It was only after I'd finished – and they'd stopped laughing – that I found out I was the only new player to do it.
LEE TRUNDLE, Bristol City striker, 2007

INTERVIEWER: Is there any music you like from the Czech Republic?

PETR CECH: There's a group named Support Lesbians who are one of my favourite bands.
INTERVIEW with the Chelsea and Czech Republic goalkeeper in The Observer *music magazine, 2006*

When we qualified for the World Cup, me and Marcus [Hahnemann] sang some Slipknot together. The other guys were like: 'You've got to be kidding.'
KASEY KELLER, United States goalkeeper, on his liking for metal and prog-rock music, 2006

When the England team was travelling you always knew which hotel room Dave Watson was in because he took with him a radio-cassette player with big speakers, and you could hear the music all the way down the corridor. His favourite group was Status Quo.
TREVOR BROOKING on the former England centre-half in 100 Great British Footballers, *1988*

We were looking through [Beckham's] playlist in the dressing-room. There was lots of Justin Bieber, Jonas Brothers and Selena Gomez. We were expecting some cool English rock bands and hip-hop. It's nice to know even David Beckham doesn't have good taste in everything.
ZLATAN IBRAHIMOVIC, briefly Beckham's Paris St-Germain team-mate, 2013

Phil Neville loves Celine Dion and always says her music changed his life. When we were travelling around Australia in pre-season, he was listening to her music all the time.
MIKEL ARTETA, Everton midfielder, on his captain's 'obsession', 2011

It wasn't that they were playing Abba, but that the masseur was running the music... If I was a player and the masseur was playing Abba I wouldn't have let it happen.
ROY KEANE on the music in the dressing-room on becoming Ipswich manager, 2009

People say footballers have terrible taste in music but I would dispute that. In my car at the moment I've got The Corrs, Cher, Phil Collins, Shania Twain and Rod Stewart.
ANDY GRAY, Sky TV presenter and former Scotland player, 2000

Liverpool has The Beatles and Manchester has Oasis. I think Manchester has the better band.
CRISTIANO RONALDO, 2009

I hate golf and like architecture. I don't say much but I do think a lot. Which seems to surprise people who think all footballers are thick.
BRIAN DEANE, *former England striker, 1996*

I'd definitely prefer Brooklyn to be a golfer. It's a better profession than football.

VICTORIA BECKHAM, *2000*

My golf handicap is 16. I'm the only black man who can beat them. They don't want to be beaten by me.
RUUD GULLIT *on playing golf with his Chelsea colleagues, 1996*

I've learned [English] from watching cartoons. Now I've progressed to films.
GILLES GRIMANDI, *Arsenal's French defender, 2000*

Rocky is one of my favourite films. I don't know how many times I've seen it but the DVD is worn out.
STEVE SIDWELL, *Aston Villa midfielder, on why he named his son Rocco, 2009*

Q: What films do you like?
A: Quentin Tarantino and stuff like that. There's nothing better than a good bit of violence.
MARK DRAPER, *Aston Villa midfielder, in a* Big Shot *magazine questionnaire, 1995*

The Jeremy Kyle Show makes me smile. Even if they get paid, I don't understand how people can throw their lives out in front of everyone. I've even recorded it once or twice so I can put it on when I'm in a bad mood and need to laugh.
SEBASTIEN BASSONG, *Norwich and Cameroon defender, 2014*

One of the first things Arsene Wenger did at Arsenal was to make sure players couldn't get pay-per-view in hotels. If players are exciting themselves quite a few times then it's going to affect their physical condition.
TONY ADAMS, *former Arsenal captain, 2006*

I room with Robbie Keane on away trips. If we're staying in a hotel on a Friday before a game we'll watch *Trigger Happy TV* then *So Graham Norton*. After that we cuddle up together and fall asleep. There's always the temptation of pay-per-view channels in hotels, but that would be embarrassing on your room bill.
RIO FERDINAND, *Leeds defender and 'EastEnders fanatic', 2001*

My fiancée and I enjoy nothing more than getting home and watching *EastEnders* and *Corrie* on Sky+ in bed.
JERMAINE JENAS, Tottenham and England midfielder, 2010

Q: Do you watch football when you're not playing?
A: I watch highlights, but not whole games – they take too long.
DJIBRIL CISSE, Liverpool and France striker, in magazine interview, 2004

After the wheel, the PlayStation is the best invention of all time.
ANDREA PIRLO, Juventus and Italy midfielder, in I Think Therefore I Play, *2014*

Three or four of the Villa lads buy the quality papers. At Palace it was always eight *Suns*, four *Mirrors*.
GARETH SOUTHGATE, Aston Villa and England defender, 1996

I've always been right of centre [politically]. Most footballers are. When you are told to go out and tear your opponents apart, it tends to make you right wing.
JIMMY GREAVES, TV personality and former England striker, 2003

Labour. Definitely. Aren't all the players Labour?
STEVE PERRYMAN, Tottenham player, in Hunter Davies's The Glory Game, *1972; only two of the players turned out to support Labour – nine were Conservatives*

I've never voted anything but Labour in my life. And never will.
KEVIN KEEGAN, England player, 1980

Football and politics are much the same. They're both full of people who are jealous of success.
TONY BANKS MP, Labour, former Minister of Sport, 1999

Dyed hair, long hair and weird hairstyles are all strictly prohibited. All players must cut their hair short. Before becoming a soccer star you must learn to behave as a true man.
FENG JIANMING, director of youth coaching with the Chinese FA, to his country's Under-17 squad, 2004

A big difference [between English and French football] is the underwear players have. But this is France and fashion. Pink, orange, green, fluorescent – and they play wearing that too.
JOE COLE, England midfielder, after joining Lille, 2011

Q: Have you ever used public transport?
A: Yes, I've been in a taxi.

GEORGE WEAH, former Chelsea striker, in newspaper questionnaire, 2001

A crazy perception persists that a footballer must have suffered a deprived childhood, not knowing where his next meal or pair of boots was coming from, to acquire the desire to turn football into a career. That is nonsense. My passion to succeed matches anybody's. My commitment to football may be even stronger because alternative career paths would have opened up for me.
JOHN BARNES, in his autobiography, 1999

The hardcore stereotypes are still there, but there are individuals in the game... I'm still eyed with suspicion for being different.
GRAEME LE SAUX, Blackburn defender, shortly before his on-the-pitch fight with team-mate David Batty over a remark made by the latter, 1995

Footballers are pampered by fans, massaged by management, stroked by the media. They are so cosseted that any criticism becomes an insult to their manhood.
MICHAEL PARKINSON, columnist, Daily Telegraph, *2001*

Professional sport is a jungle and the higher you go, the worse it gets. They should stop talking about love of the shirt and being faithful. All that no longer exists, apart from in national teams.
NICOLAS ANELKA on quitting Arsenal for Real Madrid, 1999

They [footballers] are just like film stars. They want to withdraw inside their shells and live in a closed world. If I were boss of Paris Saint-Germain I would have put it in [Nicolas] Anelka's contract that he had to be filmed at home, eating his lunch and talking to his girlfriend. Show it on TV and watch it get a two per cent rating. Then no one would care any more and he'd be left in peace.
JEAN-LUC GODARD, French film-maker, 2002

The worst pressure I'm under is my baby crying at night.

ALAN SHEARER, Blackburn striker, playing down the 'pressure' of his £3.3m price tag, 1992

Football takes all my pressures away. The police have my passport and I'm not allowed to train with the other players, but nothing bothers me out on the pitch.
MICKEY THOMAS, Wrexham captain, as his team's FA Cup run coincided with his release on bail on charges of counterfeiting currency, 1992

Nothing scares me in football. I'm the same at home – the bills come in left, right and centre, but

I never look at them until the red ones arrive.
STEVE STONE, Nottingham Forest and England midfielder, 1995

As a player it's like living in a box. Someone takes you out of the box for training and games, and makes all the decisions for you. I have seen players – famous internationals – all stand up in an airport lounge and follow one bloke to the lav. Six of them, maybe, standing there not wanting to piss themselves but following the bloke who does. Like sheep, never asking why, because that's the way they've been trained.
GEOFF HURST, former England striker, in Brian James's Journey to Wembley, *1977*

In every squad of 20 players there's going to be the one who hates blacks, foreigners. He don't know why. He just hates 'em.
VINNIE JONES on racism in football, 1991

In France, if I go to a boutique and staff don't recognise me I see them looking at each other as if to say: 'Watch out, what's he doing in a classy place like this?' In Italy it's worse. I'd be the only black person in a nice restaurant, the only black person with a nice car. You absolutely have to be a footballer to get to the higher echelons.
MARCEL DESAILLY, Chelsea and France captain, praising the 'tolerance' he found in England, 2004

This is your workplace. You don't expect to come to work to be abused.

JASON ROBERTS, black Reading and Grenada striker, on racism in English football, 2013

When you're getting into mid-winter in England, you need a few hard white men to carry the artistic black players through.
RON NOADES, Crystal Palace chairman, in the Channel 4 documentary Critical Eye: Great Britain United, *1991; Noades said his comments were 'taken out of context'*

The players themselves are very liberal now. They've grown up in a multi-racial country. Some might do this macho thing about 'women should only be in the kitchen', but they don't mean it. You can see players with their new babies and it's often them that's doing the cleaning and changing nappies.
RACHEL ANDERSON, players' agent, 1999

Someone asked me last week whether I missed the Villa. I said: 'No. I live in one.'
DAVID PLATT, former Aston Villa striker, on life with Bari in Italy, 1991

I once took Sheffield United all the way to China and we had an opportunity to go see the Great Wall of China. Two players out of 25 wanted to go to see it. All the rest of them wanted to do was have their bloody earphones on and get their music pumped in. There's more to life.

NEIL WARNOCK, Leeds manager, 2012

My idea of an end-of-season trip is somewhere like Alicante where we can spend some time on the beach and have a few beers.

BRYAN ROBSON, West Bromwich Albion midfielder, when Albion became the first team from the West to visit China, 1978

See one wall and you've seen them all

JOHN TREWICK, Robson's West Brom colleague, at the Great Wall of China, 1978; team-mate Cyrille Regis said in 2013 that Trewick's comment was 'tongue in cheek'

Did we see the Great Wall? We practised bending free-kicks around it.

RON ATKINSON, West Brom manager, 1978

We had a nice hotel with beautiful views of the Pyramids. The FA arranged a trip to see them and came to ask us if we would like to come. I shouted through to Kitch, who was sunbathing on the balcony, to see if he wanted to go. A voice came back: 'Tell 'em we can see 'em from here.'

BRYAN KING, former Millwall and England squad goalkeeper, remembering a 1960s visit to Egypt with an FA team that included club colleague Barry Kitchener, 2013

When you come to a place like Barcelona, you think: 'Bloody hell, I wish I was back in England.'

TERRY BUTCHER, Ipswich and England defender, 1979

On my debut for Besiktas they sacrificed a lamb on the pitch. Its blood was daubed on my forehead for good luck. They never did that at QPR.

LES FERDINAND, England striker, recalling his spell in Turkey, 1995

Q: England's best supermarket?
A: Tesco and Harrods.
SLAVISA JOKANOVIC, Chelsea
midfielder, in a programme
questionnaire, 2001

Q: Last tin you opened?
A: Not tin. Bottle of wine.
MARCEL DESAILLY, Chelsea defender,
in a programme questionnaire, 2001

Just when I thought it was safe to
go to parties again and say I was a
footballer.
GARRY NELSON, striker with
numerous clubs, on Eric Cantona's leap
into the crowd at Selhurst Park, in Left
Foot Forward: Diary of a Journeyman
Footballer, *1995*

I'm the last old-fashioned centre-
half. They're all fancy dans now,
too many good-looking bastards
like Rio Ferdinand who all go out
with pop stars.
NEIL RUDDOCK, in an interview
with Loaded *magazine, 2000*

I don't speak much after a defeat.
Footballers can be murder to live
with. Every one I know is grumpy.
CHRIS SUTTON, Blackburn striker, 1994

You start hiding in your house
because you feel ashamed of
yourself.
MAGNUS HEDMAN, Coventry
goalkeeper, after a run of poor results,
2000

Q: What's the worst thing anyone
has ever said to you?
A: You're not playing.
MARK STEIN, Chelsea striker, in a
newspaper questionnaire, 1995

Football has given me riches,
popularity and privileges, but
I want even more. I live for
indescribable emotions and football
can give me those.
GIANLUCA VIALLI on leaving
Juventus for Chelsea, 1996

It's like turtles in the South Seas.
Thousands are hatched on the
beaches, but few of them reach the
water.
STEVE COPPELL, players' union official
and England player, on career prospects
for young players, 1983

Take it from me, as a failed
footballer, there is no better way to
earn a living, to be paid for what is
a hobby and a passion.
HOWARD WILKINSON, Leeds
manager, to graduates from the FA
National School, 1992

I remember knocking on the
manager's door at Sheffield
Wednesday. I said: 'Could I have
a little of your time? I don't know
whether I'm coming or going.'
'Wilkinson,' he said, 'you're
definitely going.'
HOWARD WILKINSON, Leeds manager,
on under-achieving as a player, 1992

You can't accuse footballers of failing society. They are very kind, going to hospitals and seeing kids, but in the main, the press don't seem to want to write a good word about them.
ALEX FERGUSON, Manchester United manager, 2000

Footballers are funny old buggers. As long as they've got their wage packet and car, they'll distance themselves.
STUART PEARCE, Nottingham Forest acting manager, on his team-mates' reaction to a boardroom takeover at the club, 1997

If I wasn't playing, I'd be putting slates on roofs back in Ireland. Playing has got to be better than that.
PAUL McGRATH, Aston Villa defender, 1993

EDITOR: What would you be if you weren't a footballer?
MARK FLATTS: On the dole.
ARSENAL programme Q & A with the reserve forward, 1993

Q: What would you have done if you hadn't been a footballer?
A: A funeral director. I like looking at dead bodies.
CHRIS SUTTON, Chelsea striker, in the club magazine Onside, *1999*

Q: If you weren't a footballer, what do you think you would be?
A: SAM ALLARDYCE (then a Bolton defender): A chef.
STAN BOWLES (QPR midfielder): A bookmaker.
DAVID O'LEARY (Arsenal defender): No idea.
CHARLIE GEORGE (Arsenal forward): I've never thought about it.
PETER TAYLOR (Crystal Palace winger): Miserable.
PETER REID (Bolton midfielder): A fat factory worker.
OSSIE ARDILES (Tottenham midfielder): A solicitor or professor of law.
ANSWERS to a regular questionnaire in Shoot! *magazine, 1970s–80s*

9

PHILOSOPHERS

Sometimes you look in a field and see a cow. You think it's a better cow than the one you see in your field. It never really works out that way.
SIR ALEX FERGUSON explaining why Wayne Rooney should stay with Manchester United, 2010

If the horse refuses to jump an obstacle, you have two choices. You can go behind him and apply the whip, to make him jump, but you could get kicked doing that. Or you could go around the other side of the obstacle and use a carrot, something sweet that he likes, to attract the horse to you. Both methods get the same result, but with two completely opposing emotional experiences.
CARLO ANCELOTTI, Paris St-Germain coach, on man-management, 2012

Some people can not see a priest on a mountain of sugar.

RAFAEL BENITEZ, Internazionale coach, answering Roy Hodgson's claim that the Spaniard left him with 'expensive failures' at Liverpool, 2010

Benitez took the elephant in the room and put it on the table.
GARETH SOUTHGATE, ITV analyst and former England defender, 2013

It's great to get that duck off my back.

GARY CAHILL, Chelsea and England defender, 2013

No eggs, no omelette. And it depends on the quality of the eggs. In the supermarket, you have eggs class one, class two, class three. Some are more expensive than others and some give you better omelettes. So when the class-one eggs are in Waitrose and you cannot go there, you have a problem.
JOSE MOURINHO, Chelsea manager, alleging a lack of backing in securing his transfer targets before what proved to be the last game of his first spell as manager, 2007

You always have an eye for a goal but you can lose your eye of the tiger. I've still got mine but if you lose your eye of the tiger you are not actually moving to where the ball is going.
DEAN SAUNDERS, Wolves manager, 2013

With some players, if he has a chihuahua character I can't make a chihuahua into a rottweiler. He could be a proud chihuahua but he remains a chihuahua.
PAOLO DI CANIO, Swindon Town manager, 2011

When the chips are down the top dogs usually come up smelling of roses.
NEIL WARNOCK, Queens Park Rangers manager, 2010

Edin Dzeko went down a bit theoretically there.
PETER REID, Radio 5Live summariser and former England midfielder, 2013

I can never predict my future because a big part of my future is already behind me.
GUUS HIDDINK, Paris St-Germain coach, 2013

Any regrets? Loads. But I don't drink pints of hindsight, I drink pints of Guinness.
PHIL BROWN, Hull City manager, 2010

There's too much – I don't know what the word is – scientology in the game.
DAVID PLEAT, media pundit and former manager, 2011

The one thing I don't like in life is stupidness.
RON ATKINSON, former manager, on Celebrity Big Brother, 2013

Supporters have every divine right to slag your players off.
DEAN WINDASS, media pundit and ex-Hull striker, 2011

The more you lose, the more you don't win.

ALEX McLEISH, Aston Villa manager, 2012

One door opens, another door opens.
MALKY MACKAY, Cardiff City manager, 2013

Cometh the man, cometh the hour, as they say.
CHRIS COLEMAN, TV summariser, World Cup finals, 2010

That was never a penalty in a million planets.
ALAN McINALLY, Sky TV pundit and ex-Scotland striker, 2011

Gary Neville is club captain but he's been injured – and Giggsy's taken on the mantelpiece.
RIO FERDINAND, Manchester United defender, 2009

When it becomes a two-horse race it's a different kettle of fish.

GARY JOHNSON, Bristol City manager, 2008

He's exacerbated the situation by making it worse.
STEVE CLARIDGE, Radio 5Live pundit, 2013

For us to overtake them has been a massive undertaking.
SAM ALLARDYCE, West Ham manager, 2012

If we hide behind clichés we'll be dead and buried by January.
DARREN BARR, Falkirk midfielder, 2009

At the end of the day, if you're old enough, you're good enough.
STEVE STAUNTON, former Republic of Ireland manager, 2013

There's no such thing as a must-win match – and this is one of them.
ALAN WRIGHT, Southport manager, 2013

I hate this phrase, but the judge was out on him.
MARK SAGGERS, talkSPORT radio presenter, 2011

It's one of them days when you just say: 'It's one of them days.'
IAN WRIGHT, media summariser and ex-England striker, 2013

This is a once-in-a-lifetime opportunity, but at least we've got another game on Tuesday.
MARVIN SORDELL, Charlton striker, 2013

It was a once-in-a-lifetime experience and hopefully I can repeat it on Saturday.
ALFIE POTTER, Kettering Town player, 2009

Come Saturday it's all about starting with a blank sheet of football.
BILLY DAVIES, Nottingham Forest manager, 2010

Whatever ebb and flow means, this is it.
DAVID PLEAT, Radio 5Live pundit, 2011

It's a lance that had to be boiled.
JOHN TERRY, Chelsea and England captain, 2011

Sometimes the pendulum swings both ways.
KEVIN KEEGAN, 2011

Every picture says a thousand words and that one said 'goodbye'.
KEEGAN, 2005

It's a shame [Tottenham] weren't meeting Manchester City in this moment of time a few months ago.
GLENN HODDLE, Sky analyst, 2013

The Championship is a hard league and you're playing against different opposition every week.
NEIL WARNOCK, Leeds manager, 2013

If I was me, I'd pick Lampard.
RAY PARLOUR, talkSPORT radio pundit, 2011

It's looking more and more less likely.
ROBBIE FOWLER, BBC TV pundit, 2012

It was handbags at half-mast, really.
ALAN PARDEW, Newcastle manager, after scuffling between Newcastle and Southampton backroom staff, 2013

The thing about Drogba is that he scores when he doesn't even play, if that's possible.
IAN WRIGHT, TV summariser, 2011

Stephen Carr's hunger has been superb.
ALEX McLEISH, Birmingham City manager, 2009

Arsene Wenger and I enjoy pitting our witses against each other.
SAM ALLARDYCE, Blackburn manager, 2010

[Riccardo] Montolivo has been made Milan captain – that's another fillip for his bow.
TREVOR FRANCIS, Sky pundit, 2013

When you're comfortable, and you think you're comfortable, it's uncomfortable.
ROY KEANE, ITV pundit, 2011

Sometimes you can't defend the indefensible.
MARK LAWRENSON, BBC pundit, 2011

Correct me if I'm not mistaken.
LAWRENSON, 2011

Question marks will have to be answered.
STEVE CLARIDGE, BBC TV pundit, 2011

As long as you hit the target they go in, if the keeper don't make a save.
IAN HOLLOWAY, Crystal Palace manager, 2012

A talking goalkeeper is a big asset.
JIM BEGLIN, ITV summariser, 2011

My passion for football is second to anyone.
RAY WILKINS, former England captain, 2011

People call it Armageddon but I think it's worse than that.
TERRY BUTCHER, Radio Scotland, 2011

The interesting thing about Nani is that he has two feet.
RAY WILKINS, 2011

It was really difficult for us playing in the midday sun with that three o'clock kick-off.
DAVID BECKHAM after captaining England to victory over Paraguay, World Cup finals, 2006

London's up there with Madrid and Milan but Glasgow's unique, along with Liverpool and Newcastle.
GEORGE GRAHAM, *former Arsenal, Tottenham and Leeds manager, 2011*

Without Laurel and Hardy, Laurel wouldn't be Hardy.
IAN HOLLOWAY, BT Sport *summariser, 2013*

If you're a burglar, it's no good poncing about outside somebody's house, looking good with your swag bag ready. Just get in there, burgle them and come out. I don't advocate that obviously, it's just an analogy.
HOLLOWAY, *Blackpool manager, after defeat by Crystal Palace, 2009*

Sometimes there are mysteries in our game that are difficult to rationalise.
ARSENE WENGER *on why Thomas Vermaelen had struggled to establish partnerships in Arsenal's defence with Laurent Koscielny and Per Mertesacker, 2013*

When you're dealing with someone who has only a pair of underpants on and you take them off, he has nothing left. He's naked. You're better off trying to find him a pair of trousers, to compliment him rather than change him.
WENGER *on the need to encourage flair, 2007*

That Mourinho should emerge as victor in the battle of tactical wits says a great deal about the brutal syzygism of opposed footballing fates.
BARNEY RONAY, *columnist,* The Guardian, *2013*

It is necessary to wear the sandals of humility and not let this win go to our heads.
ANTONIO LOPES, Vasco da Gama *coach, after beating Manchester United, 2000*

If it is just the case that you need a first XI and three or four more players, then why did Christopher Columbus sail to India to discover America?
CLAUDIO RANIERI, Chelsea *manager, 2004*

When the seagulls follow the trawler it is because they think sardines will be thrown into the sea.
ERIC CANTONA *addressing the media after escaping jail for his 'kung fu' attack on an abusive fan during Manchester United's visit to Crystal Palace, 1995*

If a Frenchman goes on about seagulls, trawlers and sardines, he's called a philosopher. I'd just be called a short Scottish bum talking crap.
GORDON STRACHAN, *former Leeds team-mate of Cantona's, 1995*

Playing against a footballer with no attacking intent is like making love to a tree.
JORGE VALDANO, *sporting director of Real Madrid, 2006*

The moral of the story is not to listen to those who tell you not to play the violin but to stick to the tambourine.
JOSE MOURINHO, Chelsea manager, 2005

Young players are like melons. Only when you open and taste the fruit are you 100 per cent sure that it's good. Sometimes you have beautiful melons but they don't taste good. Other times they're ugly but the taste is fantastic.
MOURINHO, 2007

People worship God when they worship footballers because football is His creation.
DELIA SMITH, Norwich director, 2006

'If' is the biggest word in football, son.
SIR BOBBY ROBSON, Newcastle manager, to a conjecturing reporter, 2004

In football, things happen now and again.

SVEN-GORAN ERIKSSON after a Sol Campbell 'winner' for England was disallowed v Portugal, European Championship finals, 2004

Sometime in the season we will have unluck, as you say.
ERIKSSON after his Manchester City

side's fortuitous derby win over United, 2007

We need a point as soon as possible, the tooter the sweeter.

ROBSON at Newcastle, 2002

We showed great bouncebackability.
IAIN DOWIE, Crystal Palace manager, 2004

We can do better footballistically.
ARSENE WENGER, 2004

The decisions decided a lot of things, but I'll leave other people to decide.
DAVID O'LEARY, Aston Villa manager, bemoaning the referee's role in a 3–0 defeat at Doncaster in the Carling Cup, 2005

The proof of the pudding is in the rankings.
KENNY DALGLISH, former Scotland player, on his country reaching a highest-ever placing of 14th in FIFA's world rankings, 2007

It's all about putting square pegs in square holes.
STEVE McCLAREN, England manager, 2006

Extra time probably came at the wrong time for us.

MARK HUGHES, Blackburn manager, after defeat by Chelsea in the FA Cup, 2007

At 2–0 down I'd have given my right arm for a draw, but I'm glad I didn't as I wouldn't have been able to clap the fans at the end.
GARY PETERS, Shrewsbury manager, 2006

We weren't beaten today, we lost.
HOWARD WILKINSON, Sunderland manager, after his side scored three own goals v Charlton, 2003

I can't tell you what's going to happen tomorrow – only today. And I can't even tell you what's going to happen today.
DAVID PLEAT, Tottenham caretaker-manager, 2004

The door is always open until it is closed.

HOPE POWELL, England women's coach, on selection for the World Cup, 2007

At the time it happened, I regretted it in hindsight.
JOEY BARTON, Manchester City midfielder, 2006

Rightly or wrongly, we've been wronged.
CHRIS COLEMAN, Fulham manager, 2007

Hard work is never easy.
JOHN TOSHACK, Wales manager, 2006

I definitely want Brooklyn to be christened, though I don't know into which religion.
DAVID BECKHAM after the birth of his and Victoria's first child, 2000

I'd rather be a footballer than an existentialist.
ROBERT SMITH, singer-writer with the rock group The Cure, 1991

Like the Tibetans I have learned to understand myself, even if you never fully can.
EMMANUEL PETIT, Arsenal and France midfielder, 1999

One minute you can be riding the crest of a wave and the next minute you can be down. It's a funny old game. It's a great leveller, and you can't get too cock-a-hoop about things. It's an old cliché but you've got to take each game as it comes and keep working at it. In playing or management, you're only as good as your last game.

BILLY BONDS, *West Ham manager, 1990*

In terms of a 15-round boxing match, we're not getting past round one. Teams will pinch your dinner from under your noses. If you don't heed the warnings, you get nailed to the cross.
GORDON MILNE, Leicester manager, 1983

It's no use crying into our soup, or milk for a phrase. We've got to get our heads up and take it on the chin.
DANNY WILSON, Sheffield United manager, 2013

My ankle injury has been a real pain in the arse.
DAVID PRUTTON, Southampton midfielder, 2007

The Achilles heel that has bitten us in the backside all year has stood out like a sore thumb.
ANDY KING, Swindon manager, 2005

We were done by our Achilles heel, which has been stabbing us in the back all season.
DAVID O'LEARY, Aston Villa manager, after Manchester City equalised in stoppage time, 2006

Steve McClaren will have a pair of sharp, canny shoulders to listen to.

DAVID PLATT, *former England player, 2006*

We've got to roll up our sleeves and get our knees dirty.
HOWARD WILKINSON, Sunderland manager, 2002

The big monster called relegation is there, ready to bite us on the arse.
STEVE COPPELL, Crystal Palace manager, 2000

Keith Curle has an ankle injury but we'll have to take it on the chin.
ALAN BALL, Manchester City manager, 1995

I've got irons in the fire and things up my sleeve.
STEVE McMAHON, Swindon manager, 1997

I have other irons in the fire, but I'm keeping them close to my chest.
JOHN BOND on leaving the Manchester City manager's job, 1983

John Spencer's hamstring is making alarm bells ring in his head.
CRAIG BROWN, Scotland manager, 1996

If someone in the crowd spits at you, you've just got to swallow it.
GARY LINEKER quoting the advice of ex-Leicester manager Gordon Milne, 1995

I felt a lump in my throat as the ball went in.
TERRY VENABLES, England coach, 1996

We can only come out of this game with egg on our faces, so it's a real banana skin.

RAY STEWART, Stirling Albion manager, on facing non-league opposition in the Scottish Cup, 2001

If we think they'll be easy meat, we'll end up with egg on our faces.
TERRY DOLAN, Bradford City manager, 1989

Obviously for Scunthorpe it would be a nice scalp to put Wimbledon on their bottoms.
DAVE BASSETT, Wimbledon manager, 1984

I've sown a few seeds and thrown a few hand-grenades. Now I'm waiting for the dust to settle so I can see how the jigsaw pieces together.
GARY JOHNSON, Yeovil manager, 2004

Although we're playing Russian roulette, we're obviously playing catch-22 at the moment.
PAUL STURROCK, Plymouth Argyle manager, 2003

I had a contract offer on the table but it was swept from under the rug.
CHRIS PERRY, West Bromwich defender, after Iain Dowie's arrival as manager hastened his exit at Charlton, 2006

If we can bring some silverware to the club that would be a nice little rainbow at the end of a dark tunnel.
TERRY McDERMOTT, Newcastle coach, 2005

It's a vicious circle. Once the bandwagon starts rolling it's a snowball effect. Obviously you've got to take it with a pinch of salt.
MICHAEL OWEN at an England media briefing after press criticism of David James, 2004

You can't switch the lights on every time and we didn't smell that one coming. The car was in neutral and we couldn't put it in drive.
GLENN HODDLE, Tottenham manager, after a home defeat, 2003

No one wants to commit hara-kari and sell themselves down the river.
GARY LINEKER, England striker and captain, explaining the dearth of goals at the European Championship finals, 1992

We climbed three mountains and then proceeded to throw ourselves off them.
BILLY McNEILL, Celtic manager, after beating Partizan Belgrade 5–4 but losing on aggregate, 1989

If you can't stand the heat in the dressing-room, get out of the kitchen.
TERRY VENABLES, England coach, 1995

The cat's among the pigeons and meanwhile we're stuck in limbo.
BERNIE SLAVEN, Middlesbrough striker, after Colin Todd's demise as manager, 1991

The tide is very much in our court now.
KEVIN KEEGAN, Manchester City manager, 2004

We miss Maine Road but we don't really miss it.
KEEGAN after City moved to a new stadium, 2003

Goalkeepers aren't born today until they're in their 30s.
KEEGAN, 2003

Argentina are the second best team in the world and there's no higher praise than that.
KEEGAN, then England manager, 2000

Argentina won't be at Euro 2000 because they're from South America.
KEEGAN, 2000

At this level, if five or six players don't turn up, you'll get beat.
KEEGAN after some Manchester City players 'went missing' at Villa Park, 2002

England have the best fans in the world, and Scotland's are second to none.
KEEGAN, 1999

Young Gareth Barry, you know, he's young.
KEEGAN, 2000

Our squad looks good on paper, but paper teams win paper cups.
HOWARD WILKINSON, Sunderland manager, 2002

A lucky goal or the run of the ball can be triggers, but they can only be triggers if you have gunpowder.
WILKINSON at Sunderland, 2002

We had a very constructive discussion at half-time, then decided to give it the full bollocks.
RON ATKINSON, Aston Villa manager, 1993

Their goal unsettled us, and no matter what you say at half-time, there's always that little bit of toothache in their minds.
STEVE COPPELL, Reading manager, 2004

If you take liberties with the opposition they'll pull your trousers down.
BILLY BONDS, West Ham manager, 1991

If you don't believe you can win, there's no point in getting out of bed at the end of the day.
NEVILLE SOUTHALL, Everton and Wales goalkeeper, 1990

At the end of the day it's all about what we do on the night.
BRYAN HAMILTON, Northern Ireland manager, before game v Germany, 1996

At the end of the day it's not the end of the world.
JIM McLEAN, Dundee United manager, after UEFA Cup final defeat v Gothenberg, 1987

There is a rat in the camp trying to throw a spanner in the works.
CHRIS CATTLIN, Brighton manager, 1983

We want to go upwards, not stand still and go backwards.
CHRIS ROBINSON, Hearts chief executive, 2004

It doesn't matter what happened – we got the three points and that's all that counts.
WAYNE BRIDGE, Chelsea defender, after victory v Arsenal – in the Carling Cup final, 2007

Our back four was at sixes and sevens.

RON ATKINSON, Aston Villa manager, 1992

There are 0–0 draws and 0–0 draws, and this was a 0–0 draw.
JOHN SILLETT, Coventry manager, 1989

It's 60–40 against him being fit but he's got half a chance.
GLENN HODDLE, Wolves manager, 2006

Five per cent of me is disappointed while the other 50 per cent is just happy we've qualified.
MICHAEL OWEN after England finished second in their group, European Championship finals, 2004

We must have had 99 per cent of the match. It was the other three per cent that cost us.
RUUD GULLIT after Chelsea lost to Coventry, 1997

We're not here just to make up the numbers. We're here to just stay in the league.
PAUL JEWELL, Wigan manager, preparing for Premiership life, 2005

We're a second-half side. The problem is the second halves aren't long enough.
DELIA SMITH, Norwich director, 2004

It was a game of two halves, and we were rubbish in both of them.
BRIAN HORTON, Oxford United manager, 1990

In cup competitions, Jack will always have a chance of beating Goliath.
TERRY BUTCHER, Sunderland manager, in his programme column, 1993

The FA Cup touches so many people. It's a fair bet that, by the end of today, players you have never heard of will be household names – like that fellow who scored for Sutton United against Coventry City last season.
BOBBY CAMPBELL, Chelsea manager, in his programme column, 1990

The first goal was a foul, the second was offside, and they would never have scored the third if they hadn't got the other two.
STEVE COPPELL, Crystal Palace manager, explaining defeat by Liverpool, 1991

If corner-kicks hadn't been invented, this would have been a very close game.
NEIL WARNOCK, Sheffield United manager, after a 4–1 defeat at Newcastle, 2000

We were in an awkward position against Yugoslavia in that in order to win we needed to score more goals than they did.
JOSE ANTONIO CAMACHO, Spain coach, 2000

If we played like that every week, we wouldn't be so inconsistent.
BRYAN ROBSON, Manchester United captain, 1990

I just wonder what would have happened if the shirt had been on the other foot.
MIKE WALKER, Norwich manager, claiming refereeing decisions went against his side v Manchester United, 1994

My players ran their socks into the ground for Manchester United.
ALEX FERGUSON, 1997

If I was still at Ipswich, I wouldn't be where I am today.
DALIAN ATKINSON, Aston Villa striker, 1992

Germany are a very difficult team to beat. They had 11 internationals out there today.
STEVE LOMAS, Northern Ireland captain, 1999

If I played for Scotland, my grandma would be the proudest woman in the country if she wasn't dead.
MARK CROSSLEY, English-born goalkeeper (who later represented Wales), 1995

The World Cup is every four years so this is going to be a perennial problem.
GARY LINEKER, TV football presenter, 1998

You never know what could happen in a couple of one-off games like these.
GRAEME SHARP, former Scotland striker, before the play-off fixtures v England, 1999

Even when you're dead, you shouldn't lie down and let yourself be buried.
GORDON LEE, Everton manager, 1981

It was a draw, so in the end we didn't win.

DAVID BECKHAM to a TV interviewer after Manchester United drew with Croatia Zagreb, 1999

Football matches are like days of the week. It can't be Sunday every day. There are also Mondays and Tuesdays.
GEORGE WEAH, Milan and Liberia striker, 1995

We had enough chances to win the game. In fact we did win it.

ALEX SMITH, Aberdeen manager, 1991

When their second goal went in, I knew our pig was dead.
DANNY WILLIAMS, Swindon manager, after they lost an FA Cup tie to West Ham, 1975

Having players you've sold come back and score against you is what football's all about.
ALEX FERGUSON, Manchester United manager, 1992

The missing of chances is one of the mysteries of life.
SIR ALF RAMSEY, England manager, 1972

Being given chances and not taking them, that's what life is all about.
RON GREENWOOD, England manager, 1982

Always remember that the goal is at the end of the field and not in the middle.
SVEN-GORAN ERIKSSON to his England squad, 2002

Too many players were trying to score or create a goal.
GERARD HOULLIER, Liverpool manager, after home defeat by Watford, 1999

It was a Limpalong Leslie sort of match.
PETER SHREEVES, Tottenham manager, after win v Coventry, 1985

It was a bad day at Black Rock.
SHREEVES after Spurs' 5–1 defeat v Watford a fortnight later, 1985

What's the bottom line in adjectives?
SHREEVES after home loss to Coventry,
1985

We threw caution to the wind and came back from the dead. Well, it is Easter Monday.
GLENN HODDLE, Swindon player-manager, after they came from 4–1 down to win 6–4 at Birmingham, 1993

He was flapping about like a kipper.
JOHN BARNWELL, Notts County manager, on Nicky Law's costly handling offences v Tottenham, 1989

We held them for 89 minutes and then they kippered us.
DOGAN ARIF, Fisher Athletic manager, after defeat by Telford, 1989

You get it [the ball] in the bollocks, in the nose, in the gob, and I don't care if it knocks out their ruddy crowns. I've got lads more than prepared to get in the kipper. But you do not turn your back and let it hit you up the arse and spin up into the top corner.
MICK McCARTHY, Wolves manager, after a member of his defensive wall broke ranks and deflected a Watford free-kick into the net, 2007

You must kill the bull or you haven't done nowt.
DANNY BERGARA, Stockport's Uruguayan manager, 1992

It was a mistake as big as a house.
RENE HIGUITA, Colombia goalkeeper,

after his error let in Cameroon's Roger Milla for a goal, World Cup finals, 1990

This for me is without exception possibly my last World Cup.

RAY WILKINS, England midfielder, en route to Mexico, 1986

The unthinkable is not something we're really thinking about at the moment.
PETER KENYON, chief executive of Manchester United, on the possibility of being eliminated from the Champions League, 2000

The new manager has given us unbelievable belief.
PAUL MERSON, Arsenal midfielder, on Arsene Wenger's impact at Highbury, 1996

I'm not a believer in luck, but I do believe you need it.
ALAN BALL, Manchester City manager, 1996

Sometimes we are predictable, but out of that predictability we are unpredictable.
JOHN BECK, Cambridge United manager, 1991

He's such an honest person it's untrue.

BRIAN LITTLE, Aston Villa manager, on midfielder Ian Taylor, 1996

That's understandable and I understand that.
TERRY VENABLES, England coach, 1996

That is in the past, and the past has no future.
DAVID PLEAT on losing the Sheffield Wednesday manager's job, 1997

The road to ruin is paved with excuses.
BOBBY GOULD, Coventry manager, after defeat by Leeds, 1993

I'm told we need a big name. Engelbert Humperdinck is a big name but it doesn't mean he can play football.
RAY HARFORD, Blackburn manager, 1996

We're a First Division club in every sense of the word.
NAT LOFTHOUSE, Bolton president, when the club languished in the Third, 1992

My team won't freeze in the white-hot atmosphere of Anfield.
RON SAUNDERS, Aston Villa manager, 1980

REPORTER: What are your impressions of Africa?
GORDON LEE: Africa? We're not in bloody Africa, are we?

EXCHANGE between journalist and the Everton manager in Morocco, 1978

The plastic pitch is a red herring.
GRAHAM TAYLOR, Aston Villa manager, after losing FA Cup tie at Oldham, 1990

We're halfway round the Grand National course with many hurdles to clear. So let's make sure we all keep our feet firmly on the ground.
MIKE BAILEY, Charlton manager, as his team chased promotion, 1981

Professional and amateur football have as much in common as a strawberry milkshake and a skyscraper.
HARALD SCHUMACHER, West Germany goalkeeper, in Blowing the Whistle, 1987

You can't compare English and German football. They're like omelette and muesli.
ERIK MEIJER, Dutch striker, leaving Liverpool for Hamburg, 2000

There's no question of us playing for the draw. As we say in Germany: 'We will be going for the sausages.'
JURGEN ROBER, Hertha Berlin coach, before a game v Chelsea, 1999

The wall we had before Bochum scored from that free-kick looked as if it was built by Andy Warhol.
ULI HOENESS, Bayern Munich general manager, 2001

The players still had Christmas cake in their feet.
SERGIO CRAGNOTTI, Lazio president, after defeat by Napoli, 2001

I can see the carrot at the end of the tunnel.
STUART PEARCE, England defender, on recovering from injury, 1992

No one hands you cups on a plate.
TERRY McDERMOTT, Newcastle assistant manager, 1995

Statistics are just like mini-skirts – they give you good ideas but hide the most important things.
EBBE SKOVDAHL, Aberdeen manager, 2001

We're now arithmetically, not mathematically, safe from relegation. There's neither algebra nor geometry involved in the calculations.
TOM HENDRIE, St Mirren manager, 1999

Never in the history of the FAI Cup had a team wearing hooped jerseys lost a final in a year ending in 5.
HOME FARM (Dublin) programme notes, 1985

Which Spanish side did John Toshack take over after leaving Sporting Lesbian?
QUIZ QUESTION in a Leek Town programme, 1999

The transfer market has changed because of the Bosnian ruling.
JOE KINNEAR, Wimbledon manager, 1998

I expect the Croats to come out... Oh dear, I better not say fighting, had I?
PETER SHREEVES, Tottenham manager, before a match v Hajduk Split from war-torn Croatia, 1991

If players won't die for this club, then I don't want them.

ALEX MILLER, Hibernian manager, 1990

Our guys are getting murdered twice a week.
ANDY ROXBURGH, Scotland coach, on the hectic schedule in British football, 1991

I'd shoot myself if I had the bottle.
VINNIE JONES after being sent off for the 10th time, 1995

I'd hang myself but the club can't afford the rope.
IAIN MUNRO, Hamilton Academical manager, 1995

The shoot-out is like shooting wee ducks at a fairground to try to win a prize.
ALEX SMITH, Aberdeen manager, after winning the Scottish Cup on penalties, 1990

Being top won't change much. It'll probably rain tomorrow and the traffic lights will still be red.
HOWARD WILKINSON, Leeds manager, on leading the league for the first time in his career, 1991

I feel like Korky the Cat, who has been run over by a steamroller, got up and had someone punch him in the stomach.
WILKINSON after Leeds' FA Cup defeat by Arsenal, 1993

When one door opens, another smashes you in the face.
TOMMY DOCHERTY on his dismissal as manager of Preston, 1981

You are always one defeat away from a crisis. On that basis, we're in deep shit.
JOHN GREGORY, Aston Villa manager, during a losing sequence, 1999

If we beat Real [Madrid] it will be a nationwide orgasm.
JESUS GIL, Atletico Madrid president, before the derby, 1995

Dani is so good-looking that Villa didn't know whether to mark him or bonk him.
HARRY REDKNAPP, West Ham manager, on his Portuguese signing, 1996

We let the convict out of jail, and we know what they are like when they get free.
HOWARD WILKINSON, Leeds manager, after 3–0 defeat by VfB Stuttgart, 1992

Rotherham reminds me of Bermuda. It's small so you bump into the same people two or three times a day.
SHAUN GOATER, Rotherham and Bermuda striker, 1993

I never heard a minute's silence like that.

GLENN HODDLE, England manager, at Wembley after Princess Diana's death, 1997

I never realised Lincoln was a seaside town.
BRIAN LAWS, Scunthorpe manager, after losing on a liberally sanded 'beach' of a pitch, 2003

Q: Which TV programme would you most like to appear in?
A: *Thunderbirds.* I'd like to fly in Thunderbird II.
KEVIN KEEN, West Ham midfielder, interviewed in club programme, 1992

Claim to fame outside soccer: I once put together an MFI wardrobe in less than four days.
TERRY GIBSON, Coventry striker, 1985

There is nothing going on in the world at the moment that I find distressing or have a view on.
MICHAEL OWEN, 1999

I'm only 33 but my hair is 83.

ANDY RITCHIE, balding Oldham striker, 1994

The trouble with you, son, is that your brains are all in your head.
BILL SHANKLY to unnamed Liverpool player, 1967

I don't like being on my own because you think a lot and I don't like to think a lot.
PAUL GASCOIGNE on the TV documentary Gazza's Coming Home, *1996*

I know more about football than about politics.

HAROLD WILSON MP, Labour Prime Minister, 1974

I thought the No. 10, Whymark, played exceptionally well.
MARGARET THATCHER MP, Conservative, after the FA Cup final, 1978; Trevor Whymark was listed in the programme but did not play

It's like going to a different country.
IAN RUSH on life in Italy with Juventus, 1988

How can you tell your wife you are just popping out to play a match and then not come back for five days?
RAFAEL BENITEZ, Liverpool manager, on Test cricket, 2005

In programme notes there is a great deal of clap trap where subconsciously people tend to become excuse worthy. I have often said to the players that there is talking and doing. Today will be a day of doing. At least we know the macabre has a habit of flourishing in different settings.
COLIN MURPHY, Lincoln manager, from his programme column 'Murph's Message', 1989

I happen to believe no one can work miracles and it strikes me that applies even to people like Holmes and Watson, the Marx Brothers, Bilko, Inspector Clouseau or Winston Churchill. All these had immeasurable qualities but I don't know whether any of them had the attributes to be able to win promotion for Lincoln City FC with all the injuries and suspensions we have had.
MURPHY from 'Murph's Message', 1988

What you call football is like cricket to us.
ANDY WILLIAMS, American pop singer, 2002

We are now into a new season and I have no doubt that George and Mildred are delighted to be selling their cheese rolls in the Fourth Division... If we all remember that the fires of war should have some good feelings then we shall not be far short at the finish.
MURPHY after Lincoln won promotion back to the Football League, 1988

Music soothes the savage breast. The cobra has been tamed. Losing. A losing sequence, namely three games, always appears to put doubts in people's minds irrespective of the club's predicament and the doubting Thomases doubt no more and the judges become experts. The cobra

has an excellent habit of wriggling free and indeed Gordon Hobson wriggled three at Burnley.
MURPHY, 1988

Footballers are no different from human beings.

GRAHAM TAYLOR, England manager, 1992

People get mad over football, people enthuse over it, people exultate, and people sadly even have started fighting and destructing over it.
MURPHY, 1988

REPORTER: It was a funny game, Jim.
JIMMY SIRREL: Human beings are funny people.
EXCHANGE between journalist and the Notts County manager after a match at Arsenal, 1982

I don't make predictions and I never will.
PAUL GASCOIGNE, 1997

There's not a word to describe how I feel, but I'm just ecstatic.
MARY PHILIP, Arsenal women's player, after the team won the UEFA Cup, 2007

10

FANS

I'm such a big Man United fan, I moved out of Manchester.
JOHN COOPER CLARKE, poet, 2013

We have been asked by the FA to remind all supporters about the dangers of flares and polytechnics.
MARGARET BYRNE, Sunderland chief executive, in instructions to fans travelling to the derby at Newcastle, 2014

This place will be under riot police control. Body search and personal belongings check will be in place. Fans are not allowed to bring drinks, poles, flares, weapons and celery.
TRAVEL ADVICE to Chelsea fans on the government website before their visit to Sparta Prague, Champions League, 2013

I look forward to hearing from the silent majority.

ALEX McLEISH, Aston Villa manager, after fans called for his departure, 2012

REPORTER: What would you say to the young Barca fan who cried for the first time tonight?
GUARDIOLA: Welcome to the club. That's the beauty of sports. Sometimes you laugh, sometimes you cry.
EXCHANGE at the press conference by Pep Guardiola, Barcelona coach, after

Chelsea knocked his side out of Champions League semi-final, 2012

I'm going [to watch Manchester United] as a supporter now. Instead of suffering with the team, I'm suffering or enjoying it with the fans.
SIR ALEX FERGUSON after retiring and becoming a director, 2014

Last night at approximately 10.30 a man from the Crumpsall area of north Manchester rang 999 in a drunken state demanding to speak to Sir Alex Ferguson. Obviously it can be a sad and depressing moment when your team lose a game. However, can we all please remember that 999 is to be used for emergencies only.
STATEMENT by Greater Manchester Police in the wake of David Moyes' United team being knocked out of the Capital One Cup by Sunderland, 2014

This is a bloke who has cheated on his own wife several times with whores, right, who now wants to leave one of the world's great clubs for money. And he's saying that the England fans – who've suffered, who've taken years of misery yet still turns up at games – and he's giving us a lecture on loyalty?
FRANK SKINNER, comedian and West Bromwich Albion fan, on the BBC TV show Have I Got News For You *after Wayne Rooney criticised England supporters for booing the team, World Cup finals, 2010*

It's the same at every club. They all want their club to buy Ronaldo and let them in for free. People say 'Let kids in for free'. Why should we let kids in free? One woman asked me to do a deal for students. She said her son can't afford to come. Then get a bloody job... (But) the worst scroungers are those who can afford to pay, and that includes pop stars. There's no such thing as a complimentary ticket; it's just paid for by someone else.
KEN BATES, Leeds and former Chelsea chairman, 2011

I'll often read fans' online forums, just to get an idea of how the supporters of a club feel about a certain manager or their chairman. Often I'm staggered by the high numbers of nutters who are roaming free out there.
JEFF STELLING, presenter of Sky's Soccer Saturday, *in* Jeffanory: Stories from Beyond Soccer Saturday, *2012*

These are people who have no friends...who spend 10 hours a day on the internet and have no one to talk to. The internet is a powerful tool. People are bringing down the government in Egypt by going on the internet, so it can be used for good. But three or four abusive idiots on a football messageboard do not speak for the majority.
GORDON STRACHAN, former Celtic manager, on the 'keyboard cowboys' he claimed were 'hijacking' football, 2011

I was watching a TV programme about accents where they said the Birmingham dialect was the most difficult to understand, so I couldn't make out what they were saying.
RAFAEL BENITEZ, Liverpool manager, after receiving verbal abuse from Aston Villa supporters, 2008

If anyone near me starts playing a vuvuzela at Stamford Bridge next season, I shall take it off them, upend it to use as an enema funnel and administer a dose of hot Bovril to the miscreant.
'BLUEBOY', Chelsea fan, on a World Cup online message board in The Guardian, *2010*

Oh my actual God...the donkey-botherers [Blackpool] are 2–0 up thanks to two of the worst refereeing decisions ever!
SIMON BLACKBURN, Blackburn-supporting leader of the Labour group on Blackpool council, on Facebook, 2011

Football supporters would sing Saddam Hussein's name if he scored a few goals for their team.
HARRY REDKNAPP, Queens Park Rangers manager, 2013

Those who don't get behind the team should shut the hell up or they can come round to my house and I will fight them.
IAN HOLLOWAY, Queens Park Rangers manager, 2004

Places like this are the soul of English football. The crowd is magnificent, singing: 'Fuck off, Mourinho.'

JOSE MOURINHO, Chelsea manager, at Sheffield United, 2006

The people chanting 'Taylor out!' were the same ones singing 'Give us a wave' when we were two up on Everton.
GRAHAM TAYLOR, Aston Villa manager, 2002

Football chanting is a kind of animal, impulsive instinct, a natural upswelling of rhythmical thinking and feeling. Chants can be bracingly vulgar, but they can often be very funny and sometimes quite ingenious.
ANDREW MOTION, Poet Laureate, 2009

I have a bank manager, a solicitor, an agent, and I would never dream that I could do their job better than them. Football is probably the only job where totally unqualified people think they know everything.
PETER TAYLOR, Hull manager, on fan pressure at his previous clubs, 2003

There are two sorts of fans – those that understand what we have been doing at this club and those who do not.
GERARD HOULLIER, Liverpool manager, after hostile graffiti was sprayed on the training-ground walls, 2004

Football isn't a game to hate the opposition. It's a game we all love.
HARRY REDKNAPP, Portsmouth manager, after his team's fans applauded Arsenal's players warmly during a 5–1 defeat, 2004

I expected abuse, but I also got a hamburger and about £4.50 in change.
GARY NEVILLE, Manchester United captain, on objects thrown at him at Liverpool, 2006

I got an email from a British soldier in Afghanistan. He tells me he wears a Pompey shirt under his uniform, and that he's just read we lost 5–0 to West Brom and the players didn't try. He says: 'When I go out on a mission, I don't know if I'm coming back. But I'm committed to my mission. Are you committed to yours, Mr Chairman?' I almost cry.
MILAN MANDARIC, Portsmouth chairman, 2003

Men have two passions. One is in bed and the other is watching their football team.
DAVE WHELAN, Wigan chairman, 2005

A man can change wives, political parties or religions, but he cannot change his favourite football team.

EDUARDO GALEANO, Uruguayan poet, journalist and football fan, 1995

The only loyalty in football is between the supporter and his club. That will never die.
STEVE COPPELL after leaving the Crystal Palace managership, 2000

Football is the only subject that can induce a bloke to swank about his fidelity.
HARRY PEARSON, author and Middlesbrough fan, in The Far Corner: A Mazy Dribble Through North-East Football, *1994*

I have measured out my life in Arsenal fixtures, and any event of any significance has a footballing shadow. When did my first real love affair end? The day after a disappointing 2–2 draw at home to Coventry.
NICK HORNBY, author, in Fever Pitch, *1992*

It was good that Ron died while his beloved Arsenal were top of the Premier League. Even he knew there was no point in waiting round for them to win the league.
CHRIS PICKARD, friend and ghostwriter to 'Great Train Robber' Ronnie Biggs, at Biggs's funeral, 2014

Can you believe [Adrian Chiles] took me aside and very seriously said: 'Just leave the West Brom stuff out?' To me, that's a red rag to a bull.
LEE DIXON, ITV pundit, on teasing Albion-supporting anchor Chiles, 2013

I'm a season-ticket holder at Tottenham Hotspur. I've been trying to get Matt [LeBlanc] along to a game – but he can't even get the hang of the name. He calls them 'Chutney Hooplas'.
STEPHEN MANGAN, actor, on his American co-star in the comedy-drama Episodes, *2012*

I bought an executive box at Swansea when they played Yeovil and we had eight adults and 14 kids in there. Next day we went to watch my brother play for Port Talbot against Cwmbran. We paid our 50p each to stand around the pitch with 80 others. And my boy, who's four, said: 'Dad, where's our box?'
JOHN HARTSON, Swansea-supporting striker with several clubs, 2006

They were moving my furniture out of my house and the removal blokes told me that about four or five people drove by, wound their windows down and said: 'Take it to a lay-by and burn it.'
IAN HOLLOWAY, Leicester manager, on the bitter reaction of Plymouth fans to his departure, 2007

The chairman told me our fans were doing the Congo up and down the train.

RUSSELL SLADE, Leyton Orient manager, after FA Cup victory at Swansea, 2011

[Charlton's] fans revelled in it, abused us and even did the bloody conga. In retrospect, of course I regret calling them morons. Imbeciles would have been more appropriate.
SIMON JORDAN, Crystal Palace chairman, in his Observer column after Palace were relegated from the Premier League following a draw at Charlton, 2005

Every thousandth person created, God unhinges their heads, scoops out their brains and issues them to football clubs as supporters.
MIKE BATESON, Torquay chairman, 1996

There's often talk about supporters winning representation on the board of their clubs. What's anyone doing on the board who isn't a fan in the first place?
MATTHEW HARDING, Chelsea vice-chairman, 1996

There's a fine line between loyalty and madness, and I'm not sure which side he's on. I think it's madness.
GARY ROWELL, former Sunderland player, on a fan who changed his name to Gary Sunderland AFC Lamb (and cited Rowell as his favourite-ever player), 2002

I heard this bloke in the stand shouting 'McGraw [Allan, manager], we're fucking sick of what you're doing to Morton, buying bastards like Gahagan.' Two minutes later I scored the winner and as I ran back I heard the same guy shouting: 'Yesssss, Johnny boy, gies another one!'
JOHN GAHAGAN, Morton player, 1990

Things worth knowing: That Association Football is becoming notorious for disgraceful exhibitions of ruffianism. That the rabble will soon make it impossible for law-abiding citizens to attend matches.
SCOTTISH ATHLETIC JOURNAL, 1887

A northern horde of uncouth garb and strange oaths.
PALL MALL GAZETTE describing Blackburn Rovers fans in London for the FA Cup final, 1884

There is no real local interest to excuse the frenzy of the mob, since the players come from all over the kingdom and may change their clubs each season.
C.B. FRY'S MAGAZINE *on crowd trouble, 1906*

Miserable specimens…learning to be hysterical as they groan or cheer in panic unison with their neighbours, the worst sound of all being the hysterical scream of laughter that greets any trip or fall by a player.
LORD BADEN POWELL, founder of the Boy Scouts, describing football spectators in Scouting for Boys, *1908*

If they knew more about football than we do, there would be 50,000 players and 22 spectators.
BILL McCRACKEN, Newcastle and Northern Ireland player, on being barracked, 1911

Generally he is short of stature, anaemic-looking, with a head too big to suggest it contains only brains, a high shrieking voice, reminiscent of a rusty saw in quick staccato action. He is blind to every move initiated by the Swansea Town players, but his attention to a faulty clearance or badly placed pass is microscopic.
CYGNET, columnist in Swansea's Sporting News, *on barracking at the Vetch Field, 1921*

Why not covered accommodation for spectators, dry ground to stand on and a reduced admission if possible? Many a wreath has been purchased by standing on wet ground on Saturday afternoons.
LETTER to the Birmingham Mail, *1905*

A policeman called me at home. Friday night again. He'd caught a dozen courting couples in the stand and asked me what to do with them. I told him to fix the bloody fence and board 'em in. Best gate of the season it would've been.
FRED WESTGARTH, Hartlepools manager, 1957

Q: What will you do when Christ comes to lead us again? A: Move St John to inside-right.
CHURCH SIGN and answering graffiti on Merseyside, 1965

Football crowds are never going to sound like the hat parade on the club lawns of Cheltenham racecourse. They are always going to have more vinegar than Chanel.
ARTHUR HOPCRAFT, author, The Football Man, *1968*

When I'm warming up their fans' veins are popping out of their necks. It's like I've done something to their family or something.
STEVEN TAYLOR, Newcastle defender, on Sunderland supporters, 2012

The renaming of Newcastle's stadium is old news. For us Sunderland fans its name changed years ago – it will always be Sid James Park.
LETTER to The Guardian *after St James' Park was rebranded Sports Direct Arena, 2011*

If you want comedy, farce or pantomime, go to Newcastle. It's been that way since 1947.

SID WADDELL, TV darts commentator and Newcastle supporter, 2008

Make sure the Sky cameras don't catch you snivelling into your scarf or blubbering into your best mate's shoulder.
NEWCASTLE UNITED official website request for fans to 'show dignity' before the game that led to their relegation, 2009

Well done Mary Poppins!
BANNER by Sunderland supporters 'congratulating' Newcastle's acting manager Alan Shearer on taking them down, 2009

I heard recently that, on average, Alex Ferguson receives two turds in the post each week. What I want to know is, who's sending the other one?
LETTER to Viz *magazine, 2009*

They tend to start off with things like 'Dear Stupid' or 'Dear Big Head'. One man wrote to me, beginning: 'Dear Alfie Boy'.
SIR ALF RAMSEY on his postbag, in Arthur Hopcraft's The Football Man, *1968*

My favourite [letter received] is one which said: 'You, Smith, Jones and Heighway had better keep looking over your shoulder. You are all going to get your dews.'
EMLYN HUGHES, Liverpool captain, 1977

The only point worth remembering about Port Vale's match with Hereford on Monday was the fact that the attendance figure, 2,744, was a perfect cube, 14 x 14 x 14.
LETTER from 'Disillusioned Supporter' to Stoke-on-Trent's Sentinel *newspaper, 1979*

Girls have sent me suggestive pictures and said what they would like to do to me. I'm absolutely shocked by their suggestions.

Then I get Sarah [Whatmore, his girlfriend] to act them out.
JAMES BEATTIE, Southampton and England striker, 2003

I got some girl's knickers through the post the other day but I didn't like them. To be honest, they didn't fit.
JAMIE REDKNAPP, Liverpool midfielder, 1995

Funny stalkers, scary stalkers, every kind of stalker. One woman turned up at my place every day for two weeks and just left different pairs of underpants for me in the mail-box. Luckily, they were always brand new.
DAVID BECKHAM on life as a Madrid galactico, 2004

I got the ball in the middle of the field and a voice in the centre stand shouted out: 'Give it to Taylor.' So I gave it to Taylor. Five minutes later, I got the ball again and the same voice shouted: 'Give it to Matthews.' So I gave it to Matthews. A couple of minutes later, I got the ball again, but this time there were three Arsenal players around me. So I looked up at the stand and the voice came back: 'Use your own discretion.'
STAN MORTENSEN, former Blackpool and England player, in Robin Daniels' Blackpool Football, *1972*

Everyone had a rattle and they went just to enjoy the game. If that sounds a rose-tinted or nostalgic memory, I'm sorry, but it's true. Then, for me and my dad, it was a cheese roll at a little café up the road, the 106 bus and then the 227 back to Poplar.
HARRY REDKNAPP, Queens Park Rangers manager, on his boyhood trips to watch West Ham, in Always Managing: The Autobiography, *2013*

It's gone now, mainly because of hooliganism. I wouldn't dare walk about now, in my old outfit, in another town. They'd be after me, wouldn't they? Around 1963, I could feel some spectators were getting out of hand.
SYD BEVERS, leader of the 'Atomic Boys', a group of Blackpool fans who attended games in fancy dress, 1972

Five Newport County supporters were arrested after they turned up at a Kidderminster Harriers match in drag. About 150 visiting fans arrived in the town but 40 went to the Oxfam shop and bought women's clothes. 'I don't know whether this is a new style, or what it is,' said Superintendent Peter Picken.
REPORT in the Worcester Evening News, *1989*

There was this male MP who was found dead in stockings and suspenders. He was also wearing a Manchester City scarf but the police kept that bit quiet so as not to embarrass the relatives.
BERNARD MANNING, comedian and City supporter, 2000

I've got three kids and I think all fathers must be anti-hooligans. That's the least they can do. It's their duty as parents.
BRIAN CLOUGH, *Nottingham Forest manager, interviewed in* Shoot! *magazine, 1980*

I vowed I'd never go to a football match again after getting hugged on a terrace by a man who had soiled himself when England scored against Germany in the qualifiers for the 2002 World Cup.
ALEX JAMES, *Blur bass guitarist, 2010*

The Spurs fans, marching and shouting their way back to the station, banged on the windows of the team coach as it threaded its way through the crowds. 'Go on, smash the town up,' said Cyril [Knowles], encouraging them.
HUNTER DAVIES, The Glory Game, *1972*

The club call us hooligans, but who'd cheer them if we didn't come? You have to stand there and take it when Spurs are losing and the others are jeering at you. It's not easy. We support them everywhere and get no thanks.
TOTTENHAM FAN *quoted in* The Glory Game, *1972*

I'd like to kill all the Arsenal players and then burn the stand down.
TOTTENHAM FAN, *as above*

The only answer is for decent supporters, and they are in the majority, to become terrace vigilantes. A few thumps on the nose would soon stop these silly youngsters.
ALEC STOCK, *Fulham manager, 1975*

No one likes us, we don't care.
SONG *by Millwall fans to the tune of* 'Sailing', *1980s*

Apparently they couldn't find one decent Millwall supporter.
DENIS HOWELL MP, *Labour, Minister for Sport, complaining about an 'unbalanced' investigation into hooliganism by BBC TV's* Panorama, *1977*

Really good Millwall supporters, right, they can't stand their club being slagged down, you know, and it all wells up, you know, and you just feel like hitting someone.
MILLWALL FAN *quoted in Roger Ingham et al*, Football Hooliganism: The Wider Context, *1978*

At 6.45 the Millwall supporters were taken under escort towards the stadium. As they passed a public house, a group of 30 to 40 males came out, and bottles and glasses were thrown and pub windows smashed. After a while it became apparent that both groups were from Millwall and each thought the other were Bristol City supporters.

REPORT *from the National Criminal Intelligence Unit after a match at Ashton Gate, 2001*

The shaven-headed fellow guest sitting next to me turned out to be a wealthy publisher of pornography and a supporter of Millwall. So that was nice. Feeling a bit like the Queen, I tried to take a polite interest by asking questions such as: 'And do you find that takes up a lot of your time?'

LYNNE TRUSS, Times *feature writer, on dining out after the 1997 Italy v England World Cup qualifier, in* Get Her Off the Pitch: How Sport Took Over My Life, *2010*

Few moments in my life rival the experience of attending my first game, of being instantly exploded into the screeching Hogarth sketch wired to the national grid that was match day at the old Den.

DANNY BAKER, *broadcaster and journalist, on watching Millwall for the first time aged five,* Radio Times, *2012*

I'm happy with the job I've got, but I'd love to have played left-back for Millwall.

BOB CROW, *RMT union leader, 2012*

What you don't want to do is replace the image of Millwall, which is one of hostility, pride and belligerence. Frankly, your fellow

supporters don't give a flying fuck for anyone else in the league or any sort of political correctness.

ROD LIDDLE, *broadcaster, journalist and Millwall fan, arguing against trying to turn the club into a 'family' club like Charlton, 2006*

He told me I was a dead man and that I wouldn't get out of The Den alive. Then he said I was fat. I said: 'Have you looked at yourself lately?'

KEVIN PRESSMAN, *Sheffield Wednesday goalkeeper, on being confronted by a pitch invader at Millwall, 1995*

If Cantona had jumped into our crowd he'd never have come out alive.

ALEX RAE, *Millwall midfielder, after the Frenchman's Selhurst Park fracas, 1995*

I have a lot of good moments but the one I prefer is when I kicked the hooligan. I did not punch him strong enough – I should have punched him harder.

ERIC CANTONA *interviewed about the 1995 incident in* FourFourTwo *magazine, 2010*

I must have done all right for them to gob all over me.
STEVE JONES, Bournemouth striker, after running a gauntlet of Birmingham fans, 1994

The most violent offenders should be flogged in front of the main stand before home games. I feel so strongly on this that I'd volunteer to do the whipping myself.
ALLAN CLARKE, Leeds manager, 1980

I know it sounds drastic but the only way to deal with hooligans is to shoot them. That'll stop them.

BOBBY ROBERTS, Colchester manager, 1980

There are more hooligans in the House of Commons than at a football match.
BRIAN CLOUGH, Nottingham Forest manager, 1980

I met these football fans smoking in a non-smoker on the railway, so I said: 'Put it out...put it out.' And they did. I think they're far less dangerous than dogs.
BARBARA WOODHOUSE, dog trainer and TV personality, 1980

What comes next – water cannon, guards, tanks and consultant undertakers to ferry away the dead?
SIMON TURNEY, Greater London Council official, on Chelsea's proposed electric fence, 1985

You can't turn a fire extinguisher on fans. It'll only inflame the situation.

JOHN BALL, West Ham safety officer, after their followers were doused at French club Metz, 1999

There have always been hooligans. In Germany they were in the Gestapo and in Russia they were in the KGB.
HOWARD WILKINSON, Leeds manager, after violence by his club's fans at Bournemouth, 1990

What's the first word to come into your head when I say 'British soccer fan'? It was 'subhuman', wasn't it? I rest my case.
PHILADELPHIA INQUIRER, doubting the wisdom of the United States staging the World Cup, 1990

There were three countries in the world whose presence would have created logistical and security problems, so we're very pleased they won't be coming: Iraq, Iran and England.
ALAN ROTHENBERG, chairman of the US World Cup committee, 1994

Every British male, at some time or other, goes to his last football match. It may very well be his first football match.
MARTIN AMIS, novelist, reviewing a book on 'football' hooliganism, 1991

English fans are brilliant. In England, when you ask someone which club he supports, it means something. The guy supports a club for his whole life, whatever the ups and downs. In France, there's no loyalty. If you're not top of the league, the fans go to another club.
ERIC CANTONA, newly signed to Leeds, on hearing England fans had rioted in Sweden, 1992

I hope [England] are on the first plane back from Deutschland. They've got the players to do well, but they're not my team. I'm from the People's Republic of Mancunia. I'll have to leave if they win it. The country will be full of Cockneys going on about it for years.
MANI, Primal Scream and former Stone Roses bass guitarist, before the World Cup finals, 2006

They eat sausages and eggs for breakfast, drive on the left, play baseball with an oar, set times for drinking and think they are the best.
ARTICLE in the Portuguese newspaper 24 Horas on the 'ridiculous' England fans before Portugal v England, European Championship quarter-final, 2004

Football matches are now the substitute for the old medieval tournaments. They are aggressive and confrontational by their nature. It's perfectly natural for some of the fans to be obstreperous.
ALAN CLARK MP, Conservative, defending rioting England fans, World Cup finals, 1998

Now that we don't have war, what's wrong with a good punch-up? We're a nation of yobs. Without that characteristic, how did we colonise the world? With so many milksops, left-wing liberals and wetties around, I rejoice that some people keep up our historic spirit.
DOWAGER MARCHIONESS OF READING, aged 79, after hooliganism by England fans, World Cup finals, 1998

The people kicking up a fuss in Marseilles are true fans. They feel passionate enough about the England team to go out and fight for them.
ELLIS CASHMORE, sociology professor, 1998

The fans all had the complexion and body scent of a cheese and onion crisp, and the eyes of pit-bulls.

MARTIN AMIS on his experience of watching Queens Park Rangers, 1991

The disrespect shown by the English fans to our national anthem was wrong. It shows that the countries who are said to be advanced culturally are actually behind.
SENOL GUNES, Turkey coach, after whistling and booing during his country's anthem at Sunderland, 2003

It's not surprising some fans behave badly when you realise how little consideration they receive from the clubs.
COLIN SMITH, Chief Constable, Thames Valley Police, 1990

Football violence is like smoking. If you try it once and hate it, you don't do it again. But if you try it once and like it, it's bloody hard to give up.
DOUGIE AND EDDY BRIMSON, self-confessed Watford hooligans, in their book Everywhere We Go, 1996

The terraces are the very last bastion of our once male-dominated culture, where boys can grow up and act like men...scream, shout, abuse, swear, even cry if we like without feeling like some effeminate twat.
DOUGIE BRIMSON, Watford fan and author of A Geezer's Guide to Football: A Lifetime of Lads and Lager, 1998

Like other infections, new strains of football hooliganism are developing that are clever, resilient and increasingly resistant.
BRYAN DREW, National Criminal Intelligence Service spokesman, 2001

Football is not about people setting out to watch a match and never returning home.

PETER RIDSDALE, Leeds chairman, after two of the club's fans were stabbed to death in Istanbul, 2000

Even the hooligans had a good time and enjoyed the party. Maybe the cannabis relaxed them.
JOHAN BEELAN, Dutch police chief, on the behaviour of England fans in Eindhoven, 2000

We don't welcome yobs in any form, but that isn't to say we're against tribal loyalty. And our tribe aren't half fearsome when they want something.
KARREN BRADY, Birmingham City managing director, 2002

The English stick their psychos in Broadmoor, while the Welsh put theirs in Ninian Park.
FULHAM FANZINE There's Only One F in Fulham, *awarding Cardiff supporters 0 out of 10 in their Best Fans poll, 1995*

I went over to take a kick where the Chelsea fans were and they started chucking sticks of celery and sweetcorn. It made me laugh to think of them popping into greengrocers' shops on the way to Wembley.
RYAN GIGGS after the FA Cup final, Manchester United v Chelsea, 1994

My arms withered and my body was covered with pus-like sores, but no matter how bad it got I consoled myself by remembering that I wasn't a Chelsea fan.
IAN HOLLOWAY, Queens Park Rangers manager, returning to work after illness, 2005

I made a two-finger gesture towards the fans to show that I'd scored twice, and that must have been misinterpreted.
PAUL PESCHISOLIDO, West Bromwich Albion striker, after a confrontation with Port Vale supporters, 1997

Helping fuel soccer riots for 40 years
SLOGAN advertising Strongbow cider in the United States, 2003

The Scotland fans' ability to smuggle drink into matches makes Papillon look like a learner.
SCOTTISH POLICE FEDERATION spokesman, 1981

We do have the greatest fans in the world, but I've never seen a fan score a goal.

JOCK STEIN, Scotland manager, World Cup finals, 1982

Communism v Alcoholism
SCOTTISH BANNER at Soviet Union v Scotland, World Cup finals, 1982

Let all France have whisky on its breath.
LYRIC from the Scotland World Cup song 'Don't Come Home Too Soon', by Del Amitri, 1998

Drinking alcohol can be dangerous as it leads to drunkenness.
UEFA HANDBOOK offering advice to fans at the European Championship finals, 2004

The kind of commitment Scots invest in football means there's less left for the more important concerns.
WILLIAM McILVANNEY, novelist and journalist, in a feature on Scottish independence, reprinted in Surviving the Shipwreck, *1992*

When Patrick Kluivert scored, it was the same feeling as when Mel Gibson got hung, drawn and quartered at the end of *Braveheart.*
DOMINIK DIAMOND, broadcaster and Scotland fan, after a late Dutch goal v England eliminated Scotland from the European Championship finals, 1996

We'd never support a Great Britain football team, even if there were 11 Scots in it.
HAMISH HUSBAND, Association of Tartan Army Clubs spokesperson, after talk of entering a GB side in the 2012 Olympic Games, 2005

We dream of beating the English, not playing in the same team as them.
GORDON McQUEEN, former Scotland defender, 2005

Get intae them! Get intae them!
CHANT by Scotland fans as Scotland kicked off against no opposition after Estonia refused to agree to switch the kick-off time, 1996

One team in Tallinn, there's only one team in Tallinn.
SONG by Scotland fans when Estonia failed to turn up for a match v Scotland, 1996

Most Scotland supporters have woken up to the fact that wearing the kilt is probably the easiest way in the world of attracting the opposite sex.
HAGGIS SUPPER, *Scotland fanzine, 1999*

Rangers fans were friendly to me. The most hostility I got [playing for Celtic] was being pelted with snowballs when I went to take a corner at Aberdeen.
STILIYAN PETROV, Aston Villa, Bulgaria and former Celtic midfielder, 2006

There was a jersey with a childish scrawl which read: 'To Saint Tommy, now up in heaven, please say hello to the rest of the saints. Especially Saint Petersburg.'
DAILY TELEGRAPH *report on tributes outside Celtic Park when ex-manager and player Tommy Burns died shortly before Zenit St Petersburg beat Rangers, Uefa Cup final, 2008*

Who are the people? We arra people!

RANGERS FANS *call-response chant, 1960s*

Ibrox really is a special place. It's incredible the bond fans have with parts of the ground. They can remember the day [Jim]

Baxter passed from here or there, and from where Gazza [Paul Gascoigne] scored. I remember at training spotting little burnt areas. These were from people who had sneaked in at night and sprinkled the ashes of former fans on the pitch.
SANDY JARDINE, former Rangers defender, 2012

If Rangers go out of business, who are the Celtic fans going to hate?

LETTER to The Herald after Rangers went into administration, 2012

The Glaswegian definition of an atheist: a bloke who goes to Rangers–Celtic match to watch the football.
SANDY STRANG, Rangers supporter, in Stephen Walsh, Voices of the Old Firm, 1995

Celtic have all the cool people supporting them. Rangers have me and Wet Wet Wet.
ALAN McGEE, ex-manager of Oasis and record-label proprietor, 2005

In football a day is a decade and the game before is another history. But it's different in Old Firm matches – the fans love you if you play shite in other matches but great against Celtic.
MIKEL ARTETA, Spanish midfielder with Rangers, 2004

After I joined Celtic I was walking down a street in Glasgow when someone shouted: 'Fenian bastard.' I had to look it up. Fenian, that is.
MICK McCARTHY, Yorkshire-born Republic of Ireland manager, 1996

I'm a small, balding, ex-Communist, Celtic-supporting Catholic and Unionist. Therefore everyone seems to hate me.
DR JOHN REID MP, Labour, Secretary of State for Northern Ireland, 2001

I would rather watch Celtic than be a bishop.
RODERICK WRIGHT after relinquishing his post as Bishop of Argyll, 1996

I'm not a violent man but when you see the first flash of green or a Republic of Ireland jersey, something inside of you snaps.
RANGERS SUPPORTER, interviewed on Channel 4 documentary Football, Faith and Flutes, 1995

They call themselves Protestants. But they say that just because they want to be different from Catholics. Most of them are atheists.
CELTIC SUPPORTER on Football, Faith and Flutes, 1995

In Glasgow half the football fans hate you and the other half think they own you.

TOMMY BURNS, Celtic midfielder, 1987

For a while I did unite Rangers and Celtic fans. There were people in both camps who hated me.
MAURICE JOHNSTON on his spells on either side of Glasgow's great divide, 1994

I hear that couples sometimes arrive at the Mersey derby together but wearing opposing colours. If you did that in Glasgow you'd get lynched.
JOHN COLLINS, Everton and former Celtic midfielder, 1998

It angers me to see Rangers or Celtic fanatics getting all steamed up in the name of religion when most of them have never been near a church or a chapel in years.
DEREK JOHNSTONE, Rangers player, in Rangers: My Team, *1979*

Do you want your share of the gate money, Jock, or shall we just return the empties?
BILL SHANKLY to opposing manager Jock Stein after visiting Scots threw bottles when Liverpool beat Celtic in the European Cup-Winners' Cup, 1966

After the match against Inverness Caley [Celtic lost 3–2] I felt I was caught up in the Kosovo war, not a damaging football result. Some so-called fans covered my car in spit and shouted obscenities at me... It was Stone Age stuff from reptiles.
IAN WRIGHT, Celtic and former Arsenal striker, 2000

We were thrown to a veritable wild horde. It was a meeting of warriors where neither weakness nor nonchalance had a place. It was a test in the pure British tradition.
FABIEN BARTHEZ, Monaco goalkeeper, on the atmosphere at Rangers, 2000

Sigmund Freud once described humour as being as incongruous as a buckled wheel, but he never played the old Glasgow Empire on a wet Monday night after both Rangers and Celtic had lost on the Saturday.
KEN DODD, comedian, 2002

When I was a lad I saw Hearts beat Kilmarnock in the 1962 League Cup Final. As John Cumming, the captain, lifted the trophy, my dad lifted me up just like the cup and said: 'There'll be many more days like this.' Only 36 years later, and the next time Hearts won anything, I took my father to the 1998 Scottish Cup Final and we beat Rangers. Sitting behind us was John Cumming.
ALEX SALMOND MSP, Scottish National Party leader, 2011

Our Reason, Our Inspiration, Our Pride: 96
BANNER by Liverpool fans commemorating the 96 who died in 1989 at Hillsborough, Champions League final in Athens, 2007

The dignity with which the families have sought justice is a lesson to us all. They are the best of us and will never walk alone.
JOHN BISHOP, comedian, on donating £96,000 to the Hillsborough Family Support Group, 2014

Very positive outcome. 23 years waiting for the truth, next step justice.

KENNY DALGLISH, Liverpool manager at the time of the Hillsborough tragedy, welcoming the Independent Panel's report which confirmed a cover-up by police and exonerated Liverpool fans, 2012

It is too little, too late. He's a low-life. A clever low-life...but a low-life.
*TREVOR HICKS, chairman of the Hillsborough Family Support Group, on the apology from ex-*Sun *editor Kelvin MacKenzie for stories that Liverpool supporters robbed victims, 2012*

There were two disasters at Hillsborough – one on the day and one afterwards: there was a contrived, manipulated, vengeful and spiteful attempt to divert the blame.
HICKS, 2012

I can't quite get my head around why people come to football matches with that first and foremost on their minds. It's not getting at the players, it's getting at families. Neither they nor I can imagine the pain those people have gone through.
JOE JORDAN, former Manchester United striker, calling for life bans on United fans who taunted Liverpool supporters by singing 'Always the victims, it's never your fault,' 2012.

I wanted to say to [Liverpool's American co-owner] Tom Hicks: imagine if it was your family – which is what Liverpool Football Club are to most people – it is like you are raping all of them at once over a long period of time and getting away with it.
IAN McCULLOCH, singer with the band Echo and the Bunnymen, 2010

Scouse people are very respectful. If they see me walking my dogs in the park, they say: 'Alright Nando, lad.' And that is all. I like that.
FERNANDO TORRES, Liverpool and Spain striker, 2009

Sinatra would kill to sing here.
BILL SHANKLY, Liverpool manager, hails the Kop, 1964

We don't need to give away
flags for our fans to wave. Our
supporters are always there with
their hearts, and that is all we need.
It's the passion of the fans that
helps to win matches, not flags.
RAFAEL BENITEZ, Liverpool manager,
criticising Chelsea (who he later joined as
interim manager), 2007

Roman's got his roubles, Glazer's
got his dollars. All we want from
Rafa [Benitez] is five Euros.
BANNER as Liverpool won their fifth
European Cup, 2005

The missus thinks I'm working
And I've lied to the gaffer
Coz I'm here in Istanbul
With Stevie G and Rafa
BANNER by Liverpool supporters in
Istanbul, Champions League final, 2005

Joey ate the Frogs' legs
Made the Swiss roll
Now he's Munching Gladbach
BANNER in praise of Liverpool defender
Joey Jones, European Cup final, 1977

For those watching in blue and
white, this is what the European
Cup looks like
BANNER at the Liverpool v Chelsea
Champions League semi-final, 2007

Forget the Beatles and the other
groups. The Kop is the real
Liverpool sound. That's real
singing.
SHANKLY, 1965

My eyes water when they sing
'You'll Never Walk Alone'. I've
actually been crying while playing.
KEVIN KEEGAN, Liverpool and
England striker, 1974

'You'll Never Walk Alone' was one
of my dad's favourite songs. He's
no longer with us and I was singing
it with them.
IAN HOLLOWAY, Blackpool manager,
when his team visited Liverpool, 2010

I always knew Liverpool fans were
special. The motto 'You'll Never
Walk Alone' is really lived by the
fans. It's a club where you feel
you're not alone.
ROY HODGSON on his appointment as
Liverpool manager, 2010

Ever since I came here, the famous
Anfield support hasn't really
been there. There was a problem
with the owners, and with Kenny
[Dalglish] being so popular and
the job going to me, so I've had
to live with that. I have to hope
the fans will become supporters
because we need support. We're not
deliberately losing games.
HODGSON, 2010; he was sacked at the
start of 2011

Feel for United. I remember how
hard it was to win our 4th one.
JOHN BISHOP, Liverpool-supporting
comedian, tweeting after Manchester
United were knocked out of the
Champions League, 2013

MUFC defending titles, LFC defending racism
BANNER in the United end at Anfield after Liverpool players and management rallied to support Luis Suarez following allegations that he racially abused United's Patrice Evra, 2012

We're not racists, we only hate Mancs

BANNER on the Kop, Liverpool v Manchester City, 2012

I love going back to Anfield. You know you're going to get dog's abuse and you'll get wags behind you who say things that make you chuckle.
MARK HUGHES, Stoke City manager, on taking his new club to Liverpool, 2013

You're uglier than Camilla
BANNER by Juventus supporters at a match v Liverpool, Champions League, 2005

Owned by Americans. Managed by a Spaniard. Watched by Norwegians.
BANNER by Everton fans at the derby with Liverpool, 2008

I love Evertonians. They're like Liverpudlians, except they're Evertonians.
DAVE WHELAN, Wigan Athletic chairman, 2013

Superman wears Tim Cahill pyjamas
BANNER by Everton fans, 2009

Twenty-three years of silver and we're still top, ta-ra Fergie.
BANNER by Manchester United fan Pete Molyneux at Sir Alex Ferguson's last game as manager, 2013

Three years of excuses and we're still crap, ta-ra Fergie.
BANNER by the same fan when Ferguson's results were disappointing, 1989

United and City. Linked by geography, separated by success.
BANNER by Manchester United supporters, 2011

MUFC – Not Arrogant: Just Better
BANNER by United fans, 2012

How many people does it take to make a banner? One. And maybe two to hold it.
RAFAEL BENITEZ, interim Chelsea manager, when a 'Rafa Out' banner was unfurled at his first game in charge, 2012

Kim Jong-il thinks I'm at work!

PLACARD in the crowd at North Korea v Brazil, World Cup finals, 2010

Attack, attack, for feck's sake attack

BANNER by Northern Ireland fans at the home defeat by Estonia, 2011

Can you win? Otherwise I'll get teased at school. Thanks, Filippo.
BANNER by nine-year-old Internazionale fan at San Siro, 2012; Inter lost 3–0 to Bologna

Milan, keep on winning, so I can make fun of Filippo at school. Samuele & Alice.
BANNER at subsequent AC Milan v Cesena game, 2012

Wanted: A worthy rival for a decent Clasico
BANNER by Barcelona fans during a match v Real Madrid, 2012; Barca had lost once in 12 meetings

Mourinho, stay!
CHANT by Barcelona fans as their team again beat Real, 2012

We'll be in Seville. You'll be watching The Bill.
BANNER by Celtic fans, aimed at Rangers' supporters during build-up to the UEFA Cup final, 2003

We dream of playing in the shirt. Today God chose you. Play like we dream.
BANNER by Manchester City fans, 2004

Victoria! Betray him with me!
BANNER by Switzerland fans against Beckham's England, European Championship finals, 2004; other Swiss supporters held up placards saying 'And me'

You can stick the league title up your arse
BANNER by AC Milan fans at the celebration of their Champions League triumph, 2007; the slogan, mocking Inter Milan's Serie A title, was unwittingly unfurled by vice-captain Massimo Ambrosini

Mum, get the pasta on!
BANNER by Italy fans as Sweden and Denmark fought out the 2–2 draw which would eliminate the Italians, European Championship finals, 2004

We've come to get our bicycles back
BANNER by Netherlands supporters at the match against West Germany, 1988; the Nazis had confiscated the Dutch people's bikes during the Second World War

Jesus is a Wiganer

BANNER by Wigan fans after Jesus Seba was signed from Zaragoza, 1996

Brazil would pick Le Tiss
BANNER by Southampton fans protesting against his omission from the England squad v Brazil, 1995

Paul McGrath limps on water
BANNER by Derby fans in praise of the injury-blighted defender, 1997

We don't need Viagra to stay up

BANNER by Charlton fans, a month
before their team were relegated, 1999

**Our husbands think we're
shopping in Dublin**
BANNER by Republic of Ireland fans in
Portugal, 1995

Sex and Drugs and Oranje Goals
BANNER at Dutch matches, Euro 2000

The Silence of the Rams
SLOGAN on anti-Derby T-shirt sold
outside Nottingham Forest ground, 1993

**Sex. Beer. Football. Have I
forgotten something?**
SLOGAN on Denmark supporters' T-shirts,
European Championship finals, 2004

Join City and you're dead
GRAFFITO on Manchester's Nike store
after Wayne Rooney said he wanted to
leave Manchester United, 2010

**I looked out and saw 30 blokes
with their hoods up. I wasn't going
to invite them in for tea.**
ROONEY on how United fans gathered
outside his home after he sought a meeting
with Sir Alex Ferguson to express disquiet
about the club's ambitions, 2010

**I don't really think it's much fun
when 50,000 spectators are singing
'Posh Spice takes it up the arse'
every weekend.**
VICTORIA BECKHAM on the TV
documentary Victoria's Secrets, 2000

**I thought I had seen it all when it
comes to the fickleness of football
folk. Then I heard the Spurs fans
singing: 'There's only one Alan
Sugar.'**
MICK McCARTHY, Millwall manager,
1994

**We seem to be lumbered with the
'Inger-lund, Inger-lund, Inger-lund'
chant. That may be boring but at
least everyone knows the words.**
HELEN JOSLIN, Football Supporters'
Association official, as England
reached the semi-finals of the European
Championship, 1996

**It took me a long time to
understand that the song they sing
about me was not trying to bully
me. People explained to me that it
was more an expression of love.**
PER MERTESACKER, Arsenal
and Germany defender, on his club's
supporters' song 'We've got a big fucking
German', 2014

**You fill up my senses
Like a night game at Yeovil
Like the Johnstone's Paint Trophy
Like an empty old Lane
Like the Steel City derby
In the old Third Division
Oh Sheffield United, you fucked up
again.**
BARNSLEY fans' re-working of 'Annie's
Song' after their neighbours' relegation,
2011

His name is Rio and he watches from the stand.
SONG by West Ham fans to the tune of Duran Duran's 'Rio' after their ex-player Rio Ferdinand was banned for missing a drug test, 2004

Stayed on the telly, you should've stayed on the telly.
SONG by Newcastle fans to Alan Shearer as the Match of the Day *pundit led the team to relegation as interim manager, 2009*

When you're sat in row Z, and the ball hits your head, that's Zamora.

SONG by Fulham supporters to the tune of Dean Martin's 'That's Amore' about striker Bobby Zamora, 2009

He's fast, he's red, he talks like Father Ted, Robbie Keane.
SONG by Liverpool fans about the Republic of Ireland striker, 2009

He's big, he's red, his feet stick out the bed, Peter Crouch.
SONG by Liverpool fans about the club's towering forward, 2005

Your teeth are offside, your teeth are offside, Luis Suarez, your teeth are offside.
SONG by Manchester United fans to the tune of 'Sloop John B' about Liverpool's Uruguay striker, 2013

Chelsea, wherever you may be, keep your wife from John Terry.

SONG by Chelsea supporters to the tune of 'Lord of the Dance' after Terry's alleged affair with Wayne Bridge's ex-partner, 2010

John Carew, Carew, he likes a lap-dance or two, he might even pay for you, John Carew, Carew.
SONG by Aston Villa fans to the tune of 'Que Sera, Sera' after the Norway striker was fined by the club for reportedly being in a lapdancing club the night before a match, 2008

City of Culture, you're having a laugh.
SONG by West Bromwich Albion followers at Hull, 2014

Feed the Goat and he will score.
SONG by Manchester City fans in honour of Shaun Goater, 1999

Feed the Pope and he will score.
SONG by Port Vale fans in homage to Tom Pope, 2013

Are you watching, Macclesfield?
SONG by Manchester City fans on the club's relegation to the third tier (as nearby Macclesfield were promoted to the same division), 1998

You can stick your Head and Shoulders up your arse.

SONG by Newcastle fans to Manchester City and England goalkeeper Joe Hart, who advertised the shampoo, 2013

Does your boyfriend know you're here?
SONG by visiting supporters at Brighton, 2012

You're too ugly to be gay.
RESPONSE by Brighton fans, 2012

It wouldn't be described as 'banter' if the taunts and chants were about skin colour. Something would have been done by now to stop it.
JOINT STATEMENT by Brighton & Hove Albion Supporters' Club and the Gay Football Supporters' Network, 2013

You're just a shit Chas and Dave.
SONG by Tottenham fans to Liam and Noel Gallagher at a Spurs v Manchester City game, 2009

You're just a fat Maradona.

SONG by Stoke supporters to Manchester City's Carlos Tevez, 2009

Strawberry blond, you're having a laugh.
SONG by Queens Park Rangers crowd to Crystal Palace's ginger-haired Ben Watson, 2008

He's got a bird's nest on his head.
SONG by West Ham fans to Everton's Marouane Fellaini, 2009

Here for the shot put, we're only here for the shot put.
SONG by Leeds supporters as their team trailed Rotherham 4–1 at the Don Valley Athletics Stadium, 2008

You can stick your flat-pack wardrobes up your arse.
SONG by Northern Ireland fans at a match v Sweden, 2007

We all agree, Easter is better than Christmas
SONG by Milton Keynes Dons supporters after Jermaine Easter scored v Stockport on Boxing Day, 2010

When the Hibs go up to lift the Scottish Cup, we'll be dead, we'll be dead
SONG by Hibernian fans after defeat in the Scottish Cup final extended their run without success in the competition to 110 years, 2012

5–1, even Heskey scored.
SONG by England fans reminding their German hosts of the rout in Munich in a 2001 qualifier, 2006

Are you Tamworth in disguise?
SONG by Burton Albion fans as Manchester United were held 0–0 in the FA Cup against the non-league side, 2006

Is that all you bring away?
SONG by MK Dons fans to 9,000 visiting Wolves supporters, 2014

We all live in an Orange submarine.
SONG by Netherlands fans, European Championship finals, 2004

Who let the Frogs out?

SONG by Leicester fans to Arsenal's French-dominated side, 2003

Deep-fry yer vodka, we're gonna deep-fry yer vodka.
SONG by Rangers fans to Zenit St Petersburg supporters, Uefa Cup final, 2008

Deep-fry yer pizzas, we're gonna deep-fry yer pizzas.
SONG by Scotland supporters in Italy, 2007

Live round the corner, you only live round the corner.
SONG by Chelsea supporters to Manchester United's supposedly London-based following, 2004

Crying on the telly, we saw you crying on the telly.
SONG by Manchester United fans to Chelsea supporters soon after the London club's exit from the Champions League, 2004

What's it like to stink of fish?
SONG by Millwall fans on the visit of Grimsby, 2003

Cedric, Cedric, show us Uras.
SONG by Falkirk fans to the club's French defender Cedric Uras, 2007

He's fat, he's round, he's given us a ground, John Prescott, John Prescott.
SONG by Brighton fans after the Deputy Prime Minister approved the plan for a new stadium at Falmer, 2005

Peter Shilton, Peter Shilton, does your missus know you're here?
SONG by Arsenal North Bank to the Nottingham Forest keeper after a tabloid revealed he had been caught in a compromising position in a car late at night, 1980

We all agree, *Emmerdale*'s better than *Brookside*.
SONG by Halifax fans during FA Cup tie v Marine on Merseyside, 1992

We all agree, Asda is better than Harrods.
SONG by Charlton fans at Mohamed Al Fayed-owned Fulham, 1999

You must've come on a skateboard.
SONG by Nottingham Forest fans to Yeading's 60 followers, FA Cup tie, 2006

There's this staunch Stoke City fan who's getting some earache from his missus. 'You'd rather go and watch Stoke than take me out,' she complains. 'Correction,' he replies. 'I'd rather go and watch Port Vale than take you out.'
PETE CONWAY, Potteries comedian and father of singer Robbie Williams, 1991

You dirty Northern bastards.

CHANT by Plymouth fans to Watford supporters, FA Cup quarter-final, 2007

Come and have a go if you think you're hard enough.
CHANT by Manchester City supporters when boxer Ricky Hatton, a City fan, took his seat at a match for the first time since winning the IBF world welterweight title, 2007

UNITED FANS: We want 10! We want 10!
IPSWICH FANS: We want one! We want one!
CHANT and response during the closing stages of Manchester United's 9–0 win, 1995

It wasn't so much the death threats or the vandalism, but when you sit with your family in the directors' box and hear a couple of thousand people chanting 'Gilbert Blades is a wanker', then you feel it's time to go.
GILBERT BLADES, on resigning as Lincoln chairman, in Anton Rippon's book Soccer: The Road to Crisis, *1982*

I always answer letters from supporters. It's the death threats I object to.

REG BURR, Millwall chairman, 1990

I understand and sympathise with their strong feelings, but I cannot accept their conservatism or parochialism.
ROBERT MAXWELL, Oxford chairman, on opposition from Oxford and Reading fans to his proposed merger of the clubs as Thames Valley Royals, 1983

You can't force people to sit down, even if they have a seat. They want to sing, and unless you're Val Doonican you can't do that sitting down.
KEVIN KEEGAN, Newcastle manager, speaking against all-seated stadia, 1992

In 10 years' time they will be sitting in the stand, watching the match, and their children will say: 'Daddy, did you really stand over there, in the wind and the rain? And did the man behind you urinate in your back pocket? And did you have a pie from that awful shop and a pint of beer thrust in your hand on a cold day?' The kids just will not understand.
SIR JOHN HALL, Newcastle chairman, 1995

The World Cup in America was a throwback to the 1950s, in the way that 'rival' supporters enjoyed mixing with each other. The only trouble I saw was at a concert in the Dodgers Stadium.
RON ATKINSON, ITV pundit and Aston Villa manager, 1994

The atmosphere in the USA isn't right. The American public look at a game as a day out to eat hot-dogs and popcorn. In Europe the fans can't eat because their stomachs are tight with tension.
ANTONIO MATERRESE, Italian FA president, 1994

The tension felt by football fans during penalty shoot-outs can trigger heart attacks and strokes in male spectators. The day Holland lost to France in Euro 96, deaths from heart attacks and strokes rose by 50 per cent.
DR MIRIAM STOPPARD, 2002

It may have been an awful night, but the meat-and-potato pies were brill.

'AWAY TRAVELLER', columnist in Crewe Alexandra supporters' newsletter after a visit to Halifax, 1983

It's bad enough having to go and watch Bristol City without having things stolen.
JUDGE DESMOND VOWDEN QC, sentencing a man who stole from a City fan's car, 1984

It is the right of every Englishman to fall asleep if he wants – particularly if he is watching Arsenal.
JUDGE MICHAEL TAYLOR quashing a fan's conviction for drunkenness after he dozed off during a match, 2004

I knew my days were numbered when I was warming up behind the goal at Parkhead and one of our fans shouted: 'Kinnaird, we like the Poll Tax more than we like you.'
PAUL KINNAIRD, Partick Thistle player, on his time with St Mirren, 1992

Football fanzines are a case of successful cultural contestation in and through sport.

JOHN HORNE, *Staffordshire Polytechnic lecturer and co-author of a paper on fanzines in* Sociology Review, *1991*

The only time I turn my pager off is when I'm watching Burnley.
ALASTAIR CAMPBELL, *press secretary to Prime Minister Tony Blair, 1999*

The worse the team, the better the fanzine.

JOHN HORNE, *sociology lecturer, 1991*

Look Back in Amber
HULL CITY *fanzine title, 1990s*

Dial M for Merthyr
MERTHYR TYDFIL *fanzine title, 1990s*

Hyde! Hyde! What's the Score?
PRESTON *fanzine title, 1990s; the name refers to North End's 26–0 win v Hyde in 1887*

And Smith Must Score!
BRIGHTON *fanzine title, named after the TV commentary to Gordon Smith's last-minute miss in 1983 FA Cup final, 1988*

Sing When We're Fishing
GRIMSBY *fanzine title, 1988*

City Till I Cry
MANCHESTER CITY *fanzine title, 1999*

I make all sorts of excuses at work to avoid missing a Burnley game. I've had several aunties die in a season. After a game with Norwich was rained off, my boss said: 'I see your aunt's funeral was postponed due to a waterlogged pitch.'
DAVE BURNLEY, *Staffordshire-based Burnley fan who changed his surname by deed poll, 2009*

They're not happy in Burnley unless they're moaning. You could win 5–0 and they still wouldn't be happy. They're good folk, but they'll moan about owt.
STAN TERNENT, *Burnley manager, 2003*

He has very broad musical taste, anything from Elgar and Bach to Genesis and Supertramp. He also supports Arsenal, but then nobody's perfect.
BRIAN PEARSON, *secretary to the Archbishop of Canterbury, Dr George Carey, 1990*

I will die a Catholic. I will die an Arsenal fan. And I will die a Tory.
CHRIS PATTEN, *former chairman of the Conservative Party, 2000*

When we won the league in '89 it was the most cosmic thing that had ever happened. Better than any orgasm ever.
EMMA YOUNG, *Arsenal fan, quoted in Tom Watt,* The End: 90 Years of Life on Arsenal's North Bank, *1993*

The Prime Minister will be aware that there are two great football clubs in north London – Tottenham Hotspur and Enfield Town.

DAVID LAMMY MP, Labour, at Prime Minister's Questions, 2010

To celebrate Arsenal's defeat in Europe, 10 per cent off everything.

ADVERT by the food retailer World of Kosher in the Jewish Chronicle, *2004*

I do hate Arsenal. With a passion. No money in the world would ever tempt me to play for them.

TEDDY SHERINGHAM, Tottenham player and fan, 1996

Q: Which TV programme would you switch off? A: Soaps and Luton on *Match of the Day.*

VINNIE JONES, childhood Watford fan, in Chelsea programme questionnaire, 1991

Q: If you could go back in time, where would you go?
A: Wembley 1967, QPR's finest hour.

PETE DOHERTY, Babyshambles singer, in Guardian Weekend *magazine questionnaire, 2007*

If your woman sleeps with your best mate, it's over. If the Rs' manager Ian Holloway slept with my best mate, QPR would still be my team.

DOHERTY, 2005

Football feeds the soul. [Manchester] United have fed mine a damn sight more than acting ever will. Acting has never been my dream. I'd give it up tomorrow to play just once for United.

JAMES NESBITT, Irish actor, 2003

I support West Bromwich Albion. I hate people who support teams like Chelsea. You have to support a proper club and follow them through everything.

GORAN IVANISEVIC, Croatian tennis player, 2007

When I was a boy kicking a ball in the streets of Belfast my favourite team were Wolves. It was around the time of their great games against the continentals and me and my friends used to play Wolves v Spurs.

GEORGE BEST in John Roberts' book Fall of a Superstar, *1973*

To John Hutley from your wife! Happy 30th wedding anniversary. Enjoy the match because you're going to pay for it later! Love, Jane.

MESSAGE on Millwall's electronic scoreboard, 2008

Jack, Are the Villa really more important than our marriage? It's over, Jess.
BANNER *draped over a bridge near Villa Park, 2008*

My life won't be complete until I'm at Villa Park. I want to be rooting on the claret and blue to a magnificent win over those suckers like Stoke City or Wolverhampton Wanderers or Queens Park Rangers.
TOM HANKS, *Hollywood screen actor, after seeing Villa for the first time against Portland Timbers in the US, 2012*

I like Aston Villa because the name is just so sweet. It sounds like a lovely spa.

HANKS, 2003

I still support the Villa but I don't like football as much as I did because the game has been tailored to the wine-bar fraternity. The culture has gradually been eradicated.
NIGEL KENNEDY, *classical violinist, 1997*

Villa have actually stopped scattering people's ashes on the pitch because some players were put off the idea of doing sliding tackles, but they've made an exception for me. It would be hilarious to be cremated wearing a Villa kit, even if I was 80.
KENNEDY, 2004

You lose some, you draw some.

JASPER CARROTT, *comedian/actor, on being a Birmingham City fan, 1979*

Any man who is paid to serve his country should never try to gain financially. That may seem an old-fashioned idea, but I am very patriotic at every level. I adore my county cricket team, Somerset, and my football team, because I support the greatest team in England, Bristol Rovers.
JEFFREY ARCHER, *author and Tory politician, during the Spycatcher case, 1987*

It says on my birth certificate that I was born in the borough of West Bromwich, in the district of West Bromwich. I said all right, all right, I'll support the bloody Albion – no need to twist my arm.
FRANK SKINNER, *comedian, 1995*

My great heroes are Sir Stanley Matthews and Dave Beasant.
JUNE WHITFIELD, *comedy actress and Wimbledon supporter, 1988*

Q: What was the first gig you ever went to?
A: Wolves 2 Moscow Dynamo 1 on 9 November 1955.
ROBERT PLANT, Led Zeppelin singer, interviewed in Q magazine, 1993

As much as I love women and music, my first love will always be football.
ROD STEWART, pop singer, former Brentford trialist and Scotland fan, 1995

Q: What's the worst thing anyone's ever said to you? A: Do you support Sheffield Wednesday?

SEAN BEAN, actor and Sheffield United director, in Guardian Weekend magazine questionnaire, 2007

Q: If you could bring something extinct back to life, what would you choose?
A: Sheffield Wednesday's chances of winning anything ever again. I've got more chance of seeing a dinosaur singing 'Show Me the Way To Go Home', pissed, in our garden.
RICHARD HAWLEY, pop singer-songwriter, also in Guardian Weekend, 2011

Famous Carlisle United fans: Melvyn Bragg (unless he's in London, then he's an Arsenal supporter) and Hunter Davies (unless he's in London, then he's a Spurs fan).
TOTAL FOOTBALL magazine, 1995

You folks may be rightly proud of your title 'Football's Fairest Crowd', but for my part I would like to see a lot more partisanship in favour of Chelsea. All too many people come to Stamford Bridge to see a football match – instead of to cheer Chelsea.
TED DRAKE, Chelsea manager, in his programme column, 1952

I collected Chelsea programmes for years, took them to New York with me when I moved there. But when I arrived and unpacked, I discovered they had all been stolen. It was very sad.
VIDAL SASSOON, hairdresser, 1988

[Fidel] Castro called the victory by the Cuban volleyball team over the US a 'sporting, psychological, patriotic and revolutionary triumph'. At Chelsea we're quite happy to settle for three points.
SEBASTIAN COE, former athlete and Chelsea fan, 1990

When I called Coventry supporters a bunch of wankers, it was the best 15 grand I ever spent.

IAN WRIGHT, *Arsenal striker, recalling one of the fines he incurred, 1999*

Leeds supporters began their revolt against [prospective owner Massimo] Cellino on Friday evening, gathering in the Elland Road car-park, preventing the Italian's taxi from reaching him for a while. Cellino's minicab was chased round and round, leaving the taxi company, Stanningley Cars, to issue a plea via Twitter for fans to desist as their driver was running out of petrol.

HENRY WINTER, Daily Telegraph *football correspondent, after Cagliari owner Cellino reputedly sacked Leeds manager Brian McDermott before actually owning the club, 2014*

When you've just bought a club and go straight to the pub, that's Cellino.

SONG *by Leeds United fans in honour of Massimo Cellino, to whom initial hostility* had abated, 2014; *he had visited the Old Peacock by Elland Road on his first day as owner*

Fans travelling to Elland Road should ridicule their abhorrent adversaries.

ADVICE on the official Manchester United website, 2003

If you ask any Leeds fan, they like it when they hear rival clubs chanting disrespectful things about them.

RICHARD NAYLOR, Leeds *captain and boyhood fan, 2010*

Do they hate us? You go to take a corner at Elland Road and you've got 15,000 horrible skinheads in their end yelling murder at you.

RYAN GIGGS on Leeds fans, 1994

When I was younger I used to get abuse off the Leeds fans, who sang things like: 'There's only one spotty virgin.'

GIGGS *on 'enjoying the ferocity' of away crowds towards Manchester United, 2009*

After Rio Ferdinand's transfer I saw a T-shirt at Leeds that said 'Traitors' and had my name and Joe's [Jordan], then Eric Cantona and Rio. And that's 25 years after I left. Some of the people wearing it weren't even born when I left.

GORDON McQUEEN, *a centre-back who also left Elland Road for Old Trafford, 2003*

We'll take our fair share of support down there [to Gillingham]. We'll take support whether it's Kent or the Arctic Circle.
KEVIN BLACKWELL, Leeds manager, on his club's first away match after relegation from the Premiership, 2004

Mr Stanley Heathman, married with five children, said they had never been in any doubt that they would be liberated. It was just a matter of how and when. He astonished one soldier by asking: 'Can you tell me – have Leeds been relegated?'
POOLED DESPATCH by journalists covering the Falklands War, 1982

It's often said that no club have a divine right to be in the First Division. Well, we bloody have.
THE HANGING SHEEP, *Leeds fanzine, 1988; Leeds had been in the Second for six years*

The accused claimed he was the reincarnated brother of Conan the Barbarian, that he was turning into an elk and had played for Leeds United. A defence psychiatrist said he was mad.
COURT REPORT, Daily Telegraph, *1988*

Man offers marriage proposal to any woman with ticket for Leeds v Sheffield United game. Must send photograph (of ticket).
ADVERT *in* Yorkshire Evening Post *as Second Division title race came to the boil, 1990*

I even judge people's characters according to whether they support Manchester United.

ARDAL O'HANLON, Leeds-supporting comedian and actor, 2001; his father, the retired Irish politician Dr Rory O'Hanlon, is a Manchester United fan

I don't expect people to change the team they support easily. I've supported Leeds United all my life and always will.
NASSER HUSSAIN, England and Essex cricket captain, on suggestions that British-based Asians should support England, 2001

I told my lads that if they signed for Man United they would have to keep their shirts in their garage.
MARCUS WALMSLEY, Leeds fan, whose eight-year-old twins turned down United for Leeds, 1999

You always knew when it was derby week [on Merseyside]. The postman would say: 'We'll be ready for you.' Then the milkman would come

round: 'You're in for it Saturday.'
Then it would be the taxi driver.
You never got away from it.
GORDON LEE, *former Everton*
manager, in Brian Barwick and Gerald
Sinstadt, The Great Derbies: Everton v
Liverpool, *1988*

I'd like to have been born Bob Latchford and then become Nye Bevan when I was too old to play football.

DEREK HATTON, *Everton fan and*
former Labour councillor in Liverpool,
1988

My father and mother had a mixed
marriage: Liverpool and Everton.
There were always rucks. I can't
believe they're still together.
PETER REID, *Leeds manager, 2003*

I've never seen a fight [among
fans] at a derby game. Shouting
and bawling, yes. But they don't
fight each other, and that says a lot
for them.
BILL SHANKLY, *Liverpool manager,*
1973

If I found out a candidate was
a closet Man United supporter
I would have to think very hard
about voting for them.
ADRIAN HENRI, *poet, painter and*
Liverpool fan, during the General
Election, 1992

The fans keep waiting for
something to go wrong. I call it
City-itis. It's a rare disease whose
symptoms are relegation twice
every three years.
JOE ROYLE, *Manchester City manager,*
as the club chased promotion, 2000

I inherited two fatal flaws from
my father: premature baldness and
Manchester City, neither of which I
can change.
HOWARD DAVIES, *former deputy*
governor of the Bank of England, 1996

I was in a bar in Manchester
after watching City and these
people wanted me to sign their
programmes. One wanted me to
put: 'You can bank on City for
promotion.'
NICK LEESON, *City fan and the trader*
who brought down Barings Bank, 1999

Have we got any Man United fans
in the audience? Course we have –
we're in Hammersmith. Every gig
I do there's a United fan. They're
like rats – you're never more than
three metres away from one of the
bastards.
JASON MANFORD, *comedian and*
Manchester City fan, on tour, 2009

I didn't watch the 1968 European Cup final. I never watch any match I think United might win.
MANCHESTER CITY fan on the TV programme Manchester United Ruined My Life, *1998*

Our new guitarist and bassist have to have nice taste in shoes and a good haircut, and not be a Man United fan. If they can do that, they're sorted.
LIAM GALLAGHER, City-supporting singer with Oasis, 1999

I'm too involved in show business to get involved as a City director. If I did spend money on football, I'd buy Old Trafford and put houses on it.
BERNARD MANNING, comedian and City follower of 65 years, 1999

The Stone Roses will re-form the day Man City win the European Cup.

MANI, United-supporting bass guitarist with Primal Scream, 2005; the band reunited in 2012

If we win I'll jump off the stand roof with a parachute. If I lose I won't bother with the parachute.

MIKE SUMMERBEE, City fan and ex-player, before the derby against United, 2006

I want to get a box at Man United and a Range Rover Sport, and [wife] Catherine wants a new carpet for the upstairs landing.
GARETH BULL, Nottinghamshire builder, after winning £41m on the EuroMillions Lottery, 2012

United fans come up to me and say: 'Thanks for giving me the best night of my life.' They usually add: 'But please don't tell the wife.'
OLE GUNNAR SOLSKJAER, former United striker, on his 1999 Champions League-winning goal, 2009

United, Kids, Wife – In That Order
BANNER displayed by Manchester United fans, 2007

'Not for Sale' seems a curiously outdated slogan, given that United have measured their lives in price tags for as long as anyone can remember.
PAUL HAYWARD, Daily Telegraph sports writer, on the fans' protests against the take-over by American billionaire Malcolm Glazer, 2005

United fans have no gratitude. They are a bunch of miserable, hypocritical, whingeing bastards. These are the people who are too stupid to acknowledge the part [former chairman] Martin Edwards played in making United the biggest club in the world.

TONY WILSON, *TV presenter and United fan, dissenting from hostility towards new owner Malcolm Glazer and his family, 2005*

United fans might support France, Argentina, China... We've got a Scottish manager, we're historically a Catholic club and England are deemed to be Protestant, Queen and country, and all that bollocks. I reckon 80 per cent of United fans don't support England. You wouldn't take a St George flag to Old Trafford. You might even be confronted.
RICHARD KURT, editor of United fanzine Red Issue, *2003*

When we go away, there are all the supporters' coaches from places like Dover and Falmouth. I had never even heard of Falmouth. I like that passion. It seeps into you.
ALEX FERGUSON on Manchester United's nationwide following, 1995

Q: How many Man United fans does it take to change a lightbulb?
A: Three. One to change the bulb, one to buy the 2007 lightbulb-changing commemorative DVD and one to drive the other two back to Devon.
'QUICK QUIZ' in The Sun, *2007*

Fans can get very snooty about football. So a couple of ponces from Hampstead support Man United? Good luck to them.
PAUL WHITEHOUSE, comedian, actor and Welsh-born Tottenham fan, 1999

The further you go from home, the more of the sad bastards there are. Kent is full of them. Half the kids who go to my lad's school take their dinner in a Stretford Sam lunch box, tucked away in a Fred the Red rucksack.
MANCHESTER CITY fanzine, King of the Kippax, *on United fans, 1999*

I love Newcastle, I love that raw passion. I remember being there once and hearing newspaper vendors shouting: 'Sensation! Andy Cole Toe Injury!' Most people use the word 'sensation' for 'Major Resigns' or 'Aids Spreading Over Country'. It's unbelievable. Glasgow's like that.
ALEX FERGUSON, 1995

With all those replica strips in the stands, coming to Newcastle is like playing in front of 40,000 baying zebras.

DAVID PLEAT, Sheffield Wednesday manager, 1997

Ed Balls has developed the doctrine of never making a commitment to anything ever at any time other than to support Norwich City Football Club.
CHARLES CLARKE, former Labour MP, accusing the Shadow Chancellor of the Exchequer of sitting on the fence, 2013

During the kerfuffle over Michael Heseltine's pit closures, Brian Clough led a march past my surgery, which is a short walk from the City Ground. Forest were heading for relegation at the time and I threatened to lead a counter-march past the ground.
KENNETH CLARKE MP, Conservative, Nottingham Forest fan, in Football and the Commons People, *1995*

I've got this tattoo on my arm that says '100 per cent Blade'. When we were filming the steamy scenes in *Lady Chatterley's Lover*, Ken Russell used to hide it with a strategically placed fern.
SEAN BEAN, actor and Sheffield United supporter, 1996

I did my grieving when I was kicked out of the band. Frankly, I'm more concerned about how Port Vale get on in the FA Cup tonight.
ROBBIE WILLIAMS as Take That broke up hours before Vale beat Everton, the Cup holders, 1996

Do you want me to buy a left-back or help to save children's lives? Are

people dying as a result of Port Vale's troubles? No.
WILLIAMS on why he donated money to a children's hospice rather than invest in Vale, 2003

Supporting a second team in the Premier League is like Yasser Arafat saying he has a soft spot for Judaism.
NICK HANCOCK, TV presenter and Stoke City fan, 1997

Can anything be done about entertaining us after the kick-off?

STOKE SUPPORTER during discussion of pre-match entertainment at the club's AGM, 1999

What a nightmare. I'm a Tottenham fan and I get cuffed to you.
TONY ADAMS, Arsenal captain, on what was said by the prisoner handcuffed to him following his arrest for drink-driving, 1998

When socialists fall out, the Tories rejoice. When Sheffield Wednesday supporters fall out, the gods weep.
ROY HATTERSLEY, Wednesdayite and ex-deputy leader of the Labour party, 2000

All that Sheffield has talked about for months is football. If there is a pit closure, or a factory goes down the pan, the MP has to get involved, so why shouldn't we use our influence to try to save this club?

JOE ASHTON MP, Labour, Wednesday fan and former director, responding to accusations of interfering in the club's affairs by arguing that Danny Wilson should be relieved of the manager's job, 2000

I genuinely do struggle to understand why some people seem to have suffered a mini emotional collapse following our relegation. Bitter disappointment and hurt I can understand, but the fathers and grandfathers of some of our complainants were able to show far greater resilience under far worse conditions [in World War II].

TERENCE BROWN, West Ham chairman, 2003

Anyone who has had to support the Labour Party these past five years knows what it's like to be a West Ham fan. There is a great similarity in the 'Oh, fucking hell', head-in-hands response you have to what they do, the own goals and ridiculous defeats.

BILLY BRAGG, singer-songwriter and socialist, 1991

You need players with big balls at West Ham. The one thing I ask

before signing is can you handle 35,000 crowds because they're gonna give you stick. 'Oi mate, you're fat, you've got big ears, a fat arse, a big hooter. You're ugly. I'll do your bird a favour when I see her down the pub.'

ALAN PARDEW, West Ham manager, 2004

Will the owner of a horse attached to a rag-and-bone cart in the visitors' car park return to his vehicle immediately.

ANNOUNCEMENT at Cardiff City when West Ham were the visitors, 2004

As an ex-Southampton player I'd normally have got stick, but in the circumstances I was seen as doing Pompey a favour. The supporters did sing 'We've got a Scummer in our goal', but with affection.

DAVE BEASANT, veteran goalkeeper, helping out Portsmouth during an injury crisis, 2003

They're very jealous of Portsmouth's history, both as a city and a club. What have they got? King Canute, who got his feet wet. The *Titanic*, which sank. Saints may have a nice new stadium at St Mary's, but there's a Pompey shirt buried under the centre circle. I know because I saw it put there.
MIKE HANCOCK MP, Liberal Democrat, 2003

Trying to explain why we hate Palace is like trying to explain why grass is green. We just do.
ATTILA THE STOCKBROKER, poet-ranter and Brighton fan, 1995

Everyone talks about what people like David Beckham and Graeme Le Saux have to put up with. But I can assure you it's far worse in the First Division than the Premiership. When a visiting player gets a red card, it's the highlight of the day for some home supporters. They jump up and down with delight as though they have just won the game.
IAN WRIGHT, former England striker, on life with Burnley, 2000

At the Worthington Cup final, when there was trouble on the pitch, with Robbie Savage involved, there was this guy behind me yelling: 'Savage, you cheating, long-haired, gypsy Welsh cunt.' I had to turn to him and say: 'Oi mate, less of the Welsh.'
PAUL WHITEHOUSE, comedian, actor and Welsh-born Tottenham fan, 1999

If it was one of our meat pies, it could have done more damage than a brick.

ANDY RITCHIE, Oldham manager, after food was thrown at the referee during an FA Cup match v Chelsea, 1999

Q: What's the craziest request you have ever had from a fan? A: Can you do your brother's autograph?

CARL HODDLE, Barnet midfielder and brother of Glenn, answering a Sun *questionnaire, 1995*

When Saturday comes, a hell of a lot of lads go home with a hard-on.
JULIE BURCHILL, writer and critic, claiming a homo-erotic motivation for male football fans in her book Burchill on Beckham, *2001*

Show me a man who loves football and nine times out of 10 you'll be pointing at a really bad shag.
BURCHILL in Burchill on Beckham, *2001*

Diehard football fans are much more optimistic about their sex appeal after a victory.
DR MIRIAM STOPPARD claiming football could induce hormonal change, 2002

I listened to a phone-in recently and heard people saying 'Ferguson's lost the plot' or 'Wenger can't do this or that.' It's completely illogical. I don't go where electricians work saying 'you've wired this wrong', but people are free to say we know nothing about our profession.
COLIN CALDERWOOD, Nottingham Forest manager, 2008

You won't get me flicking on a [football] phone-in. I'd rather listen to a game of chess on the radio. Phone-ins are platforms for idiots.
JOE ROYLE, Manchester City manager, 2001

There's a new breed of flash young executives who think they've got the right to call to account anyone in the world.
RON GREENWOOD, England manager, after the Wembley crowd booed his team v Spain, 1981

Football's getting too polished and nice and trendy now. You get media people in London saying: 'Football's the new rock 'n' roll.' For all us working class, football's a way of life, always has been.
SEAN BEAN, actor and Sheffield United fan, 1996

I went with two friends to watch Forest's game at Barnsley. It cost over £60 to watch the football equivalent of what French farmers have been feeding their cattle.
LETTER to Nottingham's Football Post, *1999*

Some people come to Old Trafford and I don't think they can spell football, let alone understand it. They have a few drinks and a prawn sandwich and don't realise what's going on out on the pitch.
ROY KEANE, Manchester United captain, on the club's corporate supporters, 2000

The man in the street has been pushed aside for the corporate fan.
MARTIN O'NEILL, Leicester manager, 1999

The average working lad can't understand or relate to the money involved in the game, but he'll go along with it if he believes it will make his team better.
ALEX FERGUSON in interview with Racing Post, 1999

They sit and admire the stadium, waiting to be entertained as if they were at a musical. We have lots of visitors for whom it's a weekend holiday, and that's no use to me or the players.
FERGUSON on Manchester United's changing support, 1997

There is an element of people coming to Old Trafford for the first time, looking around the place and forgetting there is a game on.
FERGUSON urging 'control' of corporate supporters, 1999

If you listened to the fans you wouldn't have a club. I spend 40 per cent of my working life here for nothing. So I'm going to listen to someone who pays £15 on a Saturday? Leave it out.
BARRY HEARN, Leyton Orient chairman, 1999

Why hasn't anyone taken me to a soccer game? There must be some English boy who wants to take me, for God's sake. I'll just have to cry and hope that someone will take me.
GWYNETH PALTROW, American actress, 2000

I'm looking for a woman but I keep landing on the same big old bloke.
STUART PEARCE, Manchester City manager, after jumping into the crowd to celebrate a goal in the derby defeat of United, 2006

11

BOARDROOM

It's disappointing when you go to a club, like Liverpool last season, and there isn't a soul in the boardroom. Eventually two or three lads came in, including the one that works for the BBC, Alan Hansen, to represent Liverpool. There are so many foreign owners that the heart and soul has gone out of quite a few clubs.
DAVE WHELAN, *Wigan Athletic chairman, 2013*

Hull City is irrelevant. My dislike for the word 'City' is because it is common. City is also associated with Bristol, Leicester, Manchester and many other clubs. It's a lousy identity.
ASSEM ALLAM, *Egypt-born owner of Hull City, on his plan to rename the club Hull Tigers, 2013*

They can die as soon as they want, as long as they leave the club for the majority who just want to watch good football.
ALLAM *on City Till We Die, a fans' group campaigning against the name change, 2013*

If he wants us to play in pink fairy dresses, he's entitled.
STEVE BRUCE, *Hull manager, on criticism of Allam, 2013*

When I took over the club, which was facing a winding-up petition, I told the FA and the fans I was doing so as a businessman, that I would be running a business. Nobody said: 'Go away, we want somebody who runs it as a football club.'
ALLAM, *2013*

If I were the owner of Manchester City I would change the name to Manchester Hunter – you need power. In time I would suggest names for all the clubs called City, but I do not have the time.
ALLAM, *2013*

No way I will change [Cardiff's shirts] back to blue under my ownership. Perhaps they can find an owner who likes blue, pay up and buy me out. I go somewhere and build another red club. In Asia, red is a colour of success, festivity, joy. After we changed it, that same season we got promoted.
VINCENT TAN, *Malaysian owner of Cardiff City, after continued protests by supporters against his changing the club's colours from the traditional blue and white to 'lucky' red and black, 2014*

One day people will apologise to me for what they've done. I'm supposed to be the Bond villain, but actually I'm James Bond.
TAN *on the demonstrations against him, 2014*

I don't understand why Cardiff and Swansea are big rivals and why they are so upset with each other. They are from the same nation.

TAN before Wales' first Premier League derby, 2013

I came to your town. I saved your club. I put in a lot of money. I took it up after 51 years into the Premier League. Supporters, it is your club. Why then do you have to do stupid things and be influenced by people who have done things that are not right for the club?

TAN addressing Cardiff fans in a BBC TV interview, 2014

Today, it's very difficult for the owner of a British club to be British. You can't compete when Arabs have a well of oil gushes at the bottom of their garden. I won't say their money has ruined the game, but it's now very difficult for an Englishman to compete.

SIR DOUG ELLIS, Aston Villa life president and former chairman, 2013

Where they find some owners now, I don't know. I remember the first guy they brought in at Portsmouth from Saudi Arabia somewhere. He looked like they pulled him off the stall outside. He looked like the only Arab who didn't have oil in his garden.

REDKNAPP, Tottenham manager, 2012

They keep coming up with these people – someone sitting up there eating a big hamburger with holes in his jeans.

REDKNAPP, on changes in ownership at his former club Portsmouth, 2010

When the Glazers took over here there was dissatisfaction, so there have always been pockets of supporters who have their views. But I think the majority of real fans will look at it realistically and say it's not affecting the team. We've won four championships since they've been there, one European Cup.

SIR ALEX FERGUSON on why Manchester United supporters should back the club's American owners, the Glazers, 2012

I'm sorry about that [the formation of FC United]. It is a bit sad that part, but I wonder just how big a United supporter they are. They seem to me to be promoting or projecting themselves a wee bit rather than saying 'at the end of the day the club have made a decision, we'll stick by them'. It's more about them than us.
FERGUSON on FC United of Manchester, the semi-professional club formed by United fans in protest against Malcolm Glazer's ownership, 2006

The new owner will regret it because I warned him the statue was a lucky thing. I said 'You will pay with blood for that' because it was something loved by people. It was a big mistake but he paid for it now. He's been relegated and if he wakes up he'll ask for Michael Jackson again and I'll say 'No way.'
MOHAMED AL FAYED, former Fulham owner, linking the club's demotion from the Premier League to the removal of the Michael Jackson statue by Shahid Khan, 2014

I'm stunned. They asked about my criminal record. I should have asked about theirs. The English don't know how to run football. There's no transparency.
MASSIMO CELLINO, owner of Italian club Cagliari and convicted fraudster, after his attempt to buy West Ham United failed, 2010

I pay millions and millions at clubs and they [the courts] say I tried to screw them over for a small amount. It's stupid. I could pay that tomorrow. I am not a dishonest crook. If I made a mistake it was not on purpose.
CELLINO after failing the Football League's 'fit and proper person' test in his attempt to buy Leeds United, 2014; he had been found guilty in Italy of avoiding £325,000 import tax

I didn't try and do anything bad to Leeds, to anyone, I just wanted to do something good. I'm so shocked and ashamed that I feel like I will jump from the window right now.
CELLINO, as above

What do you think they're smoking over there at Emirates?

JOHN W. HENRY, American principal owner of Liverpool, on Arsenal's £40,000,001 offer for Luis Suarez, 2013

I never said I was an expert in football clubs. I was just a fan, although a very wealthy fan. But I'm not so wealthy now.
MIKE ASHLEY, Newcastle owner, after relegation from the Premier League, 2009

The club was taken over by people who didn't know what they were doing. Football will find you out so quickly, it's horrifying.
MALCOLM MACDONALD, former Newcastle centre-forward, 2009

Our season is not beyond my wildest dreams because they usually involve Elle Macpherson.
PAUL DUFFEN, Hull City chairman, during the club's first-ever season in the top flight, 2009

Ask me to name five of our team and I couldn't. They're all bloody nice guys but I don't mix with them so I don't know them well. I don't go into the dressing-room. They can walk out of the showers and then I feel I've got an inferiority complex.
BERNIE ECCLESTONE, Formula One magnate and then co-owner of Queens Park Rangers, 2010

[Club chairmen] need to wake up from their coma and join me in this fight with the Premier League and the FA. They can come and have lunch with me at Harrods, where I can serve them stags' testicles from my Scottish estate, Balnagown. We all need big balls in this business.
MOHAMED AL FAYED, Fulham chairman, 2009

I was primarily duped. My advisers were duped, the bank was duped, the shareholders were duped. We've all been duped. I always remember someone said: 'Does it pass the sniff test?' [Craig Whyte] was Scottish, he wasn't a foreigner, he was supposedly a Rangers supporter, he had the money. There is a Stock Exchange offer document there. If you can't believe that, what can you do?
DAVID MURRAY, former Rangers chairman, on selling his majority shareholding to Whyte, 2012. Whyte placed the club in administration, and was found by the Scottish FA to be 'not a fit and proper person' to run a club

I've said my piece and will now slip back into semi-anonymity. It's time for my wife to be seen with me in public without having to wear a burkha.

TURNBULL HUTTON, Raith Rovers chairman, on his criticism of the proposal to parachute the re-formed Rangers into the First Division, 2012

Thank God some of these chairmen haven't got the atomic-bomb button because the world would have been blown up by now. They get knee-jerk reactions, thinking about the transfer window. They think: 'Do we want this? It might be better to give someone else the transfer window so we can bring players in.'
IAN HOLLOWAY, Blackpool manager, 2011

The chairman's got just one job in a football club – choosing the manager. Get that right and everything else falls into place.

BRIAN CLOUGH in retirement, 2001

A chairman once had the effrontery to talk to me about football. I used a bit of Anglo-Saxon, which I was prone to lapse into, and told him to piss off.
CLOUGH, as above

Everyone was sad, including the fan who used to wait for me every week as I walked down Braemar Road. Eventually I lost my temper and suggested he go forth and mutiply. He did and I never saw him again.
GREG DYKE, FA chairman and non-executive chairman of Brentford, on their 2007 relegation, 2013

I will stab myself in the arse with a sausage if we win the league.

LOUIS NICOLLIN, Montpellier president, before the club won their first French championship, 2012

I will cut off [the players'] testicles and eat them in my salad.
MAURIZIO ZAMPARINI, Palermo owner and president, after poor results for the Sicilian club, 2003

I received my resignation by email.
DENNIS TUEART, former Manchester City and England winger, on being ousted as a City director after Thaksin Shinawatra's takeover, 2008

The most amazing men in football are the Premiership chairmen. Your heroes might be on the pitch. Mine are in the boardroom.
DAVID GOLD, co-owner of Birmingham City, to the press, 2002

I had a tweet from someone who said, 'It's not your club, it's the fans' club.' I tweeted back, 'You're absolutely right. The club belongs

to the fans. Only the debts belong to me.'
GOLD, West Ham co-chairman, 2011

I don't give a fuck about football protocol and the other club owners. They want me to sit and have lunch before the games. Fuck that. I don't go to football to drink Chardonnay in the boardroom with those tossers. I go to win games.
SIMON JORDAN, Crystal Palace chairman, 2004

I see other clubs' chairmen as the enemy. I want to go in there and beat them up.

JORDAN, 2006

A fortunate few clubs are richer than ever... All too often the source of this wealth is individuals with little or no history of interest in the game, who have happened upon football as a means of serving some hidden agenda. Having set foot in the sport, seemingly out of nowhere, they proceed to throw pornographic amounts of money at it.
SEPP BLATTER, president of FIFA, football's world governing body, 2005

I don't really believe that foreign billionaires get involved because of their love of English football.
DELIA SMITH, TV chef and majority shareholder in Norwich City, 2007

Call me old-fashioned, but we don't need his money and we don't want his sort. They only see an opportunity to make money. They know sweet FA about our football, and we don't want these types involved.
PETER HILL-WOOD, Arsenal chairman, on reports of interest in the club by American businessman Stan Kroenke, 2007

I couldn't have sold to a foreigner. I didn't want an ex-Siamese prime minister here, thank you very much. This is an English club.
SIR JACK HAYWARD, former Wolves owner-chairman, after selling to Liverpudlian Steve Morgan, 2007

The only sure way to make a small fortune from football is to start with a big one.

JEFF RANDALL, BBC business correspondent, 2003

Football is a shambolically run business, run by greedy and vain people who seem only to act in self-interest. And none of them seems to realise that if they carry on the way they are going, they will destroy the business.
TOM BOWER, investigative reporter, in his book Broken Dreams: Vanity, Greed and the Souring of British Football, *2003*

That was a nasty era in my life... I met some very horrible people in that industry and it made me very guarded and suspicious.
SIR ALAN SUGAR on his time as Tottenham owner, 2005

Alan Sugar was one of my better chairmen. He knew nothing about football, but it's often the ones who think they know the game that are the problem.
GERRY FRANCIS, former Tottenham manager, 2011

Time was when you couldn't name a football club chairman let alone recognise one in the street. They were grey-suited men who drank white wine in the bowels of the stand and watched unrecognised from the best seats. Nowadays there is an egotistical breed of chairman who think they know it all.
JIMMY GREAVES, former England striker, in his Sun *column, 2003*

[Roman] Abramovich didn't speak English. There was an interpreter. I wasn't totally convinced he was the real thing. I'd Googled him, but he just didn't appear anywhere. Nobody knew anything about him. So I wasn't sure whether it was a scene from *Candid Camera* and that suddenly Jeremy Beadle was going to jump out at me. But we did the deal in just 10 minutes... I suggested he spent £20m on players. He spent £140m in six weeks. It was the biggest change I've seen in English football.
TREVOR BIRCH, Chelsea's chief executive in 2003, recalling how Roman Abramovich bought the club that year, 2013

Abramovich knows nothing about football. I already have his sword sticking into me... Even if I win the European Cup, I'll be sacked.
CLAUDIO RANIERI, Chelsea manager, on the club's new Russian billionaire owner, 2004

Abramovich spat on Russia by buying Chelsea. He abandoned our teams, which need support.
YURI LUZHOV, Mayor of Moscow, 2003

If he [Abramovich] helped me in training we would be bottom of the league. And if I had had to work in his world of big business we would be bankrupt.
JOSE MOURINHO, Chelsea manager, 2005

We passed like ships in the night. He was a huge yacht, I was a little rowing boat.

GRAEME LE SAUX *recalling leaving Chelsea as Abramovich arrived, 2006*

Mr Abramovich is almost like one of the lads, if a billionaire can be.
JOHN TERRY, *Chelsea captain, 2005*

He's a real Chelsea fan. When we lose a difficult match, he's sulking and there are tears in his eyes.
BRUCE BUCK, *Chelsea chairman, on Abramovich's 'devotion', 2007*

Malcolm Glazer risks plunging [Manchester] United into a financial meltdown that would make what happened at Leeds look like the equivalent of missing an HP payment on the telly.
SEAN BONES, *spokesman for Shareholders United, a group opposed to the American tycoon's takeover at Old Trafford, 2005*

[Malcolm] Glazer is a guy who looks more like he should be propping up a bar somewhere, or perhaps a bar owner. I just hope he has the humility to let other people make the decisions. People who know about football.
ERIC CANTONA, *former United player, 2005*

Mr Lerner was pleasantly surprised that I knew some things about American football, though he may have suspected I'd done a bit of homework the night before.
MARTIN O'NEILL, *Aston Villa manager, on the club's American chairman Randy Lerner, who also owned the Cleveland Browns gridiron franchise, 2007*

It's not my club, it's the fans' club. I'm just here as the maintenance man.
MILAN MANDARIC, *Portsmouth owner and chairman, 2004*

If you made a lot of money selling biscuits, buy our club.
SONG *by West Ham fans (to the tune of the Club biscuit advert), after Icelandic entrepreneur Eggert Magnusson bought into the club, 2006*

The story of the most popular football club chairman ever.

SLOGAN *on a video about Peter Ridsdale's reign at Leeds, 2001*

All this home-grown talent we've nurtured means we want them to stay to win trophies with Leeds United. They are not for sale. We're a public company and my responsibility is to the shareholders. But the responsibility is also to win things.
PETER RIDSDALE *as Leeds challenged for top place in the Premiership, 2000*

I have no intention of running away. When I go I would like to think that Leeds will be flying again.
RIDSDALE *on being barracked at what proved to be his last home game before resigning, 2003*

We lived the dream.
RIDSDALE *on the spending he sanctioned when David O'Leary was manager, 2003*

Leeds United may have lived the dream, but I inherited the nightmare.
PROFESSOR JOHN McKENZIE, *Ridsdale's successor, 2003*

But whose dream was it? The fans bought it, of course, but the real dream was that the people behind Ridsdale thought they were going to make oodles of money. Football was never meant to be like that.
JOHN GILES, *former Leeds player, after Ridsdale resigned, 2003*

Had we not invested, we wouldn't have had five years of going to Madrid and Milan and Barcelona.

The fans want a successful team. For five years we've delivered that, then got it wrong. Should we have spent so heavily? Probably not.
RIDSDALE, *2003*

Peter has had a nice ride and been very well paid for his time at Leeds. It's not as if he's going to end up in a grotty little bedsit.
SIMON JOSE, *co-founder of Leeds United Independent Fans' Association, on Ridsdale's departure from the plc and club boards, 2003*

The Leeds programme has a team-sheet so glossy that it is impossible to write on it. They should have given Peter Ridsdale chequebooks like that.
DAVID HOPPS, *sports writer, reporting in* The Guardian, *2005*

There are no more goldfish. I ate them with my tuna sandwich at lunch.

GERALD KRASNER, *Leeds chairman, 2004; the goldfish kept by Ridsdale became a symbol of Leeds' free-spending ways*

I want to show people who criticise me that I can run a football club

well. Leeds was a dream come true, but Barnsley's even more exciting.
RIDSDALE on taking control at the South Yorkshire club, 2003

When I left Leeds I had two options – to jump off the top of a tall building or to cope. I decided to cope.

RIDSDALE on succeeding Sam Hammam as Cardiff chairman, 2007

The last word to the various moaners... What have you done? Bellyached about the new club colours, admission prices and everything else that has come into your little heads... If you don't want to support the club jolly well stay away and take your money with you instead of hanging round here.
KEN BATES, then Oldham chairman, in his club's programme on the 'silly people' who had suggested a boycott of matches, 1966

If I was in Ken Bates's shoes I would wake every morning praying to God and thanking him that Pini Zahavi put £19m in his pocket [by bringing Roman Abramovich to Chelsea]. He is history as far as English football is concerned.
PINI ZAHAVI, Israeli football agent, on the 'revolting character' Bates, 2005

When Ken Bates jumps in the water, the sharks jump out.
DAVE ALLEN, Sheffield Wednesday chairman, on the former Chelsea chairman's interest in taking over at Hillsborough, 2004

Let us leave the EEC, abolish human rights laws, take TV sets, pool tables and phones out of prisons, bring back corporal and capital punishment, slash benefits and put single mothers into hostels instead of giving them council flats. Finally, if we chucked out all the illegal immigrants and asylum seekers there would be enough jobs for everyone.
KEN BATES, now the Monte Carlo-domiciled Leeds chairman, in his programme column, 2011

There's nothing else in life except soccer and a good woman. I've got a good woman so I need the soccer.
BATES on why he bought control of Leeds United, 2005

It's better than lying in bed, drinking gin and tonic and waiting to die.
BATES on coping with the financial problems at Leeds, 2006

If I had my time over again, I'd be a general or a bishop.

BATES, 2005

Bates always had to be one up on you. If you told him you'd been to Tenerife, he'd say he'd been to Elevenerife.

DAVID SPEEDIE, former Chelsea striker, 2003

We see a lot of Ken Bates. He'll always have a laugh and a joke with you. At your expense, obviously.

GRAEME LE SAUX, Chelsea defender, 2000

Ken Bates here. I understand you're richer than I am, so we'd better get together.

BATES, Chelsea chairman, in call to wealthy supporter Matthew Harding, 1994; Harding put in £24m over the next two years

The difference is that Bates appears to think Chelsea is his club, while Harding's attitude is that it's our club.

ROSS FRASER, chairman of Chelsea Independent Supporters' Association, as the Bates–Harding rift worsened, 1995

When David Mellor is prepared to put money into the club – or even pay for his own tickets – he will be entitled to his opinion.

MATTHEW HARDING after Mellor, a Conservative MP, criticised him while hosting a radio phone-in, 1995

I'm not star-struck around players. How could I be? I'm the biggest star here.

BATES, 1997

Has any chairman since Mao had more faith in his own opinions than Ken Bates? If laying down the law was an Olympic sport, the Chelsea chief would be staggering under the weight of gold medals.

ALEX FERGUSON in his autobiography, 2000

Some fans said: 'We don't want a bloody Londoner running Leeds.' I said: 'You've got a problem then, haven't you? Nobody in bloody Leeds wants to run Leeds, do they?' I see all these bloody millionaires with money coming out of their ears. Talk about long pockets and short hands.

BATES after six months as Leeds chairman, 2005

Ninety-nine per cent of the letters and emails [from fans] are supporting us. That's as good as Saddam Hussein got – and he was fiddling the figures.
BATES after beating off other bidders to buy debt-ridden Leeds back from the administrators, 2007

Why have I bought Birmingham City? Because football is good for society.

DAVID SULLIVAN, Daily Sport *publisher, 1993*

When I used to watch Roy Rogers on his white horse, Trigger, he never lost. He always won because he was the good guy. The bloke on the black horse with the mask, the baddie who killed, raped and pillaged, always got beat. I want that to continue here.
DAVID GOLD, Birmingham chairman and Sullivan's co-owner, 2002

I played with Johnny Haynes. It was at snooker, but hey, I played with him.
GOLD on his spell as a Fulham youth player, 2002

The chairman, Doug Ellis, said he was right behind me. I told him I'd sooner have him in front of me where I could see him.
TOMMY DOCHERTY after being fired as Aston Villa manager, 1970

When Tommy [Docherty] does his rounds of after-dinner speaking, he uses me at every opportunity. Greavsie [Jimmy Greaves] calls me 'Deadly' and lads in the street shout: 'Oi, Deadly!' As long as Aston Villa's name is attached to it, I don't mind. If you operate at a high profile, you have to accept criticism.
DOUG ELLIS, Villa chairman, 1991

To be fair, although there's been 11 Villa managers in roughly 30 years, there's only been seven I've sacked.
ELLIS, 1999

Aston Villa is the reason I get up every day and the day I'm not mentally able to hold my own with all the young whipper-snappers in this business is when I'll call it a day.
ELLIS at 77 years old, 2000

This is my life. I kick every ball and sign every cheque.
ELLIS, 2000

The trouble with our chairman is that he's living in a time warp.
JOHN GREGORY, Villa manager, 2000; he later had to make a public apology to Ellis

They're building another stand at Villa Park. They're going to call it 'The Other Doug Ellis Stand'.
KEN BATES, Chelsea chairman, in Jason Tomas's book Soccer Czars, *1996*

Six months [after trying to buy Chelsea] he bought Fulham, having discovered that he was a lifelong Fulham supporter.
BATES on Mohamed Al Fayed buying control of Chelsea's neighbours, 2002

The trouble with Fayed is that he doesn't understand British traditions and institutions. I mean, he took over Fulham and made them successful.
ANDY HAMILTON, comedy writer, on BBC Radio 4's News Quiz, *1999*

It's ironic that it's left to me to save the England team when no one will let me have a UK passport.

FAYED after agreeing to let Fulham manager Kevin Keegan coach England part-time, 1999

This is a message for possibly the best supporters in the world. We need a 12th man. Where are you? Let's be 'avin' you!
DELIA SMITH, Norwich City co-owner, in an impromptu loudspeaker appeal to fans during half-time v Manchester City, 2005

Delia, back in the kitchen, luv.
POSTING on the BBC football message board after her outburst, 2005

I would prefer death to relegation.

DAVID McNALLY, Norwich chief executive, 2014

A few weeks before I left Southampton, the team went clay-pigeon shooting. I was ready to fire, looking through the sight, when the chairman [Rupert Lowe] came into view. It was very tempting, I can tell you.
JIM MAGILTON, Ipswich midfielder, 2004

Swing Lowe
Swing Rupert Lowe
Swinging from the Itchen Bridge
SONG by Southampton fans, 2006

We will not be pushed around by a bunch of north London yobbos.
RUPERT LOWE as Tottenham courted Southampton manager Glenn Hoddle, 2001

How much have I put in? I wouldn't get much change from £75m, but I'd only have given it to the government on my death. I might as well spend it and give the people of Wigan some pleasure while I'm at it.

DAVE WHELAN, *Wigan chairman-owner, after the club completed their rise from the Northern Premier League to the Premiership, 2005*

You can spend your life in smart restaurants, but I've done all that. To be honest, I'd rather have a burger and a cup of Bovril.

GREG DYKE, *former director general of the BBC, before his first match as Brentford chairman, 2006*

My mum rang up when she heard I wanted to take over the club and said: 'Oh son, don't.' Only an 11-year-old boy would want to get into something like this. You have to have that mixture of romantic and businessman. I know it's a risk, but I can't think of anything I'd risk more for.

BILL KENWRIGHT, *theatre director, on his bid for control of Everton, 1998*

I remain the father of Wimbledon and wanted to be their hero. I have a lot of love and happiness for AFC Wimbledon. We are together in mind.

SAM HAMMAM, *former Wimbledon FC owner, on the fans' 'breakaway' club, 2003*

We will serve sheep's testicles as a delicacy in the boardroom. There are plenty of sheep in Wales so it's right that they should make some representation at Ninian Park.

HAMMAM, *having left Wimbledon and taken over at Cardiff City, 2000*

Alex Ferguson told me I was mad buying Cardiff and gave me the address of a good psychiatrist.

HAMMAM, *2000*

Sometimes you need to employ someone who is a poacher turned gamekeeper. They know how the hooligans think.

HAMMAM *after it was revealed that the Cardiff chairman's bodyguard was a convicted 'football' hooligan, 2002*

I'd rather die and have vultures eat my insides than merge with Crystal Palace.

HAMMAM, *Wimbledon chairman, on reports of a possible merger of the two Selhurst Park-based clubs, 1992*

I just hope I can grab the heart of this man [Kjell-Inge Rokke] and make him understand. The man lives in a world of accountants, not football. I must make him love us. We must show him our legs and cleavage to make him fancy us.
HAMMAM on Wimbledon's Norwegian co-owner, 1999

Every time we lose, I feel like running a warm bath and slashing my wrists.
SIR JACK HAYWARD, Wolves chairman, 2003

When my son [Jonathan, Wolves chairman] asks me for more money to buy another player, I tell him: 'This is blackmail.' He says: 'Do you want to get into the Premiership?' I say yes. Then he says: 'Do you want to win the FA Cup?' I say yes. Then I say: 'Oh, go and buy him then.'
SIR JACK, 1995

A friend has described me as the village vicar of football-club chairmen, which I rather liked, but I've discovered there are people in the game who would slit your throat for tuppence.
JONATHAN HAYWARD, Wolves chairman and Northumberland farmer, 1996

I don't want Wolves fans to think I'm off my trolley, but Dermot Reeve [Warwickshire's cricket captain] is the kind of character I'm looking for as manager.
JONATHAN HAYWARD, Wolves chairman, 1995

I've never taken a penny out of Wolves and never want to. I only want an emotional return, not a financial one. If I go and stay with the team on a Friday night, I settle my own bill. When I eat in Sir Jack's [restaurant at the ground], I pay. I don't take a salary like some chairmen and I don't draw any expenses. That's why I was upset by this fan's remark, though I have to say that the letter he handed me was nicely typed and obviously thought out.
SIR JACK HAYWARD, stung by a supporters' criticism, 2000

I only hope Tony Adams plays because he's the only name I know. All these Viallis, Vieiras and Viagras. I prefer old-fashioned names like Cullis and Wright.
SIR JACK before Wolves' FA Cup semi-final v Arsenal, 1998

They thought the Golden Tit – me – would go on for ever.

SIR JACK on his £60m outlay on players and ground improvements, 1997

My friends in America say I must love it [owning his home-town club] but unless we're 6–0 up with 15 minutes left I hate it.
SIR JACK after Wolves again failed to reach the Premiership, 2002

Elton John and myself developed a relationship – it's a bit dangerous saying that about us, isn't it? For a period I was his reality.
GRAHAM TAYLOR, Watford manager, on his pop-star chairman, 2000

'Candle In The Wind' remains one of my favourite songs. But Elton and I had this agreement that I would tell him nothing about music if he told me nothing about football, and it worked well.
GRAHAM TAYLOR, 1991

I used to have to tour when I didn't really want to, to be able to afford to buy a centre-forward.
ELTON JOHN on his days of bankrolling Watford, 1995

An overview of my career is usually: glasses, homosexuality, Watford Football Club, tantrums, flowers. But the music was pretty phenomenal.
SIR ELTON JOHN, 2007

Beware of the clever sharp men who are creeping into the game.
WILLIAM McGREGOR, founder of the Football League, in League Football and the Men Who Made It, *1909*

The ideal board of directors should comprise three men – two dead and the other dying.

TOMMY DOCHERTY, manager with numerous clubs, 1977

I'm drinking from a cup today. I'd like a mug but they're all in the boardroom.
DOCHERTY, 1988

A man who gives himself up to football, body and soul, will take risks and get himself entangled in such a way as he would never consider in the conduct of his own business.
SIR FREDERICK WALL, FA secretary, in his book Fifty Years of Football, *1935*

We shall all be rich one day when we've got a BUPA hospital and a hotel on this ground.
ERNIE CLAY, Fulham chairman, 1979

I've still got my old school report. It says I was dyslexic, backward, mentally deficient and illiterate – all the qualifications you need to be a football club chairman.
GEORGE REYNOLDS, Darlington chairman, 2000

The biggest fans in the world are the chairmen, not the blokes on the terraces. Real fans? What does 'real' mean? A real fan is someone who works really hard for nothing, gives up all his time for nothing, worries all the time, and on top of that lot, puts in his own money.
BARRY HEARN, Leyton Orient chairman-owner, 2001

I'd always thought of chairmen as tight bastards. Now I can only applaud them for the money they put in and the abuse they take.
BARRY FRY in praise of his Peterborough chairman, Peter Boizot, 2000

I had hair when I became chairman. Not any longer.

PETER HILL, Hereford chairman, on using his toupee 'to wipe away my tears' after relegation from the league, 1997

Nowadays chairmen seem to live in Spain. That bloke who was at Forest [Irving Scholar] lived in Monaco. I often wonder how people like that got into football. You can't love football and live abroad, because you miss the one thing you want to watch, your team.
BRIAN CLOUGH, former manager, 1999

I have spoken to more than one chairman who has told me the quality they look for on a manager's CV is an ability to affect the share price.
HOWARD WILKINSON, FA technical director, 1999

Football attracts a certain percentage of nobodies who want to be somebodies at a football club.
BRIAN CLOUGH, Nottingham Forest manager, 1979

Football hooligans? Well, there are the 92 club chairmen for a start.
CLOUGH, 1980

I've never been so insulted by anyone in football as this little upstart puppy.
DENIS HILL-WOOD, Arsenal chairman and Old Etonian, responding to Clough, 1980

I am struck by the parallels between the disorder which characterises the approach of some football boardrooms and the disorderly behaviour of a minority of the game's followers.
NEIL MACFARLANE MP, Conservative, Minister for Sport, 1983

Let club directors make a hash of the affairs of their own teams, but spare England the catastrophe of their attentions.
LEN SHACKLETON, journalist and former England player, on the committee

of club directors who selected the national team, 1958

Soccer is run by second-rate conmen. Petit bourgeois, frustrated small businessmen. It's a tragedy, because football is very important socially.
EAMON DUNPHY, Republic of Ireland midfielder, 1973

Have you ever had an octogenarian English comedian at training before – apart from FA committee members?
NORMAN WISDOM, comic actor, to Sven-Goran Eriksson in Albania, 2001

We don't recognise any supporters' organisations... I never go to supporters' dinners; it only costs a fiver or so, but then they think they own you. I never accept money from supporters' organisations; they hand you a couple of cheques for a few thousand and the next thing you know they are demanding a seat on the board. My ambition is for the club to function completely without any money coming through the turnstiles at all. That is the road to Utopia.
BOB LORD, Burnley chairman and butcher in the town, 1974

One wonders today what some businesses would be like if they were run on the same haphazard lines as most football clubs still are. The amateur director has been kicked out of most industrial and commercial boardrooms. But not in football.
DEREK DOUGAN, Wolves striker, in Football as a Profession, *1974*

Football is an emotional game and that's where it's different from your average major business.
DAVID SHEEPSHANKS, Ipswich chairman, 2001

When I was a director of Sheffield United for six months, the chairman told me normal business standards didn't apply in football. It was the most stupid advice I ever had.
MIKE WATTERSON, Derby chairman, 1982

Normal business principles don't apply in football.

LIONEL PICKERING, publisher and Derby chairman-owner, 1992

Industries go to the wall every day... Football's a business, it's no different, and it is not going to be run by the blazer brigade any more. It needs to be run as a business by businessmen.
SIR JOHN HALL, Newcastle chairman and advocate of a closed-shop, two-division Premier League, 1995

I entered as just A.N. Other, a member of the board, simply to do a job, i.e. finance director. No loyalty or love, but a cold, clinical job. I ended up falling in love like the rest of you, which became the most expensive love life man can imagine.
REG BREALEY, Sheffield United chairman, in message to supporters, 1990

People tell me: 'You must have better things to spend your money on.' But I have no desire for huge yachts in Monte Carlo. I'm just a homely boy from East Northants who enjoys doing what I do.
MAX GRIGGS, chairman of Rushden & Diamonds and the Doc Martens footwear empire, on ploughing millions into the then non-league club, 1995

Wolves, Derby, Blackburn: these fans with money pour it in, the club lights up, then it fizzles away. Doesn't work. End of story.
KEN BATES, Chelsea chairman, 1995

Football clubs are great community institutions, to which supporters feel a huge sense of belonging. But the reality is that they are owned by private businessmen, using the clubs for their own purposes, who can ride roughshod over them. And the authorities are absolutely incapable of monitoring the game.
PETER KILFOYLE MP, Labour, on the ownership of Everton, 1999

I went out to buy a car for the missus and came back with a football club that cost me £5m just to clear the debts.
GEORGE REYNOLDS, Darlington chairman, 1999

We're trying to get rid of the assumption that football clubs are the preserve of white, middle-class men in camel coats, sipping champagne and using the game as an extension of their own egos and virility.
DAVE HELLIWELL, leader of Calderdale Council, after it bought control of Halifax Town, 1990

I've heard claims that I'm using Mafia money. Soccer clubs are in such a mess right now that you could buy them out of Brownie funds.
ANTON JOHNSON on becoming Rotherham chairman, 1983

Football directors are nobody's friends except when there are Cup final tickets to give away.

ROY HATTERSLEY MP, Labour,
Sheffield Wednesday supporter, in
Goodbye to Yorkshire, *1976*

When I came to Manchester from
the north-east aged 15, I didn't
know what a director was or what he
did. My dad would have explained it
as someone who didn't work.
BOBBY CHARLTON on joining the
Manchester United board, 1985

The Super League idea has about
as much chance of getting through
as there is of Arthur Scargill
admitting he needs a wig.
ERNIE CLAY, Fulham chairman, a
decade before the launch of the Premier
League, 1982

A few of us want to discuss super
leagues but all the rest can talk
about is the price of meat pies.
DAVID MURRAY, Rangers chairman,
on his Scottish League counterparts, 1992

Sir Harold Thompson, the
chairman of the FA, treated me like
an employee. These Arab sheikhs
treat me like one of them.
DON REVIE, United Arab Emirates
coach and former England manager, 1979

I flew to Paris for the Real Madrid
final with the Liverpool directors,
and a more disagreeable bunch
of people I've rarely encountered.
I'd sooner take my chances with a
bunch of so-called hooligans. They
talked about players as if they were
below-stairs staff. Their attitude

towards them was so patronising it
was almost Victorian.
JOHN PEEL, disc jockey and Liverpool
fan, 1987

[The board] was full of furniture
removers, insurance brokers and
clueless fogies, living in a Scotch-
and-soda, curled-up-sandwiches
world of self-congratulation.
ROBERT PLANT, Led Zeppelin singer
and Wolves fan, on why he resisted
attempts in the 1980s to lure him on to
the Molineux board, 2002

You could put his knowledge of
the game on a postage stamp. He
wanted us to sign Salford Van Hire
because he thought he was a Dutch
international.
FRED EYRE, former assistant manager
of Wigan Athletic, on a powerful director,
1981

When I asked Michael [Jackson]
to become a director, he said:
'Oh wow, do you realise I know
nothing about sport?' I said: 'You
don't have to.'
URI GELLER, spoon-bending psychic
and joint chairman of Exeter City, on
trying to lure the American pop singer on
to the board, 2002

The man who sacked me at
Fulham was Sir Eric Miller, the
property developer who shot
himself. Shows how he reacted to
pressure, doesn't it?
BOBBY ROBSON, Ipswich manager,
1981

Even I could manage this lot.

SAM LONGSON, Derby chairman, after the final parting with Brian Clough, 1973

Sacking a manager is as big an event in my life as drinking a glass of beer. I would hire 20 managers a year if I wanted to – 100 if necessary.
JESUS GIL, president of Atletico Madrid, 1989

One chairman told me his club had only had 23 managers since the war. I said: 'Why, man, the war's only been over four weeks.'
LAWRIE McMENEMY, England assistant manager, soon after the Gulf War, 1992

I don't walk past him every day and ask if I've got his full support. But the other night he bought me a sandwich at the reserves' match and that's a real show of affection from our chairman.
STUART PEARCE, Manchester City manager, on his chairman John Wardle, 2007

When I arrived here the board said there would be no money and they have kept their promise.
DAVE BASSETT, Sheffield United manager, 1994

There just aren't enough raving lunatics out there with chequebooks.
MICHAEL KNIGHTON, Carlisle chairman-owner, on struggling to sell the club, 2000

For years I've been saying that football should be run by football people. Then along came Franny Lee at Manchester City. Oh well, back to the drawing board.
JIMMY GREAVES, former England striker, in his Sun column, 1995

I've played in the World Cup, sweated out multi-million-pound business deals, I've trained some good horses and I'm a father. But 90 minutes at Maine Road can make me feel like an old dish-rag.
FRANCIS LEE, Manchester City chairman, 1997

I've survived two heart attacks and Stan Flashman. And Stan was the worst of the three.

BARRY FRY, Birmingham manager, recalling a turbulent relationship with his former chairman at Barnet, 1995

I'm sick of people telling me to relax. They can stick my heart up their arses.

JESUS GIL, *Atletico Madrid president, on seeing them lose to Villarreal soon after having a pacemaker fitted, 2003*

Bill Bell: chairman and business entrepreneur, dedicated to making Port Vale the No. 1 team in the Potteries. Bill also wants to find the lost city of Atlantis, be the first man to walk the Channel, and skateboard up Mount Everest.
THE OATCAKE, *Stoke City fanzine, derby-day edition, 1989*

What entitles you to question Alex Ferguson on football matters?
QUESTION *to chief executive Martin Edwards at a Manchester United plc meeting, 1999*

United have begun to think 'class' is something that comes with big office suites and flash cars. That great club is slowly being destroyed. And I blame one family for the ruin. The Edwards family, the master butchers of Manchester.

HARRY GREGG, *former United goalkeeper, after his sacking as a coach at the club, 1981*

How can anyone praise Martin Edwards at Manchester United? He has twice tried to sell the club to the enemies of football, Robert Maxwell and Rupert Murdoch. How can he look anybody in the eye and say he loves the club when he has been trying to make 60 million quid selling it?
BRIAN CLOUGH, *1999*

Even the most brilliant manager could not deal with Manchester United as long as the club is run from the chairman's [Martin Edwards] office the way it is.
MICHAEL CRICK *and* DAVID SMITH, *authors, in the book* Betrayal of a Legend, *1989*

Peter Swales wore a wig, a blazer with an England badge on it and high-heeled shoes. As a man he really impressed me.
MALCOLM ALLISON, *ex-Manchester City manager, on the club's former chairman in Jeremy Novick,* In a League of Their Own: Football's Maverick Managers, *1995*

Peter Swales likes publicity. He wears a card round his neck saying: 'In case of heart attack call a press conference.'
TOMMY DOCHERTY *on the Manchester City chairman, 1982*

I gave up football the day I went back to Maine Road and saw the chairman [Peter Swales] signing autographs.
MIKE SUMMERBEE, former City winger, 1988

The trouble was he had no repartee with the fans.

PETER SWALES, City chairman, after sacking Mel Machin as manager, 1989

My chairman, Robert Maxwell, they ought to let him run football.
JIM SMITH, Oxford United manager, 1983

I threatened to quit over the sale of Dean Saunders, but Maxwell sacked me. He told me: 'No one resigns on the Maxwells.'
MARK LAWRENSON on his time as Oxford United manager, 1993

Maxwell has the posture and manners of the dominant male.

DR DESMOND MORRIS, author of The Naked Ape and co-director of Maxwell's at Oxford, 1983

I have played football since I was a toddler. Left wing, as you would expect. I was very fast.
ROBERT MAXWELL, Oxford chairman, 1985

If a supporter asked me about that [lending £1.1m to Tottenham to buy Gary Lineker], I'd tell him to get stuffed. What I do with my money is my business. Haven't I already done enough for Derby? They were in the knacker's yard when I was invited to help them.
MAXWELL, by now Derby chairman, on the club's 'transfer freeze', 1990

There are still some things that baffle me about the bloke [Maxwell]. Like why he loves seeing his mug across the back pages, because Robert Redford he ain't.
BRIAN CLOUGH, Nottingham Forest manager, 1987

Robert Maxwell has just bought Brighton and Hove Albion, and he's furious to find out that it's only one club.
TOMMY DOCHERTY as Maxwell tried to add to his portfolio of clubs, 1988

I like a challenge. If I'd been a woman I would have been pregnant all the time because I can't say no.
ROBERT MAXWELL on his interest in 'saving' hard-up Tottenham, 1990

Robert Maxwell's record is exemplary... He has always been prepared to invest heavily in

football at a time when others are turning their backs on the game. Some people seem to doubt him, but they don't know the man.
IRVING SCHOLAR, Tottenham chairman, on Maxwell's bid to take control, 1990

I feel like the guy who shot Bambi. I'm not an egotistical loony.

ALAN SUGAR, Tottenham chairman, on the fans' reaction to his attempt to sack Terry Venables as manager, 1993

It has been the ultimate roller-coaster ride, but I hope that whoever takes this club over has as much success as I enjoyed in my first five years here. Obviously I wouldn't wish the last three on anybody.
MICHAEL KNIGHTON, Carlisle chairman, on his plans to sell the club and their latest last-day escape from relegation out of the league, 2000

From parks football to Carlisle to Milan, we all aspire to The Dream. Robert Maxwell dubbed me a Walter Mitty figure, but that's fine because this is the industry of dreams and I'm the greatest dreamer alive.

KNIGHTON, Carlisle chairman and ex-Manchester United director, 1995

Q: How did you feel when Darlington got a wild-card entry back into the FA Cup?
A: I always felt we'd get it. I had a chat with Him upstairs the night before. Got through to him even though he's ex-directory.
GEORGE REYNOLDS, Darlington chairman, after his club were readmitted to the Cup following Manchester United's withdrawal, 1999

I'm a great believer in God. He has always been very kind to me. I say to him: 'Can you get your finger out and give us some help?'
REYNOLDS, 2000

I won't turn my back on this club, and we will be successful, we will be profitable. I will turn it around. But I won't be travelling to Exeter to watch a pile of shite.
REYNOLDS after his wife criticised the Darlington players at a public meeting, prompting them to walk out, 2002

At other clubs the directors probably get worried if things aren't going well, and they don't like people coming up to them criticising in pubs and at parties. That doesn't influence me at all. If people start telling me what's wrong with the team, I just say: 'Look, why don't you fuck awff?'
PATRICK COBBOLD, Ipswich chairman, 1981

You ask what constitutes a crisis here. Well, if we ran out of white wine in the boardroom.
COBBOLD, 1982

At Ipswich, the chairman drank a bottle of champagne when we won. When we lost he drank two bottles and thought we'd won.
SIR BOBBY ROBSON, Newcastle and former Ipswich manager, 2003

If eventually I'm kicked out, I'll just go back to buying a season ticket.
PETER RIDSDALE, Leeds chairman, 2001

A chairman's place is in the directors' box, not on the terraces.
DAVID WILLMAN, Merseyside police chief superintendent, after Ridsdale left his seat at Everton to confront Leeds fans chanting against coach Brian Kidd, 2002

I knew it was going to be a red-hot atmosphere when I looked up and saw everyone in the directors' box singing and jumping up and down.
GARY NEVILLE, Manchester United defender, after winning at Rangers in the Champions League, 2003

I'd rather have a big crowd than the TV money. I know what it's like to be roared on.
NIALL QUINN, Sunderland chairman and ex-player, on spurning an offer to have their match v Derby on TV and sticking to a 3pm kick-off, 2007

I've been chairman of a soccer club. I know how to lose.
ELTON JOHN before the Oscars ceremony, 1996

Being part of this football club is the fullest experience you can have of being alive.
DELIA SMITH, TV chef and Norwich City director, 2002

I came down last week to watch United play Port Vale. By the time I got home I was chairman again and looking for a new manager. My wife said: 'I'm taking you to the hospital to get your head examined.'
DEREK DOOLEY on his surprise return to the boardroom at Sheffield United, 1999

The locals are starting to accept me. Maybe when we've delivered the Champions League in 2026 they will say: 'He's all right.'
KEVIN HEANEY, multi-millionaire chairman of Truro City, on plans to take the Cornish club from the Toolstation Western League to the Football League in 10 years, 2007

12

REFEREES

Referees, like most of us, are human beings.

PIARA POWAR, *executive director of Football Against Racism in Europe, 2013*

He can't even control his kids so I wonder how he can even control a game of football.

KAY WEBB *on her husband Howard before he refereed the World Cup final, 2010*

I struggle with the fact that Howard Webb didn't see it [an incident involving Mario Balotelli and Scott Parker], but then again he didn't see six studs land on someone's chest in a World Cup final, not to be too harsh on him.

GRAHAM POLL, *former Premier League and World Cup referee, 2012*

I would concede there was a sense of relief when [Manchester] United played well and won, particularly at Old Trafford. I knew if they didn't win there was every chance of seeing and, more importantly, hearing [Sir Alex] Ferguson and reading his comments about me in the papers the next day.

POLL *in his* Daily Mail *column, 2014*

All referees knew that Fergie's standing in the game – and the fact that he was at the biggest club – meant that when he unleashed the hairdryer on a referee there were inevitable headlines.

POLL, *as above*

Some referees don't like it. They don't like the truth but I just told him how bad he was in the first half.

SIR ALEX FERGUSON *on confronting Mark Clattenburg at half-time, Manchester United v Bolton, 2007*

I've never had a player come to me in the past 15 years and say a referee has sworn at them during a game, ever. So that's where I stand: I don't believe it.

FERGUSON *after Chelsea's John Obi Mikel alleged racial abuse by Clattenburg in a match v Manchester United, 2012; Clattenburg was cleared*

All look the same those mixed-race boys.

STAN COLLYMORE *tweeting after referee Andre Marriner mistakenly sent off Arsenal's Kieran Gibbs after Alex Oxlade-Chamberlain had handled the ball, 2014*

It's very difficult to be a referee and I respect them. The players play too quickly; the players are always trying to cheat because football is cheating. Of course nobody likes it when the referee whistles against your team when it is wrong, but a lot of time he whistles and gives you an advantage that maybe you didn't have.

MANUEL PELLEGRINI, *Manchester City's Chilean manager, 2013*

It is well known that the big clubs, especially at home, but often away too, get the big shouts. I am not questioning any referee's integrity, it's human nature. It's always been like that and it never changes.
PETER COATES, *Stoke City chairman, 2014*

It's going to be a long, hard season for me with these people [referees]. I had this with Blackpool. Certain clubs get fouls and others don't.
IAN HOLLOWAY, *Crystal Palace manager, after defeat v Tottenham, 2013*

Why haven't they got cameras? The officials can speak to each other easily enough now. Why aren't we using laptops that are linked up and can give a decision in five seconds? A chimpanzee could do it – with not much training. We might as well go back to being cavemen, grab our girl by the hair, drag her into the cave whether she wants to come in or not because we may as well live in that age.
HOLLOWAY, *Blackpool manager, after losing to Crystal Palace, 2009*

We have to accept there is a match played on the pitch with its own facts, and another that happens at the same time – the match shown by television – that has facts that might be slightly different from the other game.
PIERLUIGI COLLINA, *Italian former international referee, on the debate over using TV technology to help the match officials, 2012*

It's a multi-million-pound business, not a game any more. Our decisions have an economic value. And the use of technology could become part of the drama, as it has in tennis, cricket and rugby. In football, though, we just turn a blind eye.
MARK HALSEY, *retired Premier League referee, 2013*

Wouldn't it be nice to get referees with balls the size of melons instead of peanuts sometimes?

DARRAGH MacANTHONY, *Peterborough chairman, tweeting about referee Tony Bates, 2011*

And tonight's match referee is... oh dear God... Davy Malcolm.
P.A. ANNOUNCER *before Ballymena United v Glenavon in Northern Ireland, 2010*

On a different day, the referee might have been throwing yellow cards around like a man with no arms.
GEORGE ANDREWS, *Signal Radio reporter, after a bruising Stoke v Everton game, 2012*

'Ref gives brilliant penalty' is not a great headline for the back pages, but Alex Ferguson attacking an assistant referee will always generate headlines.
DAVID ELLERAY, *former Premier League referee, 2013*

There's a saying in football – 'You'll never see a racehorse refereeing a match.'

GRAHAM POLL *on the 'mistaken' obsession with fitness, 2009*

You're out there with 22 multi-millionaires who you have to control with a whistle and two – sometimes three – cards.
POLL, *on quitting the game, 2007; a year earlier he had been cut from the World Cup after cautioning Croatia's Josip Simunic three times*

All the next season the crowds sang 'World Cup, and you fucked it up', and they were right. That hurt. I heard it and it cut me every time.
POLL *reflects on the Simunic error after retiring, 2007*

Football is shit. Football is nothing. Your family is what matters and you're a really nice guy.
CARLOS SIMON, *Brazilian referee, to Poll after his error in Stuttgart, 2006*

Anyone who craps in Graham Poll's toilet can't be all bad.
JEFF WINTER, *former Premier League referee, after Leicester's Robbie Savage admitted using Poll's loo, in* Who's the B*****d in the Black?, *2006*

Two more, he only gets two more.

SONG *by Colchester fans as Poll showed a yellow card in his first game after the World Cup, 2007*

More men have been on the moon than have refereed a World Cup final, yet I was there, in Japan last year, as the fourth official when Brazil beat Germany to win the tournament. That was utopia.
HUGH DALLAS, *Scottish referee, 2003*

I became a referee because I did not play football that well.
URS MEIER, *Swiss referee at European Championship finals, 2004*

It's almost like playing, but without the ability.
GRAHAM POLL *before refereeing the FA Cup final, 2000*

Refereeing is a very cut-throat business. A player can play in a cup final on the left or right of midfield. There's only one position for a referee.
JEFF WINTER, former Premiership referee, 2006

I'm back refereeing in the Argentine League and receiving as much shit as ever.
HORACIO ELIZONDO, World Cup final referee, denying he had been offered a job in the Argentinian government, 2006

The fourth official was my guardian angel.
ELIZONDO on Spanish official Luis Medina Cantalejo, who spotted and alerted him to the butt by Zinedine Zidane of France on Italy's Marco Materazzi, World Cup final, 2006

I was very pleased to see him [Elizondo] again. It was a great pleasure. He sent me off, sure, but he just did what he had to do.
ZINEDINE ZIDANE, retired France captain, on meeting Elizondo a year after the Argentine sent him off in Berlin, 2007

At Stoke once an elderly lady was waiting by the dressing room after the game. She said: 'Mr Knight, I'm 74 and a grandmother, and I'd just like to say you're the worst

fucking referee I've ever seen.' Certainly put me in my place.
BARRY KNIGHT, Football League referee, 2005

Hijo de puta! (Son of a whore!)
DAVID BECKHAM to the referee's assistant who flagged for a penalty against Real Madrid at Murcia, 2004; he was sent off

I do get abuse. You get 'Oh fuck off' but 'Fuck you' is more common. I say 'Fuck you as well' and away we go.
GRAHAM POLL at the World Cup finals, 2006

[Graham Poll] is good for games like these because he makes so many mistakes that people get angry and it motivates them.
JOSE MOURINHO, Chelsea manager, on the plus side of 'a referee we have no luck with' after a match v Manchester United, 2007

[Marcus Merk] is always against us. He must have been let out of prison to referee this match.
MOURINHO, then Porto coach, on the German referee after a match v Deportivo La Coruna, 2004

It was a definite penalty – the Portsmouth player had hold of his shirt. I'll just have to go home and kick the cat. He's called Referee.
GARY JOHNSON, Bristol City manager, 2008

We've got the drug-testers here today. I assume they'll ignore the players and go straight to the officials.
MICK McCARTHY, Wolves manager, after a controversial home defeat by Birmingham, 2007

Usually I like to get kissed before I get screwed.

McCARTHY, as above, 2007

Sir Alex Ferguson once complimented me on my handling of a game against Nottingham Forest. Three weeks later – after I'd refereed Manchester United v Fulham – he pulled me aside and said: 'Well, Jeff, back to normal. Fucking business as usual.'
JEFF WINTER, retired Premiership referee, 2004

The ref was a big-time homer, more interested in his rub-on suntan.
DAVID MOYES, Everton manager, on Winter, 2003

I've no qualms about playing in Uriah's charity golf events, although I might be tempted to wrap my five-iron around his neck.
DAVE JONES, Wolves manager, on Uriah Rennie's 'diabolical' handling of a game v Bolton, 2004

How the mega-rich male model referee slipped out of Molineux in his luxury Mercedes after a day of mayhem
HEADLINE in Wolverhampton's Express & Star after the Rennie controversy, 2004

I feel like a hunted animal and I'm scared to let my children leave the house. I don't want to live like that. I won't even go out on a pitch again. I'm too frightened. It's not worth it. Unfortunately, that's the way football looks today.
ANDERS FRISK, Swedish referee, on quitting the sport after receiving threats following criticism by Chelsea manager Jose Mourinho, 2005

These are not highly paid people like the players. They are basically people who have another job. It's unfair to put them in a situation where they have to go into hiding.
WILLIAM GAILLARD, UEFA director of communications, on Frisk's resignation, 2005

Shame on the Swiss referee, the Emmental-eating appeasement monkey who ruined the lives of millions of honest yeomen bearing their simple flag.
JUSTIN CARTWRIGHT, novelist, after Urs Meier refused England a last-gasp winner over Portugal, European Championship finals, 2004

Urs cheated on me and it sounds like he has cheated on England.

FRANZISKA MEIER, former wife of Urs Meier, 2004

Ninety-five per cent of the people who've watched the replay know it's not a penalty. Unfortunately the referee is one of the other 5 per cent.
NEIL WARNOCK, Sheffield United manager, after Rob Styles awarded Liverpool a spot-kick, 2006

In rugby it's accepted that the referee is right even when he's wrong, that you don't argue. The old saying is true: rugby is a game for thugs played by gentlemen, whereas football is a gentlemen's game played by thugs.
GORDON MILES, president of Warwickshire Society of Rugby Union Referees, 2005

The FA has accepted dissent. Everyone, especially the media, has bought into this entertainment-at-the-expense-of-sportsmanship ethos. We've forgotten what the game is about. It's childlike.
TONY KENNEDY, rugby referee, on the round-ball game's disciplinary problems, 2005

Respect is a two-way thing. You get some referees who call the police when you approach them.
STEVE BRUCE, Wigan Athletic manager, 2008

In rugby, you prevent things happening by continually talking to players. They call us 'Sir', not 'Ref'. There's no backchat; they know they'll be penalised. In football, all the refs are prima donnas.
ALAN GOLD, secretary of the Essex Society of Rugby Union Referees, 2005

Don Revie used to tell us to go in hard with the first tackle, because the referee would never book you for the first one. We used to call it the freebie. I'd go in hard, pick 'em up, say sorry to the ref and sometimes you hardly saw that player again.
NORMAN HUNTER, former Leeds and England defender, 2004

By the time referees are finally experienced enough to understand the teams and what the players are trying to get away with, it's time for them to retire.
RAFAEL BENITEZ, Liverpool manager, 2004

You can buy vibrating socks and electronic flags, but you can't buy experience. You can learn from others, but if you try to copy, it will be a bad copy.
KIM MILTON NIELSEN, Danish international referee, 2005

I don't want to be remembered for sending off David Beckham. I'll always be the man that sent him off even though it was in 1998 and so much has happened since.
NIELSEN, 2005

My dad used to referee me when I was a kid. I remember him booking me – and asking my name.
KEVIN KYLE, Coventry striker, 2006

Referees should arrive by the back door and leave the same way.

ALAN HARDAKER, Football League secretary, 1964

The trouble with referees is that they know the rules but they don't know the game.
BILL SHANKLY, Liverpool manager, during a referees' 'clampdown', 1971

Next thing we'll be giving our handbags to the linesmen before we skip on to the field.
MIKE SUMMERBEE, Manchester City winger, 1971

A good ref is one that doesn't chicken out – who'll give a penalty against Liverpool in front of the Kop.
DAVID CROSS, Coventry striker, 1975

The basic training of referees is appalling. They tested my eyesight by getting me to stand at one end of a small room, facing a wall chart showing red, yellow and blue kits. Some guy pointed to one shirt and said: 'What colour's that?' I replied 'Red' and he said, 'You're in.'
GORDON HILL, Football League referee, in Give a Little Whistle, *1975*

I got the impression that few toilets were used more than those in the referee's room.
JACK TAYLOR, World Cup referee, in World Soccer Review, *1976*

Mr Martinez was slow to realise that the Dutch invented the clog.
DAVID LACEY, football writer, reporting in The Guardian *on the Holland v Italy match, 1978*

'Referee, what would you do if I called you a bastard?' one player enquired politely. 'I'd send you off,' I replied. 'What would you do if I thought you were a bastard?' was the next question. 'There's not a lot I could do,' I answered. 'In that case, ref, I think you're a bastard,' he said, turning smartly on his heel.
PAT PARTRIDGE, Football League referee, in Oh, Ref!, *1979*

The referee must have felt like the President of the United States at the time of the Cuban missile crisis.
HOWARD WILKINSON, Leeds manager, after a game v Manchester

United was postponed because of a waterlogged pitch, 1992

It's getting to the stage where we hate referees and they dislike us.
KENNY SANSOM, Arsenal and England defender, 1983

People say we've got the best referees in the world. I shudder to think what the rest are like.

MARTIN BUCHAN, Manchester United defender, 1983

There's no rapport with referees these days. If you say anything you get booked. If you don't they send you off for dumb insolence.
JACK CHARLTON, Sheffield Wednesday manager, 1983

We had a Mauritian referee against Paraguay. Mauritius is a lovely island, but they don't play football.
EVARISTO MACEDA, Iraq coach, World Cup finals, 1986

There was a murderer on the pitch – the referee.

OMAR BARRAS, Uruguay manager, on the Italian official who sent off one of his players after 40 seconds against Scotland, World Cup finals, 1986

Then my eyesight started to go and I took up refereeing.
NEIL MIDGLEY, FA Cup final referee, 1987

We may be useless, but we are not cheats.
DAVID ELLERAY, referee, to Arsenal defender Tony Adams, who had called him a 'fucking cheat', 1989

David Elleray was that far away he would have needed binoculars. It's about time we use the means to sort these things out rather than relying on some bald-headed bloke standing 50 yards away.
NEIL WARNOCK, Sheffield United manager, after losing an FA Cup tie at Southampton to a penalty, 2001

I gave him 10 out of 10 after our Worthington Cup tie at Colchester this season and [Southampton manager] Glenn [Hoddle] will probably give him 10 this time. It means he'll average about five for the game.
WARNOCK, as above

The referee is available for Christmas pantomime or cabaret.
KEITH VALLE, tannoy announcer, as Bristol Rovers and Wigan players left the pitch, 1989

I have nothing against the visually handicapped as such, but I am surprised they are allowed to referee at this level.
THE SOUP, *Kidderminster Harriers fanzine, 1989*

We are stage managers, not performers.
ALAN GUNN, FA Cup final referee, 1990

I'll have to stop that. I don't think the Italian referees appreciated being patted on the head or the bum.
PAUL GASCOIGNE, early in his Lazio career, 1991

Thank God the referee and his linesmen are all out there together, otherwise they could have ruined three matches instead of one.
TOMMY DOCHERTY, working as a radio pundit at Old Trafford, 1992

It takes some believing for a ref to mix up two players as different as we are. I'm 5ft 8in and white, he's 6ft 4in and black.
TONY SPEARING, Plymouth Argyle defender, after he was booked in mistake for Tony Witter's foul, 1992

I'm 27 years old and yet the referee tells me I'm not allowed to swear.
VINNIE JONES, Wimbledon midfielder, after being dismissed for foul and abusive language, 1992

The referee has got me the sack. Thank him for that.

GRAHAM TAYLOR to a linesman and the FIFA official as England lost to the Netherlands and failed to qualify for the World Cup finals, 1993

It was lucky that the linesman wasn't stood in front of me as I would have poked him with a stick to make sure he was awake. I only hope he has woken up in time for his drive home this evening.
IAN HOLLOWAY, Queens Park Rangers manager, after defeat by Bristol City, 2002

The perfect referee does not exist. It's one man against 90,000 people and 22 actors, and a percentage of decisions will always be wrong.
GUIDO TOGNONI, FIFA spokesman, defending standards at the World Cup finals, 1994

The official today was a muppet.
IAN WRIGHT, Arsenal striker, after being booked at Norwich, 1994

In fairness, the referee had a complete cerebral failure.
RICK HOLDEN, Oldham winger, after defeat at Southend, 1995

My certain feeling is of being raped week in, week out, by referees and it just cannot go on.

SAM HAMMAM, Wimbledon owner, 1995

I do swear a lot, but having played abroad I can do it in a language different from the referee's.
JURGEN KLINSMANN, Tottenham and Germany striker, 1995

My wife, who was in the stand, told me that at one stage the entire row in front of her stood up and gave me the V sign. I asked her what she did and she said she didn't want them to know who she was so she stood up and joined in.
NEIL MIDGLEY, retired referee, recalling his First Division debut in Derick Allsop, The Game of Their Lives, 1995

I played full-back in rugby union, wicketkeeper in cricket and goalkeeper in football. The positions in which you stand out. Refereeing is like that. We're very much loners.
PHILIP DON, Premier League referee, 1995

Why should I allow a referee to do things which destroy my life? When managers make mistakes they get sacked. [David Elleray] is probably going home in his car now thinking about where's he going to referee next week.
JOE KINNEAR, Wimbledon manager, 1995

I've seen harder tackles in the half-time queue for meat pies than the ones punished in games.
GEORGE FULSTON, Falkirk chairman, 1995

I have to hand it to Manchester United. They have the best players – and the best referees.
SAM HAMMAM, Wimbledon owner, 1995

Most jobs get easier as you get more experienced. I've been a local government officer for 20 years and it's getting easier. This [refereeing] is getting harder. The pressure has increased, the pace is greater. There's so much money involved, so much at stake.
STEPHEN LODGE, Premier League referee, 1995

You can't think that one decision by you could be worth millions of pounds. If you think about the financial implications when you see a possible penalty, it will disturb your concentration and you may make a wrong call.
KIM MILTON NIELSEN, Danish World Cup referee, 2005

Can anyone tell me why they give referees a watch? It's certainly not for keeping the time.
ALEX FERGUSON after Graham Poll added 'only three minutes', Manchester United v Everton, 1996

In England the referees either shoot you down with a machine-gun or don't blow their whistle at all.
GIANLUCA VIALLI after his Premiership debut for Chelsea, 1996

My motto is 'perfect preparation prevents poor performance'.
MIKE RILEY, Premiership referee, 2007

I do like Selhurst Park. There's a Sainsbury's next to the ground so it's an ideal chance to get some weekend shopping out of the way.
DAVID ELLERAY, Premier League referee, 1996

I love my job. I get a buzz when I say 'Play on' and a goal results. I think: 'God, I made that.'

ALAN WILKIE, Premiership referee, 1998

I made the gesture [punching the air] because the referee loves to see the ball in the net after he has played an advantage. It proves he was right.
MIKE REED, Premiership referee, after appearing to celebrate Patrik Berger's goal for Liverpool v Leeds, 2000

If we're going to have sponsored referees, maybe we could approach Optrex or the Royal National Institute for the Blind.
PAUL DURKIN, Premiership referee, 1998

There are occasions when you say to yourself: 'I need to give a yellow card here and re-establish my authority.' That's when it gets like teaching. When it gets a bit lively, you need a sacrificial lamb.
DAVID ELLERAY, Premiership referee and Harrow School housemaster, 1998

This referee [Mike Reed] is so poor that I'd have been booked just getting off the bus.
NORMAN HUNTER, Radio Leeds summariser and former Leeds and England defender, 1998

Professional referees may help but it won't necessarily bring better positioning, better eyesight and more courage.
MARTIN O'NEILL, Leicester manager, 1998

I understand that [Everton manager] Walter Smith described the ref as diabolical. I didn't think he was as good as that.
JIM SMITH, Derby manager, 1999

There's no point asking a referee for an explanation of his action. You get that in the report a couple of weeks later, when everyone has got the right story. The boys in black have time to organise a story, make sure it's right and then send it out. Yet I have to try to give instant explanations.
GORDON STRACHAN, Coventry manager, alleging a conspiracy by match officials after defeat at Liverpool, 1999

I tried to talk to the ref but it's easier to get an audience with the Pope. If I'm in London again and I get mugged, I hope the same amount of people turn up – there were six police officers, four stewards and a UN peace-keeping observer.
STRACHAN after controversy at Arsenal shortly before resigning as Southampton manager, 2004

I don't know why they don't have the bookings before the start so that we can get on with the game. You know they are coming.
DAVID O'LEARY, Leeds manager, complaining of over-zealous refereeing by Mike Reed at Tottenham, 1999

I tried to have a word with him after the game but he wouldn't speak to me. He's untouchable. He should have been a policeman.
JOHN GREGORY, Aston Villa manager, on referee Jeff Winter after defeat at Leicester, 1999

Referees act almost like policemen, and the fourth officials are becoming jobsworths. They are reporting managers up and down the country for stepping outside the technical area.
GREGORY, 1999

The referee was bobbins. If you need that translating, it means crap.
DAVE JONES, Southampton manager, 1999

It is a great profession being a referee. They are never wrong.

ARSENE WENGER, Arsenal manager, 1999

That linesman is as dangerous as a monkey with two pistols. He always seems to ruin the show.
GREGORIO MANZANO, Real Mallorca coach, blaming a referee's assistant after two of his team were sent off in a 4–0 defeat v Barcelona, 2003

I don't think we should have shoot-outs. We should have a shoot-the-ref shoot-out. After that penalty, the referee should have been shot.
JOHN GREGORY, Aston Villa manager, after a last-minute penalty awarded to West Ham, 1999

Referees should be wired up to a couple of electrodes and they should be allowed to make three mistakes before you run 50,000 volts through their genitals.
GREGORY after David Elleray awarded a penalty against Villa at Sunderland, 1999

The ref was a disgrace. He got three things right – the kick-off, half-time and full-time.

ANDY RITCHIE, Oldham manager, 1999

It doesn't seem to matter how hard we try, we still get a slagging for trying to do the job as honestly as we can. It would be very interesting one Saturday if we decided not to turn up until 3.30pm.
PAUL DURKIN, Premiership referee, 1999

The radio link will be a great help once we get used to it, but I'm still not sure where to put my microphone.
STEVE DUNN, Premiership referee, after a trial run with an earpiece and microphone, 1999

Sometimes, privately, I say, 'The referee was crap today,' but not publicly. Managers have a responsibility to protect the referee. You have to believe he gives his best. Good and bad decisions even themselves out.
ARSENE WENGER, 1999

In the tunnel I say to David Elleray: 'You might as well book me now and get it over with.' He takes it pretty well but he still books me.
ROY KEANE, Manchester United captain, 2000

They were like a pack of wolves. I've never seen so much hatred on players' faces. It looked as though they were trying to put pressure on Andy D'Urso so that he wouldn't send off Jaap Stam as well as giving the penalty decision.
KEITH COOPER, referees assessor and ex-referee, after United players pursued Andy D'Urso, 2000

If the ref had stood still we wouldn't have had to chase him.
ROY KEANE, United captain, on the D'Urso incident, 2000

When linesmen come to check the nets when I'm warming up, I'll usually say: 'I'm a referee too, so I know what you've got to put up with.' Referees could do with more help from us; players could sometimes be more honest with officials.

STEVE HARPER, *Newcastle goalkeeper and referee in the Peterlee & District League, 2000*

The penalty decision put us back in the game. The player should have been sent off, but Mr Harris didn't know who the player was who had handled. The ref did get the minute's silence right before the game, though.

JOHN GREGORY, *Aston Villa manager, after a controversial game v Tottenham, 2000*

My players wouldn't take a throw-in for that sort of money.

GORDON STRACHAN, *Coventry manager, on learning that Gerald Ashby's match fee was £200, 1998*

I can't understand why the ref wasn't more sympathetic. After all, we used to go to the same bookies.

STEVE CLARIDGE, *Portsmouth player-manager, after his team incurred two red cards v Fulham, 2001*

[David] Elleray went around with his arms folded like a schoolteacher. Which, of course, he is.

SIMON JORDAN, *Crystal Palace chairman, 2001*

I've got no friends among the players. You're doing a job of work and so are they.

STEPHEN LODGE, *Premiership referee, 2001*

When Paolo Di Canio pushed over the referee [Paul Alcock], if the referee had been a player he'd have been booked for diving.

BARRY DAVIES, *TV commentator, recalling a 1998 match between Arsenal and Sheffield Wednesday, 2004*

I'd like to smash the ball into a referee at 200 miles an hour and see if he can get out of the way.

BOBBY ROBSON, *Newcastle manager, criticising Nolberto Solano's dismissal for handling, 2001*

You cheated us. It was impossible to miss that handball. You deserve to go and referee in Afghanistan. If you made the same mistake there, you'd get shot.

ROBERT NITA, *Rapid Bucharest player, picked up by the TV microphones after match v Arges in which Constantin Fratila denied his team two penalties, 2001*

What makes a sane and rational person subject himself to such humiliation? Why on earth does anyone want to become a Premiership referee?
LORD HATTERSLEY, Sheffield Wednesday supporter, 2002

I believe when the referees are enjoying their recreation on the sunbeds, or swimming up and down the pool and talking together in their free time, there is an agenda with Alan Smith. They all have their little chats and jump on him very, very quickly.
DAVID O'LEARY, Leeds manager, after Andy D'Urso sent off Smith in an FA Cup tie at Cardiff, 2002

This is what happens when you have village referees in the World Cup.
CHRISTIAN VIERI, Italy striker, after England's Graham Poll and his assistants denied the Azzurri two goals v Croatia, World Cup finals, 2002

We weren't lucky – it was the Irish who had a flower up their backsides. What the referee did makes you want to kill him. He crushed us. And as for the linesman, he's got a spring-loaded arm.
JOSE ANTONIO CAMACHO, Spain coach, on the Swedish referee after beating the Republic of Ireland on penalties, World Cup finals, 2002

We were unlucky that we ran into a referee who ought to be thinking more about his diet than his refereeing.
ALESSANDRO NESTA, Italy defender, on the Ecuadorian referee for their defeat by South Korea, World Cup finals, 2002

I never talk to the media after a match. Anything you say is on your head, and the media certainly aren't there to help referees.
MIKE RILEY, Premiership referee, 2007

People say a good referee is one the fans don't notice but that's a myth. If a referee has to give three penalties in a match, then he is going to be noticed. That doesn't mean he's not a good referee.
PIERLUIGI COLLINA, Italian referee, shortly before officiating in the World Cup final, 2002

Collina says: You're off...to Comet.
SLOGAN on an advert using Signor Collina to promote the electrical store, 2004

It was like 20 mates at a holiday camp. We used to do Arthur Askey impressions. And nobody missed the bingo nights.
GRAHAM POLL on referees' conventions in his autobiography Seeing Red, *2007*

13 WOMEN

Did you hear charming Karren Brady this morning complaining about sexism? Do me a favour, love.
RICHARD KEYS, co-presenter of Sky's coverage of Wolves v Liverpool, unaware that he was being recorded, 2011

Apparently, a female lino today, bit of a looker.
ANDY BURTON, Sky reporter, to Keys' co-presenter Andy Gray, Wolves v Liverpool, 2011

I can see her [assistant referee Sian Massey] from here. What do women know about the offside rule?
ANDY GRAY, as above

Well done to the lady lineswoman.
CHRIS KAMARA, Sky summariser, when Massey called a tight offside correctly, 2011

What a decision from the woman linesman.

PAUL MERSON, Sky studio pundit, on Massey's intervention, 2011

@KellyCates Phew am exhausted. Just read about something called 'the offside rule.' Too much for my tiny brain. Must be damaged from nail polish fumes.
TWEET by Cates, Kenny Dalglish's daughter, 2011

Nice one lads. Would you like me to pop down and explain the concept of an own goal?
LETTER from a female reader to The Guardian *after the comments by Keys and Gray, 2011*

What really upsets me is the fact only females in our industry are judged by their gender. It never would have occurred to me that they had those views, whether public or private. It almost makes it worse that they're speaking off-air, because they would never have had the brass neck to say it publicly. I don't believe it's just banter.
KARREN BRADY, West Ham vice-chairman and broadcaster, after Keys and Grays left Sky following the Sian Massey episode, 2011

There have been times when I've spoken to managers and they said they weren't comfortable talking to a girl about football. They just thought I was someone's PA, or there to make cups of tea.
GEORGINA LILLIS, football agent, 2013

When I go to games I always get asked: 'Which one is your boyfriend?'
LILLIS, as above

I like footballers' bodies and their lives, but I'd never marry one. Most are very shallow.
MICHELE ZUANNE, Spanish model who had dated Atletico Madrid player Diego Costa, 2014

This is football. What I would say to any wife or girlfriend is 'This is what's paying the bills.'
CURTIS DAVIES, Hull City defender, when the wife of ex-West Bromwich Albion colleague Shane Long tweeted that a transfer to Hull 'isn't worth the stress', 2014

My wife's the boss. Things don't happen just like that but if she says to me 'Honey, I want to go to Paris St-Germain,' then I will have to take that into consideration.
EDEN HAZARD, Chelsea and Belgium midfielder, 2014

I'm afraid there's always a problem when you let the wives tell footballers what to do.

THIERRY ROLAND, French TV pundit, after Beckham spurned Paris St-Germain, reputedly at Victoria Beckham's insistence, 2012

Trying to understand why my hubby's on the bench now #ridiculous.
MELISSA JOHNSON, wife of Wolves captain Roger Johnson, in a tweet, 2012

What's happening? F*** all and its starting to wind me up!! Sort it out Harry [Redknapp] for f*** sake.
KIMBERLY BENTLEY in a tweet about speculation concerning husband David's future at Tottenham, 2011

To survive in football management you need a good wife and a stable home life to come back to.
JOE MERCER, Coventry director and former England interim manager, 1980

There's a Burton's [menswear shop] 10 minutes from where we live. She probably thought it was there.
HARRY REDKNAPP, Queens Park Rangers manager, on claims that he was overlooked as England manager because his wife did not want to live near Burton-upon-Trent and the FA's St George's Park training centre, 2013

[Wife] Sharon was a wreck, crying her eyes out. I thought at first she was re-watching the last episode of Downton Abbey.
NEIL WARNOCK on his sacking as Queens Park Rangers manager, 2012

I accepted the FA's charge of improper conduct and paid a £2,000 fine. In fact, my behaviour cost me a grand total of £2,012 because I also had to pay a £12 fine to my wife Kim after initially telling her that I hadn't sworn at the ref.
IAN HOLLOWAY, Crystal Palace manager, 2013

We had a flat here but we had to get out, and Tony [Pulis] has moved in. I'm not sure if he's got my old car, but he's not having my woman.
HOLLOWAY *on being succeeded by Pulis after his dismissal by Palace, 2014*

There are sections of the crowd who complain but it's why they come to the ground. These fellas get shit off the wife all week and they come to football to let it out.
KEVIN NOLAN, *West Ham captain, 2012*

Choosing between City and Liverpool to take the title is like choosing which bloke nicks your wife.
GARY NEVILLE, *2014*

I'm really proud of my medals. No one can take them away from me. Not even my ex.

RAY PARLOUR, *former Arsenal and England midfielder, 2012*

[Pascal Chimbonda] was good for one season at Wigan. Now he moans more than my ex-wife.
ALAN McINALLY, *Sky TV summariser, 2009*

Q: Most dangerous opponent?
A: My ex-wife.
FRANK WORTHINGTON, *England striker, in a magazine questionnaire, 1975*

If there's anyone luckier than a footballer, it's a footballer's wife. She has all the money and prestige but none of the pressure.
GORDON STRACHAN, *Southampton manager, 2003*

I got really glammed up. The whole Millwall team turned up. I felt like a proper footballer's wife then.
NATALIE RUDD, *model and girlfriend of the Stoke and ex-Millwall player Peter Sweeney, recalling her 21st birthday party in* Nuts *magazine, 2005*

Q: What do you set the video for?
A: It has to be *Footballers' Wives*. I like the show's gritty realism.
IFFY ONURA, *Sheffield United striker, in a programme questionnaire, 2003*

We do have occasional pangs about those 80 or 90 little girls there must be running around playgrounds lumbered with the name Chardonnay.
BRIAN PARK, *executive producer of the ITV drama series* Footballers' Wives, *2004*

I was recognised too much [in Liverpool] and sometimes women would suddenly climb all over me.
MAROUANE FELLAINI, *Everton and Belgium midfielder, on why he moved house to Manchester, 2013*

It is very easy in England to find a girl who wants to be with you for the wrong reasons.
WOJCIECH SZCZESNY, Arsenal and Poland goalkeeper, 2012

The truth is some women will do anything to crack on with footballers. Some birds will buy you drinks all night, strip for you, get shagged with other people in the room and do all sorts of tricks.
RIO FERDINAND, Manchester United and England defender, in Rio: My Story, *2006*

The England players didn't like [Eriksson]. He started to pull their birds.

EAMON DUNPHY, Irish TV pundit, 2010

If you say you want to grow up and marry a footballer, everyone slags you off, but if you said you wanted to marry Johnny Depp or Leonardo DiCaprio, that'd be all right.
ABBEY CLANCY, model and wife of England striker Peter Crouch, on the 'myth' that she set out to marry a footballer, 2010

Any maid I allow into my house must know how to clean, how to iron, and be grossly ugly. There are pretty and ugly maids in this world. Women with footballers must always hire ugly.
EVANGELINA ANDERSON, Argentinian model and wife of Argentina defender Martin Demichelis, after her former partner, footballer Maxi Lopez, was cleared of making lewd advances to a maid, 2010

These women don't cook for their husbands, they don't clean, they have all the handbags they want, but they never do a day's work. What kind of aspiration is that?
CHERYL COLE, pop singer and then wife of England player Ashley Cole, 2008

I told the players that they might never get the opportunity to reach a big final again, so they should go out there and do it for their wives, girlfriends – or both for that matter.
PAUL JEWELL, Wigan Athletic manager, on the Carling Cup semi-final v Arsenal, 2006

With this ring I thee WAG
HEADLINE in the Daily Mail *as four England players prepared to marry on the same day, 2007; WAGs was the media acronym for the wives and girlfriends of the England squad at the 2006 World Cup*

I don't know where they will stay, it's not my concern. I'm hoping there will be a virus.
FABIO CAPELLO, England manager, when asked about the WAGs' movement at the World Cup finals, 2010

You undertake to John, Toni and *OK!* magazine that you will not photograph or otherwise record any part of the wedding and/or reception.
WORDING *on the invitation to the wedding of John Terry and Toni Poole, 2007*

I've sold my wedding pictures to *The Kop* magazine for a pound.
JAMIE CARRAGHER, *Liverpool and England defender, on his marriage to Nicola, 2005*

How can you tell the difference between the species of English woman and the majority of German women? They spend more cash on clothes in 10 minutes than ours do in a lifetime.
BILD ZEITUNG, *German newspaper, on the England WAGs at the spa resort of Baden Baden, 2006*

I think shopping is their favourite thing to do. And they enjoy the cafes and bars, too.
BRIGITTE GOERTZ-MEISSNER, *head of tourism in Baden Baden, 2006*

Tell all the WAGs we've got a brand new shopping centre in Plymouth.
IAN HOLLOWAY, *Plymouth Argyle manager, 2007*

Apparently, more young women are getting into debt because they shop like a footballer's wife. If I heard of anyone doing that, I'd tell them to get a grip.
COLEEN McLOUGHLIN, *Wayne Rooney's partner and prolific shopper, 2006*

I would like to bring in another two players. I like shopping. Maybe I have become a woman.

PAOLO DI CANIO, *Swindon Town manager, 2012*

Priorities have changed for footballers and they are being dictated to by their wives and girlfriends... Greed will always be part of the game, but this side of it, with the women running the show, worries me.
ROY KEANE, *Sunderland manager, complaining he had missed out on signing certain players because their partners wanted to be near the big shopping cities, 2007*

If they don't want to come [to join Sunderland] because their wife wants to go shopping in London, it's a sad state of affairs. To me, that player is weak because his wife runs his life.
KEANE, *as above*

They're famous for doing nothing. They take advantage of their partner's position. I didn't seek out Darren because he's a footballer. I've got my own career.
JAMELIA, pop singer and partner of Millwall striker Darren Byfield, on the World Cup WAGs, 2006

I don't know what the fuss is about the England players' wives. They look ugly to me.
VRATISLAV LOKVENC, Czech Republic striker, European Championship finals, 2004

A team-mate at Marseille once told me: 'Ah, English footballers, fantastic. But ugly wives.' I'm pleased to say we've caught up with the Continent. These days, players' lounges are like beauty pageants.
TONY CASCARINO, former Republic of Ireland striker, in his Times *column, 2005*

Wives of old were quiet, sensible girls next door. Now they're feisty, independent socialites... Most are fun-loving, bubbly and far smarter than the stereotype. It's an environment with shallow elements, certainly. The percentage who've had hair extensions, breast enlargements and so on is probably higher than the national average. The wives of the older pros see the younger girlfriends and don't want to be outshone.
CASCARINO, as above

It was his weekend off. He can do what he wants. Do you spend time with your girlfriend? Do you go to the cinema with her? Would you like her to kiss you now and then? That's what Artur [Boruc] has done. I still go to the cinema with my wife and still kiss her. She doesn't like it, but there you go.
GORDON STRACHAN, Celtic manager, to journalists after his goalkeeper was seen 'out on the town', 2008

I did a 24-hour sponsored silence for Children In Need and if I hadn't had my girlfriend to talk to, I think I would have struggled.
ANTON FERDINAND, Sunderland defender, 2008

At 9am on Saturday, he [Ray Parlour] called me. I told him I was in bed... He said: 'Kal, I'm leaving.' I said: 'What, Arsenal?' And he said: 'No, you.' I said: 'Let's talk about this – tell me why you're leaving.' He said coolly: 'I can't talk now. I'm at the hotel and I've got a game this afternoon and have to concentrate.'
KAREN PARLOUR, ex-wife of the then Arsenal midfielder, after being awarded a substantial divorce settlement, 2004

Andy Goram and Miriam Wylie split after less than two years of marriage when she found a woman's footprints on the ceiling of their Shogun 4x4.
REPORT in the Scottish Sun, *2003*

How [Garry Flitcroft] was naive enough to think he could pledge eternal love to a lap dancer without having the whistle blown to his wife escapes me.
VANESSA FELTZ, television personality, after Blackburn captain Flitcroft failed in a legal bid to prevent the press reporting his allegedly serial philandering, 2002

If we did get promoted there would be a tear in my eye and my wife would hammer me. I didn't cry at my wedding or the birth of my children and she has warned me not to cry or I'll be in trouble.
MARC BIRCHAM, Queens Park Rangers player, before losing to Cardiff in the Second Division play-off final, 2003

I have to use my maiden name for work. Sometimes I even pretend my husband does something else for a living. When I taught at the Law Society in Madrid, for example, I told my students I was married to a plumber.
VICTORIA McMANAMAN, wife of former England player Steve McManaman, 2006

When I was first with Steve as a teenager, people couldn't believe it when I wanted to go to university. They said, 'Go on, give it up, do nothing.'
VICTORIA McMANAMAN, as above

If my husband made a brilliant save in Europe the headline would never read: 'Husband of artist makes fantastic save.' When I was short-listed from 300 to 30 artists from 22 countries and won a prestigious award, my headline was: 'Footballer's wife is good at art shocker.'
SUSAN GUNN, artist and wife of former Scotland goalkeeper Bryan Gunn, 2006

It's seven years today, my anniversary [as manager], and it was my birthday yesterday, so it's been a great weekend for me. I'd better be careful with the missus otherwise I'll probably put her in the club.
NEIL WARNOCK, Sheffield United manager, 2006

I told Cathy I had a match, but she wasn't having any of it. She said it was a friendly and that I had to help her to pack because we're moving house.
SIR ALEX FERGUSON on how his wife stopped him attending Manchester United's pre-season game at Dunfermline, 2007

Of course I didn't take my wife to watch Rochdale as an anniversary present. It was her birthday. Would I have got married during the football season? And anyway it wasn't Rochdale, it was Rochdale Reserves.
BILL SHANKLY, Liverpool manager, 1966

I take my wife Lesley to watch midweek matches. She's in the studio audience tonight. It's one of the rare times I've taken her out somewhere she doesn't need to wear an overcoat.
GORDON STRACHAN, *Southampton manager, on BBC TV's* Onside *show, 2002*

Basically, he [Bill Nicholson] doesn't think women have any place in football. I never saw him play for Spurs and I'm not allowed to go to see them now. I feel an outsider, really, as if I was a member of the opposition.
GRACE NICHOLSON, *wife of the then Tottenham manager, in Hunter Davies's* The Glory Game, *1972*

When I lose I've got to talk about it. I go home and relive it with the wife. She just nods and says yes or no.
NORMAN HUNTER, *Leeds and England defender, 1973*

It takes a lot to get me excited. Ask my wife.

ROY KEANE, *Sunderland manager, after they beat Tottenham on returning to the Premier League, 2007*

When I said that even my missus could save Derby from relegation, I was exaggerating.
PETER TAYLOR, *Derby manager, 1982*

My wife knows more about football than any other woman I know... Many occasions I have said to her: 'Come on, luv, I'll take you out for a meal,' and she'll look disappointed and say: 'You know that Wimbledon Reserves are playing.'
ALEC STOCK, *former manager, in* A Little Thing Called Pride, *1982*

My wife has been magic about it.
JOHN BOND *when the story of his affair with a Manchester City employee broke following his resignation as manager, 1983*

John Bond has blackened my name with his insinuations about the private lives of football managers. Both my wives are upset.
MALCOLM ALLISON, *Bond's predecessor as Manchester City manager, 1983*

We hope to revive the old tradition of the husband going to football on Christmas Day, while the wife cooks the turkey.
ERIC WHITE, *Brentford official, 1983*

My idea of relaxation: going somewhere away from the wife.
TERRY FENWICK, *QPR captain, in a* Match *magazine questionnaire, 1986*

My wife says it would be better if there was another woman. At least then she would know what she's up against. But she says: 'How can I compete with football?'
DON MACKAY, *Blackburn manager, 1988*

The only threats I've had this week have been from the wife for not doing the washing-up.

HARRY REDKNAPP, Southampton manager, before the derby against his previous club Portsmouth, 2005

Only women and horses work for nothing.

DOUG ELLIS, Aston Villa chairman, 1983

Q: At home, when was the last time you ironed a shirt?
A: I pay my wife to do that.
MARK ROBINS, Leicester striker, in a programme questionnaire, 1995

John Hollins was a mistake. He has a very strong wife. It might have been better if I had made her manager.
KEN BATES, Chelsea chairman, 1995

What does my wife think of me still being in management? She doesn't talk to me. Well, she does, but she knows it's pointless.
SIR BOBBY ROBSON answering questions by Dutch journalists about being a manager at the age of 71, 2004

My wife was hoping I'd get the sack so we could retire down to Cornwall with the children.
NEIL WARNOCK, Sheffield United manager, 2005

The reason I'm back is that the wife wants me out of the house.
KENNY DALGLISH on returning to management with Blackburn, 1991

I married a girl who was very easily told: 'If you marry me, you're marrying football.'
GRAHAM TAYLOR, England manager, 1992

Whether or not we win against Germany, I will stay away from all of you for seven days. I have to sleep with my wife.
LUIZ FELIPE SCOLARI, Brazil coach, to the media on the eve of the World Cup final, 2002

I would rather my wife got injured than my players.
JEAN TIGANA, Fulham manager, 2002

You can tell how a team's doing by the state of the wives. Second Division wives always need roots touching up.
MRS MERTON, played by Caroline Aherne, on TV's The Mrs Merton Show, 1995

If it wasn't for Tracy, I'd be an 18-stone alcoholic playing for Penicuik Athletic.
ANDY GORAM, Rangers and Scotland goalkeeper, paying tribute to his second wife, 1995

I used to stand up and glare around when fans were giving Geoff stick. Norman Hunter's mum used to lash out with her handbag when people booed her Norman.
JUDITH HURST, wife of Geoff Hurst, in Brian James's book Journey to Wembley, *1977*

I'd look out of my bedroom window and see friends of mine kissing some girl. I'd say: 'Can't I go out for half an hour?' My mum said: 'One day you will thank me.' I thank her every day.
JERMAIN DEFOE, Tottenham and England striker, on his mother Sandra, 2012

When I get home from training, my mum's there, in my face. She's there 24/7. I don't know where she gets her knowledge from. At first she wouldn't come to the games, but then she saw how much I liked it and really got into it. Now she thinks she's Jose Mourinho. Some of the stuff she's telling me, the manager is telling me as well. She really knows about the game and how to play, what to do.
RAHEEM STERLING, Liverpool and England winger, 2013

I'm more scared of my mum than of Sven-Goran Eriksson. She'd always give me a clip round the ear if she thought I wasn't doing right.
WAYNE ROONEY quoted in England's Hero *by Sue Evison, 2004*

I gave [the teenaged Cristiano Ronaldo] an Arsenal shirt with his name on it. I'm disappointed that I seduced only his mum.
ARSENE WENGER on how he persuaded Ronaldo's mother he should join Arsenal as a teenager but not the Portuguese winger, 2008

The mother's the secret. I say always: 'Get the mother.' There's always danger with the father. He tries to live his life through the boy. But the mother? No, she won't do it that way. She's 'My boy, I want more of this for my boy.'
SIR ALEX FERGUSON, Manchester United manager, on wooing young players to Old Trafford, 2013

When I leave Damien Duff out of the side, my 84-year-old mother rings to ask me why. She kills me for it.
CLAUDIO RANIERI, Chelsea manager, 2003

My mum would kill me if I wore gloves in a game.

MATT JARVIS, West Ham and England winger, 2013

He's not joining Pisa for the simple and most important reason that his mother decided that days ago.
BRIAN CLOUGH, Nottingham Forest manager, on speculation that son Nigel was Italy-bound, 1988

I will no longer take penalties for Ghana. My mother advised against penalties, and since she is no more, I have to heed her advice.
ASAMOAH GYAN, Ghana striker, after missing a crucial extra-time spot-kick v Uruguay, World Cup finals, 2010

When I was at Inter Milan I used to call my mum to resolve every little problem. Here I have to deal with things on my own.
MARIO BALOTELLI, Manchester City and Italy striker, 2012

My mum actually taught me how to knit. I knitted my teddy bear a jumper, but I couldn't round off.
DAVID JAMES, Portsmouth and England goalkeeper, 2009

REPORTER: Is it true you said you would tackle your own grandmother if necessary?
BILL SHANKLY: Don't be stupid. She would have more sense than to come anywhere near me.
EXCHANGE at press briefing, 1965

Is [Roberto] Soldado a donkey or what? My old grandmother could have scored the one he just missed.
LORD SUGAR, former Tottenham owner, on Twitter during Dnipro v Spurs,

Europa League, 2014

Football is all very well as a game for rough girls, but it is hardly suitable for delicate boys.
OSCAR WILDE, 1890s

Football reminds me of the Nuremberg Rally. It's so aggressive. Great men with bald heads, roaring and screaming. Why should anyone welcome that?
MICHELE HANSON, Guardian Women writer, in Match of the Day *magazine, 1998*

Women should be in the kitchen, the discotheque and the boutique, but not in football.
RON ATKINSON, Sheffield Wednesday manager, 1989

What are women doing here? It's just tokenism for politically correct idiots.

MIKE NEWELL, Luton manager, on referee's assistant Amy Rayner, 2006

Who's cooking your tea?
STAN TERNENT, Burnley manager, to referee's assistant Wendy Toms, quoted in his autobiography Stan the Man, *2003*

The Italians are a gayer set of lads, who love life and their girlfriends… They think the English boys are slightly mad putting sport before the ladies.
EDDIE FIRMANI *on his move from Charlton to Sampdoria, in* Football with the Millionaires, *1960*

To score in front of 70,000 fans at San Siro is like finding a place in a woman's heart. No, it's better.
NICOLA BERTI, *Inter Milan midfielder, 1988*

I don't think my girlfriend would be too happy to hear I've been chasing Totti round Rome.
JONATHAN WOODGATE, *teenage Leeds defender, on the prospect of facing Roma's Francesco Totti, 1998*

Blimey, you're the first bird I've met with an FA coaching badge.
RON ATKINSON *to a female journalist who asked about Sheffield Wednesday's long-ball game under his predecessors, 1989*

Women who talk about football tactics, it's beautiful. I find that fantastic. And you know what a 4–3–3 is, right?
LAURENT BLANC, *Paris St-Germain coach, after a question by a female Swedish journalist, 2013*

My wife Cristina often complains about my tactics. She keeps telling me I should stick with the players who won the last match. Explaining my rotation system to her is much harder than telling Arjen Robben that he'll have to settle for a place on the bench.
PEP GUARDIOLA, *Bayern Munich coach, 2014*

Well, they're allegedly football reporters but they haven't got a ghost of a clue what's going on on the field… One can be a woman in print without it noticing; you can't see the lipstick or smell the perfume. But when it comes to a woman asking questions on TV… I would find it difficult to listen to a Miss Motson banging on… You'd never trust a woman with something as important as a football result.
BRIAN GLANVILLE, *veteran football writer, on female journalists covering football,* The Times, *1998*

I am from the old school when football press boxes and commentary positions were men-only locations and the thought of a female commentating on football was abhorrent. It is an insult to the controlled commentaries of John Motson, Mike Ingham and Alan Green that their domain is threatened by a new arrival whose excited voice sounds like a fire siren.
STEVE CURRY, Daily Mail *football writer, on the appointment of Jacqui Oatley to* Match of the Day, *2007*

If there really are men who prefer football to girls, I've never met any.

SHARON KNIGHT, 19-year-old Miss Stoke-on-Trent, 1990

I hate football. I think most women do. It's not the sort of sport I'm interested in. I prefer the indoor sort of games.
CYNTHIA PAYNE, Streatham 'Madam', 1990

The Old Firm are like two old girls in Sauchiehall Street raising their skirts to any league that walks past.
KEITH WYNESS, Aberdeen chief executive, on the possibility of Rangers and Celtic quitting the Scottish League, 2002

If a woman suggested that the simplest way of brightening up football was by making the goals a bit bigger, they would say she didn't understand the game and why didn't she go off and practise her netball.
NIGELLA LAWSON in her Evening Standard column after FIFA president Joao Havelange suggested widening the goals, 1990

We now have three ladies on the board. Say something, ladies! You're always talking at home. Say something now!
SEPP BLATTER, FIFA president, after a third woman was elected to the world governing body's executive committee, 2013

The only place for women in football is making the tea at half-time.
RODNEY MARSH, former England player, 1997

[Australia's Moya Dodd] is good, and good-looking.
BLATTER addressing the Asian Football Confederation delegates before Ms Dodd was elected in the above vote, 2013

Being part of #mufc history is something I am proud of! Special shout to the dinner ladies!
RIO FERDINAND tweet, 2013

They are nice people with a part to play but at the end of the day they are tea ladies who do not understand the game.
TREVOR STEELE, Bradford Park Avenue chairman, resigning after two women directors were elected to the board, 1990

Doing well in football is like childbirth – it doesn't happen overnight.
BRIAN CLOUGH, Nottingham Forest manager, 1991

Q: What has been your biggest thrill in life?
A: When my wife Norma told me she was pregnant and signing for Newcastle.
ALBERT CRAIG, Partick Thistle midfielder, in a Sun *questionnaire, 1994*

Why not treat the wife to a weekend in London and let her go shopping on Saturday afternoon while you go and watch the Latics play West Ham?
OLDHAM ATHLETIC programme, 1991

A football team is like a beautiful woman. When you do not tell her, she forgets she is beautiful.
ARSENE WENGER, Arsenal manager, 2004

You've certainly tried to go out with a girl but find she has chosen someone else. You don't commit suicide.
WENGER after Arsenal's attempt to sign Luis Suarez from Liverpool was unsuccessful, 2013

I've always believed in treating the ball like a woman. Give it a cuddle, caress it a wee bit, take your time, and you'll get the desired response.
JIM BAXTER, Rangers and Scotland player of the 1960s, 1991

Leaving a club is like leaving a woman. When there's nothing left to say, you go.
ERIC CANTONA after leaving Leeds for Manchester United, 1992

Footballers are the worst gossips – they're worse than women.
LEE CHAPMAN, Leeds striker, 1992

We defended like women.
JOE ROYLE, Oldham manager, after 5–2 defeat by Wimbledon, 1992

[Fernando] Torres and [Jan] Vertonghen were at each other's throats all game, like a couple of girls – pulling each other's shirts and pushing each other.
ROBBIE FOWLER, BBC TV pundit, on Final Score, *2013*

Next time I'll learn to dive maybe, but I'm not a woman.

THIERRY HENRY, Arsenal striker, after defeat by Barcelona in the Champions League final, 2006

If we're not careful we'll be playing in high heels and skirts and playing netball.
STEVE BRUCE, Birmingham manager, alleging over-zealous refereeing, 2006

Footballers are turning into women. You'd never have got away with anything like that when I was playing.
GORDON RAMSAY, TV chef and former Rangers youth-team player, on reports that top players were shaving their body hair, 2005

The strip was a bloody stupid colour. I think one of the directors' wives must have chosen it.
DAVID PLEAT, Luton manager, on the end of his club's tangerine and navy kit, 1992

Women run everything. The only thing I've done within my house in the past 20 years is recognise Angola as an independent state.
BRIAN CLOUGH, 1992

Every girl I ever went out with I took on the North Bank at least once. They never wanted to go twice.
LAURENCE MARKS, comedy writer and Arsenal fan, in Tom Watt, The End: 80 Years of Life on Arsenal's North Bank, *1993*

I loved football. I played in the morning and in the afternoon. Even when I went to bed with my wife I was training.
DIEGO MARADONA after his last match for Argentina, 1994

Our last Prime Minister was a woman. The head of the Royal Family is a woman. And the head of Birmingham City is a woman.
KARREN BRADY, Birmingham City managing director, on why she believed men and women 'receive equal treatment in society', 1993

I met much more [male] chauvinism working for the *Sport*. I've always had the 'I bet she's shagging the boss' remarks.
BRADY, 1995; her 'boss' at the Sport and Birmingham was David Sullivan

I know everybody thinks I earned this job between the sheets, but I'm not bonking him.
BRADY on her relationship with Sullivan, 1994

I am probably more male than most men. I was brought up going to watch boxing and football.
BRADY, 1995

I will tell you straight away, before you ask me: I have never slept with a footballer, never gone to dinner with one and never seen one naked in the dressing room. OK. Now we can start.
PAOLA FERRERA, Italian TV football presenter, before being interviewed, 1994

I didn't get too many women running after me. It was their fucking husbands who'd be after me.
CHARLIE GEORGE, former Arsenal player, recalling his 1970s heyday, 1995

Q: What's the craziest request you've ever had from a fan?
A: A male fan once asked me for my wife's phone number and when my next away match was.
FRANCIS BENALI, Southampton player, in Sun *questionnaire, 1995*

Could you take Eric's sliding tackle from behind? Football. It's a girl's game.
DAILY STAR *advertisement, 1995*

Q: Who's your dream woman?
A: Jennifer Lopez with the personality of Kathy Burke.
JASON McATEER, Blackburn midfielder, in newspaper questionnaire, 2000

We want women to come to football don't we? I think they're bloody pretty, a damn sight prettier than any bloke I've seen. You talk to women about footballers and what do they like – they like legs and yet our shorts are getting longer. We should go back to the days when half your arse was hanging out.
IAN HOLLOWAY, Queens Park Rangers manager, 2005

What's wrong with letting a load of young ladies see a good-looking lad take his shirt off?
HOLLOWAY on referees booking goalscorers for celebrating by removing their shirts, 2005

After all, this is not a game for little ladies.

PLACIDO DOMINGO, opera singer, defending Spain's rugged tackling during the World Cup finals, 1994

If I had my way, today's Premiership fixture between Motherwell and Ross County would have been cancelled. That's because Fir Park should have been torched on Thursday in order to cleanse the stadium after it played host to women's football.
TAM COWAN, Daily Record *columnist and Motherwell fan, after Scotland's 'girlies' beat Bosnia-Herzegovina 7–0, 2013*

I need to find a woman who is strong, quick and athletic, like Venus Williams. It doesn't matter whether she can play football – she can learn that. Ideally it would be a very tall, blonde and beautiful Norwegian.
LUCIANO GAUCCI, president of Perugia, announcing the Italian club's desire to field a female player in Serie A, 2003

I'm pleased with the way the girls battled back from a 2–0 defecate.
ROD WILSON, Lincoln Ladies manager, as quoted in a press release, 2009

The more beautiful game.

SLOGAN on Football Association billboards at Women's European Championship finals, in England, 2005

The future is feminine.

SEPP BLATTER, *general secretary of FIFA, football's world governing body, after the Women's World Cup, 1995*

Some of the girls can do things men would find very difficult. When I coached at the Centre of Excellence, one girl had a trick I'd never seen any professional do. I tried to work it out and gave up after 10 minutes. And they're physical when they want to be. They'll have a dig in and kick people – they're just the same [as the men].
KEVIN KEEGAN, *England (men's) manager, 2000*

I don't care for women's football, especially when they distract me by running round in those tight shirts. I've watched it on TV and they're not suited to it. I like my women to be feminine, not sliding into tackles and covered in mud.
BRIAN CLOUGH, *2000*

Women's football is a game that should only be played by consenting adults in private.
BRIAN GLANVILLE, *journalist, 1990*

I thought I would watch some of the ladies' football at the Olympics. What a disappointment. The game they played was 20 years out of date. They did not spit every two minutes. They did not dive. They did not feign injury. There was no arguing with the referee. There was no amateur dramatics. And no really nasty tackles.
LETTER *to* The Independent, *2004*

If you look at the England team, they only use the pretty girls on [promotional] posters, the ones that don't look like lesbians. They want to advertise the sport as not being associated with lesbians, when they should be doing more to make people feel comfortable about being gay.
ANDIE WORRALL, *gay Manchester City Ladies and Wales goalkeeper, 2008*

Let the women play in more feminine clothes, like they do in volleyball. For example, they could wear tight shorts.
SEPP BLATTER, *head of FIFA, the world game's ruling body, 2004*

There's always been that stereotyping of female footballers as butch, dykey and unattractive, so maybe it's just best left alone.
HOPE POWELL, *England women's coach, on lesbians in football, 2005*

It's ridiculous that some people think playing [women's] football will make you a lesbian. If you're gay, you're going to be gay whether you play football or tiddlywinks. I'm out and I've never had any problems. In the teams I've played for recently, everyone is out.
WORRALL, *as above*

I made up lies about having a boyfriend or acted a certain way because I felt that's how I had to act and be accepted by the modern world. I wasn't happy doing that because I was always lying – to myself as well.
CASEY STONEY, England women's captain and Arsenal Ladies defender, on coming out, 2014

Men say things like: 'Oh, they're just a bunch of dykes.' I hate the fact that there are girls who would love to play but don't because the image of women's soccer is so bad.
JULIE FOUDY, United States captain, 1995

There's still the blinkered view that all women footballers have thighs like joints of ham and make rugby players look like Flake adverts.
MARIANNE SPACEY, Arsenal and England striker, 1995

When I go to functions I love glamming it up, putting a gown on. People do a double take and are like: 'Oh my God, it's you!' When I wear skirts they go: 'I didn't know you had legs.' What do they think I play football with every week?
SPACEY, now Fulham player-coach, 2003

My sister's the girlie one who goes to him for hugs. But with me he says: 'You all right, son?'
NATASHA DOWIE, Liverpool Ladies striker, on her father Bob, 2013

Arsenal Ladies would do really well against [Tottenham's men]. I'm sure they would get a point.
CESC FABREGAS, Arsenal midfielder, in a Loaded *magazine interview, 2008*

The coach [Gaute Haugenes] told me at half-time that he was substituting me because it was against the rules to have 12 people on the pitch.
KATIE CHAPMAN, Fulham and England midfielder, on how news of her pregnancy was broken to team-mates, 2002

We just don't like the males and females playing together. Anyway, it's not natural.
TED CROKER, FA chief executive, 1988

The men under-perform but still keep their massive pay checks while the women's side has all its financial support stopped. The Charlton board continue to sit in their lovely Laura Ashley offices and drive their fast cars, but the little girls who dreamt of playing for Charlton and England are told the girls' section is no longer going to exist.
DANIELLE MURPHY, Charlton Athletic and England midfielder, after the London club closed their women's team following relegation for the men, 2007

Some referees in women's football are avuncular, enthusiastic and fair. Some use the game to prove that they can control women.
ALYSON RUDD, Leyton Orient Ladies striker and Times columnist, 1994

I've no objection to women referees provided they're good. My only concern is that a dishy referee will have players swarming round her and protesting against decisions.
JOHN RUDGE, Stoke City director of football, 2000

I've been told off for smiling when I show the red card.

WENDY TOMS, the first woman to referee at Conference level, 1996

The court said it was unusual for a husband to complain about his wife spending too much time on football.
TOMS after her divorce, 1991

Stick to playing netball.
CHANT by Kidderminster Harriers fans to Toms, 1999

I saw someone eyeing me in the pub. I asked him: 'Do I know you?' He said: 'You should. You sent me off today.'
SONYA HOME, referee, 1995

Everyone thought to a man that it was a penalty, but not a woman.
PAUL JEWELL, Ipswich manager, on the performance of referee's assistant Amy Fearn, 2012

I've played netball, but never football. I couldn't kick a ball to save my life.

AMY RAYNER, 21, on her rise from officiating in the Rugeley Boys League to being fourth official at First Division matches, 1999

I am not sexist but...how can they make accurate decisions if they have never been tackled from behind by a 14-stone centre-half, or elbowed in the ribs or even caught offside?
JOE ROYLE, Manchester City manager, attacking the appointment of Wendy Toms as an official for the Worthington Cup final as 'politically correct', 2000

It's bad enough with the incapable referees and linesmen we have, but if you start bringing in women you have a big problem. This is Championship football. This is not park football.
MIKE NEWELL, Luton manager, criticising referee's assistant Amy Rayner, 2006

We are now getting PC decisions about promoting ladies. It does not matter whether they are ladies, men or Alsatian dogs. If they are not good enough to run the line then they should not get the job.
GORDON STRACHAN, *Coventry manager, complaining about a female assistant referee, 1999*

I knew it wasn't going to be our day when I arrived at Montrose to find we had a woman running the line. She should be at home making the tea or dinner for her man after he has been to the football.
PETER HETHERSTON, *Albion Rovers manager, on Scotland's first female referee, Morag Pirie, 2003*

I love women. I prefer their company to men's. Men are boring arseholes with nothing to talk about apart from football, and I don't like football.
LEMMY, *leader of the rock group Motorhead, 1998*

Where's the girls, then? Where do we find them? Where's the shag?
STAN COLLYMORE *in Leicester City's hotel at La Manga, as quoted by a businessman guest, 2000*

Five minutes after a game, everything is all right. After the 1999 Champions League final when Bayern lost to Manchester United, I had to comfort my girlfriend. She was much more upset than I was.
LOTHAR MATTHAUS, 2000

Will I ever play in Italy? Never say never in life. I do gladly travel there, like I did last summer, because there are the most beautiful and sexiest girls in the world.
CRISTIANO RONALDO, 2009

Attempts on goal are like going to a nightclub. You could speak to 50 girls, but if you're going home on your own, it's no good is it?
ROY KEANE, *Ipswich manager, 2010*

To put it in gentlemen's terms: if you've been out for a night and you're looking for a young lady and you pull one, some weeks they're good-looking and some weeks they're not the best. Our performance today would have been not the best-looking bird, but at least we got her in the taxi. She weren't the best-looking lady we've ended up taking home, but she was very pleasant, so thanks very much and let's have a coffee.
IAN HOLLOWAY, *Queens Park Rangers manager, after a win over Chesterfield, 2003*

I love England, one reason being the magnificent breasts of English girls. Women are ultimately all that matters in life. Everything that we do is for them. We seek riches, power and glory, all in order to please them.
EMMANUEL PETIT, *French midfielder, 1998*

It's incredible that she has left me. Only recently I paid £7,000 to make her breasts bigger – and now this.
MO IDRISSOU, Hanover striker, on his ex-girlfriend, 2004

I know women are stronger than we are. But I play the football, I make the money.
DAVID GINOLA, Tottenham winger, 2000

When I first came to England I was amazed at the way women behave. From London to Newcastle to Leeds to Manchester, I saw women vomiting in streets. In France the women will drink only a little bit because they have to drive their husbands home.
GINOLA, 2003

I don't even understand offside so I'm not likely to understand a Manchester United contract.
VICTORIA BECKHAM as David renegotiated his deal with the club, 2002

What I love most about Norway is you ladies. Back home I'm used to fat and hairy women journalists.
DIEGO MARADONA in Oslo, 2006

After the game, Sheila, who was sitting right in line, told me the ball had crossed the goal line. She's a very honest person and that was good enough for me.
RAFAEL BENITEZ, Liverpool manager, on taking his secretary's word that Luis Garcia's 'ghost' goal v Chelsea was valid, Champions League semi-final, 2005

I would like to be a woman, though I don't know why.

DJIBRIL CISSE, France striker, on owning a Jean Paul Gaultier dress, 2003

14

MEDIA & ARTS

When you shake hands with the devil you have to pay the price. Television is God at the moment. When the fixtures come out, they can pick and choose because they want the big teams on TV.
SIR ALEX FERGUSON, Manchester United manager, 2011

A night without a game of football on television leaves me a little bit disillusioned. England is a good country because it gets dark early in winter, you go home and you're in an environment where you want to watch television. My wife understands my passion and is ready to pay the price.
ARSENE WENGER, Arsenal manager, 2009

They just talk drivel. Whoever is winning is great, whoever isn't winning isn't. It's banal. And also semi-literate at times. They never criticise in an intelligent way. Anything that's not banal is said to be an outburst. They've created this cartoon world where everyone talks like [Gary] Lineker and says nothing.
EAMON DUNPHY, Irish TV match summariser and journalist, on the Match of the Day *pundits, 2013*

So many sofa experts in this game... Absolutely no idea about football what so ever!
GLEN JOHNSON, Liverpool defender, tweeting on criticism of their 3-3 draw at Crystal Palace after leading 3-0, 2014

When I first retired I had my dad at the back of my head saying: 'This is too easy. You can't do this. Get a proper job. You can't be a Gary Neville or an Alan Hansen. You can't be a journalist! Go out at 5am and come back at midnight.' I thought it was money for old rope.
TONY ADAMS, former Arsenal and England captain, on the ex-player pundits, 2013

I saw Alan Hansen on *Match of the Day* doing a piece about Aston Villa's young defence. He thought: 'I'll pick on their ages.' It's irrelevant. I lifted a trophy at Arsenal at 21. If you're 21 and good enough, it doesn't matter. I don't respect Alan because he has never put his head on the block [as a manager]. For me to do punditry in the early days would have felt very hypocritical.
ADAMS, as above

[Alan] Hansen thinks every goal ever scored is a defensive error. When you don't understand football you can stop a tape anywhere running up to a goal and find a mistake. [Gary] Lineker goes: 'Oh, all right then.' [Mark] Lawrenson simply underlines or puts inverted commas round what Hansen says. It's all happy families. They need to be challenged.
MICHAEL ROBINSON, former Liverpool striker and Spanish TV summariser, on his 'comfy' BBC equivalents, 2005

They [the Belgian media] are filth. They smell of shit as they torture themselves. Fortunately their criticism is erased by the praise of international connoisseurs Gary Lineker and Alan Hansen.
ROBERT WASEIGE, Belgium coach, during the World Cup finals, 2002

Worse than the overpaid boys in shorts are the overpaid commentators in long trousers. They have 'analysis' where they watch bits over again in a manner that suggests short-term memory loss may be an issue.
SANDI TOKSVIG, Anglo-Danish broadcaster, writer and humorist, 2010

It looks like nobody at the BBC is ever going to tell Alan Shearer that 'he has went' is not English.
WHEN SATURDAY COMES *magazine, 2008*

I never liked pundits before I became one.
ALAN HANSEN on becoming a fixture on Match of the Day, *1994*

You win nothing with kids.
HANSEN on Match of the Day *after a youthful Manchester United lost 3–1 at Aston Villa on the season's opening day, 1995; United went on to win the Premiership*

Nothing's black or white in our country – you're either brilliant or you're hopeless.
ALAN SHEARER, Match of the Day *studio pundit, 2010*

I wouldn't trust some of these people to walk my dog.
ROY KEANE, Sunderland manager, on Sky Sports' summarisers, 2008; Keane later became an ITV pundit

The BBC is considering a red-button version of the World Cup without the constant annoying drone – or just stop employing Mick McCarthy.
LOOK AWAY NOW, *Radio 4 sports comedy show aired as TV viewers complained about the noise made by vuvuzelas in South Africa, 2010*

Jamie Carragher, the only man who can make John Bishop sound like Brian Sewell.
ANDY DAWSON, Daily Mirror TV critic, after Carragher joined ITV's panel, European Championship finals, 2012

Collymore: to arrogantly and aggressively drown out the opposing view in an argument by droning on and ruddy on in a Brummie accent.
ENTRY *in the web-based Urban Dictionary, taken from the BBC TV programme* Charlie Brooker's Screenwipe, *2007*

Usually it takes a bottle of Bacardi and a gallon of Coke to get John [Giles] out of his seat.

EAMON DUNPHY, *Irish TV pundit, on his fellow panellist Giles, 2001*

I should rather like the *Match of the Day* theme tune played at my funeral.
CARDINAL BASIL HUME, *Newcastle fan, 1986*

Cudicini is like a rabbit with headlights.
DAVE BASSETT, *Sky summariser, 2006*

The keeper was like a rabbit in the headlines.
BOBBY GOULD, *talkSPORT pundit, 2010*

He's got to put his name in the headlights.
DANNY MURPHY, *BBC pundit, 2014*

If Walcott scores it's a different kettle of story.
ADRIAN CHILES, *ITV anchor, on Ukraine v England, 2013*

The South Koreans threw the kitchen sink at them, or whatever the Korean equivalent of a kitchen sink is.
CHILES, *World Cup finals, 2010*

As a child, Poland's Jakub Blaszczykowski watched his father murder his mother, but he's bounced back.
CHILES, *European Championship finals, 2012*

Murder on the Gdansk floor.
GARY LINEKER, *BBC TV presenter, European Championship finals, 2012*

Pele did say an African team would win the World Cup before 2000 – I think it's going to be longer.
ALAN SHEARER, *BBC TV pundit, on Ghana's quarter-final exit, World Cup finals, 2010*

Sky gets its money from prescription payers.
MARTIN KEOWN, *broadcaster and former England defender, 2008*

I can see England winning tonight, but I can also see them losing.
LEE DIXON, *ITV summariser, before*

England's crucial World Cup qualifier in Ukraine, 2013

I mean the Scots, they can talk for England, can't they, the Scots.
NEIL WARNOCK, TV pundit, 2013

We've given the lad some stick for diving but since then he's come on leaps and bounds.
BILLY DODDS, pundit on BBC Scotland's Sportscene, *2013*

My gut feeling is they will do all right. Why? I have no idea.

ROBBIE SLATER, Fox Sports Australia football expert, on West Bromwich Albion's prospects for the new season, 2013

On *Soccer Saturday* you don't see any goals, or even shots on goal. You don't see any real action. It's just like watching West Brom.
JEFF STELLING, Sky anchor, 2005

So the status quo is pretty much as it was.
STELLING on Soccer Saturday, *2008*

David Goodwillie got that goal, so it's probably a good thing that I've got to press on.
STELLING, as above

Fernando Torres is a certain starter. Is he starting, Alan?
STELLING, 2009

They'll be dancing in the streets of Total Network Solutions.
STELLING in what became a catchphrase used after victories by Welsh Premier League club TNS, 2000s

Barnet's Tommy Fraser has not been sent off. And I want to make it very clear that the information that he did came from our wire service, because Tommy is related to Frankie Fraser, the famous London gangster.
STELLING, 2011

For Arsenal, the sight is in end.
DAVID PLEAT, ITV summariser, at the Champions League final, 2006

Cristiano Ronaldo has been compared to George Best. The incomparable George Best.
PLEAT summarising a Manchester United match, 2007

If it doesn't go right tonight, Wenger has another leg up his sleeve.
GLENN HODDLE, Sky TV pundit, during the first leg of Arsenal's Carling Cup semi-final v Spurs, 2007

Aston Villa literally metaphorically had their pants pulled down.
DION DUBLIN, BBC TV pundit, 2013

That's literally opening a team up and putting them to the sword.
NIALL QUINN, Sky TV pundit, 2012

I watched the United v Reading game with my jaw literally hitting the floor.
IAN WRIGHT, media pundit, 2012

Harry [Redknapp] is going to be literally, literally pulling his hair out.
JOHN SCALES, ESPN summariser, 2011

Jan Koller was literally, literally up his backside there.
ANDY TOWNSEND, ITV summariser, 2008

In his youth Michael Owen was literally a greyhound.
JAMIE REDKNAPP, Sky summariser, 2011

Arsenal have been literally passed to death.
JAMIE REDKNAPP, 2011

Gareth Bale literally has three lungs.
JAMIE REDKNAPP, 2010

The linesman needs shooting for that. Not literally, but he at least needs a good telling off.
MATT LE TISSIER, analyst on Sky's Soccer Saturday, 2011

Everton are literally a bag of Revels.
PAUL MERSON, Sky studio pundit, 2011

Alex McLeish will have had kittens – literally.
CHRIS COLEMAN, TV summariser, 2011

Liverpool have literally come back from the grave!
CLIVE TYLDESLEY, ITV commentator, at Liverpool v AC Milan, Champions League final, 2005

You can literally see what the players are thinking.
ALLY McCOIST, TV summariser, World Cup finals, 2010

Fabregas literally carries 10 yards of space around in his shorts.
RAY WILKINS, TV pundit, 2011

Losing by six goals can certainly take the steam out of your sails.
WILKINS, 2011

On this surface it flies into the roof of the net.
MICHAEL OWEN, BT Sport pundit, 2013

It's like trying to put a needle through a small hole.
ALAN SMITH, *Sky pundit and ex-Arsenal and England player, 2008*

McLean's been like a fresh of breath air.
ROY KEANE, *ITV pundit, 2012*

Bogdan should be playing for whatever country he comes from.

PHIL THOMPSON, *Sky pundit, 2012*

This is a roller coaster of a feast.
MARTIN TYLER, *Sky TV commentator, 2011*

He's an American, qualified to play for Wales because he has a Welsh grandmother, who was on the bench against Switzerland.
GUY MOWBRAY, *BBC TV commentator, World Cup finals, 2010*

Another good run by Dani Alves, like a leech.
CLIVE TYLDESLEY, *ITV commentator, 2013*

Slow motion doesn't reflect the speed at which that happened.
TYLDESLEY, *2011*

Damien Duff is not George Best, but then again, no one is.

TYLDESLEY, *2002*

There are times now when the missing Real Madrid player is very visible.
PETER DRURY, *ITV commentator, on Real Madrd v Barcelona, 2011*

Getting out of the bottom three is Wolves' main objection.
MARK LAWRENSON, Match of the Day *studio pundit, 2011*

Newcastle are absolutely besotted by injuries.
LAWRENSON, *2012*

James Morrison is a player [England manager] Roy Hodgson should be taking a keen interest in.
GARTH CROOKS, BBC TV Final Score *analyst, 2012; Morrison had 23 Scotland caps*

That showed a total lack of disrespect from the player.
CROOKS, *2011*

I've just watched the replay and there is absolutely no doubt – it's inconclusive.
CROOKS, *2012*

Michael Owen will get double figures this season – or at least 10, possibly more.
CROOKS, 2012

Most of Michael Owen's goals have come in the past.
DAN WALKER, BBC TV Football Focus *presenter*, 2012

Anyone can beat anyone else in this league and to prove this there were seven draws yesterday.
DON GOODMAN, *Sky pundit*, 2008

Rooney's carved out such a partnership with Tevez. It's telescopic at times.
TIM SHERWOOD, *Setanta Sports summariser*, 2008

He has feathered a few ruffles.
IAIN DOWIE, *Sky pundit*, 2011

The turning point in the game was how they defended through the match.
GARY NEVILLE, *Sky analyst*, 2011

[QPR chairman] Tony Fernandes is in that goldfish bowl and he's swimming against the tide.
NIALL QUINN, *Sky analyst and ex-Sunderland chairman*, 2013

A few South Americans in this Porto team. Three Romanians and three Portuguese. We should be in for some Samba action tonight.
DAVID PLEAT, *ITV summariser*, 2008

And so we say au revoir to Italy.
PLEAT, *ITV pundit, World Cup finals, 2010*

The butterflies will certainly be jangling.
GABBY LOGAN, *BBC TV anchor*, 2012

Ghana would love a goal to put the icing on the cake they already seem to be eating.
MARTIN TYLER, *Sky commentator, World Cup finals*, 2010

I wish somebody would elbow someone. It'd give us something to talk about.
MICK McCARTHY, *BBC TV summariser, on Brazil 0 Portugal 0, 2010*

There's a real lack of inexperience in the South African team.
STEVE McMANAMAN, *ESPN summariser, World Cup finals*, 2010

It was a toughicult match for Upson to come into.
ALAN SHEARER, *BBC TV analyst, World Cup finals*, 2010

It could be a problem for Germany if Schwarzsteiner isn't fit.
DENNIS IRWIN, RTE Sport pundit, on Bastian Schweinsteiger, World Cup finals, 2010

The altitude must have dropped or something.
RONNIE WHELAN, RTE Sport pundit, World Cup finals, 2010

Franck Ribery is not the flavour of a lot of people's eye.
CRAIG BURLEY, ITV co-commentator, World Cup finals, 2010

Man City have got quite a run of genteel games coming up.
BURLEY, 2012

One-nil is never a lead.

EFAN EKOKU, ESPN summariser, World Cup finals, 2010

United will break caution to the wind.
GLENN HODDLE, Sky summariser, 2010

Ledley's gone out on a limb with his knee.
HODDLE, 2011

Didier Drogba's had malaria, so he's not 100 per cent fit for whatever reason.
HODDLE, 2010

Liverpool are looking for the good feel factor.
CHARLIE NICHOLAS, Sky studio summariser, 2011

The Old Firm match is a one-off – and there are seven of them this season.

NICHOLAS, as above

Chelsea have got an Achilles heel. They don't like it when the boot's on the other foot.
KEVIN KEEGAN, ESPN summariser, 2010

In the end, class telled.
KEEGAN, 2012

Kalinic was as calm as a cucumber there.
CHRIS KAMARA, Sky summariser, 2010

Karl Henry was sent off for a deliberate red card.
KAMARA, 2012

Sandro is holding his face. You can tell from that it's a knee injury.
DION DUBLIN, BBC TV analyst, 2013

I think Southampton will finish above teams that are well below them.

PAUL MERSON, *Sky studio panellist summariser, 2013*

If you get Adel Taraabt in the side he can do something out of the extraordinary.
MERSON, 2013

Steven Fletcher cost a lot of money, though it weren't a lot of money, Jeff, if you know what I mean.
MERSON, 2012

You don't want to bite your nose off to spite your face.
MERSON, 2011

Today will open the title race wide back up.
MERSON, 2011

That shot moved like... I was going to say a shop, but the shop's shut.
MERSON, 2011

He's got his 50p head on.
MERSON after a striker missed several chances from headers, 2011

Drogba fires a 35-year-old free kick.

MERSON, 2010

Liverpool were all mishy-mashy. I know that's not a word, but it should be.
MERSON, Sky TV summariser, on Arsenal's 6–3 win in the Carling Cup, 2007

[Robin] Van Persie is the right player for them – he can open a can of worms.
MERSON, 2006

Too many players looked like fish on trees.
MERSON on England's performance in a defeat by Croatia, 2006

The pitch is full of white snow.
MERSON, 2010

He hasn't had a kick, apart from two headers.
ROBBIE SAVAGE, BBC pundit, World Cup finals, 2010

You cannot have Guatemalan referees at a World Cup. Name me a club in Guatemala.
SAVAGE, as above

Let's see if we can lip-read and hear what he said.
LEE DIXON, ITV summariser, 2012

Ireland need fresh impotence.
PHIL BABB, Sky pundit, 2011

Rooney's goal record speaks without saying.
DWIGHT YORKE, Sky pundit, 2011

United set their stool out early in the season.
YORKE, as above

Somehow, under Ferguson, United papered over the craps.
JAMIE REDKNAPP, Sky summariser, 2014

Reading have shot themselves in the foot and committed suicide.
JOHN SALAKO, Sky summariser, 2011

Vidic got raped by – sorry, got taken apart by – Torres in that one game at Old Trafford.
GRAEME SOUNESS, Sky analyst, 2012

He's like a squid, he's all arms and legs.
SOUNESS, 2013

There's nothing more horrible than a big galoot coming up your backside with no protection.
MATT LE TISSIER, Sky TV pundit, 2005

Hakan Yakin plays with Young Boys in Berne.
JONATHAN PEARCE, BBC TV commentator, World Cup finals, 2006

Ljungberg desperately wants to suck in Cocu.
ANDY TOWNSEND, ITV summariser, 2004

Ian Evatt has gone down easier than my daughter.
DAVE BASSETT, Sky pundit, 2006

Joaquin scuffed that shot with his chocolate leg.
MICK McCARTHY, Sunderland manager, working as a TV pundit at Spain v Greece, European Championship finals, 2004

The Dutch have tasted both sides of the coin now.
ANDY TOWNSEND, ITV summariser, as the Netherlands beat Sweden in a shoot-out, European Championship finals, 2004

Colour-wise it's oranges v lemons, with the Dutch in all white.
CLIVE TYLDESLEY, ITV commentator, at Netherlands v Sweden, 2004

They're wearing the white of Real Madrid and that's like a red rag to a bull.
DAVID PLEAT, TV summariser, as Chelsea prepared to face Barcelona, 2006

Senegal will be kicking themselves because they've shot themselves in the foot.
EFAN EKOKU, TV pundit and former Premiership striker, 2006

Alan Shearer has banged it through a gap that wasn't even there.
PAUL WALSH, Sky TV summariser, 2005

You could have driven a Midnight Express through that Turkish defence.
TERRY VENABLES, ITV summariser, 2003

These Iraqis don't take any prisoners.
RON ATKINSON for ITV at the World Cup as the Iran–Iraq war raged, 1986

And the German stormtroopers are arriving at the far post.
BARRY DAVIES, BBC TV commentator, 1992

2–0 is a cricket score in Italian football.
ALAN PARRY, ITV commentator, 1990

Great striking partnerships come in pairs.

NIGEL SPACKMAN, Chelsea player, working as a Sky TV pundit, 1994

And that's a priceless goal, worth millions of pounds.

ALAN PARRY, ITV commentator, on Champions League final, 1995

The Belgians will play like their fellow Scandinavians, Denmark and Sweden.
ANDY TOWNSEND, ITV pundit, World Cup finals, 2002

Germany benefited there from a last-gasp hand-job on the line.
DAVID PLEAT, ITV summariser, after Torsten Frings handled the ball v United States, World Cup finals, 2002

JOHN MOTSON: Bramall Lane is a fantastic place, and I believe one of the only grounds to host an FA Cup final and Test cricket.
MARK LAWRENSON: Stay in last night did you, John?
EXCHANGE during BBC TV coverage of a Sheffield United v Middlesbrough match, 2009

PRESENTER: You dropped your head when Pele announced your name. Was that relief?
CRISTIANO RONALDO: No, I was just checking my flies.
EXCHANGE during Portuguese TV coverage of Ronaldo's FIFA Player of the Year award, 2009

INTERVIEWER: Your eyes are streaming – are you all right?
MEL CHARLES: I'm OK. I've just got clitorises in my eyes.
EXCHANGE after an early floodlit game on TV, 1960; the Arsenal player suffered from cataracts

GARY LINEKER: Trevor Brooking is in the Sapporo Bowl. What's it like, Trevor?
TREVOR BROOKING: Well, it's a bowl-shape, Gary.
EXCHANGE during BBC coverage of a World Cup match in Japan, 2002

PAUL GASCOIGNE: I've never heard of Senegal before.
DES LYNAM: I think you'll find they've been part of Africa for some time.
EXCHANGE on ITV after the Senegalese victory v France, World Cup finals, 2002

GARY LINEKER: Do you think Rio Ferdinand is a natural defender?
DAVID O'LEARY: He could grow into one.
EXCHANGE during BBC TV's World Cup coverage, 2002

My programme has been switched to accommodate David Beckham and his boyfriends chasing an inflated sheep's pancreas round some field in Portugal.
JEREMY CLARKSON, presenter, on the BBC TV motoring show Top Gear, *2004*

Always on the television is Rangers, Celtic, Celtic, Rangers, Rangers, Celtic, and other teams only get on the television one or two times, but only if they play against the Celtic.
CSABA LASZLO, Hearts' Hungarian manager, 2009

There's too much football on TV. You don't want roast beef and Yorkshire pudding every night and twice on Sunday.
BRIAN CLOUGH, former TV pundit, 2003

It was when old ladies who had been coming into my shop for years started talking about sweepers and creating space that I really understood the influence of television.
JACK TAYLOR, Wolverhampton butcher and World Cup referee, 1974

The governing body of football: television.

MIKE INGHAM, BBC radio football correspondent, 1991

It looks like a night of disappointment for Scotland, brought to you live by ITV in association with National Power.
BRIAN MOORE, ITV commentator, during Brazil v Scotland, World Cup finals, 1990

Poland v England, 7pm tonight, followed by *Female Orgasm*, 10.50pm tomorrow.
ADVERT for Channel 5, 1999

One old lady phoned to say that the fireworks made her cat bolt out of the door and she hadn't seen it since.

BRIAN TRUSCOTT, Southampton secretary, on BSkyB's pre-match extravaganza, 1992

There are already millions of camera angles showing everything, and referees even have things in their ears now. Pretty soon they'll be going out on to the pitch with a satellite dish stuck up their arses.
IAN WRIGHT, former England striker and TV presenter, 1999

PRESENTER: 'A good goal was scored by Ronaldo.' Is the verb active or passive?
CONTESTANT: He scored, so that's active to me. Yeah, definitely active.
EXCHANGE on Sky1's Are You Smarter Than A 10-Year-Old?*, 2011*

For all my so-called obsession, I'm terribly conscious that football can start to eat you up a bit, and I try not to let it.
JOHN MOTSON, BBC TV commentator, 2002

There! He blew the whistle! Norway has beaten England 2–1 at football and we are the best in the world! England, the home of the giants! Lord Nelson! Lord Beaverbrook! Sir Winston Churchill! Sir Anthony Eden! Clement Attlee! Henry Cooper! Lady Diana!
BJORGE LILLELIEN, Norwegian TV commentator, 1981

Maggie Thatcher, can you hear me? I have a message for you in your campaigning. We have beaten England in the World Cup! As they say in the boxing bars around Madison Square Gardens in New York, your boys took a hell of a beating!
LILLELIEN, as above

MIKE CHANNON: We've got to get bodies in the box. The French do it, the Italians do it, the Brazilians do it.
BRIAN CLOUGH: Even educated bees do it.
EXCHANGE on the ITV World Cup panel, 1986

What's this? Ninety minutes on the clock and Manchester United haven't scored. They have to score, they always score…

Sheringhaaaaammmmm!
CLIVE TYLDESLEY, ITV commentator,
Champions League final, 1999

There are some people on the pitch. They think it's all over. It is now!

KENNETH WOLSTENHOLME,
BBC TV commentator, as Geoff Hurst
completed his hat-trick in England's win
over West Germany, World Cup final,
1966

England are sizzling in Shizouka
and after this the sausages will be
sizzling back home.
JOHN MOTSON, commentating on
Brazil v England, World Cup finals,
2002; throughout the tournament Motson
referred to what viewers might be having
for breakfast

Actually, none of the players
is wearing earrings. [Jacob]
Kjeldberg, with his contact lenses,
is the closest we can get.
EXTRACT of Motson commentary from
his book, co-authored with Adam Ward,
Motson's National Obsession: The
Greatest Football Trivia Book Ever,
2004

[John Motson] is a guffawing
whining-voiced clown, anally

obsessed with meaningless
statistics.
TONY PARSONS, Daily Mirror
columnist, 2006

One man's commentary is another
man's pain in the arse.
BARRY DAVIES, BBC TV
commentator, 1990s

I want to stay in football. What
else can I do? I do media and that
farting around, but there's no
passion there. Who wants to sit and
commentate on Middlesbrough
v Everton? Where's the job
satisfaction in that?
STUART PEARCE, former England
captain, facing retirement as a player, 2003

You won't see me in 20 or 30 years'
time, sitting and slagging off an
England performance. Shoot me if
you do.
FRANK LAMPARD, England
midfielder, on the TV panel's criticisms of
the team at the World Cup, 2006

A Premiership manager said to me:
'If I lose my job, I think I'll do
what you do.' That's the attitude.
They think it's easy. It's not.
TONY CASCARINO, talkSPORT
radio pundit, 2004

Ferguson refusing to speak to
MUTV is like Joseph Stalin
blanking Pravda.
DAVID LACEY, Guardian football
writer, on Manchester United's defeat by
Norwich, 2005

I'm trying to tell you the positive things. So I'm getting to the point where I might whack you over the head with a big stick, you bad, negative man.
GORDON STRACHAN, Southampton manager, to a Sky interviewer after a third successive defeat, 2004

You want to take your rose-scented glasses off, mate.
ROBBIE SAVAGE, co-presenter, to a caller to Radio 5Live's 606 programme, 2013

We shouldn't blame the Panama programme for the World Cup bid failing.
GRAHAM TAYLOR, 5Live pundit, after a Panorama *programme, 2010*

They've got that six-man wall that makes it hard for a team to impregnate.
WILLIE MILLER, Radio Scotland summariser, 2013

Then Rooney scored after a fluid exchange with Giggs.

SIMON BROTHERTON, 5Live commentator, 2009

They had a complete lack of desire, hunger, passion, steel – any adjective you care to use.

DARREN FLETCHER, 5Live commentator, 2013

He couldn't hit the old proverbial with a barn door.
IAN PAYNE, 5Live presenter, 2011

He's not renowned for his trademark headers.

BRIAN MARWOOD, media pundit, 2011

Most players will tell you they don't want to lose the opening game.
MARK BRIGHT, 5Live summariser, European Championship finals, 2012

If England do get through it looks like they'll be playing Germany or Siberia.
MIKE PARRY, talkSPORT radio presenter, World Cup finals, 2010

Today it's the big one – Holland against The Netherlands.
PADDY McKENNA, RTE 2fm radio presenter, World Cup finals, 2010

Newcastle just don't get beat. They've only been beaten four times.
STEVE CLARIDGE, 5Live pundit, 2010

When you lose a goal so early, you've always got an uphill mountain.
CLARIDGE, 2011

I saw a defeat coming when they went 3–0 down.
DAVID PLEAT, 5Live summariser, 2013

It's all pumps blazing as we go to the wire.
PLEAT, as above

When you've got a mountain to climb you may as well throw everything into the kitchen sink.
PLEAT, 2011

I think they'll have to throw the kitchen sink at them now. Maybe not the whole sink, with all the plumbing – maybe just the taps for now.
PLEAT, 2009

He hit the ball unerringly past the post.
PLEAT, 2010

Neither team has really taken the baton by the scruff of the neck and put their stamp on it.
NIGEL WORTHINGTON, 5Live pundit, 2012

I've never seen that tattoo on James Collins's back before. Mind you, why would I have ever seen his naked back?
JACK WOODWARD, Aston Villa Radio commentator, 2011

He will probably claim his quote was lost in transfusion.
ALAN BRAZIL, talkSPORT presenter, 2011

I've got my doubts, no doubt about it.
BRAZIL, 2011

Manchester United started out like a train on fire.
BRAZIL, 2010

Migueli, the Barcelona defender, nicknamed Tarzan as they say in Spanish.
BRAZIL, 2010

Villa are making a great challenge for the so-called top four.
BRAZIL, 2009

Let's hope it's not just a case of sore grapes.
BRAZIL, 2008

Sir Alex Ferguson is Manchester United. If you cut him he bleeds red.
BRAZIL, 2004

And Roy Keane's face punches the air.

BRAZIL, 2003

One moment I'm playing football and the next – whack – I wake up in hospital unconscious.
BRAZIL, 2003

Arsenal are doing just enough, which just isn't enough.
MARTIN KEOWN, 5Live summariser, 2010

Why didn't Robben just pull the trigger and shoot himself?
KEOWN, European Championship finals, 2012

It's turning into a war of nutrition in midfield.
KEOWN, 2013

I've just been praising Michael Dawson, then he makes a terrible pass. Hope I haven't put the plock on him.
BOBBY GOULD, talkSPORT pundit, 2010

Adam Johnson was a revolution when he came on.
GOULD, as above

I can't wait to see what happens – we're all abating.
GOULD, 2011

Ngog couldn't score last season, there's no definition about that.
GOULD, as above

Fellaini has put a spanner in the wheels.
GOULD, as above

Harry Redknapp is not in his technical dug-out.
GOULD, as above

I wanted to conceive all my energy.
GOULD, 2012

I'm what you call a country pumpkin.

GOULD, as above

The papers are portraying Rafa as a parrot, just like they did when they showed Graham Taylor as an onion.
GOULD, as above

[Former Burnley chairman] Bob Lord was well reputated within the game.
GOULD, as above

They're living in land cuckoo land.
GOULD, 2013

United losing confirms Chelsea as the big containers now.
GOULD, as above

The referee has misinterpretated that.
GOULD, as above

Jamie O'Hara has been brilliant on the recordings I've seen of him on the radio.
GOULD, as above

I was expecting a bit more aliveness.
GOULD, as above

I'm Coventry born and bred, and I played for them, so that's where my liaisons lie.
GOULD before Arsenal v Coventry, FA Cup, 2014

Villa have got their tails between their teeth.
TOM ROSS, BRMB radio commentator, 2011

I haven't seen so many grown men hugging and kissing since I watched Brokeback Mountain with the missus.
ROSS after Portsmouth scored v Aston Villa, 2008

It's like I always say, if you want to buy a ticket you have got to win the raffle.
TONY BROWN, BRMB pundit, 2011

He picked the postage stamp over the wall with aplomb.
TIM FLOWERS, 5Live pundit, 2011

His legs have gone and it's time to hang them up.
JOHN HARTSON, 5Live summariser, 2011

If my gran had had cojones, she'd have been my uncle.
STAN COLLYMORE, talkSPORT summariser, 2011

That could be the carrot on the top of the cake.
COLLYMORE, as above

Matty Jarvis had acres of time there.
COLLYMORE, 2012

A lot of people are jumping on the moral background.
MICK QUINN, talkSPORT pundit, on Wayne Rooney swearing into a TV camera, 2011

It was nice to hear Ray Wilkins speaking so articulate.
QUINN, 2012

Pitches today are like snooker carpets.
QUINN, 2012

If QPR go into the Championship, the players will be like rats jumping over a ship.
QUINN, 2013

Paul Gallagher's right foot is like a hammer today – you could peel carrots with it.
IAN STRINGER, BBC Radio Leicester reporter, 2011

The Us are playing all in leather. Leather? I meant yellow.

NEIL KELLY, Radio Essex reporter, covering Colchester United, 2008

Arsenal's touch and movement are amazing. I hope the listeners are watching this.
CHRIS WADDLE, BBC Radio 5Live summariser, at Bolton v Arsenal, 2007

This World Cup has got a very international feel about it.

JIMMY ARMFIELD, 5Live summariser, 2006

In technical terms, that's what I call a dinky-do.
ARMFIELD on 5Live after Ruud Van Nistelrooy chipped a goal for Manchester United, 2004

I'm not saying he's going to field a weakened team. It just won't be as strong.
MARK LAWRENSON, 5Live summariser, 2007

Most players would give their right arm for Jason Wilcox's left foot.
LAWRENSON on 5Live, 1996

And Vegard Heggem, my word, he must have a Honda down his shorts.
TERRY BUTCHER, Radio 5Live summariser, on Liverpool's Norwegian defender, Euro 2000

What a goal! One for the puritans.

COMMENTATOR on Capital Gold radio after Dennis Bergkamp scored for Arsenal v Newcastle, 2002

What I said to them at half-time would be unprintable on radio.
GERRY FRANCIS, Tottenham manager, to Radio 5Live after his team came from behind to beat West Ham, 1995

Sorry, but I've had a really busy day today. I've been playing in a golf day for a boy seriously injured in a car accident. I had to drive like a lunatic to get here.
RAY HOUGHTON, talkSPORT radio pundit, apologising for being late on-air, 2004

Don't ever call me a bottler on the radio with all those thousands of people listening.
JAMIE CARRAGHER, Liverpool and England defender, calling a talkSPORT phone-in after the host questioned his appetite for continuing to play for his country, 2007

I read the newspapers every day and I can tell you that you are always great managers. How many games have you managed? I promise you if you manage one I will sit in the stands and chant: 'You know what you are doing.'

ARSENE WENGER after his substitutions prompted chants of 'You don't know what you're doing' and questioning by reporters, 2012

Friends of the press. I am leaving. Congratulations.
LOUIS VAN GAAL, departing Barcelona coach, to the media with whom he had a difficult relationship, 2000

There's a glass of champagne for each of you. Here, let me pour it. I've got the police waiting at the end of the road to breathalyse you all.
SIR ALEX FERGUSON to the media at his final pre-match briefing before retiring as Manchester United manager, 2013

There have been some times when I have not agreed with what people have written, and when you write positive things I tend to dismiss them. I've never held a grudge. It's not my style.
FERGUSON to the press before retirement, 2013

The media was different when I started. That's a difficult job given the pressure journalists are under with modern TV, the internet, Facebook and all the other nonsense.
FERGUSON, as above

You lot had me out of the door three years ago. You had me in a bath-chair down on Torquay beach.
FERGUSON addressing the press, 2009

You've enthralled me all season with your honesty, integrity – and nonsense.

FERGUSON to reporters, 2009; one replied: 'Likewise'

If you ever predict my team right, I'll give you a free weekend up in Loch Lomond. And I'll make sure the midges are out for you.
FERGUSON to the media, 2008

Let people get *The Beano* or *The Dandy*, or some Agatha Christie novels. There's plenty of reading material out there, Jesus Christ.
FERGUSON when reporters argued that the public wanted to read about Wayne Rooney, 2008

Jesus Christ. How do you lot come up with this stuff? It's Korky the Cat, Dennis the Menace stuff. Do you read Lord Snooty?
Which comic is it you guys work for these days?
FERGUSON to reporters who asked about United's supposed interest in Charlton's Darren Bent, 2006

I'm here to discuss Manchester United, not one player. You want a headline, I want a team performance.
FERGUSON, as above

I love you all. I've come to spread peace!
FERGUSON greeting to the media before the Champions League final, 2008

I should have recognised that voice. Hearing it is like having poison creep all over my body.
FERGUSON to a Daily Mirror reporter, 2013

Sir Alex was very convivial. So I chanced a joke to him that it was the longest he'd spent talking to the press in years. At first he laughed but five minutes later in the corridor outside he growled: 'I'll remember you.'
BARRY FLATMAN, Sunday Times tennis writer, on Ferguson's appearance at one of Scottish tennis player Andy Murray's US Open press conferences, 2012

I try to be honest. Some of you don't write it the way I say it.

DAVID MOYES, Ferguson's successor at Manchester United, addressing a press conference, 2014

We've all talked the same nonsense over the years. Everything you tell the press is a lie.
JAMIE CARRAGHER, Liverpool and England defender, 2012

You weren't allowed to speak to the press when I was playing. If you got caught, you got a fine of a week's wages, which was about £7.
HARRY REDKNAPP, Tottenham manager and former West Ham winger, 2012

You are not my friend, you are a journalist. If you invited me to dinner then I would not attend.
JOSE MOURINHO, Internazionale coach, to a Sky Italia reporter who criticised him, 2008

MOURINHO (to reporter): Maybe you should pick the team.
REPORTER: If you gave me part of the nine million euros you earn, I would.
MOURINHO: It's not nine, it's 11, and with sponsors it comes to 14.
EXCHANGE at an Inter Milan press conference, 2008

You're looking for shit. You're looking for trouble. Fuck you.
SAMIR NASRI, France midfielder, to reporters after his country's elimination, European Championship finals, 2012

If I had been suspended any time I insulted a journalist, I would not

have made many appearances for the national team.
MICHEL PLATINI, UEFA president and former France captain and coach, on suggestions that Nasri should be banned for his behaviour to reporters, 2012

Why should I waste my time talking to people who are clearly less intelligent than me?
FABIO CAPELLO, Real Madrid coach, on the media, 2007

Gentlemen, if you want to write whatever you want to write, you can write it because that is all I am going to say. Thank you.
STEVE McCLAREN, England manager, before walking out of the press conference after criticism of the team's performance in beating Andorra, 2007

Whoever that [reporter] was I'd like to pull his pants down and slap him on the arse like I used to do to my kids.
IAN HOLLOWAY, Queens Park Rangers manager, after stories claiming defender Danny Shittu was about to be sold, 2005

The press in Barcelona are always there. They want to come home and sleep with you.
THIERRY HENRY, Barcelona, France and former Arsenal striker, 2007

You're such nice people. Sometimes I wonder who writes all the articles.
SVEN-GORAN ERIKSSON to journalists at an FA get-together, 2004

A very nice bunch of bastards.

GRAHAM TAYLOR, England manager, describing the English press pack in Norway, 1993

I've always said there's a place for the tabloid press in football. They just haven't dug it yet.
TOMMY DOCHERTY, former manager, 2005

English football is as advanced in the stadiums as it is backward in the press. Football and tits are mixed up in the tabloids. If a girl says 'I am a footballer's girlfriend' they all think it's true. Anything goes and you cannot defend yourself.
MARIO BALOTELLI, Italian striker with Manchester City, on being linked with Big Brother *contestant Sophie Reade, 2010*

I have started collecting press cuttings to make an album. Out of 100 things that are written about me, at most five are true.
BALOTELLI, 2012

[Football journalists] are just about able to do joined-up writing.
SIR ALAN SUGAR, former Tottenham owner, 2005

As soon as I arrived in England I didn't like the press. They have never judged me on how I play football; they judged my attitude. The media said I dived, moaned, postured, they said I was racist, everything. They have never spoken well of me.
LUIS SUAREZ, Liverpool and Uruguay striker, 2014

REPORTER: What do you think of Tottenham?
JOHNSON: Come on! Are these real questions? I couldn't give a shit to be honest. Is that it, yeah? Cheers.
INTERVIEW with Wolves captain Roger Johnson, post-match, 2012

If you feel hard done-by, you want to tell the truth about something that happened in the game. If someone asks you a question, you're emotionally imbalanced at that time and you feel an urge to tell the truth. You become a victim of that. There are people out there waiting for you to drop your guard. Journalists can catch you.
KENNY SHIELS, Greenock Morton manager, announcing his decision not to give post-match interviews, 2014

When a dog three months old is the front page of a newspaper in this country, you cannot believe the things you read.
JOSE MOURINHO, Chelsea manager, after being arrested by police over the quarantine status of his Yorkshire terrier, 2007

I've had players arguing their worth based on the marks out of 10 they get in *The Sun*. The media and football live off and need each other. The papers get used by football people day after day. Circulation tarts that they are, they love it and beg for more.
SIMON JORDAN, Crystal Palace chairman, 2006

You fucking sell your papers and radio shows off the back of this club.

SIR ALEX FERGUSON banishing the press after reporters raised an issue he had insisted was off the agenda, 2003

They [the press] have a hatred of Manchester United. It's always been there. It goes with the territory.
FERGUSON on a press conference he curtailed after 74 seconds, 2005

You always feel with the press that they don't really want to know about the football side... There was a time when sports journalism was about what happened in the 20th minute, how the goal was scored, how good the final pass was. Now a team loses and it's another headline about the manager's future.
FERGUSON, 2004

The thing I don't enjoy [about English football] is the way the media talk about us. I feel as if the knives are being aimed in our direction while the flowers are in another.
JOSE MOURINHO in his first season at Chelsea, 2004

If you ask me if I've lied to the press I must honestly say yes, but I had a clear conscience because it was for a good cause. I speak to the player beforehand and say: 'This is the story we're going to give.'
ARSENE WENGER, Arsenal manager, 2010

They say Alf Ramsey was hounded out by the press, but they were pussycats compared to now. It doesn't matter who you are, or what your character is, they're going to pick you to bits. With me it was tactics, with Don Revie it was too dour. He was a great guy but they didn't like him. Ron Greenwood was too nice. With Sven-Goran Eriksson it was what happened off the pitch. They will always find something.
KEVIN KEEGAN, former England manager, 2007

The worst opponent the England team has is the media... [Their] treatment makes certain players I know question the value of playing for their country. Is it really worth the hassle?

PETER SCHMEICHEL, former Denmark and Manchester United goalkeeper, 2001

Many Swedes think the English press is crazy. To instigate such a story, making such an effort and working for six months to set it up – what's the point? What Sven said was quite boring. It was a classic Sven moment.
ERIK NIVA, football writer with Swedish paper Aftonbladet, *on the 'fake sheikh' sting by the* News of the World, *2006*

There are **20** reporters outside my house now. If that is part of another culture, it isn't part of mine.
LUIZ FELIPE SCOLARI, Portugal and former Brazil coach, on why he turned down England, 2006

If someone talks about my private life, I'll give them a good punching. I'm not interested in suing. I like to sort things out my way.
SCOLARI at a press briefing, 2006

We always have to win but even when we win, they are not happy because we didn't put on a show. If we put on a show, they are not happy because we didn't score six or seven goals. If we score six or seven goals, then they say that the opposition was no good.
DUNGA, Brazil coach, on his country's media, World Cup finals, 2010

I'd love someone in America to write a story like that about me [Graeme Souness reputedly leaving Blackburn to manage Tottenham]. You don't sue for 10 thousand, you sue for 10 million. Press in England is fantasy, fiction, exaggeration.
BRAD FRIEDEL, *Blackburn's American goalkeeper, 2004*

The press in England make from a little mosquito a big elephant.
RUUD GULLIT *at Chelsea, 1997*

It's part and parcel of being a footballer these days. I think a few of the lads would have liked to have seen a couple of them [the paparazzi] eaten by the lions.
JOE COLE, *England midfielder, on the attentions of photographers during a safari trip with Fabio Capello's squad in South Africa, World Cup finals, 2010*

Not only the cows are mad in England. The English press is also infected.

EL MUNDO DEPORTIVO *newspaper after 'Spain-bashing' stories before the European Championship quarter-final, 1996*

As it was the media who had tipped us to win, I thought one or two of their jobs might be in jeopardy. Not likely. It was me they were after.
BOBBY ROBSON, *former England manager, recalling failure in the 1988 European Championship finals in* Against All Odds, *1990*

During Scotland's 1974 World Cup in Frankfurt, my English colleagues – remember, 'Britain' didn't qualify for that one – labelled us 'fans with typewriters'. Here's an update: the English Brat Pack are hooligans with computers.
JIM BLAIR, *columnist in Scotland's* Daily Record, *after press vitriol aimed at Graham Taylor, 1992*

Now, if you could just let us have your names and those of your newspapers, we'll know who to ban.
KEN BATES *ending his first press conference as Leeds chairman, 2005*

We've got crash-bang-wallop journalism now where you're either the best in the world or the worst. You have letter pages, phone-ins, websites and TV polls on football. Everyone thinks managing is fantasy football. They say 'I'll take him off' or 'I'll get him for £8m'.
JOE ROYLE, *Manchester City manager, 2001*

For the press, you're either brilliant or you're crap. We didn't win so it was crap. That's how they work.

TEDDY SHERINGHAM, England striker, after 0–0 draw v Croatia, 1996

The shrewdest players never take any notice whatsoever of good press or bad press.
MALCOLM ALLISON, Manchester City coach, 1971

A lot of people in football don't have much time for the press; they say they are amateurs. But I say: 'Noah built the Ark, but the *Titanic* was built by professionals.'
ALLISON, back as City manager, 1980

Reporters can make or break footballers. The reverse can rarely be said.

MALCOLM MACDONALD, Newcastle player, 1974

Mistrust of the press is a standard feature of any international footballer.
PETE DAVIES, author, All Played Out: The Full Story of Italia 90, *1990*

I have been let down so often, read so much that wasn't remotely true, that I now find it difficult to trust anyone who shows up with notebook and pen.
JOHN HOLLINS, Chelsea manager, 1988

People have perceptions on you and they're based on portrayals written by guys who've never had five minutes with you. Why get worked up about it?
SOL CAMPBELL, Arsenal and England defender, 2005

Theatre critics and film critics do know what the mechanics of a production are. Most football writers don't. So players tend to despise journalists. On the other hand players are flattered by their attention... So you have contempt and at the same time a slight awe at seeing your name in print.
EAMON DUNPHY in his book Only a Game?, *1976*

Players always get upset when old pros criticise them in the papers. You just think: 'What an old git. He doesn't know what he's talking about.'
ALAN SMITH, Daily Telegraph columnist and ex-Arsenal and England striker, 2004

I have to make a living just like you. I happen to make mine in a nice way. You make yours in a nasty way.
SIR ALF RAMSEY, England manager, to journalists, 1973

Reporters want a quick answer to something I might want all Saturday night and all Sunday to get somewhere near.
HOWARD WILKINSON, Sheffield Wednesday manager, 1983

I read the papers and they said we played badly last week. I thought we were fantastic, so it shows how much I know.

DAVID O'LEARY, Leeds manager, 1999

I've had enough of this bullshit. After every game some smart-ass journalist tells us what we've done wrong. The way you're reporting is an impudence. It's pure crap. We've played badly but you guys are sitting comfortably, having downed a few beers, and asking us why we haven't thrashed Iceland 5–0.
RUDI VOLLER, Germany coach, addressing the media after a 0–0 draw in Reykjavik, 2003

After that performance I have to say to you: I have a gun and a licence and I wouldn't mind blowing their brains out.
MICHAEL ADOLF ROTH, Nuremberg president, to reporters after defeat by Lubeck, 2003

This is the last day I speak to you. I never cared what you write anyway. You can say what you want about me as a player, but when you offend me as a person – well, I'm more of a man than all of you put together.
CHRISTIAN VIERI, Italy striker, to his country's media at the European Championship finals, 2004

You have to remember I have managed in Italy and it's much, much worse. In this country, the journalists want to kill you some of the time. In Italy, all of the time.
CLAUDIO RANIERI, Chelsea manager, on whether he felt 'pressure' from the media, 2004

You lot [the media] are amazing. You moan and claim we never say anything interesting. What on earth do you want? Of course we tell you we're behind the manager. Do you seriously expect us to say anything different?
LUIS ENRIQUE, Barcelona midfielder, after sacking of coach Louis Van Gaal, 2003

I am ashamed of the [French] press. I am dealing with dishonest, incompetent yobs. I hope the public can figure that out.
AIME JACQUET, France coach, after criticism of him and his team en route to winning the World Cup, 1998

You shouldn't be training your lenses on our bedroom windows. I don't think the French people care

whether Fabien Barthez sleeps in boxer shorts or underpants.
WILLY SAGNOL, France defender, in a tirade against photographers at their base in Germany, World Cup finals, 2006

It's nice to be stabbed in the front for a change.

TERRY VENABLES, Australia coach, on the open antipathy of the media down under, 1997

I've always understood that criticism from the media is part of football. There is a simple answer to it. If you don't like it, don't read it. Nobody makes you look at it. I didn't realise for five days that I'd been called a turnip because I hadn't seen *The Sun*.
GRAHAM TAYLOR, sports journalist's son and former England manager, after goalkeeper David James was branded a donkey, 2004

You smell blood, don't you?
RUUD GULLIT to media before defeat at Southampton which provoked his dismissal by Newcastle, 1999

I never speak, according to the newspapers. I just storm and blast.
KEN BATES, Chelsea chairman, 1990

They were Rotherham feelers, writing in a Rotherham paper for other Rotherham feelers, so bugger impartiality.
BILL GRUNDY, television presenter, recalling his earlier career as a football reporter, 1975

Shame fills the heart of every right-thinking Englishman. How could our lads play like that? How could they let us down so badly?
LEADER in The Sun *after England opened the World Cup with a draw v Republic of Ireland, 1990*

They couldn't play, sneered the critics. They couldn't string two passes together. How wrong the world was.
LEADER in The Sun *after England's semi-final exit v West Germany, 1990*

A van-load of John Barnes arrived on the scene.
LINE from a Press Association report about England fans rioting in Marseilles as mis-heard over the phone by a copy-taker, 1998; it should have read 'a van-load of gendarmes'

YOU DIRTY SCHWEIN!

HEADLINE in the Daily Mirror *after Bayern Munich's Bastian Schweinsteiger was sent off at Manchester United, 2014; Bayern banned the paper from the second leg*

Yes! Now we are going to sort out the little English girlies

HEADLINE in the Berlin BZ newspaper before Germany's 4–1 win over England, World Cup finals, 2010

Zidane appears and leaves Beckham in his underwear
HEADLINE in Spain's Marca *newspaper after the France captain's two late goals beat England, European Championship finals, 2004*

I turned Ronaldo on with my Tesco knickers – exclusive
HEADLINE in the News of the World *after allegations that Cristiano Ronaldo 'romped' with prostitutes, 2008*

Swedes 2 Turnips 1
HEADLINE in The Sun *after England lost to Sweden, 1992*

I'm beginning to wonder what the bloody national vegetable of Norway is.
GRAHAM TAYLOR, England manager, before game in Oslo, 1992

Swede 1 Beetroot 0
HEADLINE in The Times *over pictures of Sven-Goran Eriksson and a red-faced Sir Alex Ferguson after City beat United in the Manchester derby, 2007*

KRANKIES 0 KRANKL 2
HEADLINE in the Daily Record *after Scotland lost to Hans Krankl's Austria, 2003*

WE IN!
HEADLINE in Newsday, Trinidad & Tobago newspaper, *after the Caribbean islands qualified for their first World Cup, 2005*

Nil–Nil Desperandum
HEADLINE in the Independent on Sunday *after England's barren draw v Macedonia, 2006*

NORSE MANURE!
HEADLINE in the Scottish Sun *after Scotland drew 0–0 in Norway, 1992*

YES! WE'VE LOST!
HEADLINE in the Daily Mirror *after England lost at home to Scotland but still qualified for Euro 2000, 1999*

Queen in brawl at Palace
HEADLINE on match report in The Guardian, *1970; Crystal Palace had a player called Gerry Queen*

I'll spill beans on Swindon
HEADLINE in Today *newspaper about allegations of corruption, 1990*

Yanks rate Arsenal as exciting as a slice of cold pizza
HEADLINE for Evening Standard *story on Arsenal's impact in Miami tournament, 1989*

Super Caley Go Ballistic, Celtic Are Atrocious
HEADLINE in the Scottish Sun *after Inverness Caledonian Thistle won at Celtic, 2000*

United supporter to be next Pope
HEADLINE in Newcastle's Evening Chronicle *on report that Cardinal Basil Hume was likely to be elected to the Vatican, 1981*

The Quakers are likely to be without Greg Blundell tomorrow as the striker struggles with a dead calf.

STORY *about Darlington in the* Northern Echo, *2007*

Next week Newton Heath have to meet Burnley, and if both play to their ordinary style it will perhaps create an extra run of business for the undertakers.
REPORT in the Birmingham Daily Gazette, *1894; Newton Heath, soon to become Manchester United, sued for libel and won a farthing in damages*

Nobody could ask Fonteyn or Nureyev to give their normal, flawless interpretation of Swan Lake on Blackpool sands; only spectators with elastic imaginations could have expected an authentic game of football on a treacherous, frost-bound pitch.
ERIC TODD, Guardian *football writer, reporting on Manchester City v Leeds, 1969*

I kept wondering which side had soiled their underpants more with the fear of making a mistake.
PAUL BREITNER, *former West Germany captain, reporting on* England 1 Germany 0, Bild *newspaper, at Euro 2000*

I'm not going to speculate on speculation.
DAVID PLEAT, *acting Tottenham manager, on reports that Giovanni Trapattoni would be the club's next manager, 2003*

What the fuck's a rhetorical question?
STEVE BRUCE, *Birmingham manager, to a press conference, 2004*

Strictly off the record, no comment.

COLIN MURPHY, *Lincoln manager, 1983*

How can you lie back and think of England
When you don't even know who's in the team?
BILLY BRAGG in his song 'Greetings to the New Brunette', 1986

It's coming home, it's coming home
It's coming, football's coming home.
OPENING of the England song 'Three Lions' by David Baddiel, Frank Skinner and the Lightning Seeds, 1996

Three lions on the shirt
Jules Rimet still gleaming
Thirty years of hurt
Never stopped me dreaming.
CHORUS of 'Three Lions', 1996

You got to hold and give but do it at the right time
You can be slow or fast but you must get to the line.
JOHN BARNES rap on the New Order/England squad World Cup single, 'World In Motion', 1990

Ossie's going to Wembley
His knees have gone all trembly.
TOTTENHAM FA Cup final song, 1981

He's football crazy
He's football mad
And the football it has robbed him
Of the wee bit sense he had.
SONG by Scottish folk duo Robin Hall and Jimmy MacGregor, 1960

When it comes to managers, we surely got the champ

When Docherty and Ormond left to join some other camp.
We had to get a man who could make all Scotland proud
He's our Muhammad Ali, he's Alistair MacLeod.
ANDY CAMERON, Scottish comedian, on the hit single 'Ally's Tartan Army', 1978

Olé Ola
Olé Ola
We're gonna bring that
World Cup home from over tha'.
ROD STEWART song for Scotland's World Cup campaign, 1978

'All I want for Christmas is a Dukla Prague away strip.'

TITLE of a song about Subbuteo by Half Man Half Biscuit, 1986

He looked into my eyes
Just as an airplane roared above
Said something about football
But he never mentioned love.
KIRSTY MacCOLL, pop singer, in a song co-written with Jem Finer of the Pogues, 1991

I fell in love with football as I was later to fall in love with women: suddenly, inexplicably, uncritically, giving no thought to the pain or disruption it would bring with it.

NICK HORNBY, author, in his autobiographical, football-based book Fever Pitch, *1992*

'But I don't see what football has got to do with being mayor.' She endeavoured to look like a serious politician. 'You are nothing but a cuckoo,' Denry pleasantly informed her. 'Football has got to do with everything.'
ARNOLD BENNETT in his novel The Card, *1911*

To say that these men paid their shillings to watch 22 hirelings kick a ball is merely to say that a violin is wood and catgut, that *Hamlet* is so much paper and ink. For a shilling the Bruddersford United AFC offered you conflict and art.
J.B. PRIESTLEY in the novel The Good Companions, *1929*

I'm a schizofanatic, sad burrits true
One half of me's red, and the other half's blue
I can't make up my mind which team to support
Whether to lean to starboard or port
I'd be bisexual if I had time for sex
Cos it's Goodison one week and Anfield the next.
ROGER McGOUGH in 'The Football Poem', 1975

So. Farewell
Then, Sir Alex.
Yes. You were
Britain's most successful
Football manager.

It was never a penalty
That was your catch phrase.
It was a definite penalty
That was another.
E.J. THRIBB, Private Eye *magazine, on Sir Alex Ferguson's retirement, 2013*

The night Stan Cullis got the sack
Wolverhampton wandered round in circles
Like a disallowed goal
Looking for a friendly linesman.
MARTIN HALL, poet and songwriter, on the 1964 dismissal of Wolves' most successful manager in 'The Stan Cullis Blues', 1974

'Anything you say may be used in Everton against you,' said Harry. And it was.

JOHN LENNON in In His Own Write, *1964*

When it comes to talking football with you, I might as well be teaching a dog to do a three-card trick.
'D.I. FRED THURSDAY', played by Roger Allam, trying to engage the young Morse in conversation about the 1966 World Cup final in Endeavour, *ITV crime series, 2014*

And that, boys, is how to take a penalty. Look one way and kick the other.
BRIAN GLOVER, playing the games teacher Sugden in the film Kes, 1969

I could have been a footballer but I had a paper round.
YOSSER HUGHES, played by Bernard Hill, in Alan Bleasdale's television drama series Boys from the Blackstuff, 1981

The sturdie ploughman, lustie, strong and bold
Overcometh the winter with driving the foote-ball
Forgetting labour and many a grievous fall.
ALEXANDER BARCLAY in Fifth Eclogue, 1508

Am I so round with you as you with me
That like a football you do spurn me thus?
WILLIAM SHAKESPEARE in Comedy of Errors, 1590

LEAR: My lady's father! my lord's knave! you whoreson dog! you slave! you cur!
OSWALD: I am none of these, my lord; I beseech your pardon.
LEAR: Do you bandy looks with me, you rascal! (Striking him)
OSWALD: I'll not be strucken, my lord.

KENT: Nor tripped either, you base football player.
WILLIAM SHAKESPEARE in King Lear, 1608

How the quoit
Wizz'd from the stripling's arm!
If touched by him
The inglorious football mounted to the pitch
Of the lark's flight, or shaped a rainbow curve
Aloft, in prospect of the shooting field.
WILLIAM WORDSWORTH in 'The Excursion', 1814

Then strip lads and to it, though sharp be the weather
And if, by mischance, you should happen to fall
There are worse things in life than a tumble in the heather
And life itself is but a game of football.
SIR WALTER SCOTT on the occasion of a match between Ettrick and Selkirk, 1815

Then ye returned to your trinkets; then ye contented your souls
With the flannelled fools at the wicket or the muddied oafs in the goals.
RUDYARD KIPLING in 'The Islanders', 1902

15

FAMOUS LAST WORDS

They're not going to lose it –
they've already won it.
*ALAN HANSEN on Liverpool's hopes
of a first Premier League title in 24
years, on BBC TV's Football Focus, 2014;
two weeks later Manchester City were
champions*

We're in a very exciting cup-tie
with a massive, massive feeling of
joy at the end of it.
*SAM ALLARDYCE, West Ham
manager, before the first leg of their
Capital One Cup semi-final v Manchester
City, 2014; West Ham lost 6–0 (9–0 on
aggregate)*

I never understand why clubs
change managers so quickly...
It seems so stupid. United will
[stand by David Moyes]. You don't
even need to go down that road.
Everybody knows what Manchester
United is; it's absolutely 100
percent. Manchester United have
always been that way.
*SIR ALEX FERGUSON, Manchester
United director, January 2014; Moyes
was sacked in April*

We gave away two terrible goals
but prior to that we passed the ball
brilliantly well, kept the ball and
had great control of the game.
*DAVID MOYES, Manchester United
manager, after a 2-0 loss at his previous
club, Everton, 2014; he was sacked within
72 hours*

I certainly don't have any plans
at the moment to walk away from

what I believe will be something
special and worth being around for
all to see.
*FERGUSON in his Manchester United
programme column, 2013; three days
later he announced his retirement*

Christ almighty, I wouldn't sell Real Madrid a virus, let alone Cristiano Ronaldo.

*FERGUSON in December 2008;
Ronaldo joined Real in July 2009*

I don't think he's a boy to go
abroad. The first chance he gets,
he goes back to his family in
Wales.
*HARRY REDKNAPP, Tottenham
manager, playing down reports of
Gareth Bale joining Barcelona, 2012;
within a year he had signed for Real
Madrid*

The name of Balotelli never came
into my thoughts. He is a rotten
apple and could infect every group
where he goes, even Milan.
*SILVIO BERLUSCONI, AC Milan
owner, when asked if he would consider
buying the striker from Manchester City,
2013; Balotelli joined Milan later that
year*

Mario Balotelli costs as much as the Mona Lisa. No team in Italy could afford him.
MINO RAIOLA, Balotelli's agent, 2013

Neymar is the kind of guy who could perform at the Bolshoi Theatre if he were a ballet dancer or win an Oscar if he were an actor. I want him to stay at Santos until he is 80 years old. I'll even offer his son a contract. As for Barcelona buying him, they can go and harvest potatoes in Catalonia.
LUIS ALVARO RIBEIRO, president of the Brazilian club Santos, 2012; Neymar joined Barcelona in 2013

I want to say something about my commitment to Arsenal because there have been many stories in the media lately. I am committed to Arsenal, and that's how it is, despite people [in the media] making up stories... I am committed, I am captain – fans should not believe everything they read.
ROBIN VAN PERSIE pledging himself to Arsenal, October 2012; he left for Manchester United the following August

The Michael Jackson statue will stay. He can't go, he is here, it is part of the deal, it is history, it is listed. You can't change otherwise I will come and take your moustache in public. He knows that.
MOHAMED AL FAYED on selling Fulham to Shahid Khan, 2013; Khan had the statue removed within three months

This Is Anfield. So what?
HEADLINE in Spain's Marca newspaper before Liverpool hosted Real Madrid, Champions League, 2009; Real lost 4–0

'Impossible' is just a word that weak men use to live easily in the world they were given, not daring to explore the power they have to change it. 'Impossible' is not a fact, it is an opinion. 'Impossible' is not a declaration, it is a challenge. 'Impossible' is potential. 'Impossible' is temporary. 'Impossible' is nothing.
DANI ALVES, Barcelona and Brazil defender, before his club met Bayern Munich, Champions League, 2013; Bayern won 4–0 (7–0 on aggregate)

No, I haven't resigned, and I've no idea why it is being suggested that I have. This is an outrage; an absolute liberty for people to be putting around this kind of rumour on the internet. It's not true, there's not a chance I will resign. Why should I? I have a year left on my contract.
HARRY REDKNAPP, Tottenham manager, 2012; he was sacked within 48 hours

I've just heard there's a lot of rubbish on Radio 5 that I'm walking out. I'm not leaving. I've got a job to do, especially for these fans. They're the best in the country.
REDKNAPP, Portsmouth manager, 2004; he promptly joined Southampton

533

Portsmouth is my club – I feel an immense sense of loyalty and unfulfilled ambition. I could have left but I would have felt a great sense of betrayal. So they're stuck with me now. This will be my last job in football.
REDKNAPP, Portsmouth manager, 2008; he later managed Tottenham and Queens Park Rangers

The club [Newcastle] is allowing all the major players of the team to go. Seriously, do you think it is the fault of the players? Andy, Nobby [Kevin Nolan] etc. This club will never again fight to be among the top six again with this policy.
LUIS ENRIQUE, Liverpool defender, in a tweet condemning his previous club, Newcastle, 2011; Newcastle finished fifth while his new club finished eighth

Chelsea is a big club with fantastic players and every manager wants to coach such a big team. But I would never take that job, in respect for my former team at Liverpool, no matter what. For me there's only one club in England, and that's Liverpool.
RAFAEL BENITEZ, Liverpool manager, 2007; in 2012 after 'the phone didn't ring for 18 months' he became Chelsea's interim manager

I haven't heard anything in reference to Michael [Laudrup] and neither have we met, or discussed, or done anything about Michael. A couple of us did actually meet up on Sunday to have a cup of coffee like we normally do. That's as simple as it was. That's where the first rumour came from. It's difficult for me to say anything because there's nothing to discuss.
HUW JENKINS, Swansea City chairman, 2014; within a fortnight the club's Danish manager had been sacked

I had the privilege to meet Mr Khan over the summer and, straight away, I felt he was a really thorough, amicable man who's very successful in business. He doesn't do anything knee-jerk.
RENE MEULENSTEEN, Fulham manager, 2014; the club's owner Shahid Khan sacked him after 76 days

Every club has this. Even Man United had this with Sir Alex Ferguson in the old days. But they continued and started winning and winning. Billy Davies is doing the right job.
FAWAZ-AL-HASAWI, Nottingham Forest owner, two days before the derby against Derby County, 2014; Davies was sacked after a 5-0 defeat

I will never run the club by mob rule – never have and never will. There's only one judge and that's me. Over the years there have been plenty of calls for managers' heads and I've never bowed to them. I'm not about to change my policy now... Getting behind the manager is the only option people have. And that includes me.

KARL OYSTON, *Blackpool chairman, as pressure mounted on manager Paul Ince, 2014; Ince was fired 13 days later*

The owners understand the difficulties and don't panic if we lose games. When all the rumours about me losing my job started they reassured me. They said, 'You go on, take us to the Premier League.'
SVEN-GORAN ERIKSSON, Leicester manger, shortly before his dismissal, 2011

I've never responded to hotheads who want to sack somebody. I don't think it's ever worked – look at Sheffield United.
JOHN RYAN, Doncaster Rovers chairman, 2011; the following day Doncaster parted company with Sean O'Driscoll and named Dean Saunders as manager

I know that he [David Beckham] is leaving Los Angeles Galaxy, but we are not interested.

CARLO ANCELOTTI, Paris St-Germain coach, 29 December 2012

[Beckham] can help the team have a great season. I'm very happy that he has joined the club.
ANCELOTTI as Beckham joined PSG, 2 February 2013

Never, never, never, never. Nothing, never, never, never. Not now. Not ever.

FLORENTINO PEREZ, Real Madrid president, denying his club's interest in Beckham shortly before signing him, 2003

I want to stay at United. There's been lots of stuff in the media about me and Real, but my feelings for Manchester, the club, the players, the fans and staff, are as strong as ever.
DAVID BECKHAM dismissing reports he would join Real, weeks before he did, 2003

Beckham will never play for this club again.
FABIO CAPELLO, Real Madrid coach, when Beckham set up a deal with Los Angeles Galaxy, 2007; Beckham won back his place and helped Capello's side win La Liga

The proof that our technical staff was correct not to retain [Beckham] has been borne out by every other technical staff in the world not wanting him, even though he was out of contract. He will be an average cinema actor living in Hollywood.
RAMON CALDERON, Real Madrid president, January 2007; by May he was calling Beckham 'a truly great professional' and exploring ways to prevent his leaving

We go to Wembley not as tourists but as warriors singing our own song.
PAOLO DI CANIO, Swindon manager, before the Johnstone's Paint Trophy final, 2012; his team lost to Chesterfield

One club I would never consider joining is Manchester United.

ALAN SMITH, Leeds striker, 2002; after signing for United in 2004 Smith said he had 'learned that you never say never'

We would never sell Wayne Rooney. That would never come about, because any club would have to pay a king's ransom for a player like him.
BILL KENWRIGHT, Everton deputy chairman, 2004; Rooney joined Manchester United later that year

One thing that has pleased me is in Ladbrokes, we're not one of the three favourites to get relegated – and they don't normally get it wrong.
DEAN SAUNDERS, Wolves manager, in February, 2013; Wolves suffered a second successive relegation in May

I've never been sacked before and I will not be sacked here.
SAUNDERS, as above; he was sacked in May

I've never played in Spain and never will. This is my last contract.
THIERRY HENRY, Arsenal striker, rejecting Barcelona to re-sign for a further four years with the Gunners, 2006; he joined the Catalan club a year later

As long as he [Arsene Wenger] is here then I will be here – it's just as simple as that.
HENRY pledging allegiance to Arsenal in April, 2007; he left in June

Mr Chairman, I think that the second half will be a damage-limitation exercise for your team.

MICHEL PLATINI, *UEFA president*

and former France captain, to Liverpool chairman David Moores when Milan led Liverpool 3–0 in the Champions League final, 2005; Liverpool won the trophy on penalties

The bookies are offering odds that I'll be out before Christmas. I've told my mates to have a bet because there's no way I won't be here then.
PAUL GASCOIGNE on becoming manager of Kettering, 2005; he did not make it to Christmas

You simply do not sack Bobby Robson.

FREDDY SHEPHERD, Newcastle chairman, 2004; within days he dismissed the veteran manager, saying there was 'no room for sentiment'

I'm sick of every Tom, Dick and Harry getting linked with my job every day. Well ding dang doo. It's my job, I own it and it's up to anyone else to take it off me.
IAN HOLLOWAY, Queens Park Rangers manager, 2005; a month later he lost his job

The Blackburn job is just more speculation. I have no plans to leave the Wales post. I'm a Welshman, who is as proud today of being national team manager as he was on the day he was appointed.
MARK HUGHES, Wales manager,

the day before taking over from Graeme Souness at Blackburn, 2004

If anyone ever hears that Kevin Keegan is coming back to football full-time, they can laugh as much as I will. It will never happen. That is certain.
KEVIN KEEGAN, later to become England manager, on going to live in Marbella, 1985

I'm not interested in the England job, so I hope no one has had a bet on me.
KEEGAN a week before being named interim national coach, 1999

If I am to lose this job they will have to take it away from me.
KEEGAN weeks before resigning as England manager, 2000

I'm not a person who goes into deep depression after a defeat. I try to remain upbeat. I'm realistic enough to know that results are often unpredictable and things don't always work out as one would wish.
KEEGAN in his programme notes before match v Germany, 2000; England lost 1–0 and Keegan resigned minutes later

Week by week the team's getting better. And I always enjoy the second half of the season.
BRIAN McDERMOTT, Leeds United manager, before Christmas, 2013; in the new year McDermott was sacked, then reinstated, as Leeds fell from the Championship's top six to the lower reaches

At least you know you're alive and not half-dead from all the emotion. Now that it has all come good, it's a lovely feeling. See you all next season.
JIM RYAN, Luton Town manager, after his team's escape from relegation, 1991; the next day he was sacked

I must be barmy to think of leaving this club. I've got the best job in football. In the final analysis, I couldn't turn my back on people who have been so good to me.
RON ATKINSON, Sheffield Wednesday manager, after spurning Aston Villa's advances, 1991; he joined Villa within a week

I believe Big Ron to be one of the top three managers in the country.
DOUG ELLIS, Villa chairman, three weeks before sacking Atkinson, 1994

Let's kill off the rumours that Ossie Ardiles's job is on the line. If he ever leaves it will be of his own volition.
SIR JOHN HALL, Newcastle chairman, three days before dismissing the Argentinian, 1992

If Alan Sugar thinks he can just walk in and take West Bromwich Albion's manager, I'll be down that motorway in my car like an Exocet to blow up his bloody computers.
TREVOR SUMMERS, West Brom chairman, on Tottenham's interest in Ossie Ardiles, 1993; Ardiles duly became Spurs' manager

We hope Peter Reid will see this club through to the next century.
PETER SWALES, Manchester City chairman, after Reid signed a three-year contract, 1993; he was sacked within six months

I am a very happy man and every day I wake up with a smile because it is a thrill to go to work. I know one day I will be sacked. That is inevitable. But I won't cry – I'll just say I did my best and move on.
RUUD GULLIT shortly before his dismissal by Chelsea, which he disputed vehemently, 1997

Ideally, I'd like to pop my clogs punching the air while celebrating the Blues' winning goal at Wembley in the year 2130.
BARRY FRY, days before his sacking as manager of Birmingham, 1996

All the speculation surrounding Birmingham has been off-putting... I'm extremely happy here. I want to manage in the Premiership and I'd love to take Crystal Palace there. End of story.
STEVE BRUCE, Palace manager, shortly before making Birmingham his fifth club in four years, 2001

Peter Taylor needs three or four seasons with us, then he can become the next England manager.
JOHN ELSOM, Leicester chairman, 2000; he sacked Taylor within a year

Ideally, I would like David O'Leary to be at this club for life.

PETER RIDSDALE, Leeds chairman, 2000; he fired the Irishman as manager within two years

Of all the great clubs I've worked with, none has had the infrastructure, commitment and potential of Leeds. The team have all the necessary qualities to become the country's best for years to come.
TERRY VENABLES on taking over as Leeds United manager, 2002; Leeds would finish the season selling off key players and narrowly avoiding relegation, Venables having already been sacked

My team just played like spoilt children who think they are great players for whom the victories will simply arrive… Today, if I was the president, I would dismiss the coach and line the players up against a wall and give them all a kick up the backside.
MARCELLO LIPPI, Inter Milan coach, after his team lost at home, 2000; he was sacked within 48 hours

I congratulate the president for making the decision not to sack me.
LLORENC SERRA FERRER, Barcelona coach, after defeat by Liverpool in the UEFA Cup, 2001; he was fired within 48 hours

Rio Ferdinand is going nowhere. Where does he think he is going – into thin air?
PETER RIDSDALE, Leeds chairman, insisting they would never allow their captain to join Manchester United, 2002; the £29.1m deal went through within days

I might even agree to become Rangers' first Catholic if they paid me £1m and bought me Stirling Castle. Let me spell out where I stand. I am a Celtic man through and through and so I dislike Rangers because they are a force in Scottish football and therefore a threat to the club I love. But more than that I hate the religious policy they maintain.
MAURICE JOHNSTON, then with Nantes, in Mo: An Autobiography, *1988; within a year he had joined Rangers*

It's a complete fabrication. You can run that story for 10 years and it still wouldn't be true.
BILL McMURDO, Johnston's agent, ridiculing reports that Rangers wanted to sign his client, 1989; within days he moved to Ibrox

I like Nottingham. It's a bit like Ireland. My heart is with this club. My present contract has another three years to go, and I did have another one of three years in mind, but now I fancy something a bit longer.
ROY KEANE professing allegiance to Forest, 1993; six months later he was with Manchester United

I want to reassure fans that Luis Figo, with all the certainty in the world, will be at Nou Camp on 24 July to start the season.
LUIS FIGO, Portugal captain, a fortnight before forsaking Barcelona for their bitter rivals Real Madrid, 2000

There's no chance of Sol leaving for Arsenal. He's a Spurs fan and there's not a hope in hell of his playing in an Arsenal shirt.
DAVID BUCHLER, Tottenham chairman, weeks before Campbell defected to Highbury, 2001

The talk about Manchester United is an honour, but I'm happy at Fulham. I don't get angry about things. Life is too beautiful for that. And Chris Coleman is a great man. He's just perfect. I can't think of anybody who has impressed me more.
LOUIS SAHA shortly before he reputedly began not talking to Coleman, Fulham's manager, for refusing to let him talk to United, 2004; he soon moved to Old Trafford

My son will not go to Chelsea. Over my dead body will he go there. Old Trafford is the only place he wants to play. If he can't play there he would rather stay at PSV and play in their reserves than join Chelsea.
HANS ROBBEN, father of Arjen Robben, a month before the PSV Eindhoven winger joined Chelsea for £13.5m, 2004

The [Michael] Essien case is closed. He will remain at Lyon. They behaved to us as if we were just country bumpkins with our berets and baguettes. England may have won the Olympics, but Chelsea will not get Essien.
JEAN-MICHEL AULAS, Lyon president, 10 days before selling the Ghanaian midfielder to Chelsea for £24.4m, 2005

Are you trying to tell me there's a bigger club than Everton? Do me a favour. Wayne Rooney is going nowhere.

BILL KENWRIGHT, Everton vice-chairman and owner, when asked whether

Rooney might eventually join 'a bigger club', 2003; he moved to Manchester United within a year

I am desperate to be the first Brazilian to play for Manchester United. All the biggest stars – like Pele, Ronaldo, Roberto Carlos and Rivaldo – wanted to be the one. But now I know it's going to be me. When I close my eyes, my subconscious is red and I can't stop seeing myself as a Red Devil.
RONALDINHO, Brazil striker, days before spurning United in favour of Barcelona, 2003

We'll probably get more fans than if we'd signed Ronaldo.
NEIL WARNOCK, Bury manager, expecting a rush of Asian spectators after signing Indian international Baichung Bhutia, 1999; his first appearance drew 3,603

I don't consider signing Stan a risk at all. He'll enhance the dressing-room spirit because he's a bright lad.
MARTIN O'NEILL, Leicester manager, a week before Collymore was prominent in the spraying of a Spanish hotel lobby with a fire extinguisher, 2000

I would lie in front of a tank for the guy [Alex Ferguson]. Now that I'm here they will have to chase me out with wild animals.
MARK BOSNICH, Manchester United goalkeeper, 2000; within months, Ferguson gave him a free transfer

There's as much chance of [Frank] McAvennie moving as there is of Rangers beating us 5–1 tomorrow.

BILLY McNEILL, Celtic manager, 1988; Celtic lost 5–1 and McAvennie eventually left

What reputation do Holland have anyway? They didn't qualify for the last World Cup, and they're in the play-offs, so it's not a great record, is it?
JAMES McFADDEN, Scotland striker, before a two-leg play-off with the Dutch for a place in the European Championship finals, 2003; Scotland lost 6–1 on aggregate

Bergkamp? He's fucking scared, that guy. He won't get on a plane. Van Bronckhorst? How good is he? Get at him. Put him on his arse!
GRAHAM WESTLEY, Farnborough manager, to the Conference club's players as they prepared to face Arsenal in the FA Cup, 2003; Arsenal won 5–1

They are just another English club. It doesn't make any difference if we're playing Sheffield United or Manchester United. All English clubs play the same way.
RONALD KOEMAN, Barcelona and Netherlands sweeper, before the European Cup-Winners' Cup final v Manchester United, 1991; United won 3–1

Oh, it's OK, it's only Ray Parlour.

TIM LOVEJOY, Sky fanzone commentator and Chelsea supporter, seconds before Parlour's spectacular goal for Arsenal against his team, FA Cup final, 2002

I've signed a contract with the Dutch national team until 2006, so I can win the World Cup not once but twice.
LOUIS VAN GAAL, Netherlands coach, 2000; the Dutch failed to qualify for the 2002 finals, after which Van Gaal resigned

I will wage my watch on Italy to beat France, and it's a gold Cartier. They will leave France by the wayside.
DIEGO MARADONA at the World Cup finals, 1986; France won 2–0

There is no limit to what this team can achieve. We will win the European Cup. European football is full of cowards and we will terrorise them with our power and attacking football.
MALCOLM ALLISON, Manchester City coach, 1968; City went out in the first round to unfancied Fenerbahce of Turkey

You can mark down the 25th June 1978 as the day Scottish football conquers the world.
ALLY MacLEOD, Scotland manager, before presiding over a shambolic first-round exit from the World Cup finals in Argentina, 1978

The only trouble Spurs will have is finding the place.

JIMMY GREAVES, broadcaster and ex-Tottenham striker, before Spurs' FA Cup tie at Port Vale, 1988; Third Division Vale won

You can rest assured it will not happen again. Last year's defeat by Sutton United was our inoculation against that.
JOHN SILLETT, Coventry manager, the day before his team's FA Cup defeat by Fourth Division Northampton, 1990

Before City got their first we could have been 3–0 up. I turned to my physio and said: 'I think I'll have a cigar. If we keep this up we'll get double figures.'
MALCOLM MACDONALD, Huddersfield manager, after a 10–1 defeat at Manchester City, 1987

The players are under no pressure to get a result, so you never know what might happen.

TOMMY GEMMELL, Albion Rovers manager, before an 11–0 defeat by Partick Thistle, Scottish Cup, 1994

If we were getting murdered every week, I'd be panicking. As it is, I'm not anxious.
DANNY WILSON, Sheffield Wednesday manager, before an 8–0 defeat at Newcastle, 1999

You don't get many opportunities in your career to have a real crack at the FA Cup, but we're at home, in the quarter-finals, so why not?
STEVE BRUCE, Birmingham manager, before a 7–0 home defeat by Liverpool, 2005

I'm waiting for [Marcel] Desailly. I excel myself against blacks.
HRISTO STOICHKOV, Barcelona's Bulgarian striker, before European Cup final, 1994; Milan won 4–0 and Desailly scored

Whatever the result, the players, directors, staff and of course the supporters of Kidderminster will have had a terrific day out.
BIRMINGHAM CITY programme welcome to Kidderminster Harriers, FA Cup tie, 1994; the non-league side won 2–1

England fans will be talking about their 1–0 win for years.
CLIVE TYLDESLEY, ITV commentator, moments before France scored twice to win 2–1, European Championship finals, 2004

There's only one team that's going to win now and that's England. I hope I'm not tempting providence there.
KEVIN KEEGAN, working as an ITV summariser, moments before Dan Petrescu's winner for Romania, World Cup finals, 1998

After tonight, England v Argentina will be remembered for what a player did with his feet.

ADVERT by Adidas featuring David Beckham, who kicked Diego Simeone and was dismissed, World Cup finals, 1998

The bagpipes will scare the stupid bandana off David Beckham. I reckon there's one or two of their players that will crack under pressure. We've got more soul than England. They just take it for granted that they'll come up here, do the business and go away again. It's not like that for us.
JOHNNY MARR, Edinburgh Tartan Army, before England's 2–0 win over Scotland at Hampden Park, 1999

All that stuff about the foreigners and their superior technique is a media myth as far as I'm concerned. I was playing for England 10 years ago when we were getting all that, and we went to Spain and beat them 4–2.
TONY ADAMS, Arsenal captain, on the eve of 4–2 defeat by Barcelona, 1999

This could be the most boring cup final in history.

JOHAN CRUYFF, former Netherlands captain, before Liverpool beat Alaves of Spain 5–4 to win the UEFA Cup, 2001

I have no doubts whatsoever that Germany will thrash England and qualify easily for the World Cup. What could possibly go wrong? The English haven't beaten us in Munich

for a hundred years. I'm convinced we're headed into another golden age of German soccer.
ULI HOENESS, former Germany player, on the eve of England's visit, 2001; England won 5–1

Apart from Oliver Kahn, if you put all the players in a sack and punched it, whoever you hit would deserve it.
FRANZ BECKENBAUER, former Germany captain and coach, in the early stages of the World Cup finals, 2002; within a fortnight Germany had reached the final

Zidane and Vieira? They're only names. I think we can win this game.

BERTI VOGTS in Paris before his debut as Scotland manager, 2002; France won 5–0

My friends are coming over to Korea and Japan for the group stages but my family are not planning to visit until the final week of the tournament.
MARCEL DESAILLY, France defender, before his country's defence of the World Cup, 2002; France did not survive the first round

Sometimes in such a Herculean struggle an outside body can

influence the outcome. God, once again, will decide this match. And we will win it.
JUAN SEBASTIAN VERON, Argentina midfielder, before the meeting with England in the World Cup finals, 2002; England won

I doubt this game will be a 0–0 draw. You don't see many goalless draws these days. The way football is now, if you're not scoring at one end then you're likely to be letting them in at the other.
KEVIN KEEGAN, Manchester City manager, before a 0–0 draw with Tottenham, 2003

I think I've had only a couple of bookings in the last dozen games, which is good for me. I had better not say any more or I'll probably be sent off tonight.
ROY KEANE quoted in Dublin's Evening Herald *before being dismissed playing for the Republic of Ireland v Russia, 1996*

I've never stopped learning since I came to Inter. When I was young, I was a bit soft-headed, stupid sometimes. Having a family has settled me down. The older you get, the more you learn to take it. I feel more in control.
PAUL INCE in Milan, 1996; he was sent off in his next match

Go out there and drop hand-grenades.
KEVIN KEEGAN, England manager,

to Paul Scholes before a match v Sweden, 1999; Scholes was sent off

You have to be careful or you end up on the front page of the *Daily Record.*
DONALD FINDLAY QC, Rangers vice-chairman, on taking the stage at the Ibrox social club to sing sectarian songs, 1999; he resigned after being exposed by the Daily Record

I know now that the public and press are out there waiting for me to take responsibility and live differently.

JERMAINE PENNANT, Birmingham winger, 2005; the next day he was sent home from training after reputedly turning up drunk

Q: What's your favourite drink?
A: A couple of years ago the answer would have been 'everything'. But now I like Diet Coke.
GASCOIGNE interviewed by a Guardian *football website, 2005; a few days later alcohol was given as a reason for his losing the Kettering job, 2005*

Q: Favourite drink?
A: Beer. No, I mean Coke.
Q: Most prized possession?
A: My car.
EIRIK BAKKE, Leeds and Norway
midfielder, in a programme interview,
2003; he was soon convicted of drink-
driving

If Roy has said he might play for
Ireland again, someone must have
caught him just after he'd had his
Christmas pudding.
SIR ALEX FERGUSON, 2004; within
three months Keane announced his desire
to resume playing for the Republic

Rooney is incredible, the best
attacker in the world. Give him
space and he will kill any defender.
And the amazing thing about him
is that he is never injured.
SVEN-GORAN ERIKSSON, England
coach, before the European Championship
finals, 2004; Rooney broke a foot early in
the quarter-final

ACKNOWLEDGEMENTS

All journalists who have stood outside a stadium in the cold and damp or risen at an unearthly hour to attend a manager's weekly pre-match 'presser', waiting to elicit precious 'nannies' (nanny goats: quotes) from determinedly tight-lipped managers and players, can take as read my admiration and gratitude.

Special thanks go to Chris Davies, Ian Herbert, Kenny MacDonald, Steve Nicholson, Ged Scott and Martin Smith for their interest and input.

My gratitude also goes to the colleagues whose support and advice have helped me throughout my career in journalism. Richard Williams, a stylishly authoritative essayist on sport and music, gave me my first writing job when he was editor of *Time Out* and continues to be an inspiration. Charlie Burgess, Simon Kelner, Paul Newman, Neil Morton, Marc Padgett and Chris Maume are among the editors who indulged me at *The Independent*, where the comradeship of Patrick Barclay, Jonathan Foster, Trevor Haylett, Joe Lovejoy, Glenn Moore, Tim Rich, Steve Tongue, Sam Wallace, Henry Winter and many more was always appreciated.

Prior to my move to the *Indy* I was proud to serve *The Guardian*, the paper my parents took when I was a child, where it was an education to work alongside fine colleagues and friends such as Steve Bierley, Russell Thomas, Ian Ridley and Jeremy Alexander.

I am also indebted to a journalist whose reports planted the idea that I could combine my interest in football with the pleasure I found in playing with words. Eric Todd was the *Manchester Guardian*'s football correspondent and later *The Guardian*'s senior northern sportswriter. His work was full of humour and the sense that there was more to a game than its chronology. Covering a drab 0–0 draw between Arsenal and Liverpool, he filed a single paragraph and told his editor: 'That's more than it was worth and that's all it gets.' I revered him all the more when I learned that, like me, he was from Leeds. Todd died in 2000, aged 90, but is not forgotten.

Thanks, finally, to Andrew Goodfellow of Ebury Press and to my editor Anna Mrowiec for keeping alive a project conceived by Roddy Bloomfield and the late Peter Ball three decades ago; to my family, Julie, Ellie and Joe, for their love and support; and to my mother Gwen and my dear late father Roy.

INDEX